ALSO BY MELVIN I. UROFSKY

Dissent and the Supreme Court

Louis D. Brandeis: A Life

Money and Free Speech: Campaign Finance Reform and the Courts

Lethal Judgments: Assisted Suicide and American Law

*Division and Discord: The Supreme Court
Under Stone and Vinson, 1941–1953*

Letting Go: Death, Dying, and the Law

A Conflict of Rights: The Supreme Court and Affirmative Action

A March of Liberty: A Constitutional History of the United States

A Voice That Spoke for Justice: The Life and Times of Stephen S. Wise

We Are One! American Jewry and Israel

American Zionism from Herzl to the Holocaust

Letters of Louis D. Brandeis (with David W. Levy)

THE
AFFIRMATIVE
ACTION
PUZZLE

THE
AFFIRMATIVE
ACTION
PUZZLE

*A Living History
from Reconstruction to Today*

MELVIN I. UROFSKY

PANTHEON BOOKS, NEW YORK

All rights reserved. Published in the United States by Pantheon Books,
a division of Penguin Random House LLC, New York, and distributed in Canada
by Penguin Random House Canada Limited, Toronto.

Pantheon Books and colophon are registered trademarks of
Penguin Random House LLC.

Library of Congress Cataloging-in-Publication Data
Name: Urofsky, Melvin I., author.
Title: The affirmative action puzzle / Melvin I. Urofsky.
Description: First edition. New York : Pantheon Books, 2020.
Includes bibliographical references and index.
Identifiers: LCCN 2019016086. ISBN 9781101870877 (hardcover : alk. paper).
ISBN 9781101870884 (ebook)
Subjects: LCSH: Affirmative action programs—United States—History.
Affirmative action programs in education—United States—History.
Discrimination—Government policy—United States—History. Minorities—
Government policy—United States—History.
Classification: LCC HF5549.5.A34 U76 2020 | DDC 331.13/30973—dc23 |
LC record available at lccn.loc.gov/2019016086

www.pantheonbooks.com

Jacket photograph by MirageC/Moment/Getty Images
Jacket design by Adalis Martinez

Printed in the United States of America
First Edition

2 4 6 8 9 7 5 3 1

Pour toute la famille

CONTENTS

INTRODUCTION

The story is told that in a small shtetl in eastern Europe, two peasants got into a fight, and decided to take the matter to the rabbi to resolve the issue. The first farmer went into the rabbi's study, poured his heart out, and when he finished, the rabbi said, "My son, you are right."

Then the second man came in, and with equal fervor told his story, at the end of which the rabbi said, "My son, you are right."

As soon as the second man went out the door, his wife, who had been listening to all this, said in exasperation, "How could you do this? How could you tell both men that each is right?"

To which the rabbi replied, "My dear, you are also right."

This anecdote is the clue to my own feelings about affirmative action. Over a quarter century ago, I wrote a book about the only case the Supreme Court has ever decided concerning affirmative action for women, and I began that study with the same story. I was conflicted when I finished writing it and to some extent remain so to this day. On the one hand, only a bigot would oppose opening wide the doors of opportunity to groups that had previously been excluded because of race, ethnicity, gender, or disability. Having said that, I believe the real question is how to achieve this goal. There are many ways that corporations that once had lily-white male workforces have been able to develop plans to recruit capable women and minority members to work for them, and in doing so tapped into resources of talent they had previously ignored. Other firms, however, took what they thought would be the easy way, setting up quotas for how many African Americans they would hire, how many women, how many Hispanics, and so on. The use of quotas, even if the firms often used the euphemism of "goals," offended many people, and as we shall see, this opposition ran across the political spectrum, from liberals to conservatives.

Opposition to affirmative action proved still stronger when colleges, universities, and professional schools adopted numbers-driven plans, even after they rephrased their goal from affirmative action to compensate for past discrimination to programs intended to achieve current diversity in their classrooms. As someone who has taught at the college and university level for many years, I value diversity, and I and many other teachers could tell countless tales about how much better a class can be when there are people in it who personally relate to the issues under discussion.

While the goal of diversity is praiseworthy, how one gets there matters a great deal. Some schools, like some corporations, managed the process carefully, while others, at least initially, just set up quotas. In public universities, this constituted state action, and thus opened the schools to lawsuits under the Equal Protection Clause of the Fourteenth Amendment. Here again, affirmative action, even if called diversity, aroused both support and condemnation that ranged from stalwart liberals to equally stalwart conservatives. It also split longtime allies, such as the Jewish community and its longtime support of African Americans seeking civil rights.

Ed Koch, the three-time mayor of New York (1978–1989), is a good example of how one could be conflicted about such programs. Peter L. Zimroth, who served as corporate counsel in Koch's administration, recalled,

> Koch deeply believed several things. One is that the whole idea of quotas was an anathema. He was a poor, Jewish person growing up in the city. He believed, I think, that people, anybody, who had the drive and the will to accomplish something had a fair chance to accomplish it. He saw the way quotas kept people down, so he had a very strong opposition to quotas; I think he believed it would diminish the achievements of people who could achieve. If the currency was that anybody who was black or Hispanic got a job through affirmative action, it would just debase their achievements. On the other side, I think he also believed it was a necessity, both politically and morally, to have a diverse government and have a city where there were, in fact, opportunities; that you had to make opportunities for certain people. . . . Both were sincerely held beliefs.

Unlike many authors on this subject, I have not attempted to make a case for or against affirmative action; this is not a polemic on either side. What I have tried to do is not only provide a historical context but also look at how affirmative action affected politics, the economy, higher education, the law, and the groups involved. While we normally associate African Americans with affirmative action and diversity, women and other racial and ethnic minorities have also played a significant role, and sometimes the goals of one group have conflicted with those of another. Who benefited and who suffered is not an easy question, nor is one that asks whether affirmative action succeeded. Similarly, what effect did affirmative action have on its intended beneficiaries—people of color, women, the disabled? The answer in all three cases depends on whom you ask. For example, both Clarence Thomas and Sonia Sotomayor were admitted to the Yale Law School under its affirmative action program. For many years, Justice Thomas claimed that the experience humiliated him, while Justice Sotomayor praised it for giving her a chance she might not have otherwise had. There are, as I said, arguments on all sides. The subject itself is a great puzzle.

There is also an important distinction to be made between what I and others have labeled "soft" versus "hard" affirmative action. The former is about doing away with barriers, of opening doors to groups previously kept out, of genuine outreach. The latter involves quotas, programs that are run either primarily or strictly by the numbers. As we shall see, Title VII of the 1964 Civil Rights Act, the section that banned discrimination, involved only the soft version. Hubert Humphrey, the floor leader for the bill in the Senate, constantly reassured skeptics that Title VII did not include quotas, and in fact specifically banned them. Despite these assurances—and the specific wording of the law itself—government officials in the 1960s and 1970s forced quota-driven programs on government contractors, universities, and other entities receiving federal money, even after the high court declared quotas unconstitutional in the *Bakke* case.

WHAT IS AFFIRMATIVE ACTION? In 1981, the U.S. Commission on Civil Rights defined it as having three components. First, it is remedial: affirmative action denotes efforts that take race, sex, and national origin into account for the purpose of remedying past and present discrimination and its effects. Second, affirmative action seeks ultimately to bring about equal opportunity: it assumes that "race, sex, or national origin [must be considered] in order to eliminate considerations of race, sex, or national origin," that "because of the duration, intensity, scope and intransigence of the discrimination women and minority groups experience, affirmative action plans are needed to assure equal employment opportunity." Third, affirmative action specifies what groups are to be considered part of the "protected class" covered by its policies.

While nearly four decades old, this definition is still useful: affirmative action takes seriously the discrimination certain groups have suffered; it attempts to overcome those prejudices and provide equal opportunity; and it defines who is covered.

This definition, while correct in many ways, does not take into account the methods by which these goals can be met or that its definitions are indiscriminate in distinguishing the different and often unique problems that various groups have faced and which in turn require discrete solutions. The discrimination faced by African Americans is no doubt the best known—slavery, then Jim Crow, and then an endemic racism that still permeates much of American life. This is far different from the prejudice against women or Hispanics or the disabled. The definition also speaks the language of a hard affirmative action, hinting that the government would enforce any remedy, although failing to specify what those remedies might be.

What is missing from the definition is the fact that over the half a century since Kennedy and Johnson started the program, it has constantly been in flux. As one scholar noted, "It is both transient and permanent, precarious and enduring. The history of the policy is complex and shifting." While nearly all proponents of affirmative action have said that it is a temporary measure that will no longer be needed once its goals have been accomplished, those goals have not been achieved; sexism and racism are still with us; and whether one reads an old-fashioned newspaper or gets information on a handheld device, affirmative action stories are still with us.

The definition also does not take into account a basic conflict between affirmative action and the American tradition of individual merit. Both supporters and detractors acknowledge that the victims of injustice belong to some group—African Americans, Hispanics, women, and others. We do not discriminate against Anne because she is vegan; she suffers because she is a woman. Similarly, we may not like that Josh is not a good soccer player, but he faces discrimination because he is black. It is the group characteristic that causes discrimination, and so affirmative action is aimed at somehow helping Anne and Josh, not for their individual quirks, nor even for their individual merits, but because they belong to a group that has suffered from prejudice.

As a result, government, universities, and private corporations have built programs targeted to benefit blacks as a group, women as a group, Hispanics as a group. Unlike Europe, however, we do not have a tradition of group rights in the United States. From the beginning of our nation, success has been predicated on individual merit, and the rights of the individual have been protected. The Fourteenth Amendment's Due Process and Equal Protection Clauses, the bases of many of our freedoms, use the word "person." Nowhere is a group mentioned.

While many countries have some form of affirmative action, Lincoln Caplan argues persuasively that the form remedial programs have taken in the United States makes it a "peculiarly American institution." First of all, its goal is an ideal, one that includes not just the erasure of discrimination but also a correction of decades, even centuries, of bias against people of color, women, and other minorities. Second, affirmative action from the beginning has been a product of trial and error as politicians, interest groups, and the courts have weighed in on how its goals can best—and legitimately—be achieved. Third, affirmative action is not an end in itself, or even a principle. It is a range of means to an end, the goal of equal opportunity or, more recently, diversity.

To this we can add that nearly everyone—both those in government who enforced a hard program of goals and quotas and the different groups that supposedly benefited from them—saw affirmative action as temporary. Initially, the rationale behind the softer version—that is, banning prejudice and opening the gates of opportunity so all could enter—assumed that within some unspecified period of time enough people of color, women, and other groups would have succeeded in the private sector or at the university and that after that a new equilibrium would be established making further affirmative action unnecessary. Even those who backed the hard rules requiring goals and quotas believed the day would come when they would no longer be needed. In the Michigan Law School case (2003), Justice Sandra Day O'Connor wrote, "We expect that 25 years from now the use of racial preferences will no longer be necessary," a comment most observers thought naive even then. Her comment, however, did reflect what the Court had said in prior decisions, that even narrowly tailored plans should not last forever.

Professor Stephen L. Carter of the Yale Law School, a self-acknowledged "affirmative action baby," writes that when he looks around his classroom,

> I realize that the bright and diverse students of color I see before me have a shot, and a good one, at being the last members of the affirmative action generation—or, what is better still, the first members of the post–affirmative action generation, the professionals who will say to a doubting world, "Here are my accomplishments, take me or don't take me on my merits."

Carter wrote those words more than twenty-five years ago, and Yale Law and many other professional schools still need special programs to create the diverse student body that Carter and his colleagues cherish and idealize.

The rationale of affirmative action most frequently cited is the remediation of past discrimination. No one can deny the long history of racism, sexism, and other forms of discrimination in the United States, and those who advocate strong forms of affirmative action argue that it is not enough to stop current discrimination (even if that were possible) but that efforts must be made to erase the effects of past prejudice. The most quoted expression of this view came from President Lyndon Baines Johnson:

> You do not take a person who, for years, has been hobbled by chains and liberate him, bring him up to the starting line of a race and then say, "you are free to compete with all the others," and still justly believe that you have been completely fair. Thus it is not enough to just open the gates of opportunity.

Those who oppose hard affirmative action believe that in fact it is enough to outlaw the various forms of discrimination and then allow all Americans to be judged solely on their merits. They for the most part do agree on what has been called the soft form, or, using Johnson's example, taking off the chains.

Different forms of discrimination, however, may require a wide range of remedies. Getting women into previously all-male colleges and professional schools, for example, proved far easier than getting people of color into previously all-white companies or universities. Discrimination against African Americans included consigning them to inferior schools, which would not make them ready to compete against white students for jobs or seats in college. Women, especially white women, went to the same schools as their brothers and came as ready as their brothers to do well in a job or in law school.

Remedying past discrimination also depends on if the person has been a direct or indirect victim. For example, even conservative jurists on the high court have agreed that if a petitioner can show direct suffering from active discrimination, he or she is entitled to a remedy. A district court found that the Alabama Department of Public Safety had engaged in intentional racial discrimination in hiring and promotion, and as a remedy the court ordered that every time a white was hired or promoted, a qualified black had to be hired or promoted, until the effects of the discrimination had been eradicated. The U.S. Supreme Court affirmed, with the majority concluding that even under a strict scrutiny analysis the plan seemed the only way to remedy an ongoing discrimination.

As Dean Erwin Chemerinsky of Berkeley Law argues, the debate often hinges on how one defines past discrimination, and usually those who back affirmative action plans and those who oppose them cannot agree on a definition. Many groups in the past have suffered discrimination in this country, including nearly every immigrant cohort that came to these shores—Irish, Italians, Jews, and of course, most recently, Asians and Hispanics. Some managed to overcome prejudice and succeed. Are they, too, owed some form of reparation? And who will bear the cost of affirmative action plans? Surely the brunt will fall most heavily on white males who can in no way be held responsible for discrimination that existed years or even decades before their birth.

Yet affirmative action, whether in its soft or hard form, must be sensitive to past discrimination and the burden it places on the current generation of people of color and other minorities. Even if all white males were totally innocent of any form of discrimination (which is hardly the case), the fact remains that African Americans, Hispanics, and many women still labor in the shadow of Jim Crow and other forms of prejudice. They need role models to show them how to succeed in a system for which they may be ill-prepared. They, just as white students, need to be exposed to diversity in the classroom; many have come from small southern towns or big-city barrios and have had little or no exposure to peers of a different color in a setting of equality. They need to be better represented in the government. One of the great accomplishments of the 1965 Voting Rights Acts was that within a few years white southerners found they had to deal with black sheriffs, aldermen, mayors, and state representatives.

Still another goal of affirmative action, according to Dean Chemerinsky, is to enhance the wealth and services available to minority communities. Getting more African Americans into medical school will, as experience shows, increase the number of doctors who practice in black neighborhoods. Set-asides for minority-owned businesses will divert more government money to owners of small businesses and their employees. Although this argument has been put forward by practically all civil rights groups, the high court has never accepted affirmative action as a legitimate form of wealth transfer. Justice Lewis F. Powell Jr. argued that merely training more black doctors would not necessarily result in more doctors actually practicing in minority communities. The goal might better be achieved, he suggested, by offering incentives for doctors to work in underserved areas.

THE LITERATURE ON affirmative action is immense, and continues to grow, because, as some scholars argue, no other issue divides Americans more. Some of this literature is more philosophical than analytical, involving moral and/or ethical reasons to support or oppose affirmative action. While I note some of these arguments, for the most part I have chosen not to take part in that dialogue; the debates in the courts, in legislatures, and in the popular press are more than sufficient in this investigation.

Nor, more than half a century after Lyndon Johnson gave his speech about taking the chains off a runner, has the issue abated. One can pick up a newspaper and often find the story of a company boasting about its fair employment practices ("Minorities Getting Slice of Contract Pie, MGM Says") or how well it treats its minority workers ("Intel Diversity Report Shows No Pay Gap Between Its Male, Female Workers"). Some colleagues, aware I was working on this book, asked how I would bring it to a close, because every day there is a newspaper article dealing with the subject in one form or another.

It will be plain to the reader that while I support many of the goals of affirmative action, I am far less sympathetic to some of the means used to reach those goals. I strongly favor what I have called the "soft" version, throwing open gates of opportunity, actively recruiting women and minorities, and making sure that once hired or admitted to a school, they do not suffer discrimination because of their race or gender. I am not enamored of the "hard" version, which is numbers-driven. Many liberals as well as conservatives oppose quotas. The supposedly more idealistic notion of goals, of trying to get a student body or a workforce "that looks like America," sounds wonderful. But if, as an example, we say that African Americans make up 12 percent of the population, then we need an entering class in which one out of eight admits is black, that to me constitutes a quota. I also am very suspicious when we get a "goal" of between 8 and 12 percent of a particular group, because the lower number is in effect a quota. We will have 8 percent, and if we get more, that's good too. And yet, I must also admit that in some circumstances only a numbers-driven plan has any chance of breaking down long-established racial and gender barriers. As Justice Harry Blackmun and others have said, in order to get past race and gender, we have to take race and gender into account.

It will also be clear that I suspect many of the statistics that show affirmative action has either succeeded or failed. There is no question that today we have a larger African American middle class than in the 1960s and that women, while still shut out of many of the Fortune 500 boardrooms, have nonetheless done well in business and the professions. On the other hand, the latest news indicates that African American students in many schools are not finishing their undergraduate degree in six years; many are not finishing at all. It is also beyond doubt that racism and sexism are still very much with us, as events during the 2016 presidential campaign and the first two years of the Trump administration have clearly shown.

What I have tried to eschew is a blanket endorsement or condemnation of affirmative action, primarily because compensatory programs or efforts to achieve diversity are rarely simple and straightforward. There are so many different plans, some of which have worked and others that have not. Some are relatively simple, and others far more convoluted. I said earlier that I remain conflicted, but after the research and writing of this book, I think I have a better understanding of why that is so. Affirmative action can be neither praised nor condemned in the abstract; rather, judgments must rely on context.

In the Michigan cases (discussed in chapter 16), the Supreme Court struck down the affirmative action plan used by the undergraduate college because it was crude and made race the determining factor in the admissions process. The court upheld the law school plan because it took many considerations, including race, into account, but did not make race the primary reason for admitting a student. Discussion about affirmative action at a general level, making all plans either good or bad, is futile. We all believe, or at least I hope we do, that at the very least discrimination in employment and education should be banned. That does not mean, however, that we can ignore the legacies of racism and sexism and other prejudices; at times a stronger affirmative action might be needed, and at others would be unnecessary. Some of the techniques that have been utilized in the name of creating greater opportunity are questionable at best, while others can and should be easily defended.

In other words, everything depends on context, but the problem is that a person of color or a woman or a person with a physical disability may view that context differently than I do, or a legislator, or a judge, or a blue-collar white male worker does. If we are to understand affirmative action—what brought it into being, what it has accomplished or failed to accomplish, which plans have been good and which bad—then we really have to make those judgments on an individual basis. This book is not a panegyric for or against affirmative action but an effort to provide a context in which we can make sense of parts of this puzzle.

Gaithersburg, Maryland

PART I

FROM KENNEDY TO REAGAN

CHAPTER I

AFFIRMATIVE ACTION
BEFORE KENNEDY

It is plain that the Fourteenth Amendment was not intended to prohibit measures designed to remedy the effects of the Nation's past treatment of Negroes. The Congress that passed the Fourteenth Amendment is the same Congress that passed the 1866 Freedmen's Bureau Act, an Act that provided many of its benefits only to Negroes. . . . After the Civil War our Government started several "affirmative action programs."

—THURGOOD MARSHALL

Studies of affirmative action often begin with either John F. Kennedy's Executive Order 10925 or the more important one by Lyndon Johnson a few years later. However, some forms of affirmative action—programs that would open opportunity or provide benefits for groups hitherto excluded—go back to Reconstruction following the Civil War. The phrase itself, though, was never used to describe these programs, nor did there exist a coherent set of governmental policies designed to attack racism and economic discrimination.

In the Civil Rights Act of 1866, Congress declared that "all persons within the jurisdiction of the United States shall have the same rights in every State and Territory, to make and enforce contracts, to sue, be parties, give evidence, and to the full equal benefit of all laws and proceedings for the security of persons and property as is enjoyed by white citizens." The law also empowered the president to use the national armed forces, if necessary, to implement these provisions and made it a federal crime to interfere with a person's exercise of civil rights.

President Andrew Johnson had no intention of using these powers, and in fact vetoed the bill, characterizing it as illegal because it contained "a distinction of race . . . made to operate in favor of the colored and against the white race." Johnson also attacked the measure as race legislation that would encourage a life of wasteful laziness for southern blacks. Johnson's veto message is worth examining, because in it one can hear the same arguments against affirmative action that will be common a century later.

Johnson disliked the citizenship provision, because it immediately made citizens of former slaves while European immigrants had to wait several years to qualify through naturalization. This "proposed a discrimination against large numbers of intelligent, worthy and patriotic foreigners in favor of the negro." He opposed federal enforcement of the rights given the freedmen, because it affords "discriminatory protection to colored persons." These arrangements "established for the security of the colored race safeguards which go infinitely beyond any that the General Government has ever provided for the white race. In fact, the distinction of race and color is by the bill made to operate in favor of the colored and against the white race." In response, Congress passed the measure over Johnson's veto. Unfortunately, no president in the rest of the nineteenth century used any of these powers, nor did any of them try to enforce the rights embedded in the Fourteenth and Fifteenth Amendments to the Constitution. Congress passed additional civil rights legislation in 1870, 1872, and 1875 and utilized the occupation army as well as the Freedmen's Bureau to try to give former slaves access not only to political rights but to economic opportunities as well.

As Congress took steps to provide the former slaves with opportunities previously denied to them, we also see the first indications of what will later be called "white backlash" and "reverse discrimination." A Florida slaveholder fumed that those who abolished slavery wanted to "give the nigger more privileges than the white man." In 1874, the *Chicago Tribune* ran an editorial in opposition to proposed federal legislation prohibiting racial discrimination in public accommodations. Titled "The Nigger School?," the editorial asked, "Is it not time for the colored race to stop playing baby?" Justice Joseph Bradley in the *Civil Rights Cases* accused blacks of seeking preferential treatment by demanding the end of caste-like exclusions. "When a man has emerged from slavery," he lectured, "there must be some stage in the progress of his elevation when he takes the rank of a mere citizen and ceases to be the special favorite of the law."

Opposition from whites also greeted the proposed Fifteenth

An 1868 etching of a soldier protecting former slaves under the aegis of the Freedmen's Bureau, the first federal agency established to help African Americans.

Amendment, which gave blacks the right to vote, and this opposition came not only from the South. Senator James Doolittle of Wisconsin argued that if the former slaves could vote, they could be voted for, and "if they can be voted for, they can be elected members of the legislature, . . . members of the Senate of the United States; generals in your army and . . . they might perhaps in the end elect some Negro as President of the United States."

In addition to constitutional amendments and civil rights statutes, Congress established the Bureau of Refugees, Freedmen, and Abandoned Lands, commonly called the Freedmen's Bureau. At its beginning, the agency helped both newly freed slaves and white war refugees with housing, employment, food, legal advice, and education, things that could easily be seen as part of a more modern general welfare program. The original charter ran only one year, but by the time it came up for renewal in 1866, its sole clientele were African Americans, and one scholar claims that its activities "most prefigured the race conscious remedies enacted in the 1960s and after." The bureau continued to operate under the aegis of the U.S. Army. Its task became harder as southern opposition increased, and it finally went out of business in 1872.

Frederick Douglass, the runaway slave who became an abolitionist leader, is often cited for the proposition that Negroes did not want any special treatment. In lectures to white audiences, he would ask

Frederick Douglass in 1870, at age fifty-three. A runaway slave who became a powerful abolitionist orator, he said he wanted no favors for his race, and certainly not until after they had attained education and political rights.

them to let blacks sink or swim on their own and say that character, not color, was all that mattered. "Do nothing with us," he declared, "and if the Negro cannot stand on his own legs, let him fall also." But at the same time, he argued that before the black man could be judged on his own merits, the handicaps of years of slavery, little or no education, and lack of experience in self-government had to be erased. Special federal legislation for safeguarding the rights of the freedmen had to be maintained until they were no longer needed. "We certainly hope that the time will come when the colored man in America shall cease to require special attention," Douglass declared. "But that time has not yet come, and is not even at the door."

Nor would it be in his lifetime, or in those of his children. In 1883, the Supreme Court severely limited congressional power to protect the former slaves, and thirteen years later approved racial segregation under the rubric of separate but equal in *Plessy v. Ferguson*. By then, however, the abolitionists and their desire to see justice as well as freedom for the former slaves had passed from the scene. Whites in the North, while they opposed slavery, did not believe African Americans were their social or intellectual equals, and were perfectly happy to let the southern states work out whatever system of racial relations they wanted. Where there had been some protest against the Court's civil rights decision in 1883, there was scarcely a peep outside black-owned newspapers following *Plessy*. Race relations played no part in the nation's policy-making dialogue for the next forty years, until the Great Depression.

THERE IS A TENDENCY, especially in these early years, to focus solely on the African American experience. The modern women's movement and agitation by Latinos, the disabled, and the LGBT community were all in the future. There is one incident during World War I, however, that deserves a brief look.

We are familiar with Rosie the Riveter and the tens of thousands of women who flooded into defense plants during World War II. What is not as well known is that a similar development occurred a quarter century earlier in World War I. Because the United States had a much shorter involvement (less than nineteen months) and sent far fewer troops overseas, the available pool of male workers dried up more slowly. But dry up it did, especially after the passage of the 1917 Draft Act. We have a case study that highlights not so much the efforts of management to hire women as the hostility of all-male unions to even letting women work as conductors on street railways during the emergency.

Not only had conductors and motormen traditionally been the highest-paying positions on street railways, but the jobs had been reserved exclusively for men. Men also filled most of the laboring positions, although some women worked as ticket sellers. By January 1918, however, streetcar companies in nearly every big city began hiring women as conductors, or as a New York firm called them, "conductorettes." Before long, women conductors became a common sight in New York, Detroit, St. Louis, Baltimore, and other cities. In May 1918, the Kansas City Railway Company acknowledged a shortage of two hundred men for its car service and informed its riders that the only way to maintain service would be by hiring women conductors as "a war measure" and acknowledged this meant at least until the end of the war.

Prior to the war, about half of all streetcar employees belonged to the Amalgamated Association of Street, Electric Railway, and Motor Coach Employees of America. In May 1918, the executive board of the union announced its unalterable opposition to the employment of women as conductors or motormen—even on a temporary basis. At the beginning of August 1918, the U.S. Employment Service (a wartime agency set up to match available labor to unfilled jobs) announced a shortage of 36,000 skilled workers for northern Ohio. The Cleveland Street Railway Company president hired 190 women to begin work as conductors and made it clear that this constituted a wartime measure.

The local chapter of the association immediately challenged this act and threatened to pull its men out on strike. The company responded that no man would be replaced by a woman and that all men would retain their seniority rights. The union demanded an investigation by the National War Labor Board, which issued contradictory reports. We need not go into all the twists and turns, except to note that no matter what the company or the National War Labor Board suggested, the union fought against any plan that allowed women to work on the cars, and even went on a three-day strike at the beginning of November, practically crippling the city. A month later the National War Labor Board issued a ruling supporting the women workers and ordering the company to put them back to work. Again the union struck. Only the relatively quick return of men in uniform to their civilian jobs ended the matter.

The opposition of all-white, all-male unions against allowing women, people of color, or other groups to get jobs in "their" industry would be an ongoing characteristic of union attitudes toward affirmative action five decades down the road.

THE EXTENT OF THE Great Depression can only partially be told by facts. Between 1929 and 1932, industrial production dropped more than half, while business construction fell from $949 million to a scant $74 million. Steel plants, the backbone of industry, ran at 12 percent of capacity, and the stock market, which had stood at 452 on 3 September 1929, bottomed out at 52 in July 1932. The greater tragedy, of course, involved the unimaginable toll of human suffering—thirteen million unemployed, two million homeless and riding the country in boxcars, people living in tar-papered shacks dubbed Hoovervilles, and families fighting outside the back doors of restaurants for scraps of food.

There is debate over whether Franklin D. Roosevelt's New Deal solved the Depression, but at the very least various New Deal agencies and programs fed people, provided jobs, and perhaps most important of all gave Americans hope. But the Roosevelt administration, with a few exceptions, paid little attention to the misery of black Americans. It is not that blacks did not get any help; most of the legislation declared there would be no discrimination based on race, color, or creed—only it did not quite work out that way.

One example is the Civilian Conservation Corps (CCC), which provided young men between the ages of seventeen and twenty-eight with work, food, and shelter. The men planted trees, worked on flood control projects, wore uniforms, and got three meals a day. By August 1935, the CCC had over 500,000 enrollees, of whom 50,000 were black. Nearly all the African Americans lived in segregated camps, worked in subordinate positions, and were supervised by white officers.

Two of the most popular New Deal programs, the 1933 Home Owners Loan Corporation and the 1934 Federal Housing Administration (FHA) helped numerous families either to hold on to their houses or to move from rental status to home ownership. Both agencies not only supported segregated neighborhoods and racial covenants but encouraged them. From its inception, one scholar wrote, the "FHA set itself up as the protector of the all-white neighborhood. . . . Racism was bluntly written into the FHA official manual" and blocked Negroes, Asians, Mexicans, and indigenous peoples from buying into white neighborhoods.

The centerpiece of the New Deal, the National Industrial Recovery Act (NIRA), included a federally established minimum wage. Employers, in order to pay their white employees the new rate, could fire their black workers who had been paid far less. The National Recovery Administration (NRA), the agency set up to implement the NIRA, established numerous labor codes, but excluded over three million blacks who worked as domestics, farmworkers, or unskilled laborers, and permitted wage differentials between black and white workers. It is little wonder that in the ghettos the NRA meant "Negro Removal Act" or "No Rights at All."

Some New Deal agencies proved more sympathetic than others. Harold Ickes, a longtime champion of civil rights, headed the Public Works Administration (PWA) and hired Robert Weaver (later to be secretary of housing and urban development in the Johnson administration) as his adviser on race relations. Weaver persuaded Ickes to require that all PWA construction contractors hire the same percentage of black workers as recorded in the 1930 census for each city. In a similar vein, David E. Lilienthal set hiring and training quotas for the Tennessee Valley Authority (TVA). Although the TVA worked primarily in southern states, and the PWA had many southern projects, Ickes and Lilienthal managed not to offend southern congressmen. There were, after all, very few African American engineers at the time, nor were there many skilled tradesmen. While blacks benefited from the hiring plans, most wound up working as unskilled laborers.

The term "affirmative action" appeared for the first time in federal law in the 1935 National Labor Relations Act, commonly known as the Wagner Act. The law gave federal blessing to workers to organize and bargain collectively and created the National Labor Relations Board (NLRB) to investigate and resolve alleged unfair labor practices, with a mandate to "take such affirmative action . . . as will effectuate the policies of this Act." Here again, the phrase does not mean what it did later, namely, a program seeking to employ members of minority groups; the beneficiaries would be workers wanting to unionize. The National Association for the Advancement of Colored People (NAACP) and other civil rights groups had lobbied for an antidiscrimination amendment, but that idea had no chance in a southern-dominated Congress.

The Wagner Act recognized unions as the workers' sole bargaining agents, and as a result African Americans were effectively kept out of skilled work by the all-white trade unions of the American Federation of Labor (AFL). The craft unions in the AFL building trades earned their reputation as the most hostile to blacks by barring them completely from skilled construction work. Although the industrial-based unions in the new Congress of Industrial Organizations (CIO) appeared more welcoming to minorities, national leaders soon discovered that they had to tread carefully so as not to lose white members unwilling to give up the advantages they had in jobs, education, housing, and legal rights. When the AFL and CIO merged in 1955, the commitment to fighting for the interests of black workers disappeared, and the former CIO unions soon became "part of the white labor establishment in privileging whiteness."

One could find an occasional bright spot, such as in 1935, when Harry Hopkins asked his all-male staff at the Works Progress Administration (WPA) if they should pay women the same wages as men. All of them said no, with one exception. Aubrey Williams, head of the National Youth Administration, alone said they should be paid equally. Hopkins wanted to know, "What makes you think you could get away with it?" Williams responded that he did not care if he could "get away with it," but he believed it the right thing to do. To this Hopkins said, "Do you know who disagrees with you? The Secretary of Labor—a woman!" The first female cabinet member in history, Secretary of Labor Frances Perkins, favored tradition. But Williams insisted, and Hopkins agreed. Women who worked for the WPA got the same wages as men, but few women worked in skilled or professional jobs. Moreover, women seeking certification for WPA employment had to show that their families included no able-bodied males.

A few—very few—New Deal measures contained provisions barring discrimination. The Hatch Act of 1939, which restricted federal workers' political activities, declared it unlawful to deprive "any person of any employment . . . made possible by an Act of Congress . . . on account of race, creed, or color." A 1940 measure extending the merit system to several newly created federal agencies had a similar clause, and that same year Roosevelt issued Executive Order 8587 prohibiting racial discrimination in the federal service. Despite the fine wording, the administration did little to enforce either the legislative provisions or the executive order, and as one scholar noted, "the policy of nondiscrimination was more a sentiment than a reality."

Recent scholarship has found the origins of the civil rights movement in the New Deal years, and especially in the Roosevelt administration's willingness to use the powers of the federal government to effect social and economic as well as political change. According to Dean Risa Goluboff of the University of Virginia School of Law, because of southern power in Congress the Civil Rights Division (CRD) of the Justice Department could not fight "separate but equal" or any other state-sponsored form of discrimination. It could and did attack working conditions on southern farms that in many places approached the status of peonage, a form of near slavery that the Supreme Court had earlier declared unconstitutional. By using the Thirteenth Amendment's Enforcement Clause, the CRD successfully helped black farmers break discriminatory labor contracts. Moreover, the willingness of the Congress of Industrial Organizations to accept black members, and to help African Americans organize, forms another part of what Goluboff and others call the "long civil rights movement." The political and ideological changes wrought by the New Deal in the 1930s and 1940s, slight as they might have been, led directly to the judicial and legislative victories of the 1950s and 1960s.

The National Association for the Advancement of Colored People, founded in 1909, for the most part had little to do with the labor-centered efforts of the CRD and fought its economic battles in the courts trying to secure equal pay for black teachers. This made a great deal of sense, because many NAACP members belonged to the middle-of-the-road black middle class or professional groups. Yet well before the Montgomery bus boycott of 1955–1956, men and women such as Ella Baker and Robert Williams, who came from far more activist backgrounds, worked in the South to defend victims of discrimination, organized interracial trade unions, pushed for social and sexual equality between blacks and whites and men and women, and insisted upon the rights of blacks not just to vote but to run for office. Other activists fought economic and social discrimination in the North.

Certainly the economic position of African Americans at this time cannot be described as anything other than depressed, with the vast majority trapped in poverty and no roads open out of that trap. When Gunnar Myrdal published *An American Dilemma* in 1944, most blacks lived in the South and on the land as laborers or sharecroppers; only one southern black farmer in eight owned his own land. Nationally, only one in twenty black men engaged in nonmanual, white-collar work of some sort; most labored in low-paid, insecure, manual jobs. Six in ten African American women were household servants who often worked twelve-hour days for pitifully low wages. In 1951, 47 percent of blacks and other minorities had an annual income of under $3,000, compared with 17 percent of whites. The median annual income for minorities stood at $3,171, that of whites at $6,107.

There is no claim for affirmative action or anything that even faintly resembled it during these years; that would come much, much later. Because we too often see civil rights primarily as a legal and legislative battle, with an emphasis on the eradication of state-sponsored segregation, we need to remember that from the beginning economic opportunity and the elimination of discriminatory labor practices played an important role in the black struggle.

INTERESTINGLY, THE Supreme Court heard its first affirmative action case in 1938, although neither the justices nor anyone else recognized it as such. Despite the near-total dominance of Jim Crow in the southern states, northern blacks saw the beginnings of an organized resistance to racial discrimination. By the end of World War I, some journalists were writing about a "New Negro" who "was not content to move along the lines of least resistance." The older generation of black leaders like Booker T. Washington passed from the scene, replaced by new leaders not averse to confrontational tactics. A number of cities saw campaigns in the black community of "Don't Buy Where You Can't Work" and the beginnings of demands that white-owned establishments hire blacks in proportion to their numbers in the community, a key element of later affirmative action.

The Sanitary Grocery store chain (which became Safeway) operated over two hundred stores, a warehouse, and a bakery in the District of Columbia and employed both whites and African Americans. The chain opened a new store on Northwest Eleventh Street, a white neighborhood, and advertised for persons "familiar with the trade in the vicinity." All the people with such qualifications turned out to be Caucasian, and the New Negro Alliance (NNA) demanded that the chain hire blacks in managerial and sales positions not only in the new store but in other outlets as well. When management refused, on the grounds that to do so would require firing white employees, the NNA picketed the store with signs saying "Do Your Part! Buy Where You Can Work! No Negroes Employed Here!" Sanitary sought an injunction against the NNA and secured one in the lower court. The NNA then appealed to the U.S. Supreme Court, which heard the case in early March 1938 and handed down its decision three weeks later.

Justice Owen J. Roberts, speaking for a 6–2 majority, vacated the injunction on the grounds that legitimate picketing was protected from judicial interference by the Norris-LaGuardia Act. He then went on to say,

> The desire for fair and equitable conditions of employment on the part of persons of any race, color, or persuasion, and the removal of discriminations against them by reason of their race or religious beliefs is quite as important to those concerned as fairness and equity in terms and conditions of employment can be to trade or craft unions or any form of labor organiza-

tion or association. Race discrimination by an employer may reasonably be deemed more unfair and less excusable than discrimination against workers on the ground of union affiliation.

The Court did not go into the merits of the NNA arguments on proportional hiring; it did not have to, because it could resolve the matter on simpler labor law grounds.

WITH THE APPROACH OF American involvement in World War II, defense industries began adding workers, most of whom were white. Racial prejudice in both the defense companies and the labor unions kept blacks on the lowest rung of unskilled and janitorial employees. The president of North American Aviation declared that company policy barred hiring Negroes as mechanics or aircraft workers. When African Americans tried to join the union so they could work at the Boeing plant in Seattle, the head of the union declared that his men had "been called upon to make many sacrifices for defense and had made them gladly, but this is asking too much." Other industries

A. Philip Randolph, the influential head of the Brotherhood of Sleeping Car Porters, who threatened a march on Washington in 1941 unless President Roosevelt acted to give more defense jobs to black people.

had similar policies. The president of Standard Steel in Kansas City announced, "We have not had a Negro worker in twenty-five years, and we do not plan to start now," a view held by many employers.

Black leaders wanted Roosevelt to take more positive action, and A. Philip Randolph, the head of the Brotherhood of Sleeping Car Porters, threatened a march on Washington in early July 1941. He succeeded in mobilizing African American leaders and organizations across the country and declared that as many as 100,000 people would attend. Not only would the march demonstrate the extent of black anger with continued discrimination in the defense industry; it would be a demand that Roosevelt do something about it. Randolph and his colleagues well understood that given the southern dominance of Congress, no chance existed for any meaningful legislation. They wanted the president to act through an executive order.

Roosevelt opposed the march from the beginning. Any strong statement on his part risked alienating southern congressional leaders whose support he needed. The existence of 100,000 blacks in Washington could easily lead to rioting and bloodshed, and the president remembered how Herbert Hoover had felt compelled to call out the army to disperse the bonus marchers in 1932, and they only numbered 43,000. Moreover, rioting and violence could easily spread across the country. The most urgent item on the president's agenda involved getting the country ready should it be drawn into the war, as he believed it would be. Congress had barely approved a draft act the year before and had only recently passed the Lend-Lease Act to help Great Britain. While Roosevelt understood the gravity of Randolph's demands, he had other problems that seemed to him far more serious. Worst of all, 100,000 people protesting racial prejudice would undermine the administration's arguments about the dangers of fascism and racism in Germany.

The president first sent a letter to the co-chairs of the Office of Production Management, which oversaw all federal government defense contracts, reiterating the administration's opposition to discrimination. Because such a letter had no force, the march leaders told Roosevelt it would not do. He then sent Mayor Fiorello La Guardia of New York and Mrs. Roosevelt, both known as friends of civil rights, to try to dissuade Randolph from going ahead, but to no avail. The president had no choice but to meet with Randolph and Walter White of the NAACP, less than two weeks before the planned protest. One week later, Roosevelt issued Executive Order 8802:

Now, Therefore, by virtue of the authority vested in me by the Constitution and the statutes, and as a prerequisite to the successful conduct of our national defense production effort, I do hereby reaffirm the policy of the United States that there shall be no discrimination in the employment of workers in defense industries or government because of race, creed, color, or national origin, and I do hereby declare that it is the duty of employers and of labor organizations, in furtherance of said policy and of this Order, to provide for the full and equitable participation of all workers in defense industries, without discrimination because of race, creed, color, or national origin.

To implement this policy, Roosevelt created the President's Committee on Fair Employment Practice (FEPC) to investigate complaints of discrimination not only by defense contractors but by federal agencies as well. For the first time since Reconstruction, the country had a federal agency devoted exclusively to minority problems.

The FEPC, however, only had power to investigate, and even if it found discriminatory practices, it could only publicize them. It could not force employers to change their hiring procedures. Nonetheless, by exposing racial discrimination by some of the biggest defense contractors in the country, the FEPC, through publicity, had some success in helping black workers. Although the FEPC managed to keep on operating through most of the war, in 1945 southern opposition in Congress led to its demise. The government no longer had any administrative mechanism to investigate discrimination in government contracts, while the Civil Service Commission took over the responsibility for ensuring equal opportunity in federal agencies. Little progress had been made.

Because much of the nation's defense manufacturing took place in the North, a massive migration of blacks from the South went north to cities like Detroit seeking work. The exodus had actually started before World War I, and altogether some 6 million blacks moved northward between 1910 and 1960, one of the greatest internal migrations in the country's history. Of this number, some 1.4 million moved north and west during the 1940s. The migrants sought to escape the legally enforced apartheid south of the Mason-Dixon Line, but they quickly encountered equally strong racial discrimination, especially in employment. Whites and their unions controlled the defense plants' workforce and were willing to allow blacks only in the low-paying unskilled and janitorial jobs. Black men were almost totally excluded from the great bulk of war industries. "Discrimination is the rule practically everywhere."

When blacks challenged white-only practices, they met with bitter opposition. In 1944, for example, Philadelphia narrowly avoided a race riot when white transit workers struck to protest the desegregation of job classifications and the promotion of some blacks in the Philadelphia Transportation Company. In complaints that would become familiar a quarter century later, whites charged that Negroes were unfairly taking their jobs. In Philadelphia as elsewhere, transit companies—in fact most companies—classified certain jobs by race. Bus drivers, motormen, and conductors were white men's jobs; blacks worked as porters and car cleaners. No black man, no matter his intelligence or ability, could work in a white man's job. To avert the crisis in Philadelphia, Roosevelt ordered the seizure of the company and called out the National Guard to maintain order.

UNLIKE IN WORLD WAR I, American participation in World War II lasted much longer—nearly four years—and involved more than fifteen million men. The pool of unemployed men shrank almost overnight as those with skills found jobs in defense industries and others joined the armed forces. Once again, the economy demanded that women go to work. In some communities, Roosevelt declared in 1942, "employers dislike to employ women. In others they are reluctant to hire Negroes. . . . We can no longer afford to indulge such prejudices or practices." The government started the "Rosie the Riveter" campaign, urging women to get out of the house and into defense plants. According to some studies, approximately six million women entered the workforce, about two million of them in defense-related industries. By the end of the war, almost nineteen million women were working, the highest number in American history.

In World War II, the American public supported women workers. A few months after Pearl Harbor, a poll reported that 68 percent of the public and 73 percent of women favored drafting single women between the ages of twenty-one and thirty-five for training in war jobs. As one writer noted, the key word was "single," for even during the war most Americans expected mothers to stay at home with their children. While the federal government and some plants set up day-care centers, many of the women workers had just graduated from high school and were unmarried.

A 1943 picture of Jessie May Turner, a "Rosie the Riveter," who was among thousands of women who took over jobs in defense industries when men went off to war.

The Gallup poll also asked whether women replacing men in factories should be paid the same wages as men. Seven out of ten men said yes, while 85 percent of women as well as the Roosevelt administration endorsed equal pay. The War Labor Board issued an order directing that equal wages be paid to women who performed "comparable quality and quantity of work" as men. Just as with government regulations regarding African Americans, the rule seems to have been honored more in the breach than in practice. At the end of the war, women left defense industries in droves, making way for the veterans returning from overseas. While the example of Rosie the Riveter seems not to have affected women's ideas in the years immediately following the war and had no impact on postwar government policy, it would be a powerful example when the women's movement of the 1960s began.

IN THE NORTH, New York became the first state to ban racial discrimination in employment with the 1945 Ives-Quinn Act. Predictably, racists there condemned the statute. Nonetheless, within a short time, more than twenty states passed laws barring discrimination in government employment, with half of the statutes specifically mentioning race and religion, although none required proportionality in hiring. Before long it became common for state governments to have antidiscrimination clauses in contracts with private businesses. The enforcement of these clauses, however, varied widely, but the agencies did collect data that proved useful later. By the mid-1950s, these state agencies as well as civil rights advocates had decided that the principal problem in minority employment was no longer in hiring but in promotion and that a major stumbling block to promoting African Americans was union rules regarding seniority. The seniority system would time and again pit minority aspirations against entrenched union rules, rules that the unions had fought hard for in the 1930s and 1940s.

Only a few years later, the Supreme Court heard what appeared to be a labor case but again involved what would soon be called affirmative action. In 1947, a group of black and white protesters in a predominantly black neighborhood picketed a Lucky grocery store in Richmond, California. They carried signs that read, "Lucky Won't Hire Negro Clerks in Proportion to Negro Trade—Don't Patronize." The protesters wanted Lucky's managers to hire blacks until their proportion of the workforce equaled the proportion of black patronage—about 50 percent.

Lucky secured an injunction against the picketers from a state court, but the protesters kept on marching and declared the First Amendment protected their activity. The California Supreme Court held the picketing illegal, because its goal of proportionate employment would violate the state's common law. "If Lucky had yielded to the demands of the petitioners, its resultant hiring policy would have constituted, as to a proportion of its employees, the equivalent of both a closed shop and a closed union in favor of the Negro race." If the picketers succeeded in their demand, then "other races, white, yellow, brown and red, would have equal rights to demand discriminatory hiring on a racial basis."

This idea seemed to alarm the justices of the U.S. Supreme Court as well. Felix Frankfurter spoke for a unanimous bench in upholding the California decision. "To deny California the right to ban picketing," he wrote,

> would mean that there could be no prohibition on the pressure of picketing to secure proportional employment on ancestral grounds of Hungarians in Cleveland, of Germans in Milwaukee, of Portuguese in New Bedford, of Mexicans in San Anto-

nio, of the numerous minority groups in New York, and so on through the whole gamut of racial and religious concentrations in various cities. . . . The differences in cultural traditions instead of adding flavor and variety to our common citizenry might well be hardened into hostilities by leave of law.

The arguments made in the *Hughes* case, both in the state tribunals and in the high court, anticipate nearly all the arguments that would be made in later affirmative action cases. Beyond that, the idea of quotas by itself divided opponents of racism and for some seemed worse than racial discrimination itself. Although a local branch of the NAACP helped sponsor the picketing against the Lucky stores, some members of the national organization expressed their discomfort. The protest "appeared to condone a quota system" that could easily backfire on blacks in areas without large numbers of Negroes. Moreover, they claimed, quotas were at variance with the principles of equality and merit for which the NAACP stood.

This internal debate within the NAACP, in fact within the African American community, went far beyond the Sanitary stores in the nation's capital or the Lucky stores in California. Throughout the 1930s, black groups sponsored boycotts and picketing in a number of cities demanding either that Negroes be hired in all-white stores if there was significant black trade or that more Negroes be hired proportional either to the population or to the business they did with targeted stores.

Within the black community, however, leaders disagreed on what should be done. W. E. B. Du Bois and others argued that the development of strong black institutions, fostering the preservation of African American cultural identity, provided the best way to achieve a non-racist society. The notion of "double consciousness" captured the Du Bois strategy: black Americans should identify as both African and American, and the dismantling of racism should not require the cultural assimilation of black values into white social norms.

Others, like Walter White and Roy Wilkins of the NAACP, also wanted to destroy racial segregation, but they wanted "inclusion" rather than pluralism for black people. The long-term existence of separate all-black institutions stood against their goal of a color-blind society. Bayard Rustin, who would later be an adviser to Martin Luther King Jr., said he looked forward to the day when Harlem would cease to exist as a segregated, identifiable black neighborhood. Blacks should be assimilated into the larger culture.

THE DEBATE HAD PICKED UP steam during the war, when it became clear that despite the need for manpower, the armed forces had no desire to allow African American inductees to serve except in segregated units or, in the case of the navy, as mess attendants. The famed African American historian John Hope Franklin wanted to join up and saw an ad that the navy needed personnel to handle paperwork, men who could type, operate simple business machines, and perform other office chores. He rushed down to the recruitment office and said he could do all those things. "The recruiter looked at me with what appeared to be a combination of incredulity and distress," Franklin recalled. "He simply said I was lacking in *one* qualification and that was color."

Robert Byrd, later to be a powerful senator from West Virginia, loathed the very idea of any colored person serving in the armed forces. "Never in the world," he wrote to the rabid racist senator from Mississippi Theodore Bilbo,

> will I be convinced that race mixing in any field is good. . . .
> I am loyal to my country and know but reverence to her flag,
> BUT I shall never submit to fight beneath that banner with a
> negro by my side. Rather I should die a thousand times, and
> see this old glory trampled in the dirt never to rise again, than
> to see this beloved land of ours become degraded by race mon-
> grels, a throwback to the blackest specimen from the wilds.

The black experience in World War I, with the overt racism in the army and the navy, left black leaders wary of supporting another war where they would again be marginalized. W. E. B. Du Bois wrote in July 1940 that while he was sorry for all the brutality and bloodshed in Europe and Asia, "the hysterical cries of the preachers of democracy for Europe leave us cold. We want democracy in Alabama, Arkansas, in Mississippi and Michigan, in the District of Columbia." Now was not the time to be silent. "A lily-white navy cannot fight for a free world. A jim crow army cannot fight for a free world. Jim crow strategy, no matter on how grand a scale, cannot build a free world."

Nor was Du Bois alone. In November 1941, the black press car- ried stories about the treatment of Negroes in the army—race riots at Fort Oswego, fighting at Camp Davis, Jim Crow conditions elsewhere. When the Office of War Information put out a pamphlet, *Negroes and the War,* it soft-pedaled the discrimination rampant in the military and recounted the insults hurled at Jesse Owens at the 1936 Olympics in Berlin and included a reminder that Joe Louis, "*our* champion," had knocked out the German champion. Despite great efforts to get the Roosevelt administration or the leaders of the military to abandon segregation, nothing happened.

The military made no bones about its policies, but one point is worth noting. The strength of the Negro personnel in the army would be maintained "on a general basis of the proportion of the Negro population in the country." Black officers would be assigned to "Negro units officered by colored personnel," but because there were so few black officers, whites led most of these units. There would be no effort to change the policy of segregation where it existed. What no one, either in the upper echelons of government and the military or among black leaders, foresaw was the impact of military service upon young black men.

Black recruits often found themselves, for the first time in their lives, provided with adequate food and decent shelter. There were no differentials in pay between black and white soldiers. Because so many southern blacks and whites were illiterate, both the army and the navy set up "Special Training Units" to teach basic skills such as the ability to write a letter, read signs, use a clock, and do basic arithmetic. Of the black soldiers and sailors in these special units, fully 90 percent were assigned to regular units at the end of their schooling. Seven in ten went on to receive advanced training, and half of this group applied after the war for assistance under the GI Bill. Although they faced a great deal of prejudice, many of them managed to go to college under the bill, thus creating a large number of not only literate but educated African Americans. We need not go into greater detail here except to say that when black veterans returned home after service, they refused to accept the old segregated order anymore. While military service did not create the civil rights movement of the 1940s and 1950s, it played an important role in its development.

FOLLOWING THE ARMISTICE that ended World War I in November 1918, the Wilson administration rushed pell-mell to demobilize the men it had drafted to serve in the armed forces as well as the thousands of men—and some women—who worked either in government agencies or in war-related industries. A much different story occurred after World War II ended with Japan's surrender in early September 1945. Despite a great clamor to bring the boys home, the Truman administration worked to make sure demobilization went smoothly. There was no army of occupation in 1918; in 1945, Allied troops stayed on in Germany, Italy, and Japan. War industries had actually started tooling back in 1944; the production of fighter planes, for example, was curtailed because the air force could not train pilots fast enough to keep up with production.

Perhaps the biggest difference is how the government and the country treated the veterans. On 22 June 1944, Franklin Roosevelt signed into law the last great New Deal measure, the Servicemen's Readjustment Act, commonly known as the GI Bill. As one scholar has noted, the GI Bill "was arguably the most massive affirmative action program in U.S. history." It provided training for needed labor force skills, financial help during job searches, small loans for starting up businesses, educational benefits including tuition and living expenses, one year of unemployment compensation, and, perhaps

Levittown, Pennsylvania, one of many communities built primarily for veterans with financing from the GI Bill, but all of them excluded blacks.

most important of all, low-interest home loans, the last of which triggered the massive postwar building boom. The original program (which later included veterans of the Korean War) ultimately extended benefits to sixteen million ex-servicemen. It is undoubtedly an affirmative action program, because it aimed at and disproportionately helped an identifiable group—white male veterans.

Aside from a desire to help the men who had fought for the country, practical reasons supported the measure. Many businessmen and government officials feared that the war had only temporarily stopped the Depression. The eleven million servicemen returning home constituted one-fourth of the American labor force. With war industries cutting back and letting people go, something had to be done to keep soldiers from turning overnight into an army of the homeless and the unemployed.

In addition, veterans benefited from another form of affirmative action through outright employment preferences in local, state, and federal agencies. Veteran preferences were not only never hidden but also well advertised. Veterans would take the civil service examination, which, of course, had been designed to ensure merit hiring. The federal and state governments would then add ten points to the scores of disabled veterans or their wives, and five points to the scores of nondisabled vets. Moreover, if after the bonus points had been added a tie existed between a veteran and a nonveteran, the veteran would be hired.

The GI Bill did not specifically advocate discrimination but, as might be expected, was interpreted differently for blacks than for whites. The historian Ira Katznelson argued that "the law was deliberately designed to accommodate Jim Crow." Because local white officials directed the programs, many black veterans did not benefit. Of the first sixty-seven thousand mortgages insured by the GI Bill, for example, fewer than a hundred had been taken out by nonwhites. In addition, many banks and mortgage companies simply refused loans to black applicants.

By 1946, only one-fifth of the 100,000 blacks who had applied for educational benefits had registered for college. Because the major southern universities remained segregated, black servicemen looking to go to college had few choices other than the historically black colleges and universities. Unfortunately, these schools came under increased pressure as rising enrollments and strained resources forced them to turn away an estimated 20,000 veterans. The historically black colleges were already the poorest and served, to most whites, only to keep blacks out of white schools. Their resources became stretched even thinner when veterans' demands necessitated a shift in the curriculum away from the "preach and teach" course of study that had been the traditional fare for black students.

Nonetheless, although black veterans encountered many obstacles that white veterans did not, the bill greatly expanded the population of African Americans attending college and graduate school. In 1940, enrollment at historically black colleges—the schools most black college students attended—had been slightly over 1 percent of total U.S. college enrollment. By 1950, it had increased to 3.6 percent. Aware of the pressure on black colleges, Congress in the Lanham Act of 1946 provided federal funding for the improvement and expansion of black colleges. Many of these gains took place in the North, but with 79 percent of the African American population living in southern states, the educational gains were not evenly distributed.

About twenty thousand black veterans attended college by 1947, albeit in predominantly black colleges. For those who managed to get an education, they, like the white veterans, became doctors, lawyers, teachers, and engineers and entered the black middle class. Moreover, given the paucity of opportunities that blacks had before the war, the GI Bill, for all its flaws in implementation, made a very big difference for African Americans who did take advantage of it. A study by the Veterans Administration in 1950 found that the participation rates of 14,571,000 white and 1,308,000 nonwhite veterans were almost identical, 73 and 75 percent, respectively. Another study found the participation rate was especially high among black veterans who had taken part in the army's Special Training Units. "Imagine the excitement of men who could afford higher education under language that called it their right," the president of Spelman College, Johnnetta Cole, recalled in 1994.

THE HISTORY OF THE civil rights movement is a complicated one, involving all the various aspects of our society, and is the subject of many books. The story of affirmative action for African Americans is one part of the larger struggle for equality, but from the beginning black leaders understood the importance of educational and economic opportunity. Just after World War II, Thurgood Marshall identified employment discrimination as one of the two most significant problems facing his people; the other was the right to vote. "When

Thurgood Marshall (right) *and Spottswood W. Robinson III in* 1953 *before arguing* Brown v. Board of Education, *the landmark case decided the following year that struck down racial segregation in schools as unconstitutional.*

those problems are solved," he predicted, "other questions will settle themselves."

Marshall hardly stood alone in this view. Because of the majestic cadences of Earl Warren in *Brown v. Board of Education*—"In the field of public education the doctrine of 'separate but equal' has no place"—and of Martin Luther King Jr. in 1963 on the steps of the Lincoln Memorial—"I have a dream"—we often lose focus on a major goal of the civil rights movement, namely, economic opportunity. The August 1963 March on Washington had been billed from the beginning as a march "for Jobs and Freedom." At the time of his death in Memphis in 1968, King was spending most of his time trying to fight the poverty endemic in the black community.

Much of the NAACP litigation in the 1930s and 1940s centered on making southern states live up to the "equal" part of the "separate but equal" formula. Between *Brown* and the passage of the 1964 Civil Rights Act and the 1965 Voting Rights Act, the public heard little of the economic aspect of civil rights. It seemed that the courts as well as the efforts of civil rights activists focused on striking down racial segregation and making African Americans equal, at least in the eyes of the law. Before economic problems could even be addressed, the apartheid system that kept millions of African Americans in subservience had to be torn down.

Harry Truman, unexpectedly thrust into the White House in April 1945, faced a multitude of crises after taking office. Black Americans had few expectations of the former senator from Missouri and were not surprised when he did not fight for a permanent FEPC. He then astonished everyone when in December 1946 he appointed a distinguished panel to serve as the President's Commission on Civil Rights to recommend "more adequate means and procedures for the protection of civil rights." After noting the many restrictions on people of color, the panel urged that every person, regardless of race, color, or creed, have access to equal opportunity in securing education, decent housing, and jobs. The report also recommended antilynching and anti-poll-tax laws, a permanent FEPC, and strengthening the Civil Rights Division of the Justice Department. The report defined the nation's civil rights agenda for the next generation.

Few blacks expected much from the new president, a product of a southern Democratic machine. But Truman, in a courageous act, sent a special message to Congress on 2 February 1948 calling for prompt implementation of the commission's recommendations, only to be met by southern threats to kill any such proposal. Aware that he could not win the legislative fight, Truman used his executive authority. He bolstered the Justice Department's Civil Rights Division and directed it to assist private litigants in civil rights cases. He appointed William Hastie, the first black judge on a federal appeals court, and named several African Americans to high positions in the administration. Most important, by executive orders later that year, the president ordered full racial integration in the armed forces.

In July 1948, Truman issued Executive Order 9980, establishing the Fair Employment Board within the Civil Service Commission, charged with receiving and investigating complaints of discrimination in federal employment, but only on appeal from departments and agencies following their own efforts at adjudication. Within a short time, the board members realized that the number of complaints they received did not truly reflect the level of discrimination in federal employment. They learned that many minorities feared retaliation if they spoke out, and so the board began running workshops in an effort to set up better communications with minority groups and encourage them to apply for federal jobs.

While the Fair Employment Board did what it could to reduce discrimination in the federal bureaucracy, the question remained of what to do about private employers. What little progress had been made during the war grew out of the influence the government had on private companies with federal contracts. Admittedly, the gains proved too little and did not last long after the hostilities stopped, and southerners in Congress had succeeded in killing off the FEPC. Truman recognized he would not be able to get any fair employment legislation through Congress, so he created, through another executive order, the Committee on Government Contract Compliance in December 1951. Made up of representatives from agencies with large government contracts, it did very little. One commentator said it functioned largely as a "study group."

Against this backdrop, the NAACP's Legal Defense Fund (LDF) intensified its efforts. It won cases attacking segregation on interstate railroads, on buses, and in amusement parks, the all-white primary, and restrictive covenants. The most important case in many ways involved the effort by the University of Texas to keep Heman Marion Sweatt out of its law school. After Sweatt applied in 1946, the federal district court gave Texas six months to establish a separate law school. The state created the School of Law for the Texas State University for Negroes, a makeshift classroom in an Austin basement, with plans to enlarge it. While the physical plant and library had grown by the time Marshall and the LDF carried the case to the Supreme Court, there was one thing that the members of the Court knew—what makes a good law school. Chief Justice Fred Vinson listed some of them—reputation of the faculty, experience of the administration, position and influence of the alumni, standing in the community, tradition, and prestige. A unanimous Court rejected the Texas claim that it had provided anything near an equal facility and for the first time ever ordered a black student admitted to a previously all-white school on the grounds that the state had failed to provide equal separate facilities. Thurgood Marshall called the Texas opinion "replete with road markings telling us where to go next." Next would be the five school cases from Delaware, Virginia, South Carolina, Kansas, and the District of Columbia, which the Court combined in *Brown v. Board of Education of Topeka, Kansas* in 1954.

In that case, Chief Justice Earl Warren spoke for a unanimous Court, declaring "that in the field of public education the doctrine of 'separate-but-equal' has no place. Separate educational facilities are inherently unequal." J. Harvie Wilkinson, a federal judge on the Court of Appeals for the Fourth Circuit, called the decision "humane, among the most humane moments in all our history. It was, with the pardonable exception of a footnote, a great political achievement, both in its uniting of the Court and in the steady way it addressed the nation."

The promise of *Brown I,* however, was greatly eviscerated in *Brown II,* which ordered that desegregation should proceed "with all deliberate speed" and triggered several years of racial unrest and occasional violence in the South. Hundreds of school districts dragged their feet, and the LDF did not have the resources to take each one into federal court. Even when local attorneys volunteered their services or the LDF sent in one of its own attorneys, it cost plaintiffs approximately $15,000 ($125,000 in current dollars) to take a desegregation suit through federal courts. As a result, as late as 1961, few school districts, especially in the Deep South, had faced a school desegregation suit. The intolerance, the violence, the overt racial hatred, led the southern-born scholar C. Vann Woodward to lament that "the lights of reason and tolerance began to go out under the insistent demand for conformity [and] a malaise of fear spread over the region."

Although the Eisenhower Justice Department, headed by Herbert Brownell, had filed an amicus brief urging the Court to strike down segregation, President Dwight Eisenhower said little publicly but fumed privately that *Brown* "had set back progress in the South at least fifteen years. . . . Feelings are deep on this, especially where children are involved. . . . We can't demand perfection in these moral things." When officials at the University of Alabama defied a court order to admit Autherine Lucy, the president said, "I certainly hope that we could avoid any interference." The university remained segregated for seven more years.

Events finally forced Eisenhower to act. In the fall of 1957, Governor Orval Faubus, previously considered a moderate, called out the Arkansas National Guard to prevent black children from attending Central High School in Little Rock. When he withdrew the troops on court order and black students again tried to attend, a mob attacked the school and drove them off. The defiance of a federal court order meant Eisenhower could no longer sit by and watch passively. He sent in a thousand paratroopers and federalized ten thousand Arkansas National Guardsmen to protect the black students and maintain order. The chief executive who had desperately wanted to avoid the entire civil rights issue, and who for three years following *Brown* had failed to provide leadership, outraged the South by becoming the first president since Reconstruction to use federal troops to enforce black rights.

IT WOULD BE UNFAIR to say that Eisenhower did nothing, because in fact he tried to continue the government's nondiscrimination policy. After Eisenhower's election in 1952, several members of Truman's Government Contract Compliance Committee resigned, and the status of the committee remained in limbo until the following August, when the president issued Executive Order 10479 replacing Truman's committee with the new Government Contract Committee. To elevate the importance of the new committee, Eisenhower named his vice president, Richard M. Nixon, to serve as chair. The executive order also strengthened the nondiscrimination clause that had become standard in all government contracts by requiring contractors to post notices at work sites acknowledging their agreement to provide employment without discrimination based on race, color, national origin, or religion. Nondiscrimination also applied with respect to promotions and transfers. Overt failure to comply could lead to cancellation of the government contract, but this committee, like its predecessors, only had power to investigate and publicize its findings, not to enforce nondiscrimination. In general, employers paid no more heed to the antidiscrimination clause during the Eisenhower years than they had under Truman.

Toward the end of the Eisenhower administration, Vice President Richard Nixon reported that overt discrimination was not as prevalent as believed but that employers were not very interested in establishing a policy of positive nondiscrimination that would allow qualified minority and women applicants to be hired and promoted on the basis of equality. Eisenhower did not act on Nixon's report, but his successor did.

CHAPTER 2

KENNEDY AND JOHNSON

In response to James Farmer's call for "compensatory preferential hiring," Vice President Lyndon Johnson, chairman of President Kennedy's Committee on Equal Employment Opportunity, said, "Yes, it is a good idea, but don't call it compensatory. Call it 'affirmative action.' It's moving the nation forward! It is going out of our way to bring minorities in that have been excluded! That is positive affirmative action!"

On 8 November 1960, the American people elected John Fitzgerald Kennedy president of the United States, but by a very close margin, 120,000 votes out of 68 million ballots cast, and the black vote might have made the difference between victory and defeat. Kennedy's Catholicism alienated many southern Protestants, costing him about 17 percent of the then-normal Democratic vote in the South. He won more convincingly in the northern states, where Republican Catholics crossed over to vote for him and African Americans rallied to him after he and his brother interceded over the jailing of Martin Luther King Jr.

A Georgia court had locked up King on 24 October. Sargent Shriver, Kennedy's brother-in-law, learned of this and also that Coretta Scott King was pregnant and in a state of near hysteria. When Shriver told Kennedy about the Kings, the candidate immediately called Mrs. King. An incensed Robert Kennedy put in a call to the Georgia judge asking him to grant King bail. When the Reverend Martin Luther King Sr. learned of the Kennedys' intercession, he told newspapermen that he had thought he could never vote for a Catholic but that the phone call to his daughter-in-law had changed his mind. The senior King's endorsement received wide play in the African American press. More than 70 percent of African Americans voted for Kennedy, providing him the winning margin in several states.

As a candidate, Kennedy could not ignore the growing fervor of the civil rights movement, and after his election no domestic struggle occupied his presidency more. Kennedy had never been a strong advocate of civil rights during his fourteen years in Congress, nor had he really known many African Americans, certainly not on a social level. He later admitted that he had rarely given much thought to the issue, nor had it mattered very much in his races for the House and Senate; Massachusetts had a relatively small black community. His political sense told him that because southerners controlled the key committees in Congress, to get ahead he should do little that would antagonize them. By the mid-1950s, the NAACP and other civil rights organizations viewed Kennedy with great suspicion, and when he attended a civil rights gathering, the audience roundly booed him. Kennedy walked a narrow path so as not to alienate southern voters and asked Lyndon Johnson of Texas to be his running mate, a move that seemed to placate the South yet made black leaders even more wary. It was one thing to talk about and promise civil rights measures during a campaign—something that southern Democrats grudgingly accepted as a political necessity—and another to actually get meaningful legislation through Congress. Both Kennedy and the South understood that quite clearly.

Once in office, he needed to act against racial discrimination for a variety of reasons—moral, political, and international. In this latter area, he, like Eisenhower, understood the difficulty of wooing Third World countries; one could hardly point to Soviet human rights violations while police beat black protesters in Montgomery and other southern cities. At the same time, he understood that the vast majority of white Americans—even while sympathetic to civil rights—had other priorities on their minds. A Gallup poll showed civil rights next to last in a long list of problems the public thought Congress should address. Kennedy needed southern votes if he had any hope of putting through other reforms, such as Medicare and an increase in the minimum wage, measures that would also help black Americans.

Kennedy did not mention civil rights in his inaugural and soon after made clear that he would propose no civil rights legislation in his first year. At the most, he would consider a piecemeal approach to some of the more urgent problems through executive action, but rejected a proposal by Roy Wilkins of the NAACP for a sweeping

Martin Luther King Jr., the acknowledged leader of the civil rights movement, whom President Kennedy kept at arm's length in the early months of his administration.

executive order. He did appoint Harris Wofford a civil rights adviser on his White House staff, although he used him primarily as a buffer between the administration and black leaders. Martin Luther King Jr. had to wait until the fall of 1961 before he received an invitation to the White House to meet privately with the president.

Nonetheless, Kennedy did begin to act. Noticing an all-white Coast Guard unit in his inaugural parade, he pressured the academy to recruit blacks, a step that greatly impressed Wilkins. More important, he gave Attorney General Robert Kennedy full authority to use the Justice Department to press for desegregation and to protect civil rights activists.

He also surprised black leaders with a host of smaller gestures. He appointed some forty African Americans to top posts, including Robert Weaver as administrator of the Housing and Home Finance Agency (later to become the cabinet-level Department of Housing and Urban Development) and Andrew Hatcher as deputy White House press secretary. He named five blacks to the federal bench, including Thurgood Marshall to the important Court of Appeals for the Second Circuit in New York. "Kennedy was so hot on the Department heads, cabinet officers, and agency heads," recalled Wilkins, "that everyone was scrambling around trying to find himself a Negro in order to keep the President off his neck." Simeon Booker, a national reporter for *Ebony*, was admitted to the presidential news pool, a first for any Negro paper or magazine. The joke in Washington was that every government department was sending out posses to recruit African Americans to avert the wrath of the White House. The searches, however, yielded a surprising success. The number of blacks in the middle grades of civil service increased 36.6 percent from June 1961 to June 1963, and in the top grades by 88.2 percent.

Civil rights leaders fully understood the realities of Washington politics, and that although they might hope to get legislation through the House, it would certainly die stillborn in the Senate. They wanted Kennedy to act, even if only through executive action. Martin Luther King Jr. publicly stressed measures that the president could take. Even the NAACP, normally oriented toward legislative and judicial action, joined in. On 6 March, Kennedy issued Executive Order 10925, establishing the President's Committee on Equal Employment Opportunity, and named Vice President Lyndon Johnson as its chair.

Order 10925 differed from its predecessors in a number of ways. It replaced both committees created by Eisenhower, the Government Contract Committee and the Committee on Government Employment Policy, and merged their responsibilities. The order specifically stated that "a single governmental committee should be charged with responsibility for accomplishing [all equal employment opportunity] objectives."

Kennedy also picked up on what Richard Nixon had said in his report on the Government Contract Committee, that employers would be unwilling to change their normal practices. So the new order went beyond just prohibiting discriminatory practices to requiring positive action to enlarge fair employment opportunities. "It is the policy of the executive branch of the government to encourage by positive measures equal opportunity for all qualified persons within the Government." In many ways, this is the first instance of a governmental commitment to affirmative action as we know it today. Kennedy also responded to a growing perception about the ineffectiveness of just processing complaints, because many minority workers would be afraid to file a complaint lest they lose their job. To avoid that problem, Kennedy put the onus on the employer to do away with discrimination.

The order required government contractors to take positive steps to ensure equal opportunity: "The contractor will not discriminate against any employee or applicant for employment because of race, creed, color, or national origin. The contractor will take affirmative action to ensure that all applicants are employed, and that employees are treated during employment, without regard to their race, color, creed, or national origin." The rule also applied to promotion, pay, and training. Employers had to post advertisements in conspicuous places indicating their adherence to the new policy. Moreover, much to the dismay of some labor leaders, 10925 recognized the role of unions in perpetuating discriminatory practices and required them to comply with the new policy.

Another part included what the historian Ruth Morgan has called the "carrot and stick provisions." The order established sanctions and penalties for failure to conform, and these included termination of any contract "for failure to comply with the nondiscrimination provisions" as well as the exclusion of such an employer from securing any further government contracts. However, certificates of merit would be given to employers and unions following "the purposes and provisions of this order."

Kennedy surprised civil rights leaders not only by the speed with which he had the executive order drafted—only six weeks after he took the oath of office—but by the fact that he invoked the full weight of his office to enhance the prestige of the new committee and the policy it would enforce. Kennedy signed 10925 at a highly publicized ceremony in the White House, attended by several civil rights leaders. The presidential decrees of previous chief executives had usually been brief and technical, often signed into the *Federal Register* with no fuss and without any accompanying statement. Kennedy, on the other hand, used the occasion to emphasize his administration's initiatives on behalf of civil rights. The next day Kennedy issued a public statement calling the new committee a "vastly strengthened machinery" that he intended would "ensure Americans of all colors and beliefs will have equal access to employment within the government, and with those who do business with the government."

Despite the administration's effort to portray 10925 as a major step for civil rights, most observers recognized it as modest, having more symbolism than substance. Professor Hugh Graham described the order as containing a "vague and almost casual reference to 'affirmative action.'" Moreover, if asked to define what "affirmative action" meant in the order, many people—including civil rights activists— would have said that it stood as a shorthand for procedural fairness; that is, all applicants for a job, black or white, had to be treated equally. Kennedy's speechwriter said he added the word "affirmative" simply because he wanted "to give a sense of positiveness" to what employers should do.

The President's Committee on Equal Employment Opportunity had some successes. A little over six weeks after its establishment, a group of southern textile suppliers agreed to end discrimination when the committee pointed out that their contracts included antidiscrimination clauses and that these would be enforced. After meeting with Secretary of the Army Elvis J. Stahr Jr. and Assistant Secretary of Labor Jerry B. Holleman, the firms agreed to the conditions.

However, for all the hoopla with which Kennedy signed the order, it had many similarities to the Truman and Eisenhower directives. Like them, the committee had no statutory status and no budget of its own. As an interagency creation, it relied on the budgets of the federal agencies associated with it, and absent statutory authority the committee had limited enforcement power. Although in some instances it could act to negate contracts, most of the time the staff would investigate and advise, as it did with the textile suppliers, and then leave it to the appropriate contracting agency—in this case the army—to enforce the contractual bans against discrimination.

How successfully did the committee battle discrimination? One view is that it proved disappointing. It issued a "Plans for Progress" whereby private corporations would sign an agreement with the committee promising to hire more blacks. Dozens of companies did so, but the head of the Plans for Progress, Robert Troutman, greatly exaggerated the success of the endeavor. The NAACP called Plans for Progress "one of the great phonies of the Kennedy administration's civil rights program," a view echoed by *Business Week,* and Troutman resigned under fire in 1962. Part of the problem involved numbers. Where Troutman might have claimed a 100 percent increase in black workers, that meant nothing if the actual numbers went from one to two. In Alabama, for example, despite the existence of numerous federal agencies and contractors, black employment by the federal government amounted to 0.001 percent of the workforce. All the same, a later accounting of the 103 companies who signed on to Plans for Progress showed an increase in the percentage of black employees from 5.1 to 5.7 percent within the first two years. That represented a gain of 40,938 jobs filled by minorities out of 341,734 vacancies—more than double the representation of black workers hired by these companies prior to Plans for Progress.

Nonetheless, in comparing the work of the Eisenhower and Kennedy administrations for a study by the Twentieth Century Fund, Michael Sovern found the Kennedy committee far more effective in investigating and resolving discrimination complaints. To give one example, the NAACP claimed that a federal agency had made a mockery of the president's order by awarding Lockheed Aircraft a $1 billion jet plane contract despite its discriminatory employment practices. Lockheed planned to manufacture the aircraft at its plant in Marietta, Georgia, whose employment policy limited African Americans to unskilled or semiskilled jobs and totally excluded them from the company's apprenticeship program. The plant had segregated cafeterias, drinking fountains, and restrooms and a segregated union. Within seven weeks of the committee receiving the complaint, the president of Lockheed signed an agreement promising extensive reforms in recruitment, employment, and training of qualified minorities. Mobil Oil in Beaumont, Texas, Avco Corporation in Richmond, Indiana, National Aniline in Chesterfield, Virginia, and other companies also agreed to end discriminatory practices in their plants. Overall, however, the results were uneven, and although a number of companies signed plans, implementation proved negligible in many instances.

The president's actions represented a delicate balancing of priorities. Although by the numbers Democrats enjoyed healthy majorities in both the House of Representatives (252–163) and the Senate (65–35), that did not indicate a working majority for the administration's plans. As Harris Wofford later explained, "The Republican-conservative-southern Democratic coalition could probably muster a majority in the House, and successfully filibuster in the Senate." In addition, southerners chaired and thus controlled most of the standing committees in each house. Kennedy believed that Congress would not pass civil rights legislation. Moreover, if he fought for such a measure, it would adversely affect other proposals on his agenda.

Kennedy understood, as did civil rights leaders, that no matter how much the government tried to eradicate racial discrimination, the real key to progress involved private-sector employment, decent-paying jobs that would pull black America out of poverty. In 1961, 57 percent of black families had incomes of less than $5,000, compared with 25 percent of white families. At the other end of the spectrum, only 8 percent of black families had annual incomes over $12,000, compared with 24 percent for whites. The median income for black families was $4,321 a year, that of whites, $8,109. By the early 1960s, the black unemployment rate was 11.2 percent, more than double the white rate of 5.1 percent. In testimony before Congress in support of the president's plan to cut taxes and stimulate the economy, Secretary of Labor Willard Wirtz detailed the deteriorating economic status of the black community and warned that "it will be a hollow victory if we get the 'whites only' signs down, only to find 'no vacancy' signs behind them."

Black frustration also exploded in ways that Kennedy had not anticipated and could not control, such as the Freedom Riders in the summer of 1961 and the violent assaults on them, the escalating protests involving tens of thousands of blacks in 1962, and then the confrontation with Governor George Wallace over admitting Negroes to the University of Alabama. Wallace's defiance and the outbreak of violence on the Tuscaloosa campus led the president to federalize the Alabama National Guard. On 11 June 1963, Kennedy went on national television and gave one of the greatest speeches of his life, setting forth the plight of black people in the United States. If the Negro could not enjoy the full and free life that all of us want, "then who among us would be content to have the color of his skin changed and stand in his place? Who among us would then be content with the counsels of patience and delay?" This was "a moral issue—as old as the scriptures and as clear as the American constitution." He would within a few days ask Congress to make the commitment to the proposition "that race has no place in American life or law."

On 19 June, Kennedy submitted a civil rights bill to Congress. On 28 August, a quarter million people gathered in front of the Lincoln Memorial in a march for both jobs and civil rights. That fall, congressional leaders declared that while there might be a fight, the time had come to enact a civil rights bill. Then, on 22 November, an assassin's bullet ended John F. Kennedy's life.

HAD AFFIRMATIVE ACTION been limited to what Kennedy called for in his executive order, it is unlikely that the issue would ever have become as divisive as it did. In essence, the government proposed a "soft" program, featuring nondiscrimination and open opportunity. It called upon private employers and unions involved in government contracts to end racial discrimination, to hire qualified people without regard to the color of their skin, to pay them the same as they paid white workers, and to provide them with equal opportunities for training and promotion—steps that all but the most rabid bigots would have conceded to be not only fair but necessary as well.

The conservative historian Herman Belz, a strong critic of later affirmative action policies, nonetheless praised Executive Order 10925. While noting that it had the political purpose of serving a key Democratic constituency, he wrote that "it also had integrity as a genuine equal opportunity program consistent with traditional equal rights principles. It expressed the widely held view that to achieve the goal of equal employment opportunity it was necessary to do more than proscribe discriminatory practices." The main idea, according to Belz, was to open channels of communication between employers and minority communities, providing not only job opportunities to would-be workers but a broader recruitment base for employers.

Thomas Sowell, an African American conservative and, like Belz, later a vociferous critic of affirmative action, also approved of the Kennedy plan. Affirmative action, he wrote, referred to various activities, such as monitoring lower-level hiring officials to ensure the fairness of their hiring and promotion decisions, and spreading information about job opportunities to encourage previously excluded groups to apply, "after which the actual selection could be made *without regard* to group membership." Sowell approved of Kennedy's order that federal contractors take affirmative action to ensure that all employees, once hired, be treated fairly and without regard to race.

If all companies had followed the "soft" version of affirmative action, the kind praised by Belz and Sowell, there would have been no need for the book you are reading. There would have been fewer court cases, far fewer federal rules regarding goals and quotas, no break between former civil rights allies, and no political campaigns built on opposition to affirmative action. It did not happen that way, in part because of facts on the ground that Belz and Sowell ignored.

CIVIL RIGHTS ACTIVISTS understood what Richard Nixon had learned and written in his last report as head of Eisenhower's equal opportunity committee, that while some examples of overt and malicious discrimination could be found, the most formidable barriers to black access to jobs consisted of habitual employer preference for white workers and unthinking assumptions bred by decades of exclusion. This statement, however, needs to be tempered by the realities of African Americans with limited education and skills, conditions that had been created by decades of bias and discrimination.

One study found that half of southern whites and 45 percent of northern whites believed at the time of the Birmingham struggle in 1963 that blacks already had "as good a chance" as whites "to get any kind of job for which they are qualified." As early as 1956, more than half the whites in one survey believed "companies give Negroes a good break" in hiring. At the same time, 70 percent of this same group also said that their own companies did not open up certain types of jobs to blacks. Less than one in four whites believed that employers should follow the same rules in evaluating black and white applicants. Whites not only maintained that blacks lacked adequate qualifications; half of them opposed any special training for them.

Many white employers simply assumed white entitlement and black incapacity. A 1962 survey of Atlanta businesses found unthinking bias prevalent in all types of stores. "This is just a sales and service office," explained one corporate official as to why there were no blacks. "We don't have any manufacturing in Atlanta." Some of the responders told the pollsters that "their work was extremely technical," implying that it was too technical for any black person. One manager ridiculed the notion of a black salesman in a firm catering to white customers.

Labor unions proved even more implacable to demands for racial equality. In the early 1960s in Pittsburgh, to take one example, African Americans made up 17 percent of the population, but only 4.7 percent of construction industry workers, and of these two-thirds held unskilled labor or plastering jobs. In the wake of civil rights demonstrations and orders from the Pennsylvania Human Relations Commission, the city's seven all-white locals slowly started admitting blacks to membership and apprentice training, but only four minority applicants took the apprenticeship exam. Of that group, two passed, and one of them left the program. That example would be true of most other cities in the United States. The U.S. Commission on Civil Rights concluded that "most international unions have failed to exhibit any profound concerns over civil rights." Although there were a few bright spots where local unions actively sought black members, for the most part union officials promised to end discrimination and then did nothing to achieve that goal. Most unions out and out refused to provide any information on their racial composition.

Around this time, the Census Bureau released a study documenting the relative economic deterioration of African Americans since the end of World War II. Black income hovered at about 55 percent of white income, and in the South nonwhites made only a third of the earnings of whites in similar occupations. Although there had been an upward spurt during the war, Herman Miller, the economist who did the study, ascribed most of the gain to those blacks who had migrated north rather than to any overall improvement in job opportunities. "In most states," Miller concluded, "the nonwhite male now has about the same occupational distribution relative to whites he had in 1940 and 1950."

Kennedy had tried to address the problem in part through the executive order and in his Keynesian tax bill. If a tax cut stimulated the economy, then a rising tide would float all boats. But he had also realized that the order by itself could do little to address the rampant racism black workers faced everywhere and wanted stronger statutory means to attack the prejudice. Lyndon Johnson, who, unlike Kennedy, came from a dirt-poor background, determined to do something about both the poverty and the racism.

BEFORE ROBERT KENNEDY had put in his call to the Georgia judge asking that bail be granted to the Reverend Martin Luther King, he called the party's vice presidential candidate to see if there would be repercussions in the South. Johnson replied, "Tell Jack that we'll ride it through down here some way, and at least he's on the side of right." Johnson, according to Arthur Schlesinger Jr., had to play the race card to some extent in Texas politics, but in fact had no racial prejudices. In 1956, he had been one of only three southern senators who refused to sign the so-called Southern Manifesto attacking the Supreme Court and its rulings in *Brown*. (The other two were the liberals Estes Kefauver and Albert Gore Sr. of Tennessee. The liberal hero William Fulbright of Arkansas signed the manifesto.) Milo Perkins, a top official of the Farm Security Administration in the 1940s, said that Johnson "was the first man in Congress from the South ever to go to bat for the Negro farmer." Moreover, Johnson learned a great deal from his work on the president's committee, experience that would translate into backing and then expanding not only Kennedy's civil rights proposal but also his own War on Poverty.

Five days after Kennedy's assassination, Lyndon Johnson addressed Congress and the nation. "All I have," he said, "I would gladly have given not to be standing here today." He reminded members of Congress that at his inaugural Kennedy had said, "Let us begin." Now Johnson told them, "Let us continue." Although Kennedy had been more concerned with foreign affairs when he took office, Johnson emphasized domestic matters, labeling them the "dreams" that Kennedy had pursued—education for all children, "jobs for all who seek them," care for the elderly, and above all "equal rights for all Americans whatever their race or color."

> No memorial or oration or eulogy could more eloquently honor President Kennedy's memory than the earliest possible passage of the civil rights bill for which he fought so long. We have talked long enough about equal rights in this country. We have talked for one hundred years or more. It is time now to write the next chapter and write it in the books of law. . . . The time has come for Americans of all races and creeds and political beliefs to understand and to respect one another. So let us put an end to the teaching and the preaching of hate and evil and violence.

Designed to calm the jittery nerves of the American people, the speech also marked the beginning of the most expansive social welfare program since the New Deal. Unlike Kennedy, who never really understood how to deal with Congress, Johnson had been, as one biographer called him, the "master of the Senate." He knew how the legislative branch worked and what had to be done to make a bill into a law, and he used those skills to get a civil rights bill enacted. The effort took up most of his time and effort for the first six months of 1964 and showed Johnson to be the most adept president at handling Congress since Franklin Roosevelt's first term.

The Civil Rights Act of 1964 banned racial discrimination in privately owned accommodations for the public, such as restaurants, hotels, and movie houses, and authorized the attorney general to eliminate de jure racial segregation in public schools, libraries, hospitals, and other public places. The carrot and the stick in the bill could be found in the section declaring that schools and other feder-

Lyndon Baines Johnson signing the Civil Rights Act on 2 July 1964, surrounded by civil rights and congressional leaders. The Reverend Martin Luther King Jr. is standing directly behind the president.

ally assisted institutions would lose federal funds if they continued to discriminate. The attorney general could also bring suits on behalf of parents complaining about school discrimination, and the federal government would assume the legal costs.

Title VII—the heart of the bill—forbade discrimination in employment and originally specified the categories of race, color, religion, and national origin. The House Rules Committee chairman, Howard Smith of Virginia, opposed the bill and thought if he added sex to the proscribed categories, that would sink it because liberals would not want to give up the special status women enjoyed under protective legislation. Instead, the House overwhelmingly adopted it, and Title VII, with sex in it, made it to the Senate. The provision for the Equal Employment Opportunity Commission (EEOC), also an afterthought, made it out of the House as well. Johnson oversaw every aspect of the Senate deliberations and defeated a three-month filibuster by southerners led by Richard Russell of Georgia. The Senate ended the filibuster on 10 June and then a short time after passed the entire bill 73–27. Johnson signed it into law on 2 July 1964.

The act had eleven titles—or subsections—covering education, public accommodations, and voting rights (although this was a minor section, which would be more fully covered in the Voting Rights Act of 1965) and expanding the powers of the attorney general. It coordinated the efforts of federal agencies to end segregation, and under the threat of losing federal funds unless they made a "good faith, substantive start," hundreds of southern school districts finally began to desegregate. Using its commerce authority, Congress prohibited racial discrimination in restaurants, hotels and motels, filling stations, and soda fountains and mandated equal access to parks, pools, and sports venues.

The bill did not—and could not—cure all the evils of segregation and discrimination overnight; racism was too deeply embedded, especially in the South, for that to happen. Many employers as well as labor unions ignored the provisions on job discrimination, and de facto racial discrimination remained widespread in schools and housing in the North as well as the South. The law did nothing to better the economic conditions of black people; it was a liberal, not a radical, measure and aimed to promote legal, not economic or social, equality.

Not all objections to the measure came from white southerners. The act empowered the federal government far beyond any similar peacetime measure and brought forth objections from libertarians, complaints that would be heard time and again in the debate over affirmative action. Restraints against discrimination interfere with freedom of association and reduce the choices normally available to individuals. Professor Richard Epstein of the University of Chicago argued, "An antidiscrimination law is the antithesis of freedom of contract, a principle that allows all persons to do business with whomever they please for good reason, bad reason, or no reason at all." Robert H. Bork, then a professor at Yale Law School, declared that whenever "the morals of the majority are self-righteously imposed upon a minority, the discussion we ought to hear is of the cost in freedom that must be paid for such legislation."

Epstein, even though he remained a critic of the law, later conceded, "So great were the abuses of political power before 1964 that, knowing what I know today, if given an all-or-nothing choice I should still have voted in favor of the Civil Rights Act in order to allow federal power to break the stranglehold of local government on race relations." Thomas Sowell, in analyzing the law's text, found that Congress had declared itself in favor of equal opportunity and opposed to racial favoritism. The problem, he wrote, lay not in the wording of the Civil Rights Act but in how federal administrative agencies and the courts would misconstrue it.

The 1964 Civil Rights Act remains an important legislative

achievement. The Supreme Court immediately upheld its provisions, and the Johnson administration enforced it vigorously. It would take time, but eventually thousands of schools, hospitals, and other public institutions abandoned apartheid. African Americans would be able to eat in restaurants, go to movies, stay in hotels, and enjoy other amenities long denied them.

Although it is unclear exactly how much the law affected black earnings, there is no question that the economic position of African Americans increased significantly at this time. Between 1959 and 1969, mean annual earnings by black men increased by 49 percent, while equivalent earnings for whites rose 26 percent. In the decade following passage of the law, the annual earnings of full-time black workers increased from 63 percent to 73 percent of white workers, while among black women the ratio rose from 68 to 90 percent. By 1971, the percentage of African Americans living in poverty (income of under $3,000 a year) had been cut almost in half, from 35 percent to 19. Some scholars believe that this surge in black income reflected the dismantling of racial job barriers in the South. Unfortunately, the progress slipped off after 1973 because of a declining national economy and a shift from manufacturing to service-based employment.

Civil rights groups recognized and applauded Lyndon Johnson for what he had accomplished, but they also knew that much remained to be done, especially in making Title VII a reality.

By the time Congress enacted the civil rights law, both the President's Equal Opportunity Committee and the National Labor Relations Board had exposed racial quotas against blacks in the workplace, whether sponsored by employers or by unions or, more likely, by both. These quotas seemed a relic of the past, a lingering symbol of bigotry. No one defended them. Yet even before the passage of the law, some liberals advanced the idea of "benign" racial quotas to compensate for years of discrimination.

Much of this thought came from the Congress of Racial Equality (CORE) and its head, James Farmer. CORE and other civil rights groups grew more militant, spurred on in large measure by the Freedom Riders and the sit-in movement. Between 1961 and 1963, CORE's chapters in the North escalated their picketing and boycotts to include retail chains, banks, construction, and some manufacturers. In one of their biggest victories, the A&P grocery chain in 1964 made an agreement with CORE that 90 percent of its new employees for the following year would be nonwhite.

*James Farmer in 1964. The head of the Congress
of Racial Equality, Farmer advocated boycotting
businesses that refused to hire minorities.*

The boycott as a weapon against job discrimination gained
momentum in Philadelphia in the early 1960s. A loose federation of
some four hundred black ministers used their pulpits to preach—and
quite effectively—for the black community and sympathetic whites
to boycott particular products of companies such as Pepsi-Cola, Brey-
ers Ice Cream, Tasty Baking Company (maker of Tastykake), Esso,
and other oil companies. Twenty-four firms agreed to specific hiring
goals for African Americans, and this success soon led other groups to
adopt the tactic in Boston, New York, and Detroit. CORE chapters
quickly grasped how the boycott could serve as a uniting as well as
a recruiting device.

Gordon Carey, CORE's national program director, explained how
the organization had changed its plans on the national level. "Heretofore, we used to talk simply of merit employment, that is, hiring
the best qualified person for the job regardless of race." Now CORE
spoke of "compensatory" hiring. "We are approaching employers
with the proposition that they have effectively excluded Negroes

One of the earliest sit-ins took place in Nashville, Tennessee, between February and May 1960. Led primarily by college-age students, these peaceful protests forced not only lunch counters but many other racially segregated eateries and public institutions, such as libraries, to desegregate.

from the work force for a long time and that they now have a responsibility and obligation to make up for past sins." One CORE activist noted a spreading conviction that "after three hundred years of discrimination . . . there is obviously no immediate solution that does not involve some kind of 'preferential hiring' system."

Other—and more militant—groups did believe in quotas and began pushing for them. The Reverend Nelson Dukes of the Fountain Street Baptist Church in Harlem demanded that New York City give Negroes 25 percent of all jobs on city contracts, "or else the dikes will break." The following week pickets from the Dukes group stopped work on a city construction project in Harlem, and Dukes upped the demand to 25 percent of all state construction jobs as well. Interestingly, the contractor for the Harlem project seems to have had no objection to a quota; he just wanted to get back to work. In 1963, the New York City Commission on Human Rights had urged "preferential treatment" of "qualified" blacks for "a limited period" to close the gap. Color consciousness, the commission had declared, "is necessary and appropriate."

Not all civil rights proponents bought into this. When Whitney

Young asked the Urban League's national board to adopt a policy of preferential hiring, he ran into a firestorm of criticism from local affiliates. Wendell Freeland, president of the Pittsburgh chapter, warned that there would be an "adverse reaction" to any such policy. The Urban League's public would ask, "What in blazes are these guys up to? They tell us for years that we must buy [nondiscrimination] and then say, 'It isn't what we want.'" In the end, Young had to back down, but in public he would not or could not conceal his private convictions.

The NAACP also opposed quotas. Jack Greenberg, who had been one of the Legal Defense Fund lawyers working on *Brown,* said that civil rights groups "do not aim to perpetuate their group interest since the group interest itself is to eliminate the socially enforced group identity." A theory of group rights, he went on, cannot guarantee equality for individuals, and individual equality had always been the NAACP's goal. Race-conscious affirmative action is based not on individual rights but on group rights, a concept that most civil rights activists had earlier dismissed.

Labor unions, of course, did not support quotas, and in reading the civil rights bill, they did not find any there. Andrew Biemiller, a lobbyist for the AFL-CIO, insisted that the measure "does not require 'racial balance' on a job" and did not give any race the right of preferential treatment. More important, it did not "upset seniority rights already obtained by an employee." Biemiller said that it would be inconceivable to the entire labor movement if the government approved of "righting ancient wrongs by perpetuating new ones."

During congressional hearings on the civil rights bills proposed by Kennedy in 1963 and the Johnson measure the following year, opponents claimed that Title VII—the heart of the bill that prohibited racial discrimination in employment—would compel employers to hire and/or promote blacks regardless of their qualifications to avoid racial imbalance. Senator John Stennis (D-Miss.) sarcastically agreed that backers of the bill did not want a quota system. They "do not dare put [quota provisions] in the bill," because "such proposals draw blood and a quick response" in the North, where they were opposed, but that is what they really wanted. Proponents responded that the bill aimed to eliminate current and future discrimination, not rectify past wrongs. Hubert Humphrey, who led the fight in the Senate, declared that "contrary to the allegations of some opponents of this title, there is nothing in it that will give any power [to any agency or court] to require hiring, firing, or promotion of employees in order to meet a racial 'quota' or to achieve a certain racial balance." In fact, Title VII prohibited preferential treatment for any particular group. Senator Thomas H. Kuchel (R-Calif.) backed Humphrey and averred that "the bill now before us is color blind."

Title VII itself is quite clear. It shall be an unlawful employment practice for an employer

(1) to fail or refuse to hire or to discharge any individual, or otherwise to discriminate against any individual with respect to his compensation, terms, conditions, or privileges of employment, because of such individual's race, color, religion, sex, or national origin; or

(2) to limit, segregate, or classify his employees or applicants for employment in any way which would deprive or tend to deprive any individual of employment opportunities or otherwise adversely affect his status as an employee, because of such individual's race, color, religion, sex, or national origin.

In looking at the congressional debate, one does not find mention of affirmative action. Supporters of the bill went out of their way to argue that the measure prohibited not only discrimination against blacks but discrimination against whites, women, or people of any particular religion or national origin. Despite the clear wording of the proposal, white supremacists kept insisting that Title VII would lead to wholesale dismissal of white employees so that blacks could take their place. As for quotas or preferential hiring based on minority status, the wording of the law is quite clear:

Nothing contained in this subchapter shall be interpreted to require any employer, employment agency, labor organization, or joint labor-management committee subject to this subchapter to grant preferential treatment to any individual or to any group because of the race, color, religion, sex, or national origin of such individual or group on account of an imbalance which may exist with respect to the total number or percentage of persons of any race, color, religion, sex, or national origin employed by any employer area, or in the available work force in any community, State, section, or other area.

But did the bill's backers really mean what they said, or were their denials merely tactics to divert attention from what opponents claimed was the real purpose of Title VII? Professor Randall Kennedy suggests that "their disavowal of preferential treatment was an authentic representation of early-1960s white racial liberalism of a certain sort—a perspective commendably opposed to invidious discrimination." But, he noted, that perspective underestimated "the barriers that would continue to ensnare racial minorities" even after the passage of the Civil Rights Act.

TWO DECADES BEFORE passage of the civil rights law, Thurgood Marshall had said that if African Americans could get jobs and the vote, everything else would fall into place. If the Civil Rights Act took some major steps to allowing blacks into the labor market, the Voting Rights Act of 1965 gave them the vote, and in places where for decades they had been disenfranchised. With the backing and protection of federal marshals and the help of civil rights organizations, tens of thousands of blacks registered throughout the South. The impact of this registration quickly made itself felt, with dozens and then hundreds of African Americans elected to local and state offices.

The enactment of the Civil Rights and Voting Rights Acts put into legislation nearly all of the demands that had been made by activists for the prior three decades: the outlawing of segregation in schools, state and local institutions, and public accommodations; the right to vote free from the restrictions that the white South had used to keep African Americans away from the polls; and federal agencies empowered to enforce these laws. The Voting Rights Act destroyed the political choke hold on southern blacks, and in the six southern states covered by the new law, the percentage of registered voting-age blacks jumped from 24.4 in 1964 to 60 by 1969. By 1970, almost a million new black voters had been added to the voting lists. White southern politicians recognized that in many districts and states, African American voters held the balance of power, and a new breed of southern governor came to power—Jimmy Carter in Georgia, Reubin Askew in Florida, and Bill Clinton in Arkansas. They openly welcomed the end of segregation and actively sought the vote of blacks. Even George Wallace of Alabama began to court black voters in the mid-1970s, asking forgiveness for his earlier racist stands.

Following his landslide victory in the 1964 election, which gave

Democrats enormous margins in both the House and the Senate, Lyndon Johnson pushed through legislation creating the agencies for his War on Poverty, providing greater federal aid to education, Medicare, and other measures. The man who had come to political maturity in the New Deal viewed his Great Society as the completion of the unfinished agenda of his hero, Franklin Roosevelt. But where Roosevelt had shown little interest in helping minorities, Johnson wanted to do a great deal. Several historians have suggested that Johnson truly believed in equality and did so as a matter of moral principle. To Johnson, wrote one scholar, "equal rights were a personal thing, not a piece of legislation." Moreover, in the time he had served as head of the Kennedy committee, he had heard the demands for some form of compensatory opportunity, and as can be seen in the story that begins this chapter, he supported affirmative action even before becoming president.

On 4 June 1965, Johnson gave the commencement address at Howard University, which he called "To Fulfill These Rights." After lauding all the gains that had been made by Negroes in breaking the chains of apartheid, he went on:

> But freedom is not enough. You do not wipe away the scars of centuries by saying: Now you are free to go where you want, and do as you desire, and choose the leaders you please. You do not take a person who, for years, has been hobbled by chains and liberate him, bring him up to the starting line of a race and then say, "you are free to compete with all the others," and still justly believe that you have been completely fair. Thus it is not enough just to open the gates of opportunity. All our citizens must have the ability to walk through those gates.
>
> This is the next and the more profound stage of the battle for civil rights. We seek not just freedom but opportunity. We seek not just legal equity but human ability, not just equality as a right and a theory but equality as a fact and equality as a result.

Although the rhetoric is uplifting, there are no particulars. Clearly Johnson did not mean that all the runners should finish the same; the purpose of a race is to win it. Did it mean some form of compensatory action? Did it mean that the government would impose some guidelines that private companies and unions would have to follow? A little more than three months later, Johnson issued Executive Order 11246.

ON 2 DECEMBER 1964, Johnson had asked Hubert Humphrey, the vice president elect, what the best way would be to coordinate the functions of the various federal agencies involved in civil rights. In the weeks that followed, Humphrey spoke to agency heads as well as civil rights activists and scholars and sent Johnson a recommendation that he establish the President's Council on Equal Opportunity. Just as Vice President Johnson had chaired Kennedy's committee, so Humphrey suggested he should chair this one. Johnson acceded, and in Executive Order 11197, issued at the beginning of February 1965, he established the council. He did so, however, with great reluctance, sensing that the Humphrey plan would be ineffectual. On the critical matter of government contract compliance, for example, it did little more than shift responsibility from one interdepartmental committee to another. Additionally, civil rights activists had begun pressuring the administration to do something to speed up the pace of desegregation of southern schools. There is also a sense that simple politics played a role, because shortly after Johnson established the council and named Humphrey to chair it, the vice president began publicly voicing objections to Johnson's Vietnam policies. Civil rights groups expressed dissatisfaction with Humphrey's leadership of the council, adding to Johnson's displeasure. Johnson soon shut Humphrey out of National Security Council meetings and began rethinking how to implement equal opportunity in federal contracts, a plan that would not include his vice president.

On 24 September 1965, Johnson issued two executive orders. Number 11246 shifted responsibility for government employment policy to the Civil Service Commission. The secretary of labor received the task of overseeing nondiscrimination in employment by government contractors. The secretary not only had the power to investigate complaints but, if he found them to be true, could cancel contracts for failure to comply with the equal opportunity policy. If a company or individual had a contract canceled, then they could be barred from getting future contracts. The directive also covered federally assisted construction projects, such as roads or buildings. Executive Order 11247 revoked the earlier order creating the President's Council on Equal Opportunity and placed responsibility for Title VI of the Civil Rights Act (the enforcement provisions) with the attorney general.

Johnson later issued an additional order amending 11246 to include gender discrimination. In 11246, Johnson also created the Office of Federal Contract Compliance (OFCC), a group representing the Civil Service Commission and the Labor Department.

There are a few noteworthy aspects of 11246. First, its length and specifics make it read more like a piece of legislation than a simple presidential proclamation. Second, in its details it gave the secretary of labor more authority than had been granted by the Civil Rights Act to the Equal Employment Opportunity Commission established by that law. Most important, the order not only restated the provision calling upon employers to not discriminate (§ 202-1) but required them to take affirmative action as a condition for approval of federal contracts (§ 301). What this actually meant is not spelled out, and could be interpreted as simply opening the factory gates to any qualified person, regardless of race, all the way up to going out and recruiting black applicants and then giving them some sort of preferential status in hiring.

Johnson probably did not have the latter interpretation in mind but seems to have been more concerned with creating an effective means to carry out the mandate of Title VII. The president wanted a high level of coordination within the government and also wanted to avoid battles between the federal agencies in Washington and the Democratic organizations in the big cities. The wording for "affirmative action" is taken directly from Kennedy's Executive Order 10925 but is in fact mentioned only once in the Johnson order. The impetus behind both 11246 and 11247 appears primarily concerned with stripping authority away from a liberal (and in Johnson's view a disloyal) vice president heading an interagency council with no statutory authority and giving it to departments and individuals who had authority vested in them by law.

Did Johnson—or Kennedy for that matter—have a clear idea of what the phrase "affirmative action" meant in practice? One colleague has suggested that Kennedy favored a "soft" form of affirmative action, while Johnson might be categorized as "soft plus." Neither man argued for what would later be called "hard" action. In the mid-1960s, what constituted affirmative action? Did it merely mean that employers had to take positive steps to ensure lack of discrimination in hiring and promotion, opening doors that had hitherto been closed to minorities and then acting solely on an individual's qualifications and abilities? Or did it mean actively recruiting African Americans and then giving minorities preferential treatment, perhaps even set-ting up quotas? Certainly the 1964 Civil Rights Act did not mandate such a policy, and in fact declared that nothing in Title VII "shall be interpreted . . . to grant preferential treatment to any individual or to any group because of the race, color, religion, sex, or national origin of such an individual or group." In addition, numbers of minorities in the factory as compared with numbers in the general population could not be taken into account, per section 703(j).

There did not seem to be any consensus among Johnson's advisers. In January 1964, as Congress began dealing seriously with the civil rights bill, a White House staffer circulated a statement on the mean-ing and scope of affirmative action. This "relatively new concept" meant "positive or firm or aggressive action as opposed to negative or infirm or passive action." Here again there is no clear articulation of either what the staffer meant or what the administration wanted. During the remainder of Johnson's administration, various officials both in the White House and in various agencies alternated between insisting on race-neutral policies and calling for some form of com-pensatory justice. It also mattered whether there had been earlier and deliberate discrimination. Then, according to Secretary of Labor Willard Wirtz, "it is not enough for that employer or union now to just stop discriminating. There is an affirmative responsibility to counteract the effects of that previous policy." On another occasion a little later, Wirtz declared that he did not support job preference. "Any talk or thought about a quota kind of employment . . . would be terribly, terribly misguided."

Edward Sylvester, the director of the Office of Federal Contract Compliance, also sent mixed signals. Where Kennedy's executive order to end discrimination covered contractors and subcontrac-tors with federal government business in excess of $50,000 a year, Johnson's order set a much lower bar—$10,000 annually. Moreover, employers with fifty or more employees and contracts greater than $50,000 had to implement plans to increase the hiring of underrep-resented minorities and women. Sylvester insisted that "there is no fixed and firm definition of affirmative action." All he could offer in, as he put it, "a general way" was that the phrase meant "anything you have to do to get results." At a gathering of contractors in 1967, he declared that "we really prefer that the contractor determine himself what affirmative action he can take."

Not everyone in the administration shared this ambivalence. Daniel Patrick Moynihan, then a special assistant secretary for research and policy planning in the Labor Department, early on argued for a "hard" affirmative action, one that gave minorities preferential treatment. Negroes, he told Wirtz, "are asking for unequal treatment. . . . It may be that without unequal treatment in the immediate future there is no way to achieve anything like equal status in the long run." Anthony Rachal, a special assistant to the chairman of the U.S. Civil Service Commission, answered critics who warned that an aggressive interpretation of Executive Order 11246 would destroy the merit system. "This is not the case," he declared in 1968. "The intent is to make the merit system whole—a true merit system, one which recognizes that all groups . . . are competent and worthy and that their inclusion . . . is essential to the mandates of the merit system."

SOME FEDERAL AGENCIES took seriously the idea of an aggressive affirmative action policy and during the remainder of the Johnson years worked out the administrative details of how to implement various policies. Some departments vigorously pursued minority recruitment and outreach programs. Representatives of the Labor Department visited colleges that had a significant minority enrollment in an effort to have African Americans and women apply for jobs. The department also reached out to minority organizations, advertised job openings in minority media, and established an internal "upward mobility" program to help lower-level employees qualify for higher-level positions. Similar programs could be found in other departments as well. During both the Kennedy and the Johnson administrations, federal agency heads took seriously the task of getting more minorities hired. The Equal Employment Opportunity Commission, created under Title VII, had been tasked with advising employers how they could meet the nondiscrimination mandate of the Civil Rights Act. The EEOC took the job description it had been given and ran with the ball.

While some people, especially civil rights groups, paid attention to the EEOC, other concerns grabbed the public's attention. Despite assurances that victory in Vietnam would soon be achieved, the war went on and on, with no light at the end of the tunnel. Opposition to Johnson and the war increased, with clashes between demonstrators and police growing more violent. The picture of a young girl crying over the body of a student shot by a National Guardsman at Kent State University became a poster for the antiwar movement. By the time he left office, Johnson had committed over 500,000 troops to the war.

Ironically, as it seemed to many, just as the civil rights movement won great victories in the 1964 and 1965 laws, black anger and frustration erupted in dozens of northern cities in 1966 and 1967. There were 38 riots in 1966, the most serious in Chicago, Cleveland, and San Francisco that left 7 people dead, 400 injured, 3,000 arrested, and more than $5 million in property damaged by fire and looting. The following year there were 164 uprisings, 33 serious enough to require the intervention of state police and another 8 that led to calling out the National Guard. The two biggest riots, in Newark, New Jersey, and Detroit, Michigan, lasted nearly a week and left more than 60 people dead, hundreds injured, and thousands of buildings burned or looted. When the riot finally died down in Detroit, Mayor Jerome Cavanagh said, "It looks like Berlin in 1945."

Nothing seemed to go well for Johnson. While Medicare, civil rights, voting rights, and other parts of his Great Society program would eventually improve the lives of many Americans, at the time critics could point not just to the urban unrest but to the quagmire in Vietnam, the rising crime rate, and a Supreme Court whose due process revolution, they charged, favored the criminal over the police. In 1964, Johnson had won the greatest electoral landslide in decades, and his coattails carried in large majorities of Democrats in both houses of Congress. By early 1968, it looked as if he not only might be defeated in the November election but might be challenged—and successfully—for the Democratic nomination. On 31 March, Johnson announced to the nation that he would not seek reelection to the presidency; the following January, he and his wife returned to their Texas ranch, leaving Richard Nixon in the White House and affirmative action still undefined.

CHAPTER 3

AFFIRMATIVE ACTION
SPREADS—AND MUTATES

In 1964, we declared that no account should be taken of race, color, national origin, or religion in the spheres of voting, jobs, and education. . . . Yet no sooner had we made this national assertion than we entered in an unexampled enterprise of recording the color, race, and national origin of every individual in every significant sphere of his life. Having placed into law the dissenting opinion of Plessy v. Ferguson *that our Constitution is color-blind, we entered into a period of color- and group-consciousness with a vengeance.*

—NATHAN GLAZER

The anti-preferential hiring provisions {of Title VII} are a big zero, a nothing, a nullity. They don't mean anything to us.

—EEOC STAFF MEMBER

Both John Kennedy and Lyndon Johnson favored what has been termed "soft" affirmative action, programs that would open the doors of opportunity—whether in industry, education, or government—to minorities that had hitherto been excluded. This would be achieved in part by federal law to ensure that national, state, and local governments as well as private employers did not discriminate against minorities, especially African Americans. Nothing in either the Civil Rights Act or Executive Order 11246 went beyond this goal.

Early discussion of what should be done to fight discrimination centered on the importance of color-blind and sex-blind rules for all employment decisions. Race and sex should be irrelevant, and employers should seek merit, especially in places they had not previously looked. People often quoted Martin Luther King Jr.'s hope that his children and all people would be judged not "by the color of their skin but by the content of their character." Many reformers, however, soon came to believe that equal opportunity was not enough.

As Richard Epstein has charged, "The ink was scarcely dry on the Civil Rights Act of 1964 when a very different set of goals and objectives came to dominate the civil rights movement: affirmative action for protected groups." Instead of punishing employers who discriminated against blacks and women, the law gave immunity to employers, both public and private, who took race and gender into account in making hiring and promotion decisions. Even before Johnson left office, affirmative action had taken on a life of its own, and representatives of disadvantaged groups called for hiring quotas and workforce demographics that mirrored the local population. Conservatives as well as some figures in the civil rights and women's movements denounced "hard" affirmative action as a threat to the equality rationale that had previously been the dominant motif in their movements. Nonetheless, within a short time, when people spoke about affirmative action—positively or negatively—they meant the "hard" version.

THE IMPETUS FOR a "hard" affirmative action predates Johnson's Howard University speech. The U.S. Civil Rights Commission in its 1961 report on employment had singled out the apprenticeship programs in many industries as being both racially discriminatory and too small to even replace the mainly white workers who retired. Much of the funding for apprenticeship programs came from the Department of Labor's Bureau of Apprenticeship and Training, which supported programs in twenty-two states with 150,000 apprentices. The bureau worked closely with the Construction Industry Joint Council, composed of representatives from eighteen national building trades unions and all the major contractor associations. The history of that relationship emphasized collegiality among all three parties—the government agency, the unions, and the contractors—and the bureau had traditionally seen its role as a promoter, not as a policeman. In fact, before a congressional subcommittee in 1962, the bureau's director explicitly declared that he did not want enforcement power regarding alleged discrimination in apprentice programs.

This began to change in the early 1960s, with the advent of a new chair of the House Education and Labor Committee, Adam Clayton Powell Jr. (D-N.Y.). Powell's committee had the responsibility to monitor Labor Department programs, and like the Kennedy administration in general it grew more responsive to civil rights activism and less concerned about the traditional labor union constituency. Following Kennedy's pledge to move against discrimination in apprenticeship programs and after consulting with Powell, Secretary of Labor Willard Wirtz in June 1963 set out new selection standards for apprenticeship programs and immediately provoked a storm of protest from the construction industry—unions and contractors alike—that the new criteria would impose a racial quota system.

The unions and the contractors clearly understood Wirtz's announcement, despite its bureaucratic language. First, future admis-

Adam Clayton Powell Jr., who represented Harlem in the House of Representatives, became chair of the House Education and Labor Committee in 1961. He immediately began pushing for traditionally all-white unions to accept African Americans into federally financed apprenticeship programs.

sion to the programs would be made on merit standards alone, and in cases where special lists had existed before, they must now be "disregarded to the extent necessary to provide opportunities for current selection of qualified members of racial and ethnic minority groups for a significant number of positions." This meant that the traditional "sponsorship" system no longer applied, by which an existing member of the union had to sponsor someone for the apprenticeship program. This practice, whereby a father sponsored his son or another family member, dated back to the medieval guild system.

The second provision required taking "whatever steps are necessary, in acting upon application lists developed prior to this time, to offset the effect of previous practices under which discriminatory patterns of employment have resulted." Labor unions immediately raised the specter of quotas. The Building and Construction Trades Department of the AFL-CIO, along with the rest of the industry, wanted to know exactly what this meant. What constituted a "significant number" of jobs for minorities? What did it mean that contractors had to "offset" the effects of prior discrimination? Union officials charged that the language not only contradicted the administration's talk about nondiscrimination but actually invited a "veiled quota system."

The third provision called for nondiscrimination in all phases of any apprenticeship program. Behind the seemingly innocuous phrasing existed the enforcement stick. If unions refused to adjust their programs, the Labor Department could "deregister" a program, meaning that contractors would no longer be allowed to pay apprentices lower wages than journeymen, and apprentices in a deregistered program would lose their draft deferments. In addition, the President's Commission on Equal Employment could terminate federal contracts with a deregistered construction company.

Did the Wirtz directive require quotas? It certainly seemed that way, although the secretary denied it. The firestorm of protest from both labor unions and the construction industry—both with powerful friends on Capitol Hill—led the Labor Department to withdraw the regulations, revise them, and then issue a new version in December 1963. The new regulations eliminated entirely the phrase "significant numbers" as well as the offset provision. No further word about quotas appeared.

About this time, it appears that, as Whitney Young pointed out, a number of companies quietly instituted some form of racially preferential hiring practices, although none came forward to boast about it. Businesses associated with Plans for Progress—the device chosen by the Committee on Equal Employment Opportunity chaired by the then vice president, Johnson—announced that sixty thousand new employees had been hired in the summer quarter, of whom one out of four were black. It seemed to Young that given the low number of African Americans employed by these companies in the past, they could not have gotten that many new hires without some form of preferential program, which probably included quotas. This pattern—of companies covertly employing preferential practices but not admitting it publicly—would make it very difficult in the future to get any sort of realistic measurement of how successful nondiscrimination law and affirmative action had been.

IN MANY WAYS, the civil rights movement that had begun with the founding of the NAACP in 1909 came to an end in 1965. The cases that led up to *Brown v. Board of Education* in 1954, *Brown*'s progeny in the decade that followed, the 1964 Civil Rights Act, and the 1965 Voting Rights Act achieved what civil rights activists had been demanding—the end to state-sponsored segregation and the ability to vote freely. Racial discrimination has, of course, continued in various forms right up to the present, but it has been privately sponsored. The dislike of some whites against people of color, bias as King and others recognized, was a type of discrimination that cannot be banned by law.

The courts have used the Civil Rights and Equal Pay Acts as a commitment to rooting out any form of discrimination against members of protected classes, most notably women and African Americans. To this end, various courts have struck down standard industry practices such as the use of sex-linked mortality tables for pensions and insurance; they have given a very narrow reading to what constitutes a BFOQ, a bona fide occupational qualification, which could be used to restrict opportunity for minorities; and at least early on, they applied disparate-impact tests where it could be shown statistically that minorities suffered even in the absence of overt discrimination.

The problem, at least from the African American point of view, was that all the cases and state laws and even the federal statutes did not, in terms of jobs and social well-being, do that much to improve the economic well-being of either the community or the individual. In part, this dissatisfaction reflected a rising level of expectation among northern blacks following the defeat of Jim Crow and a frustration that it had not significantly changed their status. Here one finds a definite disjoint between perception and reality. In the eight years between the time Kennedy took office in 1961 and Johnson left, the portion of Americans living below the poverty line dropped from 22.2 percent to 12.6 percent. Great Society programs such as the Elementary and Secondary Education Act did much to improve the quality of the nation's poorest schools while at the same time reducing school segregation. Medicaid and Medicare, both part of the 1965 Social Security Act Amendments, extended health care to millions of poor and elderly people.

Stephan Thernstrom and Abigail Thernstrom, who have been among the leading academic critics of affirmative action, argue that the pace of economic progress for African Americans was due in large measure to the great migration that brought millions of blacks north and away from state-sponsored Jim Crow. In fact, they claim, economic progress was more rapid before the civil rights legislation of the 1960s. In 1940, 43 percent of black men worked on farms, mainly as tenants, sharecroppers, or simple laborers, at very low wages. By 1960, this number had fallen to 14 percent. "The huge black agricultural proletariat was well on its way to vanishing." Conversely, in 1940 only one in ten black men had any kind of white-collar or skilled labor job, a basic component of being middle class. By 1960, this group had expanded to one in four. The economic position of black women also improved dramatically. In 1940, six out of ten worked as low-paid household help, and twenty years later this number had been cut to one in three. Many black women moved into positions hitherto barred to them, such as clerical and sales work. Black men in 1960 earned an average of two and a half times what they had earned on the eve of the war. The Thernstroms believe that the greatest economic advance of the African American community came before affirmative action and had far more to do with the migration of blacks northward and the healthy state of the American economy.

However, even they concede that economically all was not well in the black community. In 1940, the black unemployment rate exceeded that of whites by only 15 percent. In 1950 this had risen to 84 percent, and by 1960 it stood at more than double the white rate, 10.2 percent as against 5 percent. Moreover, despite the significant progress the Thernstroms record, they admit that "blacks remained far behind whites economically." In 1960, blacks earned 40 percent less, on the average, than whites, and were more than three times as likely to live in families with incomes below the poverty line (39 percent versus 12 percent). While the Thernstroms note that several factors influenced these figures, such as levels of education, "discrimination in the labor market played a part as well. That was especially true in the South."

In a Harris poll taken in 1963, more blacks (30 percent) listed employment discrimination as affecting them than mentioned any other form of discrimination; educational discrimination at 11 percent placed a distant second. Over half believed they received less pay for the same work as a white man would get. In another poll that year, 58 percent of African Americans cited equal job opportunity as the highest priority for immediate government action. In a third 1963 poll, blacks rated the right to hold the same jobs as whites highest among "rights wanted by almost all Negroes."

Even with the passages of the 1964 and 1965 laws, civil rights leaders had become aware that "abolishing legal racism would not produce Negro equality." Bayard Rustin wrote that the civil rights movement had undergone "an evolution calling its very name into question." The movement was "now concerned not merely with removing the barriers to full *opportunity* but with achieving the fact of *equality*." In a similar vein, James Farmer of the Congress of Racial Equality noted that "we can no longer evade the knowledge that most Negroes will not be helped by equal opportunity. These are staggering problems for which the traditional CORE program of anti-discrimination is ill-equipped."

What had happened? Why had the phenomenal success of the civil rights movement led so many of its leaders to see it as a hollow victory? In part, the frustration stemmed from a realization that some of their basic assumptions had simply been wrong. The NAACP, CORE, the Southern Christian Leadership Conference, and the Urban League had all assumed that once the legal supports for Jim Crow had been destroyed, a "natural society" would emerge that would be color-blind and would soon create an integrated and equal America. Suddenly this utopian vision appeared to be just that—utopian and highly oversimplified. True, state and local governments and private corporations could no longer legally treat people of color as a form of inferior species, but economic facts, unlike segregation laws, would not disappear overnight. The Civil Rights Act would not, in the short term, affect a black unemployment rate twice that of whites, or the fact that because of poor education so many employed blacks worked in the lowest-paying jobs. The leitmotif of the civil rights organizations prior to 1965 had been that if racially discriminatory laws and practices could be eliminated, then the individual model of equal opportunity would soon lead to greater economic and social mobility. They ignored a fact that had long been known: a merit-based economy guarantees that many people—those least qualified educationally or occupationally—will be stuck at the bottom. Black leaders now had to deal with the fact that a century of Jim Crow in the South and discrimination in the North had left many African Americans poorly educated and lacking job skills. And once they and their allies began focusing on results, the troubles were inevitable.

In 1965 and 1966, two reports circulated within the government that painted an even more pessimistic view of black life in the United States. Daniel Patrick Moynihan, an academic sociologist then employed in the Labor Department to help develop policy for Johnson's War on Poverty, had gathered a whole variety of economic and social statistics about African Americans. He then focused on

The former professor Daniel Patrick Moynihan in 1974. Under both the Johnson and the Nixon administrations, he pushed for social programs to help black families and later became an influential senator from New York.

what is normally accepted as a prime criterion of social stability and progress—the family. Nearly one in four urban black women who had ever been married were now divorced, separated, or deserted, a rate three times that of white urban women. As a result, one black family in four was fatherless, and more than half of all black children would live in broken homes by their eighteenth birthday. One-fourth of all Negro babies born in America were illegitimate, compared with a 3.07 percent rate for whites. More than half of all blacks subsisted on Aid to Families with Dependent Children for some period in their childhood. At the same time, the birthrate for urban ghetto-dwelling blacks was 40 percent higher than for whites.

The intention of the report, Moynihan later explained, had been not to indict the black family but to use it as "the best point . . . at which to measure the net, cumulative plus or minus impact of outside forces on the Negro community. All the abstractions of employment, housing, income, discrimination, education, et al. come together here." That might have been its intent, but many black activists condemned it as one more example of blaming the victims for their problems. It seemed to say, according to some critics, that if only blacks would take control of their lives, embrace monogamy, and nurture their children, all would be well. But where would the jobs come from? Who would provide better schools, medical care, and the other necessities of life that middle-class white families took for granted?

The year after publication of the Moynihan Report came another government document, the Coleman Report, the result of an obscure provision in the 1964 Civil Rights Act that mandated a study "concerning the lack of availability of equal educational opportunities for individuals by reason of race, color, religion, or national origin in public educational institutions at all levels in the United States." James Coleman, a sociologist at Johns Hopkins University, surveyed four thousand schools and 600,000 students and found— much to his surprise, indeed shock—little difference between black and white schools when it came to physical plant, curricula, and teacher characteristics. However, a significant gap between black and white achievement scores began in the first grade and widened on up through high school, and the level of expenditures had little relation to student success. The data seemed to contradict a long-held shibboleth among professional educators that student accomplishment improved as the community spent more money on school buildings,

equipment, and teacher salaries. The presence of children from afflu-
ent families seemed to be the only characteristic that had any direct
causal relationship to student achievement (as evidenced in standardized test scores).

Despite the grandeur that marked the passage of the Civil Rights
and Voting Rights Acts, the black community, especially in the
North, struggled with social and economic problems that legislation
could not fix. Five days after passage of the Voting Rights Act, blacks
began rioting in the Watts section of Los Angeles. On 11 August,
police arrested an African American motorist for drunk driving. A
minor roadside argument quickly escalated into a fight, and the community exploded in six days of looting and arson. An overwhelmed
Los Angeles Police Department needed the help of four thousand
members of the California National Guard to restore order, but not
before the riots left thirty-four dead and $40 million in property
damage.

Governor Pat Brown asked the former CIA director John McCone
to investigate the causes of the outbreak. The McCone Commission
report, issued in December 1965, identified the root causes as high
unemployment, poor schools, and inferior living conditions for African Americans in Watts. In addition, the community resented the

*Devastation in the Watts area of Los Angeles, 13 August 1965, one of many cities
ravaged by riots spurred on by anger and frustration in racial ghettos.*

passage of Proposition 14, an amendment to the state constitution sponsored by the California Real Estate Association that in effect repealed the Rumford Fair Housing Act.

Over the next few years, racial riots broke out across the country. One scholar counted 290 "hostile outbreaks" from 1966 to 1968, leaving 169 persons dead, seven thousand wounded, forty thousand arrested, and hundreds of millions in property damage, nearly all of it in the black ghettos.

There is no claim that affirmative action had any causal effect on the rioting over those three long, hot summers. Rather, reports on nearly all of the riots take note of high unemployment, poor housing, lack of jobs, discrimination, poor schools, and in general a sense that the benefits of both national prosperity and civil rights activism had not gone to the people of the urban ghettos in the North. Certainly the uprisings played into the hands of the growing conservative movement in the United States, which looked on the disturbances, as well as the opposition to the Vietnam War, the women's movement, and the cultural revolution of the young and the hippies, as signs of the fraying of the American social fabric. For others, the riots signaled that redressing the evils of racism and reversing the legacy of Jim Crow could no longer be delayed.

THE CIVIL RIGHTS MOVEMENT, that is, those groups and activists who had led the fight against Jim Crow and whose greatest accomplishments had been the Civil Rights and Voting Rights Acts, had no game plan for what they would do next. King and others, it is true, had already marked economic improvement as the next step, but aside from Whitney Young's abortive call for a Marshall Plan for African Americans, nothing specific came out of a movement already in the process of fragmenting. In city after city, when civil rights leaders tried to intercede to bring order, the rioters ignored them. The comedian and civil rights activist Dick Gregory was shot in the leg trying to restore order in Watts.

Although southern racists saw King and others as radicals, he and his followers had actually preached nonviolence and supported legislative and judicial means to secure the specific changes they wanted. Now that they had achieved those goals, what next? James Farmer, former head of CORE, in 1966 described the civil rights movement as "reeling" and said that the major organizations "didn't know where they were going or what to do at that point." A. Philip Randolph, the beloved leader of the Brotherhood of Sleeping Car Porters, declared that "the civil rights movement is undergoing great frustration and fragmentation at the present time." Martin Luther King's last book, published in 1967, had the title *Where Do We Go from Here: Chaos or Community?*

The Johnson administration, well aware of the frustration in the black community, had no one to talk to, no one putting forth specific proposals that would rally African Americans. In many ways, the debate over affirmative action in the years to come would be played out without the traditional civil rights groups and their leaders affecting the discussion. Government agencies, at both the state and the national levels, private businesses, and the courts would determine the manner and impact of affirmative action. Moreover, other minority groups such as women and Latinos began demanding affirmative action benefits as well.

IF AFFIRMATIVE ACTION had no causal relation to the riots in the mid-1960s, the opposite is not true: the riots spurred the Johnson administration to urge businesses to go out and recruit Negroes for jobs. During the riots, representatives of the administration reported back regularly on the absence of black faces either in the police forces or in the National Guard units trying to regain control. Attorney General Ramsey Clark told the president that "the deployment of military forces composed almost entirely of whites heightened the tension and anger in the Newark riot area."

The National Advisory Commission on Civil Disorders, known as the Kerner Commission, appointed by Johnson to study the causes of the riots, also took seriously the need for affirmative action in both the police and the National Guard. While African Americans made up approximately 10 percent of the population, they made up only 1.15 percent of the Army National Guard and 0.6 percent of the Air National Guard. Johnson passed this information on to Secretary of Defense Robert McNamara, noting, "This is a matter of highest urgency and I know you will give it your immediate attention."

But police and to some extent the National Guard were creatures of the state, not of the national government, and in many places— not only in the South—local white officials had no desire to see more black policemen. When federal officials pointed out the lack of black faces in the Newark, New Jersey, police force, and how this had been a hindrance in trying to put down the rioting, the mayor of Newark,

Hugh J. Addonizio, said he would try to get the money to promote one Negro lieutenant to captain.

In the wake of the riots, several Great Society programs targeted inner-city blacks, and by 1966 blacks constituted over half the people involved in the federal government's antipoverty efforts. One job program, supposedly color-blind on its face, had an 81 percent black participation rate in 1968, while six out of ten persons employed in the Job Corps were black.

But no matter how large the federal government grows, and even if it is the single largest employer in the country, the vast majority of men and women work in the private sector. Great Society programs could reach only a limited number of people; moreover, should administrations change, another president or another Congress could kill the Great Society agencies or seriously reduce their funding. Business leaders heard both from their peers and from the government what they should do. A *Harvard Business Review* article titled "To Prevent a Chain of Super-Watts" painted a grim picture of what could happen to business interests from either rioting or government response to rioting that would place increased control of business decisions in the hands of the government. The Ad Council and the National Alliance for Businessmen produced a public service campaign asking business "to give jobs to ghetto blacks before their businesses burned down."

The logic that hiring Negroes could somehow control black violence seems to have been fairly widespread. *U.S. News & World Report* reported on companies like Jersey Bell in Newark hiring black high school dropouts who failed the normal application tests, or Standard Oil of California taking on black employees with an arrest record to work at their service stations. The aim, according to the writer, "would be to ease discontent that has brought violence and destruction to many of America's big cities in recent summers."

In Detroit, one of the cities hardest hit by rioting, the need to hire African Americans through affirmative action programs made good sense. An officer of a utility company admitted that this practice could be seen as reverse discrimination, "but such steps are required to convince the Negroes that we are serious and want them to apply for work with us."

The administration watched this activity closely, encouraging it and even setting up special programs to facilitate hiring people who lacked job skills. Early 1968 saw the creation of Job Opportunities in the Business Sector (JOBS), which involved partially subsidized on-site training in private businesses. JOBS worked with the National Alliance of Business—which Johnson had helped organize—to secure promises of employment openings from private firms. After a year and a half, 150,000 people had been hired, 75 percent of whom were black.

One could go on with other examples of private businesses adopting some form of affirmative action in the 1960s, and while the Johnson administration certainly encouraged them to do so, much of the time self-interest proved a very strong incentive. Paul Gorman, the president of the Bell System's Western Electric Company, told a reporter that "if cities continue to deteriorate, our investment will inevitably deteriorate with them." Although initially many of the jobs that became available to blacks were unskilled, eventually some of these men and women showed promise and received promotions. As more and more African Americans went to college or trade school, they found that companies that had once shut out black applicants now happily took them. This is not to say that the riots and the Johnson administration led American businesses to suddenly end discrimination against minorities. But the 1960s saw a start, and what we need to keep in mind is that often private companies adopted affirmative action—even in its "hard" form—for sound business reasons.

Later, when the Reagan administration opposed affirmative action, private businesses remained free to hire as they saw fit, and usually this meant keeping the door open for minorities. In the midst of the Reagan years, Marion Sandler of Golden West Financial explained why the company had instituted an affirmative action plan for Hispanics. "The whole country is moving away from being white, Anglo, and Protestant to polyglot," especially in places like Texas and California where Golden West did business. "You have to recognize what's happening and be part of it." Golden West and other companies understood that the huge potential market of Hispanic and African American customers would be lost if only white faces staffed their banks.

Richard Epstein, a consistent critic of governmental efforts to establish affirmative action, nonetheless applauded what the private sector had done. "There should be no legal obstacle against the practice," he wrote, "no matter how extensive or overt, of affirmative action by private institutions if they are willing to pay the costs of implementing any such programs, whether these costs are large or small." More and more private businesses adopted plans, not because the government told them to do so, but because such plans made sense from a business point of view.

ALTHOUGH JOHNSON in his 1965 Howard speech had talked about going beyond just outlawing discrimination, there is little evidence of what he meant or hoped to do. He certainly wanted to increase the pool of workers available for jobs or students for college to include more African Americans, women, and other minorities. But Johnson, like Kennedy before him, espoused a "soft" form of affirmative action.

In Johnson's second term, two government agencies began developing affirmative action policies that clearly went beyond the "soft" view. In Executive Order 11246, Johnson had created the Office of Federal Contract Compliance, and the 1964 Civil Rights Act established the permanent Equal Employment Opportunity Commission. In the executive order, contractors had to not only hire without discrimination but also take affirmative action. What that meant would depend on what the OFCC and EEOC decided it meant. These two entities almost from the beginning adopted the "hard" interpretation of affirmative action, one that went further than merely opening a door to actively bringing in minorities and giving them preferential treatment.

One should keep in mind that Title VII of the 1964 Civil Rights Act specifically forbade the use of group-based, equal-results approaches in civil rights enforcement. There could be no requirement of "preferential treatment to any individual group" because of race, color, religion, sex, or national origin, or on account of "an imbalance which may exist" in their numbers or percentages relative to the community demographics. The EEOC legal staff, after months of research on what Title VII allowed and forbade, came to the conclusion that "by the explicit terms of section 703(j), an employer cannot be found in violation of Title VII simply because his use of minority groups does not mirror their representation in the community." All an employer had to do was post notices and not discriminate in hiring or other employment practices. Nonetheless, before long employers had to do more.

The OFCC, established by executive order and housed in the Department of Labor, spent much of its first two years developing new forms by which to measure compliance by federal contractors with a nondiscrimination policy. Not until 1968 did the OFCC finally institute a coherent plan. First, when entering the bidding process for a federal contract, companies had to "submit such information as the Federal Highway Administration or the Director of the Office of Federal Contract Compliance requests," specifically statistics on the number of minority members in the firm's workforce. The Labor Department identified groups to be included in the employment census—"Negroes," "Orientals," "American Indians," and "Spanish Americans." If the information of the low bidder appeared satisfactory, a contract would be awarded; if not, the agency moved on to the next low bidder or re-advertised the contract.

As one attorney who tried to work in this system noted, "The deficiencies were legion." Neither contractor nor compliance officer had any clear idea what an acceptable plan should contain. As a result, different agencies—and even different officers within the same agency—could approve or reject a plan without reference to any accepted baseline. Some officers believed that affirmative action simply meant "more." Contractors might find that a plan that had been approved for one bid might be disapproved for another on the grounds that repetition did not constitute affirmative action; there had to be "more" minorities.

In 1966, Edward Sylvester, the OFCC's first director, announced that contractors who wanted to bid on $125 million in school and hospital construction projects in the Cleveland area had to provide affirmative action plans that "have the result of assuring that there was minority group representation in all trades on the job in all phases of the work." Although Sylvester did not mention quotas, the idea of proportional representation could not be missed. One contractor offered to provide a "manning table" that would indicate the specific number of minority workers to be hired in each trade. The OFCC awarded the contract and began urging manning tables on all other firms bidding for contracts in the Cleveland area.

Sylvester at all times emphasized results-oriented affirmative action that shied away from specific numbers. Years later, he told a reporter that "the average business guy wants to know what to do. You've got to give him numbers. They'd say, 'Tell me what you want and when.'" One OFCC compliance officer explained that all one had to do was "take the employer to the cliff and say, 'Look over, baby.'" Over the cliff lay cancellation of a contract. Because the OFCC knew that federal laws prohibited quotas, it deliberately avoided detailing what the affirmative action numbers should be. It wanted affirmative action to be vague and imprecise, because it believed it would be successful that way. Sylvester declared, "We really prefer that the contractor determine himself what affirmative action he can take." The obligation, he told a meeting of government contractors, would vary according to the situation, "from day to day, from place to place, from escalation to escalation," depending on the local labor market. Affirmative action, he concluded, "is anything that you have to do to get results."

THE STORY OF THE Equal Employment Opportunity Commission is far more complex, but in the end it too managed to subvert the prohibitions in Title VII and implement a "hard" affirmative action. There seems to have been confusion from the start about exactly what the EEOC should be, what it should do, and what powers it had. Originally, a proposal that had come out of the House Education and Labor Committee in 1963 had envisioned a regulatory agency like the Federal Trade Commission (FTC) or the National Labor Relations Board. These agencies had been created to enforce *public* rights so that citizens would be protected by the government against tainted foods or union-busting employers. They could investigate complaints, issue cease-and-desist orders, hold quasi-judicial hearings, and if necessary as a last recourse take alleged malefactors to court. The idea behind the FTC and NLRB, dating back to the Progressive and New Deal eras, was that of efficient control of the product market through administrative action. Had this template been kept, not only would the EEOC have been a powerful entity, but it would have had already existing agencies as a model, complete with administrative law and procedures it could have adapted.

This proposal, however, never made it into the 1964 bill because of opposition from southerners and conservatives, both of whom opposed having another powerful federal agency, especially one with a mission to combat racial discrimination. The EEOC that emerged had a responsibility for enforcing an *individual's* right to nondiscrimination. Where the Federal Trade Commission, for example, wanted to protect all citizens against shoddy or dangerous articles, and could act with or without an individual complaint, the EEOC had the task of enforcing an individual's *private* right to nondiscrimination. Moreover, it could investigate and attempt to resolve individual complaints, but without the power to adjudicate problems. For example, if a company discriminated against blacks (or women) and, say, ten minority employees had received lower wages than white employees in similar positions, all ten would have to file an individual complaint, and the EEOC had no power to go against the employer. Liberals condemned the EEOC as a toothless agency that could only react to discrimination; a 1966 study referred to the EEOC as a "poor enfeebled thing."

The EEOC got off to a bad start; a few days after it moved in to its offices, Watts erupted. Theoretically, the agency's jurisdiction would grow so that in three years it would cover 358,000 companies employing 30.6 million workers, including 16 million members of fifty-two thousand union locals. Congress appropriated $5.2 million for its first year, an amount smaller than that of the Office of Coal Research. The Federal Crop Insurance Corporation had a larger staff than the EEOC's 314 people. The budget had been derived on the assumption that the agency would process only 2,000 complaints the first year; instead, it received 8,854. Within ten years, the number of complaints rose to 77,000.

After the passage of the 1964 act, Johnson had a lot on his plate—the war in Vietnam, the election that fall, and then getting the new Congress to enact his Great Society programs. As a result, he did not appoint the five members of the EEOC until June 1965, delaying the start-up organizational planning for a year. As chair he chose a "name": Franklin D. Roosevelt Jr., a former member of Congress and a weak administrator who really had no interest in the agency; Roosevelt resigned before the end of his first year to run—unsuccessfully—for governor of New York. Rumors said that the younger Roosevelt spent most of that first year on his yacht. Subsequent agency heads also did not last very long.

Into this administrative morass and leadership vacuum stepped the Rutgers University law professor Alfred W. Blumrosen, a man who combined a passion for justice with a sharp criticism of existing state and federal civil rights enforcement. Between 1965 and 1967, Blumrosen led the organization of the EEOC and then served as its first chief of conciliation and director of state-federal regulations. He had been at the agency only two weeks when he proposed that the federal government organize a uniform national standard for reporting compliance. "The history of the period 1945–1965," he explained, "makes it clear that the use of numerical standards is necessary if there is to be significant improvement in the employment opportunities. Milder medicine will not work."

The EEOC during these early years is a case study in bureaucratic aggrandizement. It took a nonexistent congressional mandate and turned it into a powerful tool to advance civil rights in the work-place. In the absence of leadership from the five EEOC commission-ers, Alfred Blumrosen had the freedom to shape the EEOC and its mission in the image he thought it should have. "Creative admin-istration," Blumrosen later wrote, "converted a powerless agency operating under an apparently weak statute into a major force for the elimination of employment discrimination." He led the EEOC in interpreting the terms of the Civil Rights Act "liberally" rather than literally. African Americans needed more and better jobs, and the EEOC should see that they got them.

To give but one example of Blumrosen's creativity, Title VII had prohibited the EEOC from requiring employers to submit statistics on the racial makeup of their workforce in any state that had a Fair Employment Practices Commission, which almost all states had out-side the South. Blumrosen decided that the intent of Congress had been to prevent duplication; that is, an employer should not have to file both a state report and a federal one. So, according to Blumrosen, the EEOC could require such a report unless the state Fair Employ-ment Practices Commission had done so, and as it turned out, none of them did. He admitted there was a problem with this interpreta-tion, in that "it required a reading of the statute contrary to its plain meaning." But, as he said, no one in Congress objected, and a national reporting system came into being—something Blumrosen had from the outset said was badly needed. Companies with a hundred or more employees had to report on the racial and gender composition of their workforce at each occupational level.

The database Blumrosen started would prove one of the EEOC's most important tools. Some record keeping regarding minorities already existed, such as minority populations in schools under court-ordered desegregation and the various Bureau of Labor Statistics sur-veys on labor trends. But race and gender played only a minor role in the latter's work. EEOC needed records that covered not only industries but geographic areas as well. EEOC staff wanted data that would be industry specific, such as the distribution by race or sex in the aerospace industry or retail trades in New York. By 1967, the EEOC had the core of what would become a very large database, one that proved indispensable in its future work.

The inclusion of gender in these reports makes a great deal of sense to anyone aware of the extent of sex discrimination in recent American history, but in 1965 the modern women's movement was still aborning. The National Organization for Women (NOW) would not be founded until a year later, and Johnson's Executive Order 11375, amending 11246 to include sex discrimination, would not be issued until October 1967. Why then did the EEOC include gender in its demands for employment statistics? Title VII did prohibit sex discrimination, but at the time most people focused on racial prejudice. Much of the credit goes to Sonia Pressman.

Pressman and her family had fled from Germany in the 1930s, and in America she had gone to Cornell and then to the University of Miami Law School. She would be a founding member of NOW and of Federally Employed Women and became the first woman attorney in the EEOC's Office of General Counsel. She worked on documenting disparities in employment patterns that would indicate discriminatory intent. In 1966, she drafted an influential memorandum suggesting the EEOC could use statistical data of an employer's workforce as legal evidence of discriminatory patterns. This, of course, fit right in with Blumrosen's ideas, and he readily agreed with her that because Title VII banned gender discrimination, the data they gathered should include women.

As an example of how little most government bureaucrats thought of prejudice against women, the Budget Bureau reviewed the EEOC after two years and criticized the growing backlog in processing complaints. In its first eighteen months, the EEOC had received 15,000 complaints and had earmarked 6,040 for investigation, but the small staff had been able to process only 3,319. By the time the five commissioners had reviewed the files and the five-person conciliation staff had conducted confidential negotiations with employers, the EEOC could claim only 110 closed cases after twenty-one months. The Budget Bureau found that the EEOC was devoting only a third of its funds to its main function, identifying and resolving discrimination complaints. The Budget people found one potential source of relief. They noted with surprise that a third of the complaints charged sex discrimination and suggested that the EEOC concentrate on the racial complaints. "Less time [could] be devoted to sex cases, since the legislative history would indicate that they deserve a lower priority than discrimination because of race or other factors."

BOTH DETRACTORS and defenders of the EEOC agree that the agency bears the onus or deserves the credit for establishing a federal policy of "hard" affirmative action. It also amazes commentators that the agency could do this at a time when it had no power to issue cease-and-desist orders or take alleged violators to court. Its statutorily limited powers included investigating individual complaints, making findings of reason to believe discrimination existed, and then conciliating disputes between employer and complainant. The commission could also issue procedural interpretations of Title VII and file amicus curiae (friend of the court) briefs in individual cases. Yet, as Herman Belz charged, "the EEOC revised the basic principles of employment discrimination law and began the transformation of equality of opportunity into equality of result."

To get there, the EEOC literally had to ignore not only the wording of Title VII but its legislative history as well. Support of conservatives as well as of labor unions for Title VII rested on assurances that past discriminatory practices would not be an issue. The EEOC would be starting on a clean slate, its actions confined to current and future practices of discrimination. This ban on retroactivity had been southern focused, to assure the South that the EEOC would neither be investigating nor prosecuting employers for Jim Crow–era discrimination.

The problem for proponents of an equal-results standard is that it sealed off the historical argument necessary, indeed crucial, to an effects test. A number of civil rights activists had said that discrimination resulted less from the prejudices of a specific employer than from the general sociocultural environment in which institutional racism flourished. The statistics that Alfred Blumrosen wanted would show not only current employment numbers but also past practices. But how could the EEOC document discrimination if legally its history only began in 1965?

The EEOC had to somehow (1) substitute a historical-based effects test in lieu of the intent standard in Title VII; (2) gather the statistics to show not individual discrimination but a "disparate impact," that is, the result of past and present practices had a greater effect on excluding blacks (and women) than on whites; and (3) devise remedies that would make job distribution proportional to minority populations. But where could it find the statutory authority to do so, because only Congress or the federal courts could change the clear meaning of Title VII's limits on the EEOC?

The historian and sociologist Hugh Davis Graham termed the EEOC a "subversive bureaucracy." As a *permanent* government agency, it had advantages over the *temporary* government of either the president, his appointees, or even the Congress, which changed, sometimes a great deal, every two years. The EEOC would be expected to formulate rules and regulations, which it would then apply, and in doing so it sought both leverage and freedom to maneuver well beyond the limits imposed in its founding statute.

It appears that almost from the beginning the leaders of the EEOC, both the commissioners and the influential staff members such as Blumrosen, favored a far more aggressive posture than Title VII provided. In August 1965, a month after the EEOC opened its office, Lyndon Johnson called a White House conference on employment discrimination. EEOC commissioners and staff, as well as major civil rights groups, agreed that discrimination should be defined as a pattern of social and economic disadvantage caused by both employment practices and related social institutions. Clearly this made individual case-by-case conciliation totally irrelevant. The conference approved Blumrosen's plan to gather nationwide statistics that included numbers of minority employees. The EEOC could then use these figures to publicize both geographic areas and individual firms that had underrepresented minorities in an effort to shame them into hiring more minorities. Although no mention of class-action lawsuits could be found in Title VII, the White House conference blessed the idea of the EEOC helping lawsuits based on racial disparity in the workforce. This disparity would establish a prima facie charge of discrimination and throw the burden of proof onto the employer.

This approach clearly ran counter to the words of Title VII and what the debate in Congress had indicated those phrases meant. Instead of starting a tabula rasa in 1965, the EEOC would take into account past practices. Herman Edelsberg, the EEOC executive director, reported one year later that the commission saw discrimination not as "an act of individual malice but more an element of a pattern of customary conduct." Individual employers might not intend to discriminate, but "traditional attitudes and patterns of conduct in business . . . may have the effect of barring minorities from employment opportunities as surely as overt discrimination itself." He went on that simply expanding recruitment—the heart of "soft" affirmative action—would not produce the "results that are needed." Where patterns of discrimination existed (and this would be shown by looking at historical data), the EEOC wanted "specific results, immediate hiring and promotion of Negroes," not proposals for equal opportunity in the future. He assured civil rights leaders that "the name of the game in EEOC is jobs."

More and more, the EEOC shifted its emphasis from the Title VII–mandated individual reconciliation to overt pressure on employers to hire minorities. Clifford Alexander, the EEOC chairman, declared in 1968 that we "here at EEOC believe in numbers . . . our most valid standard is in numbers in a variety of categories, not just total numbers. The only accomplishment is when we look at all those numbers and see a vast improvement in the picture." The only word missing, but certainly implied, was "quotas."

Had the EEOC stuck to the very narrow confines of its statutory mandate, it would have remained a "poor enfeebled thing." How could it handle thousands and thousands of individual cases without any real power to force employers to cease discrimination? How could it determine what constituted a discriminatory practice without reference to what had happened prior to 1965?

When the Kerner Commission held hearings on employment discrimination in October 1967, it heard testimony that buttressed the EEOC's view on what needed to be done. Governor Otto Kerner opened the meeting declaring that on the testimony they had heard so far, employment constituted the most urgent need of the inner-city black community. A crisis existed, the status quo did not work, and so the commission welcomed new ideas.

The final report of the Kerner Commission in 1968 fully adopted the disparate-impact approach as the best means of determining the existence of racial discrimination. In fact, the document is sometimes given credit for legitimizing affirmative action ideas, especially the notions of disparate impact, systemic discrimination, and proportional hiring. Moreover, the report reached a wide audience. The first edition of thirty thousand copies sold out in three days, and eventually millions of copies of both the hardback and the paperback editions circulated around the country. It received endorsements not only from civil rights stalwarts like King and Young but also from the black power advocate H. Rap Brown.

The report also contributed to the fact that by 1968 the EEOC's interpretation of Title VII enjoyed wide acceptance in the civil rights community and, to a limited extent, in the larger community as well. The 1965 cutoff date had been unceremoniously discarded. The commission had created one of the largest databases in the country, which gave industry and geographic information on the numbers of minorities and women employed and at what level. An emerging legal doctrine championed by the commission, and welcomed by plaintiffs' lawyers, rested on a statistical analysis showing disparate impact, which, once established, threw the burden onto the employer, without regard to the individual intent required by Title VII. More and more, an affirmative action based on numbers, whether described as quotas or not, seemed well on the way to becoming the norm.

CHAPTER 4

NIXON AND THE PHILADELPHIA PLAN

Incredible but true, it was the Nixonites who gave us employment quotas.

—*FORTUNE,* AT THE TIME OF NIXON'S DEATH IN 1994

Richard Nixon was the strongest president on affirmative action—up to that point.

—JAMES FARMER, CIVIL RIGHTS LEADER

When I was a plumber, it never occurred to me to have niggers in the union.

—GEORGE MEANY, PRESIDENT OF THE AFL-CIO

More than two decades after his death, the mention of Richard Nixon immediately conjures up the derogatory epithet of "Tricky Dick," the southern strategy designed to thwart desegregation, the secret bombings of Cambodia, the "enemies" list, the Watergate scandal, and his resignation in 1974 to avoid impeachment. Yet almost as soon as objective scholars began looking at the Nixon years, they found puzzling contradictions to the view that he was the Darth Vader of American politics. The Nixon administration created the Environmental Protection Agency, began the withdrawal of American troops from Vietnam, reopened American relations with mainland China, established wage and price controls to tamp down inflation, set up the Office of Minority Business Enterprise (OMBE), moved from a draft to an all-volunteer army, expanded the reach and power of the Equal Employment Opportunity Commission, and, despite his campaign rhetoric, set up an expansive affirmative action program that Johnson had failed to do during his tenure.

A complex man who could swing from strong support of a program to opposing it, Nixon's opposition to discrimination, his pragmatism, and his political instincts all influenced his approach to affirmative action. He had learned about discrimination during his years as vice president, and when he took over the Oval Office, he not only recognized a need to open the building trades to minorities but saw significant political advantages in doing so. Affirmative action in his administration began with Nixon's leadership, but when he lost interest, it freed willing bureaucrats to apply their own standards.

NIXON'S SUPPORT FOR black entrepreneurship emerged during the 1968 campaign, as part of his response to the urban riots sweeping the nation. On the one hand, he condemned the violence and pledged that his would be a law-and-order administration. On the other, he believed that racial tensions could be healed if ghetto residents had economic opportunities. Recognizing that minorities had been in large measure frozen out of the market, Nixon had called for "black capital ownership." Although African Americans made up about 12 percent of the population, they owned only 4 percent of the businesses in the country, and those firms produced less than 1 percent of all sales and assets.

Nixon had no illusions about solving black America's problems through minority entrepreneurship, and he understood the enormous problems facing such a program. "*Any* small business has a 75% chance of failing," he told Secretary of Commerce Maurice Stans, "and a *minority* small business has a 90% chance of failing." High crime rates also made ghetto businesses risky. A little over six weeks after his inauguration, Nixon signed Executive Order 11458, establishing the Office of Minority Business Enterprise within the Commerce Department. Stans also set up, under the already existing Small Business Administration (SBA), an agency to provide loans to minority-owned small-business investment companies and by 1972 had established some fifty programs. Although the office disclaimed that it awarded grants based on race alone, in fact the funds only went to minorities.

The idea certainly had merit. The low level of minority business ownership resulted from many factors—shortage of capital, lack of managerial skills (because blacks had been shut out of white-owned businesses where they could have learned), and competition from larger and better-financed white firms. Minority-owned businesses had a high failure rate, and according to some commentators the black community in general held business in low esteem.

The OMBE had no program budget and no authority but was directed to "coordinate" the efforts of some 116 existing programs in twenty-one different agencies. Nixon proposed no transfer of federal programs or agencies, and he asked for no new funds from Congress. As a result, the OMBE, with a staff of ten and no budget of its own, had to seek funds from other agencies. To the dismay of Leonard Garment, the White House staff member in charge of minority affairs, the creation of the black-oriented OMBE triggered a turf war with a section of the Small Business Administration headed by a Hispanic, Hilary Sandoval. All in all, the OMBE initially looked like a cheap trick, designed to placate civil rights activists. "Nothing much is happening," commented Clarence Mitchell of the NAACP, while Whitney Young lamented, "Black capitalism is a shambles."

Eventually, Congress did appropriate money for the OMBE in 1971 and increased that amount the following year. Within a few years, the government made grants, loans, and guarantees to minority businesses valued at nearly $250 million. In addition, many federal procurement contracts required that a certain amount be set aside for minority businesses, and this number rose from a very modest $8 million in 1969 to $243 million in 1972.

With the establishment of the OMBE, as Terry Eastland noted, "runners of other colors appeared alongside the black runners." In the reporting forms used by the agency, minorities included, along with blacks, American Indians, Puerto Ricans and other Spanish-speaking Americans, Asian Americans, Eskimos, Aleuts, and eventually women as well.

The program had mixed results. On the one hand, it helped establish forty-five of the largest Hispanic-owned businesses in the country between 1969 and 1976, and 30 percent of black businesses between 1969 and 1971. Spurred on by the federal example, private industry created the National Minority Purchasing Council, which led to some $50 million in new business for minority firms in 1969 and far more than that in later years. The number of businesses owned by African Americans grew from 163,000 when Nixon took office to 195,000 in 1972, and their gross income increased by more than 50 percent.

Some of that gain can be attributed to high inflation, but by 1972 only twenty-six black-owned businesses had annual sales exceeding $5 million. The income of the top one hundred black businesses combined would have earned them a ranking of 284 on the Fortune 500 list. Moreover, during the entire Nixon administration the growth of government loans to nonminority businesses grew far more rapidly than loans to African-American- and Hispanic-owned companies. Nonetheless, minority business owners prospered under Nixon as they had not under Kennedy and Johnson.

RICHARD NIXON MIGHT NOT have had the fire in his belly that marked Lyndon Johnson's championship of civil rights, but in his own way he wanted to improve the lot of African Americans and other minorities. In the latest biography of him, John Farrell notes that Nixon not only met civil rights activists while he was vice president but impressed them with his sincerity; Martin Luther King thought highly of him, as did other civil rights leaders.

In his first year in office, in addition to setting up the OMBE, he not only reaffirmed the policy of equal employment opportunity in the federal government supported by past presidents but went a bit further, requiring all agencies and departments to establish affirmative action programs. In forwarding the order to department and agency heads, the White House noted a recent report by the Civil Service Commission regarding the lingering problem of discrimination in federal employment. The government must, Nixon said, "through positive action, make it possible for our citizens to compete on a truly equal basis for employment and to qualify for advancement within the federal service."

In his memoirs, the White House aide John Ehrlichman described Nixon as believing strongly that "the majority of Americans did not support open housing, affirmative action . . . , the Equal Employment Opportunity Commission, and other federal civil rights activities." Two factors, however, motivated the president in his plan to improve the economic lot of minorities: his service as Eisenhower's vice president chairing the Government Contract Committee, and that men among his trusted advisers convinced him that the only way to avoid continued racial strife such as the urban riots of the past few years lay in somehow finding a way for African Americans to get out of poverty and work their way into the middle class. Chief among these advisers was his choice for secretary of labor, George P. Shultz.

Left to right, *President Richard Nixon, George Meany, president of the AFL-CIO, and Secretary of Labor George Shultz in the Oval Office in March 1969. Although Nixon originally had little interest in labor matters, Shultz not only persuaded him to adopt affirmative action, but argued it would be politically advantageous to him.*

An experienced labor negotiator and dean of the University of Chicago Graduate School of Business, Shultz, like many Republicans at the time, had conservative economic views but liberal social ideas. Nixon later called him a "bulldog," an academic intellectual whose calm demeanor masked an iron determination. For Nixon, the Labor Department originally mattered little because it had an overwhelmingly Democratic constituency, so he welcomed the recommendation of his economic adviser, Arthur Burns, that Dean Shultz would do fine as secretary of labor.

At the end of 1968, Secretary-designate Shultz delivered the presidential address at the Chicago meeting of the Industrial Relations Research Association. The country faced many problems, he said, but at the top stood the question of race and employment. Until recently, labor economists like himself had mostly ignored the "appalling unemployment experience of black teen-agers," an exclusion he termed dangerous. Without spelling out specifics, Shultz called for "special measures" and for government incentives to persuade employers facing the "explosive" situation of racially skewed unemployment. Employers, he declared, "cannot conduct business as usual."

Shultz also knew, although he did not mention it in his talk, about the rampant racism in the craft unions. The industrial unions that had been part of the CIO had slowly begun the racial integration of their organizations. But the men—and they were nearly all men—of the skilled trades unions of the AFL continued to exclude minorities, despite the calls of national leadership to open their ranks to minorities. Shultz decided to launch his attack on the construction unions, which had for years excluded minorities from all but the lowest-paying and most menial unskilled jobs.

The racism of the major construction trades unions proved difficult to dismantle. In October 1961, the U.S. Commission on Civil Rights had issued a lengthy report charging that "most international unions have failed to exhibit any profound concern over civil rights problems." Existing federal law, the report charged, "has little impact on the discriminatory practices of labor organizations." One year later, the NAACP president, Roy Wilkins, lamented that a "Negro worker needs the patience of Job, the hide of an elephant, plus a crowbar to get into Mr. Meany's own union—the plumbers."

The Democratic administrations of Kennedy and Johnson, despite calling for affirmative action in federal contracts, did little to actually force the unions to integrate. In Nixon's first year in office, before he could put any plans into effect, union discrimination triggered several protests across the North. Racial disputes delayed construction projects at the University of Washington, Tufts, and the State University of New York at Buffalo. In other places, black demands for admission into unions led to white backlash. Pittsburgh's mayor pressed construction unions to admit African Americans, and white workers descended on city hall brandishing American flags and "Wallace in '72" and "We Are the Majority" placards. A government probe of union bias in Chicago brought rank-and-file members onto the streets. "I had to wait my turn getting my apprenticeship," one worker told a reporter. "Why should these guys be given special consideration just because they happen to be black?"

The administration also knew that the NAACP planned to institute lawsuits to halt construction of government projects unless the builders hired qualified blacks. At a news conference, Roy Wilkins described the building trades unions as the "last bastion against employment of Negro workers as a policy." Blacks wanted a just share of the $80 billion planned construction in the coming year. Before long, lawsuits would be filed in Buffalo and Chicago seeking injunctions to prevent federal, state, and local officials from spending any construction money until procedures ensured that minorities could obtain jobs. In addition, the Legal Defense Fund filed a complaint with the Department of Housing and Urban Development to suspend further work on the Model Cities Program in Charlotte, North Carolina, until an affirmative action program had been put in place in accordance with the provisions of the Model Cities Act.

Shultz took over Labor at a difficult time. The holdover head of the Equal Employment Opportunity Commission, Clifford Alexander, had refused to tender his resignation to the new president. In Congress, a subcommittee of the Senate Judiciary Committee headed by Edward Kennedy had begun investigating a $9.4 million contract with three southern textile mills, from which the Pentagon had failed to get written assurances and plans for affirmative action before awarding them contracts. The blatant anti-union as well as racially discriminatory policies at J. P. Stevens & Company had even evoked the ire of Republican members of the subcommittee, with Senator Everett Dirksen of Illinois attacking the EEOC and the Office of Federal Contract Compliance for failing to do their jobs.

A few weeks after taking office, Nixon met with Shultz and Secretary of Housing and Urban Development George W. Romney, and the three men discussed what each recognized as a bastion of racial discrimination—"the restrictive practices of construction unions." Shultz noted that of the 1.3 million construction workers in the United States, only 106,000 were black, and 80 percent of those worked in the lowest-paid categories of unskilled labor. There were only 5,000 African Americans among the 130,000 building apprentices in the country. The problem was even more acute with minority construction contractors. At the time, the nation had approximately 870,000 general and specialty contractors, of which fewer than 2,000—or two-tenths of 1 percent—were black. Because minority contractors faced a host of problems, including inadequate sources of financing and bonding, they had been restricted to small projects that allowed little opportunity for growth.

Shultz decided that the Labor Department would take the lead. He told one union leader, "I am deeply interested in civil rights matters and feel the Department of Labor can—and should—play a significant role in assuring equal opportunities to all Americans." Labor also housed the Office of Federal Contract Compliance, and soon after he took office, Shultz threatened to withhold government contracts from southern textile mills that failed to implement a "reasonable program of affirmative action."

Shultz went to the Oval Office and presented a revised version of the Johnson-era Philadelphia Plan. Ehrlichman, who sat in on the meeting, recalled that Shultz appealed to the president's solicitude for jobs, the Quaker virtue of hard work, and giving African Americans a chance to move into the middle class. According to Ehrlichman, the Shultz proposal appealed to Nixon because it apparently constructed "a political dilemma for the labor union leaders and civil rights groups," with civil rights activists wanting more and the unions hating the whole idea. "Before long, the AFL-CIO and the NAACP were locked in combat over one of the passionate issues of the day and the Nixon Administration was located in the sweet and reasonable middle." Shultz, no political neophyte, also understood the partisan virtues of tying together the tails of the Democratic-voting black laborers and the lily-white construction unions.

This all had to be done carefully, and that spring Shultz reorganized the Department of Labor, a not unusual activity for a new secretary, especially one who had such superb administrative skills. He created a new position, assistant secretary for wage and labor standards, and filled it with Arthur A. Fletcher, a former professional football player, an entrepreneur, a civil rights activist, and—what made him most attractive to the new administration—an African American Republican. Shultz gave Fletcher responsibility for revising the Philadelphia Plan.

The history of blatant racism in the construction trades and the refusal to allow any minorities to work except at the lowest-paid and the most menial work struck both men as requiring far more than gentle persuasion. Philadelphia seemed a good place to start. As Fletcher later recalled,

> It had sixteen craft unions servicing the construction industry. And the vast majority of the members of some unions even had the same type of surname: Polish or Italian or Irish and so on.

President Nixon and Arthur Fletcher, his point man on affirmative action, in December 1971. One of a very small number of African American Republicans at the time, Fletcher became an ardent advocate of compensatory programs that he credited with creating a black middle class.

If you didn't have that type of name, you didn't participate. In essence, public taxes were being used to take care of a family clan called a union. So I asked the question, Are we in the business of taking care of the Kawaski family? In the Philadelphia area we even found Italians with green cards who couldn't speak English, let alone read or write a word, sentence, or paragraph—yet who were working on federal contracts. At the same time, those same unions and contractors were saying they couldn't find qualified blacks.

Fletcher found that when contractors signed agreements with the government, they agreed to abide by the specific terms of the contract, that is, nature and number of deliverables, deadlines for sections as well as the final product, and cost. They agreed to fair employment provisions only *after* the contract had been signed, thus making it a voluntary agreement and one not enforceable as part of the contract. Fletcher concluded that the only way to get around this problem was to specify a "reasonable percentage of the working hours in a given contract be earmarked for minorities and women. It didn't specify the number of minorities and women to be hired under a given contract, only the number of hours." This pedantic exculpation fooled no one, because everybody recognized that all you had to do was divide the total number of hours by forty to determine how many women and minorities needed to be hired.

Shultz and Fletcher agreed that the pilot project would be in Philadelphia. During the Johnson administration, the head of the OFCC, Edward Sylvester, had explored several areas to see where a strong affirmative action plan might work. The agency had tried to establish programs in St. Louis, San Francisco, and Cleveland, but Sylvester ran into trouble in all three cities from both the employers, who complained that they could do nothing because of union contracts, and the unions themselves, which bitterly opposed affirmative action. Philadelphia seemed a better opportunity, especially because the "City of Brotherly Love" had a very troubled history of racial animosity.

The AFL-CIO Council, in an effort to integrate the area's construction locals, negotiated an agreement with local builders and city officials that added six—*six!!*—black workers: one steamfitter, one plumber, two sheet metal journeymen, and two electrical apprentices. In protest, the twenty-two-hundred-member Steamfitters Local 420 withdrew from the Philadelphia Building and Construction Trades Council. When the city's NAACP protested by picketing a school construction site, violence broke out, and thirty-nine of the protesters wound up in the hospital. In addition, the metropolitan area's minority population had grown from 18.3 percent in 1950 to 26.7 percent a decade later and 33.5 percent in 1970. Minorities constituted one-third of the Greater Philadelphia population, and unions opposed having even a token handful admitted to their ranks.

Another fact that figured heavily in the choice of Philadelphia is that the federal government had committed $550 million in school construction in the five-county area that made up Greater Philadelphia, and the city had another $250 million, primarily in federal grants, for construction of libraries, school dormitories, and a new U.S. Mint going up on Franklin Square, part of the Independence National Historical Park. There would be some outcry from the builders at government demands that they hire minorities, because they depended on the union hiring halls for their workers. The main opposition would come from twenty-two building trade locals, many of them virtually all white.

Fletcher announced the Revised Philadelphia Plan in June 1969. All federal contractors on projects exceeding $500,000 had to show good faith in hiring minorities, defined as Negro, Oriental, American Indian, and Spanish surnamed. After consultation with contractors in the Philadelphia area, the OFCC would establish numerical ranges for employment of these groups, with the focus on African Americans. The iron trade unions, for example, would have to hire between 5 and 9 percent blacks in 1970, with these ranges increasing each year afterward. Although the wording could have been interpreted to cover all federal contracts all over the country, the Labor Department did not have the staff to enforce that large an area. Instead, it covered the five counties in eastern Pennsylvania that made up the metropolitan Philadelphia area. Employers who declined to show good faith in meeting these targets could lose their contracts. In effect, the plan would work because of the big stick wielded by the government—show good faith, hire minorities, or lose the contracts and never get another one. In Philadelphia, the goal would be to increase minority employment by federal contractors from 4 percent to 26 percent between 1969 and 1973.

There is a certain irony here, in that the Labor Department took advantage of a shrinking pocket of discrimination in construction unions outside the South to create a permanent regime of federal social control on all government contractors. The various civil rights laws, both state and federal, as well as court orders, had in fact accelerated the desegregation of unions that, according to some scholars, had become well advanced by 1969. In the more progressive unions that had been in the Congress of Industrial Organizations, African Americans made up a reasonable percentage of the 4.5 million members of large industrial unions such as auto, chemical, steel, and rubber workers. The trade unions of the former American Federation of Labor, which had 9 million members in 1969, still resisted allowing in minorities to what had essentially been a father-son monopoly, and this discrimination proved strongest in the building trades. Nonetheless, by 1969 African Americans made up 11 percent of the population and 8 percent of the construction trade unions. Even in Greater Philadelphia, most of the seventy-five thousand workers in construction unions in 1967 belonged to integrated locals, as did twenty-eight thousand in building trade locals. These numbers, however, are somewhat misleading. Black workers, as a rule, were new to union membership, and therefore found themselves at the bottom of seniority ladders. There seems to have been little wage discrimination, though, between black and white workers at the same level.

The Labor Department focused on six locals with five thousand members that practiced blatant discrimination. The plumbers and electrical workers had token minority membership, while the structural steamfitters had six blacks out of eight hundred members; the sheet metal workers and elevator constructors had no minorities at all. Taking on these "bad apple" locals, according to Hugh Graham, allowed Shultz to accomplish two goals: speed minority access to good jobs in cities that had suffered racial rioting, and build what had heretofore been a minor cabinet department into a regulatory powerhouse.

Although the Revised Philadelphia Plan emphasized "goals" and "good faith efforts," just about everyone regarded them as quotas, and it ran into immediate opposition. The AFL-CIO's president, George Meany, attacked it as a "completely unacceptable" quota program. The Senate minority leader, Everett Dirksen, at a meeting in the White House told Nixon, "As your leader in the Senate, it is my bounden duty to tell you that this thing is about as popular as a crab in a whorehouse." He warned the president that it could split the party and that he himself would not be able to support the scheme.

George Meany charged the administration with making unions the whipping boy and trying to score "brownie points" with civil rights groups. Union lobbyists descended on the capital, bringing enormous pressure to bear on members of Congress. The reception among black leaders could be described as "lukewarm" at best, and in his memoirs Nixon wondered "whether the black leadership was not more interested in dramatic tokenism than in the hard fight for actual progress."

By the end of October 1969, the administration had awarded contracts that put the plan in effect for six construction unions in the Philadelphia area. Eventually, the administration extended the Philadelphia Plan to New York, Pittsburgh, Seattle, Los Angeles, St. Louis, San Francisco, Boston, Chicago, and Detroit.

Was it a quota system? Later, both Shultz and Fletcher said as much. The secretary commented, "We found a quota system [in the construction industry]. It was there. It was zero." Fletcher reminded reporters that the "way we put a man on the moon in less than ten years was with goals, targets, and timetables." Both men distinguished "quotas," which required a set number or a fixed ratio of

African Americans, and "goals," which merely established numerical ranges and were not set in stone. Of course, the lower number in a "range" is essentially a quota.

In the fall of 1969, both organized labor and various contractor organizations put aside their normal differences and lobbied against the Philadelphia Plan. They found an unlikely alliance with conservative southern Democrats and pro-business Republicans who normally fought anything proposed by labor. Moreover, some civil rights groups joined them. Clarence Mitchell, the chief lobbyist for the NAACP who had fought all his life for color blindness, termed the Philadelphia Plan a "calculated attempt coming right from the President's desk to break up the coalition between Negroes and labor unions." Everett Dirksen, who had insisted on a ban on quotas as the price for his support of the Civil Rights Act, threatened to rally the appropriations committees to deny funding for the plan.

Then Dirksen died in September, and Senator Sam Ervin of North Carolina, took over the fight; in mid-December, the Senate, by a vote of 52–37, passed an amendment to a minor hurricane relief bill to the effect that no congressional appropriation could be used to finance any contract the comptroller general ruled violated a federal statute. The White House now called on House Republicans to defeat the measure, and led by Gerald Ford, they did so. The Senate dropped its efforts, and Congress adjourned for its Christmas recess. With the battle won, the Labor Department solicitor general, Laurence H. Silberman, noted, "we went on to spread construction plans across the country like Johnny Appleseed."

Even before the House vote, the Labor Department had issued Order No. 4, signed by the OFCC director, John Wilks; its language seemed to apply to *all* federal contractors: "The rate of minority applicants recruited should approximate or equal the ratio of minorities to the applicant population in each location." While contractors would set their own hiring goals, Order No. 4 made clear that these goals had to reflect the minority percentage of the local population. Order No. 4, like the Fletcher announcement of the Philadelphia Plan the preceding June, had not been preceded by any hearings, nor had it been published in the *Federal Register* for the customary notice-and-comment procedure that usually accompanied agency rule making. In early February 1970, Shultz issued a revised Order No. 4 requiring *all* federal contractors, not just those in the construction industry, to file an affirmative action plan within 120 days of signing a contract.

The contractor would have to identify all job categories and then determine in which areas there was "underutilization" of minorities. This would be followed by a detailed plan, including specific goals and timetables. Failing to take corrective action, as determined by the OFCC, could lead to cancellation of the contract and barring that firm from doing any future business with the government.

HISTORIANS HAVE DISAGREED widely about why Nixon, who earlier in his career had fought against expanding government into social welfare fields, became such an ardent advocate of affirmative action. Many believed, as Clarence Mitchell charged, that Nixon did it only for political purposes, to pit two pillars of the Democratic Party—union workers and African Americans—against each other. If so, the strategy eventually worked, with many union members becoming "Reagan Democrats" a few years later. Because almost everything Nixon did in his career reflected political considerations, there is a certain amount of truth in this charge. But all politicians, especially presidents, take into consideration what political impact their statements and policies will have. Nixon was for the most part an astute politician who looked around him and took into account what he saw happening in the country. While his "southern strategy" led the administration to do no more than what the courts required in terms of school desegregation, he seems to have believed that the ultimate answer to black unrest lay in providing jobs and creating a black middle class. Nixon claimed that the Philadelphia Plan carried few political benefits, and he told Maurice Stans, "Politically, I don't think there are many votes in it for us, but we'll do it because it is right." In fact, according to Hugh Davis Graham, the plan divided both parties in Congress and fueled a growing controversy about "reverse discrimination." Ultimately, the quota plan split the Republicans so badly that in 1980 the party's conservative wing, led by Ronald Reagan, repudiated Nixon's affirmative action policy completely.

If Nixon really believed in affirmative action, on what basis did he and his administration do so? The language of the "soft" affirmative action proposals of John Kennedy and Lyndon Johnson, as well as the 1964 Civil Rights Act, had been firmly grounded in a nondiscriminatory tradition of equal individual rights. The outreach programs that called for aggressive recruiting of minorities did not violate this tradition; rather, they augmented it by bringing in more talented people who could then compete for jobs or places in college. "Hard" affirmative action, on the other hand, rested on notions of group rights and compensatory discrimination. It gave preference for protected classes, not for individuals, and it ran directly against the ideal of individual opportunity that had long been a staple of American classical thought, an ideal shared in varying degrees by both Republicans and non-southern Democrats.

Although some of the older civil rights leaders like Clarence Mitchell decried a quota-driven plan, many minorities saw in it a way to move forward. Traditionally, civil rights organizations, like the NAACP's Legal Defense Fund, went to court to seek an injunction against discrimination, and it often proved difficult to demonstrate that the actor, even the state, had intended to discriminate. Professor Graham gives a whole litany in which discrimination of some sort existed, even if it had not been intended: "Job tests and promotion criteria favored better educated employees, career incentives favored male employees, seniority disadvantaged recently hired workers, English language routines favored native speakers, the architecture hindered the disabled."

Aside from the difficulty of proving intent, even showing that certain practices had a disparate impact on minorities required painstaking research. The Supreme Court ruled in *Griggs v. Duke Power Company* (1971) that an ostensibly neutral standard for employment or promotion could violate Title VII if it had a racially disparate impact not justified by business necessity. In that case, a unanimous Court ruled that a test given to job applicants had no relation at all to the tasks required by the positions but effectively blocked African Americans, nearly all of whom lacked even a high school diploma. While this precedent helped in a number of cases to strike down irrelevant requirements, again this required civil rights groups to fight the discrimination on a case-by-case basis and to prove disparate impact. It is no wonder that in the late 1960s civil rights advocates grew dissatisfied with the slow pace and heavy burden of dismantling discrimination.

Affirmative action—or compensatory justice, as some of its defenders termed it—did not look at any particular company's past or current practices. It focused on near-future results. Affirmative action plans, like that in Philadelphia, did not say, "You are bad because you have kept minorities out of your jobs." Rather, it said you now have to hire minorities so that by a certain time a certain portion of your workforce—call it goals or quotas—will consist of previously excluded minorities. Instead of the traditional progressive goal of protecting citizens from past harm, such as fraudulent securities or unsafe drugs or polluted water, affirmative action could be applied by the government as part of its social regulation. Just as the Environmental Protection Agency could order firms to reduce their air or water pollution by so much within a certain time, so the various equal opportunity agencies in the government could order employers to increase the number of their minority workers within a given period.

At the time, many Republicans supported hard affirmative action, albeit for a variety of reasons. For Nixon and his close aides, it might prove a way to ease racial tensions in the cities and move minorities into the middle class. They also took great satisfaction in splitting the civil rights groups and labor unions. Others might have believed, as did Secretary of Labor Shultz, in the moral imperative of affirmative action as a means of compensating minorities for past discrimination and giving them a chance to compete more fairly. Attorney General John Mitchell, hardly a liberal, argued that to remedy the results of past discrimination, it might be necessary to use race-conscious plans.

IN AMERICA, as Alexis de Tocqueville said many years ago, all public issues wind up in court, and affirmative action proved no exception. It made its first appearance in 1970 and has continued to be litigated ever since.

The Philadelphia Plan put contractors in a squeeze. On the one hand, their collective bargaining contracts with the construction trade unions required that they hire union members sent from union hiring halls on the basis of seniority. On the other, the government threatened to cancel lucrative contracts unless they hired sufficient minority workers. So the contractors sued the Labor Department in the federal court for the Eastern District of Pennsylvania, in front of Judge Charles R. Weiner, a Democrat appointed to the bench by Lyndon Johnson in 1967. Weiner had been one of the leaders in the Pennsylvania state senate, where he had enjoyed good relations with civil rights organizations.

The contractors relied on the 1964 Civil Rights Act, with a legislative history showing that the draftsmen of that law had consistently and specifically rejected racial classifications, ratios, quotas, and anything that would favor one group over another. The law prohibited them from discriminating against "any individual with respect to his compensation, terms, conditions, or privileges of employment, because of such individual's race, color, religion, sex, or national origin." Moreover, Congress had not authorized the executive to make exceptions to this very strong and specific ban on employment discrimination. The Labor Department replied that the Philadelphia Plan did not set quotas, but rather established flexible goals and timetables. Contractors had to make a good faith effort to reach those goals but would not automatically forfeit their contracts if they failed to do so. It also argued that the president had sufficient authority to implement the plan without specific congressional approval.

Judge Weiner sided completely with the government, rejecting each of the contractors' arguments and concluding, "The destiny of minority group employment is the primary issue and the Philadelphia Plan will provide an equitable solution to this troublesome problem."

The contractors appealed the decision to the Third Circuit, where a three-judge panel unanimously confirmed Judge Weiner's decision, although here Judge John J. Gibbons (appointed by Nixon to the appellate court in late 1969) had to do a little fancy legal footwork. In their appeal, the contractors claimed that Title VI of the Civil Rights Act, the statutory basis for the presidential orders, commands that "no person in the United States shall, on the grounds of race, color, or national origin, be excluded from participation in, be denied the benefits of, or be subject to discrimination under any program or activity receiving federal financial assistance." This had been the title by which southern schools, threatened with a cutoff of federal money, had finally begun to desegregate. Critics of the bill claimed it gave the president dictatorial control over the federal budget. The contractors argued that the Philadelphia Plan violated not only Title VII (a claim rejected by the district court) but Title VI as well.

To sidestep whether Nixon in fact relied on Title VI for his authority, Judge Gibbons simply held that Title VI did not apply to executive orders. Because the use of the phrase "affirmative action" had first appeared in Kennedy's Executive Order 10925 in 1961, it predated the Civil Rights Act, and the Philadelphia Plan did not derive its authorization from Title VI. The Supreme Court denied certiorari, in effect affirming the lower-court rulings. The Philadelphia Plan, and its numerous progeny, remained safe for the moment.

———

WITH THE PHILADELPHIA PLAN safe and Order No. 4 expanding the reach of government-mandated affirmative action programs, leadership shifted from the White House to lower-level officials in the federal bureaucracy. The Labor Department pressed goals on businesses with contracts exceeding $50,000 a year and extended the scope of the order to include women. While Shultz remained at Labor, he, and then his successor, James D. Hodgson, sought to encourage unions, businesses, and civil rights groups to establish affirmative action plans in states and local communities, a form of voluntary Philadelphia Plan in which federal money would not be involved. By the time Nixon left office, nearly sixty such hometown plans could be found across the country.

During the 1970s, the EEOC began applying numerical hiring ranges for women and minorities in the private sector. Nixon lobbied Congress not only to increase the EEOC budget but also to give the agency more enforcement power. Originally, the EEOC could only investigate complaints and try to arrange conciliation; in 1972, Congress gave the EEOC power to litigate and to bring suits against employers charged with hiring bias. The new chairman, William H. Brown III, used this new power to pressure private corporations—even those with no government contracts—into adopting affirmative action plans. By mid-decade, goals, proportional representation, timetables, and even quotas had entered the conversation in corporate suites.

Clearly many companies adopted affirmative action reluctantly, for fear of losing lucrative federal contracts. Once they had begun, however, corporations discovered, or at least rationalized, other reasons for their policies. John M. Stafford, head of the Pillsbury Company, said, "It has become clear to us that an aggressive affirmative action program makes a lot of sense." A company like Pillsbury had many minority customers who could be driven away if they believed that the company discriminated. A 1983 survey of fifty major federal contractors conducted for the Center for National Policy Review indicated that all had accepted affirmative action as "an integral part of today's corporate personnel-management philosophy and practice." B. Lawrence Branch, the director of equal employment for Merck, admitted that the pharmaceutical giant would not have initiated an affirmative action plan without the government's prodding, but now "we don't need the government involved in this—affirmative action is a way of life here."

To avoid the explicit language of Title VII, the various government agencies adopted what Herman Belz decried as the "underhanded and indirectly coercive tactics" of the Philadelphia Plan, as codified in the Federal Executive Agency Guidelines on Employee Selection Procedures issued in 1976 by the Justice Department, the Labor Department, and the Civil Service Commission. The guidelines forced employers to engage in preferential treatment through the so-called bottom line method of Title VII enforcement, which said proof of nondiscrimination would be found in the bottom line of a company's employment rosters—how many minorities, how many women, and the ratio of these groups to the general population.

Within the government, goals and timetables also became the new norm. On 11 May 1971, the U.S. Civil Service Commission sent a memorandum to department and agency heads titled "Use of Employment Goals and Timetables in Agency Equal Employment Opportunity Programs." The commission set forth a new strategy to ensure equal opportunity in hiring for federal positions. "The establishment of goals and timetables is a useful management concept and should be used where they will contribute to the resolution of equal employment opportunity problems." The memo clearly negated what had been a core value of the civil rights movement and of the commission since its inception as a wartime agency in 1941: a color-blind policy of nondiscrimination. According to one scholar who worked there, the commission had been very much opposed to this new policy and adopted it only after it became obvious that not to do so would jeopardize its dominant role in federal personnel policy. In other words, it played catch-up to what the Labor Department and the EEOC had done, and within a short time it too hired on an affirmative action basis. In at least one area, the employment of African American lawyers, the plan clearly succeeded. By 1975, there were more than five hundred black attorneys working for the federal government, compared with about fifty a decade earlier.

IN HIS MEMOIRS, Nixon wrote that "getting the plan written into law turned out to be easier than implementing the law. There were some initial successes, but I was disappointed that we received only lukewarm support from the national black leaders, who tended either to minimize the results we had achieved, or to complain that we had not gone far enough."

The plan seems to have been successful in hiring minority workers, as is shown in the following table:

Philadelphia Plan Goals for Utilization of Minorities in Construction Work

| | GOALS AND TIMETABLES | | | | ACTUAL GOALS ACHIEVED | |
	1970	1971	1972	1973	Dec. 1971	July 1972
Ironworkers	5–9%	11–15%	16–20%	22–26%	19.8%	19.0%
Plumbers, Pipefitters	5–8%	10–14%	15–19%	20–24%	14.3%	15.3%
Steamfitters	5–8%	11–15%	15–19%	20–24%	14.2%	15.0%
Sheet metal	4–8%	9–13%	14–18%	19–23%	10.4%	13.5%
Electrical	4–8%	9–15%	14–18%	19–25%	9.2%	18.2%
Elevator Constructors	4–8%	9–13%	14–18%	19–23%	9.8%	15.0%

At the end of July 1972, the goals for hiring minority workers seem to have been met in five of the six categories where the Labor Department found trade unions had systematically barred minorities, and in that last category—sheet metal workers—it looked as if the goal would be met by the end of the year. Moreover, in the six months between December 1971 and July 1972, one finds a significant increase in the minority workforce in nearly all categories. The problem is, as noted before, that aside from important lily-white locals many of the smaller locals had already admitted blacks. While the numbers improved, we have no basis of comparison for what it might have been without the plan.

Various studies indicate that the labor market position of minorities improved after 1971, far more than what would have been expected based on earlier trends and general business conditions. While there has not been extensive research on the impact of the OFCC and EEOC, what there is suggests that both have been important factors in the growth of minorities in the workforce, and at a higher level than would have been predicted without the agencies. One study found a great deal of conflicting data and concluded that the "glowing rhetoric" about black achievement might not be completely warranted.

A Rand Corporation study conducted by two economists believed unsympathetic to affirmative action nonetheless concluded that "affirmative action has resulted in a radical reshuffling of black jobs in the labor force." Black male employment shifted toward firms covered by the EEOC, and as a result there had been an increase of black men in managerial and professional jobs. This, in turn, had a positive effect on the wages of young black workers. A study by the OFCC in 1984 indicated that companies covered by government affirmative action rules showed more favorable gains for minorities and women between 1974 and 1980 than in nonfederal contractors. The latter, of course, remained subject to the nondiscrimination command of Title VII, but not to the affirmative action requirements. During this six-year period, total employment grew by 8.2 percent, while that of minorities increased 20.1 percent, although female employment grew only 2.2 percent. Moreover, federal contractors showed fewer minorities and females in the lowest-paying jobs and significant growth in managerial positions. Another study also found that while the OFCC requirements greatly helped black workers, they had less impact on nonblack minorities and women. In this study as well, the greatest gains came in higher-paying managerial, professional, and craft positions.

While these studies showed relatively little gain for women, another one conducted by the Bureau of National Affairs of 114 firms in a representative cross section of American industry found that women had achieved at least first-level managerial positions in nine out of ten firms, and higher executive-level jobs in about half. In this study, women did far better than minorities. An executive search firm found that in companies it represented, women made up about 2 percent of senior executives, a low number but one several times what it had been only a few years earlier. While government-sponsored affirmative action programs seem to have had a significant impact on blue-collar and even middle-management hiring, they apparently had little effect on the executive suites.

Did affirmative action work? It all depends on with whom you speak. "There's one simple reason to support affirmative action," declared a writer in 1995. "It works. The black middle class has grown only when a strong economy has been complemented by affirmative action programs." Arthur Fletcher, the head of the Labor Department's affirmative action program, claimed that one-third of black Americans used the civil rights acts and presidential orders "to position themselves in middle-class America. One-third of black America has made it in the last twenty years—the life of the document, affirmative action." The only ones who did not make it, he charged, were those who did not try.

Not all American businesses wholeheartedly endorsed the philosophy behind affirmative action, and some surely went along only out of fear of losing government contracts. In fact, the threat of federal retaliation has always been more potential than actual. Although the OFCC and its counterparts in fifteen other federal agencies supposedly monitored a quarter of a million firms, in the ten years after the adoption of the Philadelphia Plan, they blacklisted only nine companies. However, although the government rarely used this power, contractors knew it existed. As one of them put it, "If you've got the atom bomb, you don't have to drop it to make your point."

The economics writer Alan Farnham noted a quarter century after the Civil Rights Act that "the mortar binding CEOs to affirmative action—a compound of social conscience, fear, and self-interest—appears strong. Some CEOs believe fervently that the programs are the best way of righting past wrongs. Others half-heartedly endorse them because, like eating oatmeal, it's the right thing to do. Still others fear the penalties for backsliding."

That thousands of firms adopted affirmative action programs as a result of the Nixon administration's initiatives is indisputable, but how much these programs have helped minorities and women is greatly disputed, and it is a topic that we shall return to throughout this book. While one can get fairly good figures for particular firms, it is impossible to get numbers across the board because one cannot tell in how many instances women, blacks, and other minorities might have been hired even in the absence of affirmative action plans. As more women and minorities began going to college in the 1960s, companies had a wider pool of qualified individuals from which to choose.

One thing is undeniable. The great push for a hard affirmative action began not in the liberal administrations of John Kennedy and Lyndon Johnson but under the unlikely leadership of Richard Milhous Nixon.

CHAPTER 5

PREJUDICE PERSISTS,
AFFIRMATIVE ACTION GROWS

*However pleased I was with my own persistence in landing a sales job at
Xerox after being twice turned away, I always knew my career wasn't
just about me. My professional life was as much a part of the civil rights
struggle as the bus boycotts and lunch counter sit-ins of a few years earlier.
The first few black salesmen at Xerox . . . entered doors opened by the
defiant struggles of our forebears against injustice.*

—A. BARRY RAND

The fifteen years following the passage of the Civil Rights and
Voting Rights Acts proved difficult in many ways for African
Americans, and yet at the same time clear gains could also be seen.
Depending on how one interpreted the often contradictory statis-
tics, life for black Americans had either dramatically improved, had
remained more or less the same, or perhaps had even slipped a bit.

Great Society programs undeniably improved opportunities north
of the Mason-Dixon Line, and eventually south of it as well. The
Justice Department and the Equal Employment Opportunity Commission energetically enforced Title VII, and within a few years after
the Voting Rights Act tens of thousands of black men and women
who had been barred from the polls registered to vote and then did
so, eventually electing hundreds of African American officials at the
local and state levels, and even to Congress.

But what next? Essentially the two great civil rights laws embodied just about everything that activists had been advocating
for decades. Efforts by southern states to continue Jim Crow met
stiff resistance not only from the Justice Department but from the
courts as well. Having secured legal equality—or as much as could

be gotten through legislation and judicial decisions—minority leaders turned to their other great objective, jobs. This would prove extremely difficult, and for reasons that often involved the legacy of decades of discrimination, poor housing, inferior education, and a culture of poverty.

Affirmative action plans in both the public and the private sectors expanded significantly, but the endemic racism faced by people of color did not abate. For every story of African Americans getting jobs or into schools that had previously been closed to them, there are other accounts that made clear the deep-seated and persistent prejudice that constituted the legacy of three centuries of slavery and segregation. Nowhere would this prove as troubling as in job markets controlled by labor unions.

MERELY BECAUSE THE Supreme Court had ruled segregation illegal in 1954 did not mean that the South would quickly or voluntarily dismantle the decades-old apartheid system known as Jim Crow. So Vincent Whylie decided to move north, where he, like many African Americans before him, believed he could make a better life. An experienced wire lather by trade and a member of an AFL-CIO union in Daytona Beach, Florida, he moved with his wife and five daughters to Brooklyn in 1962. Wire lathing—installing frameworks for buildings—is a hard job, and Whylie did not expect it to be any easier in New York; in fact, it might be even more difficult. In an often hazardous occupation, one worked mostly outdoors during months of rain, sleet, cold, and snow. He expected, however, that as a union member he would at least get decent pay, security, and a future. But Local 46 of the Wood, Wire, and Metal Lathers, which controlled all aspects of the trade in the city, had six thousand members—all white—and no interest in admitting blacks, even one with a transfer card from a sister local.

Whylie turned for help to the NAACP, which assisted him in getting on a post office building project. He soon lost it, however, on the pretext of a layoff, only to see a white man hired in his stead. He went to the New York Human Rights Commission, which found "gross discrimination" and ordered Local 46 to admit him at once. The union stonewalled, and in 1970 a desperate Whylie wrote to President Nixon for help: "I have fought with the Union in every way . . . even gone on bended knees, but without success." While the dispute dragged on, his children sometimes went without food, he had nearly lost his home, and because of the turmoil he "became very ill and had to have a major operation." He only wanted, he told the president, "a chance to earn a decent living so that I will not have to rear my children on Welfare."

Whylie's experience explains why, as one observer noted, "today there are fewer Negro plumbers or electricians than Negro Ph.D.s." The director of the Chicago Urban League declared, "Exclusion in the craft unions is so complete that segregation would be a step forward." Moreover, Whylie's story was far from unusual, although the building trades seemed a logical place for employment. Hiring essentially began anew with each project, so low turnover and seniority—factors that often kept African Americans out of factory jobs—did not play a role. In the 1960s, Great Society programs funded dozens of building projects in America's cities, jobs that at least geographically should have been available to inner-city minorities. Under Johnson's Executive Order 11247, federally funded jobs should have had at least some form of affirmative action, but this tended to be truer in defense than in civilian projects. Publicly funded all-white construction projects in the inner cities infuriated the minority population, which justly decried a labor apartheid as strict as anything they suffered in the South.

Much of the money for this building came from the Great Society Model Cities Program, which aimed not only at revitalizing decrepit urban areas but also at providing jobs for the residents of those communities. Yet time and time again, African Americans would be excluded by union rules that essentially kept the jobs in the family. One asbestos workers' local required applicants to have written recommendations from three current members and a majority vote from the membership in a secret ballot, as well as four years' experience as a "helper," a job restricted to "sons or close relatives living in the households of members."

While today it is easy to condemn this type of exclusion, the pattern itself goes back to the guilds of the Middle Ages, when skilled craftsmen, whose only "property" consisted of their knowledge, would pass down their expertise from father to son, just as the landed nobility handed down their estates to their eldest sons, or a shop owner would train up his son to take over the business. The modern union movement in the United States began in 1886 with the founding of the American Federation of Labor, and well into the 1930s it faced intense opposition from governments at all levels, as well as from ultraconservative courts. Not until the New Deal did many of the anti-union laws fall; following World War II, unions came into their own, enjoying the greatest prosperity they had ever known. It is little wonder that union members tried to keep a good thing going for themselves and their sons. When black workers picketed a construction site chanting, "Jobs Now!" many white workers reacted furiously: "Some of us waited half our lives for a job, and they want jobs now." A common white interpretation of black protest was "They want *our* jobs," and there was an element of truth in this reaction.

Civil rights leaders since the 1940s had argued that before African Americans could take their place as equals in American society, they needed two things—votes and jobs. The 1965 Voting Rights Act gave them the ballot; jobs proved a lot harder. In the spring of 1969, the Boston United Community Construction Workers, an organization of about 350 black workers with experience in the building trades, sent a "black tester" to five federally funded construction sites reportedly suffering labor shortages. The tester, a black carpenter with five years' experience, was turned down at all five sites, according to the Urban League, because lily-white unions, with the consent of the contractors, controlled all hiring.

Theoretically, seventeen construction trade unions had reached agreement on an affirmative action plan in the summer of 1968 in order to comply with the provisions of the Model Cities Act. In practice, according to civil rights groups, the plan was a sham, designed to perpetuate tokenism by excluding all but a handful of minorities. Herbert Hill, the labor director for the NAACP, wrote to Secretary of Housing and Urban Development George Romney threatening that if the Labor Department approved these "agreements," then the organization would have little choice but to go to court.

Civil rights leaders claimed that having a job meant far more than earning the money needed to feed, clothe, and shelter one's family. Herbert Hill argued that unemployment led to perceptions of injured manhood among black men, seen as emasculated by racism. The NAACP executive told a congressional subcommittee that "jobs in the building trades are for men." In the "highly important symbolic sense," these were "male jobs," and such "manly jobs" with "high status implications" were "especially important for Negro men." In 1967, a study showed how some poor black men's inability to secure any but menial and intermittent jobs as laborers undermined their marriages, ruined relations with their children, took away their self-respect, and left them to the mercies of street corner society.

Bias against blacks was not confined to the building trades, and even when big companies accepted the need for affirmative action, discrimination remained. Thirteen years after Congress enacted the Civil Rights Act, black unemployment ran at 15.5 percent, twice the rate for whites. African Americans made up 10.8 percent of the workforce, and in every occupational category save one they were underrepresented: white-collar jobs (7.5 percent), professional/technical (8.3 percent), managers/administrators (4.5 percent), sales (4.2 percent), and clerical (9.8 percent). Only in blue-collar work, much of it unskilled, did they exceed their share of the national population (12.3 percent). There were a number of reasons given, including the aging of the inner-city workforce, the move of many businesses to the suburbs or beyond, inadequate education for anything but unskilled labor, poorer health among inner-city dwellers, prison records among a higher percentage of ghetto youth, and frequent lack of a stable family pattern—all factors that had been picked up by the Moynihan Report. But for most civil rights leaders, the basic cause remained the same—racial discrimination.

The continued lack of progress in closing the gap between black and white workers led to a cottage industry of economists trying to explain the cases. Theoretically, the two races should have worked together harmoniously, with whites having capital to invest in business, and blacks having labor needed for such enterprises. The problem, as the economist Gary Becker wrote, is that the white community has "a taste for discrimination," which undermined what should have been a rational economic partnership. Economists could not find a workable equation for their statistics-driven models to figure out how much this very noneconomic factor affected an otherwise "rational" economic theory.

Thomas Sowell, one of the leading black critics of affirmative action, took a different approach. Human capital, he wrote, is not money or material ownership; it is "the vital accumulation of knowledge, skill and organizational experience." Not only are black people poor in terms of material objects, but "their share of the human capital of the country is even more desperately small." Sowell went on to argue that while poor education accounted for some of this poverty, a much greater cause could be found in the lack of experience and tradition in the African American community. Ideas such as punctuality, efficiency, and long-term planning are little use to a people who have been limited to menial jobs for generations. As a result, these traits—so critical for success in our society and economy—are totally lacking in the vast majority of black families. The "knowledge of specifically who, where, and how to get things done is very unequally distributed and constitutes a tremendous handicap to the poor in a highly complex society."

PART OF THE PROBLEM of understanding African American economic life in the 1970s in general, and affirmative action in particular, is that the black community is not monolithic, and in some areas visible progress could be seen. For example, affirmative action in the chemical industry seems to have succeeded in increasing not only the number of African Americans but also the percentage working in skilled, professional, or white-collar positions. Although not enough time had passed so that blacks could be found in significant numbers in all levels of work above unskilled labor, the analysis expected that would happen. An important reason why lay in the enormous expansion of the chemical industry starting in the 1960s. As noted before, in growth industries needing labor, affirmative action programs had the best chance of success.

Law provided another area of growth for African Americans. Harvard had graduated its first black lawyer—George Lewis Ruffin—in 1869, and other northern law schools had accepted some African Americans from time to time, but the legal profession—and the law schools—had remained overwhelmingly white. The desegregation of southern law schools in the late 1950s and early 1960s, as well as active recruiting of minorities by northern schools, had led to a visible increase in black lawyers by the mid-1970s.

Any clear-eyed examination of African American employment in the 1970s would find that despite some gains blacks still faced enormous prejudice in the job market. For example, because African Americans were often the last hired, seniority rules dictated that in a recession they would be the first fired. An examination of the "last hired, first fired" rule found that roughly half the difference between white and nonwhite employment rates could be accounted for by fairly objective labor market factors but that the other half could only be accounted for by racial considerations. While firms with affirmative action plans and plant-wide, rather than job-specific, seniority systems cushioned layoffs for some minority employees, any major reduction in the workforce impacted African American far more heavily than Caucasian employees.

In an article titled "An Economic Bill of Rights," the authors noted that "for black people in American society no factor is as consistently, and consciously, ever present and powerful as the fact of race and racial discrimination." This bias infects and affects every social, economic, and political aspect of their lives, including choice of residence, occupation, schools, and relations with police and public officials. While all groups, including African Americans, had benefited from the economic growth of the 1960s, people of color had reaped the fewest rewards. There might be more black professionals, such as doctors and lawyers, and there might even be a recognizable and growing black middle class, but by all objective economic standards African Americans still lagged behind other groups in the economy. Despite Title VII, executive orders, and the EEOC, true equality of opportunity did not exist for those in the black community.

NONETHELESS, WHEREVER ONE looked in the late 1960s and the 1970s, one could find affirmative action programs in government, from the federal level down to cities and towns, in academia, and in the corporate world. For some of these entities, affirmative action programs resulted from lawsuits based on Title VII; in other cases, the desire to secure federal contracts made some minority hiring plan a necessity; and some private companies acted, if not out of altruism, at least from a recognition that prior employment practices could no longer be justified.

A good example of the latter is the Xerox Corporation, which twice refused to hire A. Barry Rand, a well-qualified African American. Rand went to a job fair in Washington and managed to get the room numbers of companies doing interviewing. He knocked on the doors of seven companies that interested him and persuaded each recruiter to give him five minutes to explain why they could not afford not to hire "a surefire moneymaker like me." He got seven job offers, one of which came from Xerox, which he chose.

The company's founder, Joseph C. Wilson, and its then president, C. Peter McColough, responded to the report of the National Commission on Civil Disorders, set up after the race riots of the mid-1960s, which accused white institutions of creating, maintaining, and condoning discrimination against blacks. Wilson and McColough recognized that Xerox stood guilty as charged and decided to do something about it. In late 1968, they sent out a memo condemning racism and announcing that the company would now seek diversity in its workforce through aggressive minority recruitment. This letter went to all managers, in production, sales, and service, bluntly announcing that Xerox shared in the responsibility for a race-divided nation and noting how few African Americans worked there. The company did not hire its first black sales rep until 1967. In 1964, Xerox had employed about 300 minority workers out of a total workforce of more than 11,000. Ten years later, minority employment had risen to 8,000 (of whom 4,300 were black) out of a worldwide workforce of 54,300. By the early 1990s, minorities constituted 27 percent of Xerox U.S.A.'s employees—14 percent black, 7 percent Hispanic, and 6 percent Asian. In some ways, this part of the affirmative action plan was the easiest, because of the massive growth of the company in the 1960s and 1970s. If one had to describe it, Xerox had a "soft" affirmative action plan. It opened doors, actively sought out minority applicants, did not deprive any white men of jobs, and never established goals or quotas.

This did not happen overnight, and hiring minorities only addressed part of the problem. A corporate culture had to be changed, one in which qualified minority members found themselves passed over for promotion or assigned to poorer areas while white sales reps got the best territories. It took a long time, with constant pressure from the top and minority members learning that they had to speak up when they believed they had been discriminated against. By the time Barry Rand—one of the first African Americans hired as a sales rep—wrote about Xerox in the early 1990s, he had spent his entire career at the company and had personally seen not only the changes but the effort needed to make those changes.

IT WOULD BE NICE TO SAY that corporate America had a sort of religious experience, and like Paul on the road to Damascus the scales fell from their eyes. In many instances, it took lawsuits to force companies to cease discriminating.

Companies having or seeking federal contracts, of course, had been required to have affirmative action plans since the Johnson administration, and the Office of Federal Contract Compliance in the Department of Labor enforced this requirement vigorously. Many companies established plans initially to comply with the federal requirement, but once in place they eventually became part of the corporate culture. As the plans proved successful, company officials discovered that hiring minorities brought some good publicity. As an example, the aerospace industry, recipient of some of the largest federal contracts, began hiring minorities under pressure from the federal government. In 1966, aerospace, an outgrowth of aircraft production, had total sales of $24.2 billion, making it the largest manufacturing industry in the country. It employed 1,298,000 people, and the federal government purchased nearly three-fifths of its output.

At that time, minorities constituted less than 5 percent of the workforce, and a study of the industry in the following years showed that aggressive efforts by aerospace companies had brought thousands more African Americans into the job ranks. But aerospace faced a daunting challenge in that many of its jobs required technical skills that in turn required advanced education or training. Professor Herbert Northrup of Wharton, who did the study at the behest of the Ford Foundation, noted a shortage of black workers possessing these skills. In addition, many aerospace plants had located in the suburbs—no doubt an inducement for white engineers and others who lived there, but it presented a logistical challenge to minorities in the inner cities who lacked the means of transportation to get to these plants.

Faced with a possible loss of lucrative contracts from their biggest customer, many companies "have adopted an unwritten policy of outright preference. Give jobs to the Negro if he is available." Northrup expected that as more minorities realized that aerospace firms would now hire them, there would be more applications from a growing number of black college graduates, as well as in-plant training programs for skilled jobs. These would take time, however, but industry officials seemed optimistic about recruiting and maintaining a significant minority presence.

Businesses do not respond well to generalities, but they do respond to specifics. As one article put it, "Businessmen like to hire by the numbers." The Nixon plan, while not specifying quotas, did want goals and timetables, and businesses now had something specific to work with, and hundreds, indeed thousands, of firms began the often painful process of self-examination, of looking at their past hiring practices and recognizing that they had, consciously or not, excluded minorities from employment and promotion. In little more than a decade, affirmative action became a way of life for many large corporations. Once embarked on the program, through either fear of losing federal contracts or an awakened social conscience, corporations began discovering or at least rationalizing reasons for their policies.

One should not suppose that all American businesses endorsed the philosophy behind affirmative action or that, on the other hand, they went along only out of fear of losing government contracts. In fact, the threat of federal retaliation had always been more potential than actual. For whatever reason they chose, companies adopted affirmative action plans out of social conscience, self-interest, or fear of losing federal contracts. Once the plans were in place, companies never jettisoned them.

THE EQUAL EMPLOYMENT Opportunity Commission seemed to grow more forceful with each decision, but certainly its most important case involved one of the nation's largest employers, the American Telephone and Telegraph Company. Prior to its breakup in the early 1980s, AT&T, commonly known as Ma Bell, enjoyed a virtual monopoly over all telephone services in the United States, including local as well as long-distance service and providing equipment, right down to the phones in an office or kitchen. In 1970, the EEOC petitioned the Federal Communications Commission (FCC) to reject a large long-distance rate increase sought by AT&T, on the grounds that the company engaged in "pervasive, system-wide, and blatantly unlawful discrimination in employment against women, blacks, Spanish-surnamed Americans and other minorities." The EEOC claimed that Ma Bell violated the Civil Rights Acts of 1866 and 1964, the Equal Pay Act of 1963, and the fair employment practices acts of several states. AT&T, according to the EEOC, had for the past thirty years suppressed women workers, and "women as a class have been excluded from every job classification except for low paying clerical and telephone-operator jobs."

In the spring of 1972, the Department of Labor intervened and took over negotiations, which came to fruition on 29 December of that year. The government proposed, and the company accepted, an out-of-court settlement, confirmed as a consent decree three weeks later. Under the arrangement, AT&T would make $15 million—the largest single award ever made until then—in onetime payments to thirteen thousand women and two thousand minority men. The settlement also required the company to pay an additional $30 million in immediate pay increases for thirty-six thousand women and minorities whose advancement in the system had been hampered by discrimination. In a follow-up settlement in 1974, the telephone company agreed to pay $30 million more in back pay and wage increases for an additional twenty-five thousand female and minority management employees.

The EEOC and the Labor Department also insisted that the company adopt an affirmative action plan, with specific hiring and promotion targets, including goals that would see the increase of women and minorities in every job classification, and this included employing males in previously all-female jobs. Conversely, women and minorities would now be eligible for what had been the all-male and nearly all-white service and management positions. All women with college degrees hired since 1965 would be immediately assessed to determine if they qualified for higher-level jobs and, if so, would be enrolled in a specific development program to prepare them for promotions into higher management positions.

The company did fulfill its commitments. It set rigorous goals and immediate targets in fifteen job categories to be met during the first year, and other goals after that. Within four years, the company reported that it had reached 99.3 percent of its objectives. The agreement also stipulated that if this initial affirmative action campaign did not meet the goals, AT&T would be free to depart from normal selection and promotion standards so it could vigorously pursue its hiring and promotion goals. This meant, among other things, that AT&T could promote women or minorities over equally or even marginally better-qualified white males who had seniority.

As would often be the case, the EEOC and the Labor Department failed to take into consideration the contracts that AT&T had with several large unions, especially the powerful Communications Workers of America (CWA). The CWA, like all unions, valued seniority, and its contract with the telephone company made clear that promotions had to be based on seniority. The consent decree did not take the unions' interests into account and gave AT&T authority to ignore its contractual obligations to the CWA and other unions.

Daniel McAleer had a $10,500-a-year job as a representative who handled orders for telephone service in the Washington, D.C., Long Lines Division. When he saw an opening in a better-paying job, he sought the promotion, but the company awarded it to a woman, Sharon Hulvey. The two had roughly equal qualifications, but Hulvey had less seniority and had scored slightly lower on the company's evaluation scale; she got the job because of AT&T's new affirmative action program. McAleer claimed he had been discriminated against because of sex and sued, asking for the promotion, differential back pay, and $100,000 in damages. The CWA joined his suit, claiming that the consent decree—to which the union had not been a party—undermined the union's ability to secure employment rights to jobs and promotions under the existing collective bargaining agreement.

Judge Gerhard A. Gesell ruled on 9 June 1976 that McAleer had been a faultless employee who became the innocent victim through an unfortunate but justifiable use of affirmative action. He awarded McAleer monetary compensation as damages but not the promotion, because the discrimination that had led to the consent decree would be perpetuated if Hulvey did not keep the position. He concluded,

> The Consent Decree was necessary only because of AT&T's prior sex discrimination. . . . Since McAleer had no responsibility for [that] discrimination, it is AT&T rather than McAleer who should bear the principal burden of rectifying the company's previous failure to comply with the Civil Rights Act of 1964. An affirmative award of some damages on a "rough justice" basis is therefore required and will constitute an added cost which the stockholders of AT&T must bear.

Judge Gesell cut right to the heart of the matter, and his reasoning would become a key argument in the debate over affirmative action. McAleer had *not personally been responsible* for the discriminatory practices of his employer, so why should he be penalized for AT&T's behavior? At the same time, to give McAleer the position would only perpetuate the very practices that had led to the lawsuit.

Although McAleer lost his case, three of the unions representing AT&T workers appealed the consent decree, claiming it to be "an improper and illegal devise to remedy the effects of past discrimination." Observers thought it might be a good case for the Supreme Court to enunciate its views on the legality or even the constitutionality of affirmative action. The high court, though, refused to take the case and gave no reason for its decision. The Court of Appeals for the Third Circuit, however, in upholding the plan said, "The use of employment goals and quotas admittedly involve tensions with . . . equal protection. But the remedy granted by the district court (in approving the plan) is permissible because it seems reasonably calculated to counteract the detrimental effects a particularly identifiable pattern of discrimination has had."

THE EEOC MIGHT have been the single most powerful force pushing for the expansion of affirmative action programs, and the impetus came during the Nixon administration. Aside from the Philadelphia Plan, the 1972 Civil Rights Act gave the agency the power to launch lawsuits on its own. The agency also benefited from President Jimmy Carter's reorganization reforms.

Carter won 94 percent of the black vote in the 1976 election, and civil rights leaders expected a great deal from him, more, in fact, than he could possibly deliver. For the most part he followed through on the Democratic Party's traditional commitments and began by opening up important government positions to minorities and women. He named blacks to high posts, such as Andrew Young as ambassador to the United Nations, Clifford Alexander as secretary of the army, Wade McCree as solicitor general, Drew S. Days III as assistant

President James Earl Carter in 1979. Carter appointed more minority members and women to federal office than any president before him.

attorney general in charge of the Civil Rights Division of the Justice Department, and U.S. attorneys in five states, including the first ever in a southern state. He also selected women for his cabinet, Patricia Roberts Harris (an African American) for Housing and Urban Development, Juanita Kreps for Commerce, and in 1979 Shirley Hufstedler for the newly created Department of Education. Because Congress created 152 new federal judgeships in 1978, Carter appointed a total of 258 new judges in four years to federal district and appeals courts, more than any of his predecessors. His nominees included 29 women (including Ruth Bader Ginsburg to the D.C. Court of Appeals), 28 blacks (three times as many as Lyndon Johnson), and 14 Hispanics. Perhaps one of his most important appointments was that of J. Clay Smith Jr. to the EEOC in 1978. Smith added sexual harassment to the list of civil rights violations that could trigger EEOC intervention. The very conservative Phyllis Schlafly charged that Carter had "an ideological litmus test plus a race/sex quota." They all had to be "liberal, pro-abortion, pro-feminist Democrats."

There would be no great civil rights laws such as those passed in the Johnson administration a decade earlier, but what happened during the Carter presidency, according to the historian Hugh Davis Graham, had a great impact—the "quiet mobilization of a comprehensive regime of civil rights regulation, wherein federal agencies extended affirmative-action requirements to virtually all business firms, educational institutions, and state and local governments receiving federal contracts or grants."

Despite all Carter did for women and minorities, they expected so much more from him. The president's adviser, Stuart Eisenstadt, noted that women, labor unions, African Americans, and other groups had unrealistically high expectations, so that no matter what Carter did, no matter how many women and minorities he appointed to high office, he could never satisfy their demands. Women's groups blamed Carter for the failure of the Equal Rights Amendment (as if he could control state legislatures), Jewish groups thought he was too tough on Israel (even though he personally brokered the peace deal between Israel and Egypt), and for all the people of color he appointed to important offices, they wanted more.

Carter's rhetoric after he became president only increased the expectations of civil rights groups. In mid-1978, he told the heads of government departments and agencies that he had a strong commitment to affirmative action, although he favored flexible programs using goals rather than quotas. "It is through such programs that we can expect to remove the effects of discrimination and ensure equal opportunities for all Americans." The president believed that the programs already in place sufficed but did not operate effectively; the problem lay in bureaucratic inefficiency in implementing those programs. Carter explained that the problem was not that "program goals are unworthy; it is not that our public servants are unfit. What is at fault is the unwieldy structure and frequently inefficient operation of the government; the layers of administration, the plethora of agencies, the proliferation of paperwork." In his inaugural, Carter had told the American people that he had "no new dream to set forth for the country." Rather, he urged "a fresh faith in the old dream."

In 1978, the former navy engineer turned to solving the problem by reorganizing government and improving the efficiency and effectiveness by which federal agencies monitored compliance with affirmative action guidelines. On 23 February, Carter submitted Reorganization Plan Number 1 to Congress, a plan that concerned itself solely with equal employment opportunity. Enforcement of fair employment laws, orders, regulations, and rules—now spread across eighteen separate government agencies—would come under the authority of the EEOC, which would become the principal governmental agency for fair employment enforcement. Contract compliance, a responsibility in eleven different bureaus, would be consolidated in the Department of Labor. The president called his proposal "the single most important action to improve civil rights in the last decade." The consolidation of equal employment activities under the plan created the "foundation of a unified, coherent Federal structure to combat job discrimination in all its forms."

In the next three years, Carter issued five executive orders implementing the plan. None of them proved controversial, because they all dealt with primarily administrative matters. On 30 June 1978, Executive Order 12067 gave the EEOC the coordination of the entire federal equal opportunity program. The Civil Service Commission had been responsible for enforcing equal employment opportunity within the federal government; that function now went to the EEOC. Administration of the Equal Pay and Age Discrimination in Employment Acts shifted from the Department of Labor to the EEOC. The year before, Carter had appointed the civil rights activist Eleanor Holmes Norton to head the EEOC; the reorganization plan gave her and her agency vastly more power.

A little over three months later, Carter issued another order aimed at enforcing fair employment standards, the consolidation of government contract compliance from eleven agencies into the Department of Labor. Here Carter substantially amended Lyndon Johnson's plan, which had left much of contract compliance to those bureaus issuing the contracts. The details and rationale for this move had not been spelled out in the reorganization plan Carter had sent to Congress, but he informed the legislature that critical elements of his overall proposal would "be accomplished by executive order rather than by the organization plan." Two other executive orders shifted even more responsibilities to the EEOC.

The final executive order dealing with fair employment vested the attorney general with the coordination of the implementation and enforcement of all federal laws mandating nondiscrimination. Under the order, the Office of the Attorney General would become a central clearinghouse for any legal action required to enforce anti-discrimination laws. Although there were now fewer agencies tasked with enforcement responsibilities, Carter wanted the government to speak with one voice regarding the meaning and implementation of affirmative action and equal employment requirements. For the Department of Labor and the EEOC, this meant that before they could issue any directives, they had to run them past the attorney general to ensure consistency in federal policy. This executive order, issued just two days before the 1980 presidential election, had little effect, because Ronald Reagan swamped Carter in the vote, winning all but a handful of states.

In the long run, Carter's emphasis on building a responsible federal bureaucracy with powers to enforce fair employment and affirmative action helped minorities and women, but it lacked political sex appeal. No one could get very excited about an executive order dealing with administrative responsibilities. But even if he had wanted to do so, Carter had limited opportunities to do something dramatic, such as Johnson's civil rights and voting rights laws or Nixon's Philadelphia Plan. Although the Democrats enjoyed substantial majorities in both the Senate and the House of Representatives, Congress was in no mood to take direction from the White House after the experiences of the Vietnam War and the Watergate scandals. The legislature had had enough of "imperial presidents"; in Carter, Congress had a man who by nature did not want to do anything extravagant and who focused more on fixing problems than charting new directions.

In the 1976 campaign, Carter had consistently emphasized issues of mismanagement and government waste and promised to make the government work more efficiently. In many ways, he accomplished that in the field of fair employment, but it brought him few if any political dividends. For those opposed to affirmative action, he went too far; for civil rights activists, he did not go far enough.

One aspect of Carter's administration that has received relatively little attention is the work of his secretary of the army, Clifford Alexander. He put a hold on a list of officers proposed for promotion to general. He later related that he was troubled "because no black colonels had been promoted, even though many had achieved that rank and served with distinction." He ordered the board that handled promotions to look at the records of eligible black colonels to determine if they had been given lesser assignments or evaluated negatively by officers who were racially prejudiced. Once race-related blemishes were expunged, black colonels with otherwise sterling records emerged as strong candidates for promotion, one of whom was Colin Powell. Alexander, interestingly, refused to describe what he did as affirmative action and insisted it was nothing more than commonsense fairness.

JIMMY CARTER, HOWEVER, did see one major piece of equal opportunity legislation passed on his watch. Congressman Parren J. Mitchell (D-Md.), the chair of the Congressional Black Caucus, offered a set-aside provision as an amendment to the Public Works Employment Act of 1977. Under his proposal, at least 10 percent of the $4 billion appropriation for public works had to go to minority business enterprises (MBEs), and he defined minorities as "citizens of the United States who are Negroes, Spanish-speaking, Orientals, Indians, Eskimos, and Aleuts." Moreover, subcontracts had to go to companies headed by minorities even if they were not the lowest bidder, as long as the higher amount of their bid resulted from inflated costs due to past discrimination. At the time, Mitchell's amendment attracted little notice or opposition, yet it surely ranks as an important legislative achievement regarding affirmative action.

Credit for the measure belongs to Mitchell and a civil rights coalition in Congress that included John Conyers of Detroit and Augustus Hawkins of Los Angeles, as well as liberal white allies, including Don Edwards of California, all of whom had the blessing of the Speaker of the House, Thomas "Tip" O'Neill. The Mitchell group and their

Representative Parren J. Mitchell, Democrat from Maryland, in 1974. A few years later, he would write the government set-aside program, which over the decades proved a great benefit to minority- and women-owned businesses.

staff documented a strong record of past discrimination that had prevented minority participation in major federally funded projects. In 1972, the House Subcommittee on Small Business Administration had blamed the difficulties that minority businesses had on past "social standards." In January 1977, the committee found that rather than overt racial bias "we more often encounter a business system which is racially neutral on its face, but because of past overt social and economic discrimination is presently operating, in effect, to perpetuate these past inequities." Large—and mostly white—firms held great advantages over smaller, minority-owned businesses in terms of experience in bidding, securing bonding, and reputation, all of which mattered when government officials examined bids with an eye not only to cost but to expectations of satisfactory completion. The record built up by this committee would prove consequential in court challenges to the law.

Congress overwhelmingly approved the set-aside amendment with practically no discussion. Neither house held any hearings; the House of Representatives accepted Mitchell's floor amendment by voice vote; and then, with Carter's enthusiastic backing, Congress approved the public works bill by large majorities in the House and the Senate. Later in the year, both houses by a voice vote gave statutory approval to the SBA's program for deprived groups, requiring each federal agency to establish an Office of Small and Disadvantaged Business Utilization to implement the MBE program. The White House, which had been under attack from civil rights groups, seized on the MBE set-aside as a major victory for affirmative action, even though other than the president's approval of the idea the executive branch had done little to develop the policy.

THE MBE PROVISION instantly roused the ire of established contractors in almost every field, because it not only would reduce their profits but also would entail seeking out and subcontracting one-tenth of the work to relatively unknown and unproved firms. In later years, after the program had been in effect for a while, the second consideration more or less disappeared. Prime contractors built it into the proposals, and by then MBEs had had enough experience to be able to get bonding, submit viable bids, and have a reputation for completing the work. In the fall of 1977, however, after the government had issued regulations as to how the MBE provision would be implemented, several associations of construction contractors and subcontractors, and a firm that did heating and air-conditioning work, filed a suit alleging that they had sustained economic injury because of the MBE requirement and that it violated the Equal Protection Clause of the Fourteenth Amendment and Due Process Clause of the Fifth Amendment. Both the federal district court and the Court of Appeals for the Second Circuit upheld the law, and the contractors appealed to the Supreme Court. The high court heard the case in November 1979 and handed down its decision on 2 July 1980.

Speaking through Chief Justice Warren Burger, the 6–3 majority ruled that Congress's spending power is as broad as its regulatory authority. In other words, the legislature's pursuit of public policy through the MBE provision (an exercise of the spending power) was legitimate provided the same pursuit would have been permissible under the regulatory power. Congress could have regulated prime contractors' awarding of subcontracts through the Commerce Clause on the grounds that the perpetuation of discrimination through subcontracting would have a negative effect on interstate commerce.

The Court also upheld Congress's use of ethnic criteria as constitutional. It was not under-inclusive for specifying only certain minority groups, because its purpose was to cure the effects of past discrimination against these groups. Nor was it over-inclusive for naming groups that could not be justified by the effects of past discrimination, because it did not apply to MBEs that could not show that their higher bid resulted from the effects of past discrimination.

The majority opinion also noted the record that the sponsors, Congressman Mitchell and his allies, had built up. Congress had not acted arbitrarily, Burger noted, but had relied on a record of past discrimination that it had the power to address. The Court would not question that record but would defer to Congress as to the wisdom of the plan. "Here we pass, not on a choice made by a single judge or a school board, but on a considered decision of Congress and the President." While the Court would not defer to the legislature or the executive on a constitutional question, it would defer to the considered policy judgment of those branches, especially when supported by a convincing factual record.

The justices in the majority did not really delve into the question of equal protection or due process considerations, which Justice Potter Stewart in dissent thought should have governed the case. After the appointment of more conservative justices by Ronald Reagan and George H. W. Bush, it would be those issues that would determine the outcome of many affirmative action cases.

EVEN BEFORE THE Carter reorganization, the EEOC not only fought to get companies to adopt affirmative action plans; in a 1974 handbook, it spelled out exactly how firms should initiate programs. It is worth looking at the details that the EEOC said would be necessary.

A. Issue Written Equal Employment Policy and Affirmative Action Commitment
B. Appoint a Top Official with Responsibility and Authority to Implement Program
    1. Responsibilities of the Affirmative Action Manager
    2. Responsibilities of Other Department Heads and Managers

C. Publicize Affirmative Action Program
1. Internally
   a. Managers and Supervisors
   b. All Employees
   c. Union Officials
2. Externally
   a. Regular Recruitment Sources
   b. New Recruitment Sources
   c. Subcontractors, Vendors, and Suppliers
D. Survey and Analyze Minority and Female Employment by Department and Job Classification
1. Identify Present Areas and Levels of Employment
2. Identify Areas of Underutilization and Concentration
3. Determine Extent of Underutilization
E. Goals and Timetables
1. Develop Long Range Goals
2. Set Annual Intermediate Targets
3. Identify Causes of Underutilization
F. Develop and Implement Specific Programs to Achieve Goals
1. Recruitment: Personnel Procedures
2. Selection Standards and Procedures
   a. Job-Related, Validated Standards
   b. Application Forms and Pre-employment Inquiries
   c. Testing
   d. Interviews
   e. Rating of Selection Standards
   f. Affirmative Action Records to Monitor the Selection Process
3. Upward Mobility System; Assignment; Job Progression; Promotion; Transfers; Seniority; Training
4. Wage and Salary Structure
5. Benefits and Conditions of Employment: "Fringe" Benefits; State "Protective" Laws; Pregnancy and Maternity
6. Layoff, Recall; Discharge; Demotion; Disciplinary Action
7. Revision of Union Contract; Membership; Referrals; Seniority; Maternity Leave; Other Benefits
G. Establish Internal Audit and Reporting System to Monitor and Evaluate Progress in Each Aspect

H. Develop Supportive In-House and Community Programs
    1. Training for Supervisors
    2. Support Services

There are several items worth noting in this outline. First and foremost, although the word "quota" is not used, there is no escaping the fact that the EEOC expected an employer to set goals and targets. Whatever might have been the intention of the drafters of Title VII, a decade later the leading government agency charged with fostering equal opportunity believed "goals" and "targets" necessary. The lower limit of a "goal" or the specific number of a "target" is, of course, a quota.

Second, for a company, especially a large company, implementing a plan would require more than a few people in the personnel department. A "Top Official," someone with authority, would have to oversee the program, and he or she would need recruiters, analysts, and people at every level of the organization to spend at least part of their time working to recruit, hire, keep, and promote women and minorities, and also be there to make sure that if a worker did not do a good job, demotion, transfer, or even firing would be based on a documented performance record. Implementing affirmative action would not be cheap.

Third, there is an indifference to and apparent naïveté regarding labor unions and their history. Unions, as we have seen, had in many cases been as guilty of racial discrimination as the rest of society, but now they faced a powerful federal agency that seemingly said, "We do not care about seniority and all the other benefits of union membership." Contracts had to be reconfigured so that newcomers—groups that had often been excluded from even belonging to unions—could be accommodated and promoted over union members with greater seniority and a better claim to those jobs. The assumption that management could just renegotiate these provisions seems foolhardy to say the least, and much of the backlash against affirmative action came from blue-collar workers who believed that they had to bear the costs of the nation's efforts to rectify its past sins.

This plan, it should be noted, does not envision the hiring of token African Americans or women. Although there are numerous allegations that companies would hire a woman, or a black, or preferably a black woman, to sit at the reception desk and do little other than be on display, the EEOC is telling companies to hire people because of their qualifications for the job. While the "goals" and "targets" are the key to so-called hard affirmative action, there is a great deal of the "soft" version here as well. Find out which minorities, including women, are underrepresented in the company's workforce, and then go look for those groups. Recruit, test, train, and then hire, with, of course, race and gender being important considerations. But if a person, once hired, did not work out, could not do the job, or caused disruption, then the company could dismiss that employee, provided it could document nonracial and non-gender reasons for the firing.

Finally, this outline made very good sense to the personnel officers who worked for corporate America and to academics who taught personnel management in business schools. Essentially, if a company set up an affirmative action plan according to EEOC guidelines—and followed that program in good faith—then it would be immune to suits by civil rights groups or disgruntled employees, it would be eligible for federal contracts, and its diverse workforce would be good for the company image.

DID AFFIRMATIVE ACTION plans succeed? That all depends on how you define success, but for the most part in the 1970s and 1980s many companies, universities, and governmental agencies adopted plans designed to increase the number of women and minorities in their workforces. Once programs became established and hiring a woman or an African American or a Hispanic no longer seemed exotic, these groups became part of the labor pool on which businesses drew to fill vacancies. Conversely, as companies that previously discriminated began hiring more women and minorities, and word got around that if you were black or Hispanic or female you could get jobs at these firms, more women and minorities applied.

The problems of discrimination did not disappear. It would be unrealistic to assume that decades of a corporate culture that excluded women and minorities would be cured overnight by what amounted to the injection of a wonder drug. Courts would continue to hear cases of real and alleged discrimination, as well as cases from white males claiming that in order to hire minorities, companies had discriminated against them. Women, more so than blacks and other minorities, might have found it easier breaking the initial barriers, but that first step in many cases proved difficult. In some places, the hostility proved extremely nasty.

Shannon Faulkner applied to the Citadel, a state military academy in Charleston, South Carolina, and the school accepted her on the assumption that "Shannon" was male. When she showed up, the officials refused to enroll her, and she went to court, which ordered her admitted with the class entering in 1995. Once enrolled, she endured five days of brutal harassment and then resigned. The male cadets erupted into cheers and jeers, which the national media carried, all making the cadets look like the bigoted male chauvinists they were. Not until the U.S. Supreme Court ordered the Virginia Military Institute to admit women did the Citadel finally and grudgingly follow suit.

Even today, with women in state legislatures and Congress, in the military, in the highest ranks of academia, and on the Supreme Court, the phrase "glass ceiling" represents the bias still facing them.

But did people think affirmative action worked then? One researcher examined the U.S. Census reports for 1970 and 1980, a task made more difficult by the fact that the Census Bureau had changed some categories and had trouble identifying Hispanics, not all of whom had Spanish-sounding surnames and could have been white, black, or brown. The Census Bureau had twelve categories of occupation. At the top, it grouped "professional, technical, and kindred," and this group included physicians, college faculty, air traffic controllers, engineers, lawyers and judges, and librarians. Level 5, "Craftsmen and kindred," included carpenters, electricians, aircraft mechanics, millwrights, and telephone repairmen. Level 12, "Private Household Workers," included cooks, maids, and nannies in private houses. The income level, in general, was highest at Level 1 and lowest at Level 12.

Between 1970 and 1980, the percentage of African Americans increased in Levels 1–6 and decreased in Levels 7–12; that is, more African Americans could be found in the professional and skilled occupations in 1980 than ten years earlier. In some areas, the percentage increase is quite striking. Blacks showed a 39 percent increase in the top two levels, and a 47 percent increase in Level 4, clerical and kindred, which included bank tellers, mail carriers, secretaries, and receptionists. The decreases could be found in categories that included unskilled workers, service employees, and household help.

Employers in both the public and the private sectors faced many of the same problems, especially discriminatory practices that kept women and people of color out of certain jobs—generally the higher-paying, more stable, and more prestigious positions. In the late 1960s, public opinion and public policy began to change. Government employers tended to hire more women and minorities and to pay them more than did private-sector companies. But while public employers seem to have had better hiring practices, evidence showed that in the public sector women and people of color remained at a disadvantage compared with white men.

Over time, studies of both federal and state practices (excluding the southern states) showed a remarkable similarity. White women workers seem to have made the greatest gain in the federal workforce following the implementation of affirmative action in the Johnson administration, but black workers—both male and female—did not do notably better. Starting in the mid-1970s, when record keeping became more sophisticated (prior to then, the government classified all nonwhite people as "black"), one could find clear gains in white-collar jobs going to white, Asian American, Hispanic, and black women, with white women gaining the most. Although black men also showed higher numbers, they clearly lagged behind women.

A similar pattern emerged in state government, although it appears that the federal government made a greater effort to comply with the Equal Pay Act of 1963. While more women moved into higher echelons of state government, the majority of the elite positions remained occupied by men, who received higher salaries than did women. In the California state government, women earned 60.4 percent of what men earned in 1975 and ten years later still lagged behind, although the number had climbed to 74.3 percent. In one study of agency heads, women held only 2 percent of such positions in 1964, but a quarter century later held 18 percent, and their salaries nearly equaled those of men. In all positions in states outside the South, women and minorities made significant gains in the early 1980s.

All these studies came with numerous caveats. For example, when women and children provided the primary constituency for an agency—such as social welfare or child protection—more women would be hired. In bureaus enforcing civil rights, blacks found greater opportunities. Those states that had more urban, liberal, and better-educated populations had less workforce segregation of women and minorities. Also, when governors rather than independent boards appointed agency heads, women could circumvent the glass ceiling.

In California, interestingly enough, state agencies were required to submit affirmative action plans for the first time following an executive order by Governor Ronald Reagan in 1974, the same man whose presidential administration the following decade would oppose affirmative action. These plans proved to be very effective. State and local governments became big employers of white and black women and black men; black women made up only 2.7 percent of private-sector employment, but more than 6 percent of state and local workers. White men's share of employment in state government dropped by nineteen percentage points from 1970 to 1990, and by 11 percent in local governments. Latinos showed the greatest growth in public-sector work, with men adding four percentage points and women eight.

AGAIN, DID AFFIRMATIVE ACTION work? All studies of African American economic life during this period show marked advancement. For example, the percentage of black males employed in white-collar jobs rose from 12 in 1960 to 30 in 1990, compared with percentages of 36 and 47 for white males in that period. The percentages for black females rose from 18 to 58, compared with those for white females of 58 and 73. The problem with these numbers, of course, is how much can be attributed to affirmative action, how much to the good economic times that created millions of new jobs, how much to civil rights laws, and how much to the growing number of minority high school and college graduates?

Despite all the studies done, there is no simple answer. It is impossible to get accurate figures because in many instances blacks and other minorities might have been hired even in the absence of a plan. The best numbers come from those firms or agencies that admittedly had discriminated in the past, and where blacks or women entered the job force only because of affirmative action. One can find specific examples—a particular company or even an industry, a college or university, or even a government agency—in which one can say that without the affirmative action plan there would have been far fewer women or minorities.

A number of economic studies over the years all find basically the same thing—that affirmative action, whether in hiring or in minority set-asides, worked. In exclusively financial terms, the benefits of the policy have seemingly far outweighed the costs. There are many success stories, and one could give example after example, study after study, but the controversy over affirmative action is not about successful programs or whether the dollar costs are outweighed by the benefits. For every study that views affirmative action positively, one can find a critic who points to nondollar issues. Critics can come up with their own numbers to show that the programs have not worked that well and have only helped a small number of people. For example, in 1970, 31.5 million women held jobs, and they earned on the whole only 59.2 percent of men's salaries. By 1985, the number of working women had grown to 51.1 million, and the salary gap had closed somewhat to 65 percent. A breakdown of these numbers, however, indicated that white women entering the job market in 1980 were actually further behind the wages of comparable white men than they had been in 1970, despite the alleged success of affirmative action. A 1985 study by the National Research Council reported that sex segregation in employment had remained fairly stable since 1900. Despite some changes after 1975, the segregation index still remained at 60, which meant that 30 percent of workers would have to move in to job categories dominated by the opposite sex just to even the numbers out. Moreover, in its study the council found that overall women still earned only 60 percent as much as men.

Numbers are important, but they really do not tell us why affirmative action is so divisive an issue. One can understand why women and minorities, especially African Americans, who had been shut out of schools and jobs because of their gender or race would welcome programs that tried to remediate the effects of that past discrimination. The backlash against affirmative action is not about numbers at all. It is about how we view what equality in America means.

CHAPTER 6

MARCO DeFUNIS, ALLAN BAKKE, AND BRIAN WEBER

The Constitution is both color-blind and color-conscious. To avoid conflict with the Equal Protection Clause, a classification that denies a benefit, causes harm or imposes a burden must not be based on race. In that sense, the Constitution is color-blind. But the Constitution is color-conscious to prevent discrimination being perpetuated and to undo the effects of past discrimination. The criterion is the relevancy of color to a legitimate government purpose.

—JUDGE JOHN MINOR WISDOM

In America, as Alexis de Tocqueville said many years ago, all public issues wind up in court, and affirmative action proved no exception. The justices had avoided the issue in the case challenging the Philadelphia Plan, but eventually they had to confront the problem of what form of compensatory justice—if any—the country owed to minorities who had been discriminated against for decades, indeed centuries. Moreover, unlike the attack on the Philadelphia Plan sponsored by a group of builders, each case that came to the high court in the 1970s had an individual and identifiable plaintiff, a white male complaining about what opponents of affirmative action condemned as "reverse discrimination." The failure of the justices to devise a workable jurisprudence reflected the growing division within the country over the merits or liabilities of affirmative action.

Marco DeFunis graduated magna cum laude and Phi Beta Kappa from the University of Washington in 1970, with a grade point average of 3.6 out of 4.0; he received no grade under an A minus in his last two years. The son of a Sephardic Jewish family, he taught

Sunday school at his synagogue while an undergraduate and also worked between twenty and forty hours a week for the Seattle Parks Department. He wanted to be a lawyer, applied to several schools, and gained admission at two public law schools, Idaho and Oregon, as well as at two private schools. He did not, however, receive an offer from either Boalt Hall, the prestigious University of California law school at Berkeley, or from the University of Washington Law School. He wanted to stay in Washington and reapplied in 1971 and, after again being denied admission, learned about the affirmative action plan adopted by the law school.

When Charles E. Odegaard became president of the University of Washington in 1958, he had looked around and asked, "Where are the black faces?" He then led the faculty in the development and implementation of a process that took race and ethnicity into account. The university, Odegaard declared, is "in pursuit of a state policy to mitigate gross underrepresentation of certain minorities in the law school and in membership in the [state] bar."

The PFYA (predicted first-year average) score seems to have been the most important standard, and it was based on previous academic records and LSAT results. With the highest possible score an 81, all applicants with a PFYA of 77 or higher received automatic admission, while scores of 74.5 or less would be rejected. The admissions committee, however, treated two groups differently. Students who had at one time been admitted but had then been called up for military service were automatically accepted. The other group consisted of applicants from four specific minority groups—African Americans, Hispanic Americans, Native Americans, and Filipino Americans.

The files of whites and non-preferred minorities (such as Asian Americans) went to the full committee. The application forms for the preferred minorities went into a separate pile, to be read by an African American student and a faculty member who had experience in the university's program for disadvantaged students. The subcommittee then returned their evaluations and the files to the full committee, which read them separately from those of the other applicants. Instead of comparing the qualifications of the minorities against the entire pool, the committee compared minority students against other minority students, and the highest ranking of these were admitted under a program in which the law school had established a goal of between 15 and 20 percent minority enrollment, in order to achieve a "reasonable representation" of minorities.

Marco DeFunis filed the first "reverse discrimination" suit when he was turned down by a law school while minorities with lower scores were accepted.

When DeFunis applied in 1971, 1,600 applicants vied for the 150 seats available for the first-year class. He had a PFYA of 76.23, which put him in the middle group that the applications committee reviewed twice; the committee first put him on a waiting list and then in July 1971 formally rejected him. Minorities made up only 4 percent, or 64, of the total applications, yet of the 150 admitted, 44 came from the minority pool, with most of them scoring below the 74.5 automatic rejection level for nonminorities. DeFunis had a better PFYA than 74 applicants who had been admitted, including 38 of the special minority group. Twenty-nine white applicants with higher PFYA scores than DeFunis were also denied admission.

Upon learning this, DeFunis hired a lawyer, Josef Diamond, who filed a lawsuit charging the University of Washington Law School with reverse discrimination in violation of the Constitution. Diamond argued that the university's plan constituted a racial classification prohibited by the Fourteenth Amendment's Equal Protection Clause, and he quoted from Justice Harlan's *Plessy* dissent that "the

Constitution is color-blind and neither knows nor tolerates classes among its citizens." The university, he claimed, could not show any compelling interest in using racial qualifications for admission, and preferential treatment for minority groups in the law school plan violated Marco DeFunis's right to equal protection.

The Washington State attorney general, Slade Gorton, represented the university and claimed that the law school indeed had a compelling interest, namely, overcoming the lingering results of three centuries of slavery and racial discrimination. African Americans made up less than 2 percent of the lawyers practicing in the country in 1970. The university wanted to end the vestigial "badges of slavery" that still attached to people of color.

Gorton had the burden of proving that Washington had a "compelling interest" because the Supreme Court had set the bar for any sort of racial classification very high. In cases involving economic regulations, the government only had to show a "rational basis" between the purpose of the law and how it operated, a standard so low that unless a specific constitutional prohibition existed, the courts would nearly always find the government program legitimate. But for a protected class such as race, there had to be a compelling interest, and the burden lay upon the government to prove it.

The attorney general characterized the policy as a "benign" form of discrimination, one that had the purpose of admitting formerly excluded groups into the law school. He also claimed that the school had a compelling interest in diversity among the student body. The Constitution, Gorton claimed, prohibited only invidious discrimination, and the law school's affirmative action plan did not rise to that level, because it was neither arbitrary nor capricious.

Here we have the first airing in the courts of arguments that will be heard over and over again. Affirmative action is a form of discrimination against whites and violates their constitutionally protected right to equal treatment. Against this would be the claim that after centuries of rank discrimination that excluded minorities from jobs, schools, and elsewhere, a benign discrimination violated neither the Fourteenth Amendment nor the Civil Rights Act.

The state's arguments did not impress Judge Lloyd Shorett of the Superior Court for King County. Marco DeFunis had been the victim of racial discrimination and denied his right to equal protection. After *Brown v. Board of Education,* Shorett concluded, "the Fourteenth Amendment could no longer be stretched to accommodate the needs of any race. . . . The only safe rule is to treat all races alike." Shorett ordered that DeFunis join the law school's entering class in September 1971.

The law school admitted DeFunis reluctantly, and because Judge Shorett's decision relied on a fundamental constitutional argument, Gorton was able to bypass the state court of appeals and go directly to the Washington Supreme Court, which heard arguments in May 1972 but did not hand down a decision until 8 March 1973. The judges clearly recognized the importance of the issue, and one reason for the delay seems to have been disagreement within the court, with two concurring and two dissenting opinions. The state's high court found a compelling state interest, namely, ending racial imbalance in the legal profession. "Where the purpose is to promote integration and to undo the effects of past discrimination it is not per se violative of the equal protection clause." The dissenters accepted DeFunis's argument that the Constitution had to be color-blind and held that "racial bigotry will never be ended by exalting the political rights of one group or class over that of another."

ALTHOUGH DEFUNIS HAD by now finished two years of law school, his ability to enroll for the final terms depended on the discretion of the university administration. By the time the state supreme court denied him a rehearing, the U.S. Supreme Court had already adjourned, and the justices had headed out for their summer vacations. Josef Diamond applied to William O. Douglas (as the justice responsible for the states in the Ninth Circuit) for a stay of the Washington court decision until the Supreme Court reconvened and could decide whether to accept DeFunis's appeal. Douglas granted the stay, leaving Judge Shorett's order in effect, and that September Marco DeFunis enrolled for his third year of law school.

Diamond filed his appeal to the high court in August, and in his brief he posed two questions that he believed the justices needed to answer:

—Does the affirmative action program violate the Fourteenth Amendment's Equal Protection Clause by giving preference to certain minorities?
—Does the plan violate Title VI of the 1964 Civil Rights Act because white applicants are required to meet different

and more stringent admission standards than do persons of other races?

Slade Gorton, as is usual when representing the side that had won in lower court, asked the justices to either dismiss the case or affirm the decision of the Washington Supreme Court. However, if they decided to take the case, then they had only one question to answer: "May the University of Washington Law School constitutionally take into account, as one element in selecting from among qualified candidates for the study of law, the race of applicants in pursuit of a state policy to mitigate gross under-representation of certain minorities in the law school, and in the membership of the bar?"

The justices met in conference on 19 October 1973, and the question immediately arose whether an actual case or controversy existed. The Court would not hear arguments for another few months, and the decision would probably not come down until late spring, by which time DeFunis would be close to graduation. To resolve this issue, they asked both sides to file supplemental briefs on whether the case was now moot, that is, in effect already settled. Four justices—Chief Justice Warren Burger and Associate Justices William Rehnquist, Harry Blackmun, and Potter Stewart—would have dismissed for mootness. Lewis Powell also leaned toward dismissal but wanted to see what the two sides said in their supplemental briefs.

Diamond and Gorton responded quickly, and both argued against mootness. Diamond claimed that lifting the injunction did not guarantee that the university would allow DeFunis to finish his third year. Moreover, the case was capable of repetition, in that other white males would be stymied in their attempts to get into law school by the university plan. Gorton agreed that the important constitutional question of the legitimacy of an affirmative action plan had to be answered so that the university would know whether it could continue with its plan. He also indicated that the university would allow DeFunis to finish his third year.

Under the rule of four, it takes the votes of four justices to grant cert, that is, to accept a case on appeal. William Brennan, Thurgood Marshall, and Byron White wanted to take the case, but they needed one more vote. William O. Douglas, although he had granted the stay order, had doubts, especially about the mootness question. His law clerk that term—Ira Ellman—convinced him that the case was not moot, because, as he presciently wrote, "the controversy will continue and is a recurring one." If the Court dismissed the case as moot, "I think it would be fairly obvious that all the Court is doing is ducking the issue." Douglas agreed, and added his vote to grant cert.

Although the *DeFunis* case is rarely studied now, overshadowed by Allan Bakke's suit four years later, it drew a great deal of attention at the time. The split in the civil rights camp could be clearly seen in the amici (friend of the court) briefs, with the Southern Christian Leadership Conference and the NAACP backing the university plan, and the Anti-defamation League of B'nai B'rith and the Jewish Rights Council siding with DeFunis. In addition to the Jewish groups, the AFL-CIO, the U.S. Chamber of Commerce, and the National Association of Manufacturers filed briefs opposing the plan. In response, twenty-two amicus briefs urged the Court to uphold the plan, and these included Harvard University, the Legal Aid Society, the American Indian Lawyers Association, the Association of American Law Schools, and the Mexican American Legal Defense and Educational Fund. All argued that affirmative action programs like that at Washington provided the only means for overcoming the nation's continuing discrimination against blacks and other minorities.

If the justices wanted to deal with affirmative action, *DeFunis v. Odegaard* certainly gave them the opportunity. All the briefs, both those by the litigants and those by the amici, argued that substantial questions of constitutional as well as statutory interpretation existed. Those siding with DeFunis claimed that the use of race to determine law school admission violated the Equal Protection Clause of the Fourteenth Amendment. The Constitution is a color-blind document that bars all discrimination based on race or heritage. The civil rights groups backing the law school asserted that color blindness in the United States had always been a fiction and that the Constitution permits reasonable uses of racial classification, especially to remedy the long-term effects of discrimination.

Moreover, this case highlighted what many critics of affirmative action had now been arguing for nearly a decade. Marco DeFunis had played no role in the historical discrimination against people of color yet would now have to pay a price for the sins of society. This was not a case of "soft" affirmative action, of throwing open the gates of opportunity wider so that people hitherto excluded could now enter. "Hard" affirmative action had goals and quotas, as did the Washington Law School plan, and it was a zero-sum game. To admit one person of color under the plan meant that another person, equally or perhaps even better qualified, would be rejected. Marco DeFunis provided the Court with the opportunity—if it wished to take it—to rule on the legitimacy of affirmative action plans.

The Court scheduled oral argument for 26 February 1974. The day before, Chief Justice Burger received a letter from Josef Diamond that his client had just registered for his final quarter of law school. When the justices came to the bench, they all knew that no matter what they decided, Marco DeFunis would graduate. For at least four justices, the issue of mootness seemed paramount. Although the Court has from time to time reached out to decide bigger issues than those in the case before them, for the most part the general rule is to decide, usually on as narrow a ground as possible, the case based on the facts before the justices. If in fact the *DeFunis* case was now moot, then no real case or controversy existed—even if capable of repetition—and the suit could be dismissed.

On the trial day, not only were all of the seats inside the courtroom filled, but according to newspaper reports dozens of lawyers and students stood outside in the Great Hall. During oral argument, the justices interrupted both Diamond and Gorton repeatedly, wanting details on how the program worked, how DeFunis had done, why the program did or did not violate the Equal Protection Clause.

When the justices met in conference the following Friday, it quickly became apparent that they were divided both on the issue of mootness and on whether the law school program violated the Equal Protection Clause. Initially, four justices—Burger, Stewart, Blackmun, and Rehnquist—believed the case moot because DeFunis would soon graduate. Four other justices—Brennan, White, Marshall, and Douglas—wanted to decide the case on its merits, although they did not agree on how the merits should be defined or how they would vote. Lewis Powell thought the case "probably moot" but believed race could be taken into account and tentatively affirmed the ruling of the Washington Supreme Court, but he wanted to think about it some more. Two weeks later he informed the brethren that he would join with those who believed the case moot.

Chief Justice Burger assigned the opinion, which would be issued as a short and unsigned per curiam (by the court), to Potter Stewart. DeFunis, the opinion noted, was registered for his last term and "will receive his diploma regardless of any decision this Court might reach on the merits of the case." Therefore, a determination of the legal issues "is no longer necessary to compel that result and could not serve to prevent it." The controversy between the parties "has thus clearly ceased." The case would be remanded to the Supreme Court of Washington "for such proceedings as by that court may be deemed appropriate."

There were two dissents. The shorter, by Justice William Brennan, and joined by Douglas, White, and Marshall, argued that the case had not become moot, that important issues had been raised, and that in disposing of DeFunis's claim as moot, "the Court clearly disserves the public interest. . . . Few constitutional questions in recent history have stirred as much debate, and they will not disappear. They must inevitably return to the federal courts and ultimately again to this Court." There is little doubt that had the Court decided to reach the merits, Brennan, White, and Marshall would have voted to sustain the law school's affirmative action plan. Not so Justice Douglas.

Arguably the most liberal member of the Court in the twentieth century, Douglas wrote a blistering opinion opposing the university's

Justice William O. Douglas, arguably the most liberal justice of the twentieth century, who wrote a blistering dissent in the DeFunis *case attacking affirmative action.*

plan. After detailing how the law school program worked (a subject almost entirely missing from the per curiam), Douglas tore into the Law School Admission Test, which he denounced not only as racially biased but as nearly useless as an indicator of how well a person would perform in law school. ("I personally know that admissions tests were once used to eliminate Jews. How many other minorities they aim at I do not know.") If the school had used its numerical index, the PFYA, in a straightforward manner, one might complain that it served poorly as an indicator of potential success. But it had not. "To the contrary, the school appears to have conceded that by its own assessment—taking all factors into account—it admitted minority applicants who would have been rejected had they been white."

Douglas went on to write a paean to cultural pluralism and individual accomplishment, and "the key to the problem is the consideration of each application in a racially neutral way." The melting pot, that old metaphor of what happens to immigrants coming to America, "is not designed to homogenize people. . . . It is a figure of speech that depicts the wide diversities tolerated by the First Amendment under one flag. Minorities in our midst who are to serve actively in our public affairs should be chosen on talent and character alone, not on cultural orientation or leanings."

As for the university's argument that it needed to train minority lawyers to serve the minority population, Douglas declared, "The Equal Protection Clause commands the elimination of racial barriers, not their creation in order to satisfy our theory as to how society ought to be organized. The purpose of the University of Washington cannot be to produce black lawyers for blacks, Polish lawyers for Poles, Jewish lawyers for Jews, Irish lawyers for Irish. It should be to produce good lawyers for Americans."

Interestingly, Douglas did not claim that DeFunis had been deprived of any constitutional right. That question had not been fully answered by the facts submitted, and he would send the case back to the state court to determine if in fact there had been a violation of the Equal Protection Clause.

Marco DeFunis did graduate from the University of Washington Law School in 1974, and after working a few years at a large law firm, he and a friend, David Balint, opened their own practice in Seattle, specializing in personal injury law. He became a pillar of the Seattle Jewish community and appeared to have been in excellent health when, on 17 January 2002, he suffered a fatal heart attack while running on the indoor track at the Jewish Community Center. He was two weeks shy of his fifty-third birthday.

As Justice Brennan predicted, the issue would not go away. Even as the *DeFunis* case worked its way through the courts, another white male, twelve hundred miles to the south, decided to sue the University of California after an affirmative action program denied him admission to medical school.

THE MEDICAL SCHOOL at Davis had opened in 1966, with forty-eight entering students, one of five medical schools in the California system. For its first four years, it had no system of preferential admissions for minorities, and only 3 percent of its applications came from minorities. The administration, concerned about a lack of diversity, set up an affirmative action plan in 1970. In that year, only about eight hundred minority students attended medical school in the entire United States, and four out of every five of them enrolled either at Howard University in the District of Columbia or at Meharry Medical College in Nashville.

Another consideration weighing on Davis officials involved the sudden spike in applications for medical schools, and even taken all together, the country's medical institutions did not have enough seats to handle the spate of applicants. Many of the schools, concerned about the low number of minority students, set up some form of affirmative action plan. In 1971, Davis established a special admissions program, reserving sixteen places out of a hundred for minorities, identified as African Americans, Chicanos, Asians, and American Indians.

Applications to Davis went into one of two piles. The "regular" applicants went to a committee of fifteen, twelve faculty members and three students, which evaluated them for the eighty-four seats that went to nonminority and non-disadvantaged candidates. A collegiate grade point average of 2.5 or less meant summary rejection. A special committee examined the files of those who self-identified as members of an "economically and/or educationally disadvantaged" minority group. In both the general and the special admissions programs, the school took account of undergraduate grade point average, grades in science courses, scores on the Medical College Admission Test, and results of interviews. In 1973, these factors added up to a maximum score of 500, and the following year some adjustments to the system raised the maximum to 600.

Allan Paul Bakke had been born in 1940 and stood at just under six feet, and his blond hair and blue eyes testified to his Norwegian ancestry. The son of a mailman and a schoolteacher, he had studied mechanical engineering at the University of Minnesota. To help pay for his studies, he joined the Naval Reserve Officers Training Corps, and after graduation did a four-year tour of duty with the U.S. Marines, including a stint in Vietnam. He then went to work for NASA, and while his experience did not lead him to want to become an astronaut, it did confirm his desire to become a doctor. Although by this time married and with a growing family, he began to prepare for medical school by taking courses in sciences and volunteering as a candy striper at a local hospital, an "incongruous male figure" among the female volunteers. He took the tough assignments, working with the battered victims of car accidents or fights.

In 1972 and again in 1973, he applied to medical school, without success, and he recognized that his biggest handicap was his age. Nearly all medical schools at that time believed thirty-three to be too old, because by the time a person finished medical school, internship,

Allan Bakke wanted to become a doctor but was turned down in favor of minority students with lower test scores. He sued the California system and won his case in the U.S. Supreme Court.

and residency, he would have been around forty, thus cutting off the number of years he would be able to practice. Despite good credentials, strong recommendations, and clear dedication, he was rejected by every school to which he applied. At Davis, Bakke scored 468 out of 500 in 1973, and the following year 549 out of 600. In both years, the school rejected him while admitting minority students with lower marks through the special admissions program.

Bakke sought out Reynold H. Colvin, a prominent San Francisco lawyer, who filed suit in California Superior Court to have Bakke admitted to Davis. Colvin decided not to concentrate on the very clear difference between Bakke's scores and those of the minority students who gained admission. Rather, he argued that setting aside sixteen seats solely for minorities constituted an illegal and unconstitutional racial quota, one prohibited both by the 1964 Civil Rights Act and by the Equal Protection Clause of the Fourteenth Amendment. Colvin would argue, at every stage of the process, that whatever the university wished to call its program, it remained a racial quota and therefore unconstitutional.

The University of California system assigned its general counsel, Donald Reidhaar, to defend the Davis program, because if it fell, then affirmative action plans at its other schools could also be struck down. Reidhaar claimed that preferential treatment for minorities did not violate the Constitution or the Civil Rights Act when the school used race as a positive factor to overcome centuries of slavery and race discrimination. He also argued that the sixteen slots for minorities constituted a "goal" and not a "quota," although he never explained how Davis had determined that number. Finally, he charged that Bakke had no standing to sue, because he had fallen short of the minimum scores necessary for admission to the medical school.

In June 1974, just before the *DeFunis* decision (or nondecision) came down, Colvin brought suit in Yolo County Superior Court before Judge F. Leslie Manker, a former Superior Court judge called out of retirement to hear the case because the two sitting judges were swamped with cases. Manker saw that he had to answer two questions: Was the special admissions program constitutional, and if not, should Allan Bakke be admitted to medical school at Davis by court order? In late November, Judge Manker ruled the Davis program a racial quota that violated the federal constitution, the state constitution, and Title VI of the Civil Rights Act. "No race or ethnic group should ever be granted privileges or immunities not given to every other race." Rather than order Bakke admitted, however, he ordered the school to consider Bakke's application again without regard to his or any other applicant's race; that is, he would be eligible for any of the hundred seats, not just those available to whites.

Both Reidhaar and Colvin appealed Manker's ruling to the California Supreme Court, Reidhaar because the lower court had struck down the special admissions plan and Colvin because Manker had not ordered Bakke admitted. Many people believed the California high court to be one of the most liberal in the country, and Davis and others in favor of affirmative action felt confident it would reverse the lower-court decision. They would be very disappointed.

In an opinion by Judge Stanley Mosk, the court, after carefully delineating the program as well as Allan Bakke's qualifications, declared that "the issue to be determined thus narrows to whether a racial classification which is intended to assist minorities, but which also has the effect of depriving those who are not so classified of benefits they would enjoy but for their race, violates the constitutional rights of the majority." The very phrasing of the matter clearly indicated which way the court would go.

Any classification by race, Mosk noted, involves a very stringent standard, that of strict scrutiny. Not only must the purpose of the classification serve a "compelling state interest," but the state also has to show that there are no "reasonable ways" to achieve that goal that impose a lesser burden on the rights of the disadvantaged group. He rejected the university's contention that a more lenient standard should be applied when the race discriminated against is the majority. "We do not hesitate to reject the notion that racial discrimination may be more easily justified against one race than another, nor can we permit the validity of such discrimination to be determined by a mere census count of the races." The court also rejected the university's argument that it needed to train black doctors to serve in black communities, and Mosk paraphrased Justice Douglas's dissent in *DeFunis*: the medical school should train good doctors for Americans. Mosk concluded by ordering Bakke admitted to the University of California at Davis Medical School and the university to reimburse him for his legal expenses.

By this time, emotions outside the courthouse ran high, because both proponents and opponents of affirmative action believed that the decision in Allan Bakke's case would either confirm the constitutionality of affirmative action or doom it. In San Francisco, two thousand people marched in protest. Some civil rights activists charged that the university wanted to take a fall, that it actually wanted to lose the case. Proponents of racial preference programs urged the regents of the California system not to appeal the decision, which constituted the greatest judicial defeat ever suffered by affirmative action.

The opposition of civil rights activists reflected tactical concerns. The rigidity of the Davis plan made it hard to defend, and the record did not show that Davis—a relatively new school—had ever engaged in past racial discrimination that could justify current compensatory programs. The case had never involved civil rights groups; neither Allan Bakke nor the California university system had ever gone to any of the national or local civil rights organizations to get any input. Essentially, a group of whites, mostly male, had created a case that posed great danger to affirmative action plans everywhere, and minorities, who had the greatest stake in the outcome, had no role to play.

DESPITE THIS OPPOSITION, California appealed the decision to the U.S. Supreme Court, which granted cert in February 1977 and scheduled oral argument the following October. In many ways, the Court had little choice. Unlike Marco DeFunis, who had almost finished law school when the justices heard his case, Allan Bakke, despite the ruling of the California Supreme Court, had still not been admitted, with his fate on hold during the appeal. This case could in no way be seen as moot. Moreover, the California court had written a strong opinion condemning affirmative action and banning the use of race in admissions policies that not only affected the many schools in the California system but could also influence courts in other states. University officials across the country publicly expressed their worry that a ruling in favor of Bakke would undo the "vast gains" made by minorities in colleges and professional schools in the last decade. On the day before the Court heard oral argument, the U.S. Civil Rights Commission issued a twelve-page statement endorsing affirmative action programs in professional schools.

Some sixty groups filed amicus curiae briefs, with the American Bar Association, the American Civil Liberties Union, the NAACP, the Association of American Law Schools, the Association of American Medical Colleges (AAMC), a number of universities, and the National Council of Churches all supporting affirmative action. Prominent Jewish groups, including the American Jewish Committee and the Anti-defamation League of B'nai B'rith, led the opposition. The brief from the federal government, normally given great consideration by the justices, proved to be such a mess that Lewis Powell, reflecting the views of his colleagues, dismissed it as useless.

The Court heard oral argument on 12 October 1977, and if the case had been decided on the basis of lawyerly skills, Bakke would have lost. California had brought in Archibald Cox, a Harvard law professor, former solicitor general, Watergate prosecutor, and above all experienced litigator before the high court. Bakke had stuck with Reynold Colvin, who had never argued a case before the Supreme Court. His inexperience soon showed, and he argued as if before a jury. Justice Rehnquist suggested this approach to be inappropriate, but Colvin plodded on. Finally, Justice Powell chided Colvin for belaboring the undisputed facts. "We are here—at least I am—to hear a constitutional argument," Powell said. "I would like help, I really would, on the constitutional issues." Colvin finally got the message and devoted the rest of his time to the legal arguments.

Archibald Cox arguing before the Supreme Court on 12 October 1977 on behalf of the California system in the Bakke *case. Cameras were, and still are, barred from the courtroom. The justices are,* from left to right, *William Rehnquist, Harry Blackmun, Byron White, William Brennan, Chief Justice Warren Burger, Potter Stewart, Thurgood Marshall, Lewis Powell, and John Paul Stevens.*

Although the Court heard the case in the opening weeks of the term, it would be eight months before the decision came down. Just as the country split over affirmative action, so too did the justices. While the Court mulled over the case, a Carnegie Foundation study reported that many whites believed that "the nation's debt to black people has been so fully paid that whites themselves are becoming victims of reverse discrimination." It is little wonder, then, that the justices landed on—one can hardly say they devised—one of the most unique and controversial decisions in the Court's history.

Two positions emerged during the discussion, and as John Jeffries, Powell's biographer, noted, "Both were intellectually coherent, legally tenable, and morally defensible. They were also diametrically opposed." They both relied on theories of how and when—or never at all—color consciousness in a government program could be constitutional, the very problem posed in the quotation by Judge John Minor Wisdom at the beginning of this chapter.

On the one side stood those who believed, as the first John Marshall Harlan had declared decades earlier, "Our Constitution is color-blind, and neither knows nor tolerates classes among its citizens." These words had been the mantra of the civil rights movement in the 1960s, at the heart of the cases striking down racial segregation in schools, and the rationale for the 1964 Civil Rights Act. The justices had heard this argument for more than three decades, ever since the NAACP had begun its modern attack against "separate but equal." Alexander Bickel, one of the foremost constitutional scholars of his day, had written, "The lesson of the great decisions of the Supreme Court and the lesson of contemporary history have been the same for at least a generation: discrimination on the basis of race is illegal, immoral, unconstitutional, inherently wrong, and destructive of democratic society." He opposed affirmative action as undermining this great moral standard. Now "we are told this is not a matter of fundamental principle but only a matter of whose ox is gored." By this line of reasoning, any racial classification—even for benign purposes—violated not only the Constitution but the basic underpinnings of a democratic society.

The argument on the other side claimed that the Constitution had never been color-blind, not in its origins nor even in its later developments. The purpose of the Equal Protection Clause had originally been a form of affirmative action, to help the former slaves overcome 250 years of bondage. Race, whether we wanted it to or not, mattered in America and imposed a continuing burden on people of color. As McGeorge Bundy put it, "There can be no blinking the enormous and unique set of handicaps which our whole history, right up to the present, has imposed on those who are not white." To adopt a strict color blindness would be no more than a high-minded way of refusing to right past wrongs. Centuries of oppression demanded some form of compensatory action.

While the issue before the Court would ultimately rely on legal and constitutional arguments, the justices and everyone else recognized that *Regents of the University of California v. Bakke* involved political, economic, and moral parameters as well. Upholding "hard" affirmative action, plans with quotas and timetables, might possibly move many minorities out of poverty and set them on a path into the middle class; on the other hand, it could well deprive poor whites of that same opportunity. Bakke's case made it very plain that in professional school admissions, affirmative action was a zero-sum game—admit one person only at the expense of denying another.

Granting, as Bundy noted, that people of color (and he could have added groups such as women and the disabled) had faced centuries of discrimination and therefore deserved some form of compensation, who would pay for it? It was one thing, such as a suit involving the Alabama State Police, which for years had excluded African Americans, to be ordered to hire by the numbers until the percentage of blacks on the force equaled their percentage of the population. There could be no doubt in that case who the perpetrators of racial injustice had been. But what sin had Allan Bakke or his second-generation immigrant parents committed? Was the nation's terrible legacy of racial persecution so heavy that just being a member of the majority race was enough to warrant imposing compensatory payment? Historically, the majority had discriminated against minorities, whether they be people of color, women, immigrants, or Native Americans. Was it in fact even possible to discriminate against the majority? An issue as divisive as affirmative action would also play out in the political arena, no matter how the justices answered the legal questions.

IT WOULD TAKE a small book to trace the discussions and the emergence of opinions between oral argument and the announcement of a decision eight months later. Essentially, the justices split into two groups from the start. Chief Justice Burger and Justices Rehnquist, Stevens, and Stewart believed the Davis plan violated the Equal Protection Clause and Title VI of the Civil Rights Act. Justice John Paul Stevens, who had taken Douglas's seat, insisted that because a statutory reason existed, the Court need not and should not decide on a constitutional basis. Eventually, he prevailed, and the other three signed on to his opinion.

Three justices from the start supported not just the Davis plan but all affirmative action programs—Brennan, Marshall, and White. They believed that both the Fourteenth Amendment and the Civil Rights Act allowed for transitional and targeted benign admissions programs to redress decades of discrimination against blacks and other minorities.

Two justices did not indicate their opinion until later. Lewis Powell circulated a memo in December 1977 stating that he believed race could be one factor, and a positive one, in admissions decisions, and he cited the protocol of Harvard College. The Virginia justice, who had been head of both city and state boards of education, knew more about education than any of his colleagues, and his experience led him to agree that diversity in the classroom constituted a compelling reason for affirmative action admissions plans. But there could be no quotas, no reserving a set number of seats for minorities; such plans, in his view, violated the Constitution.

This 4–3–1 status lasted until 1 May 1978, when Justice Harry Blackmun, who had been away from the Court for medical reasons, returned, and no one knew what he would do. If he joined Warren Burger, that would give the opponents of the Davis plan a majority, and Burger expected his friend to do just that. But Blackmun surprised everyone by joining the Brennan-Marshall-White group. In his memo to the brethren, he agreed that affirmative action plans met constitutional requirements and that the California courts had been wrong to invalidate the medical school program.

On 28 June 1978, Lewis Powell handed down the decision of the Court with five votes (including his) holding that race could be a factor in admissions, and with a different group of five that quotas could not. There were five other opinions, all marked "Concurring in Part and Dissenting in Part." Powell's opinion, as one might expect, was a lucid and lawyerly document in which he explored the reasons for the Davis program, why quotas could not be tolerated, and why race could be a factor to ensure diversity in the classroom. Altogether it made a strong case for affirmative action that did not utilize quotas;

Justice Lewis F. Powell Jr., who joined the Court in 1971, fashioned one of the most unique opinions in Supreme Court history in the Bakke *case, but one that would ultimately provide the guiding principle in affirmative action cases.*

its weak point lay in his decision to use the Harvard protocol as a model. Both Harvard and Davis used race or ethnic background in evaluating candidates, but the Ivy League school did not quantify its use nor set up a separate track for minority admissions. Rather, Harvard's affirmative action program, at least on its face, consisted of a case-by-case search for diversity.

Critics claimed that this amounted to a difference in form and not substance, and one did not have to be a cynic to believe that the Harvard procedure was simply a more subtle and sophisticated way to do what Davis had done so crudely. Essentially, Powell seemed to be saying, "You can do whatever you like in preferring racial minorities, so long as you do not say so."

THE PUBLIC REACTION to the decision echoed the disarray within the Court. Conservative newspapers ran headlines such as "White Student Wins Reverse Bias Case" (*Chicago Sun-Times*), while liberal papers announced, "Affirmative Action Upheld" (*The Washington Post*). *The Wall Street Journal* came closer to the truth in its headline: "The Decision Everyone Won."

Some conservative critics of *Bakke,* such as Terry Eastland and William Bennett, took a fairly balanced view and argued that the case represented two ideas about equality, one that of numerical equality put forth by the university and "the other the ideal of moral equality, as represented by the individual, Allan Bakke." The far more conservative Robert Bork, then a law school professor, angrily declared that "those who supported the UCD affirmative action plan challenged in *Bakke,* especially those on the U.S. Supreme Court, were the hardcore racists of reverse discrimination."

Not all critics could be described as conservative, and among minorities and liberals there was a widespread view that affirmative action had been severely crippled. Congressman Ron Dellums regarded *Bakke* as a "racist decision by the Nixon court." Julian Bond, an icon of the civil rights movement, charged that the decision "has reinforced the 200-year old racist and sexual quota system." Jesse Jackson called *Bakke* a "devastating blow to our civil rights struggle," while Tom Wicker worried that the validity of all affirmative action programs had been "seriously, if not fatally, undermined." The headline in the *Amsterdam News,* the leading paper in Harlem, read, "BAKKE—WE LOST."

Perhaps the most astute evaluation came from the pen of Anthony Lewis, the Pulitzer Prize–winning Supreme Court reporter for *The New York Times.* In a piece titled "A Solomonic Decision," Lewis found that the Court decision, while perhaps baffling because of the numerous opinions, nonetheless laid down some basic principles. State universities may take race into account in their admissions processes. The public and private institutions of this country have considerable leeway in how they structure affirmative action programs. They may not, however, use quotas. While the last holding is stern, the bulk of Justice Powell's decision studiously avoided absolutes, which was the problem with the California Supreme Court decision. Affirmative action not only is complicated but also can be divisive, and so the Court ruled that in the implementation of programs there should be sufficient flexibility to meet the needs of the school, the community, and minority groups. The Court had given the country permission to experiment, and if some of those efforts did not work out, or crossed the constitutional line, then the courts would be there to correct them. Meg Greenfield of *Newsweek* shared this view. She had predicted that the Court would blur the edges of the controversy while reaffirming the important principles on both sides of the debate. "You say this is fudging the issue? Fine. It ought to be fudged."

One of the functions of a Supreme Court decision is that it guides lower federal as well as state courts when they confront a similar issue. Powell's opinion in *Bakke* did not really provide that guidance, and its ambivalence has been the target of both scorn and praise. The former has come from both advocates and opponents of affirmative action, who wanted the Court to make a definitive ruling on the constitutionality of affirmative action. The praise has come from those who see the whole issue of affirmative action as wrapped in ambiguity. The greater presence of minority faces in the classroom and in the professions is due, at least in part, to the freedom Powell gave higher education to use race as a factor in admissions.

Shortly after the *Bakke* decision came down, Judge Henry Friendly of the Second Circuit, and one of the most respected jurists in the nation, wrote a note to Lewis Powell praising him for the "great service" he had "rendered the nation" with his "statesmanlike" opinion. Friendly had worried that the racial dispute had the potential to be "another Dred Scott." Solicitor General Erwin Griswold, on learning of the note, told Friendly, "I am glad you wrote to [him] . . . It seems to me that he saved the day, because a clear decision either way would have been a disaster. Thanks to him, we are free, to some extent at least, to try to work things out."

Allan Bakke would not comment on the decision, believing anything he said would make it more difficult to fit into medical school and complete his education. He started at Davis a few months later, guarded by plainclothes police officers as one hundred noisy demonstrators protested outside. He asked the university to reimburse him for his legal fees of $437,295, and when the school refused, Bakke filed suit and won a judgment of $183,089. He graduated quietly in 1981, and after gaining his license, he moved to Rochester, Minnesota, and settled into a career as an anesthesiologist first at the Mayo Clinic (where his patients later included Justice Powell) and then on the staff of Olmsted Community Hospital. Bakke has continued to this day to refuse interviews or to comment on the case.

———

DEFUNIS AND *BAKKE* both involved state professional schools, and so those race-conscious programs fell within the arc of state action subject to the Fourteenth Amendment's Equal Protection Clause. The Court, however, had not given any indication as to how it would respond to a nongovernmental affirmative action plan. It got that opportunity the following term in *United Steelworkers of America v. Weber*.

Under the prodding of the Johnson and Nixon administrations, as well as the Civil Rights Acts, unions and employers slowly began creating affirmative action plans, especially in training programs. In 1974, the Kaiser Aluminum and Chemical Corporation entered into a collective bargaining agreement with the United Steelworkers of America that covered fifteen plants. One provision aimed at eliminating the marked racial imbalance in the almost all-white craft workers by reserving for black employees 50 percent of the openings in in-plant training programs, until the percentage of black craft workers approximated that of African Americans in the local labor force. At the plant in Gramercy, Louisiana, Kaiser had until 1974 only hired craft workers with prior experience. Because blacks had long been excluded from craft unions, few could present these credentials; in 1974, only 1.83 percent—5 out of 273—skilled craft workers were black, even though blacks made up 39 percent of the local workforce.

As is usual in union labor agreements, workers applying for the training would be accepted on the basis of seniority. In the first year of the plan, Kaiser chose thirteen men for training, seven blacks and six whites. The most senior black chosen had less seniority than several white applicants who had not been selected. One of them, thirty-two-year-old Brian F. Weber, had been working at the plant as a laboratory assistant and had applied for the training program. Even though he had more seniority than nearly all the African Americans chosen, he had not been selected.

Weber decided to challenge the plan and went into federal court for the Eastern District of Louisiana. Because neither the union nor Kaiser could be considered a state actor, Weber filed suit under Title VII of the 1964 Civil Rights Act, claiming that the preference plan unlawfully discriminated against whites. The district court ruled in his favor and issued a permanent injunction against using race in selecting workers for training. Both the union and Kaiser appealed, and a three-judge panel voted 2–1 to affirm the lower-court decision, despite amicus briefs by the United States, the Equal Employment Opportunity Commission, and two of Kaiser's rivals, Reynolds Metals and Alcoa, all in favor of the affirmative action plan.

Judge Thomas Gee did not find this a hard case at all. Congress had been very explicit in forbidding racial preferences in training programs. Kaiser and the union claimed that justification could be found in Executive Order 11246 issued by President Johnson and that the agreement resulted from threats by the Office of Federal Contract Compliance. Gee dismissed this claim; executive orders, he ruled, do not take precedence over specific legislative directives. He conceded that other circuit courts had upheld quota programs initiated under 11246, but the opinions in these decisions often proved murky as the authors tried to navigate around the very clear wording of Title VII. Only Judge John Minor Wisdom dissented. He did not so much disagree with Gee's reasoning, but in his mind quota systems could be used when there had been blatant evidence of prior discrimination.

Justice William J. Brennan Jr., from the time of DeFunis *(1974) until his retirement in 1990, remained the Court's staunchest proponent of affirmative action's constitutionality.*

The Supreme Court took the case and handed down its decision in late June 1979. Justice Brennan wrote for the majority, joined by Stewart, White, Marshall, and Blackmun, and reversed the lower courts. In something of a tour de force, he somehow managed to find that the explicit wording of Title VII prohibiting racial discrimination did not foreclose private race-conscious affirmative action plans. Brennan relied on the voluntary nature of the collective bargaining agreement and declared that Weber's reliance on the statute, while "not without force," was misplaced. It is, he said, "a familiar rule, that a thing may be within the letter of the statute and yet not within the statute, because not within its spirit, nor within the intention of its makers." Therefore the law had to be read not literally but in the spirit of the authors of the Civil Rights Act who wanted to not only eliminate present and future discrimination but also wipe out the burden of past discrimination. Thus a literal reading "would bring about an end completely at variance with the purpose of the law." Brennan went back to the congressional debate in 1964 to pick out statements that would support a loose interpretation of those provisions and completely ignored very specific assurances from Congressman Emanuel Celler (D-N.Y.), chairman of the House Judiciary Committee, and Senator Hubert Humphrey (D-Minn.), the floor leaders of the bill, that Title VII meant exactly what it said: one could not discriminate in any way in employment or training on the basis of race.

The majority opinion held that affirmative action plans involving racial preference had to be transitional in nature and necessary, designed to correct statistical imbalances, not result in an absolute bar to hiring nonminority people—thus temporary, with a clear end date or goal—and allow flexibility in hiring nonminorities. The plan at the Gramercy plant met all of these criteria, and therefore fit into the area of discretion that the framers of Title VII intended.

There were two dissents, one by Chief Justice Burger and the other by William Rehnquist. The latter painstakingly went over not only the wording of the Civil Rights Act but its birthing, the debates in Congress in which the meaning of important sections of Title VII had been hammered out. He could not find any mention of, or even infer from the record, that a zone of discretion had deliberately been created. He compared the majority opinion to a scene in George Orwell's *1984* (1949), in which an official of Oceania is denouncing one of the other great powers, Eurasia, when in the middle of his speech a runner comes in and hands a slip of paper to the speaker. He glances at it and, without breaking his stride, announces that the government is at war with Eastasia!

Although rights leaders hailed the decision, for the most part, commentators believed that the Court had failed to provide a straightforward definition of affirmative action and when it could be constitutionally applied. Unfortunately for Brian Weber—and for all the workers at the Gramercy facility—Kaiser closed the plant a little over a year after the Court handed down its decision.

ASIDE FROM THE FACT THAT William Brennan was one of the most skilled justices in putting together a majority on the Court, the 1970s seem to have been a period when the justices appeared sympathetic to the idea of affirmative action. All that would change in the following decades as the conservative Reagan-Bush appointees took their seats and stalwart liberals like Brennan, Marshall, and White (who remained liberal on racial issues) retired. At a time when public attention focused so much on Bakke's case, hardly anyone noted that the Court, by denying appeal in certain cases, had taken a strong step in favor of affirmative action. Without recorded dissent, for example, the justices left standing a lower-court approval of a consent decree requiring American Telephone and Telegraph and local phone companies to hire more blacks and women, and commentators interpreted this to mean that the Court had little interest in reviewing affirmative action plans in employment.

Also, as noted in the last chapter, the Court proved supportive of another type of affirmative action, the minority business enterprise provision of the Public Works Employment Act of 1977. In the *Fullilove* decision, Chief Justice Burger held that Congress's spending power is as broad as its regulatory powers and that the implementation of a public policy—in this case the MBE provision—through the spending power was legitimate if it would have been permissible under the regulatory powers of the Commerce Clause. In *Fullilove,* Burger finally wrote what many rights activists had been waiting to hear for a long time: "We reject the contention that in the remedial context the Congress must act in a wholly color-blind fashion. . . . It is fundamental that in no organ of government, state or federal, does there repose a more comprehensive remedial power than in Congress."

———

WHAT WOULD ONE THINK in the summer of 1980 about the constitutional status of affirmative action? The Court had punted in *DeFunis,* but Justice Douglas's dissent would be quoted many times by opponents of affirmative action, and over time an increasingly conservative Court would come to agree with him that race should never be a criterion for any governmental program.

In *Bakke,* we get one of the most unusual of all court opinions, a 4–1–4 decision in which Justice Powell's compromise—race can be a factor, but there cannot be quotas—will later be seen as an appropriate way for the Court to handle an issue that would surely fire the emotions of many. It would initially sink into the mists of lost causes, and in the 1990s at least one court refused to accept it as a precedent, until Justice Sandra Day O'Connor revivified it in 2003.

Weber seemed to say that the private sector, even if goaded by federal instrumentalities such as contract compliance offices and the EEOC, had far more flexibility in designing affirmative action programs than did state governments. In many ways, *Weber* has had enormous impact, in that thousands of companies have, over the years, adopted plans that brought in minorities and women to jobs from which they had previously been excluded. Today affirmative action may be greatly restricted in some areas, such as state universities, but it is alive and well in the private sector. Of all the affirmative action decisions of the Court in the 1970s, *Bakke* might have been the most discussed and the most controversial, but *Weber* might have had the longest reach.

CHAPTER 7

CHANGING ACADEMIA

The rising middle class {of England}, if often uneducated itself, was not unaware of the advantages of education, nor was it lacking in ambition. It looked to the schools to provide, in addition to a moral and intellectual discipline, a common platform enabling its sons to associate on equal terms with those of families who, if thoroughly outdistanced in income, still diffused a faint aroma of social superiority.

—R. H. TAWNEY, *THE RADICAL TRADITION* (1964)

It has long been a commonplace that to succeed in America, a college degree or some form of postsecondary education is necessary. Moreover, various studies confirm that those with a bachelor's degree or higher will make more money during their careers than people whose education ends after twelfth grade. Thus it should be no surprise that minorities wanted access to higher education. Prior to *Brown,* the historically all-black colleges provided opportunity to some students, and while the sons and daughters of middle-class African American families could gain entrance to northern state universities and even to the Ivies, only a small number had either the resources or the educational credentials necessary for admission.

Beginning in the early 1960s, the demand for access to higher education grew. Northern private schools that had hitherto been nearly all white began recruiting minority students, and for a while the historically all-black colleges accused elite schools, such as the Ivy League, of cherry-picking, tempting the best-qualified African Americans with full scholarships and other perks. And why wouldn't a bright minority student want to go to Harvard or Princeton rather than to an essentially small, isolated, and segregated southern school?

The problem, however, had never been the children of the middle class. Their parents made sure they had the proper training to go on to college, often had the resources to pay for it, and wanted their sons or daughters to be accepted in one of the "better" schools. The demand came from those who had not had the benefit of a middle-class upbringing, who had attended starkly inferior segregated schools, and who had no tradition of higher education in their families or culture. But like earlier immigrant groups, they intuitively knew that without a college degree there would be little or no opportunity for them.

IN THE LATE 1960s and the 1970s, affirmative action in higher education meant two things: enrolling more minorities as students and hiring more women and minorities as faculty. Colleges and universities made a great and for the most part successful effort to recruit minority students, and in many instances merely letting the community know that previous barriers had been dismantled proved sufficient to get African Americans and Hispanics to apply. Some private schools aggressively went after talented black students, many of whom might otherwise have gone to historically black colleges. The Ivy League and Seven Sisters schools together in 1968 accepted 808 African American students, of whom 455 enrolled that fall. The following year these schools sent acceptance letters to 1,660 black applicants, of whom 945 enrolled. In northern state universities, blacks had long been enrolled, although not in proportion to their percentage of the population.

During the latter part of the twentieth century, the percentage of African Americans and Hispanics in undergraduate programs rose slowly so that by 1997 blacks and Hispanics enrolled in undergraduate programs bore a fairly close resemblance to their numbers in the overall population. For the most part, affirmative action at the undergraduate level rarely involved saying no to white applicants to make room for minorities, mainly because of the enormous growth of colleges and universities in these years. This did not happen, however, in graduate and professional programs. Although African Americans made up approximately 11–12 percent of the population, they were only 7.5 percent of students seeking advanced degrees. Similarly, Hispanic Americans, whose percentage of the population by the end of the century nearly matched that of African Americans, made up only 4.5 percent of students in graduate and professional schools.

William G. Bowen, president of Princeton University, and Derek Bok, president of Harvard, co-authored The Shape of the River *(1998), one of the most important studies done on how affirmative action worked in the nation's best schools.*

The most comprehensive study of how affirmative action affected undergraduate minority enrollment in American colleges and universities, *The Shape of the River,* relied on a massive database put together by the Andrew W. Mellon Foundation. It included detailed records of the characteristics, academic performance, and graduate degrees of roughly forty-five thousand students—including thirty-five hundred African Americans—for those classes that enrolled as freshmen in 1976 and in 1989. The authors of the report had vast educational experience. William G. Bowen had been president of Princeton from 1972 to 1988 and then president of the Mellon Foundation. Derek Bok had been dean of the Harvard Law School and then president of Harvard from 1971 to 1991. They supplemented the Mellon Foundation database with more detailed questionnaires regarding the class entering in 1989.

In their study, Bowen and Bok divided the twenty-eight colleges into three groups according to their degree of selectivity. Group one included only private schools, such as Princeton and Stanford. The second group had some private schools, Columbia, Northwestern, and Oberlin, but also a number of public universities. The third group consisted entirely of public universities, especially large ones such as the Universities of Michigan and North Carolina. The overall enrollment in 1989 was approximately 16,000 in group one, 39,000 in the second group, and 250,000 in group three. In 1989, roughly one million students entered four-year colleges for the first time. While we need not go into their methodology, Bowen and Bok estimated that because of affirmative action the proportion of African Americans in group one rose from 2.1 to 7.8 percent; in group two from 2.8 to 5.8 percent; and in the third group from 4.5 to 6.6 percent. Extrapolating from percentages would indicate that the number of black students entering the most highly selective schools rose from a hypothetical 300 to an actual 1,200; in group two from a hypothetical 1,100 to an actual 2,300; and in the third group from a hypothetical 13,000 to an actual 20,000. (The increase on a percentage basis in group three is smaller because the big public universities already had a substantial number of minority students.)

The increase in minority students did not happen all by itself. The great growth of colleges and universities in the latter part of the twentieth century made it easier to add a cohort of African American or Hispanic students without having to turn away qualified whites. In addition, many schools launched race-conscious affirmative action plans, spurred on in part by the civil rights movement that roiled the country in the 1950s and 1960s.

To take one example, Cornell University launched the Cornell Opportunity Program in 1964, admitting an inaugural class of ten students; the following year it took thirty-seven. Nearly all these students had been recruited from predominantly black high schools across New York State. The steering committee also recommended that the scholarship program find a new way to identify recipients, because recent research showed the usual criteria—GPA and SAT scores—did not reliably predict how well disadvantaged students would do in school. When the Opportunity Program began recruiting students at predominantly black high schools, high school transcripts and counselor recommendations played the biggest role, and the committee essentially discarded the SAT scores altogether.

Columbia University, which had been rocked by student riots in 1968, had an extensive recruiting program, but as the dean of Columbia College, Robert Pollack, told students and alumni two decades later, affirmative action should be seen as justice, not charity, and its beneficiaries included white students as well as people of color. Columbia, according to Pollack, had no trouble finding minorities with the intelligence needed to make it at the college. The challenge was to cast the recruitment net as widely as possible and to make sure that those invited to the table would be able to partake of the offerings.

Unlike the Bowen and Bok study on undergraduate enrollments of minorities, there is very little on how affirmative action affected graduate and professional schools, and at least for this period, related only to schools in highly competitive fields such as law and medicine. A 1997 report showed that if a race-blind admissions process based solely on undergraduate grade point average and the Law School Admission Test had been applied to those entering law school in 1991, approximately 90 percent of black applicants and 70 percent of all minorities would not have been admitted to the best law schools to which they applied. It also estimated that three out of four black applicants and one-half of other minorities would not have been admitted to any of the 173 law schools approved by the American Bar Association. If correct, and just those criteria had been used, then the percentage of blacks admitted to American law schools would have fallen from 6.8 to 1.6 percent, and the proportion of Hispanics from 4.6 to 2.4 percent.

Because of selectivity of professional schools, the first legal challenges to affirmative action had come in regard to a law school (*DeFunis*) and a medical school (*Bakke*). There would be no challenge to an undergraduate program until the University of Michigan turned away Jennifer Gratz in 1995.

ADMISSIONS DECISIONS TO undergraduate institutions vary enormously. Public two-year colleges for the most part will accept anyone with either a high school degree or a GED, the equivalent credential for those who at one point dropped out of high school. Technical schools and colleges, where one may wish to study engineering, look more closely at grades in certain subjects or at the math sections of the SAT and other tests. The more selective a school is, the more things get taken into account, and because admissions committees usually meet in closed sessions, it is not always clear why of two students with roughly equivalent records, one will be offered admission and the other not. The same is even truer for graduate and professional schools. Some very large schools that get tens of thousands of applicants every year have tried to quantify the process, taking some ten or twelve indicators and assigning them numerical value. In addition to the usual grade point average and standardized tests, there will be questions related to extracurricular activities (sports or school newspaper), geography (does the applicant come from an underrepresented area, an important consideration in state universities), legacy (has the applicant's parents or other relatives attended), alumni input (usually in the form of reference letters), and race. This last issue meant very little overall when schools expanded in the 1960s and 1970s, but it would become both a political and a legal controversy later.

How schools took race, gender, or ethnicity into account varied from school to school and often depended upon the type of school. For the most part, the decision of many schools to go coed at this time met with little resistance, although the logistics (bathrooms and showering facilities, athletics) often created problems. The fact that most of the women coming into these schools were initially white made a difference. White parents who might have objected to letting minority groups into "their" schools could hardly object to letting in their daughters. That the number of African American and Hispanic undergraduates increased seems not to have been the bone of contention it would later become. Except when schools went too far.

THE CITY UNIVERSITY OF NEW YORK (CUNY) dates back to 1847. According to § 6201 of the state's education law, CUNY is an "independent system of higher education" committed to "academic excellence and to the provision of equal access and opportunity for students, faculty, and staff from all ethnic and racial groups and from both sexes." In the early 1970s, the two goals of access and excellence came into conflict, and access overwhelmed CUNY at the expense of excellence.

Excellence has always been the goal of colleges and universities and is for the most part easily recognized; in addition, there are specific criteria one looks for—reputation of faculty, quality of entering students, library holdings, level of faculty research, and adequate physical plant, to name a few. There has been a continuous debate starting in the latter part of the nineteenth century over access, primarily whether higher education should be the purview of the rich and/or talented or should be open to all, albeit with some criteria for entrance. That debate, for the most part, has been settled in favor of greater access.

In 1862, Congress passed the Morrill Act to establish land-grant colleges that would teach agriculture and mechanical arts. These schools became the great state universities that are now found all over the country and that teach hundreds of thousands of students every year. In New York City, the citizenry in 1847 had approved a proposal to establish a free academy, one with a curriculum similar to that offered at Harvard or Columbia. The Free Academy, which became the City College of New York (CCNY), originally taught only males, but in 1870 a comparable school, now known as Hunter College, prepared young women to become elementary and secondary school teachers. From its beginnings with just these schools, two characteristics marked the City University of New York system: it maintained high standards, and it was free. The system not only helped to Americanize the children of immigrants but prepared them to go on to graduate school. A report in 1901 noted that City College was "practically filled with Jewish pupils, a considerable proportion of them children of Russian and Polish immigrants." By 1930, half of New York City's doctors, lawyers, dentists, and public school teachers were the children of Jewish immigrants, and many of them had gone to college in the city system. By the 1960s, CUNY had expanded to sixteen senior and community colleges, enrolling 175,000 students.

In the wake of growing civil rights activity in the 1960s, pressure began to build on CUNY to provide greater access to minority students. The system had never been segregated, but the entrance standards, especially to the senior colleges, made it difficult for black and Hispanic students from ghetto schools to gain admission. CUNY, which operated separately from the state's system, responded to these same political pressures and in 1965 adopted a ten-year plan that would be fully implemented by 1975. Under this plan, the top 25 percent of high school graduates would automatically be admitted to one of the senior colleges; the next 40 percent would be admitted to community colleges; the next 10 percent would go to special programs, while the bottom quartile would enter educational skills centers emphasizing either career programs or training for transition to college. The plan not only made sense but allowed enough time for CUNY schools to prepare for what everyone expected would be a large jump in enrollment, especially of students who might not have been previously admitted.

In 1969, however, the plan had to be scrapped. That February a group of black and Puerto Rican students demanded, among other things, that the racial composition of the next entering class at CCNY reflect the proportion of black and Hispanic students in the city's high schools. Two months later, students shut down CCNY's

South Campus, demanding that it be renamed Malcolm X–Che Guevara University. Protesters charged that CCNY discriminated against minorities and the poor, and protests soon shut down other CUNY schools. Some of the radical faculty supported student demands; on some campuses, protesters set buildings on fire, and police responded to frequent riot calls at the schools.

In light of the escalating violence, trustees and college administrators felt they had little choice but to respond to student demands. Deputy Chancellor Seymour Hyman recalled, "I was telling people about what I felt when I saw smoke coming out of [the Great Hall at City College], and the only question in my mind was, How can we save City College? And the only answer was, Hell, let everybody in."

For the next few months, administrators, protesters, faculty, students, and alumni argued about what to do next. The administration and the Black and Puerto Rican Student Committee reached agreement on a "dual admission" plan that would have admitted one-half of the freshman class from poor neighborhoods and high schools in primarily black and Hispanic areas, while the other half would be admitted based on traditional standards. The uproar over this plan forced the administration to back down, with faculty and alumni groups condemning the proposal as a quota system that would relegate minority students to a second-class status. One of the most powerful voices raised against the plan was that of the Central Labor Council of the city's trade union, which charged that the dual admission plan would not increase access for children of the white ethnic groups, especially Irish, Italian, and others, who made up the bulk of the union membership.

The CUNY administration heard the union voice and decided that any plan had to have ethnic as well as racial integration. After wrestling over the summer with how to maintain academic excellence while radically altering the student body makeup, the trustees threw up their hands, decided to move up the implementation date to 1970, and for all practical purposes abandoned any effort to secure a class that would have met existing standards. All students who had achieved a minimal high school average of 80 in academic courses or were ranked in the top half of their graduating class could attend one of the senior colleges. All other high school graduates would go to community colleges. By offering admission based on class rank, the trustees gave up any effort to set an objective standard for admission.

Students would be ranked against their peers rather than against all students seeking admission. The top half of a class at Bronx Science or Stuyvesant—the two best high schools in the city—meant something far different from the top half of a school in the barrio. Moreover, for years the state's Regents examinations had provided a gold standard in measuring academic ability; students in Albany and Syracuse and the rural parts of the state as well as in New York City all took the same subject exams, and a 92, for example, on an Intermediate Algebra Regents exam meant the same thing everywhere. Schools used the Regents exams as the basis for their college preparatory courses, and now CUNY said they did not matter. Even supporters of open admissions conceded that many of the new students would not be well prepared.

Shortly after the announcement of the plan, the editors of *The New York Times* noted that open admissions seemed to have widespread support, one of the few things that all the candidates in that year's mayoral election agreed upon. A few days after this rather optimistic assessment of widespread support for open enrollment, very large cracks appeared. The chancellor of CUNY, Dr. Albert H. Bowker, predicted there would be financial troubles, and as a result he expected campus disruptions. Black and Hispanic students began to complain that the protocols designed to get more minorities in were actually going to keep many out. Mayor John Lindsay and Comptroller Mario Procaccino demanded that the CUNY trustees guarantee that any student who would have gotten in under the old system be assured a place in the entering class; qualified people should not be shunted aside to make room for the less qualified. The head of the CCNY alumni association charged that the Board of Trustees was abetting black racism.

Then the trustees began worrying that minority students who had not been adequately educated in high school would be assigned to the community college track, thus effectively setting up a de facto segregated system. To avoid this, they expanded two programs that had been set up several years earlier by the state legislature, SEEK (Search for Education, Elevation, and Knowledge) and CD (College Discovery). Colleges that chose to participate recruited economically and educationally disadvantaged students, admitted them, and then provided counseling and compensatory instruction. There had been little fuss over SEEK and CD primarily because the numbers of students involved had been low, and thus the schools had been able to provide the necessary remedial instruction for the students to succeed.

The CUNY trustees decided to expand the 1970 SEEK freshman class by twenty-five hundred students—an 85 percent increase. It is little wonder that the CUNY faculty began voicing concerns about the resources to handle the influx and how academic standards could be maintained. Where the regular college admissions process had been designed to provide an incentive to maintain a B average, the SEEK program gave preference to students with D averages. In addition, there had been relatively little faculty input into the whole process. While the notion that faculty run a university is nonsense, there is no doubt that on academic questions the faculty voice does carry weight. By late 1969, faculty worries increased a great deal about what open enrollment would do to CUNY. Little did they know how bad it would be.

IN ONE WAY, the CUNY program worked. Within five years, the combined enrollment at all the CUNY schools did in fact reflect the racial composition of the city's public high schools. In 1969, the last year of regular admissions, CUNY undergraduates had been 13.8 percent black, 5.9 percent Puerto Rican, and 80.2 percent white and other. Five years later, blacks made up 28.8 percent of the undergraduate enrollment; Hispanics, 13.4 percent; whites and others, 57.8 percent. Aside from this statistic, open enrollment at CUNY never lived up to expectations, except of those who had predicted the worst.

Initially, some of the concerns of the naysayers about money failed to materialize. Both the city and the state provided additional money to hire both full-time and adjunct faculty, and this placated some of the faculty who had expected to be inundated with students. In the fall of 1971, 35,000 new students enrolled on the various campuses (up from 19,559 the year before), and this included 8,500 SEEK students; the city's Board of Higher Education had to rent 1.4 million square feet of space to accommodate additional classes. The fear that good students would be driven away did not materialize either. CUNY remained tuition-free, as great a lure as it had always been for poor but bright students.

Throughout that first year, one story after another appeared about how, despite the sudden jump in enrollment, CUNY and its faculty seemed to be coping well. New students did not drop out after the first semester, and in fact the retention rate of the freshman class was actually a little higher than the year before. The schools did not turn into racial or ethnic ghettos, although black students continued to complain that they were still a small minority on most campuses. One story declared that the influx of new students had given Brooklyn College "new life."

But despite the optimistic public relations releases, the story on the ground proved quite different. As one faculty member at Queens College recalled, "Many of the kids who came were unprepared for college work, due to the weaknesses of public secondary education, and so at one point the *majority* (!) of entering freshmen did not qualify for English Composition and had to take the remedial course instead—for which they received no credit." Over at Brooklyn College, one of the professors teaching the introductory political science class said, "Many of them had not been adequately prepared for college work. Even sadder, the college administration had little sympathy for them. My colleagues and I were fairly unhappy about the way the kids' college experience became a revolving door." At Hostos Community College in the Bronx, students demanded that they be allowed to graduate without having to pass a written assessment of their English skills. Although a fairly modest test, seven out of eight students failed.

Nonetheless, CUNY expanded the program and now had a total enrollment of nearly 200,000 students. A senior professor at Hunter said, "In no way has the first year's experience borne out any of the predictions of the Cassandras." There are problems, he admitted, "but over-all it's working." How well it was "working" depended on one's point of view. An investigative report on the first year agreed that while some fears had not come to pass, students admitted under SEEK and other options were barely keeping up, and if nothing else the CUNY colleges had to provide more remedial work—a great deal more remedial work.

One reason the plan seemed to work involved the makeup of the student body. At the senior four-year colleges, three out of five students admitted had high school averages above 80 percent, and only 6 percent had averages under 70 percent. At the community colleges, however, the numbers reversed, with only one out of ten having an average over 80, one out of three below 70, and more than half of the entering class between 70 and 80 percent. Also, under the plan, students with the best high school credentials could choose which of

CUNY's colleges they would attend, packing Queens and Brooklyn with mainly white, high-performing students. Officials worried that some of the two-year schools had become "educational ghettos" for poorer students.

As a result, in January 1972, the Board of Higher Education changed the admissions procedures so that while those students with averages above 80 percent would still be automatically admitted, they would not necessarily get to pick which school they would attend. The board plan assigned as many students as possible from families with an annual income below $4,000 to the better four-year colleges. "Open admissions will develop best in a heterogeneous setting, and not in colleges ghettoized by income, ethnic background, or academic preparation," according to Luis Quero Chiesa, chair of the board. Not a word was said about merit; everything relied on equality, or what the board hoped would be equality.

Then things began to go south. After two years of open admissions, one out of every two students admitted under the special provisions had dropped out. Moreover, university officials believed that by the time the first class stood ready to graduate, two-thirds of those would have left school. Robert J. Kibbee, the CUNY chancellor, nonetheless found a silver lining. "Even if only 15 or 20 percent of those who ordinarily would never have gotten a chance to go to City University obtain degrees, I would regard that as a significant accomplishment."

The initial impact of open admissions on the faculty had been eased considerably by an infusion of money that brought hundreds of new teachers into the system, some on a tenure-track basis and the majority as adjuncts. By 1974, CUNY was calling for more money from the city and the state, but none seemed to be available. The CUNY board developed a list of things it believed would help the open admissions students do better, nearly all of which cost money the system did not have. Things got even worse when the city nearly went bankrupt in 1975. At Queens, one of the senior colleges, all of the adjuncts had to be let go, "and the required courses like Composition had to be taught by full-time faculty, some of whom hadn't done it in ages, and felt dissed and downgraded by it." Not only did the English department faculty have to teach remedial writing, but so did faculty in other departments. I remember getting a phone call one day from a full professor of history at City College, begging me to help him find another job. He was teaching multiple sections of remedial writing, and the rifts within the department had become so acute that newspapers picked up the story.

In response to the fiscal crisis, CUNY officials proposed cutting costs by closing, merging, or downgrading several of the colleges. But Puerto Ricans objected to the merging of Hostos and Bronx Community Colleges; African Americans objected to turning Medgar Evers into a community college. Police officers did not want the John Jay College of Criminal Justice merged with another college, and residents of Staten Island objected to the proposed closing of its four-year college. One alternative involved the very large burden CUNY carried of remedial classes that cost $30 million a year, but when the board tried to impose some minimal standards of competency in math and reading (at the eighth-grade level!), several officials from schools with high open admissions enrollments threatened to sue.

In June 1976, CUNY could not meet its payroll and closed for two weeks. By then, the system had laid off the equivalent of thirty-six hundred full-time teaching positions, consisting of administrators, adjuncts, and nontenured faculty. The city had no money, and the state legislature believed it unfair for CUNY to remain free while the State University of New York (SUNY) system charged tuition. Only after Mayor Abraham Beame agreed to support tuition charges did the legislature provide funds allowing CUNY to reopen. In the end, the only choice available involved the abandonment of a century-and-a-quarter tradition of free public higher education. State aid would subsidize poor students, but families with an annual income of $20,000 or more would have to pay full tuition.

Students whose families could afford tuition now began looking elsewhere. The SUNY system was then in the full flower of its growth, with four major university centers and a number of four-year colleges, as well as community colleges. The number of CUNY students from the city's better schools dropped sharply, as did the number of applicants with high school averages of 85 or better. One of the costs of open admissions had been the departure of some of the best faculty who had contributed to the excellence of CCNY, Queens, Hunter, and Brooklyn. Open admissions staggered along for a few more years, but eventually the high costs of remediation, as well as the poor quality of a New York public school education, began blurring lines. In 1974, unofficial estimates put 40 percent of the city's 300,000 high school students two or more years behind grade level, with the average ninth grader fifteen months behind the national standard.

With the imposition of tuition, enrollment plummeted at CUNY from 187,334 in September 1975 to 155,040 a year later. Enrollment at Brooklyn College alone fell by more than 50 percent. In that same time frame, CUNY laid off nearly five thousand people. Rather than tighten admission requirements in an effort to regain lost excellence, CUNY colleges lowered their admissions standards and recruited even less qualified students. An in-depth analysis of the student body seven years after the great experiment began showed CUNY students to be older, more economically deprived, and more likely to be raising children of their own than one would expect at a traditional college. Where the city schools had once been the gateway of opportunity for the children of immigrant Jews, by the late 1970s Spanish had replaced Yiddish as the main non-English language in the students' background. But the school still served the needs of new immigrant groups, such as Asians, Greeks, and Italians. One report noted that what was especially different in the CUNY of today, compared with the same institution as recently as a decade earlier, was the representation of blacks and Hispanics, who had been hardly noticeable in the old CUNY.

Ever since, individual schools, as well as the CUNY system itself, have tried to develop procedures that would allow under-qualified minority students to at least get a toehold on the ladder of higher education while at the same time trying to develop some uniform policies so that all of the colleges and community colleges would be operating from the same playbook. In fact, many of the schools in the system continue to have problems. In 1997, students at Hostos Community College in the Bronx rioted because 88 percent of them had failed a written assessment test required for graduation. Herman Badillo, the vice-chair of the CUNY Board of Trustees, probed further; he found widespread grade inflation as well as a large number of students getting degrees without completing all of their requirements.

No one talks about open admissions anymore. Old-timers remember how great the CUNY system used to be, while some defenders of the system say that it is still great, and much more democratic. While CUNY may be the worst-case scenario of open admissions, other schools have tried it, and none can claim success.

CONGRESS, IN THE Higher Education Act of 1965, had not specifically called for affirmative action for minority groups, but had allocated money for remedial programs to help "disadvantaged students" do college-level work. For the most part, the disadvantaged students proved to be African American or Hispanic, and even without schemes such as open admissions, schools would have sought out students who would qualify for the federal money.

A far different story involved faculty. Executive orders from Johnson through Carter applied to contractors with fifty or more employees who received federal contracts of at least $50,000—which covered many colleges and universities—while the Equal Protection Clause also affected public institutions. Title VII applied to both public and private schools. In 1975, the Supreme Court ruled that the federal government's initiatives regarding discrimination had a dual aim: to "bar like discrimination in the future" and to "eliminate the discriminatory effects of the past." In a later case, the Court ruled that affirmative action might be appropriate even if it adversely affected other employees, because "a sharing of the burden of the past discrimination is presumptively necessary." As a result, all colleges and universities had to adjust their hiring protocols, including setting up "placement goals" that would reflect the availability of women and minorities for each type of job, although supposedly there would not be numerical quotas. Moreover, an institution's compliance with affirmative action requirements would be monitored by the Office of Federal Contract Compliance Programs (OFCCP), the same office that oversaw defense and other government contracts. Laws relating to people with disabilities (according to the Rehabilitation Act of 1973) and veterans also had to be taken into account. As one treatise on the law of higher education put it, colleges and universities were and are pulled in multiple directions by sometimes conflicting rules. Another problem involved the fact that white male faculty had the task of recruiting women and minorities, and many of them had not the slightest idea of how to do so.

Well into the 1960s, hiring in the better universities often consisted of an old boys' network. If a position in modern European history opened, the chair of the department would send a notice to historians he knew personally at other schools seeking a recommendation. Doctoral students seeking jobs would then go to the annual professional meetings, where they would meet representatives of departments looking for new faculty, with many of the interviews scheduled ahead of time. The fact that I had a well-known mentor at Columbia meant a great deal when I went for a job interview. Only if this approach did not work did a school advertise a position in one or more of the professional journals. It is little surprise, then, that in 1969, 96.3 percent of all faculty were white, 2.2 percent African American, 1.3 percent Asian American, and "Other" 0.3 percent. In universities with graduate programs, the most prestigious schools in which to work, 97.7 percent were white, 0.5 percent were African American, 1.6 percent were Asian American, and 0.3 percent were "Other." At a meeting of graduate students at one of the best history departments in the country, the professor in charge of helping place people completing their doctorates told a woman student that there was very little available for her and she ought to be looking for a husband rather than a job.

Once it became clear that the federal government expected—indeed demanded—that colleges and universities implement some form of affirmative action for faculty hires, the responses were predictable. On the one hand, those who favored affirmative action argued that excellence could be maintained and indeed increased by expanding the pool of available talent. On the other side, prominent academics worried that the heavy hand of the government would undermine the quality of schooling in the name of equality.

A good example of the latter fear came after the Department of Health, Education, and Welfare (HEW) announced on 11 February 1972 that it would withhold $13.8 million in federal contracts from Columbia University—and threatened cancellation of the contracts after 6 April—if Columbia did not produce a "satisfactory" employment program. Columbia did produce a report by December, totaling 316 pages and full of minute trivia regarding the types of people in nearly every department. As one commentator noted, in reality the report represented a vast expenditure of time and human labor to satisfy a federal bureaucracy that had acted terribly. Ten other major colleges and universities also had contractual funds withheld or threatened, and they, too, had to expend resources on detailing minutiae. This led the well-known philosopher Sidney Hook of New York University to decry the government's action and warn against the imposition of a quota system that would inevitably lead to destruction of academic integrity.

Hook did not oppose equal opportunity and had in fact been a champion of civil rights and of women for many years, or, as he put

Professor Sidney Hook of NYU, a leading liberal critic of affirmative action, who worried that letting in less qualified students would adversely affect the quality of higher education.

it, his whole life had been "testimony" against discrimination. But the integrity of the university could not be compromised. It had to be free to seek truth and to find the best men and women, of whatever color or ethnicity, to both do research and teach the next generation. "Everyone who remembers his own education," he noted, "remembers teachers, not methods and techniques. The teacher is the heart of the educational system."

Hook objected to the numbers-driven rationale used by J. Stanley Pottinger at HEW to find Columbia guilty of discrimination. While numbers can sometimes be helpful, they can also be misleading, and Pottinger and HEW's reliance on alleged statistical evidence was just that. HEW's logic, Hook wrote, "would prove that medical schools are guilty of religious discrimination because not a single Christian Scientist can be found on their faculties." It would also mean that "members of the Republican party are victims of crass discrimination in higher education because their number on university faculties, in comparison to the ratio of Republican party members in the general population, is so extraordinarily small." Such conclusions are ridiculous, Hook said, but no worse than Pottinger's use of numbers.

Moreover, despite the government's protestation, HEW really wanted universities to set up quota systems—so many African Americans, so many women, so many Hispanics in a ratio to their numbers in the population. To prove this, Hook pointed to a HEW notice to the University of Michigan in December 1970, rejecting its affirmative action plan because it failed to "achieve a ratio of female employment in academic positions at least equivalent to their availability as evidenced by applications for employment." A few months later, the government charged the University of Oregon with discrimination against minorities because out of many minority applicants only one had been accepted.

Hook went on to argue that when hiring, one should be looking not at the number of applications but at the ones with the best qualifications. Moreover, the real number is not how many people are hired but how many offers had been made. "A black candidate offered a post may have accepted a better offer elsewhere; a woman offered a Fellowship may have decided to reject it because her husband accepted a teaching post elsewhere." What Hook did not say, but could have, was that in the early 1970s universities seeking qualified women and minorities—those with doctorates or other terminal degrees—did not have a large field to choose from. The few African Americans who had made it through graduate school by then had their pick of jobs to choose from. There were a few more women available, but not that many. Both minority and women PhDs operated in a sellers' market.

This does not mean that discrimination did not exist. During the open admissions experiment at CUNY, the blatant bias against women became evident. Where it normally took seven years for a woman to gain tenure, it took only three for a man. Not a single woman served on CUNY's oversight board. At the newly established Graduate Center, designed to be the crown jewel of the system, there were only 35 women and 566 men, and all the department heads were male. Perhaps when schools went out to look for a woman, a sellers' market existed; once hired, however, they faced the same discrimination as they had previously.

Hook argued persuasively that government bureaucrats had no understanding of what made a great or even a good university. A school's reputation depended not on whether its faculty statistically represented the larger public but on the quality of those teachers and researchers. While schools should certainly be seeking talent from all groups, in some years the number of minorities hired might be greater than their percentage of the population, and in other years less. One also had to take into account other factors, such as whether the applicant would fit into the department, in terms of both collegiality and area of expertise, whether he or she had prior teaching experience, whether the record indicated that this person was involved in research. The establishment of quotas by bureaucrats would be the end of good education and had to be fought fiercely.

Columbia apparently "corrected" its affirmative action plan, for later in the year HEW allowed the contract payment to go through. According to one critic, however, whenever its vice president, William de Bary, made a new appointment, he had to prove to HEW that he had tried "in good faith" to find a woman or minority to fill the position. The well-known dean of the Journalism School, Elie Abel, complained that Columbia could not promote an assistant professor without a national search. Academic liberals, the conservative columnist John Chamberlain declared, "are suddenly waking up to the fact that quotas cannot be applied in the world of scholarship without doing violence to all the ends of education."

There is a surreal atmosphere about all this. Essentially it meant that if a job opened in the economics department, and the university said it needed to hire a woman or an African American or a Hispanic, then all white male candidates, no matter how well qualified, would have their applications thrown into a wastebasket. This happened at Virginia Commonwealth University in Richmond, when James A. Cramer, a white male in a non-tenure-track position in the sociology department, applied for a newly established tenure-track position. He discovered that his application, and that of all other males applying, had essentially been disregarded because the school wanted a woman in that job. He sued, and won, although he had to settle for a monetary award and not a job. No doubt cases like this arose at other schools as well. The whole notion of excellence as a criterion would be not just jeopardized but dismissed outright. To be sure, there would be qualified women and minorities applying, but would they necessarily be the best candidates in the pool? Apparently, that consideration meant very little to the bureaucrats at HEW. When the government had first started requiring affirmative action plans from federal contractors, the comment often heard was that businesses like numbers; that is, they wanted a specific goal. This policy, even though supposedly barred by Title VII, now permeated government offices as well.

As one professor noted, HEW's guidelines had a Kafkaesque quality. When hiring, college administrators had to, in HEW's words, "employ and promote qualified members of groups formerly excluded even if that exclusion cannot be traced to particular discriminatory actions on the part of the employer." Moreover, "benign neutrality in employment practices will tend to perpetuate the status quo ante indefinitely." As Professor Justus van der Kroef put it, the people at HEW had made it very clear to college and university administrators: hire more minorities and women or lose your funding. HEW had no interest in quality, only in numbers, and the results of this grotesque policy could be seen everywhere. For example, a department chair at Chico State College in California declared that because his was an affirmative action institution, he would not only waive doctoral requirements for minority candidates who were willing to pursue part-time graduate work but also give them greater latitude in their teaching areas.

Eventually, pressure mounted on HEW to modify its assault. Another Carnegie study in 1975 attacked the federal agency for its heavy-handed approach that had, in fact, not worked. "Seldom has a good cause spawned such a badly developed series of Federal mechanisms," the report charged. "Few Federal programs are now so near to self-destruction." Even the General Accounting Office, the federal government's watchdog agency, found that HEW had made "minimal progress" in getting colleges and universities to end discrimination. As *The New York Times* editorialized, the HEW program amounted to affirmative chaos.

One cannot help but question what the men and women at HEW could have been thinking. It is true that under executive orders, companies with fifty or more employees or that had contracts worth more than $50,000 had to have an affirmative action program. But universities are not companies, where the president or CEO can order something and the hierarchical chain of command will then implement it. Anyone familiar with university governance recognizes that there are very few areas where a directive from the president's office will have deans and department chairs standing up to say, "Aye, aye, sir!" Schools within a university, especially medicine and law, are for the most part independent fiefdoms and not terribly amenable to orders from on high.

Another consideration that HEW failed to take into account is that while openings do occur every year, a very large number of faculty are tenured, and only retirement, death, or a better job offer will move them. Many faculty receive tenure—that is, job security for life—when they are promoted to associate or full professorship in their thirties. Let us say that in a moderate-size history department, with twenty to twenty-five members, there is one whose specialty is Russia. He took his doctorate at a good university, has traveled to Russia to do research, has published, and gets good student evaluations. The department wants to keep him, and so they promote him and give him tenure and a full professorship by the time he is thirty-five. He likes the school and his colleagues, his spouse has a satisfying job in town, and the school system is very good for their children. There is every chance that he will not leave until he retires, and so there will be no opening in Russian history at that school for thirty or more years. According to the Council on Education, of all male faculty in the academic year 1972–1973, 30.3 percent were full professors, and another 25.1 percent were associate professors; in other words, over half the faculty were tenured. The only legitimate way to get rid of tenured faculty is if there is a financial crisis, when whole programs or departments may have to be ended.

Colleges and universities needed more women and minorities, but what HEW failed to recognize, and why its heavy-handed tactics failed to work, is that change in a university comes slowly. There would eventually be a larger number of women and minorities, but not until there were a lot more women and people of color completing graduate school.

NOT ALL ACADEMICS opposed affirmative action. A number of professors joined together in the Committee for Affirmative Action in Universities, which not only rejected criticism of the HEW guidelines but wanted the government to do even more in forcing universities to end decades, even centuries, of discrimination. Dr. Gertrude Ezorsky, a philosophy professor at Brooklyn College, declared that affirmative action did not require the hiring of unqualified people. Those who complained "have yet to say what the Government should do to make universities stop the historic massive discrimination against women that has been documented." The committee had been founded to oppose the Committee on Academic Nondiscrimination and Integrity, which had asked President Ford in December 1974 to "end the numbers games played by Government administrators."

In an analysis of data collected both by the federal government and by private foundations, Professor Rodney Reed of the Graduate School of Education at Berkeley found that the increase in minorities and women on university faculties in the 1970s had been slow, and they remained underrepresented almost everywhere. Until they did achieve parity, at least in terms of their percentage of the population, affirmative action had to continue. The one bright spot he identified related to the growing number of women and minorities completing graduate work. Part of the problem in the 1970s had been the dearth of people with the proper credentials. As more women and minorities completed their doctorates, affirmative action plans would be more effective.

Another defense of compensatory policies involved not the denial of the intellectual meritocracy argument but the claim that universities serve a plurality of purposes, including social service through graduated students. This view sees higher education not just as the training of the best and the brightest but also as an integral part of the community, with responsibilities to that community. This requires making sure not only that minorities have the opportunity to study at a school but also that teachers be role models for minority students and reach out to the larger society as well.

THE LAST WORD on this subject for the 1970s can be that of Tom Wicker, the astute columnist for *The New York Times*. When a report from the Carnegie Commission on affirmative action came out, it appeared to support the anger many people felt about so-called reverse discrimination. Wicker believed the anger to be misplaced: "It is like being angry at a painful treatment rather than at the wound or illness that made it necessary." He more or less agreed with the report that one answer lay in getting more minorities and women into graduate school so that the pool of qualified people would expand. That, however, would take time and might well lead to white applicants complaining that they had been discriminated against.

What had to be understood, Wicker wrote, is that the need for affirmative action "arose only because some groups—primarily white males—for years were greatly advantaged at the expense of others." Colleges and universities that for so long discriminated against women and blacks and used a merit system that favored the white middle class "are in a poor position to decry the shortage of qualified blacks and women." He could find little evidence that without the pressure of affirmative action anything would have changed.

There is no way, he said, to redress deep-seated grievances without "shaking and disarranging some who would otherwise have been preferred." But even if affirmative action is necessary as a short-term instrument, "it is still preference by race and sex, and such preferences are not finally compatible with democratic society." The only way to get past this situation, he concluded, is to speed the day when all Americans could compete for jobs solely on merit. That day, he sadly concluded, still lay in the future.

CHAPTER 8

BACKLASH AND DEFENSE

Racial quotas under any guise are repugnant to all Americans. When a proposal is made to establish racial quotas as public policy, honest men must protest. . . . We prefer the free choice of free men and we are certain that the vast majority of Americans, white and nonwhite alike, prefer such freedom.

—AFL-CIO BUILDING AND CONSTRUCTION
TRADES DEPARTMENT, 1969

It is evident that the high moral outburst of the 1960s was but a passing spasm. The memory of that period has already receded and diminished into a remote past, and black people, once again, are left to fight the battle alone. As we celebrate the tenth anniversary of the Equal Employment Opportunity Commission, we also participate in a memorial service for the Second American Reconstruction.

—HERBERT HILL OF THE NAACP, 1975

In the early 1980s, the political scientist Stanley Greenberg convened a meeting of white male blue-collar voters in the industrial heartland and read to the group a statement by Robert Kennedy: "Americans ought to honor a special obligation to black citizens who lived through the slave experience and racial discrimination." The responses caught Greenberg and his associates by surprise:

"That's bullshit."
"This happened years ago. And they talk to you about it as if it was happening right now."

"I really feel that they have had so much just handed to them. . . . Most of them are abusing it. It's where now, it's almost like a turnaround. They're getting, getting, getting, and the whites are becoming the minority."

One sees here the development of the so-called Reagan Democrats, primarily blue-collar white male workers who had once been strongly aligned with the Democratic Party; many of the same group would later vote for Donald Trump in 2016. By 1980, these workers saw Democratic campaign themes such as "fairness," "equity," and "justice" as nothing more than code words for quotas, and they saw themselves as the primary victims of affirmative action. Much to Greenberg's surprise, in repeated group encounters white fury over affirmative action topped their list of grievances and led them to support candidates, such as Reagan, who opposed affirmative action.

But opposition to affirmative action went far beyond those who believed—rightly or wrongly—that whenever an African American or a Hispanic or a woman got a job or won a place in college, it was always at the expense of a white male. The range of those condemning compensatory programs included men and women, blacks and whites, university professors and small-business owners. Like Stanley Greenberg, few people could foresee the extent and intensity of the backlash. At the same time, some strong voices could be heard praising affirmative action, even in its hard form.

AFTER LYNDON JOHNSON gave his speech at Howard University in 1965, and for most of the rest of the 1960s, soft affirmative action—the quest to open good job opportunities to minorities—seemed like a relatively conservative way to redress decades of racial injustice. Affirmative action looked tame compared with the scorn of Malcolm X for American institutions, the Black Panther Party's armed militancy, the National Welfare Rights Organization's demand for federally funded "jobs or income now," or even Martin Luther King's efforts in the last years of his life to eliminate poverty through the Poor People's Campaign. For mainstream white America, affirmative action seemed cheaper, safer, and more in keeping with traditional ideas of equal opportunity. Yet within a decade, all this had changed, and wherever one looked, one found a strong backlash.

It would be far too facile, as some have done, to blame this on racist conservatives who cleverly and effectively got the public to see affirmative action not as a quest for decent jobs and education but as a surly and radical demand for a giveaway. While it is true that racism certainly played a role in the swelling chorus opposed to affirmative action, many other considerations played a part as well. Chief among these was the heavy-handed grab for power by the Equal Employment Opportunity Commission, which blatantly ignored the plain language of the 1964 Civil Rights Act. Another is the fact that the civil rights movement that so many whites supported had emphasized color blindness. Critics constantly quoted Martin Luther King Jr., who hoped that his children would "not be judged by the color of their skin but by the content of their character."

Because opposition to affirmative action often shaded over into charges of racism, we need to keep in mind the apparent shift in public opinion that took place after 1945, leading to *Brown v. Board of Education* in 1954 and culminating in the Civil Rights Act of 1964 and the Voting Rights Act of the following year. This was far from a complete victory for the civil rights movement; pockets of overt racism remained and would resurface periodically, most recently during and following the 2016 presidential election. According to various polls, however, a majority of the country believed that African Americans should have equal opportunities in the job market. The National Opinion Research Center asked, "Do you think that Negroes/blacks should have as good a chance as white people to get any kind of job, or do you think white people should have the first chance at any kind of job?" In 1944, 52 percent of respondents thought that whites should have the first chance; by 1972, only 3 percent took this position. This, of course, meshed perfectly with the idea of a "soft" affirmative action, one that did no more than open the doors of opportunity on an equal basis to all. As governmental agencies moved toward "hard" affirmative action, with its numerical goals and timetables, public acceptance decreased. One needs to keep in mind that polling results often depended on time, place, and especially the wording of the questions.

In early 1979, a Harris poll found that seven out of ten whites favored an outreach form of affirmative action for African Americans but not quotas. An even larger majority agreed that ability and not skin color should be the criterion for getting into college or securing a job. Civil rights leaders immediately challenged the poll. Benjamin Hooks of the NAACP, for example, claimed that even if the results were true, "most whites still prefer to sit idly by while other whites nibble away at the few gains blacks have made while the Klan and the Nazi Party attack these gains openly." The same poll revealed a sharp contrast between how African Americans and whites perceived equal employment opportunity. Seven out of ten whites believed the national government stood committed to equality, but only four out of ten blacks agreed. Moreover, 93 percent of the whites in the survey thought African Americans "were getting a better break in getting jobs than they did ten years ago," a view the black community strongly rejected.

Although we now have many years of polling on affirmative action, the results over the years have always been mixed. A majority of whites and blacks, men and women, favor a soft, or "outreach," form of affirmative action for minorities and women. On the other hand, a majority is almost always opposed to any plan requiring quotas, although here the percentage of African Americans who support quotas, even if only a minority, is still larger than the percentage of whites who endorse them. As two scholars who had studied the polls concluded, little had changed between 1978 and 2006. Most Americans favored equal rights and equal opportunity but opposed preferential plans, especially those involving goals or quotas, to help particular groups. Again, much depends on how the questions are phrased.

Many conservatives did oppose affirmative action, but not all of these critics can be labeled racist. There is no question that racists attacked any program that would benefit African Americans, and this group would include not just die-hard southerners but members of most of the craft unions. Libertarians and critics of big government found much they disliked, and many academics who supported civil rights denounced programs that they believed threatened the integrity of the university as well as the quality of education. Legal and political philosophers argued that the American tradition had always emphasized individual opportunity, not group rights. While blacks appeared as the major target of the opposition, women, Hispanics, and other groups that sought to overcome past discrimination through compensatory programs also found themselves under attack. The opposition, it should again be emphasized, did not manifest itself against "soft" affirmative action. The backlash came when the EEOC began enforcing a "hard" version, replete with quotas and a philosophy of equality of results rather than equality of opportunity.

—————

RELATIVELY LITTLE national attention focused on affirmative action until the EEOC began its campaign, but by the mid-1970s there could be little doubt that affirmative action had become a major part of the national debate on public policy. The number of articles in periodicals and newspapers grew year by year, and in 1976 *U.S. News & World Report* became the first magazine to make it a cover story, with an accompanying article with the headline "Reverse Discrimination: Has It Gone Too Far?"

One study after another found affirmative action plans in higher education badly designed, unevenly enforced, and yielding poor results. According to *The Chronicle of Higher Education*, "the general feeling among many women's leaders, affirmative action officers, and some administrators is that affirmative action is not working," and these people blamed the federal government, particularly HEW's Office for Civil Rights. That office required every one of the thirteen hundred institutions of higher education receiving federal money to secure approval for their affirmative action plans, yet by December 1975, HEW had approved only thirty-one plans. Most colleges did not meet their stated numerical goals, but none suffered withdrawal of federal funds for their failure. In general, HEW had a miserable record regarding discrimination on campus. By the end of 1974, it had not resolved even one of the 616 employment discrimination complaints it had received between 1971 and 1974.

The most devastating criticism of government efforts came from the Carnegie Council on Policy Studies in Higher Education, led by the former chancellor of the University of California system Clark Kerr. Looking at programs launched between 1967 and 1979, the commission reported that "few federal programs are now so near to self-destruction. Seldom has such a good cause spawned such a badly developed series of mechanisms." Many proponents of affirmative action shared this dreary view. Mary Frances Berry, a member of the U.S. Commission on Civil Rights, blamed poorly trained officials in HEW's Office for Civil Rights who, she charged, "would not know what an affirmative action plan with a high probability of success looks like." When the director of that office, Peter Holmes, resigned under fire in late 1975, he admitted that there was "a widespread feeling that the process has become very burdensome and I wonder if it is yielding the intended results."

The real problem, according to some critics, is that affirmative action not only did not work; it *could not* work. Joseph Adelson, a professor of clinical psychology at the University of Michigan, charged that all the claims supposedly showing a great increase in minority enrollment failed to include one major number—how many graduated. At Michigan, the training program in clinical psychology in the early 1970s had adopted an ambitious one-third minority quota, and "in order to meet it admitted students recklessly." The result proved to be a very high attrition rate, with less than one in five of these special admits completing their doctorate, compared with two out of three of those regularly accepted.

Many who criticized affirmative action programs did so not because they opposed the idea of helping minorities but because they believed the programs as implemented had not worked, and the chief reason lay in the federal government's failure. Before the Supreme Court decided *Bakke* in 1978, affirmative action had strong support in groups like the American Association for Affirmative Action and the Committee for Affirmative Action in Universities, whose board members included such luminaries as John Rawls, Irving Howe, Arthur M. Schlesinger Jr., and Alfred Kazin. When Bernard D. Davis, a faculty member at Harvard Medical School, charged that the school's affirmative action program had resulted in lower standards, four hundred protesters came to picket outside his office, and both the Association of American Medical Colleges and the American Medical Association denounced his comments.

The question of merit—that is, of people qualified either to hold a particular job or to get into a prestigious college or professional school—has been a constant in the debate. Professor Davis's article essentially said that the affirmative action plan had awarded spots in one of the nation's top medical schools to people unqualified to be there; they lacked the necessary merit. Since the beginning of this country, individual ability has been highly esteemed. Individualism is at the heart of our constitutional system of rights; individuals have the right to free speech or to have an attorney or to enjoy religious freedom. Unlike European countries, the United States does not have group rights, and Jefferson's ideal of meritocracy, or government by the best qualified, has been part of our national tradition for more than two centuries.

The problem, of course, as the historian John Livingston has charged, is that meritocracy rests on assumptions that may have racist consequences. I would not go as far as he does in saying that "meritocracy tends to create an elite whose members are indifferent to racial injustice and a middle class that may even psychologically require it," but it is also clear that in order for merit to be the standard for success, there has to be a level playing field. One cannot expect a person who has suffered discrimination, attended an inferior school, and lived in poverty to compete against someone who has been the recipient of a good education and enjoyed the cultural and psychological advantages of a middle- or upper-class life. Yet even recognizing this disparity, a majority of Americans believed in the 1970s and still believe that individual merit—not race or gender or ethnicity—should determine economic and educational opportunities.

The noted sociologist Daniel Bell charged that affirmative action violated the "American philosophical creed," which emphasized individual, not group, rights. While one could justify special subsidies for the poor especially in nursery schools and elementary education, he could not accept any plan that discriminated "against others." When one asks for special quotas or preferences, particularly in the cases of schools or jobs where places are limited, such a request serves to discriminate against others. And this is a much more difficult question, morally and practically, to solve.

How did African Americans feel about affirmative action? Writing shortly after a 1965 Labor Department report suggested what would become "hard" affirmative action, Professor Donald E. Smith had predicted that such a program would be regarded by the larger community as "patently unfair" and "would meet with strong objections from the Negro community itself, which would resent the official label of social or economic backwardness." Smith proved right on his first point, but African Americans held a wide variety of views, ranging from wholehearted support to a hearty antagonism.

PRIOR TO THE PASSAGE of the 1964 Civil Rights Act, African Americans most resented job discrimination. In 1963, more blacks (30 percent) listed employment discrimination as affecting them than any other type of discrimination; educational discrimination placed a distant second (11 percent). In terms of government action, three out of five blacks cited equal job opportunity as the highest priority for government action. In another poll that year, African Americans rated the right to hold the same jobs as whites highest among "rights wanted by almost all Negroes." In 1976, a poll of national black leaders asked them to choose between goals of "equality of opportunity: giving each person an equal chance for a good education and to develop his or her ability" and "equality of results: giving each person a relatively equal income regardless of his or her education and ability," 86 percent chose equality of opportunity; only 7 percent chose equality of results.

Despite numerous polls of people of color taken in the quarter century following the Civil Rights Act, one could not find any consensus among African Americans regarding affirmative action. Public opinion, especially on such a multifaceted issue, depends on how the issue is framed, and that is especially true here, where so much relies on the specific aspect of affirmative action policy that respondents are asked to consider. To take one example, in a 1984 survey, 57 percent of a sample of 1,150 African Americans agreed and 38 percent disagreed that "minorities should be given special consideration when decisions are made about hiring applicants for jobs." Yet three questions later, 72 percent agreed that "job applicants should be judged solely on the basis of test scores and other individual qualities."

Various polls showed blacks supporting programs to help minorities and women get ahead, and also opposing quotas. Other polls had a majority of black respondents supporting quotas and programs that set aside a number of openings—either in employment or in college—for groups that had been discriminated against in the past. There does seem to be some consistency in that blacks saw affirmative action most positively when quotas were not involved. They favored training programs and equal opportunity—programs that a majority of white respondents also supported—and tended to disfavor giving minorities special treatment, setting quotas, or hiring on any basis other than merit; here again, whites opposed this type of affirmative action as well.

Are these poll results contradictory? Of course they are, because attitudes toward affirmative action in the United States have been so ever since the shift away from "soft" to "hard," from opening the gates of opportunity to an effort to enforce equality of results. Understandably, minorities—especially people of color—would be more sympathetic to programs that tried to compensate in some manner for decades, indeed centuries, of discrimination. All the polls, however, indicate that as the EEOC ramped up its demands that schools and businesses set goals—which everyone knew meant quotas—a majority of black Americans wanted a fair shot at getting a good job

William F. Buckley Jr. listens sympathetically as Thomas Sowell, the leading African American critic of affirmative action, explains his opposition on Firing Line, *3 November 1983.*

or getting into school based on their merit, not their color. All they apparently wanted out of an affirmative action program was "a fair shake."

PERHAPS THE LEADING black critic of affirmative action is and has been for a long time Dr. Thomas Sowell, a senior scholar at the conservative Hoover Institution at Stanford University. Trained as an economist at the University of Chicago, Sowell has championed the free market, preferring its operation to any governmental plan for social improvement. By the mid-1970s, he was claiming that affirmative action did little good. Sowell argued that poll after poll showed that African Americans resented busing as well as affirmative action and charged that both programs had been imposed on the black community by whites who had no idea of the damage they were doing or what the black community wanted.

Little evidence existed, he claimed, that affirmative action had helped anybody; in fact, black income compared with that of whites had reached its highest level before 1970, before the EEOC had begun its push to establish quotas. The programs, he agreed, had helped a few people get jobs, but such benefits had been more than offset by the liabilities imposed, not only on employers, who had to spend millions on "reports," but on other minorities who would not get a job because the EEOC had, contrary to its goal, actually made hiring women and minorities harder.

Even Sowell conceded that merely stopping discrimination with a "cease and desist" order might not be enough; some additional affirmative steps had to be taken. If programs worked, then there might be grounds for supporting affirmative action as a national policy even while recognizing that for certain groups to benefit, others would have to suffer. Life is unfair, and we have many national policies that benefit one group at the expense of others. But Sowell claimed that affirmative action's track record in helping to alleviate social ills was even worse than that of busing to achieve integration. "The truly disadvantaged—those with little education or job experience, or from broken families—have fallen even further behind during the era of affirmative action."

Sowell was especially bitter about the experience of minority students. When some public colleges instituted "open admissions," blacks poured into those schools, and in many instances failed out almost as quickly, while driving away faculty and qualified white students. Even when colleges did provide remedial services, many minority students rejected this help as patronizing. In a 1989 book he titled *Choosing a College: A Guide for Parents and Students,* Sowell charged that even in the elite schools "the drive to get a good-looking 'body count' of black students leads the top colleges and universities to go way beyond the pool of black students who meet their normal admission standards." This may ease the conscience of white administrators, but unfortunately "many black students discover too late that the 'opportunity' to go to a big-name school turns out to be a trap."

Another influential African American critic, the Harvard Law professor Derrick Bell, believed that affirmative action, even though sought by minority groups, is really a sideshow. The proposed remedies "distract the subordinate group from the real issues of racial injustice with token benefits while the dominant whites at every level are the short and long-run beneficiaries." Bell charged that if one looks closely at minority admissions policies, for example, they usually included no more than 10 to 12 percent of the school's entering class. "Traditional admissions and hiring standards are not altered but remain oriented toward the upper middle class." And who will benefit when hostility between poor whites and their black and Chicano counterparts increases? The dominant white group, of course.

SCHOLARS AND WRITERS have grouped opponents of affirmative action under several headings, such as "color-blind liberals" and "color-blind conservatives." Racism also played a part, but when one looks at this area, it is often hard to pull out affirmative action from the wider response of whites to the civil rights movement that crested in the mid-1960s. As early as 1963—a year *before* passage of the Civil Rights Act—Murray Friedman published an article titled "The White Liberal's Retreat" in which he argued that "the liberal white is increasingly uneasy about the nature and consequences of the Negro revolt." Why? After school desegregation arrived in northern cities, white liberals realized that the African American was no longer an abstraction or just a southern problem. The rise of black nationalism and growing violence exacerbated tensions with white liberals, especially after several civil rights groups expelled white members. As Friedman noted, "In the final analysis, a liberal, white, middle-class society wants to have change, but without trouble." The liberal retreat from radical reform, Friedman noted, was not new. "To the Negro demand [for rights] 'now,' to which the Deep South has replied 'never,' many liberal whites are increasingly responding 'later.'"

Attorney General Robert F. Kennedy as early as 1962 had privately argued that the attainment of equality in the North would be harder than it then seemed in the South. The goal of civil rights activists in the South had been to eliminate official state-imposed rules that not only kept blacks and whites separated but kept people of color out of decent schools and jobs as well as the voting booth. While the elimination of these barriers would not mean full equality, the dismantling of the apartheid system would be a major step forward.

Northern cities and states in the latter part of the twentieth century did not impose legally mandated segregation. Blacks could, for the most part, vote freely north of the Mason-Dixon Line. As Anthony Lewis wrote, recounting his conversation with Kennedy, "In the North, Negroes would be demanding not removal of official barriers—which did not exist—but affirmative action by the government and people to win acceptance of Negroes in every human situation." In the North, African Americans would be struggling to make color irrelevant in the lives of men and women, and overcoming the legacy of decades of poverty and ignorance would require not neutrality on the part of society but active steps to help the black population.

White resentment in part grew out of the belief that affirmative action is a zero-sum game, that there are only so many jobs or seats in law school or in training programs, and that if an African American gets that slot simply because of his or her race, then an equally qualified or perhaps even better-qualified white person did not. Unfortunately, in some instances this proved true. Darlene Murphy, a personnel secretary at a West Coast defense contractor, had responsibility for a billboard outside the gate listing available jobs. People interested in those positions would come in, fill out the necessary forms, and then hand them to her.

> When receiving an application, I was instructed to thank the person, wait until they left, then pencil in their race in the upper right-hand corner. You see, we had "enough" whites and Hispanics at the facility; we needed more blacks. If the applicant was not black, no matter what his qualifications, the application went into an inactive file to be considered no further.

"Let's face it," she concluded, it would have been more honest to say that only blacks need apply, but "that would have been discrimination."

How often did it happen that a white male was deliberately blocked from getting a job because the employer wanted a minority? One cannot be sure; much of the record is anecdotal, and allegedly "hard data" is unreliable. For example, a telephone survey of white males had one in ten claiming they had lost a job or promotion due to affirmative action quotas. In other polls, as many as four out of ten white males believed that they or someone in their family would lose out in securing a college admission or in getting a job or promotion because of affirmative action. In the four years ending in 1983, the EEOC received more than 1,500 complaints from white males charging racial discrimination. California's Department of Fair Employment in one year received 418 job-related discrimination complaints from whites out of a total of 7,161 filings. Are these a lot, or are they, as one critic argues, underreported, because white males were reluctant to complain openly of reverse discrimination?

The animus against affirmative action was not limited to blue-collar workers. Big corporations that had hundreds of employees could make affirmative action work insofar as government required "goals." But many small businesses had a great deal of trouble complying with federal regulations that, in their context, made no sense. Jim Supica Jr. owned a modest-size bridge-building company in Lenexa, Kansas, and claimed that federal rules had created a nightmare for him. He employed fifteen men, three of them black, but the government cited the firm for not meeting the numerical goals of 12.7 percent minority group members and 6.9 percent women in one job category, truck drivers. Supica, however, employed only two truck drivers, both white males who, as he pointed out, could sue him for reverse discrimination if he fired them to hire a black or a woman. Other small, white-owned firms also complained about the unrealistic "goals" and inordinate amount of paperwork required by the government.

THERE IS ONE AREA, however, where white males, especially in unionized blue-collar jobs, had a legitimate grievance. In the great expansion of unions after World War II, unions and management had put many aspects of labor relations under contract. These provisions covered not only wages, hours, benefits, and procedures for settling disputes but also rules regarding the importance of seniority in cases where an economic downturn might require laying off some workers. This usually meant "last hired, first fired," which made perfectly good sense in a homogeneous workforce. Unions strongly defended these provisions as historic protection against management favoritism or animus against union activists.

During the drafting of the civil rights law, unions lobbied in vain to have the EEOC placed in the Labor Department and to have all the hard-won gains of the past three decades included as "civil rights." The procedures adopted for filing a civil rights complaint with the EEOC, moreover, bore no relation to the by-now-familiar methods used in industrial relations. As a result, when cases involving racial or gender discrimination arose, judges ignored labor issues such as collective bargaining, seniority, and security agreements, none of which were addressed in antidiscrimination laws.

In the 1960s, civil rights split the labor movement into two camps. On one side stood the conservative craft unions of the old American Federation of Labor, which had stoutly resisted integration of black and white locals. On the other side were the unions of the former Congress of Industrial Organizations, which had had fewer segregated unions and, compared with the craft unions, had been far more welcoming of minority workers. The CIO had for the most part accepted the original "soft" affirmative action, but both sides closed ranks in the mid-1970s when the EEOC attempted to expand affirmative action beyond nondiscriminatory hiring and promotion to include a reversal of the hallowed seniority system.

The "last hired, first fired" principle at the heart of contractual seniority provisions inevitably worked to the disadvantage of minorities and women whose past exclusion kept them low on the seniority list. Under government prodding, companies and unions had begun admitting minorities in the late 1960s and early 1970s, prosperous years that made it easy to hire new workers. But when a recession hit in the mid-1970s, many companies laid off employees, and the principle of seniority clashed with that of equal employment opportunity. For example, a survey of furloughed steelworkers at one midwestern plant in the mid-1970s found that while 11.5 percent of the total workforce was out of a job, 38 percent of black workers lost their position. In 1974, the Big Three automakers laid off 225,000 employees, and these cutbacks hit some local unions especially hard. In Linden, New Jersey, for example, General Motors let go of 2,400 workers, including all 300 women who had been hired since 1970; in Fremont, California, the following year, the company laid off 2,300 workers, including nearly all 500 of its women employees. According to a story in *The New York Times,* "Resentment among minorities and women is growing. They feel that just as they were finally getting a foot in the door of employment opportunities, it is being slammed in their faces."

If one followed the principles of a "soft" affirmative action, then little could be done when a legitimate seniority system existed. But a unanimous Supreme Court in *Griggs v. Duke Power Company* (1971) found that Title VII did not permit hiring or promotion policies— and this would include layoffs—that maintained a pattern of racial inequality, even though these policies might appear to be race or gender neutral. On the face of it, seniority is a race-neutral policy, but minorities and women had long been excluded from the workforce, so that applying normal seniority rules would inevitably mean laying off the most recently hired—people of color and women.

As one might have expected, when companies began laying off

workers, court suits followed. Lower courts tried to come up with solutions that maintained a seniority system yet also protected minorities. The "rightful place" doctrine created a constructive or fictional seniority to put minority employees in the approximate spot on the seniority list that they would have occupied had they not been the victims of bias. By using plant seniority rather than departmental seniority, black workers who had been employed in menial jobs before Title VII led the company to move them into higher-paying positions could use the years they worked as a janitor to gain seniority over a white employee who had more years in a department but not in the plant as a whole.

Presumably, Title VII holds that a bona fide seniority system cannot, in itself, constitute an unlawful employment practice, especially if it had originally been established without discriminatory intent. Once again, however, the EEOC stepped in and ignored the plain wording of the law. In April 1975, the EEOC approved layoff guidelines that would require companies to violate seniority agreements that resulted in "disproportionate" layoffs of minorities. For once, the EEOC overreached itself and had to indefinitely postpone implementation of these guidelines because of heavy criticism from other government agencies.

Lower courts came up with a variety of answers when confronted by lawsuits involving contractual seniority systems. Some appellate courts read the legislative history of section 703(h) of Title VII as indicating that layoffs made pursuant to a plant-wide seniority system that operated in a facially neutral manner were "bona fide" plans, and therefore could not be considered unlawfully discriminatory even if the results bore most heavily on minorities. However, other courts reached different conclusions. The Court of Appeals for the Fifth Circuit ruled that even a bona fide seniority system lawful under Title VII may be changed as part of a remedy for other unlawful practices. In other words, even if the system is facially neutral and operates in a neutral manner, discriminatory practices in other areas justify altering the contractual obligations. The issue would not be cleared up until the Supreme Court finally took a case directly involving a seniority system and recently hired minority and women employees in 1986. In *Wygant v. Jackson Board of Education* case, a 5–4 majority upheld a valid seniority system over efforts to give minority teachers preferences during a layoff.

These contradictory results led to greater union angst, especially after the 1974 Steel Consent Decree. The previous year a Labor Department investigation into Bethlehem Steel's Sparrows Point plant in Maryland and a federal suit against U.S. Steel's facility in Birmingham, Alabama, both found discriminatory seniority systems in place. In an out-of-court settlement, steel manufacturers paid $31 million in damages to black, Hispanic, and women workers and agreed that 20 percent of all new workers would be affirmative action hires. The leaders of the steelworkers union reluctantly accepted the decree for pragmatic reasons, because an "industry-wide lawsuit could lead to unworkable and inconsistent seniority rules, written by judges, a complete reshuffling of employees, and a severe crippling of the International."

In this area, one can clearly see a conflict of rights. Workers had fought for the better part of a century before they finally won the right to organize and bargain collectively, and the contractual seniority system satisfied the needs of both employer and employee. It provided a fair and clear rule for when companies, for whatever reason, had to lay off workers. As the historian Nelson Lichtenstein put it, union members saw the seniority system as "part of the moral economy of the work regime," representing the most important "property" interest a worker held in his job. Unionists might differ about what form "last hired, first fired" should take, but they stood steadfast in their loyalty to seniority.

For those who had worked—and often fought—for the seniority system, black demands that they be retained while whites who had worked there for years be let go merely embittered them more. They saw the gains that had been made since the New Deal washed away by a system of race and gender preferences enforced by governmental agencies that no longer cared about them.

CONVENTIONAL WISDOM HOLDS that the blue-collar white reaction to affirmative action played a major if not *the* major role in winning this group away from the Democratic Party and supporting Ronald Reagan in the 1980 election. While this is probably true on one level, public opinion polls indicate a far more nuanced situation. All whites do not speak in one voice, nor do they view civil rights in general—and affirmative action in particular—through one lens.

First, polls taken in the quarter century following the passage of the 1964 Civil Rights Act showed white Americans becoming more supportive of equal legal rights for African Americans as well as for the goals embodied in that statute. According to one study, "Some previously quite controversial issues—for example, segregation in public transportation—are not now even salient. Even on issues that are still controversial, such as school and residential integration, the increase in pro-integrationist response by whites has been steady."

Whites also believed—in general—that some programs had to be supported to improve the conditions of minorities who had suffered years of discrimination. Here again, the support was general; that is, most whites believed that something should be done to help African Americans get better jobs and more access to good housing and education. Even when asked about affirmative action, seven out of ten whites supported it provided there were no mandatory quotas.

At the same time, support for general proposals foundered upon disapproval of the specific policies. "Even when whites pass the test of racial tolerance . . . this in itself does not mean that they will support compensatory efforts on behalf of blacks." Respondents to a *Washington Post* survey agreed that much remained to be done to achieve equality for blacks, but when the subject of preferential treatment came up, support dropped precipitately. Less than one in three agreed that minorities and women should be granted special preferences as compensation for past discrimination, and a significant minority of whites believed that the pursuit of equality had gone too far.

Interestingly, support among African Americans also dropped as questions moved from a philosophical commitment for greater equality to particulars. The percentage of blacks who supported affirmative action ran twenty to thirty points higher than whites, a sort of reverse mirror of more whites than blacks who believed that things had greatly improved for minorities.

A fourth aspect to polls at this time involved white assumptions about why more blacks than whites experienced high levels of poverty. A substantial percentage of white respondents believed that poverty resulted from lack of personal responsibility exercised by the impoverished; they did not believe that racial discrimination in modern America was so bad that it would prevent blacks who wanted to get ahead from doing so.

It should be apparent that the white backlash went far beyond simple racism. A significant gap separated white and black perceptions during this time, and while many polls showed a general and significant increase in white attitudes toward tolerance and equality (an improvement that would not have occurred if all whites were simply racist), many of those whites who supported principles of legal equality, antidiscrimination, and equal treatment had a much different view toward specific policies to achieve those goals, and especially about affirmative action.

SOME WHITES—LIBERALS and conservatives alike—opposed hard affirmative action for moral and philosophical reasons, believing racial identification for jobs or school "demeaning" both to the individual and to the American democratic tradition. The nub of the moral argument is that while women, blacks, and other minorities had been discriminated against as *groups,* quota programs that benefited these groups disadvantaged *individual* white males. Moreover, not all white males would pay the price of society's desire to compensate the victims of past discrimination—only those in targeted jobs or schools. The normally liberal *New Republic* admitted that the system could not be designed so that only "oppressors" would be excluded, even if they could be identified. "The fate of young men and women is at stake, and they are classified according to their racial or ethnic identity, not according to their moral conduct."

The price is paid not only by the individual, the journal's editors argued, but by individuals who are overwhelmingly from blue-collar white groups. Affirmative action rarely affected upper-class white males; they had been well educated and had no trouble getting into good colleges or graduate schools and then beginning managerial or professional positions. Marginal candidates, on the other hand, had not been as well educated and might themselves have come from poor or disadvantaged backgrounds; these were the people who got bumped to make room for women and minorities. This resulted in the bottom groups getting not pushed up to an equality with all others but merely pushed ahead of the "next to last" group, primarily white ethnic Americans. And that, according to critics, "is grossly unfair" and "simply shifts injustice one notch up the social hierarchy leaving the basic inequalities of American society untouched."

All opponents of affirmative action, whatever their particular dislike, always wound up attacking quotas. As noted earlier, a series of public opinion polls throughout the 1970s and into the 1980s found public support for affirmative action when it involved opening the doors of opportunity and even for compensatory programs, such as additional job training, for minorities. Support turned to opposition once pollsters mentioned quotas.

Morris B. Abram, former head of the American Jewish Committee, charged that quotas created an "ethnic spoils system" pitting one group against another, and warned that it would inevitably result in an "institutionalized division of the pie of opportunity by bureaucratic decisions as to the group disadvantaged and the numbers of each group to be benefited." In a passionate and moving essay, the eminent legal scholar Alexander Bickel wrote,

> A racial quota derogates the human dignity and individuality of all to whom it is applied; it is invidious in principle as well as in practice. Moreover, it can easily be turned against those it purports to help. The history of the racial quota is a history of subjugation, not beneficence. Its evil lies not in its name, but in its effects; a quota is a divider of society, a creator of castes, and it is all the worse for its racial base, especially in a society desperately striving for an equality that will make race irrelevant.

As for past injustices, critics of affirmative action did not deny that blacks, women, and other minorities had faced discrimination, but it was neither fair nor logical to compensate present members of these groups for ills suffered by their ancestors, at the expense of other—and innocent—groups today. It simply did not follow, philosophy professor Carl Cohen charged, either "in morals or in law, that individual blacks, or Orientals, or Jews who were not damaged are entitled now to special favor in group redress."

Of course, some opponents of the civil rights movement picked up on the color-blind argument, because it proved a far more respectable way to oppose African American demands for equality. In 1963, James J. Kilpatrick, the editor of *The Richmond News Leader* and one of the champions of massive resistance, wrote an article for *The Saturday Evening Post* tentatively titled "The Hell He Is Equal" in which he argued that "the Negro race, as a race, is in fact an inferior race." The magazine decided not to publish the piece after four black girls were killed in the Birmingham, Alabama, church bombing. In the mid-1970s, Kilpatrick found color blindness to be a far better way to attack race-conscious programs while ignoring the history that had led to them. "I am getting to be like the Catholic convert," he declared, "who became more Catholic than the Pope." He told supporters of affirmative action that "if it is wrong to discriminate by reason of race or sex, well, then, it is wrong to discriminate by reason of race or sex." He labeled supporters of compensatory programs "egalitarians" and condemned them as "worse racists—much worse racists—than the old Southern bigots." In 1979, he claimed "that the bureaucrats of HEW had done more to destroy good race relations in the past ten years than the Ku Klux Klan did in a century."

Although colleges and universities, under the lash of the EEOC as well as a growing awareness of the educational benefits of diversity, had begun to admit minority students and sought out minority and female faculty, some in academia worried whether schools would have to accept unqualified students and, in order to do so, would have to lower overall standards. The larger question to some educators, however, dealt with whether colleges and universities should be in the business of trying to remedy decades of societal discrimination, the rationale of the California system in *Bakke*. A university exists to advance knowledge, and it benefits society by training the best and brightest of a new generation in the arts, humanities, sciences, and the professions. Advocates of affirmative action argued that maintaining high academic standards would mean too few educated minority members, and this would hurt the country in the long run. So too would the failure to educate the nation's brightest if resources had to be diverted to compensatory programs. John Bunzel, the president of San Jose State and later a fellow at the Hoover Institution, declared that the university "is not the Department of Health and Human Services, and should not be mistaken as an adjunct agency of the federal government in the important business of political and social reform."

THE CHARGE AGAINST affirmative action—other than in its pristine "soft" form—that riled more people than any other aspect is that it constituted "reverse discrimination." Preferential policies are an evil means to an allegedly good end; that is, one has to discriminate to correct injustice. It is impossible to say with any certainty who used the phrase first, or when, but the most influential argument on that topic came from the sociologist Nathan Glazer of Harvard. In a 1975 book titled *Affirmative Discrimination: Ethnic Inequality and Public Policy,* Glazer laid out a strong case against affirmative action, which, he charged, "now attach[es] benefits and penalties to individuals simply on the basis of their race, color, and national origin."

For Glazer, the greatness of American opportunity had been that we valued individual achievement—with each person judged on his

Professor Nathan Glazer of Harvard opposed affirmative action for many years, but eventually came around to reluctantly supporting diversity as an important issue in higher education.

or her own merits—and that our law system had created and sustained rights for individuals, not for groups. Affirmative action supposedly aided minorities, but this meant preference not for minorities in general—because all people are members of some minority—but only for certain arbitrary groups, namely, blacks, American Indians, Asians, and, in what he considered total absurdity, people with Spanish surnames. Glazer asked why these groups should be singled out for special treatment and could find no logical answer.

Like others, Glazer believed affirmative action wrong not just morally but legally as well, citing Title VII of the 1964 Civil Rights Act prohibiting any employer to give preferential treatment to any individual or group on the basis of race, color, religion, sex, or national origin. Government agencies, especially the EEOC, had not only ignored § 703(j) but bragged that the anti-preferential provisions "are a big zero, a nothing, a nullity."

In part, Glazer's position grew out of the earlier and very optimistic book he had written with Daniel Patrick Moynihan, *Beyond the Melting Pot* (1963). In it, they argued that assimilation into American society did not require that the groups they wrote about—Negroes, Puerto Ricans, Jews, Italians, and Irish in New York City—give up their specific distinctions of religion and ethnicity. Instead, each group had found its own distinctive path to success. African Americans had yet to find their path and had problems, but so had the Irish and Italians earlier. New York, the two concluded, "will very likely in the end be an integrated area."

In the foreword to the 1970 edition, Glazer and Moynihan admitted that they had assumed blacks would behave—and see themselves—as one ethnic group among many. They had not imagined that blacks would want to be treated as something wholly new, a "racial" group, and were "saddened and frightened" by it. Race and the revolts on college campuses in the late 1960s pushed Glazer and many others of the so-called New York intelligentsia to the right, and that is clear in *Affirmative Discrimination*. Government intervention to overcome the effects of discrimination represented a willful refusal by blacks to "accept the main pattern of American history," a pattern of ever-expanding inclusiveness and opportunity.

Glazer's charges, while reverberating with many critics of affirmative action, might have been stronger had he, as some critics noted, dealt with some of the basic arguments in favor of affirmative action. One held that the ever-expanding society of opportunity and inclusion had never really accepted nonwhite minorities, even in the great polyglot of New York. Glazer seems to have realized this, because in a foreword to the 1987 reissue, he seemed to be in the midst of changing his mind. It was becoming clear, he wrote, that African Americans were not being assimilated the way other groups had been. Perhaps affirmative action had some positive aspects, and he conceded that the actual conditions of the African American community perhaps warranted a system of goals and quotas. Ten years later, he acknowledged that the optimism that he and Moynihan had exalted three decades earlier did not apply to all groups, especially to blacks. The hard fact of the African American experience was and remained the refusal of other Americans to accept blacks as suitable candidates for assimilation into American life. Nonetheless, for Glazer and others, the color-blind model of American opportunity for individuals had to be protected.

NOT EVERYONE OPPOSED affirmative action, even after it began to move from a simple "open the door" format to one based on numbers. Civil rights activists argued that only preferential treatment could overcome centuries of slavery and discrimination. After the city of

Indianapolis instituted hiring goals in 1976, black representation on its police force rose to 14 percent. Barry Goldstein of the NAACP Legal Defense Fund noted that in 1970 there were about 23,000 black police officers in the country; in 1979, there were 43,000. In that same decade, the number of black electricians rose from 15,000 to more than 37,000. For Goldstein, numbers such as these showed that affirmative action worked. Daniel Maguire, a theologian and ethicist, argued that the main issue was not fairness or equality but justice. True, some quotas are unfair and treat people unequally, but society accepts certain inequalities because they are perceived as just.

The notion that the country's treatment of blacks since its founding had been so horrific that only radical measures could provide even mild compensation is found in numerous articles and op-ed pieces and is the theme that runs through a long and anguished screed by Herbert Reid in the *Howard Law Journal*. Reid's thesis, while certainly not new, could not be missed: the "past and present degeneration of the legal status of black Americans" necessitated positive action to promote opportunities for qualified members of minority groups and/or to provide special training to help them become qualified. Reid challenged the notion that the *Brown* decision and the Civil Rights Act had made for a color-blind country; discrimination still permeated every aspect of American life. He wanted an all-out defense of affirmative action in the courts and in legislatures, because the country essentially owed it to minorities to make up in the present generation at least some of the indignities visited upon their forebears in the past.

Advocates of affirmative action for the most part claimed that it had worked. According to Stephen Steinberg, a distinguished professor of sociology at the City University of New York, prior to affirmative action mandates, blacks had only token representation in the nation's core industries. Affirmative action had opened up access to mainstream occupations. Companies subject to EEOC requirements—because they had federal contracts—raised the percentage of black workers in their employ far more than companies not under EEOC scrutiny. "The occupational spheres where blacks have made the most progress—in government service, in major blue-collar occupations, in corporate management, and in the professions—are all areas where vigorous affirmative action programs have been in place."

Finally, let us not forget that some whites supported affirmative action out of a sense of guilt or felt their Christian beliefs demanded

Professor Paul Spickard found himself adversely affected by affirmative action yet continued to defend it as the right and "Christian" thing to do. He is shown here in 2007.

they do so. The "just citizen," according to Daniel Maguire, cannot be at peace while social injustice exists. Even if he is guilty of no personal offense, "he owes a debt to legal justice by the very nature of social personhood. Here the guilt is the guilt of omission, the guilt of not having done enough, of not caring enough. . . . In the matter of American racism, the white who would claim to be without such guilt is, in the phrase and spirit of the Apostle John, 'a liar.' "

Paul Spickard faced a personal test of his commitment to this Christian view of justice. Spickard, a white male, had degrees from Harvard and Berkeley in Asian history but was twice turned down for jobs because colleges wanted a minority person. "Isn't all this unfair?" he asked. Yes, he concluded, but

> my family came over on the *Mayflower* and made money in the slave trade. Doctors, lawyers, judges, and comfortable business people go back several generations in my clan. . . . I am standing on the shoulders of my ancestors and their discriminatory behavior.

Contrast my experience with that of a Chicano friend, whose immigrant father had a fourth-grade education and ran a grocery store. Without affirmative action and the social commitment it symbolizes, my friend might not have gone to Amherst, nor to Stanford Law School. . . . Our society would be poorer for the loss of his skills. . . . Affirmative action may not always be fair. But I'm willing to take second best if overall fairness is achieved. After all, for biblical Christians, fairness—often translated in our Bibles as "justice" or "righteousness"—is a fundamental principle by which God calls us to live. And affirmative action is an appropriate program aimed at achieving the godly goal of putting others' welfare before my own.

Spickard, who went on to a distinguished career in academia and is now in the history department at the University of California at Santa Barbara, reports that after publication of the article, "I received 300 pieces of hate mail from my good Christian coreligionists, and three positive letters." That is not surprising, because by the end of the 1970s the critics of affirmative action not only outnumbered the supporters but were far more vocal.

CHAPTER 9

BLACKS AND JEWS DIVIDE

So you want to know how I became a bigot? I'll tell you. The blacks have options we don't. The Jews never had a civil rights movement. We fought for everything ourselves. When my parents came over here, they didn't have signs in Yiddish and Italian, they were only in English. And those giveaway programs. I'm not getting any! This is how I became a bigot. I'm tired of it. I want equal opportunity, not this sixty-forty business.

—JEWISH WOMAN IN CANARSIE, BROOKLYN

The call for quotas, or even "goals," upset many people, but none more so than those in the Jewish community. No other group had stood so steadfastly with African Americans in their fight for equality and social justice. American Jews had no problems with affirmative action so long as it remained an outreach program, efforts devised to open the doors of opportunity and then let the best people win on the basis of merit. That had been the story of Jews in America, and they were more than willing that people of color should have the same chance at success as they had. Quotas, however, struck a primal chord of fear among Jews, and the insistence by the black community that they needed compensatory programs with quotas drove a wedge between the two former allies.

Themselves long the victims of persecution, Jews understood better than many what it meant to be deprived of a job or an opportunity because of who they were. It is little wonder, then, that Jews had been among the strongest supporters of civil rights. As early as the Birmingham struggle in 1963, Charles Silberman, an editor at *Fortune*, urged American Jews to recognize that something needed to be done to help Negroes overcome the continuing effects of

Rabbis Maurice Eisendrath and Abraham Joshua Heschel march with the Reverend Martin Luther King Jr. in February 1968 to protest the Vietnam War.

decades of discrimination. Nathan Margold had devised the plan that the NAACP had used to launch its attack on "separate but equal," while Jack Greenberg had been Thurgood Marshall's right-hand man and then his successor at the Legal Defense Fund. Herbert Hill, another Jew, had been the labor director at the NAACP for decades. Groups like the American Jewish Congress and the Anti-defamation League (ADL) were longtime civil rights allies, and prominent rabbis marched with Martin Luther King Jr. in Selma and elsewhere. As late as 1974, representatives of nine national Jewish bodies and ninety-seven local community relations groups announced that they would work with African American and Chicano groups in affirmative action plans that advanced educational and employment opportunities for minorities. But, many Jews insisted, they would oppose any form of reverse discrimination, and Jewish community leaders made clear their opposition to quotas.

IN AUGUST 1972, Philip Hoffman, the president of the American Jewish Committee, sent a letter to the two presidential candidates, Richard Nixon and George McGovern, calling on them to "reject

categorically the use of quotas and proportional representation."
Both men denounced quotas, and Nixon vowed not to tolerate them.
When some civil rights advocates criticized Hoffman, he declared
that his organization opposed any form of quotas in employment
and other facets of American life and denounced critics who said that
this meant the committee was "pulling back" on its support of civil
rights. The committee still endorsed civil rights and even affirmative action that provided greater opportunity for minorities—but
not quotas.

The Commission on Social Policy of the Synagogue Council of
America, an umbrella group of Reform, Conservative, and Orthodox Jewish congregations, urged support of affirmative action policies that increased opportunities but opposed any and all quotas.
Although Orthodox Jews tended to be less involved in social policy
matters than their Reform or Conservative brethren, even they spoke
out. Rabbi Louis Bernstein, president of the Orthodox Rabbinical
Council of America, wanted to open the gates of opportunity as wide
as possible, but the criterion for going through those gates should
be merit.

A loose coalition of business leaders, conservative Republicans,
and southern Democrats had for many years criticized government
efforts to ensure equality for minorities, especially African Americans. This time, however, the criticism came from a sector that had
long suffered discrimination itself and had advocated civil rights for
all. Never had charges of "reverse discrimination" warranted such
attention. Patricia Roberts Harris, an African American Democratic
Party activist, noted that Jewish intellectuals had long led the fight
for progressive change, and when "this group appears to have deserted
the cause of remediation for the black community . . . it is very serious." It sends a signal that this is no longer an issue that politicians
have to worry about.

The overt support given to the civil rights movement, however,
masked long-term tensions between the two groups at the local level.
In New York City, home of the largest concentrations of Jews and
blacks in the country, African Americans daily encountered Jews
as employers, merchants, landlords, teachers, school administrators,
and social workers. In the 1960s, despite the passage of the 1964
and 1965 laws, within the black community one found a growing
distrust of liberals, and Jews, "perhaps more than any other groups,
were identified as liberals in the white community." A study done

in the 1960s found that African Americans believed that, faced with black neighbors, "Jews act, in the main, like other whites." Despite the efforts of the major Jewish organizations—which all backed civil rights—both African Americans and Jews found a great gulf between the words of the leaders and the actions of the rank and file. A 2006 study of black-Jewish relations found the so-called golden age to have been a fairly thin veneer—focused primarily on ending racial discrimination—that covered serious ongoing tensions between the two.

Several events in the 1960s only exacerbated relations between the two groups. While American Jews rallied to Israel in the 1967 war, a number of black activists became radicalized and linked racial injustice in the United States to neocolonialism in the Third World and Israeli treatment of Palestinians. Moreover, they did so in blatantly anti-Semitic terms. Then came Ocean Hill–Brownsville. In the mid-1960s, of some eight hundred school principals in New York, only one was black; of the twelve hundred top administrative positions, one could find only four African Americans. In both these areas, Jews—who had begun to pour into the system in the 1930s—occupied many of the positions. In an experiment of community control, African Americans took over the Ocean Hill–Brownsville schools in Brooklyn and had numerous white teachers transferred out, leading the overwhelmingly Jewish United Federation of Teachers, headed by Albert Shanker, to strike citywide. While one could find anti-Semitic remarks on one side and antiblack slurs on the other, both Jewish and black leaders recognized that the real issue involved African American aspirations for an equal place at the table of economic opportunity. Jews had used the school system to get out of their ghettos; now blacks wanted to do the same thing.

Commentary magazine, an influential journal sponsored by the American Jewish Committee, was then in the process of abandoning its liberal roots and becoming quite conservative; the magazine became one of the chief critics of any affirmative action plan utilizing quotas. Paul Seabury, a noted political scientist, used the journal pages to praise merit, which he claimed had always been—and in fact should remain—the one criterion used to judge applicants for educational or employment opportunities. Seabury argued that what had made America great had been the belief that individuals succeeded because of ability and accomplishment and not because of status or preferment. He conceded that merit had not been a blanket rule for getting ahead but that it had proven a far better indicator of achievement than anything else. Affirmative action, especially the version that imposed quotas, not only ignored the long tradition of merit but in fact destroyed it.

That this happened, and was not just a case of crying wolf, could be seen in actions taken by the San Francisco School Board in March 1971 to eliminate dozens of administrative positions. While supposedly only 71 jobs were involved, for technical reasons 125 administrators received notice that they were in line for "deselection." The board formally established criteria for deselection, including "the racial and ethnic needs" of students, "special sensitivity to unique problems," competence, experience, and previous service. While the last three categories proved uncontroversial, the first two, without further definition, could mean anything. Then, following HEW guidelines, the board used nine categories in making its determination: Negro/Black, Chinese, Japanese, Korean, American Indian, Filipino, Other Nonwhite, Spanish-Speaking/Spanish Surname, and Other White. A state hearing officer declared that strict seniority would be followed for those classified as "Other White," but everyone in the other eight categories would be exempt from deselection. All 125 administrators put on notice fell into the category of "Other White."

The deselected administrators hired an attorney, and at a hearing their lawyer asked a representative of the school superintendent why these groups had been chosen. He answered that the categories, aside from "Other White," had all suffered discrimination and persecution in the past. Following is part of the exchange between the lawyer, asking the questions, and the superintendent's representative:

Q: Do you know that Armenians, as well as being a minority ethnic group, have had a history of persecution and disadvantage?

A: No, I never studied that.

Q: Did you ever hear of the persecution of the Armenians by the Turks?

A: Not as I recall.

Q: If the [demoted Armenian] respondent in this case says: "I am an Armenian and I want to be treated as a separate minority," what would you do with his case?

A: I would judge him to be "white" and put him in "white" because there is no specific Armenian classification. . . .

Q: Would you consider that the Jewish people were an ethnic group?

A: Yes.

Q: Do you believe there is a history of persecution and disadvantage which the Jewish people have had?

A: I have some remote knowledge of this.

Q: Now suppose one of the respondents in this case came to you and said: I am a member of an ethnic minority, one of the Jewish people, and I believe that by reason of our historical disadvantage that we would like to be treated as a separate ethnic group, what would your reply be?

A: That we have no category for you as a Jew.

In the face of intense opposition, the school board backed down and none of the 125 persons lost their jobs. Then the board tried a new ploy, proposing a plan whereby no more than 20 percent of Other Whites would be hired for or promoted to administrative positions in the first year, no more than 10 percent in the second year, and none in the following years until ethnic and racial proportions among administrators equaled that of the school population. The plan kicked up even more of a ruckus, because it not only completely ignored experience and merit but seemed based only on the ethnic or racial traits of the applicant. It said that it did not matter how good or bad an applicant was, if he was black or she was Japanese, that is all that mattered.

Six years later, the Labor Department issued a ruling that companies with government contracts had to do a survey of their employees to determine how many were American Indian, Aleut, Asian or Pacific Islander, Black not of Hispanic origin, and Hispanic. As *The Jewish Advocate* irately noted, "The punch line is that the Labor Department's definition of a minority excludes the Jewish community and other white minority groups in this country." The conservative columnist Kevin Phillips expanded on this, charging that not only would Poles, Italians, Greeks, and others be blocked out but the federal policy meant, "in essence, that blacks, Indians and Hispanics will get the gravy while white ethnics get the beans."

If anyone thought that white ethnic groups had it made, Phillips pointed to a recent study of 106 major corporations or financial institutions headquartered in Chicago. A hundred and two had no Polish directors and 97 had no Polish officers, even though Polish

Americans made up one-fifth of the city's population. A similar story held for Italian Americans, who held no directorships in 84 corporations and no officer positions in 75. For Phillips the lesson was clear: affirmative action meant reverse discrimination, and not only against Jews but against all white ethnics.

WHY DO JEWS SO FIERCELY oppose quotas? The answer lies in their history, when they were subject to the *numerus clausus,* both officially in Europe and unofficially in the United States. Starting in the nineteenth century, as the emancipation movement freed European Jews to pursue lives outside the ghetto, many countries put quotas on how many Jews could attend a university, hold a government job, or even live in a certain area. The *numerus clausus* (which means "closed number") weighed down most heavily in eastern Europe and Russia, and later in the Soviet Union. Its harshness led many young Jews to leave home and migrate either to the United States or to Palestine. In the United States, the quota system never enjoyed official status, but many of the Ivy League schools and the better medical, dental, and law schools all put a surreptitious cap on the number of Jews that would be admitted. For example, the number of Jews in Columbia University's medical school dropped from 47 percent in 1920 to 8 percent in 1940. By 1945, three in four gentiles who applied to medical schools got in, against only one in thirteen Jews. The turning point came in 1946 when Rabbi Stephen S. Wise mounted an attack on Columbia University for practicing unofficial discrimination against Jews, and petitioned the city council to withdraw Columbia's tax exemption. The school had no choice but to announce that it would no longer take religion into account in its admissions policy.

It is no wonder, then, that a program of "hard" affirmative action, especially if it had even a hint of a quota, would upset Jews. The United States had always been the *goldenah medinah,* the golden land of religious freedom and opportunity, and Jews had succeeded here well beyond what their numbers would suggest. In 1970, as the EEOC began ramping up its quota protocols, Jewish family income was 173 percent of the average American income. In 1982, Jews obtained undergraduate degrees at nearly twice the rate of the general American population. So when the EEOC began pushing a program of hard affirmative action, every single national Jewish organization protested. The brunt of the attack, however, came from a group labeled neoconservatives, or neocons. They are probably best remembered for their hawkish foreign policy stance during the George W. Bush years, but their first battle involved affirmative action. Among this group could be found the noted philosopher Sidney Hook; the sociologist Nathan Glazer; Norman Podhoretz, the editor of *Commentary;* Irving Kristol, an editor at Basic Books; Paul Seabury, a political scientist; and Daniel Patrick Moynihan, who had been an academic and a presidential adviser and would later be a senator from New York. Jews made up most of the early neocon group, with some important exceptions, such as Moynihan and Seabury, and one could find their attacks on quotas in the pages of *Commentary* and a new journal, *The Public Interest.*

Even before the EEOC ignored Title VII and began promoting quota plans, the neocons saw affirmative action in any form other than outreach as a threat to the liberal values that had sustained American Jewry. In March 1964, *Commentary* ran a forum called "Liberalism and the Negro." As moderator, Podhoretz announced that "American liberals are by now divided into two schools of thought." One believed in simply removing barriers to individual social and economic mobility, and the other treated African Americans as a group whose plight would be solved by a domestic Marshall Plan and preferential treatment in hiring. The neocons could only accept the first option, because they believed individual opportunity to be the essence of liberalism.

Daniel Patrick Moynihan sounded the most powerful alarm when he warned that if "ethnic quotas are to be imposed on American universities, Jews will be almost driven out." Others picked up on this theme, notably Milton Himmelfarb, Earl Raab, and Paul Seabury. Podhoretz warned against the reinstitution of discriminatory measures targeting Jews and raised the specter of a new anti-Semitism by which Jews must inevitably be harmed. For Podhoretz and others, affirmative action appeared a zero-sum game: if one group derived any advantage, then another group must lose by a corresponding amount. In assessing affirmative action, he bluntly declared, one had to ask, "Is it good for the Jews?"

The strongest attack came in a 1975 book by Nathan Glazer, tellingly titled *Affirmative Discrimination.* In it, he attacked the EEOC and its blatant—and he termed illegal—mandate of quotas. The proper public policy in all areas—employment, education, and housing—should not be quotas or some approximation of them but rather equal opportunity for individuals as individuals. The concept of statistical parity ran contrary to the American concern with individual claims to justice and equity. Glazer went out of his way to emphasize that he did not in any way condone discrimination or believe that antidiscrimination laws should not be enforced. He objected strongly, however, to how the EEOC had ignored clear words that forbade taking race, ethnicity, or gender into account and then required businesses and universities to do just that.

JEWISH OPPOSITION TO affirmative action went far beyond a critique by intellectuals. In his study of the mostly middle-class Canarsie section of Brooklyn with its mixed ethnic population, Jonathan Rieder found that Jews opposed affirmative action as strongly as did their Italian neighbors. Area residents viewed concepts like compensation and affirmative action as "fancy versions of robbery," with the middle class as the victims. A self-described former liberal told Rieder,

> I liked John Kennedy, and I liked the early civil rights movement. I was a liberal. I used to fight for the *schvartzes'* rights. I thought, all people have a right to public accommodations, to jobs according to ability. But, if my kid has a ninety-nine average, why should he be deprived? He has one life to lead. What's fair is fair. The *schvartzes* want to get ahead. They *should* get ahead. But not on my kid's back. Blacks are taking advantage.

Others had similar views. They, like the neocons, saw affirmative action as a zero-sum game, and any program that benefited blacks or Hispanics inevitably came at a cost to them. Many of the people Rieder interviewed said that they had once been liberal and had been supporters of civil rights. It pained them because they felt torn between a commitment to justice for all peoples, and especially for African Americans, and their opposition to affirmative action as a means of redress.

The Jews and Italians of Canarsie believed they had pulled themselves up by hard work and that society had equitably rewarded those who had brains and integrity and perseverance with success. That was the American way. Quotas, open enrollments, rioting, busing, and even demands for reparations violated a standard of justice that they and their immigrant parents had seen as the promise of America. Affirmative action seemed to bump blacks and Hispanics ahead of white groups. Sure, blacks had been slaves, but the Italians and the Jews had also suffered greatly and, at least as they saw it, they had made it on their own.

JUST AS THE PUBLIC SCHOOL systems had been an avenue of opportunity for Jews in the 1930s, the professions and academia provided that chance in the 1950s and 1960s. According to figures compiled by the Anti-defamation League, 85 percent of college-age Jews enrolled in colleges, and 47 percent of them went on to graduate or professional school. Despite the quotas imposed by the Ivy League and other schools from the 1920s until after the end of World War II, by 1975 Jews made up 10 percent of all college faculty members, and 20 percent of those teaching at elite universities, and all this when Jews made up no more than 3 percent of the total population. Unlike the corporate world, where Jews remained unwelcome for many years, the university and the professions cherished merit; an objective evaluation of achievement would reward learning and hard work. So when the neocons began warning that a quota-driven affirmative action would have a particularly onerous effect on Jewish faculty, it resonated across the academic landscape, especially among some older professors such as Sidney Hook, who had grown up in the quota era.

As affirmative action goals spread in blue-collar and some white-collar areas in the late 1960s and early 1970s, most of the Jewish agencies remained supportive; after all, their members would be minimally affected. Even when talk first started about such goals in higher education, some Jews remained sympathetic. In the early to mid-1970s, however, pushed by African American and female activists demanding faculty role models, the Ivy League and other top universities, as well as the more prestigious law, medical, and graduate schools, began aggressively recruiting minorities. The Jewish agencies started worrying. While the *DeFunis* case did not warrant a great deal of attention in legal circles, it raised a red flag among the Jewish defense organizations.

Had the recruitment been based on merit—had it been a soft affirmative action—the Jewish community groups could not have complained. They believed in merit, and if students of color had been admitted solely on the same objective criteria applied to majority applicants, that could have been accepted. After all, if a black student had a higher GPA or had scored higher on the College Boards than a Jewish applicant, that would have been in the tradition of merit that Jews esteemed. But they objected to the "preferential treatment" given to minorities. Benjamin Epstein of the Anti-defamation League later interpreted the "strong anti-black backlash" as a basic reflex of self-preservation. "Jews have said, 'Let's make sure that blacks get equal treatment, but not at our expense.'"

The Jewish organizations watched carefully but erupted in protest when HEW demanded that colleges and universities open their books to show what they were doing to hire minorities and women as faculty. This led to the Hoffman letter to Nixon and McGovern, with both candidates assuring the American Jewish Committee president that they did not favor quotas. "We cooked up a real storm," said Hyman Bookbinder, the committee representative in Washington. The results, he said a few weeks later, went "way beyond our wildest expectations, the issue of de facto 'quotaism' is being not only discussed but being tackled. Literally scores of top government officials are involved in evaluating, modifying, and monitoring the various programs. . . . We have started a full-fledged national discussion of the subject," one that, he believed, would create a new climate.

How much government officials scurried around is questionable. After all, the Philadelphia Plan stayed in place, and the EEOC did not retreat from pushing its version of a hard affirmative action, complete with goals and timetables. But the neocons certainly ramped up their attacks. Only plans that opened doors of opportunity on a color-blind and gender-blind basis met the historic criteria of the liberal tradition. Norman Podhoretz, Sidney Hook, Nathan Glazer, and others hammered continuously on the theme that true civil rights had been and remained committed to a color-blind law and governmental policy. Race-conscious programs that supposedly strove for equality and justice through quotas betrayed not only the liberal tradition but the great work of Martin Luther King Jr. and the civil rights movement.

The sociologist Daniel Bell condemned the drive for an "equality of results" as a destructive attack on the necessary "meritocracy" of postindustrial society. "What is at stake today," he wrote, "is the redefinition of equality." Paul Seabury attacked HEW and the EEOC as a group of mid-range bureaucrats trying to increase their power. Nathan Glazer believed that "Jews found that their shift against the positions of the major Afro-American civil rights organizations not only did not do violence to their principles—it defended their principles." By this he meant that Jews had long supported equal opportunity and color-blind merit and had parted company with African Americans when the latter had begun pushing for compensatory treatment. For Carl Cohen, racial preferences were simply "illegal and immoral."

The writings are replete with high-sounding tributes to justice and equal opportunity for all. What is absent is any sense that the black experience in America over more than three centuries had been so horrific that except for a very few the gates of opportunity could not be opened. Blacks who attended inferior schools could not compete fairly with the children of the white middle class who attended far better schools designed to help them get into college. While some of the traditionally black colleges provided a good education, their graduates measured up poorly against those from better universities. In business, blacks faced barriers as well. For African Americans, talk of equal access to opportunity sounded hollow, because they knew they did not have the keys to open those doors by themselves. Moreover, what the neocons described as *the* civil rights tradition had really been one of many traditions, the one that white people had always found easiest to support. But from the time of W. E. B. Du Bois and on, there had been multiple traditions of protest, of trying to secure a meaningful equality. As the sociologist Stephen Steinberg noted, the Jewish experience differed markedly not only from black Americans' but from most other immigrant groups' as well. Jews arrived in America as whites of European descent with urban experience and a level of education unusual in an era of mass industrialization. For American Jews, enforcement of antidiscrimination laws to ensure individual opportunity had proven more than enough.

The neocons and their organizational allies tried to pull the Jewish community to the right and to adopt a narrower view of equality and opportunity. On the left, however, another group of liberals read the latest developments far differently. The American Civil Liberties Union, long one of the country's leading voices of defense for civil rights and liberties, had a disproportionate number of Jews among its members and on its board. The ACLU supported the efforts of HEW and the EEOC, as well as hard affirmative action, and rejected the notion of reverse discrimination. Whites and males adversely affected by affirmative action plans "are deprived not of their rights, but of their expectations, expectations grounded in discriminatory practice."

Moreover, and to its credit, the ACLU practiced what it preached and, although exempt from any statutory commands, launched its own affirmative action plan, one as rigorous as if not more so than that pushed by HEW. According to one member of the national board, the ACLU did it "by the numbers," deliberately getting more minorities, women, and gays on the board and as officers and recruiting them for staff; within a few years, the numerical goals had been achieved. The ACLU, it should be noted, filed amicus briefs in every affirmative action case that came before the Supreme Court, always defending the plans.

THROUGHOUT THE 1970s, the neocons and the Jewish agencies intellectually and politically allied with them developed a three-pronged attack on hard affirmative action: a commitment to equal opportunity and due process to protect individual rights; upholding merit and standards of excellence; and concern that affirmative action would affect Jews adversely. While the first two points could be found in other, non-Jewish opponents of affirmative action, all three, and especially the last, resonated strongly within the Jewish community.

Jewish agencies agreed with and indeed supported equal opportunity not only for African Americans but for all groups and believed everything should be done to prepare minorities to get ahead. This progress, however, could not be achieved on the backs of others. If blacks or women received preferential treatment in a zero-sum game, then nonminorities and males would be held back, deprived of opportunities they should have been allowed to pursue. Advocates of affirmative action admitted that there might be problems for some whites, but as one liberal Catholic leader put it, "it is self-deluding to advocate the promotion of civil rights for Americans who have been economically exploited by our society, without expecting some consequences to that society."

Jews had first benefited from a merit system in the late nineteenth century when thousands of prior patronage jobs in the federal government came under the aegis of the civil service system. "The merit concept," according to the ADL's Benjamin Epstein, "was the dream that made America so meaningful to the underprivileged Jew when he came to this country." That dream, Paul Seabury explained, reflected the belief that people would advance "according to ability and accomplishment, rather than according to status, preferment, or chance." Merit, and only merit, should govern, and quotas to benefit blacks would undermine years of effort by Jews to escape the quota system.

In the 1970s, some critics claimed, one could already see the detrimental effects of abandoning merit—the elevation of allegedly less competent African Americans through preferential treatment. This argument would be repeated constantly during the long fight over affirmative action and is still heard today. Much of the claim is anecdotal, and there is very little hard evidence to prove that a minority hire almost always took place at the expense of a better-qualified white person. What is known is that many institutions, in their rush to amend centuries of discrimination, undoubtedly made some weak appointments. Moreover, because there were so few African Americans with doctorates, a fierce competition for them led universities seeking black scholars to often ignore the credentials of any nonminority candidate. The law of supply and demand worked in favor of blacks and inevitably caused resentment among whites. While a few Jewish liberals declared themselves willing to have society and the Jewish community pay this price, most did not.

The third prong reflected an age-old fear peculiar to the Jewish community, that they would be the ones to suffer from affirmative action, that their children would be deprived of places in colleges and professional schools, denied employment opportunities, and faced with discrimination in other areas of American life. At the 1972 convention of the American Jewish Committee, members agreed that Jewish agencies had to defend "Jewish interests within the broader context of defending the democratic process."

THE MALE CHAUVINISM so rampant in business and the universities had its reflection in the Jewish agencies—all headed by men. While they and the neocons lauded merit, they ignored the blatant discrimination faced by women—the rigged searches and the totally nonprofessional criteria, such as the old boy network, used to fill faculty positions. Nancy MacLean has documented the abysmal record of the leading Jewish agencies in responding to discrimination against women. Nearly all the major positions, such as chairman or executive director, were filled by men who shared the general sexist attitudes common in that era. A Detroit woman, after reading the Hoffman letter and hearing so much praise about it, pointed out that the record of Jewish agencies in recognizing female talent was "dismal." Even supposedly "enlightened groups like the American

Jewish Committee are extremely male-oriented." Just as the nation began to wake up to the growing feminist movement, women staffers complained that at committee meetings "women still play hostess and pour tea," and they would not even have this role without their husbands, fathers, or financial position. When women on the staff complained about sexist discrimination, they usually received "condescending jokes."

Bertram Gold, the longtime director of the American Jewish Committee, believed that Jewish agencies did not have to do anything for white women and distinguished "affirmative action for [white] women from affirmative action for minorities," because "a qualified female labor force exists to take advantage of the removal of discrimination" in a way that was not true of minority populations. Being white meant access to schools and resources denied to most children of color, and he claimed that white women filed more complaints about faculty hiring than members of all minority groups put together.

The Hoffman letter aroused the anger of many Jewish feminists.

Bella Abzug represented congressional districts in New York from 1971 to 1977. She had earlier suffered discrimination because of her gender and became one of the strongest voices in the fight for women's equality.

Among the most furious was Bella Abzug, who had won election to Congress in 1970 as the first Jewish female member of the House of Representatives. Before her election, Abzug had been active in the liberal civil rights coalition, the same alignment now condemned by the neocons. She attacked both the neocons and the Jewish agency leaders for ignoring the discrimination against women for so many years. "I would like to remind my brothers that in attacking affirmative action programs in higher education as producing reverse discrimination against Jews, they are talking about and speaking for Jewish *men,* not for Jewish women." Abzug knew of what she spoke, having been denied admission to the Harvard Law School for no other grounds than her sex.

IT WOULD BE GIVING too much credit to the Hoffman letter and the alleged power of the Jewish agencies to think that they and they alone caused HEW's retreat. By 1972, the Nixon administration had, despite the Philadelphia Plan, committed itself to the so-called southern strategy, designed to lure southern conservatives into the Republican Party. When pushed, HEW and the EEOC could come down hard, especially on Ivy League schools like Harvard and Columbia, and southern conservatives applauded when these alleged bastions of liberalism proved to be bastions of discrimination as well.

Black activists felt betrayed. Of all white groups, organized American Jewry had been their strongest ally. Because of their own history of persecution, Jews owned a certain moral authority on civil rights; as Eleanor Holmes Norton put it, "Jews were far and away the best whites." The vehemence of the anger in the black community took many Jews by surprise. African Americans saw the merit system lauded by the neocons as just another way to keep blacks out of jobs and out of the universities. The civil rights attorney Theodore Shaw argued that supposedly objective measures of merit reflected something other than actual ability; they reinforced the benefits of privilege, a "self-reifying process of unnatural selection that becomes enshrined as 'merit.'" Vernon Jordan spoke, he claimed, "with the bluntness of a true friend" in addressing Jewish audiences, and he told them that the issue that most divided the two communities was affirmative action. As for the argument that merit should be the determining factor in hiring and education, Jordan denied that a true merit system existed. An NAACP field director in Mississippi charged the American Jewish Committee with being out of touch with the reality of the black experience in the labor market. He kept running into white employers who claimed they would employ blacks if only they could find qualified workers. "They use the very system you endorse (merit) to keep Blacks from certain positions."

AS THE DECADE WORE ON, relations between the black and the Jewish communities seemed to disintegrate even further. In 1977, President Jimmy Carter appointed the civil rights activist Andrew Young ambassador to the United Nations, the first African American to hold that position. In July 1979, Young learned that the United Nations Division for Palestinian Rights would soon issue a report calling for the creation of a Palestinian state. Young wanted to delay the report because the Carter administration had too many other issues on its plate that it had to deal with. Young met with the representatives of several Arab countries to convince them that the report should be delayed, and they agreed on condition that the Palestine Liberation Organization (PLO) would also consent.

Andrew Young, U.S. ambassador to the United Nations in 1977, whose meeting with representatives of the Palestine Liberation Organization triggered an angry backlash in the American Jewish community and forced Young to resign.

On 20 July, Young secretly met with Zehdi Labib Terzi, the UN representative of the PLO, at the apartment of the Kuwaiti ambassador. Three weeks later, news of this meeting became public when Mossad, the Israeli intelligence agency, leaked a transcript of the conversation between Young and Terzi. The response among American Jewish groups could only be described as apoplectic, because the United States had repeatedly promised that it would not meet with the PLO until that organization recognized Israel's right to exist.

Jimmy Carter immediately announced that he had no complicity in what he termed the "Andy Young affair" and asked for Young's resignation. Young soon after appeared on several television shows, declared that he was not sorry for anything he had done, and called Israel "stubborn and intransigent." Many in the black community blamed Young's firing on the Jewish lobby for Israel.

Rabbi Arthur Hertzberg of Englewood, New Jersey, noted that Young's firing had precipitated conflict between Jews and blacks but said the real cause of the tension would be found not in debates over foreign policy but in affirmative action. In the 1950s and 1960s, American Jewish agencies had "no significant domestic agenda involving [Jewish] self-interest" but spent their energies on the civil rights movement. During the six years that he served as president of the American Jewish Congress, Hertzberg claimed that he had tried his best to defuse this issue by proposing forms of affirmative action that did not involve quotas. Forget about Andy Young and the PLO, he urged, because at some point the United States and Israel would have to deal with the Palestinians directly. Blacks and Jews needed to meet—and now—to work out an agreement on affirmative action. Hertzberg, almost alone among American Jewish leaders, supported affirmative action.

The comments of Professor Seymour Siegel of the Jewish Theological Seminary more accurately reflected community sentiment at the time. Siegel declared that no difference existed between so-called numerical goals and quotas. While the "supreme aim" of the civil rights movement in the 1960s had been to remove race as a factor, advocates of affirmative action "have reintroduced what we have been trying so long to eliminate—race as a factor—all in the name of eliminating racism." Siegel went on to argue that affirmative action lowered the self-esteem of those it supposedly helped, debased institutions of higher learning, and fostered not love and understanding but hatred and jealousy among groups. Moreover, arguments for affirmative action rested on a great fallacy, that all members of a minority have been equally victimized. "The son of a judge who is black surely is less disadvantaged than the son of a survivor of a Nazi concentration camp."

In late 1979, the editors of *Commentary* sent out a statement and a series of questions to "a group of American Jews of varying political views." The statement and questions read as follows:

> For many years now, it has been taken for granted by most American Jews that their own interests coincided with and could best be represented through the standard liberal agenda. But this axiom might seem to have been called into question by certain recent developments—the widespread support among liberals for quotas, the diminishing enthusiasm among liberals for Israel, the growing sympathy of liberals for the PLO and the paucity of liberal protest against the anti-Semitism that surfaced in the wake of Andrew Young's resignation.
>
> How seriously have these developments affected your own thinking as a Jew about liberalism? Do they warrant a reconsideration by the Jewish community in general of its traditional commitment to liberalism? Do you expect such a reconsideration to take place? If so, is it likely to result in a significant movement away from the Democratic Party in 1980?

Fifty-two respondents replied, and while they addressed all of the issues, the one that concerns us here is the first charge, that liberals had shown widespread support for quotas. This, of course, refers to civil rights as part of the "standard liberal agenda" that Jews had supported in the previous quarter century. The essays that the men and women had sent in appeared in alphabetical order, starting with Morris B. Abram, a lawyer with impeccable credentials not only as a strong supporter of civil rights but also as part of the American Jewish elite—with stints as president of the American Jewish Committee and Brandeis University, as well as U.S. representative to the United Nations Commission on Human Rights. His answer reflects what many of the others wrote.

Abram began by noting his long involvement in the civil rights movement, including his spearheading the drive to overturn the racially organized county-unit system in Georgia, which led the Supreme Court to condemn the plan as unconstitutional. The difference between liberals and conservatives, he explained, is that the former believed in equality and freedom, and the latter in status and rank. Too often, the opportunity for certain groups could be thwarted by prejudice in the marketplace and inferior education, so liberals fought for laws against discrimination. Liberals and Jews both proved sensitive to the needs of those victimized by prejudice and worked to eliminate such barriers. "Equality before the law, neutrality as to ethnicity, religion, or sex, were the proper goals of the advocates of equal opportunity." In the 1960s, Abram believed both civil rights activists and the liberal community—including most Jews—agreed on this.

He and others had supported the early "soft" affirmative action, which he saw as opening the doors to employment and education for those who had previously been excluded. Soon after, Abram claimed, the meaning changed to denote racial preferences, "first as relatively mild and unenforced goals and timetables, hardly something to be opposed by optimists, of whom liberals have their share." But this "mild" form soon morphed into demands by black activists for specific goals imposed and enforced by the federal government. This is nothing less, Abram charged, "than a demand that government should classify and treat Americans on a basis which liberals had denounced for one hundred years as contemptible and invidious. This total reversal of form was described as liberalism, and those who resisted were branded as conservatives, neoconservatives, or reactionaries."

Abram branded this view as "absurd, unfair, and counterproductive." Moreover, he objected to having the term "liberal" hijacked and used to describe positions that denied much for which liberals had fought. He still believed in the older notions of equality and freedom and could only hope that the present situation represented a temporary detour.

This notion that "what is now called liberalism" no longer reflected what so many people had believed in for so many years soon spread, especially among the neocons. Jews had become liberals, as another writer put it, not out of guilt but because liberalism "embraced and embodied the political values which protected and advanced Jewish principles and interests." The Jews had not abandoned liberalism; it had abandoned them and their beliefs.

Many of the respondents affirmed their beliefs in what they had supposed had been liberalism, but as Rabbi Eugene Borowitz explained, he had been "chastened in my hopes that government can produce greater social justice. People are not as moral or as rational as I once believed." Nonetheless, for all these disappointments, he remained committed to classic liberal beliefs. So, too, did Arthur A. Cohen, who sadly noted that "I gave up thinking of myself as a liberal" but could not bring himself to identify as a conservative.

Some of the people, it should be noted, declared that they had never thought of themselves as liberal or had moved over to the conservative side years earlier. As the author Midge Decter noted, when so-called liberalism (which she identified as the far-left wing of the Democratic Party) not only changed but did a 180-degree turn, she and many others could no longer identify with what liberalism had become. And there were others, like Leonard Fein, the editor of the Jewish bimonthly *Moment,* who claimed they did not recognize the new developments in the survey statement. He did not believe that so many liberals endorsed quotas or that they supported the PLO and had abandoned Israel. If Jewish liberals were in crisis, it was because liberalism itself was in crisis, trying to come to terms with many changes in society. The writer Nat Hentoff echoed this in some way, asking where Jews should go if they left the liberal fold—to a Republican Party headed by such exemplary figures as John Connally, Ronald Reagan, George H. W. Bush, and Howard Baker?

In none of the essays can one find the sense that all is well, that nothing needs to be done, or that traditional liberalism has remained unchanged. If the editors wanted a broad and varied portrait of American Jewish attitudes, the intellectuals they invited certainly gave it to them. Many, in fact most, still believed in classic ideas of freedom and equality and condemned not affirmative action itself but only the form in which it became a question of numbers and quotas. Even as HEW and the EEOC pushed harder and harder to implement numerical goals, they drove not just Jews but many others—liberals and conservatives—into opposition to affirmative action.

RELATIONS BETWEEN THE TWO communities never regained what both sides had seen as their former closeness. While moderates on both sides struggled to find a common ground, more often than not the conversation foundered on bitter words. Writing in 1995, Glenn Loury declared that "relations between American blacks and Jews are clearly in deep trouble" and there would be no "restoration of the golden age of black-Jewish cooperation." Loury listed issues that divided them, the first of which was that Jews had a great investment in the idea of America as a meritocratic, open society in which rewards went to those who prepare and apply themselves. Blacks, on the other hand, believe that America is a closed society in which people of color, whatever their individual merit, suffer systematic disadvantage in the competition for economic, educational, and social benefits. These two views, he believed, "are fundamentally and irreconcilably in conflict," and two decades of efforts by moderates on both sides had failed to relieve the tension. In the 1970s, the 1990s, and even today, the two groups continue to divide over this tension, which is at the heart of affirmative action.

CHAPTER 10

WOMEN AND AFFIRMATIVE ACTION

The paramount destiny and mission of a woman are to fulfill the noble and benign offices of wife and mother. This is the law of the Creator.

—JUSTICE JOSEPH BRADLEY

No longer do we have to be satisfied with philosophical discussion. . . . Quite simply, in an employment situation, women can no longer be considered one of the better cheaper acts.

—ETHEL BENT WALSH OF THE EEOC

It is true, of course, that the position of women in America has improved markedly in recent decades. Nevertheless, it can hardly be doubted that, in particular because of the high visibility of the sex characteristic, women still face pervasive, although at times more subtle, discrimination in our educational institutions, in the job market and, perhaps most conspicuously, in the political arena.

—JUSTICE WILLIAM J. BRENNAN JR.

In 1993, the New York City Fire Department issued a curious order, namely that no pictures could be taken of Brenda Berkman, a fifteen-year veteran of the force, on or off duty, inside or outside a firehouse. This proved to be one last gasp in the protest against women in what had been an all-male preserve for the department's 117-year history.

The fight had started much earlier. In 1971, Secretary of Labor James D. Hodgson issued an order calling on all federal contractors to take affirmative action to eliminate sex discrimination. That order had little effect, and in 1977 the Office of Federal Contract Compliance announced that it planned "to get tough" with building and construction contractors who failed to seek out and train women for work on everything from steel girders to bricklaying. According to Weldon Rougeau, the head of the office, parents should start talking to their daughters about going into blue-collar work instead of traditional female roles such as housekeeper, nurse, or stenographer. New York City, already under attack for its failure to give women access to traditional male jobs, announced that it would allow women to take the Firefighter Exam. But when over four hundred women passed the written portion, the city changed the standards on the physical ability test to make it practically impossible for women to meet the criteria. It took five years and a class-action sex discrimination lawsuit until forty-two women passed new, court-supervised tests and training to qualify as the city's first female firefighters. That group included Brenda Berkman, who became founding president of the United Women Firefighters and a constant thorn in the side of fire department officials as well as the male union.

One might have expected skepticism as to whether women could do the job, and whether their lesser strength might prove a problem. But male firefighters responded bitterly, trying to drive the women out, sending hate mail and death threats, refusing to talk to the women for months on end, putting up obscene antifemale graffiti in the firehouses, and not only harassing the women in general but in one case actually resorting to rape. The women, despite repeated appeals to the city government as well as public demonstrations, got no help or even support except from one group—the Vulcan Society, the organization of black firefighters, who also had fought a long and bitter fight against discrimination in the fire department.

BETWEEN THE END OF Reconstruction in 1877 and passage of the Nineteenth Amendment in 1920 giving women the right to vote, women's rights activists differed on their goals. The single-issue suffragists aimed solely at obtaining the vote; "social feminists," while also calling for suffrage, worked to secure protective legislation for women in the workplace, such as maximum hours, minimum wages, and safety regulations. After 1920, feminist fervor subsided until awakened by the civil rights movement in the 1960s, marked by the publication of Betty Friedan's *Feminine Mystique* in 1963, the establishment of the National Organization for Women (NOW) in 1966, and the first issue of *Ms.* magazine in 1972.

For purposes of affirmative action, we can point to several events—the inclusion of gender in the Civil Rights Act of 1964, President Johnson extending his executive order on affirmative action to include women in 1967, and especially Title IX of the Education Amendments of 1972, which prohibited sex discrimination in any educational program receiving federal assistance in all public and private educational institutions. That same year, the Equal Employment Opportunity Act gave the EEOC court enforcement powers. Although the initial push by the EEOC focused on African Americans, it soon added women to the demands it made upon employers.

What affirmative action meant for women differed markedly from what it did for people of color. The debate on whether government policy should seek "equality of opportunity" rather than "equality of results" had most people, including African Americans, supporting the former and opposing the latter, which often meant numerical goals and quotas. Women wanted equality of opportunity as well, in that they sought access to jobs that had formerly been restricted to men, such as linemen for the telephone company. In this sense, women and minorities both wanted to have the opportunity to get jobs from which they had previously been excluded.

A significant difference, however, existed between women and African Americans. For blacks, when the EEOC talked about equality of results, it usually meant that if a local metropolitan area had a 37 percent minority population, then 37 percent of the employees of a company with fifteen or more workers should be minority. While African Americans wanted to be paid the same as their white co-workers, they mainly wanted the chance to get hired where they had previously been excluded. For women, most of the complaints they brought to the EEOC involved equality of pay and other benefits, such as seniority and retirement. They also brought suits, especially regarding colleges and universities, about gaining entry to the faculty; blue- and pink-collar women, like black men, wanted equality of results. Women also did not have to rely solely on Title VII of the 1964 Civil Rights Act; Congress had mandated equal pay for equal work during the Kennedy administration.

Today when we talk about discrimination, the bias against African Americans heads the list; despite the election of Barack Obama in 2008 and talk about a "post-racial" America, the evidence that racism is still strong could not be missed in Donald Trump's 2016 campaign and after. But we have also learned about other prejudices—against

Hispanics, Jews, the disabled, transgendered, and especially women. "Sexism" in the 1960s had as yet no meaning in public discourse. In some ways, Howard Smith's "sex" amendment to the 1964 Civil Rights Act stole a march on history, and although it passed, very few members of Congress paid much attention to it. During 1963 and 1964, the House and Senate held hundreds of hours of hearings and produced thousands of pages of testimony dealing with racial inequality; there was not a single committee hearing or report on gender inequality. Men of power in the government, in business, and in labor unions learned to take racism seriously, but not sexism.

So in 1964 the American public, when looking at Title VII, could be forgiven if they did not pay much attention to the gender provision, and some corporate executives saw it as a joke. When *The Wall Street Journal* asked business leaders how they felt about Title VII, nearly all agreed that racial prejudice had to cease. One airline personnel executive declared, "We're not worried about the racial discrimination ban—what's unnerving us is the section on sex. What are we going to do when a gal walks into our office, demands a job as an airline pilot and has the credentials to qualify? Or what will we do when some guy comes in and wants to be a stewardess?" Even the chair of the EEOC refused to take it seriously. At a news conference, a reporter asked Franklin Roosevelt Jr., "What about sex?" to which Roosevelt responded, "I'm all for it." Shortly thereafter *The New York Times* ran a parody on the supposed "bunny problem," when a male applied for a job as a Playboy Bunny or to clerk in a corset shop. "Bunny problem, indeed!" the *Times* despaired. "This is revolution, chaos. You can't even safely advertise for a wife anymore."

The *Times* soon had reason to regret its flippant and juvenile attempt at humor. In 1972, a caucus of women employees challenged the paper's commitment to fairness. The *Times* had once boasted in an advertisement that one of its women employees, a copy editor, had a "passion for facts." Eighty women working at the paper collected "facts" and gave them to that copy editor, Betsy Wade—a member of the caucus—who documented sex-based salary inequities, limitation of women to lower-paying jobs, and failure to promote women even after years of exemplary service. In addition, women were totally excluded from nonclassified advertising sales, management, and policy-making positions. The *Times* initially ignored the petition, so the women hired a lawyer, filed charges with the EEOC, and entered a class-action sex discrimination suit on behalf of the 550 women employed by the paper.

It took six years, but eventually the women won, and the *Times* settled out of court. It paid the women for past discrimination in salaries as well as their legal costs and adopted an affirmative action plan with numerical goals for jobs previously closed to them, from entry-level to management positions. "Considering where we were in 1972," said one member of the caucus, the settlement package was "the sun, the moon, and the stars." In June 2011, the *Times* named Jill Abramson the first female executive editor in the paper's 160-year history.

The EEOC tiptoed around the ban on sex discrimination as long as it could, and many felt that the addition of sex to Title VII had been meant to cripple the commission. The EEOC would be so inundated with complaints of gender discrimination that it would have neither time nor resources to deal with more serious problems faced by racial and ethnic minorities. One of the first commissioners, Aileen Clarke Hernandez, complained that "the message came through clearly that the Commission's priority was race discrimination, and apparently only as it related to Black *men.*"

Given the practically nonexistent guidance it had received from Congress, it is small wonder that during its early years the EEOC did little—and that in a cautious, sometimes bumbling manner—about gender discrimination. It suggested that the prevalent local culture should be taken into account, which in essence permitted relegating women to lower-paying jobs. The American Newspaper Publishers Association had no problem with the ban on racially seg-regated want ads but defended the necessity for sex-specific classified advertisements, claiming that both readers and advertisers preferred the traditional single-sex listings. Moreover, according to the association, Title VII had not given the EEOC power to ban sex-specific ads. The EEOC might have continued stumbling around the gender issue except that a new and very activist feminist movement had arisen whose leaders declared that both the Constitution and the Civil Rights Act were sex-blind as well as color-blind.

About this time, the EEOC commissioner, Richard Graham, approached Betty Friedan seeking her help. One reason, he explained, that the EEOC had not responded well to women's complaints was that there were no organized women's groups lobbying the commis-

Betty Friedan's book The Feminine Mystique
(1963) helped launch the modern women's move-
ment, and Friedan became one of the founders
and leaders of the National Organization for
Women. Here she is talking to reporters in 1967.

sion the way African American groups were so effectively doing. Graham, one of the Republican members of the EEOC, as well as Aileen
Hernandez, wanted a feminist equivalent of the NAACP to push
gender discrimination issues. Friedan also heard from a young lawyer
on the staff, Sonia Pressman, who spoke confidentially to Friedan for
fear of losing her job. One of the problems, according to Pressman,
was that the women who sat on the EEOC and its advisory panels
all represented middle- and upper-class women. None of them had a
grassroots base that could bring pressure on the agency.

Graham claimed he had gone to the League of Women Voters,
the American Association of University Women, and other women's
organizations headquartered in Washington, urging them to pressure the EEOC to enforce Title VII. Appalled at the suggestion, they
told him they were not "feminists." That June, representatives from
all the state status-of-women commissions gathered in Washington,
and, mad as could be at the EEOC and the administration, they
established the National Organization for Women, with Friedan as
founding president, and Graham and Hernandez as founding vice

presidents. (Hernandez resigned from the EEOC in frustration a few years later and succeeded Friedan as NOW president.) Graham had found what he needed, a grassroots organization that could push the EEOC to pay attention to gender discrimination.

THE "AWAKENING" OF THE EEOC to gender discrimination did not happen overnight, but growing pressure from NOW and other women's advocates, as well as the undeniable facts of their own reports, gradually moved the agency to act. At first, EEOC staff and commissioners assumed that women would have the same complaints as African Americans, but this myth evaporated once they looked at the numbers. The first-year report noted that 60 percent of the complaints the EEOC received were racial but nearly all the rest— 37 percent—involved sex discrimination. Moreover, the focus of the complaints varied enormously. The major single complaint of black petitioners involved hiring discrimination (37.3 percent), while women charged discrimination in employee benefits, such as wages, pensions, and medical coverage, followed by discriminatory seniority. Only 5.6 percent complained about hiring and firing.

Both women's groups and the EEOC ran into the problem of state protective legislation laws, dating back to the Progressive and New Deal eras, designed to protect women in the workplace. These included limits on how many hours a day or week a woman could work, mandatory rest periods, and exclusion from dangerous labor, to name a few. Unwilling to enter this minefield, the EEOC announced that it did not have the power to rewrite or annul state laws and that if women did not like these statutes, they should challenge them in federal courts.

Feminist groups jumped on the suggestion and found they could get media attention by legal challenges to state laws, many of them relics of the Victorian era. NOW and others attacked a Texas law barring women from dancing in tents, a Nebraska law keeping women off juries unless the judge approved of their restrooms, and a Washington statute that prevented a married woman from filing a suit in state court unless her husband joined her in the suit. Many of these laws had not been enforced for years, but remained on the books, much to the litigating feminists' delight. One Texas law dated back to 1856 and recognized the right of a husband to kill his wife's lover if he caught them in the act, whereas if the wife did the same, she would be charged with murder. In Ohio, then a bastion of organized labor, strong unions had secured rules that barred women entirely from nineteen job categories. A *Wall Street Journal* story on these laws and the legal challenges to them began with the following lead: "Shades of suffragettes! The ladies are up in arms again. They're demanding equal rights."

By the late 1960s, one could see a divide between how minorities saw affirmative action and how women's groups viewed it. Once the issue between "equal rights" and "special protection" had been resolved, women wanted a sex-blind version of equality. At the same time, African American activists were moving from a demand for color-blind equality to a demand for race consciousness in hiring, promotion, and college admissions—all for the achievement of equal results. According to some scholars, women's groups soon became vociferous advocates for gender-specific affirmative action. While this may be true, the two movements differed significantly, and it would be a mistake to see affirmative action for women as merely a reflection of what African Americans demanded.

By 1969, the EEOC abandoned its previous ambivalence about the sex clause in Title VII and began to prosecute cases of gender discrimination with as much energy as it did instances of racial bias. As far as the EEOC was concerned, the Constitution was not only color-blind but sex-blind as well, and Title VII meant what it said. One scholar described this change as "the belated feminist conversion of the EEOC."

The record of the EEOC in the early 1970s could not have been more satisfactory to feminist groups. Under prodding from the commission, courts handed down one decision after another doing away with gender discrimination. Most of the cases dealt with blue- or pink-collar jobs and with the then common practice of advertising for jobs by gender. It took the EEOC longer to do away with gendered want ads than with "whites only" and other specific racist descriptions. But what about some jobs that were indeed gendered, that only a woman could fill, such as dancing with the Radio City Music Hall Rockettes? For this the EEOC allowed a "bona fide occupational qualification," commonly known as a BFOQ. A casting director, for example, may advertise for women to play female roles and men to play male parts, but not for a woman to be his or her secretary.

WOMEN FACED A NUMBER of challenges as well as widespread discrimination in many areas, not just in blue- or pink-collar jobs. Prior to the Civil Rights Act, a common assumption existed about which jobs men should have and which women should fill, paralleling in many ways the old assumptions about which positions should go to white men and which to blacks. The phrase "sex segregation" did not exist prior to 1964, and Title VII helped shine a light on "job ghettos" involving not only blacks but women as well. Women unionists had challenged lower wages and lesser benefits before the act but for the most part had seen sex distinctions in jobs as not only normal but, as one person put it, "sacrosanct." That men and women should hold different jobs seemed obvious and required no explanation. To break out of what feminists began to call "the pink-collar ghetto" seemed nonsensical, because nearly everyone accepted these walls. "We never questioned it when they posted female and male jobs," recalled one woman who had been active in the labor movement in the 1940s and 1950s. "We didn't realize it was discrimination." By asking why only men or only women could do certain jobs, feminists opened "foundational questions about gender."

Affirmative action seems to have been fairly successful in helping women. Feminist activists, just like their counterparts in the civil rights movement, never believed that affirmative action by itself could solve the discriminatory problems that women faced. For women (and other minorities) to succeed, there had to be not only laws against sex discrimination and affirmative action plans to open opportunities but also full employment, pay equity, unionization, and advances in education and training. Women saw affirmative action as a means to end occupational segregation, to get women out of the "pink ghetto." And that it did to some extent. The index of occupational segregation by sex, according to statistics collected by the Department of Labor, declined more in the decade from 1970 to 1980 than in any other comparable period in American history. By 1994, women made up over 47 percent of bus drivers, 34 percent of mail carriers, and 16 percent of police—all jobs that had traditionally been male and all jobs that had better pay and benefits than the usual "women's work."

At the same time, middle- and upper-class women enjoyed a great advantage over minority groups such as blacks and Hispanics. Women had been attending public universities, especially in the West and the Midwest, since the latter part of the nineteenth century. While never in large numbers, there were female doctors and attorneys, and if many white men did not know any blacks or Hispanics personally, they had wives and sisters and daughters. Unless wedded to very out-of-date notions about the "proper place" for females—namely, barefoot, pregnant, and in the kitchen—these men opposed discrimination against their womenfolk. In polls covering nearly every socioeconomic group, affirmative action for women stirred up far less hostility than it did when it involved African Americans.

Entrance into previously all-male colleges and professional schools proved fairly easy, certainly as compared with the struggles by blacks, and the emphasis is on "as compared." The ruckus at the Citadel in Charleston, South Carolina, in which boorish male cadets hounded Shannon Faulkner out of the academy—and in doing so brought down the opprobrium of the country on the school—is best seen as an outlier. When the Virginia Military Institute, after a long court fight, accepted women, the newspaper coverage consisted primarily of stories praising the school for its peaceful transition. One should also note that although there would be later problems of sexual harassment, the military academies at West Point, Annapolis, and Colorado Springs also had fairly smooth transitions when they began accepting women.

Higher education had a long history of gender discrimination, especially in the older private schools on the East Coast. They not only resisted going coed; they flat out did not hire women as faculty. It proved easier to admit women as students, and the statistics bear out the great changes that took place. Nearly every all-male college and graduate school in the country turned coeducational in the 1970s and early 1980s, increasing the percentage of bachelor's degrees going to women from 43 in 1970 to 55 in 1996. Ironically, by the turn of the twenty-first century, some colleges were putting a great effort into attracting male applicants in order to offer their female students a better social situation.

Women seeking professorial positions, however, found a much tougher row to hoe, and universities soon found both HEW and the EEOC breathing down their necks. The government agencies began their assault on academic exclusionary practices not in response to African American activists but because of a Jewish feminist. Bernice Sandler earned a PhD in counseling from the University of Maryland in 1969 at the age of forty-one. Her department refused to even consider her for one of several open faculty slots, and when she asked one of the professors why, "he was truthful, and simply said, 'Let's face it, you come on too strong for a woman.'" Dr. Sandler recalled disparaging remarks about women from some of the faculty, and that she had been turned down for what should have been a merit-based fellowship because she was married; it went to a married male because he supposedly needed it more. No woman had ever received tenure in her department, and while male students got good offers for full-time positions, women wound up in temporary or part-time positions.

Mad as she could be, Bernice Sandler became a volunteer at the Women's Equity Action League (WEAL) and began to research sex discrimination at the University of Maryland and elsewhere. While at WEAL from 1969 to 1971, she worked to enforce the 1967 executive order signed by President Lyndon Johnson that prohibited sex discrimination within organizations with federal contracts. Most universities did not have policies eliminating gender discrimination, but they did have federal contracts. Dr. Sandler filed sex discrimination complaints against 250 institutions under this executive order. With Representative Edith Green (D-Ore.), she went on to spearhead hearings that documented gender discrimination in employment and educational opportunities. These hearings led to the passage of Title IX, which removed the education exemption from Title VII, and other laws eliminating overt gender discrimination in education. Sandler's key role in the creation and implementation of this law gave her the nickname the Godmother of Title IX.

Around this time, the National Organization for Women sued Harvard and the entire State University of New York system and produced a do-it-yourself "Academic Discrimination Kit." The torrent of complaints that Sandler started, and WEAL and NOW expanded, forced HEW to act, and after a number of universities refused to cooperate in providing data on women faculty, HEW threatened them with the loss of federal contracts worth millions of dollars.

The male chauvinism so rampant in the universities could be easily identified by anyone who knew how to look, especially the rigged searches and the totally nonprofessional criteria, such as the old boy network, used to fill faculty positions. Daniel Patrick Moynihan joked to Richard Nixon in 1969 that probably "there are proportionately more women in the Marine Corps than on most university faculties." In fact, when HEW finally pressured Harvard to provide information, of 411 tenured professors in 1970, only one was female, and she held a chair earmarked for women. Two years later Ruth Bader Ginsburg became the first woman at Columbia Law School to hold a full-time position above lecturer. Studies confirmed not only

Ruth Bader Ginsburg, head of the ACLU's Women's Rights Project in 1977, litigated many of the cases that brought women greater legal equality. She would later be appointed to the high court by President Clinton in 1993.

the absence of women in faculty ranks but the scorn with which men received applications from female candidates. At Yale, faculty members gathered at the men-only Mory's to recruit new colleagues and even hold committee or departmental meetings.

As the controversy over affirmative action heated up in the 1970s, some schools found passive resistance an effective defense against demands by the federal government to hire more women. University officials as well as faculty insisted that there could be no lessening of quality just to get a colored or feminine face in front of the classroom. In part, there was still a dearth of qualified minorities and women with doctorates, and it would take two more decades before universities finally gave up that argument.

Even if women did get into the better schools, they often found lingering bias. Ruth Bader Ginsburg recalled her time at Harvard Law School, when Dean Erwin Griswold invited the dozen or so women students to his house for tea. He then asked them if they did not feel ashamed at having taken away a spot from a man who would have to support a family. Ginsburg transferred to Columbia Law School for her third year and upon graduation, despite enthusiastic recommendations from the faculty, could not get a coveted clerkship at the Supreme Court. Felix Frankfurter, who during his career had backed many black and female causes and had been the first to hire a black clerk, would not take Ginsburg for no other reason than her gender.

Ginsburg's experience remained common throughout the 1970s and 1980s, and well-educated women with professional degrees and sterling backgrounds often found it hard to get a management position or, if they did, to secure promotions as their male counterparts did. The phrase "glass ceiling" soon became common, the invisible barrier that kept women from rising into executive positions. In studying this problem, one group of management scholars found that business leaders relied on a whole slew of myths about women that they used to rationalize either not hiring them or, if hired, not promoting them:

- Women are more emotional and sensitive to the feelings of others, while men are rational and coolly objective in their relationships with others.
- Women are uncomfortable in a man's world.
- Women work as a hobby or for luxuries and, as a result, lack the ambition, aggressiveness, and dedication necessary to excel in business.
- Women have higher rates of sickness and absenteeism.
- Women do not understand statistics.

FOLLOWING THE EXAMPLE of the civil rights movement, women took to the courts to fight gender bias. Ruth Bader Ginsburg set up the American Civil Liberties Union's Women's Rights Project and successfully argued several cases in the U.S. Supreme Court that overturned state and federal laws that discriminated against women.

We need to note the wider context in which the EEOC, HEW, and the courts operated at this time. Although the Equal Rights Amendment (ERA) had first been proposed as early as 1923, it did not pass both houses of Congress until 1972 and seemed well on its way to approval when it stalled three votes shy of the thirty-eight states it needed for ratification. The media carried numerous stories about the new women's movement, and the nine gentlemen of the Supreme Court could hardly have been ignorant of women's demands for equal treatment. If nothing else, they read the papers and watched television; they were all married, and several had daughters and/

or female law clerks. It would have been impossible for them to be unaware that women had adopted the strategies of the civil rights movement and that whatever happened to the ERA, questions of women's equality would come before the Court. Ironically, it was the Burger Court, with men supposedly chosen for their devotion to judicial restraint and strict construction, that would make sex discrimination constitutionally suspect.

The justices entered the debate in a unanimous opinion in *Reed v. Reed* (1971) that invalidated an Idaho estate law giving men preference over similarly situated women as administrators of decedents' estates. Over the next several years, even as the EEOC and HEW ramped up their efforts, the Supreme Court in essence put the sense of the ERA into effect:

- In *Nashville Gas Company v. Satty* (1977), the Court held the practice of stripping pregnant women of accumulated job seniority a violation of Title VII. A few years earlier, the justices ruled that schoolteachers could not arbitrarily be dismissed or placed on involuntary leave if pregnant.
- Firms willing to hire fathers, but not mothers, with preschool children engaged in sex discrimination prohibited by law.
- The Court struck down provisions of the Equal Pay Act and Title VII exempting the military and ruled that the armed services could not deny to married women the same fringe benefits paid to their male counterparts.
- A Louisiana jury selection scheme that excluded women, similar to the Florida one earlier approved by the Court, fell afoul of both the Sixth Amendment (fair trial) and the Fourteenth (equal protection).
- A unanimous Court struck down sections of the Social Security Act that provided death benefits to a widow but not to a widower.
- In two cases, the Court adopted a "heightened" or "intermediate" scrutiny standard for gender discrimination cases. Justice Brennan had tried, and failed by one vote, to have sex and racial discrimination cases judged under the standard of strict scrutiny. This intermediate standard gave women more protection but did not place the burden on the state or the employer to prove that gender categorization did not discriminate.

THE SUPREME COURT struck an important blow for professional women in *Hishon v. King & Spalding* (1984). After graduating from Columbia Law School in 1972, Elizabeth Anderson Hishon accepted a job with one of Atlanta's premier law firms, King & Spalding, and assumed that she, like the male associates hired at the same time, would advance to partnership in five or six years if she received satisfactory evaluations. The firm assured her during recruitment interviews that associates as a "matter of course" became partners and that such decisions would be made on a "fair and equal basis." Hishon relied on these assurances when she decided to accept the firm's offer and during her years there did receive satisfactory evaluations. In May 1978, the firm considered and rejected Hishon for partnership and did so again the following year. The firm terminated her employment as of 31 December 1979.

After she left the firm, she received permission from the EEOC to sue and went to federal district court, alleging that King & Spalding had discriminated against her on the basis of her sex when it failed to make her a partner. Even though at this time the firm had fifty partners (all male) and fifty associates, it claimed that as a partnership it did not come under the various federal laws governing employment, such as Title VII of the Civil Rights Act. Hishon lost in the district court and in the Court of Appeals for the Eleventh Circuit, and some commentators thought she had little chance in the high court.

In a surprise unanimous decision, the Court ruled in Hishon's favor. The opinion by Chief Justice Warren Burger held that a partnership decision in a law firm came within the scope of Title VII, which made it unlawful for an employer to discriminate against an "individual with respect to compensation, terms, conditions, or privileges of employment" because of several factors, one of which being the gender of the individual. Hishon had relied on the promise of partnership made as an inducement during recruitment and the promise to consider her on a fair and equal basis. That promise fell under Title VII and could not be made in a discriminatory manner. In essence, Hishon had an employment contract with King & Spalding. The Court practically dismissed out of hand the firm's claim that as a partnership Title VII did not apply to it. (After this decision, Hishon and the firm agreed on an out-of-court monetary settlement, and she went to work as a partner in another Atlanta law firm.)

The announcement of the decision led several prominent women to recall their own struggles. Congresswoman Pat Schroeder (D-Colo.) reported that after she graduated from Harvard Law in 1964, not one Denver firm would interview her. "They were just not interested in me, although they were interested in my husband." Firms that did interview women "were very blunt about it. They would say, 'We just had to do this to look good. But we don't plan to hire any women.'" Schroeder said that the Harvard placement office took the masculine marketplace for granted.

Anne Jones, a former FCC commissioner, had graduated first in her class at the Boston College Law School in 1961 and told an even more horrid story of gender bias. By tradition, the top student in the graduating class got a clerkship with the chief justice of the Massachusetts Supreme Judicial Court. She did not, because, as she was told, the chief's clerk oversaw the other judges' clerks in the state, who were all men and who would resent having a woman over them. Two of the firms that interviewed her wanted to make sure she planned to use birth control. Ropes & Gray, the firm that finally hired her, started her at 15 percent less salary than her male counterparts, because they expected her to be a "casualty" to motherhood. Jones remembers telling the man who hired her, "When I am 65 years old, if I'm still Miss Jones and have never missed a day of work, will I get a retroactive increase?" He laughed.

Women not only had to be better than men to make partner, said leading women lawyers, but would be judged by different standards, especially in partnership decisions. By 1984, there were 93,000 women among the country's 612,000 lawyers. They made up 30 percent of law firm associates whose salaries averaged $50,000 but held only 5 percent of the partnerships, which at the time could be worth $100,000 and more.

One should note again that, compared with African Americans' experience, and the resentment that affirmative action stirred up against them, there seems to have been, at all levels, greater acceptance of the idea that discrimination against women was wrong. Although there would be plenty of stories about men being shut out of jobs they had qualified for so that women could be appointed (with a subtext that the women were less qualified), we have no reliable data on how often—if ever—that happened.

PART II

FROM REAGAN TO TRUMP

CHAPTER II

THE REAGAN PRESIDENCY

Just as the starting gate must be open to all, so, too, can there be no artificial adjustments at the finish.

—WILLIAM BRADFORD REYNOLDS

The idea that you can use discrimination in the form of racially preferential quotas, goals, and set-asides to remedy the lingering effects of past discrimination makes no sense in principle; in practice, it is nothing short of a legal, moral, and constitutional tragedy.

—EDWIN MEESE III

In February 1979, readers of the journal *Human Events* found a short article on affirmative action by the former governor of California Ronald Reagan. In it he praised Sears, Roebuck for suing the federal government, including the secretaries of labor, commerce, housing and urban development, and health, education, and welfare, as well as the EEOC, the Office of Federal Contract Compliance, and the Census Bureau. Sears complained that a number of federal regulations contradicted each other, making it impossible for Sears—which had over 400,000 employees—and any other company with fifteen or more workers not to run afoul of the law.

Ever since 1945, federal law had required giving employment priority to veterans of World War II, most of whom were white males. On the other hand, the various affirmative action decrees issued by different government agencies required preference for other groups. Sears had had an affirmative action program since 1968 and was proud that its minority employment had risen from 8.7 percent in

1965 to 19.9 percent in 1978, while at the managerial and executive levels the growth had been from a minuscule 1.4 to 10.5 percent. Yet no matter what it did, the company violated one federal regulation or another.

Reagan supported the company but noted that "it is hard to imagine even a court order getting those bureaucratic grand duchies in Washington to devote much energy to unsnarling red tape. But, at least it might get them to think twice before launching any more search-and-destroy missions in the business world."

In less than two years, Ronald Reagan would become president of the United States, and when he came to Washington, it certainly seemed that he wanted to get rid of affirmative action. He and his aides learned, however, that more support existed for affirmative action in Congress, in state and local governments, and among the public than they had believed. As the law professor Neal Devins put it, from 1981 to 1992 the Reagan/Bush Justice Department "fought and lost a holy war over affirmative action."

DURING THE 1980 presidential campaign, Reagan frequently voiced his support of equal opportunity for all Americans but attacked government programs that, as he charged, had been distorted by an emphasis on racial and gender quotas. Reagan believed that true civil rights consisted of racial neutrality, and he was neither the first nor the last person—liberal or conservative—to express that view. The "explicit promise" of the American social system gave every person certain inalienable rights. "This promise," he explained, "wasn't meant to be limited or perverted by special privilege, or by double standards that favor one group over another. It is a principle for eternity, America's deepest treasure." His administration stood "committed to achieving a society that is color blind, gender neutral, ethnically and religiously tolerant and diverse—in which each individual has equal dignity before the law, and an equal opportunity to compete for life's rewards solely on ability and effort regardless of sex, race, color, religion, national origin or age."

In his first news conference after taking the oath of office, President Reagan promised there would be no retreat on civil rights, and that his administration would be dedicated to equality, but that some programs, once useful perhaps, had become distorted in practice. Affirmative action programs are "becoming quota systems. And I'm old enough to remember when quotas existed in the United States for the purpose of discrimination, and I don't want to see that happen again." According to one scholar, Reagan "was determined to revise [Johnson's] Executive Order 11246, in order to eliminate the federal mandate requiring employers to adopt minority and white female hiring goals." Activists certainly believed Reagan stood ready to undo two decades of progress, not just in affirmative action but across the whole field of civil rights.

About a month after Reagan's election, a conference of mostly African American conservatives met at the Fairmont hotel in San Francisco to make recommendations on how the new administration should deal with black Americans. Although there were a few whites and liberal blacks among the fifty attendees, nearly all of them had for years opposed the agendas of the main civil rights organizations on issues such as school busing, the War on Poverty, the role the government should play in the economy, and, of course, affirmative action. Although 86 percent of black voters had cast their ballots against Reagan, the administration knew it would have to make several minority appointments, and this conference showed that some blacks not only held conservative views but opposed much of what had passed for civil rights activism in the past.

Moreover, the attendees believed that the president-elect cared about them, and he had sent his counselor, later to be attorney general, Edwin Meese to the meeting. In his talk, Meese disparaged the older, established civil rights leaders. He and Reagan had just met with a delegation that Meese characterized as "people who purport to represent the black community." The difference between that meeting and this conference, Meese declared, is significant. "They were talking about the last ten years. You are talking about the ideas of the next ten years or beyond." The men at this meeting assumed not only that they would have the ear of the new administration but that some of them would be asked to join it, in part because they had little or no connection to the leadership of the NAACP and similar organizations. Reagan did not disappoint them. Clarence M. Pendleton Jr. would chair the U.S. Commission on Civil Rights, and Clarence Thomas, then an aide to Senator John Danforth of Missouri, would be appointed first assistant secretary of education for the Office for Civil Rights and then in 1982 chair of the Equal Employment Opportunity Commission. He would fill the latter office for eight years until nominated to the judiciary.

The Justice Department, which ever since the mid-1960s had

President Reagan, with his counselor, Edwin Meese (left), *and Attorney General William French Smith II* (right), *in 1985; all three opposed affirmative action.*

been the prime governmental champion and protector of civil rights, would now be headed by William French Smith II, and the department's Civil Rights Division by William Bradford Reynolds, both highly unsympathetic to affirmative action. Smith had no prior experience with civil rights, and during his confirmation hearings several senators objected to the fact that he refused to resign from two private clubs that had membership restrictions. Smith saw his job as implementing the president's views, and in several areas the Department of Justice reversed its previous positions.

William Bradford Reynolds served as the administration's point man on civil rights in his capacity as head of the DOJ's Civil Rights Division. There is no question about how he felt regarding affirmative action, which he described as "an experiment gone awry" and having lost its moral compass. Like Smith, he believed there should be redress only for the actual victims of a discriminatory practice; if a black man or a woman had in fact suffered discrimination, that person should be compensated and made whole. The remedy should definitely not be imposing a quota on employers. Affirmative action denied those who persevered and succeeded through their own talents and efforts their victory, all in a wrongheaded attempt to achieve a "more balanced" student enrollment or a "more diverse workplace" or a "more representative" contracting force. Worst of all, it subverted the American ideal of individual accomplishment and "mocks the valiant struggle for an equal opportunity society that has defined America's domestic agenda for the last four decades."

Reynolds, like Reagan, Meese, and Smith, had no difficulty rejecting the views of the established civil rights groups. All the Reagan people agreed with Reynolds that "our country is not a group of groups; our laws protect individuals, not classes." In saying this, he also rejected a basic working assumption of every president from Kennedy through Carter, namely, that the American civil rights problem could be resolved only if seen through its group context.

THE TRANSITION TEAM responsible for recommendations on the EEOC gave more than a hint of where the administration would go. Headed by J. A. Parker, a black activist and chairman of the conservative Lincoln Institute for Education and Research, the team excoriated the agency for using affirmative action as a tool to "implement" the 1964 Civil Rights Act when the law itself specifically called for nondiscriminatory rules in the workplace. The committee made a number of recommendations, but the one most worrisome to the established civil rights group was its final comment. The wrongheaded policies of the EEOC "are not found in any legal statutes but, instead, in administrative regulations, [and] these can be altered in the same manner. Similarly, those policies which we find in error which are found in Executive Orders can be altered" by the president acting alone. By this time, the EEOC as an administrative body did have statutory status, but the laws establishing and then funding the agency did not spell out any formal affirmative action policies. An EEOC opposed to affirmative action could nullify much of the regulatory scheme built up in the 1970s, and Reagan could, with a stroke of his pen, completely undo Executive Order 11246.

Although Reagan himself never tackled 11246 directly, affirmative action found itself under assault from many directions. Under David Stockman, the Office of Management and Budget slashed appropriations for enforcement. For example, the 1983 budget for the Office of Federal Contract Compliance Programs (OFCCP) was 40 percent less than in 1980, and its personnel cut in half. Political appointees in various agencies and departments involved with civil rights worked to transform the administration's philosophical opposition to affirmative action into pragmatic measures, such as limiting the types of lawsuits that the government would institute. Career lawyers in the Civil Rights Division found themselves hampered every time they wanted to enforce the law, that is, a law that had been passed by Congress regarding the obligation of the division to enforce civil rights statutes. As one of these lawyers told a reporter, "It's the lawyers who are trying to enforce the statutes against Reynolds, who is trying to keep these lawyers, these raving liberals, down."

The Justice Department, which under Carter had invariably taken the side of minorities and women in litigation, switched sides in a number of cases, now backing the party that had been sued for discrimination. As one critic noted, when the government switches sides, especially in the case of civil rights litigation, the public image of the government lawyer is that of a "hired gun," working at the whim of politicians, and this "breeds public distrust of the legal profession and of government ethics in particular."

A somewhat different but related problem could be found at the EEOC. During the Carter years, a "rapid charge processing" system had been put in place to reduce the growing backlog of job discrimination complaints and had cut the waiting list from 126,000 in 1975 to 55,000 in 1980 to 31,000 in 1983. Then the Reagan appointees to the EEOC began to dismantle this system, and the number of unprocessed cases doubled to 61,686 by the end of Reagan's tenure. Moreover, a report released by the nonpartisan General Accounting Office charged that the commission had failed in its duty to investigate alleged discrimination. According to the report, a large majority of the complaints closed by the agency had not been fully investigated.

The Reagan-era EEOC retreated from the fight over discrimination not only because of ideological reasons but also because in the 1980s the administration cut the EEOC budget considerably. During the 1970s, the EEOC inflation-adjusted budgets grew almost 15 percent per year; the Carter administration added fourteen hundred budgeted positions, a growth of 50 percent, between 1976 and 1980. During the Reagan years, the EEOC's constant-dollar budget fell considerably, and it lost over a thousand positions, and at a time when age and gender discrimination claims rose sharply. (By 1992, only 40 percent of all cases involved race, compared with 85 percent in 1970 and 61 percent in 1980.) It is little wonder, then, that the EEOC could not keep up with its caseload.

Secretary of Labor Raymond Donovan, like others in the Reagan administration, opposed affirmative action, yet recognized that if he tried to do away with the OFCCP entirely he would run into a firestorm in Congress and from civil rights groups. He proposed new regulations that would free nearly three-quarters of the companies doing business with the federal government from the "burden" of affirmative action reports. These regulations, said Donovan, keep "the necessary safeguards for protected groups, while cutting down the paperwork burden for employers." Under the new proposals, only federal contractors having 250 or more employees and a contract worth $1 million or more would have to file documents regarding the affirmative steps they took to recruit and retain women and minorities, including goals and timetables.

There is no question that by 1981 reporting requirements had indeed become onerous. In the Labor Department, more than fifteen hundred civil servants monitored the employment practices of some seventeen thousand federal contractors with more than twenty-six million workers. If an employer had facilities in more than one location, it had to maintain a separate affirmative action plan for each, so that the seventeen thousand employers had to submit 108,000 plans and update them annually. A two-inch-thick manual explained how. At a Senate hearing, the general counsel for Johns Hopkins University displayed a two-and-a-half-foot stack of documents weighing sixty-five pounds that her university had produced in compliance with OFCCP requirements.

Ellen Shong Bergman, the director of the OFCCP, said the proposed regulations were designed to encourage voluntary compliance and to put an end to "mindless confrontations with employers who have been acting in good faith." Bergman's emphasis on voluntary action marked her two-year tenure at the OFCCP, during which, like Reagan appointees in other offices dealing with affirmative action, she rarely enforced existing rules. Nonetheless, the career civil servants at the OFCCP continued to work and actually increased the number of reviews they did annually, although some members said that the increase in numbers had been achieved by a decrease in "quality and thoroughness."

There had, of course, been suspicion by minorities during the 1980 presidential campaign about whether Reagan had any kind of commitment to civil rights, and his administration almost immediately made it apparent that while the president continued to say he believed in equality, his lieutenants—with his blessing—undercut government programs that under previous presidents had taken the lead in fighting for women and minority rights. Because the 1965 Voting Rights Act would soon be up for renewal, Reagan's initial opposition to it changed to a belief that it ought to cover all fifty states. The White House called in Arthur Fletcher, who had overseen the development of affirmative action in Nixon's time, to advise the president how to deal with what Fletcher called "the inordinate fear that is pervading the black community." At the same time that Fletcher told black leaders Reagan had abandoned the fifty-state idea, other West Wing officials declared that the president still had it on the table. The headline on the front page of *The New York Times* declared, in somewhat of an understatement, "Reagan Sends Mixed Signals on Civil Rights."

Civil rights activists felt even more threatened when, in May 1981, Senator Orrin G. Hatch (R-Utah), chair of the Senate Judiciary Subcommittee on the Constitution, opened hearings on affirmative action and indicated right from the start what he thought of the idea. He characterized the concept as "an assault upon America, conceived in lies and fostered with an irresponsibility so extreme as to verge on the malign." The hearings, Hatch hoped, would further his proposed constitutional amendment to prohibit the federal government from "making distinctions on account of race, color, or national origin." Nothing came of Hatch's proposal, but it served as one more sign that the Republicans had little intention of fostering affirmative action.

ONE THING LACKING twelve months into Reagan's presidency was a clear-cut policy on both civil rights and especially affirmative action. The Justice Department announced that it opposed two of the devices often used to enforce affirmative action policies—numerical goals and hiring timetables for women, African Americans, and Hispanic Americans. The Labor Department, however, believed strongly in the legitimacy of goals and timetables but wanted to relieve federal contractors of what the department considered intrusive government regulation and paperwork.

Another red flag to rights groups came when Reagan forced out Arthur S. Flemming, a moderate Republican, as chairman of the U.S. Commission on Civil Rights and replaced him with Clarence Pendleton, a conservative Republican from California who, like many of the Reagan cohort, opposed affirmative action as well as the agendas of the major civil rights organizations. Flemming had been an outspoken supporter of affirmative action and told a reporter that if someone wanted an agency or an educational institution to be a model of equal opportunity, it would not happen by wishing it so. He considered discrimination against women and minorities so built into the fabric of the nation that to defeat it one needed strong tools, such as affirmative action. The Reagan administration, he declared, opposed affirmative action, and he had little hope that anything would change that attitude.

At a news conference in December 1981, Reagan repeated that he fully supported equal opportunity for women and minorities. While he continued to oppose government-mandated affirmative action programs, he had no objection to voluntary action by unions and management in the private sector to provide greater opportunity for minorities. His administration, he declared, "is dedicated and devoted to the principle of civil rights," but he also believed in federalism and returning more power and functions to the states. Nonetheless, "I recognize that one of the prime responsibilities of the Federal Government is to assure that not one single citizen in this country can be denied his or her constitutional rights without the Federal Government coming in and guaranteeing those rights." Of course, Reagan made no mention of the fact that just a few days earlier William Bradford Reynolds had expressed opposition even to voluntary affirmative action and had said that he hoped to be able to convince the Supreme Court that its decision in the *Weber* case, upholding a voluntary plan, had been "wrongly decided." On the anniversary of his inauguration, Reagan told reporters, "I have been on the side of opposition to bigotry and discrimination and prejudice, and long before it ever became a kind of national issue under the title of civil rights. And my life has been spent on that side."

This might have been true, but a year after Ronald Reagan became the fortieth president of the United States, he and his administration were widely perceived to be unsympathetic, indeed hostile, to the interests of women and minorities. Benjamin Hooks of the NAACP told a Senate subcommittee that he could not point to "any action of this administration that would give any hope or comfort to minorities." The ACLU distributed a newsletter in February 1982 describing an "administration whose hostility to individual rights is relentless." A lawyer with the National Women's Political Caucus condemned Reagan's record as "absolutely deplorable." About the only positive thing that could be said, according to an Urban League official, is that "he's the glue that's bringing us together."

While civil rights groups attacked Secretary of Labor Donovan's proposal to cut down on the paperwork, conservatives attacked him for not going far enough. In fact, Donovan in a speech to the National Press Club in April 1981 had actually said, "The President and I are firmly behind affirmative action" but want to take enforcement "out of the arena of push-pull-slap-punch" and "to cut down on the damn paperwork." According to groups like the conservative Heritage Foundation and the U.S. Chamber of Commerce, the administration should have done away with the whole OFCCP and its rules and regulations, leaving businesses subject only to the rules of equal opportunity in hiring, and killed affirmative action once and for all.

One cannot characterize the debate over affirmative action as strictly a Democratic-Republican or even a liberal-conservative debate. Some moderate Republicans and conservatives believed that given the history of racism and gender bias in American history, true equality of opportunity in the future would require some compensatory programs now. To get past race, one had to take it into account. Similarly, some Democrats and liberals deplored the whole idea of group rights and found the EEOC's behavior and policies an obstacle to equality. Michael Heyman, the chancellor of the University of California at Berkeley, told a reporter that the ham-fisted behavior of some EEOC officials had undermined the faculty commitment to affirmative action at the liberal Berkeley campus. The heavy-handedness of the EEOC in the 1970s had produced a backlash among traditionally liberal people who normally supported fairness in employment and promotion. "No single development of the past fifteen years," according to the political columnist Michael Kinsley, "has turned more liberals into former liberals than affirmative action."

Throughout Reagan's first term, whatever he did in the area of civil rights failed to please some group or the other. He kept his campaign promise to appoint a woman to the Supreme Court, although liberals grumbled that Sandra Day O'Connor was too conservative and not interested in gender issues, while conservatives complained she was not conservative enough, especially on abortion.

The Justice Department cut way back on its civil rights litigation. In 1980, the Civil Rights Division had filed twenty-nine prison inmate suits; in 1981, none. In 1980, the CRD had entered twenty-two school desegregation suits; in 1981, ten. Not a single housing discrimination suit was filed in 1981, and only one the following year. This was not some stealth plan. Both Attorney General Smith and Assistant Attorney General Reynolds made it quite clear what they were doing. Smith told the American Law Institute that some resegregation had occurred but that it resulted from non-state factors: parents wanted to send their children to schools near home or had enrolled them in private schools. The Department of Justice saw no state action that required intervention. Reynolds told Congress that in future school segregation cases the Justice Department would "define the violation precisely and seek to limit the remedy only to those schools in which racial imbalance is the product of intentionally segregative acts of state officials."

Yet Reynolds had also told Congress that while the administration would not ask courts to order employers to use anything but "fair and non-discriminatory selection procedures" in deciding whom to hire, the government would "seek percentage recruitment goals for monitoring purposes. . . . These recruitment goals will be related to the percentage of minority or female applicants that might be expected to result under a nondiscriminatory employment policy." As one critic asked, What does Reynolds mean? Is he for affirmative action or not?

After initially saying he approved of the voluntary plan the Court validated in *Weber,* Reagan said that the Court had been wrong and that he disapproved of any quotas, voluntary or involuntary. Yet for all he could have done simply through executive order, Reagan reluctantly concluded it would be politically dangerous to end affirmative action, and while he took no action, his aides did all they could to undermine the program.

In the fall of 1982, Edwin Meese, Reagan's counselor, told a predominantly black audience of New Right conservatives that "President Reagan has called for a new Emancipation Proclamation." The Heritage Foundation co-sponsored the one-day gathering with the New Coalition for Economic and Social Change, the latter tracing its roots to that Fairmont hotel conference in December 1980. The New Coalition declared, "We believe the answer to black poverty lies in our black communities, and depends for success on our individual initiative and independent action—not on government." Emancipation from government, and from government programs like affirmative action, was precisely what Reagan promised, Meese told the audience.

In 1982, Reagan appointed Clarence Thomas, a conservative African American, to head the EEOC. Thomas, who had attended Yale Law School as part of its diversity plan, strongly opposed affirmative action, calling it a form of racial discrimination and every bit as wrong as segregation or slavery. In a later interview, Thomas claimed that the stigmatizing effects of affirmative action put him at a huge disadvantage when he sought work as a lawyer. In interviews with one "high-priced lawyer" after another, they did not take him seriously because they thought he had received special treatment.

Thomas disappointed civil rights groups, who claimed he had been slow to challenge employment discrimination. At his confirmation hearings for the Supreme Court in 1991, Nan Aron of the liberal Alliance for Justice charged that while heading the EEOC, Thomas "failed to demonstrate commitment to civil rights and liberties." Defenders argued that Thomas had resisted pressure from Meese and others to criticize Supreme Court rulings and to speak out more forcefully in support of the administration's efforts to roll back civil rights programs. There is no question that Thomas's opposition to affirmative action shaped his views, and he also changed the way the EEOC did business.

Before his arrival, the EEOC typically settled a large number of cases and prosecuted very few to the end. Under Thomas, enforcement concentrated on fully prosecuting suits in which clear discrimination could be proved. This policy, however, led to a jump in the backlog of cases, and it caused a minor controversy when it turned out that a two-year statute of limitations had expired on more than ten thousand age discrimination claims filed with the agency. Thomas also ran into criticism from congressmen when he abandoned the EEOC's traditional reliance on class-action suits in favor of individual ones. This clearly, however, reflected not only his personal philosophy but also that of the Reagan administration in general.

"I continue to believe," Thomas wrote in 1987, "that distributing opportunities on the basis of race or gender, whoever the beneficiaries, turns the law against employment discrimination on its head. Class preferences are an affront to the rights and dignity of individuals." In 1986, Thomas, backed by Attorney General Meese, proposed abandoning the use of hiring goals and timetables in settling discrimination suits. Such tactics, Thomas declared, "denigrate an entire class of people." Like other administration attacks on affirmative action, this one failed to gain any political traction.

AND YET . . . IN WHAT SURELY started out as an effort to discredit affirmative action, a study by the Labor Department concluded that the very type of program attacked by Reagan had proven highly effective in promoting the employment of African Americans, women, and Hispanics. In September 1981, Ellen Shong Bergman, director of the OFCCP, assigned her special assistant, J. Griffin Crump, to study the question. Given the fact that Secretary of Labor Donovan opposed affirmative action, one could fairly surmise that he, Bergman, and others fully expected the report to demonstrate the futility of affirmative action.

Instead, the study found that companies doing business with the federal government "have posted significantly greater gains in the employment and advancement of minorities and women." The study analyzed reports from 77, 000 factories, offices, and work sites, with a total of more than 20 million employees, and credited these gains to the "good-faith efforts of Federal contractors to comply with their contractual obligations of affirmative action."

Between 1974 and 1980, the rate of minority employment had grown by 20 percent among federal contractors, compared with 12 percent among companies not covered under the OFCCP. Women's participation expanded by 15.2 percent as compared with 2.2 percent in the nonfederal workforce. In addition, the study found that women and minorities experienced significantly greater upward mobility in federal contracting firms. Large numbers of blacks, women, and Hispanics who had been service workers or low-skilled blue-collar workers moved up to skilled production, craft, and white-collar jobs.

The Reagan administration did not want to hear this, and the Labor Department decided not to publish the study, claiming that it wanted to check its methodology and conclusions. Robert Follett of Welch Associates, an economic consulting firm in Santa Monica, California, who had been hired by the Labor Department to review the study, said the "methodology was appropriate" and the conclusions valid. The Labor Department, however, refused to release the study as well as another one that also found affirmative action worked, and worked very well.

(From 1984 to 1986, Harold Orlans directed a study of affirmative action in higher education for the U.S. Commission on Civil Rights, and when he concluded that compensatory programs had been successful in enrolling women and minorities, the commission buried his report as well.)

Someone with access to the Labor Department documents leaked them to the press, and to a predictable reaction. Barry Goldstein, a lawyer with the NAACP, and others crowed with satisfaction over not only the results but also the fact that the Labor Department had tried to keep both reports from the public. Surely if these findings became widely known, it would embarrass the president and the Justice Department, both of whom strongly opposed affirmative action and claimed it did not work. Even with those results suppressed, there have been a number of academic studies that all come to the same conclusion: affirmative action worked and benefited the target community, be it minority or female.

IN 1984, RONALD REAGAN ran for a second term. He and his advisers clearly recognized that he would have little support from minorities and in effect wrote them off by the policies his administration pursued.

The new staff director for the U.S. Commission on Civil Rights, Linda Chavez, recommended changes in its programs, changes, she claimed, that would show the adverse effects of affirmative action, racial quotas, court-ordered busing, and bilingual education. Reagan had managed to get rid of the old commission and after a bitter fight with Congress had created a new commission with eight members, all of whom he appointed. In a memorandum to the commission members, Chavez recommended doing away with studies regarding

Ronald Reagan and Linda Chavez, whom the president named as director of the U.S. Commission on Civil Rights, where her conservative views roused the ire of civil liberties activists. In 1985, she left the commission to become White House director of the Office of Public Liaison.

financial aid to minority students, and also opposed the commission adopting the legal theory that employers should set equal pay for jobs of comparable value, a theory championed by nearly every women's advocacy group. She also recommended that as its highest priority the commission undertake a study of "the adverse consequences of affirmative action programs on Americans of Eastern and Southern European descent." By 1987, the commission had lost almost all credibility as a defender of civil rights. An editorial in *The New York Times* said that any document coming out of that agency ought to carry a disclaimer that "despite its name, this body no longer can be relied upon to stand up for the rights of those who have legitimately felt unfairly treated, now or in the past."

In June 1984, the U.S. Supreme Court, by a 6–3 vote, upheld the vested rights in a valid seniority system against affirmative action. In 1980, Memphis had entered a consent decree—approved by the Justice Department—in which it recognized discrimination in the fire department and other city agencies. The city agreed to promote certain individuals and established interim goals of filling one-half of job vacancies and 20 percent of promotions in each job category with qualified black applicants. The decree did not contain any provisions for layoffs, but the following year, faced with budget deficits, Memphis said it would have to reduce personnel across all departments, and in doing so would follow a "last hired, first fired" rule. Because most black employees had only recently been hired or promoted, nearly all of them would be laid off. Carl Stotts, an African American fireman, went to court and got a restraining order forbidding the firing of any black employees. The predominantly white firemen's union, which had not been a party to the decree but had negotiated the seniority system, went to court to defend the system.

In *Firefighters Local Union No. 1784 v. Stotts,* Justice Byron White noted that Title VII of the Civil Rights Act specifically permitted bona fide seniority plans as justification for differences in compensation and conditions of employment, and lower courts could not ignore such plans when attempting to fashion remedies against discrimination. Neither the union nor nonminority workers had been parties to the consent decree, and therefore had not agreed to give up their rights under the system they had negotiated with the city.

Reagan administration officials crowed with delight. Clarence Pendleton of the Civil Rights Commission called the decision "a milestone in . . . limiting the use of so-called remedies such as quotas and similar devices." William Bradford Reynolds declared that the *Stotts* decision fully justified Reagan policies. Invoking the case as authority, he called for fifty-one jurisdictions to "cleanse" past consent decrees of anything even resembling quotas. Union officials, such as Albert Shanker of the American Federation of Teachers, praised what he termed "a very important decision," and said that seniority systems, with their built-in objectivity, would in the long run prove beneficial to minorities.

At the other end of the spectrum, civil rights leaders believed the case a disaster. Richard Fields, the attorney for the black firemen, said the decision would allow cities to thwart all the gains made through affirmative action. Benjamin Hooks of the NAACP bitterly complained that to uphold the "last hired, first fired" rule "is to turn our backs on the reality that such discriminatory practices have had and continue to have on excluded groups." Judy Goldsmith of the National Organization for Women worried that the decision would erode affirmative action as a remedy against race and sex discrimination.

The Reagan Justice Department immediately went into court to do battle against all affirmative action plans, citing the *Stotts* decision as the rule that lower courts had to follow. In papers filed with the Court of Appeals for the Eleventh Circuit in Atlanta, the Justice Department opposed a one-black-for-one-white promotion plan ordered for the Alabama state police, arguing that it constituted the kinds of "racial quotas" that the high court had explicitly barred in *Stotts*. Reynolds personally went to Cincinnati to try to overturn a federal district court order that barred the city's police department from laying off or demoting minority officers on the basis of seniority, and on to Newark, New Jersey, where a seniority plan conflicted with a court order preventing the city from laying off minority members. At a press conference, Reynolds announced that he planned to use the Court's language in *Stotts* to review and possibly revise "hundreds" of court orders to which the government had been a party.

Reynolds and his colleagues read far more into *Stotts* than the Court had implied. First, only three other justices fully signed on to White's opinion, robbing it of precedential value. Two justices, John Paul Stevens and Sandra Day O'Connor, concurred with the results, but not with White's exaltation of seniority systems. Moreover, White's opinion had not been a full-scale attack on affirmative action but dealt solely with the issue of seniority systems. Linda

Greenhouse, the Supreme Court reporter for *The New York Times,* pointed out that in fact the decision broke no new ground and did little more than reaffirm Title VII's protection of seniority systems. Douglas Seaver, a Boston civil rights and employment lawyer, called the ruling "fairly narrow, and not unexpected." He believed unions would be the real losers, because they would be caught between their female and minority members seeking modification of seniority rules and white males demanding full protection of their vested interests. In fact, before the year ended the Court of Appeals for the Sixth Circuit upheld a Detroit Fire Department affirmative action plan. In response to the white males who claimed they had not been hired because of their race, Judge George Edwards said that their arguments against the plan failed against the weight of the city's history of discrimination in hiring. As for the Alabama case, the appeals court approved the plan, and the Supreme Court confirmed that judgment in early 1987, even though Reagan's solicitor general argued against it.

Interestingly, at the 1984 NAACP convention, Secretary of Transportation Elizabeth Dole told delegates that there were "real opportunities" for minority groups in a construction program under the Surface Transportation Assistance Act of 1982. Her department, she claimed, had been working to increase opportunities under the act for minority-owned businesses. Secretary Dole might have been one of the few members of the administration who believed in such programs.

RONALD REAGAN STOMPED Walter Mondale in the 1984 election, winning forty-nine of the fifty states with nearly 60 percent of the popular vote. Mondale won only his home state of Minnesota and the District of Columbia for a total of thirteen electoral college ballots, the lowest number since Roosevelt had trounced Alf Landon in 1936. Mondale did get more than 90 percent of the black vote, while Reagan got 73 percent of the white male vote. If one looked at areas outside the northeastern section of the country, the Reagan percentage among white Protestant males might well have approached the percentage of black vote for Mondale.

According to Nicholas Lemann, the closest that affirmative action came to its demise occurred in early summer 1985, six months after Reagan had overwhelmingly been reelected. During his first term, several of his advisers had urged the president to replace Johnson's

Edwin Meese, the Reagan administration's leading opponent of affirmative action, being sworn in as attorney general in February 1985; left to right, Reagan, Meese, Ursula Meese, Daniel Marks (deputy executive clerk), and George H. W. Bush.

Executive Order 11246, and they now interpreted Reagan's large electoral victory as a mandate to do so. The group included the new and confrontational White House chief of staff, Donald Regan, former counselor and now attorney general, Edwin Meese, Assistant Attorney General for Civil Rights William Bradford Reynolds, and William Bennett, the newly appointed secretary of education.

But Raymond Donovan, a fellow conservative who agreed with them, had resigned his position as secretary of labor, and Reagan replaced him with Bill Brock, a moderate who wanted to protect the Office of Federal Contract Compliance Programs, one of the most powerful agencies in the Labor Department.

The obvious goal of the anti-affirmative-action officials, Johnson's Executive Order 11246, had, according to one scholar, "evolved into precisely the sort of race-conscious, group-oriented civil rights policy that Reynolds and Meese had criticized" from the start. To repeal the Johnson order would have been the administration's landmark legacy, and a draft circulated of an executive order that would completely rescind requirements for federal contractors to hire women and minorities—not just ease the paperwork burden as Donovan had done. In addition, the draft forbade the Labor Department to use statistical evidence to measure contractors' compliance with statutory prohibitions against discrimination. It should be noted that nothing in the draft would have prevented employers from using racial goals, quotas, or other forms of preference on a voluntary basis. The Labor Department, however, would no longer require federal contractors to use them.

The attorney general's plan would not by itself do away with affirmative action. Reagan, Meese, and others in the administration supported a "soft" affirmative action, namely, programs that encouraged employers to open doors of opportunity for women and minorities but eschewed numerical quotas and timetables. The Meese draft would have "each government contractor and subcontractor engage in affirmative recruitment and employment-related training programs designed to ensure that minorities and women receive full consideration for hiring and promotion." The secretary of labor would still have an oversight role, but there would be no quotas and no penalties.

The cabal overplayed its hand. Brock left Washington for a lengthy foreign trip, and in his absence Meese, Reynolds, and Bennett presented their ideas to the president. News of the plan leaked to the press, stirring up a predictable outcry, not only from civil rights groups and their Democratic allies, but from congressional Republicans and businesses.

Nearly every civil rights group objected. The NAACP, the Southern Christian Leadership Conference, the Urban League, the National Council of Negro Women, and many others all objected to the idea of voiding 11246. At the Legal Defense Fund, one attorney declared that if Reagan signed the proposed order, "it would be the most anti-civil rights step taken by a President since Woodrow Wilson issued orders requiring the segregation of offices and other facilities in Federal Government buildings."

The president of the League of United Latin American Citizens, Oscar Moran, warned Reagan that so-called "voluntary compliance [was] doomed to failure." The entire Congressional Hispanic Caucus, like the Black Caucus, opposed the draft and reminded Reagan that every president since 1965, Republican and Democratic, had sought to "strengthen these much needed provisions."

The National Organization for Women had been among the first groups to embrace affirmative action, but by 1985 support had been building among women's groups far beyond the ranks of NOW. Groups from the Girl Scouts to radical feminists and women's groups in between rallied to the cause. The League of Women Voters, always the voice of civic-minded moderates, reminded Reagan of all the good that 11246 had done, and "the dismantling of a pervasive system of discrimination takes work—and commitment."

On 18 September 1985, a bipartisan group of 125 members of Congress urged Reagan to leave 11246 in place and to retain affirmative action guidelines for federal contractors. Support for affirmative action appeared so strong that had Reagan accepted the Meese proposal, it would have embroiled him in a battle with Congress that, no matter what the outcome, would have damaged the president and his other programs.

The National Association of Manufacturers also wanted Reagan to leave the order alone, claiming that "diversity in work force participation produced new ideas in management, product development, and marketing." In a survey of chief executives of large corporations, nine out of ten respondents claimed that "numerical objectives in their company's affirmative action were established partly to satisfy corporate objectives unrelated to government regulations." In response to a question about what the companies would do if the government repealed affirmative action requirements, over 95 percent said they planned to use numerical goals regardless of government requirements.

Even simply dropping their race- and gender-based employment processes, as the draft seemingly intended them to do, would have generated serious problems. Most large companies had an entrenched affirmative action bureaucracy, and many of the people who staffed those personnel offices were women and minorities, some with close ties to civil rights groups. If these companies ended their affirmative action programs and let their personnel people go, these employees would probably not have gone quietly. If companies like IBM, AT&T, and Merck, each with extensive affirmative action programs, suddenly shut down their in-house programs, they would face a firestorm of protest and boycotts from consumers. As *Fortune* magazine noted, "Once a company has an affirmative action program in operation, it cannot stop or even retreat noticeably without stirring grievances and impairing morale among women and minorities on the payroll."

Why did the business sector—known for its perpetual opposition to government regulation—urge Reagan to leave affirmative action rules alone? While some pointed to positive results such as a better workforce and new ideas, they also wanted to preserve legal predictability. As long as the government required contractors to use goals and timetables that favored hiring and promoting women and minorities, these firms would be immune to reverse discrimination suits brought by white males. Remove the Labor Department rules and that certainty would disappear.

In addition, despite all they tried to do to get rid of the program, Meese, Reynolds, and others in the conservative coalition failed to grasp the reality of affirmative action, how it had taken hold in the two decades since 11246. Reagan might have been the most conservative president since Herbert Hoover, but he had far better political instincts. While he could to some extent write off women and minorities, he could not ignore one-fourth of Congress or the most important constituent in his political coalition—business. Moreover, the GOP had been working hard to woo conservative black Americans, and all that work could now evaporate. The Council of 100, an organization of black Republicans, reacted in dismay. The proposed changes "will be harmful and destructive to the interest of the Council of 100 members, American Blacks, and the future of our country." The board of the National Black Republican Council voted unanimously to condemn the attorney general's plan.

Even while Meese and his lieutenants bad-mouthed affirmative action and tried to derail some of its programs, they could never persuade Reagan to go that final step. Politically, his decision made a great deal of sense, and in making that choice, he had the support of business and moderates in Congress. In addition, Reagan probably knew that various public opinion polls showed that although many Americans had conflicted feelings about affirmative action, a majority of the country embraced "soft" policies even while opposing quotas.

The Meese group and others in the administration debated the merits of the draft over the summer and into the fall, in the White House, in the Justice Department, and in the press. The key confrontation took place at a cabinet meeting on 27 October. Meese, backed by Clarence Pendleton of the Civil Rights Commission and Pat Buchanan, the White House communications director, urged Reagan to sign the draft. In opposition, Secretary of Labor Bill Brock had the support of Secretary of the Treasury James Baker and Secretary of State George Shultz, as well as that of the Senate Republican leader, Bob Dole, and the House Republican leader, Robert Michel. Brock, unlike the Meese group, had for a long time been trying to make the Republican Party more appealing to minorities. He was only willing to change OFCCP guidelines to prohibit mandatory quotas but would have permitted some goals and timetables. At the end of the meeting, Chief of Staff Donald Regan, who felt that Meese had tried to do an end run around him, suggested that the president not make a decision at the moment, and consider his options. Reagan agreed and essentially let the matter die. According to Reynolds's recollection, too much political capital was being wasted on this issue and was getting in the way of other, more important things.

The opponents of affirmative action in the Reagan administration had failed to recognize that for all the outcry about reverse discrimination and the fact that no law mandated compensatory programs, plans to help minorities and women get jobs or into schools had by the 1980s become, for better or worse, part of the nation's fabric. Although some of the leading critics belonged to the Republican Party, many in the GOP supported it. When Elizabeth Dole headed the Labor Department in the George H. W. Bush administration, she held a ceremony to mark the twenty-fifth anniversary of Executive Order 11246 and presented a plaque to Edward Sylvester, the first head of the Office of Federal Contract Compliance Programs.

ALTHOUGH THEY LOST the fight to repeal 11246, Meese and Reynolds kept up the battle to weaken affirmative action during the remaining three years of Reagan's term. They did this, probably with the president's blessing, but Reagan himself became more and more distracted by the Iran-contra imbroglio and paid little attention to their efforts. Relying on their interpretation of the *Stotts* decision, the Justice Department asked a federal court to overturn a five-year-old consent decree in Buffalo, New York. The court refused. In 1975, the city had been found guilty of discriminating against blacks, Hispanics, and women who applied for jobs as firefighters or police officers. In 1979, the court had ordered minority hiring goals that would remain in effect until the percentage of uniformed personnel equaled the percentage of minorities in the city's overall labor force.

At the beginning of April 1985, the Justice Department released a list of fifty-six cities, counties, and states that it claimed now had to modify their affirmative action plans so as to end the use of numerical goals and quotas. The letter sent to all public employers declared that any program using goals and timetables violated Title VII of the Civil Rights Act of 1964. As we have seen, racial and gender goals and timetables were specifically barred by that law, but in the intervening years affirmative action plans with goals and timetables had been used in dozens of localities to remedy past discrimination.

The Justice Department under previous presidents had signed off on almost all these decrees.

Although a few localities said they would cooperate, the majority wanted to keep the consent decrees in effect. They were working smoothly by this point, and their abandonment would most likely stir up unrest among women and minorities. The Justice Department decided to make Indianapolis its test case, hoping that a win there would bring recalcitrant jurisdictions into line, although Reynolds said no one should read this filing that way. Here again, government lawyers relied on *Stotts,* a case involving a valid seniority system that had nothing to do with the situation in Indianapolis. There the consent decree had been, like that in Buffalo, aimed at ending the discrimination against women and minorities in the police and fire departments, and according to Mayor William Hudnut it had been working just fine, with far greater numbers of women and minorities in these uniformed services, a view echoed by others.

Indianapolis defended its hiring plan, and before long other cities also said they would not follow the Justice Department demands. In New York, New Jersey, Miami, Chicago, Boston, Philadelphia, and San Francisco, officials decried the Reagan administration's efforts. Philip Trapani, the city attorney for Norfolk, Virginia, told a reporter, "No community that has been through this and achieved the success we have is anxious to go back and revisit it." The Justice Department had targeted two counties and five cities in New York, and Karen Burstein, the president of the New York State Civil Service Commission, said the state had informed Reynolds of its opposition to any effort to modify plans. "You don't make the law. Courts do and we're observing the court orders. If you're not happy, come and sue us." Similar comments came from mayors and city attorneys across the country. Only San Diego agreed to go back to court and have the judge remove the quota requirements from its plan.

During this time, the Justice Department relied on *Stotts,* which lower courts recognized as inapplicable to cases not involving seniority systems. Then, in May 1986, the high court handed down a split decision involving the layoff of white teachers in Jackson, Michigan. Once again, it upheld a valid seniority system, but Justice Lewis Powell's opinion had only Chief Justice Burger and Justice Rehnquist joining him in full, and Justice O'Connor in part. Justice White concurred in the judgment but did not join Powell's opinion, while Marshall, Brennan, Blackmun, and Stevens dissented. The failure of five justices to agree on a jurisprudential rationale left this case with even less precedential value than *Stotts*.

Then, on the last day of the term, the Court handed down two major decisions that completely undercut the Reagan administration's arguments. In *Sheet Metal Workers v. EEOC,* a 5–4 Court affirmed a lower-court order mandating minority membership goals for the union, which had stonewalled the decree. The five members of the majority, as well as Justice White (who dissented), specifically went on record to decline the government's invitation "to read *Stotts* to prohibit any kind of race-conscious relief that might benefit nonvictims."

In a second case, the Vanguards, an organization of black and Hispanic firefighters, charged Cleveland, Ohio, with discrimination in the hiring, assignment, and promotion of firefighters. The city decided to negotiate a consent decree, but the primarily white firefighters' union interceded and sought to block the agreement. The court eventually entered a decree, and the appellate court upheld it. The Reagan administration joined the firefighters in their appeal to the Supreme Court. By a 6–3 vote, the high court affirmed the lower court and also declared that "the voluntary action available to employers and unions seeking to eradicate race discrimination may include reasonable race-conscious relief that benefits individuals who were not actual victims of racial discrimination." The following year the Court, again by a 6–3 vote, upheld a Santa Clara, California, affirmative action plan that aimed at getting more women into jobs previously held only by men.

With the Supreme Court specifically approving plans with goals and timetables, Meese and Reynolds found they had no leverage with any of the localities they had been pressuring. Nonetheless, they kept on soldiering, and one week after the Supreme Court handed down its decision in this case, Reynolds went into the Court of Appeals for the District of Columbia asking it to block a District plan to hire more minorities in the fire department. When asked about the Supreme Court decisions upholding such plans, Reynolds said they had "very little impact" on the case. Unfortunately for him, Supreme Court decisions carry a great deal of "impact" on lower courts.

IN THE 1988 PRESIDENTIAL CAMPAIGN, George Herbert Walker Bush pledged to uphold and provide continuity to the conservative revolution begun by Ronald Reagan. That included maintaining

Reagan's views on employment discrimination, namely, opposition to preferential treatment for women and minorities. Yet surprisingly enough, Bush enjoyed unprecedented support from African Americans in the first eighteen months of his presidency. A *New York Times/ CBS* poll in April 1990 found a 56 percent approval rating among blacks, the highest of any Republican president since Eisenhower.

This support quickly evaporated when it became evident that Bush meant what he said about quotas and affirmative action. In October 1990, he vetoed the Kennedy-Hawkins civil rights bill, in part because it allowed quotas, and the following year he nominated Clarence Thomas, an outspoken opponent of affirmative action, to replace the civil rights icon Thurgood Marshall on the Supreme Court. Yet during Bush's four-year tenure, he signed two major employment antidiscrimination measures, the Americans with Disabilities Act (ADA) of 1990 and the Civil Rights Act of 1991, which is discussed in the next chapter.

ALTHOUGH THE BUSH ADMINISTRATION claimed the Americans with Disabilities Act as a victory, the historian John Robert Greene notes that it "deserves less credit than it has to date received." There had been no provisions for the disabled in the 1964 Civil Rights Act, and a later congressional study estimated that of the forty-three million Americans with disabilities the vast majority had faced either segregation or discrimination. In the mid-1980s, the National Council on Disability had recommended passage of a statute that would, in essence, apply civil rights law to people with disabilities and in addition require governments, businesses, and schools to make reasonable accessibility accommodations. The council drafted the first version of the bill and introduced it in both houses of Congress in 1988, but in an election year neither Congress nor President Reagan had any interest.

A revised version crafted by Senator Lowell Weicker of Connecticut had been introduced by the time Bush became president. The four-part bill prohibited employers from discriminating against qualified people with disabilities, required employers to provide adequate access to their businesses for patrons with disabilities, called for expanded access to transportation services, and required the Federal Communications Commission to provide equivalent telephone services for the speech-and-hearing impaired. All new construction after July 1992 had to be fully compliant with ADA Accessibility

Guidelines. Older buildings, if possible, had to be retrofitted, and here the law recognized that some buildings would never be able to meet the accessibility requirements.

Opposition to the act came primarily from some religious groups who did not want churches and religious schools listed as "public accommodations," and they prevailed. Not so business interests who claimed that it would cost millions of dollars. The National Federation of Independent Business called the ADA a "disaster for small business." The U.S. Chamber of Commerce called the costs associated with the law "enormous" and would have "a disastrous impact on many small businesses struggling to survive."

Shortly before the scheduled vote, disability rights activists gathered in front of the Capitol, shed their crutches, wheelchairs, and other assistive devices, and in front of numerous news cameras proceeded to crawl up all one hundred of the Capitol's front steps. As they did so, they chanted, "ADA now" or "Vote now." Jennifer Keelan, a second grader with cerebral palsy, pulled herself up the stairs using mostly her hands and arms, vowing, "I'll take all night if I have to." How effective the "Capitol Crawl" might have been in influencing the vote is impossible to determine, but present-day activists consider it the most important single action responsible for passage of the ADA.

Even though the bill did not constitute an administration measure, President Bush strongly supported it. (People close to him believed he did so because one of his sons had dyslexia and had been subject to discriminatory practices in school.) He embraced it in his inaugural and soon after told a staff gathering at the Department of Health and Human Services that he considered it one of his highest domestic priorities. On 26 July 1990, he signed it into law.

The law revolutionized the way people with disabilities are treated in this country. For all the complaints of business, in most instances the cost of providing accessibility proved far less than onerous. All of us are now used to curb cuts and ramps to facilitate people using wheelchairs. Architects had little trouble designing accessibility into new buildings, although in some instances it proved impossible to retrofit older buildings. Certainly businesses have not complained when disabled people come into their stores to spend money, and employers have discovered that just a very little accommodation in the form of assistive technology has opened a new labor pool of eager and capable workers.

George H. W. Bush signing the Americans with Disabilities Act on 26 July 1990.
Joining the president are (left to right) Evan Kemp, chair of the Equal Employment
Opportunity Commission; the Reverend Harold Wilke of Claremont, California;
Sandra Parrino of the National Council on Disability; and Justin Dart of the
President's Committee on Employment of People with Disabilities.

In some ways, one can consider Title I of the ADA a "soft" form
of affirmative action, in that it prohibited employment discrimination in hiring, firing, or promoting persons with disabilities. The
law did not establish goals or timetables, but essentially did for the
disabled what the 1964 Civil Rights Act had done for minorities and
women—opened the gates of opportunity.

CHAPTER 12

THE COURT CHANGES ITS MIND

It is plainly true that in our society blacks have suffered discrimina-
tion immeasurably greater than any directed at other racial groups.
But those who believe that racial preferences can help to "even the score"
display, and reinforce, a manner of thinking by race that was the source
of the injustice and that will, if it endures within our society, be the
source of more injustice still. The relevant proposition is not that it was
blacks, or Jews, or Irish who were discriminated against, but that it was
individual men and women, "created equal," who were discriminated
against. And the relevant resolve is that it should never happen again.
Racial preferences appear to "even the score" (in some small degree) only
if one embraces the proposition that our society is appropriately viewed
as divided into races, making it right that an injustice rendered in the
past to a black man should be compensated for by discriminating against
a white.

—ANTONIN SCALIA

For all that the Warren Court did in combating racial discrimination and expanding individual liberties, it never dealt directly
with affirmative action. The first decisions on that subject came with
the Burger Court, starting with the *Bakke* case in 1978. While the
Burger Court cut back a little on the major decisions of the 1950s
and 1960s, it never overturned any of the landmark cases that made
up the so-called due process revolution of the Warren era. Moreover,
in the area of women's equality and abortion, the Burger Court went
far beyond its predecessor.

Then Ronald Reagan named four persons, including the first
woman, and George Bush added two more. By the end of Bush's

Justice William Hubbs Rehnquist, a longtime foe of affirmative action, was named to the Supreme Court by President Nixon in 1972 and then elevated to chief justice by President Reagan in 1986.

tenure in the White House, the Court had indeed become more conservative, and its earlier acceptance of affirmative action weakened considerably.

The four Reagan appointees—Sandra Day O'Connor, Antonin Scalia, Anthony Kennedy, and William Rehnquist, who was elevated to chief justice—all looked askance at affirmative action, although O'Connor and Kennedy would later modify their views. Of the two Bush appointees, David Souter turned out to be a moderate, while Clarence Thomas became the Court's most conservative member and the one most opposed to race-based compensatory programs.

President Bill Clinton would name two members of the Court, Ruth Bader Ginsburg in 1993 to replace Byron White, and Stephen Breyer in 1994 to take the seat vacated by Harry Blackmun, and they would both support affirmative action. Then an unusual thing happened: there would be no further changes on the Court for eleven years, the second-longest "natural court" in history since the early nineteenth century. During this period, Scalia and Thomas joined with the chief justice to form the conservative bloc. Ginsburg, Breyer, and Souter made up a moderately liberal group, and in the middle were Stevens, who often joined the liberals, and Kennedy, who often joined the conservatives, and O'Connor, the true swing vote.

IN JULY 1980, the Burger Court had handed down its decision in *Fullilove v. Klutznick*, which together with *Bakke* and *Weber* apparently approved affirmative action programs by the government, by private industry, and by universities. Then, during the Reagan years, much to the dismay of the administration, the Court approved several plans and consent decrees involving affirmative action. During the first term that William Rehnquist presided as chief justice, the Court heard its only case involving affirmative action for women.

In 1980, Paul E. Johnson, an employee for the Transportation Agency of Santa Clara County, California, was passed over for a promotion to road dispatcher. In compliance with the affirmative action plan it had promulgated in 1978, the county selected a woman, Diane Joyce, for the position. Both applicants were deemed well qualified, but Johnson scored slightly higher in evaluations by the all-white, all-male management team of the department. The county manager, however, aware of the fact that men held all the 238 skilled-craft positions in the Transportation Agency and upon advice of his affirmative action officer, named Joyce to the position. Johnson went to court, alleging that the promotion decision had been gender based and, as such, violated Title VII of the 1964 Civil Rights Act. Although he won in district court, the Court of Appeals for the Ninth Circuit reversed and noted that the agency's consideration of Joyce's sex in filling the road dispatcher position was lawful. At this point, Johnson had no more money for an appeal, but his lawyer put him in touch with a conservative legal defense fund, the Lakewood, Colorado–based Mountain States Legal Foundation, which filed an appeal to the Supreme Court.

The high court affirmed. The Court first of all had to resolve, according to Justice Brennan's majority opinion, "whether the consideration of the sex of applicants for the skilled-craft jobs was justified by the existence of a 'manifest imbalance' that reflected underrepresentation of women in 'traditionally segregated job categories.'" Brennan said it was and that the county had been justified in considering an applicant's sex for promotion, "in addition to a host of practical factors in seeking to meet affirmative action objectives."

Brennan posed a second question: Had the plan "unnecessarily trammeled the rights of male employees or created an absolute bar to their advancement"? The Court rejected this argument, and Brennan said that men and women had to compete for advancement, and no absolute entitlement existed. The county's plan had legitimately attempted to create a balanced workforce, not to maintain one.

Although the official vote of the Court sustained the county by 6–3, Brennan really had only five votes fully endorsing his opinion—those of himself and Justices Marshall, Blackmun, Powell, and Stevens. Justice O'Connor wanted the opinion to emphasize that only a high numerical imbalance could justify such a plan; because Brennan would not go that far, she concurred in the judgment but not the reasoning.

If there is any single document that epitomized conservative judicial opposition to affirmative action, it would be Justice Scalia's dissent in this case. He began with an appeal to read the plain language of Title VII, language "with a clarity which, had it not proven so unavailing, one might well recommend as a model of statutory draftsmanship." He went on to quote the relevant portion of Title

Justice Antonin Scalia, appointed to the Supreme Court in 1986, laid out the strongest constitutional arguments against affirmative action in his dissents.

VII, noting that sex was one of the enumerated factors that could not be used to "deprive or tend to deprive any individual of employment opportunities or otherwise adversely affect his status as an employee." The Court, according to Scalia, "completes the process of converting this from a guarantee that . . . sex will not be the basis for employment discriminations, to a guarantee that it often will."

Scalia also articulated one of the chief conservative arguments against affirmative action. While the actual victims of discrimination should certainly be compensated and given some preference to make them whole, people who had not suffered from actual discrimination should not benefit from preferential plans. The Santa Clara plan, he charged, did not remedy prior discrimination, because there had been no discrimination to remedy. The county wanted the workforce to mirror the racial and sexual composition of the county, a statistical situation that could never exist in a bias-free world. The only way to achieve that goal required quotas. And innocents like Paul Johnson would have to pay for it. Moreover, the Court then handed down another decision that went even further, *United States v. Paradise.*

Alabama, one of the Deep South states that fought hardest not only to keep segregation but also to keep African Americans out of jobs and schools, had a state trooper force almost entirely white. In 1972, a federal district court had found that for four decades the Alabama Department of Public Safety had systematically excluded blacks; the court then issued an order imposing a hiring quota and prohibiting the department from further discrimination in its employment practices, including promotions. By 1979, although a few black troopers had been hired, none had been promoted, and the district court issued a new order requiring the department to promote one qualified black for each white trooper promoted. The appeals court affirmed the plan, and the Reagan administration brought suit against the court order.

Paradise proved to be a perplexing case and the first one since *Bakke* that involved an overt quota, a fact that had roused the wrath of William Bradford Reynolds and the Justice Department. Brennan announced the Court's opinion and, joined by Marshall, Blackmun, and Powell, declared that even under a strict scrutiny analysis the relief ordered by the district court met the requirements of the Equal Protection Clause. Such relief, he maintained, (1) was justified by a compelling governmental interest in remedying decades of discrimination, (2) supported the societal interest in compliance with judgments of federal courts, and (3) was narrowly tailored to accomplish its purpose. These four justices, along with Justice Stevens, who concurred in the results, believed that the remedy adopted by the lower court fit perfectly the egregious discrimination practiced by the state and forbidden by the Constitution.

Four justices dissented, and while none of them even attempted to defend the Alabama practices, they believed that other remedies existed that would have achieved the same result without the use of quotas. They also disagreed with the majority view that the lower-court plan had been narrowly tailored and met the standards of strict scrutiny.

The two decisions, coming within a month of each other, misled some commentators into believing that the Court, "after nine years of agonizing, splintering, and seesawing on the issue," had finally come down in favor of affirmative action and would now chart a new course in support of compensatory programs. They also noted that despite the Reagan Justice Department's best efforts the Court had repulsed their argument that affirmative action, especially plans using specific quotas, violated the Constitution. While correct on the second assertion—the failure of the administration to get a court ruling sinking affirmative action—they could not have been more wrong on the claim that the Court had reached agreement on affirmative action.

From the time it heard its first affirmative action case, the Court had been unable to achieve unity on either the results or the reasoning in this area. *Johnson* had been the first case involving gender—and in fact would be the last—and Brennan had been able to pull together a majority only because of the obvious statistical inequity that existed. Similarly, the overt discrimination of the Alabama state troopers, as well as the state's blatant defiance of a federal court order, had given him enough votes to sustain what had clearly been the most far-reaching remedy the Court had ever seen in compensatory plans. All the decisions, starting with *DeFunis* in 1974, had been by divided courts, none more so than the 4–1–4 voting in *Bakke*. The justices had been reluctant, or even unable, to engage in any systematic exposition of the law of affirmative action. The divisions among members of the Court reflected the divisions in American society, making any consensus not only impossible but perhaps undesirable as well.

Law professor Robert Belton wrote soon after *Johnson* and *Paradise* came down, "The central question in the national debate on affirmative action can be stated very simply: under what circumstances, if any, is it appropriate to take into account race or sex in the allocation of public or private economic or other resources or opportunities in our society? The various responses to this basic question also can be stated simply: always, never, or sometimes." Belton argued that neither the Court nor society had been able to resolve questions of when taking race or gender into account was permissible and/or appropriate, how one defined an "innocent" class, what the criterion of "best qualified" actually meant, and how the nation and its courts can accommodate both "equality" and "diversity" within an overarching policy against discrimination.

Given these considerations, one could hardly expect the courts to be more united than the public. Affirmative action, like abortion, has been and remains a divisive issue, and just as there is no public consensus on either one, so too have the courts remained divided.

IN MAY AND JUNE 1989, an increasingly conservative Court handed down several decisions, nearly all of them by a 5–4 vote, taking a narrow view of both Title VII and 42 U.S.C. § 1981, the two bases for most employment discrimination cases. Because these decisions involved statutory interpretation—that is, how a majority of the Court read the law—Congress could override the Court by passing new legislation that explicitly spelled out that Congress meant A, and not B as the Court had said. When the Court hands down a decision based on constitutional grounds, of course, Congress does not have that option. Briefly, these are the cases that civil rights activists and their allies in Congress wanted overturned:

Patterson v. McLean Credit Union. Brenda Patterson sued the credit union claiming it had discriminated against her, harassed her because of her race, and then fired her. She based her suit on 42 U.S.C. § 1981, an older civil rights law that had been given new life by activists trying to fill in gaps left by Title VII. The 5–4 majority rejected all of Patterson's claims and ruled that while § 1981 prohibited racial discrimination in making and enforcing private contracts, it did not cover harassment on the job.

Wards Cove Packing Co. v. Atonio (1989). In a 1971 case, the Supreme Court had held that if employment qualifications, even if facially neutral, had a disparate impact and led to discrimination against a racial group, then they violated Title VII. In this case, the Court essentially abandoned the disparate-impact test and said that plaintiffs would have to show outright discrimination in hiring and promotion.

Price Waterhouse v. Hopkins (1989). Ann Hopkins, a senior manager at Price Waterhouse, had twice been proposed for partnership and turned down, apparently due to comments about her that resulted from sex stereotyping. She sued on the basis of Title VII, and the lower courts held that such reasoning constituted discrimination and found in her favor. The Supreme Court reversed and held that if an employer could show that it also had legitimate reasons to act as it did, then the burden of proof falls on the plaintiff to show that the decision resulted from discriminatory purposes.

Lorance v. AT&T Technologies, Inc. AT&T had agreed to allow women to apply for and be promoted to a category previously held only by men. One woman filed a suit that she had been discriminated against, but the lower court ruled that she had waited too long and the statute of limitations barred her suit. The clock began running at the time the new system had been adopted, even though the alleged discrimination occurred after that.

Martin v. Wilks. Seven white firefighters sued the city of Birmingham, Alabama, alleging that they had been denied promotions in favor of less qualified blacks. The suit resulted from an earlier consent decree in which the city and county agreed to promote more blacks. The district court had dismissed the suit, noting that because the white firefighters had not been a party to the decree, they could not attack it. The court of appeals reversed, and the Supreme Court agreed, holding that it was the obligation of the original parties—the NAACP and the city—to join the firefighters in their suit; otherwise they could not be bound by the decree.

Shortly after the Court adjourned, the United States Conference of Mayors met in Charleston, South Carolina, and adopted a resolution deploring the Court's recent decisions because they would undermine affirmative action. The resolution said that recent Court decisions make "it more difficult to insure equal opportunities in employment for all Americans." Mayor William Hudnut of Indianapolis, a Republican, argued that without affirmative action "the good ol' boy network" would continue to favor whites.

AT THE TIME, although George H. W. Bush occupied the White House, Democrats controlled both houses of Congress by wide margins, and they eagerly sought a law aimed at reversing the high court. Sponsored by Senator Edward Kennedy of Massachusetts and Representative Augustus Hawkins of California, the Civil Rights Act of

1990 called for the protection of employees from job discrimination by forcing employers who practiced discrimination to pay significant monetary penalties. Businesses, of course, opposed the bill because they feared it would lead to expensive lawsuits. A number of black leaders also opposed it, seeing it as a step back from earlier civil rights legislation. Bush argued that the threat of lawsuits would lead businesses to set hiring and promotion quotas to avoid litigation. In the words of the conservative Heritage Foundation, the measure "will lead inevitably to racial quotas in America." Attempts to broker an

Senator Jesse Helms (R-N.C.) and his opponent, Harvey Gantt. The 1990 senatorial race was marked by a Helms-led smear campaign focusing on affirmative action.

agreement failed, and although both houses of Congress approved the bill, Bush vetoed the measure, declaring it would "introduce the destructive forces of quotas into our Nation's employment system." The Senate failed by only one vote to override the veto.

That fall the failed civil rights act proved a white-hot issue in the congressional elections. The Republican incumbent Jesse Helms of North Carolina used it to beat off a strong challenge from Harvey Gantt, the African American former mayor of Charlotte. Helms ran an ad that showed a white man ripping up a job rejection letter, with the voice-over declaring, "You needed that job and you were the best qualified, but they had to give it to a minority because of a racial quota." David Duke, supposedly free from ties to the Louisiana Ku Klux Klan, lost his bid for a U.S. Senate seat but won 60 percent of the white vote by playing to the quota issue. In California, Pete Wilson used the same issue to successfully win the gubernatorial race. The racial bitterness in some elections led the House majority leader, Richard Gephardt of Missouri, to charge Republican strategists with "following a new trail of racial resentment" and seeking political gain by dividing whites and blacks over the issue of affirmative action.

ON 24 SEPTEMBER 1991, Senator John Danforth, a Republican from Missouri, introduced what would become the Civil Rights Act of 1991. On 30 October, the measure passed the Senate with broad bipartisan support, as it did in the House the following week. Both chambers had veto-proof majorities. Congress largely saw itself as reaffirming its original purpose and not as enacting new legislation. Although the 1991 law dealt with multiple court decisions, the corrective action was akin to what earlier Congresses had done on a variety of issues. George Bush, trying to prove to the American people that he was neither racist nor sexist, signed it into law on 21 November 1991.

The four stated purposes of the act were to (1) provide appropriate remedies for intentional discrimination and unlawful harassment in the workplace; (2) codify the concepts of "business necessity" and "job-related" enunciated by the Court in cases prior to *Wards Cove;* (3) confirm statutory authority and provide statutory guidelines for adjudication of disparate-impact suits under Title VII; and (4) expand the scope of relevant civil rights statutes in order to provide adequate protection to victims of discrimination.

In a typical Title VII disparate-treatment case, plaintiffs (those allegedly hurt by discrimination) have the initial burden of establishing a prima facie case of differential treatment. This may be as easy as showing that there are no minorities or women in low- or middle-management positions. The employer can then respond by explaining how the numbers rest on nondiscriminatory grounds, which the plaintiff will then try to show is a mere pretext. However, in some situations employment decisions might have been based on both lawful and unlawful reasons. In *Price Waterhouse,* the Court said that in these mixed-motive cases plaintiffs had a higher initial burden, namely, showing that the employer "intended" to discriminate. The Court declared that an employment or promotion decision only in part motivated by prejudice did not violate Title VII because the employer would have made the same decision absent the discriminatory factor.

The new law overturned *Price Waterhouse* and clarified the prohibition against impermissible considerations of race, color, religion, sex, or national origin in employment decisions. The complaining party need not prove intent, only that prejudice was a motivating consideration, even if other lawful values were involved.

Ever since 1971, employers could not use standards (such as a high school or college diploma) or tests of any sort unless they could show that these standards and tests were relevant to the job for which the person was applying. In *Wards Cove,* the Court said that "business necessity," as determined by the employer, would justify the use of standards and tests and that these need not be "essential" or "indispensable" to the employer's business for it to pass muster. Plaintiffs trying to establish a discrimination case had a high burden to identify exactly which standards or tests had led to disparate impact. The Civil Rights Act turned the law back to what it had been prior to *Wards Cove,* and the burden of proof now lay on the employer to show the challenged practice was in fact job related and consistent with business necessity. (The law, however, failed to define "business necessity.")

Martin v. Wilks had held that parties agreeing to a consent decree had the obligation to include all other parties who might be affected. The new law codified standards for judicial rulings affecting affirmative action and held that people who had notice of or should have known about proposed consent decrees could not then challenge the decrees on grounds that they had not been parties.

Sexual harassment, according to the Court in *Patterson,* had no remedy in either Title VII or § 1981, and in fact § 1981 only applied to intentional discrimination in the making of an employment contract, not to what happened afterward. The law now made post-contractual conduct, such as sexual harassment, subject to § 1981.

In *Lorance,* the Court ruled that in cases involving seniority systems, the statute of limitations begins to run then the system is adopted. The new law overturned this ruling and provided that where a seniority system is adopted for intentionally discriminatory purposes, the time for filing an EEOC complaint begins when (a) the employee becomes subject to the seniority system or (b) the employee experiences the injury caused by the system.

The law provided other remedies designed to aid men and women who believed they had been the victims of employment discrimination, such as allowing jury trials and punitive as well as compensatory damages. U.S. citizens working for American companies abroad now had the protection of Title VII, reversing a decision earlier that year by the high court that said Title VII did not apply. The act also prohibited "race norming" in recruitment or promotion. (Race norming refers to the practice of adjusting the scores or using different cutoff scores for employment-related tests on the basis of race, color, or gender.) Finally, the 1991 law provided for the Glass Ceiling Commission to study obstacles facing women and minorities in trying to move upward in organizations.

Although different sections of the statute deal with affirmative action, the act itself does not define what the law actually was with respect to affirmative action, or indeed the legality of affirmative action under Title VII. As one scholar noted, "The debate about its passage is almost deafeningly silent on the subject." An interpretive memorandum submitted by Senator Bob Dole and Representative Henry Hyde noted that "this legislation does not purport to resolve the question of the legality under Title VII of affirmative action programs that grant preferential treatment to some on the basis of race, color, religion, sex or national origin, and thus 'tend to deprive' other 'individuals' of employment opportunities." The law, therefore, should not in any way be seen as expressing approval or disapproval "of any judicial decision affecting court-ordered remedies, affirmative action, or conciliation agreements." Senator Edward Kennedy agreed that nothing in the bill intended to "change the law regarding what constitutes lawful affirmative action and what constitutes impermissible reverse discrimination."

THE NEW LAW SATISFIED no one. On the one hand, several provisions regarding the ability and willingness of employers to have special programs for women and minorities now gave opponents new weapons. Section 106, for example, outlawed race norming, or the adjustment of test scores to make minorities more competitive. The next part, section 107, which responded to the *Price Waterhouse* decision, could almost be read as abolishing all affirmative action. On the face of the law, it outlaws all decisions based on race, color, sex, or national origin as a "motivating factor," but affirmative action plans do in fact take those considerations seriously. It would be possible, according to a legal scholar, that in some discrimination cases employers would now have to prove the validity of their affirmative action plans.

On the other hand, the statute also created incentives for employers to engage in race- and gender-conscious plans. Here the reversal of *Wards Cove* revived the disparate-impact test and would lead employers to hire and promote minorities and women in order to have the right numbers if sued in a discrimination case. Section 108 would make it harder, if not impossible, for groups not party to a consent decree to challenge it in court such as the firefighters had done in *Martin v. Wilks.* The new provision allowing jury trials would also encourage employers not only to set up affirmative action programs but to make sure they worked properly to avoid the expenses associated with a trial.

THE 1991 CIVIL RIGHTS ACT, however, could not touch the most important case of the 1989 term, one that marked a major shift in the Court's approach to affirmative action—*City of Richmond v. J. A. Croson Co.*

To understand *Croson,* one first has to recall *Fullilove v. Klutznick* (1980), in which the Court upheld the set-aside provisions of the Public Works Employment Act of 1977. In that statute, Congress had authorized $4 billion for public works and required that at least 10 percent of each contract go to minority business enterprises, or MBEs, which Congress defined as businesses controlled by "citizens of the United States who are Negroes, Spanish-speaking, Orientals, Indians, Eskimos and Aleuts." In the eyes of their supporters, set-aside programs offered a great opportunity for minorities to enter the economic mainstream. They also assumed that MBEs would hire minority workers and buy from minority suppliers, thus enhancing an economic network the same way white businesses had done. In *Fullilove,* a fragmented Court found that Congress had the power to enact such programs under the remedial authority granted to it by the Fourteenth Amendment.

Following this decision, many state and local governments enacted similar set-aside programs to divert public expenditures to MBEs. In April 1983, the Richmond, Virginia, City Council adopted a plan that required prime contractors doing business with the city to subcontract at least 30 percent of the dollar amount of the contract to one or more MBEs; the set-aside did not apply to contracts awarded to minority-owned prime contractors. The requirement could be waived if the prime contractor could prove that no MBEs existed that met the contractual requirements, such as eligibility for bonding. The council declared that its purpose in adopting the plan was remedial "and is enacted for the purpose of promoting wider participation by minority business enterprises in the construction of public projects." The resolution defined MBEs as any business 51 percent or more of which is owned by "citizens of the United States who are Blacks, Spanish-speaking, Orientals, Indians, Eskimos or Aleuts." While no one could remember when they had last seen an Eskimo or an Aleut on Broad Street, the council thought it prudent to adopt the same language as Congress had used.

Congress, however, had done a fair amount of work gathering facts about discrimination in the construction industry before passing the 1977 law. The council relied on very few facts, but everyone "knew" about discrimination. By 1983, the general population of Richmond had become 50 percent African American, but less than two-thirds of 1 percent of the city's prime construction contracts had gone to MBEs between 1978 and 1983. The Associated General Contractors of Virginia had no blacks among its 130 Richmond-area members, and the Central Virginia Electrical Contractors Association had one black among its 45 members, but no association admitted overt discrimination. Councilman, and later mayor, Henry L. Marsh, a longtime civil rights activist, declared, "I have been practicing law in this community since 1961, and I am familiar with the practices in the construction industry in this area, in the State, and around the nation. And I can say without equivocation, that the general conduct of the construction industry in this area, in the State, and around the nation is one in which race discrimination and exclusion on the basis of race is widespread." The city's attorney assured the council that the ordinance would pass constitutional muster because it had all the elements the high court had approved in *Fullilove*—a remedial purpose, data to support the existence of discrimination (actually, there was very little data), and a plan and definitions similar to those enacted by Congress.

That fall the city invited bids to install and renovate plumbing fixtures in the city jail. The Ohio-based J. A. Croson Co. won the bid, and because 75 percent of the cost would be the cost of the fixtures, it looked for an MBE to provide all or part of them. Only one MBE said it could do it, but by the time it paid extra to get credit and bonding, it had driven the cost well above what Croson and the city had agreed upon. Croson asked the city to waive the requirement; the city refused, announced it would rebid the contract, and invited Croson to enter a new proposal. Instead, Croson sued and in the fall of 1988 wound up in the Supreme Court.

During oral argument, Justice O'Connor asked the city's attorney,

Justice Sandra Day O'Connor, the first woman on the Supreme Court (appointed in 1981), initially voted against affirmative action. She was also the "swing vote" on the Court, and in later cases cast her ballot to uphold college diversity plans.

John Payton, a longtime civil rights lawyer, what specific evidence of discrimination Richmond had to justify the set-asides. Payton had to admit that the city had no specific evidence, but such discrimination had been well documented by Congress. This troubled O'Connor a great deal, and she wrestled over the course of her tenure on the Court with the breadth of the Fourteenth Amendment's guarantee of equal treatment and the permissibility of race-based measures to atone for discrimination. Because Richmond could show no evidence, she believed the set-aside program arose from political favoritism. Blacks constituted half of the city's population and held five of the nine seats on the city council. In the opinion she wrote for a 6–3 court, she said,

> While there is no doubt that the sorry history of both private and public discrimination in this country has contributed to a lack of opportunity for black entrepreneurs, this observation standing alone cannot justify a rigid racial quota in the awarding of public contracts in Richmond. . . . An amorphous claim that there has been past discrimination in a particular industry cannot justify the use of an unyielding racial quota.

O'Connor laid out four reasons why the plan violated the Constitution: the city had failed to demonstrate a compelling governmental interest (the sine qua non of strict scrutiny); the plan had not been narrowly tailored, and while supposedly passed for the benefit of local minority businesses, MBEs from all over the country could bid; the city had failed to utilize other less discriminatory measures to address the problem; and the fact that the city had modeled its plan on that of Congress made no difference, because Congress drew its unique authority from the Enforcement Clause of the Fourteenth Amendment.

Justice Scalia concurred with the judgment but would have outlawed all affirmative action plans, and his argument, quoted at the beginning of this chapter, encapsulates the logic of those who, for completely nondiscriminatory reasons, opposed affirmative action.

Despite Justice Marshall's impassioned charge that the decision "marks a deliberate and giant step backward in the Court's affirmative action jurisprudence," the majority result did not require an end to preferential programs. "Nothing we say today," wrote Justice O'Connor, "precludes a state or local entity from taking action to rectify the effects of identified discrimination within its jurisdiction." The Court was not shutting the door on affirmative action as much as making government accountable under stricter terms and requiring actual evidence—not anecdotes—to prove discrimination.

(After the decision came down, a group of faculty at the University of Richmond Law School volunteered to help the city put together such a record, which turned out to be a relatively easy task. The city then enacted a more modest plan that avoided the problems spelled out by Justice O'Connor.)

The most important part of the ruling, joined by five justices, said for the first time that all race-conscious policies, even those designed to benefit minorities, had to be assessed by the highest judicial standard, that of strict scrutiny. Until this case, there had been no agreement on exactly what standard race-based plans should be judged—the relatively low standard of rational basis (approval if the plan made sense to a rational person), intermediate scrutiny (requiring the government to have an "important" interest, and applied mainly to cases involving gender discrimination), or strict scrutiny (the government had to have a "compelling" interest with a "narrowly tailored" remedy).

In some ways, *Croson* brought to an end a debate going back to *DeFunis* and *Bakke.* How should the Constitution look at laws and programs that differentiate on the basis of race? Should there be one standard for the older segregationist-era laws that favored whites over blacks, and another criterion for new laws that gave blacks preference in the name of historical redress? Or should there be just one standard for any race-based law, that of the first justice Harlan's "the Constitution is color-blind"? In *Croson,* a majority for the first time agreed it should be the latter: "The standard of review under the Equal Protection Clause is not dependent on the race of those burdened or benefited by a particular classification."

Municipal and state governments with set-asides—and there were many of these—now worried whether their plans might be challenged and, if so, whether they would survive. Richmond had gone too far in setting 30 percent as a standard; different localities had varying percentages. In the wake of the decision, no one knew exactly what evidence would be needed, what would be an allowable set-aside, and how pervasive discrimination could be documented. In Georgia, the state supreme court, relying on *Croson,* overturned the widely copied Atlanta construction ordinance, which had set—

and met—a goal of 35 percent, and Mayor Andrew Young called for a moratorium on construction contracts until the issue could be settled. In the decade following the decision, localities for the most part continued some form of set-aside, although a few of these wound up in state or lower federal courts; the Supreme Court took none of them on appeal.

Perhaps the most unusual reaction to *Croson* appeared in academia. The Reverend Charles Stith, president of the Organization for a New Equality, asked Professor Laurence Tribe of the Harvard Law School if he could convene on short notice a group of constitutional scholars to provide guidance to states and municipalities on what they needed to do to either protect or modify their affirmative action programs. Eighteen scholars gathered in Boston's historic African Meeting House on 30 March 1989; another twelve participated by phone.

The group accurately read what O'Connor had said in the majority opinion, that "affirmative action programs [must] be carefully designed—not dismantled. A call for fairness and flexibility in affirmative action programs should never be equated with a call for retrenchment and defeat." The case, in their opinion, did not depart from legal principles established in *Bakke, Fullilove,* and *Wygant,* namely,

1. The Equal Protection Clause does not preclude measures to bring excluded groups into the societal mainstream.
2. The Court has rejected the notion that localities have to bear the often tortuous burden of documenting specific acts of discrimination. Rather, flexible race-conscious remedial goals should be based on relevant statistical comparisons.
3. The Court has not held that set-aside programs initiated before *Croson* must be dismantled because the facts justifying such programs had not been fully developed at the time those programs were put in place.
4. In some contexts, race-conscious programs may be used not only to rectify past discrimination, but also as a forward-looking way of promoting racial harmony. The best example of this is the desegregation of schools and the efforts to achieve racial diversity.
5. Race-conscious remedies need to be both effective and fair to the entire community, and the burdens incidental to such programs should be spread equitably.

The scholars then suggested three guidelines for both government officials and the courts that would hear any challenges:

1. Attention must be paid to the pervasive effects of discrimination, especially the subtle consequences of deterring and discouraging members of minority groups from even seeking to enter the market for occupations, business opportunities, or even homes in certain neighborhoods.
2. When asking local governments to establish a factual record, it is essential not to deter voluntary efforts by forcing these governments to point fingers needlessly or to make compromising public admissions in order to establish the justification for a program.
3. While cities should be responsible for modifying their programs to fit the Court's ruling in *Croson,* they should be allowed sufficient time to engage in good faith efforts to do so.

Anthony Lewis, the longtime legal affairs correspondent for *The New York Times,* praised the scholars' statement for its measured tone and its message that the Court had not, as some of its members might have wanted, killed affirmative action. "This is a time for healing," they had said, and while difficult legal doctrines should be hotly debated, they could not obscure what is at the heart of the issue. "The remedies must be careful and fair, but they cannot yet exclude consciousness of what brought us to this point—race."

THE HIGH COURT heard two more cases in the next few years, both dealing with programs of the national government. The first, *Metro Broadcasting, Inc. v. Federal Communications Commission* (1990), concerned two types of federal set-asides; one gave special credit to minorities applying for new licenses, and the other, a so-called distress-sale program, required some radio and television stations to be sold only to minority-controlled companies. The Communications Act of 1934 had called for the FCC to award radio licenses to diverse groups, but this had meant geographic status rather than race. Starting in 1977, however, after a conference showing how few minorities owned radio or television stations, the FCC implemented plans to facilitate more minority-owned outlets. During the Reagan administration, the FCC had tried to dismantle these programs, but

Congress, in 1987, blocked the commission from spending any of its appropriated money to examine or change the policies. Under the policy, the FCC awarded Rainbow Broadcasting, whose ownership was 90 percent Hispanic, a license for a UHF facility in Orlando, Florida. Metro Broadcasting, which probably would have gotten the license absent the policy, sued the FCC, charging that the policies violated the constitutional guarantee of equal protection. The court of appeals upheld the extra credit policy but struck down the distress-sale program.

In his last opinion for the Court, Justice William Brennan managed to cobble together a 5–4 majority, joined by White, Marshall, Blackmun, and Stevens. In an endorsement of affirmative action, the Court ruled that Congress may order preferential treatment of minorities to increase their ownership of broadcast licenses. Such benign race-conscious measures, including those that do not compensate victims of past discrimination, are constitutional as long as they further important governmental objectives, in this case giving minorities a greater voice in the country's radio and television media.

The decision certainly cheered civil rights activists, who agreed with the Harvard Law professor Kathleen Sullivan that "it's a green light for many federally initiated affirmative action programs." William Taylor, a civil rights lawyer, noted that many congressionally authorized programs "are commonly race or gender specific." Conservatives like Charles Fried, the former solicitor general in the Reagan administration, called the ruling "a horrible thing because it doesn't necessarily put any black people to work." Setting aside lucrative licenses seemed to him "a ready-made source of corruption."

The enthusiastic sense of victory lasted only to *Adarand Constructors, Inc. v. Peña* in 1995. Although a very splintered decision—only Rehnquist and Kennedy joined fully in O'Connor's opinion; Scalia and Thomas concurred only in the judgment; Stevens, Souter, and Ginsburg dissented, with Breyer joining the latter two—it extended strict scrutiny review to programs of the federal government.

The federal government had authorized set-asides ever since 1977, and the program had been upheld in *Fullilove v. Klutznick* (1980). Following *Croson,* however, a white-owned company, Adarand Constructors, lost a government subcontract to a minority-owned business and sued, claiming that the racial classification violated the Fifth Amendment's Due Process Clause. Justice O'Connor held that under the Due Process Clauses of the Fifth and Fourteenth Amendments any action involving racial classification by either the state or the federal government would henceforth be judged by a standard of strict scrutiny, and that part of *Metro Broadcasting* giving the federal government greater leeway was overruled. Just as the Court had for four decades frowned on measures that discriminated on the basis of race, it now also frowned on measures that favored on the basis of race.

O'Connor, however, just as she had done in *Croson,* stated that this decision did not make all affirmative action programs, including set-asides, automatically unconstitutional. Instead, government—federal, state, or local—would have to show a record of actual prior discrimination to justify a narrowly tailored plan. "The unhappy persistence of both the practice and the lingering effects of racial discrimination against minorities in this country is an unfortunate reality, and government is not disqualified from acting in response to it."

This willingness to allow some racial classification lost her Scalia and Thomas, who argued that a government could never meet the compelling interest standard of strict scrutiny if it engaged in discrimination to compensate for prior discrimination. Under the Constitution, Scalia maintained, there can be no such thing as either a creditor or a debtor race. "We are just one race in the eyes of government. It is American."

(Despite all the rhetoric, the Court did not actually invalidate that part of a 1977 law requiring set-asides but sent it back to the district court to rehear the case and apply strict scrutiny.)

The analysis of *Adarand* that followed ranged from "this should be the end of affirmative action once and for all" to "the decision is inconsequential." *Adarand* was "very nearly beside the point" and "insignificant," because it is the world of politics, "not the courtroom, where the fate of affirmative action will ultimately be decided." Columnist George Will also attacked the decision for "settling nothing," but much to Will's chagrin President Bill Clinton and his assistant attorney general for civil rights, Deval Patrick, spoke of *Adarand* as "a setback, but not a disaster," and they dismissed what they termed "exaggerated claims about the end of affirmative action—whether in celebration or dismay."

The Justice Department noted that *Adarand* would probably have little effect. With the exception of Scalia and Thomas, who categorically opposed any and all race-based programs, a majority of the Court acknowledged that the lingering effects of racial discrimination would justify some race-based programs. One area in which the Court had given no hint involved diversity, and nothing in *Adarand* cast any cloud on affirmative action programs in universities, for example, whose goal was to diversify the student body. Another area that the Court had failed to address involved gender-based programs. The Court had earlier refused to make gender a suspect classification subject to strict scrutiny, and nothing in *Adarand* shed any light on how the justices would respond to future cases involving affirmative action for women.

Neal Devins, a law professor at William & Mary, made a strong case that *Adarand,* like nearly all the high court's decisions on affirmative action, had very little relevance to the real world. Affirmative action, for all the criticism against it, enjoyed wide support in Congress and in state governments, a proven program to enable legislators to show, in very concrete terms, what they were doing to help women and minorities. Although the Court had set some boundaries limiting the reach of some affirmative action programs, in essence these programs would continue and would be little affected. In earlier cases, Court decisions had enabled affirmative action plans to develop, and whether one thought they did good or harm, they had become established. In the private sector, many companies had adopted affirmative action plans, and no one challenged them; the Fourteenth Amendment applied to state governments, not corporations. All the cases discussed in this chapter attacked government—at the local, state, or federal level—and despite the shift in the high court, most jurisdictions still maintained some form of affirmative action to benefit minorities and women. By the 1990s, affirmative action had become part of the nation's politics, its economy, and its educational system.

THERE WOULD BE no more major Supreme Court decisions on affirmative action until 2003, but two other cases are worth a brief discussion.

In 1975, the Board of Education of the Township of Piscataway, New Jersey, developed a fifty-two-page affirmative action plan pursuant to a directive from the state board of education, which, with a supplemental 1983 document, would govern all employment decisions in the Piscataway schools, including hiring as well as layoffs. If two applicants applied for a job, the one with clearly superior qualifications would be hired. If, however, the two had equal merit and one was a minority member, then the minority person should be chosen. The policy seemed to meet the criteria in *Weber* that a policy should mirror the overall antidiscrimination purposes of Title VII and not "unnecessarily trammel the interests of [nonminority] employees." There was no past discrimination to be remedied; black employees were neither "under-represented" nor "under-utilized." In fact, the percentage of African Americans in the job category that included teachers exceeded the percentage of blacks in the available workforce.

A fairly specific state law governed decisions regarding layoffs—nontenured before tenured, and among tenured faculty in reverse order of seniority. In May 1989, the board decided to reduce by one person the teaching staff in the business department at Piscataway High School. Two of the teachers were of equal seniority, Sharon Taxman and Debra Williams. Williams was the only African American in the business department, and because the two were equal in seniority and both had good records, the board decided to keep Williams for the sake of diversity. In no other layoff had there been a question of race, and school officials testified that the decision had been based entirely on race.

Following the board's decision, Taxman sued on the grounds of discrimination. She won in federal district court, where a jury awarded her $134,000 for back pay, fringe benefits, and other costs and ordered the school board to hire her back with full seniority from the time she began work. The jury also awarded her an additional $10,000 for emotional suffering. Both sides appealed, and the court of appeals affirmed the lower court's judgment. Judge Carol Los Mansmann, a Reagan appointee, ruled that Congress intended Title VII to stop discrimination or remedy previous discrimination. Only the latter reason allows employers to use race in making employment decisions, and such a record did not exist in this case. The appeals court also rejected the board's attempt to use the *Bakke* decision as a basis for upholding diversity.

Both the school board and Taxman appealed to the Supreme Court, which granted certiorari on 27 June 1997. The board had already spent nearly a quarter of a million dollars on the case and recognized that before the litigation ended, it would cost a great deal more. Moreover, many of the amicus briefs that had been filed with the high court urging it to take the case wanted the Court to overrule two decades of precedent upon which affirmative action policies rested. At this point, several national civil rights organizations expressed their concern that an adverse ruling in the case would gut the infrastructure of affirmative action across the country. Working through the Black Leadership Forum in Washington, they contributed $308,500 to the school board for it to make an offer Taxman would accept. That money accounted for 70 percent of the settlement, which came to $433,500 plus attorneys' fees. The case now became moot, and the Supreme Court dismissed certiorari a few days later.

There were very few such cases, but even though this episode took place primarily during the Clinton administration, which was favorable to affirmative action, the civil rights groups remembered very well the hostility of the Reagan and Bush presidencies. In fact it was the Bush Justice Department that first filed the suit against the school board, and rights organizations worried that if they lost this case, which seemed very likely after the district and appeals courts had ruled, it would become a polestar for future administrations hostile to affirmative action. To be rid of that worry seemed worth the $300,000.

THE SECOND CASE proved far more worrisome to civil rights activists. Cheryl Hopwood, as Judge Jerry Smith pointed out, had a "unique background." In fact, if overcoming past hardship were counted as a plus when she applied to the University of Texas Law School, she should have been among the more qualified candidates. Her father died when she was young, and she was reared by her mother under difficult circumstances. Hopwood had worked her way through high school and then put herself through community college and California State University at Sacramento, from which she graduated with a 3.8 GPA. She had married a serviceman and given birth to a severely handicapped child (who later died) and a baby who died hours after birth. After she became a Texas resident, she did well enough on the LSAT to get into a category of applicants who were almost automatically admitted. If the university was truly seeking diversity, "her circumstances would bring a different perspective to the law school." But the school turned her down, and at first Hopwood, who is white, thought, "Wow, they must have an awfully smart class," and she wanted to know how smart. She then discovered that the school had an affirmative action policy and that African American and Mexican American students with test scores comparable to hers—and even lower—had been admitted. She decided to go to court.

The university argued that part of its mission was to increase the racial and ethnic diversity of the Texas legal profession, including law firms, the state legislature, and courts. "Law in a civil society depends overwhelmingly on the willingness of society to accept its judgment," said Michael Sharlot, dean of the law school. "It becomes harder to achieve that if we don't see members of all groups playing roles in the administration of justice." In Texas, African Americans and Mexican Americans made up 40 percent of the population, but a far smaller proportion of the legal profession. The law school affirmative action program aimed at enrolling about 15 percent of the entering class from minority applicants.

On 19 August 1994, the district court ruled that Texas could continue to impose racial preferences and that the goals of diversity and overcoming the effects of past discrimination satisfied the compelling interest part of strict scrutiny. The judge, however, ordered the school to allow Hopwood and other plaintiffs to reapply without a fee.

Hopwood appealed, and the Fifth Circuit by a 2–1 vote not only ruled in her favor but applied the *Croson-Adarand* test of strict scrutiny and found the law school admissions policy defective. Judge Jerry Smith also ruled that the decision in *Bakke,* whatever its virtues in 1978, was no longer good law for several reasons. According to Smith, if the case came before the current Court, Justice Lewis Powell's view would not command five votes. In the past, Smith claimed, the high court had only found a compelling governmental interest in remedying the effects of past discrimination, and there had never been five votes for prospective justifications, such as achieving the benefits of diversity. Because Texas could not justify its plan as a remedy for past discrimination—a blatant discrimination that Smith conveniently played down—its affirmative action plan had to fall.

The Fifth Circuit decision came down on 18 March 1996. That August, the Texas attorney general, Dan Morales, advised Texas colleges and universities to operate on a race-neutral basis. He interpreted *Hopwood* as applying to all student programs, efforts at recruitment and retention of minority students, and tutoring specifically directed toward minority students. Morales also advised the University of Texas to dismantle a $300,000-a-year minority hiring program that had helped bring numerous African American and Hispanic professors to the University of Texas campus in Austin between 1988 and 1997. Formally segregated and forced to integrate in 1950, the UT forty-seven years later could no longer consider race in its admissions decisions.

In response to *Hopwood,* the U.S. Department of Education issued guidelines declaring that *Bakke* still held for colleges and universities not in the Fifth Circuit, but those institutions in the three states covered by the circuit had to follow *Hopwood.* For schools in Louisiana and Mississippi operating under desegregation decrees from federal courts, it made no difference. In the end, only Texas would be affected.

There minority admissions plummeted. In 1995, the entering class at the law school consisted of 7.4 percent black and 12.5 percent Hispanic; in 1997, those numbers fell to 0.9 and 5.6 percent, respectively. To legally address the dearth of minority undergraduates at the University of Texas and Texas A&M, then governor George W. Bush signed into law what has become known as the Top 10 Percent Plan. Under this law, all Texas students who graduated in the top tenth of their high school class would receive automatic admission to any public college or university in the state. The plan has indeed increased minority enrollments, but it has also come under attack. Many of the poorer schools that serve minority areas may produce students who, although in the top tier of the school, are not academically prepared for college.

Although the law school appealed to the Supreme Court, the justices refused certiorari and as usual did not spell out the reasons why. Justice Ginsburg, joined by Justice Souter, entered a brief concurrence. The question raised in the initial suit, whether a public college or graduate school could use race in its admissions process, "is an issue of great national importance." However, Texas was not challenging the judgment of the lower court, and in fact the law school had ceased using the procedure in place when Hopwood had applied. Instead, Texas was challenging the reasoning employed by Judge Smith. "This Court reviews judgments, not opinions." Therefore they would have to wait until a case involving a genuine controversy addressed this important issue.

It would be nearly a decade before the Court took a university affirmative action case, and a decade after that a new Texas plan made its way to the Marble Palace.

CHAPTER 13

MEND IT, DON'T END IT—OR NOT

So let us today trace the roots of affirmative action in our never-ending search for equal opportunity. Let us determine what it is and what it isn't. Let us see where it's worked and where it hasn't and ask ourselves what we need to do now. Along the way, let us remember always that finding common ground as we move toward the 21st century depends fundamentally on our shared commitment to equal opportunity for all Americans. It is a moral imperative, a constitutional mandate, and a legal necessity.

—BILL CLINTON

Bill Clinton spoke at the Congressional Black Caucus dinner every year starting with his election to the presidency in 1992. At the caucus's awards meeting in July 2008, the members honored him as "the first black president." Clinton, who had set up his postpresidential office in Harlem, declared, "I am honored to be thought of as the first black president." At the time of his election, he had a reputation going back to his days as governor of Arkansas as being friendly and fair to minorities. Not surprisingly, rights activists hoped that after twelve years of Reagan and Bush they would finally have someone in the White House sympathetic to the needs of African Americans, women, and other groups suffering discrimination. Clinton for the most part lived up to their expectations.

He took office, however, at a difficult time. Joan Biskupic, writing in *The Washington Post,* compared racial issues to abortion as the country's most "bitter and sustained" conflicts. Another commentator, Steve Roberts, believed "affirmative action is a time bomb primed to detonate in the middle of the American marketplace." Lincoln

Caplan claimed that affirmative action had become "a surrogate for unsolved problems of race in America."

Public opinion polls in the years leading up to Clinton's presidency consistently found that between 70 and 80 percent of respondents opposed granting preferential treatment to individuals based on racial or ethnic classifications. This animus would only grow. In the last year of Clinton's tenure, a Gallup poll showed that 85 percent of Americans would vote against, and only 13 percent for, a proposition mandating racial preferences in jobs and schools. Although racism played some role in all this, studies showed that many whites, even while opposing affirmative action, still expressed support for making extra efforts to help African Americans. The intensity of feeling on both sides made it impossible for Clinton—or for any president friendly to affirmative action—to move as easily as Lyndon Johnson or even Richard Nixon had done.

ALTHOUGH CLINTON campaigned on the economy—the signs in his campaign offices read, "It's the Economy, Stupid"—in fact the recession that had begun under Bush in 1990 had started to improve by the 1992 election, although recovery remained sluggish. An estimated 4.5 million Americans had lost their jobs, many of them from the middle classes; contemporaries spoke of a "white-collar recession," and the unemployment rate reached 7.8 percent in mid-1991, the highest in ten years. Despite the underlying improvements, bad economic news dominated the headlines in 1991 and 1992, making Clinton's point even sharper.

Clinton took the oath of office in January 1993, and economic conditions, especially for African Americans, improved considerably during his two terms. The median household income for blacks increased from roughly $24,000 in 1990 (in constant 2000 dollars) to $30,400 in 2000, or by 27 percent. In the same period, median income for whites rose by 10 percent, although they still outearned blacks. The income of African American married couples, which had been 67 percent that of white couples in 1967, had risen to 87 percent by 1995. College-educated black women did very well in the workforce. Black poverty also declined from 9.8 million in 1990, affecting 31.9 percent of all blacks, to 7.9 million in 2000, or 22 percent. According to the historian James Patterson, this was a "stunning" decrease, because black poverty had hovered between 30.7 and

35.7 percent between 1970 and 1990, and all this improvement took place after 1993. At the same time, median household income for Hispanics rose by 17 percent, from $28,700 to $33,400, and for Asian Americans from $49,400 to $55,500, far above the overall rise from $38,400 to $42,200. For some commentators, the government's efforts had allowed blacks to move "into a wider range of professions and higher income brackets, creating a black middle class." Many black leaders cheered that affirmative action procedures, despite all the efforts of Reagan and Bush, seemed solidly entrenched in corporations, universities, and local governments.

Once in office, Clinton initially tended to avoid the issue of affirmative action, although he tried, as he had promised, to have a cabinet and administration that "looked like America." This policy angered conservatives, and a *Newsweek* article titled "White Male Paranoia" quoted critics who declared that Clinton's determination to appoint "the best female attorney general baldly and publicly violated the canons of fair play and equal opportunity." As one woman sarcastically noted, the appointment of Janet Reno now put the historic count of attorney generals at seventy-seven men to one woman. In the end, some feminists charged, despite all his talk about a diverse

In 1993, President Clinton named Janet Reno his attorney general, the first woman to serve in that position; the appointment stirred up conservative opposition.

administration, Clinton put too few women into the cabinet, and almost none in key White House advisory positions.

This is unfair, especially when comparing Clinton's choices with those of previous presidents. He named women to the cabinet—at Justice, Energy, and Health and Human Services—as well as to the United Nations and the Environmental Protection Agency. He appointed African Americans to Agriculture, Commerce, Veterans Affairs, and the Drug Czar's office, and Hispanic Americans to Transportation and Housing and Urban Development. Clinton's record on judicial appointments also shows a greater diversity than any of his predecessors. Nonetheless, civil rights activists, disappointed with the twelve years of Reagan and Bush, wanted more, and they kept after Clinton to do more.

One incident that had rights activists wondering about Clinton involved a promise he had made during the campaign to a coalition of gay and lesbian groups, in which he said that he would issue an executive order to end the ban on homosexuals in the military. Less than ten days after his inauguration, Clinton sent a memorandum to the secretary of defense asking for a draft of an executive order by 15 July "ending discrimination on the basis of sexual orientation in determining who may serve in the Armed Forces of the United States." The secretary should consult with the Joint Chiefs of Staff and recommend how the policy could be carried out in "a manner that is practical, realistic, and consistent with the high standards of combat effectiveness and unit cohesion our Armed Forces must maintain." At that time, the military barred gays from service and determined who they were by the simple expedient of asking. Clinton believed that there should be a separation between homosexual status and homosexual conduct during military service. So long as gays observed the armed forces regulation governing sexual conduct, they should be allowed to serve without fear of dismissal. Clinton had no idea how this memo would stir up a hornet's nest of opposition both in Congress and at the Pentagon.

From the start, a wide range of opponents, including all the Joint Chiefs of Staff and key members of Congress, resisted the idea. For Clinton, the proposal seemed simple, straightforward, and fair, but it kicked up an acrimonious controversy that lasted into July. The president then accepted a compromise worked out by Senator Sam Nunn (D-Ga.), put into effect not by an executive order but by a

President Clinton with the Joint Chiefs of Staff, who unanimously opposed allowing gays to serve in the military. From left to right, *Admiral Frank Kelso, General Gordon Sullivan, General Colin Powell, President Clinton, Secretary of Defense Les Aspin, Admiral David Jeremiah, General Merrill McPeak, and General Carl Mundy Jr.*

Defense Department directive. Military personnel would not reveal their sexual preference, and their superiors would not ask them about it. Known as "Don't ask, don't tell," the policy pleased no one. The military removed any references to sexual orientation from enlistment questionnaires and directed officers to judge the actual conduct of service men and women and not their sexual preference. The policy outraged the gay community, which had strongly supported Clinton's candidacy, and the controversy caused a twenty-point decline in the president's approval rating. "Don't ask, don't tell" did not work very well. Over the next ten years, the military discharged some ten thousand service men and women who revealed their sexual preferences. Not until 2010 did Congress enact legislation repealing the policy and allowing gays, lesbians, and bisexuals to serve openly in the armed forces.

THE TURMOIL OF "Don't ask, don't tell," as well as the Republican takeover of Congress in 1994, made Clinton wary of undertaking additional race-related initiatives. The GOP "Contract with America" included opposition to affirmative action, and in both the 104th and the 105th Congresses, Republicans introduced several bills to dismantle affirmative action. The Senate majority leader, Bob Dole, co-sponsored a repeal of all race and gender preferences in 1995 along with Representative Charles Canady of Florida. Senator Phil Gramm of Texas, who had his eye on the 1996 Republican nomination, several times attached riders to appropriations bills prohibiting minority set-asides, although not a single one emerged from committee. Efforts soon ground to a halt in the Senate, awaiting Dole's decision on whether to push forward.

On the House side, Speaker Newt Gingrich blocked consideration of a repeal measure until the Republicans could enact "empowerment" legislation to help minorities and the poor. In March 1996, Representative Canady began pushing his bill, and the House Judiciary Committee's Constitution Subcommittee approved the Dole-Canady proposal on an 8–5 vote. The purpose of the bill, he explained, would be to "prohibit the federal Government from intentionally discriminating against, or granting a preference to, any person or group based in whole or in part on race, color, national origin, or sex, in three specific areas—Federal contracting, Federal employment, and the administration of other federally-conducted programs." The bill would have also prevented the government from "requiring or encouraging Federal contractors to discriminate or grant preferences based on race or sex." The only form of affirmative action it would have allowed would have been outreach, as long as at the decision stage all contracts were awarded solely on the merits of the bidder. Between the opposition of the Clinton administration and that of corporations who did not want to offend women or people of color, the effort to roll back federal affirmative action policies went nowhere.

With a presidential campaign and election looming in 1996, and after the success of the Contract with America, Republicans began attacking affirmative action programs more energetically. As one Republican strategist put it, "It is a no-lose proposition for us." Senator Bob Dole of Kansas, the early front-runner for the Republican nomination, avoided coming right out in opposition, but in an appearance on *Meet the Press* he said, "The people in America now are paying a price for things that were done before they were born. We did discriminate. We did suppress people. It was wrong. Slavery was wrong. But should future generations have to pay for that?"

A few days after the House overwhelmingly killed a tax break that would help minority businesses buy television and radio stations, Clinton announced that the administration would review dozens of

Senator Bob Dole, Republican of Kansas, in 1984; he would lose to Clinton in the 1996 presidential contest.

federal preference programs and support changes in any found to be unfair. His senior adviser George Stephanopoulos explained that "the President wants to make sure that we stand against any attempt to use race as a wedge issue, to make sure that where there is discrimination, affirmative remedies apply and still apply." According to a Library of Congress search ordered by Senator Dole, the federal government had 160 affirmative action programs that had been written into law over a nearly thirty-year period. Clinton told the House Democratic Caucus that all of these should be looked at to ensure there is no waste or corruption, "but we have to reaffirm the best aspects of our historic commitment to equal opportunity." A day later, he reiterated his remarks, saying, "We shouldn't be defending things that we can't defend," but he believed a majority of Americans still supported affirmative action.

Clinton asked officials in his administration to answer three specific questions in evaluating federal affirmative action programs:

What are these programs? Do they work? Is there some other way we can reach any objective without giving a preference for race or gender in these programs? He hoped the review would be a starting point for a national conversation that would engage men and women, people of color and whites, and the nation's policy makers as well as its intellectual elite.

The president received the first draft of the review at the end of May. The report concluded that most hiring and other preferences based on race or sex were justified in employment and education. Problems did exist, however, with some purchasing programs that reserved federal contracts for companies owned by blacks or women. Most programs increased productivity by reducing discrimination and finding the best candidates for particular jobs. But problems existed in programs that established "hard set-asides" or rigid quotas for blacks, Hispanics, and women. These latter programs seemed to be the main cause of white male opposition, which appeared to be rising not because of affirmative action but because of a static or shrinking economy, corporate layoffs, and increasing nonwhite immigration, all of which "may fuel ugly racial sentiments, particularly in tight or transitional economic times." Clinton, already aware of white resentment and the efforts of the Republican Party to utilize it, had acknowledged this problem in a speech to the California Democratic Party in April, saying, "This is psychologically a difficult time for a lot of white males, the so-called angry white males" who feel they have been treated unfairly.

All this had taken place before the *Adarand* decision came down on 12 June 1995, and because of the review it had done, the administration could respond quickly. Even as Republicans in Congress called for complete elimination of affirmative action programs, the Department of Justice sent out a thirty-eight-page memorandum to all federal agencies, saying that any preferential programs now needed to be justified by evidence of particularized discrimination in a specific sector, rather than a general assumption of widespread racism or sexism. The memo also drew a distinction between programs required under a congressional statute, which presented a much stronger legal case—because Congress had in most of those laws held hearings documenting discrimination—than did federal programs not directly authorized by Congress. The general counsels of all federal agencies had to review any affirmative action plans within their agency to ensure that they met the new criteria; no program, however, should be suspended until after completion of the review. Once the separate administration review had been completed, Clinton met with civil rights leaders in mid-July, assuring them that while there might be changes in some programs, he remained committed to affirmative action. Meanwhile, opposition to affirmative action in Congress cooled, because Speaker of the House Newt Gingrich wanted the GOP to develop a legislative package that would benefit minorities and women, and no evidence of such a package yet existed. Republicans also worried that a strong anti-affirmative-action bill would make them look racist, sexist, and heartless.

Clinton turned to Christopher Edley, his special counsel, who had overseen the administration's review, and asked him to draft a speech, which he gave in the Rotunda of the National Archives on 19 July 1995. "Our challenge is two-fold," the president began, "first, to restore the American dream of opportunity and the American value of responsibility and, second, to bring our country together amid all our diversity into a stronger community, so that we can find common ground and move forward as one. More than ever these two endeavors are inseparable."

Affirmative action had not always been perfect, and it should not go on forever. "It should be changed now to take care of those things that are wrong, and it should be retired when its job is done. I am resolved that this day will come, but the evidence suggests, indeed screams, that this day has not come. The job of ending discrimination in this country is not over."

Despite some progress, there were too many areas of American life in which minorities and women still faced discrimination. In many instances, affirmative action had been abused or not used well, and the Clinton administration would do all that it could to get rid of such problems. But all in all, affirmative action had worked—in government, in the military, in private businesses, and in universities. And compensatory programs remained necessary in the light of discrimination that minorities and women still suffered. "The job is not done. So here is what I think we should do. We should reaffirm the principle of affirmative action and fix the practices. We should have a simple slogan: Mend it, but don't end it."

But while Clinton still supported affirmative action, federal agencies, in the aftermath of the *Adarand* decision and Republican congressional opposition, began to back off from some of their prior positions. The Pentagon suspended a contracting rule that in 1994 had led to over $1 billion in subcontracts going to minority-owned businesses. The Office of Federal Contract Compliance Programs revised its procedures on how federal contractors had to report their minority workers, a step hailed by everyone as lessening a regulatory burden. In March 1996, the administration announced a three-year moratorium on any new federal programs that reserved some contracts exclusively for companies owned by minorities or women. The stringent conditions applied to any new proposals led a senior administration official to say that "as a practical matter, set-asides are gone." Near the end of the Clinton years, the Federal Communications Commission also changed its rules, which in effect did away with the quotas that had often been disguised as goals.

In December 1997, Clinton and Vice President Al Gore, as part of the Race Initiative Outreach program, met with some of the most fervent opponents of affirmative action: Ward Connerly, the chief strategist of California's Prop 209; Professors Abigail and Stephan Thernstrom; Elaine Chao, an economist and later to be secretary of labor in the George W. Bush administration; and the Florida congressman Charles Canady, who had introduced legislation to end affirmative action. While the conservatives argued that whites had

President Clinton and Vice President Al Gore meet with civil rights leaders and opponents of affirmative action, 19 December 1997. The woman seated to the left of the vice president is Linda Chavez, and as can be seen from her expression, the discussion changed no minds.

real fears, Clinton responded that they ignored equally real fears in the black community. "The other day we had a group of African-American journalists in here," the president said. "Every man, every single, solitary one, had been stopped by the police when he was doing nothing, for no other reason than he was black." Police profiling, sentencing disparities, redlining of mortgage applications, and employment discrimination still existed. The country needed affirmative action not just to compensate for the past injustices of slavery but to tear down the systematic racism that still impacted the daily lives of African Americans.

DESPITE SOME DRAWBACKS by federal agencies, Clinton believed that affirmative action worked, and there seemed solid evidence to support that view. The Department of Labor sent out a questionnaire aimed at determining whether the policies of the Office of Federal Contract Compliance Programs had made a difference, and it turned out that the OFCCP had been quite effective. In the summer of 1994 alone, the OFCCP had negotiated a number of affirmative action settlements. To take but one example, the Honeywell Corporation agreed to a $6.5 million settlement resolving a sex discrimination case that could affect up to six thousand women. In addition to back pay, the company agreed to promote equal employment opportunity in all its plants and offices.

Other sources also seemed to agree that affirmative action had in fact made a big difference in the lives of working women and minorities but differed over how much of the improvement could be attributed to one program or another. Alfred Blumrosen, a labor law specialist at Rutgers University, argued that various government equal opportunity programs accounted for the employment of as many as five million people of color—one-quarter of people of color—in the 1992 labor force. Two economists who studied affirmative action agreed that federal contractors employed a higher proportion of women and minorities than companies without federal contracts. According to a report requested by the White House, "There is near-unanimous consensus among economists that the government anti-discrimination programs beginning in 1964 contributed to the [rise in] income of African-Americans. Nevertheless, it is difficult to draw conclusions about which specific anti-discrimination programs were most effective." There could be no question, however, that regardless of how much effect any single program had, taken together they worked.

Blumrosen also did a study for the Labor Department that found claims of reverse discrimination by white people had dropped dramatically, but despite that finding and despite these tales of success minorities and women still faced formidable barriers, among which white men's fears posed a particularly strong one. The Glass Ceiling Commission, a government agency founded in 1991, reported that despite three decades of affirmative action "glass ceilings" and "concrete walls" still barred women and minorities from the ranks of top management in American industry.

White men, constituting 43 percent of the workforce, held about ninety-five out of every hundred top management positions, defined as vice president and above. White women, who poured into the workforce in the previous two decades, took nearly 40 percent of jobs but constituted less than 5 percent of senior managers. Women had greater success getting into the ranks of middle management, defined as assistant vice president and below, and white women held close to 40 percent of those jobs. Black women held 5 percent, and black men 4 percent. The study identified the major barrier to women and minorities advancing as the fears and prejudices of white male executives on the lower rungs of the corporate ladder. In the report's own words, the barriers exist

> because of the perception of many white males that as a group they are losing—losing the corporate game, losing control, and losing opportunity. . . . Many middle- and upper-level white male managers view the inclusion of minorities and women in management as a direct threat to their own chances for advancement. . . .
>
> Corporate leaders are talking the talk of inclusion. Yet minorities and women express dismay and anger when they describe what they perceive to be innumerable obstacles to their corporate advancement. In short, there is a difference between what corporate leadership says it wants to happen and what is actually happening.

The report came after literally hundreds of interviews across the country, and while the commission reserved its recommendations for a later report, it suggested that women and minorities were not receiving the mentoring and other support that white men automatically received from other white men. They also had to combat unfounded rumors with which white men did not contend. Hispanic workers, for example, were assumed to be foreign-born and lazy, yet two-thirds had been born in the United States, and they had the highest rate of participation in the labor force of all the groups surveyed.

The Clinton people greeted this report with delight and took special care to note Senator Dole's sponsorship of the Glass Ceiling Commission. George Stephanopoulos passed around a transcript of Mr. Dole's comments at that time: "You do not have to be a brain surgeon to deduce that something is wrong out there." Secretary of Labor Robert Reich viewed the commission's report as a possible "step toward bipartisanship" on affirmative action. That would not be the case.

THE DEBATE IN THE MID-1990S was far from one-sided; it had so many voices involved that one could not say exactly what the great majority of Americans believed. If given a choice between the "soft" version, where one tried to open the doors of opportunity to hitherto proscribed groups, and the "hard" version with its numerical goals, Americans had not changed their views much in two decades. Most Americans favored the former and opposed the latter. Opponents of affirmative action condemned Clinton's commonsense and modest call for "mend it, don't end it," while proponents and civil rights groups said it did not go far enough. Largely absent were moderate voices, such as Max Frankel, the editor of *The New York Times*. People, he wrote, already favored reverse discrimination even if they did not recognize it as such. They approved of policies if they understood the objective. "Just as football teams need beefy linemen and basketball teams need giant centers," so other organizations needed diversity for a host of pragmatic reasons. "New organizations need the different insights of both women and men, blacks and whites, Catholics and Jews. When the end is recognized as beneficial and the means as measured, affirmative action will be seen as affirmative."

Several critics believed that Clinton would have to do more than piously proclaim the need to mend, not end, affirmative action, if he wished to keep the black electorate tied to the Democratic Party. Interestingly, the president did not issue his first executive order on employment discrimination until 1998—three years after the

Adarand decision and two years after Prop 209—and these did not specifically mention African Americans. Clinton's orders focused on people with disabilities, Hispanics, and homosexuals. The latter, by far the most controversial, amended Nixon's original Executive Order 11478 by adding "sexual orientation" to the list of groups that could not be subjected to employment discrimination by federal agencies. In a way it fulfilled one of Clinton's campaign pledges to the gay community. Unlike his efforts to do away with discrimination in the armed forces, he faced far less danger of a backfire here.

As expected, gay rights activists hailed the move, while congressional Republicans and conservative religious groups denounced it. Members in both the House and the Senate introduced bills to overturn the order or to prohibit agencies from using public money to enforce it. Only one of these measures, an amendment to a House appropriations bill, ever came to a floor vote, and it lost decisively in early 1998 by a wide margin, 252–176, although Republicans still controlled a majority of seats in the lower chamber.

While Clinton knew that his executive orders would have more far-reaching impact if embodied in a congressional statute, Republicans—even though they lost seats in both the 1996 and the 1998 elections—still had a majority in the House of Representatives and would never allow any of these measures—especially the one dealing with gays—to get out of committee. Nonetheless, the orders did comfort some of the core groups within the Clinton coalition, primarily organized labor, liberal Democrats, and rights groups.

The executive orders in the last three years of the administration saw a bitterly divided Republican majority in the House—ideologically conservative, demoralized, and with a razor-thin working majority, all blamed on the short tenure of Newt Gingrich as Speaker. During this time, public approval of how congressional Republicans were doing their job fluctuated between 31 and 44 percent, while the Gallup poll showed that the president's approval rating never fell below 57 percent (May 2000) and reached as high as 67 percent (March 1998). This gave Clinton some leeway in which to achieve by executive order policies he knew would be dead on arrival in Congress.

What is surprising is that given the Republican congressional victories and control of both houses of Congress during six of Clinton's eight years, as well as the popular resentment against affirmative action as seen in the referenda in California and Washington, as well as the governor's order in Florida (see next chapter), affirmative action never really bubbled up as a decisive issue.

At the end of the Clinton presidency, one scholar, Michael Hughes, summing up the mountains of polling data about race over the previous fifty years and looking to the beginning of the twenty-first century, concluded, "Two facts are clear: traditional prejudice among whites has declined, and support for policies that would reduce racial inequality has not increased." Hughes suggested that the new animus against people of color was not so much that they posed an economic, social, or political threat to whites as that blacks violated traditional American values. Essentially, in programs like affirmative action, they were seen as wanting to jump the queue and therefore did not deserve any special help. More than three decades of affirmative action had certainly done some good, but still left many questions unanswered.

CHAPTER 14

PROP 209

Race-based affirmative action is wrong because it discriminates on the basis of race. For three decades such discriminatory policies have been embraced with the hope that they would reverse the effects of centuries of racism. To a certain extent, they have. But it is time affirmative action ended. Race and gender preferences now do more harm than good.

—UC BERKELEY *DAILY CALIFORNIAN*

It's important for applicants to know that grades are important only one-half of the time.

—UC REGENT HAROLD WILLIAMS

The recession of the early 1990s hit California harder than the rest of the nation, even as immigrants from Mexico, Latin America, and Asia (many of them illegal) flooded into the state. For the first time, California residents witnessed mass layoffs of the largely college-educated middle class. The state had fewer jobs in 1994 than in 1990, and state unemployment rates ran 3 percent higher than the rest of the country, approaching 10 percent in 1993. Almost half the loss of jobs came in the aerospace industry, long a cornerstone of the state's Republican Party and a symbol of faith in continuous upward mobility.

Although California is now considered the bluest of all states, its politics had long been dominated by Republicans, with governors like Ronald Reagan, George Deukmejian, and Pete Wilson. Wilson at one time had been a moderate and supported racial preferences; as mayor of San Diego in the 1970s and early 1980s, he had developed a nationally acclaimed affirmative action program. He now built much of his campaign and program on antiwelfare and anti-immigration issues and threw his weight behind Proposition 187, a 1994 initiative that would have established a state-run citizenship screening program and prohibited illegal aliens access to the state's educational, medical, and welfare programs. Although he had been trailing in the polls, Wilson surged ahead on the strength of his support for 187 and won a second term.

On 1 June 1995, Wilson issued the "Executive Order to End Preferential Treatment and to Promote Individual Opportunity Based on Merit," and he exploited the themes of antiwelfare, anti-immigration, and anti–affirmative action in a brief, ill-fated bid for the Republican presidential nomination. But he did effect a radical change in the Board of Regents for the University of California. The regents serve twelve-year terms, and Jerry Brown, who had been governor from 1975 to 1983, had appointed primarily liberal Democrats. Their terms expired during Wilson's tenure, and he named Republican businessmen who had contributed significantly to his campaign. They stood ready and willing to end affirmative action.

California has a three-tiered system of higher education: the University of California (UC), which then had nine university campuses with 162,000 students and a $10 billion annual budget; the California State University (Cal State) system with 23 colleges; and 113 community colleges. UC dates back to the Morrill Act of 1862, and in 1868 the Agricultural, Mining, and Mechanical Arts College merged with the private College of California. In the Organic Act of 1868 chartering UC, the legislature made clear its concerns with issues of equal access, diversity, and representativeness. The legislators prohibited any form of religious bias either in admissions or on the board of trustees and showed a sensitivity to the fact that in many private eastern schools only the middle and upper classes could get an education. Section 14 of the Organic Act read,

> As soon as the income of the University shall permit, admission and tuition shall be free to all residents of the State; and it shall be the duty of the Regents, according to population, to so apportion the representation of students, when necessary, that all portions of the State shall enjoy equal privileges therein.

The diversity and equal representation sought by the bill did not constitute affirmative action as we know it today, and it is doubtful if the legislators gave much thought to the relatively small minority population in California at the time. They had greater concern about geography, because initially there would be only one campus serving the entire state. As the system expanded, the geographic problems disappeared, but after World War II it became clear that the UC system, either intentionally or not, discriminated against minorities and women. So in 1960, the regents adopted a master plan that, among other things, broadened access for minorities and included goals of helping minorities who could not meet the stringent qualifications for the flagship schools like Berkeley, Los Angeles, and San Diego. The plan initially called for a minimum of 2 percent, later raised to 4 and then 6, of students "whose ethnic or economic background has disadvantaged them." Between 1980 and 1995, minority enrollments grew from 24 to 54 percent of the student population in the UC system (with minorities including African Americans, Chicanos—Hispanics from Mexico—and Asians).

On 19 July 1995, Bill Clinton gave his talk on affirmative action in which he called on the country to "mend it, don't end it." Governor Pete Wilson denounced the president's address, charging that "he is trying to keep in place a system that will contain the virus that threatens to tribalize America, and to divide us." The next day, 20 July, the regents met in response to the governor's executive order, which directed UC to "take all necessary action to comply with the intent and requirements of this executive order."

Descriptions of the meeting that day all agree on the frenzied atmosphere, with hundreds of people trying to get into the three-hundred-seat auditorium at the regents' headquarters in San Francisco. The regents arranged for a video broadcast in a room adjacent to the auditorium that could hold five hundred. More than two hundred people and groups had requested permission to speak, and the board had invited thirty speakers to address them. The night before more than a thousand people had gathered at a San Francisco church to hear the Reverend Jesse Jackson attack the regents for planning to do away with affirmative action, and while many people said they planned on civil disobedience, the police arrested only six protesters before the regents met.

The regents had already drafted the policy SP-1, "Ensuring Equal Treatment of Admissions," and while on the face of it SP-1 banned anything that even looked like affirmative action, it nonetheless called to mind Mr. Dooley's famous dictum about antitrust law: "A law, Hinnissey, that might look like a wall to you or me wud look like a triumphal arch to th' expeeryenced eye iv a lawyer."

Section 2 read that effective 1 January 1997 "the University of California shall not use race, religion, sex, color, ethnicity, or national origin as criteria for admission to the University or to any program of study." Section 3 applied the same ban on "admissions in exception," that is, admissions outside the normal process.

But section 5 declared that "no less than 50 percent and not more than 75 percent of any entering class on any campus shall be admitted solely on the basis of academic achievement." While one can understand holding a few places for athletes, that still leaves up to one-half of all admissions to be determined by factors other than grades and standardized tests. Section 6 said nothing should be done that would jeopardize eligibility for any state or federal program, which meant that OFCCP rules regarding faculty diversity would not be affected.

Section 7 allowed universities to take "appropriate action to remedy specific, documented cases of discrimination by the University." And then, of course, came section 9:

> Believing California's diversity to be an asset, we adopt this statement: Because individual members of all of California's diverse races have the intelligence and capacity to succeed at the University of California, this policy will achieve a UC population that reflects the state's diversity through the preparation and empowerment of all students in this state to succeed rather than through a system of artificial preferences.

While SP-1 seemed to close the door on affirmative action, it really did not. In looking at the last part, as one scholar noted, one needed what Nietzsche called "ears behind their ears." Although there was a specific date for the policy to be implemented, several sections called for the establishment of advisory committees, consultation among university presidents, the faculty senate, and the regents, and for special consideration to be paid to disadvantaged youth who, despite their environment, showed signs of promise. In the last section, the regents were clearly referring to disadvantaged racial groups, even if they did not use the word "race."

THE SWISS-CHEESE APPEARANCE of SP-1 gave added incentive to a plan by two academics, Glynn Custred and Thomas Wood, who described themselves as "staunch conservatives," to put the issue of affirmative action on the ballot in 1996. They had tried to do so unsuccessfully in 1992 and 1994, but now felt they had a real chance. "Affirmative action has been losing steam with the general public," they claimed, "and we think we've hit upon the sure way to finally reverse it and restore true color-blind fairness to the United States." To get the initiative—which would forbid racial preferences in California colleges and universities—on the ballot, they would need to get one million signatures and about $1 million to finance the drive.

The two men went to the assembly leadership to see if the legislature would put the issue on a ballot. They learned that it would take a two-thirds vote in each house to do so, and the odds on that happening were very long. So they came up with what they called the California Civil Rights Initiative. Arnie Steinberg, a Los Angeles political consultant working with Custred and Wood, said he had no doubts they would raise the $1 million they needed. "We can do that. After all, we've got the polls on our side and we can raise money not only in California but all over the country."

It turned out to be more difficult than Custred and Wood had anticipated. Getting the question on the ballot required not only money and signatures but political savvy as well. Money was needed not just to pay people to canvass for signatures but, once they had the necessary numbers, for advertisements, political consultants, bumper stickers, yard signs, and all the other paraphernalia of a political campaign. They eventually lost control of the campaign to Ward Connerly, a successful businessman with close ties to Pete Wilson, who had appointed him to the UC Board of Regents.

Connerly, who is African American, declared, "I've always believed that people shouldn't be judged by their race." He shrugged off charges that he was betraying his people. "I don't make my living in the black community. I don't wear black on my sleeve. I'm already a traitor to them. What the hell else, what more can they do to me?"

Proposition 209 had several implementing sections, but the heart of it could be found in the first part:

> The state shall not discriminate against, or grant preferential treatment to, any individual or group on the basis of race, sex, color, ethnicity, or national origin in the operation of public employment, public education, or public contracting.

Although specifically mentioning the university as a state agency, Prop 209 went further than SP-1 could have; the regents had titular power over UC, but Prop 209 covered all state agencies. Moreover, although it tracks the wording in Title VII of the 1964 Civil Rights Act, there was little doubt that there would be no California version of the EEOC to ignore its plain meaning. And it would have a major effect. Not only the colleges and universities would have to change policy, but so would all the various levels of government. The state for years had had a 15 percent set-aside for minorities and another 5 percent for women. Moreover, a state constitutional provision required all government agencies to continue their affirmative action programs whatever holdings might come down from the U.S. Supreme Court or other judicial bodies unless the decisions applied directly to their plans.

A number of groups opposed Prop 209, including all of the traditional civil rights and feminist groups. President Clinton and most Democrats decried it as well, worried what it might do to California's electoral ballots in the 1996 presidential election. With polls showing a majority of people in favor of 209, would its backers also vote Republican? Senator Bob Dole, the GOP candidate, hoped so, and he campaigned in California in support of 209. The opponents, as Lydia Chávez showed, could never agree on a single statewide effort, so they began to work independently, often at cross-purposes, while the campaign by Ward Connerly ran smoothly and had more than enough money to get its message across. According to Chávez, those who package their message well and can afford to repeat it often enough will win.

The initiative drew support from across the political spectrum. Thomas Wood, the executive director of the conservative California Association of Scholars, said that he had been denied a teaching job solely because he was a white male. "I was once told by a member of a search committee that 'You'd walk into this job if you were the right gender.'" National conservatives like Pat Buchanan and William Buckley praised the initiative. Charles Geshekter, a teacher of African history at Cal State Chico, wrote, "As a liberal Democrat, I despise those who advocate preferential treatment based on genitalia or skin color. . . . I am appalled to watch sexist and racist demands for equality of outcomes erode the principle of affirmative equality of opportunity."

Ironically, in the middle of the fight over 209, the *Los Angeles Times* published a poll in March 1995 that found that the vast majority of Americans believed that racial discrimination remained an important national issue. Seventy percent of the respondents agreed that the country is not "close to eliminating discrimination." While it was no surprise that 90 percent of African Americans claimed that discrimination is not close to ending, 68 percent of white men agreed.

And yet, on 5 November 1996, the people of California adopted Prop 209 by a margin of 55 to 45 percent. With the exception of the urban areas around San Francisco and Los Angeles, the initiative won in every county in the state. At the same time, the state gave 52 percent of the popular vote and its fifty-four electoral votes to Bill Clinton, who opposed 209.

Ward Connerly gave a "victory speech" that night in Sacramento in which he said, "Tonight, my friends, we celebrate. In our hearts and minds, we dance—not in the darkness, but in the warm sunshine to the sweet music of equal treatment for all and special privileges for none."

Following passage, opponents turned to the courts to try to block its implementation. On 23 December, the U.S. district judge Thelton Henderson issued a preliminary injunction blocking enforcement, but on 8 April 1997 a three-judge panel of the Court of Appeals for the Ninth Circuit ruled Prop 209 constitutional and vacated the injunction, despite an appeal from the Clinton administration to leave the injunction in place. The Supreme Court denied cert.

WHAT ACTUALLY HAPPENED? In the immediate aftermath of SP-1, not very much. *The New York Times* sent a reporter to talk to UC admissions counselors and other campus officials. He drew the conclusion that the universities were going to do their best to ignore the regents, exactly the type of behavior that Custred and Wood had worried about.

In fact, between the time the regents adopted SP-1 in July 1995 and the passage of Prop 209 in November 1996, leaders of the UC institutions did their best either to delay implementation of the regents' policy or to find a way to circumvent it. This did not prove hard to do, in part because of the vagueness of some of the SP-1 provisions. The regents themselves decided to back off a bit and set a new implementation date of the spring of 1998, after the prestigious American Association of University Professors issued a report saying the regents had acted hastily.

At the same time, the Office for Civil Rights of the federal Department of Education completed a seven-year investigation into affirmative action policies at Berkeley, the jewel in the crown of the UC system, and concluded that the school did not discriminate against whites. Moreover, the academic quality of the student body had increased as it became more diverse. There had been no quotas, and race had been just one of the considerations taken into account in the admissions process.

Unlike SP-1, the University of California could not directly ignore Prop 209 when it became a provision of the state's constitution. Minority applications dropped for every one of the UC schools; applications from black students from California high schools dropped by 7.7 percent, and those of Hispanics by 12.2 percent. Minority applications to the UC law schools also plummeted. Boalt Hall, the prestigious law school at Berkeley, announced that only one of the 17 African American students admitted for the fall 1997 class of 270 planned to attend. The Haas Business School at Berkeley saw black student admissions drop 52 percent, and that of Hispanics 54 percent. At the UCLA Law School, the number of blacks admitted plunged from 104 to 21, and of these only 8 actually enrolled. The law professor Adam Winkler teaches a first-year class of eighty students in constitutional law at UCLA. There have been semesters, he says, "when I taught *Brown v. Board* in classes that did not have a single black student."

African American enrollment dropped from 3.8 percent of the class entering the UC system in 1997 to 2.8 in 2001 and did not reach the pre–Prop 209 level until 2010. Asian American enrollment actually increased from 36.4 to 39.8 percent, while Chicanos, after a small drop, went from 12.7 percent in 1997 to 20.7 percent in 2010. Whites also dropped, and never recovered, going from 40.2 percent in 1997 to 26.8 percent in 2010. Although some schools in the system reported an increase in minority applications, Irvine, San Diego, and Davis showed sharp declines; of all nonwhite groups, only Asian Americans held steady.

(Although many people assume that minorities accepted into college are primarily poor, the figures at Berkeley and elsewhere belie this. In the years prior to Prop 209, only a third of the black students entering Berkeley could be considered lower income; more than half had families with incomes of more than $40,000 a year, with quite a few in brackets much higher than that. This figure should not be surprising, because Bowen and Bok, in *The Shape of the River,* reported that of the twenty-eight elite schools they surveyed, just 14 percent of minority students came from homes earning less than $22,000 a year.)

According to Michal Belknap, professor of law at California Western in San Diego, minority enrollments have crept up in some schools to pre-209 levels. UC adopted a form of the Texas system, by admitting a fixed percentage of every high school in the state. Belknap thinks the system worked better in California because minority populations there are more ghettoized than those in Texas. But the record is uneven. UC San Diego has very few African American and Latino students, although freshman classes are half Asian. The greatest loser, Belknap claims, has been the Republican Party, which has been reduced to a tiny and helpless minority. With the exception of Arnold Schwarzenegger, who, while nominally a Republican, governed mainly as an independent moderate, there has been no Republican governor since Wilson. Under current California election rules, the top two candidates in the gubernatorial primary run against each other, and no Republican has made it in over twenty years.

One reason minority numbers have climbed is that many of the UC schools have figured out creative ways to get around 209. For example, Larry Vanderhoef, the chancellor at UC Davis, said, "I am not yet ready to concede that we will not be able to pursue diversity." Davis gives preference in its medical school to students who say they will practice in underserved areas. Experience has taught that students who grew up in underserved areas are most likely to return there. "Consequently, a large proportion of black and Latino students enter our medical school although race and ethnicity weren't anywhere involved." Albert Carnesale, the chancellor at UCLA, told the *Times* columnist Anthony Lewis, "You have to distinguish between means and ends. What's important here is the end, diversity. Affirmative action is just one means to that end."

All nine of the universities established some sort of program targeted at the economically and educationally disadvantaged, helping those already in school to be able to graduate and assisting high school students with preparation to get into college. The Berkeley Pledge program has undergraduate volunteers working with forty low-performing schools in four districts near the campus, all with large populations of minority and low-income children. The college students do many things, but above all tutor their charges in basic courses they will need to graduate from high school and go to college.

Nearly all schools recruited minority students more actively than before, but minorities also discovered that they could get a good education at places like Davis and Irvine without the pressure that existed at Los Angeles and Berkeley. The number of African Americans entering UC as freshmen in 2000 through 2003 was on average only 2 percent below pre-209 levels. The number of Hispanics actually increased by 22 percent, and the graduation rate for all minorities rose by more than 10 percent. Nonetheless, a 2000 study found that while overall minority numbers seemed to be rising, there were significant disparities within the system, and at the flagship schools in Berkeley and Los Angeles minority enrollments stayed low.

In 2000, a new Board of Regents adopted a policy that would broaden the factors considered in selecting students. The policy, known as comprehensive review, would grant provisional admission to the top 12.5 percent of graduating students at all the state's public high schools. The board made no bones about why it proposed the new policy: overall minority admissions had dropped, despite rebounds at some schools. Richard C. Atkinson, president of the Board of Regents, said, "The goal here is to increase diversity . . . in terms of low-income students, diversity in terms of under-represented minority students, diversity in terms of rural students."

Prop 209 also had a dramatic impact on small entrepreneurs. It had been easy to find minority firms working on many state transportation projects, said Frederick Jordan, the president of a civil and environmental engineering firm. "But all the minority firms were wiped out. In 1996 in San Francisco I could've produced ten or fifteen African-American firms that could do any kind of work. Today I can't find anybody—zero, zero." A study by the Discrimination Research Center confirmed that only a third of minority enterprises that had been certified to do business with the California Department of Transportation in 1996 were still in business following the passage of 209.

Ward Connerly for a while found himself one of the most sought-after people in the country, as foes of affirmative action wanted him to come to their states and kill race-conscious programs there. In 1995, legislation had been introduced in twenty-six states and in Congress to repeal or significantly roll back affirmative action; none succeeded. With the victory of Prop 209, opponents of race-conscious programs found new energy and hope. "We absolutely have the momentum now," said Earl Ehrhart, the Republican whip in the Georgia House of Representatives, who had been pushing a similar bill for three years. "This is no longer just some idea out in California. . . . [It's] right in the middle of the radar screen."

The dynamics of California, with a then-popular Republican governor, did not necessarily translate elsewhere. In New York, Governor George E. Pataki, also a Republican, resisted calls to eliminate affirmative action. So too did his neighbor the Republican governor of New Jersey, Christine Todd Whitman. "Government should set an example of inclusiveness for others to follow," Whitman said, and argued that the state had benefited from programs that took race and gender into account in hiring and promotions.

In some of the conservative western states, affirmative action hardly registered on the political screen because of small minority populations, and in the South a growing Republican presence had to take into account the large number of African American voters. Efforts to start local state versions of Prop 209 went nowhere in Florida, Michigan, and other states. In Congress, House Republicans backed away from their own bill, partly out of election year fears that it would alienate minority and women voters. Moreover, one of the party's stars, the retired general Colin Powell, issued a ringing defense of affirmative action.

Wade Henderson, director of the Leadership Conference on Civil and Human Rights, a coalition of groups that opposed measures like 209, dismissed talk that the tide had turned against such programs. "We believe the vote in California in no way reflects the general public's sentiment on the value and viability of affirmative action programs. Most Americans support preservation of equal opportunity, especially in the workplace."

A survey by *The Chronicle of Higher Education* in early 1998 found that the fear of a "white-out" on college campuses had state legislatures from South Carolina to South Dakota backpedaling from California-style proposals. According to the survey, there was a growing consensus that unless sufficient minority students could attend flagship universities, there would be a dearth of black leaders in the coming generation.

OPPONENTS DID WIN one victory, however, in a state north of California that had a population 86 percent white. Minorities made up only 14 percent of Washington State's people, and the biggest minority group—Asian Americans—did not qualify for most of the state's minority-directed programs. Ward Connerly's American Civil Rights Institute played a role in backing Initiative 200, which banned preferences based on race or sex in state contracts, hiring, and admissions to public colleges and universities. On 4 November 1998, voters in Washington approved Initiative 200 by a 58–42 margin, with majorities everywhere except in Seattle. Unlike 209, however, 200 did not amend the state's constitution, but simply became one of Washington's statutes and could therefore be more easily rescinded than if it had been a constitutional amendment.

Washington colleges and universities had to stop affirmative action programs. Dr. Ernest Morris, vice president for student affairs at the University of Washington, noted that in the past three decades it had graduated more than 5,000 students through its preferential admissions program. Moreover, minorities made up a small part of the university's 37,500 undergraduates and graduate students—2.8 percent African American, nearly 4 percent Hispanic, and 1.5 percent Native American. Asian Americans, who made up 19 percent of the students, were not considered an "under-represented minority." In the year after voters approved 200, the percentage of Native Americans who graduated from high school and went on to college dropped from a little over half to 38 percent.

Following approval of Initiative 200, Ward Connerly indicated that there were several states which might be possible sites for the next anti-preference campaign, including Florida, Michigan, and Nebraska. Connerly did not have to worry about one of the states he mentioned.

In 2000, Governor Jeb Bush of Florida signed an executive order ending race-based admissions at any Florida college or university. "We ended up having a system where there were more African-American and Hispanic kids attending our university system than prior to the system that was discriminatory." As part of his One Florida plan, Bush guaranteed spots in the state's eleven universities to the top 20 percent of graduates from every high school. This certainly seemed generous, even noncontroversial, compared with the 10 percent law passed in Texas under his brother. Then Jeb Bush found out that roughly two-thirds of black students who might have benefited had been so neglected in high school that they had failed to graduate with the necessary credits for admission to state universities. Florida then began pushing public schools that served minorities to provide better course offerings and do some of the things that made the Texas plan work.

Officials at the state's two premier universities, the University of Florida in Gainesville (UF) and Florida State University in Tallahassee (FSU), said that minority enrollments had been shrinking and that if the trend continued, it could diminish their standing as world-class schools. At the Gainesville campus, African Americans constituted just 6 percent of the freshman class in 2013, down from 9 percent in 2011. FSU had a 15 percent drop in black freshmen between 2000 and 2009. "There will be so few black students on our campus," said Brandon Bowen, assistant vice president for student affairs at FSU, "that prospective students [who are black] will choose not to come here because they see no one who looks like them." The provost at UF, David Colburn, admitted that school officials were very anxious. The old affirmative action laws had been working well, and "we don't want to lose any of the momentum we've had in diversifying the student body." At the time Bush issued his order, black students made up 18 percent of all freshmen at Florida colleges.

Bush's claim that there were more minorities after his edict rested upon the state's booming Hispanic population, which in turn led to a large number of Hispanic students attending Florida schools. Black students concentrated in lesser-known regional schools in the larger cities that had less stringent admissions requirements. Officials at UF and FSU said they were losing prospective minority students to the University of Central Florida in Orlando, South Florida in Tampa, and Florida International University in Miami. One student who had the grades to attend UF went to Gainesville on a visit and felt isolated. "I didn't see a lot of black people, and that made me very cautious about attending." As the number of black students dwindled, a growing sense of isolation developed among those who attended the flagship schools. In 2013, when a campus survey at UF asked whether students "felt respected on campus," half of the black students said no.

As in California, officials at UF and FSU have been trying to work around Bush's One Florida order. At UF, the administration guarantees free tuition and mentorship to three hundred first-generation students per class, and about 30 percent (ninety students) are African American. Both schools made efforts to improve the quality of life on campus for black students, but so far have not been able to determine if their plans have succeeded.

THE SUCCESS OF Prop 209 in California did, on the one hand, stir opponents of affirmative action to greater effort, and they had success in Washington State and Florida. At the same time, the dramatic drops in African American and Hispanic students at colleges and universities in those states raised the alarm of "white-outs," where the generation of college students who would become leaders in those states would have no minority members. University officials in all three states immediately began looking for ways around the bans imposed constitutionally, statutorily, or by executive order.

The NAACP, of course, reaffirmed its support of compensatory programs, which surprised no one, but there seemed to be an emerging consensus that some sort of special admissions might be necessary until urban schools did a better job for minorities, that is, until they provided first-rate preparation for college. So long as public schools serving minorities allowed them to graduate without the necessary training to succeed in getting either employment or admission to college, the country would continue to need affirmative action.

This idea even snuck into the ranks of the neocons, the former liberals who had been among the first to war against racial preferences more than twenty years earlier. The March 1998 issue of *Commentary,* once the leading journalistic voice against affirmative action, carried several articles by writers who reluctantly supported measures to increase minority enrollments.

James Q. Wilson, once a fierce foe, now grudgingly accepted affirmative action at public colleges but only at the undergraduate level; on the other hand, he enthusiastically proselytized for it in police and fire departments, arguing that these agencies must be racially representative for them to function successfully in the community.

In 1975, Nathan Glazer had written the bible of anti-preference conservatives, *Affirmative Discrimination,* in which he argued that taking race into account in college admissions and employment was both morally wrong and socially corrosive. In the late 1990s, he had a change of heart. In *We Are All Multiculturalists Now* (1997), he ruefully admitted that the melting pot no longer existed, and where earlier assimilation of all groups had been the goal, now the nation needed multicultural diversity. Those institutions that provided the gateway to social mobility and economic success, notably the nation's universities, had to be fully integrated, or else American democracy would be undermined.

John Bunzel, the former president of San Jose State University and a onetime member of the U.S. Civil Rights Commission, also had a change of heart. He had opposed quotas as early as 1972, and in 1988 had written a blistering attack on how affirmative action worked in the California system, especially at Berkeley. One might have expected him to wholeheartedly embrace Prop 209, yet he found it "troublesome," because it put a very complex issue in a stark, binary form—yes or no. "I could not accept the zero-sum formulation of [Prop 209]'s most ardent supporters that any form of race-related preferences under any circumstance is *wrong* and that Proposition 209 is *right.*"

Rather, he believed that the debate over affirmative action more often represented a collision between right versus right rather than right versus wrong. Race consciousness did not have to be bad in all forms, although zealots who took it to extremes did the people they wanted to help no good at all. Rather, a measured and prudent awareness of race could be considered a way of contributing to the larger social good. Affirmative action by itself was neither good nor bad; in practice, it required a skillful trade-off between different claims and interests. Universities had to balance their obligations to students, to different groups, to society, and not least to themselves. He then noted,

> Colleges and universities present their own special concerns. If an institution has determined it does not want an all-white freshman class, and if it is also not willing to admit students simply because they are black or Hispanic, shouldn't it be permitted the latitude to offer some sort of limited preference to promising black students with lower-than-the-highest SAT scores and high school grade point averages?

But how much lower was a difficult question, and he did not want any hard-and-fast rules here. He trusted university officials to try honestly to strike a balance between diversity and merit. He had always opposed admitting students who lacked the necessary academic preparation, but there had to be sufficient "wiggle room" for schools to seek the diversity they wanted. And race would have to be a consideration in striking that balance.

CHAPTER 15

AFFIRMATIVE ACTION
AND ELECTIONS

Before we had the right to vote, politicians publicly called us niggers. After we received the right to vote, but our numbers were few, they called us Nigras. When we reached 5,000, they called us colored. 10,000, they called us black people. Now that we have reached 50,000, they call us Commissioner Wicks, Judge Cain Kennedy, Representative Yvonne Kennedy, and Senator Figures. If you don't want to go back to square one, vote for Mims and Greenough.

—1981 RADIO AD IN MOBILE, ALABAMA

If you drove down {Interstate 85} with both car doors open, you'd kill most of the people in {District 12}.

—ANONYMOUS NORTH CAROLINA LEGISLATOR

The 1972 Democratic convention in Miami Beach saw the implementation of a set of reforms recommended by the Committee on Party Structure and Delegate Selection that had been chaired by Senator George McGovern (D-S.D.) before he decided to run for president. That committee had grown out of the turmoil at the 1964 convention, when the Mississippi Freedom Democratic Party unsuccessfully tried to gain recognition as the official delegation from that state, and the violence involving antiwar activists at the 1968 convention in Chicago. The committee made a number of recommendations, including doing away with the winner-take-all rule in primaries, but the most important, for our purposes, were quotas mandating that a certain percentage of delegates be women or members of minority groups. The new rules accelerated the trend toward grassroots politics that had been pioneered by Eugene McCarthy in 1968.

At the 1972 convention, 38 percent of the delegates were women (compared with 13 percent in 1968), 15 percent were black (5 percent in 1968), and 23 percent were younger than thirty (compared with less than 3 percent in 1968). The new rules created a number of credential challenges, and many traditional Democratic groups such as organized labor, white ethnics, and big-city machines had only a small representation at the convention. The crowning insult to the party faithful came when the delegates voted to exclude the regular Illinois delegation, controlled by Chicago's mayor, Richard Daley, and instead seated a group led by the Reverend Jesse Jackson. McGovern recognized the mixed results of the changes that he had made to the party's nominating process, saying, "I opened the doors of the Democratic Party and 20 million people walked out."

Among the rules adopted—and nobody in the Democratic Party even blinked at what all conceded to be affirmative action—one required an equal division of men and women. In some primaries, the state party simply listed all the women pledged to a particular delegate in one group, all of the men in another, with instruction to pick one or two from each group. This, in turn, led to some unforeseen situations. In late 1979, as the Democrats began getting ready for the 1980 convention, a question arose in Suffolk County, New York. The county, which takes up the eastern half of Long Island, would have five delegates, and the question was whether the delegation would be three men and two women, or three women and two men. Eventually, because party rules did not specify any procedure, the party chairman tossed a coin, and women won the toss.

Interestingly, although the Democratic convention has "come to look like America," the Republicans have not felt any need to adopt such a policy. Viewers watching the 2016 presidential conventions could not help but notice that while the Democrats had women, blacks, Hispanics, and wheelchair-using delegates, one had to look long and hard to see any but white faces at the GOP convention.

ALTHOUGH THE 1964 Civil Rights Act had a profound impact in many areas, the section on voting rights proved somewhat ineffective, so that hundreds of thousands of blacks remained disenfranchised. The total of registered blacks in Alabama, for example, had risen from 7,000 in 1947 to 110,000 in 1964, but not a single one had been able to register in Lowndes and Wilcox Counties, where African Americans outnumbered whites four to one. All told, although blacks made up about half of Alabama's population, they accounted for a very small percentage of its registered voters. To publicize the problem, Martin Luther King Jr. organized a protest march from Selma to the state capital in Montgomery. Governor George Wallace forbade the march, and when King persisted, Wallace refused to provide protection for the participants. On Sunday, 7 March 1965, Alabama state troopers attacked unarmed and defenseless men, women, and children using bullwhips, clubs, and teargas as television cameras broadcast the sickening spectacle to the nation and to the world. Lyndon Johnson federalized the Alabama National Guard to protect the demonstrators and in one of his greatest speeches asked Congress for "a simple, uniform standard which cannot be used, however ingenious the effort, to flout the Constitution." The president then paused and, looking out at Congress and the nation, said emphatically, "And we *shall* overcome."

Using all his famed persuasive skills, Johnson steered the 1965 Voting Rights Act through Congress and signed it into law on 6 August. More than any other statute, the Voting Rights Act gave

At a voting rights demonstration in Selma, Alabama, 7 March 1965.

blacks real power. Two months after a federal registrar arrived in Selma, the percentage of voting-age blacks on the rolls rose from 10 to 60; within a year after passage of the law, 166,000 African Americans registered for the first time in Alabama, and within five years the total number of black registered voters in the South more than doubled, from 36 to 65 percent of black adults in the region. Before long, these figures translated into elected black legislators, mayors, and especially sheriffs. The fact that blacks now had a powerful voice in the election of sheriffs significantly affected the way law enforcement officials treated African Americans. When southern states challenged the power of Congress to regulate local registration and elections, a near-unanimous Court upheld the law in *South Carolina v. Katzenbach* (1966). Congress amended, expanded, and renewed the act in 1970, 1975, 1982, 1992, and 2006.

THERE ARE MANY PROVISIONS to the 1965 law and its amendments, but the part that concerns us here is section 2, as amended in 1982. Section 2(a) prohibits voting regulations that "result" in denying or abridging the right to vote on account of race, and section 2(b) held that a section 2(a) violation occurred when the "totality of the circumstances" revealed that election processes were not equally open to all races and that minorities had less opportunity than other voters to participate and elect representatives "of their choice."

That year the North Carolina General Assembly adopted a redistricting plan for state house and senate seats based on the 1980 census returns. African Americans challenged the plan, claiming that one single-member district and six multimember districts prevented them from electing representatives of their choice, in violation of section 2. In *Gingles v. Edmisten* (1984), a three-judge federal district court agreed and declared that the redistricting plan diluted the power of minority voters in each of the disputed districts. Lacy Thornburg, the North Carolina attorney general, appealed directly to the Supreme Court.

The Supreme Court concurred in the district court's evaluation except for one electoral district, and in doing so for the first time upheld the notion of "vote dilution." Speaking for the Court, Justice William J. Brennan spelled out three conditions that had to be met in order to prove minority vote dilution. "First, the minority group must be able to demonstrate that it is sufficiently large and geographically compact to constitute a majority in a single-member district. . . . Second, the minority group must be able to show that it is politically cohesive. . . . Third, the minority must be able to demonstrate that the white majority votes sufficiently as a bloc to enable it—in the absence of special circumstances, such as the minority candidate running unopposed . . . —usually to defeat the minority's preferred candidate."

Under section 2 as well as the Court's opinion in *Gingles,* the states could not set up any districting scheme that left black voters in a position where they could not affect election results. For example, one could not draw districts in which there would be a white majority that could control the election results. But the states also had to take what might very well be called electoral affirmative action. They had to create districts in which black voters constituted a majority, the so-called majority-minority districts. For example, say a state covered under the Voting Rights Act had ten electoral districts, and African Americans constituted 30 percent of the population. In order to give the minority electoral power comparable to its numbers, there should be three districts in which the minority African Americans constituted a majority of the voters and could thus elect candidates of their choice. Indeed, when the high court heard two majority-minority districting cases in 1995, *The New York Times* called the question "perhaps the most basic affirmative-action issue in democracy: whether election districts can be drawn according to the race of the people who live in them."

THE RESULTS OF THE 1990 census gave North Carolina an additional congressional district, and the legislature had to draw boundary lines that would, under terms of the Voting Rights Act, meet with Justice Department approval. At the time, North Carolina had no majority-minority districts out of eleven. With an additional seat, not only did the legislature have to redraw lines to keep all the districts fairly equal in population, but it also faced pressure—both internally and externally—to make at least two of the twelve districts majority minority. Moreover, because part of North Carolina remained subject to section 5 of the Voting Rights Act, the state's congressional redistricting plan required Justice Department preclearance.

The external pressure came from the Civil Rights Division of the Bush Justice Department, and as Professor Tinsley Yarbrough suggests, some people thought that staff attorneys with no partisan interests whatsoever simply believed that the 1982 amendments to section 2 as well as the *Gingles* ruling required two majority-minority districts to guard against vote dilution. Democratic officeholders in North Carolina and other southern states, however, saw the push for majority-minority districts as part of a Bush "Max-Black" campaign, orchestrated by the Republican National Committee, to pack African American voters—the most reliable part of the Democratic electoral coalition—into a few districts, leaving other districts predominantly white, and therefore more likely to elect white Republicans to office.

Internal pressure came from the increasingly politically active African American community in the state. The Voting Rights Act and assembly redistricting in the 1980s had led to the election of a number of blacks in the North Carolina General Assembly, and in 1991 Dan T. Blue, a Raleigh attorney, became the first African American elected Speaker of the state house of representatives. But there had been no black congressman since George Henry White had served two terms and then retired in 1901. The legislative black caucus, the state NAACP, and Speaker Blue all wanted two majority-minority congressional districts.

Blue, however, remained cautious, fearful that too strong a push could lead to a white backlash, and he had the very recent experience of Jesse Helms playing on white fears to defeat the black mayor

Dan T. Blue, the first African American Speaker of the North Carolina House of Representatives, whose term (1991–1994) was marked by a tug-of-war with the Justice Department over majority-minority districting.

of Charlotte in the 1990 senatorial campaign. So he and the leaders of the state senate went into redistricting with the hope of getting one majority-minority district, and the initial plan devised by the committee appointed to do the work did just that. The First District had been represented by Walter B. Jones Sr. since 1965, but the seventy-seven-year-old Jones was expected to retire (in fact, he died in September 1992), so there would be no sitting member of Congress displaced in the new majority-minority district.

In October 1991, legislative leaders and the staff who had worked on the redistricting plan went to Washington to meet with Justice Department officials, carrying twenty large notebooks that detailed the new lines and the reasons for them. There they learned that the Civil Rights Division lawyers wanted North Carolina to have not one but two majority-minority districts. They not only wanted it; they insisted on it. As Speaker Blue later said, "We had not intended to do that," and the first thing they thought of on the way home "was that we were going to have to have huge geographical expanses to put together 550,000 people, at least 250,000 to 300,000 of them having to be minority." In December, North Carolina heard officially from the Justice Department that there would have to be a second majority-minority district.

Given no real choice, the legislative committee went back to work. Under the new plan, 43 percent of North Carolina's 1.4 million blacks now lived in either the First or the Twelfth District, and in the 1992 congressional elections blacks won in both districts. As nearly everyone recognized, however, in order to create the two districts, the drafters had been forced to ignore the traditional criteria for drawing district lines—compactness and contiguity.

The Wall Street Journal described the First District: "It wanders from the Virginia border almost to South Carolina. Two of its parts appear to be connected only by a river, with the banks on each side in other districts." The Journal described the Twelfth District as "a long snake that winds its way through central North Carolina for 190 miles, from Durham to Charlotte, scooping up isolated precincts with nothing in common save a large number of minority voters. . . . For much of its length, the district is no wider than the Interstate 85 corridor that links the two cities." When someone asked how candidates would campaign in such a monstrosity, a black member of the assembly said, "We'll just have rallies at every exit along I-85."

ALTHOUGH THERE WOULD continue to be political bickering and deal making in the Tar Heel State, the question had in fact already moved to the courts, with the GOP complaining that the redistricting scheme unfairly packed Republicans into just two districts, keeping all the others safe for Democrats. The GOP problem, as the state's attorney general noted, lay in the lack of any legal basis for such a claim.

A decade earlier, Indiana Democrats had filed a lawsuit charging that the Republican-controlled assembly had drawn legislative districts for strictly partisan purposes. The Supreme Court in *Davis v. Bandemer* (1986) required plaintiffs in a political gerrymandering case to show evidence that the scheme caused "continued frustration of the will of the majority of the voters or effective denial to a minority of the voters of a fair chance to influence the political process" over a significant number of elections. The mere absence of party representation in a legislature proportionate to party voting strength in the electorate was inadequate to establish a constitutional violation. Plaintiffs would have to show that they had been deliberately shut out of the political process.

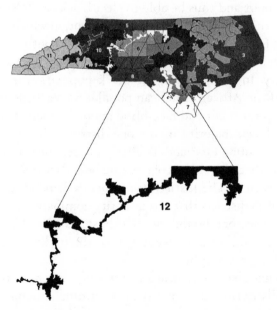

North Carolina's Twelfth Congressional District, which managed to have an African American majority but violated all the rules regarding compactness and contiguity.

A federal district court, by a vote of 2–1, dismissed the North Carolina Republican challenge on the basis of *Bandemer,* and the Supreme Court summarily affirmed, with only one justice wanting to give the case a full hearing. But if the Court would not review political gerrymandering unless the plaintiffs could meet a very high level of evidence, what would the justices do if the gerrymandering involved race rather than party? Moreover, the white majority in North Carolina had set up district lines not to minimize the black vote but to augment it, and it did so under pressure from the federal government, nominally carrying out the mandate of the 1965 Voting Rights Act that the high court had previously approved.

It had, of course, been illegal ever since *Gomillion v. Lightfoot* in 1960 to gerrymander districts to dilute minority voting strength. In *Rogers v. Lodge* (1982), the high court had approved a district-court-ordered plan to replace at-large county commissioners with single-district seats. In Burke County, Georgia, blacks constituted a majority of the total population, but only 38 percent of the registered voters. In at-large elections, the white majority easily defeated any black candidates. By ordering single-district seats, the lower court ensured that in at least some districts blacks would make up a majority of the voters and thus be able to elect black candidates.

It is one thing to ensure fair apportionment, in which local African Americans form the majority in compact and contiguous districts. Proportional representation, however, had never been a practice in this country. In many states, the black population is so scattered that even if the African American population reached 20 or 25 percent of the total, a fair and race-blind apportionment scheme might not have a black majority in any one district. The weird shapes of the North Carolina First and Twelfth Congressional Districts illustrated perfectly the problems of creating boundary lines for majority-minority districts. The Justice Department's demands that southern states establish districts that had minority domination ran against the custom that electoral boundaries within states should be contiguous and compact, and certainly went against the tradition of individual as opposed to group rights.

The Rehnquist Court heard a series of challenges to majority-minority districting, and it had to determine, among other questions, whether race-conscious districting affected individual or group rights. These cases, it should be noted, came up to the high court at the same time that the justices were taking a less sympathetic view of government-required affirmative action, and if affirmative action in hiring and subcontracting violated equal protection, it would seem that affirmative action in electoral apportionment should as well.

(In February 2018, the Pennsylvania Supreme Court ruled that the state's congressional districts, drawn after the 2010 census, violated the state constitution's Free and Equal Election Clause and ordered a new map be drawn for the 2018 election. Because the court based its opinion entirely on state law, the U.S. Supreme Court had no reason to review it. A few months later, the high court avoided decisions in two gerrymandering challenges by focusing more on technicalities than on the misapportionment itself. In June 2019, a 5–4 majority declared gerrymandering a "political question" beyond the scope of judicial resolution.)

In the 1970s and 1980s, federal courts turned back several challenges to race-conscious districting that had been adopted as a means of redressing prior discrimination, and here, as in the affirmative action cases, courts proved more sympathetic to race-based remedies in the face of proof of past discrimination. However, instead of applying the strict scrutiny standard normally used in cases of racial classification, the district and circuit courts often utilized a lower standard, deferring to congressional policy-making power exercised under the Enforcement Clauses of the Fourteenth and Fifteenth Amendments. In these years, however, enormous population shifts occurred throughout the country and in the South in particular. The 1990 census required not only North Carolina but most southern states to redraw their congressional district lines, and state legislatures, under pressure from the Justice Department to prevent vote dilution among African Americans, created majority-minority districts. When challenged in court, states responded that the Justice Department requirements constituted a compelling state interest.

The challenge to the North Carolina case came from an unlikely source, Robinson Oscar Everett, a professor of law at Duke University, the head of a successful law practice in Durham, and a former chief judge of the Court of Military Appeals. He had a specialty in military law, not voting rights, and had never argued before the Supreme Court. He had been active in the civic, political, and cultural life of Durham and of the state, was a moderately liberal Democrat, and had long enjoyed good relations with the leaders of Durham's African American community. He believed discrimination against blacks to be morally abhorrent, but he also objected to race-conscious policies beneficial to blacks. Everett found the 1991 districting plan objectionable, and he put together a team to oppose it—one of his Duke colleagues, one of his sons, an old friend, and a secretary in his firm would act as co-plaintiffs. Everett won two victories in the high court, and when further redistricting removed him and the other original plaintiffs from the disputed districts, he still believed in the idea of a color-blind constitution. So he put together a group of new plaintiffs and continued the battle.

A THREE-JUDGE PANEL dismissed Everett's suit in district court for failure to state claims upon which relief could be granted and for lack of subject matter jurisdiction, technical matters that allowed the panel to avoid dealing with the merits. The plaintiffs appealed to the U.S. Supreme Court, where they won a victory of sorts. The high court reversed the finding of the lower court, holding that in fact the plaintiffs had stated a claim under the Equal Protection Clause. Jurisdiction for the case, however, lay not in the district court in North Carolina but in the district court for the District of Columbia.

The 5–4 majority did not rule on the merits of race-conscious districting or even on North Carolina's claim that it had a compelling interest created by the Justice Department's requirements under the Voting Rights Act. Rather, it ruled only that white citizens in the state had a justiciable claim—that is, one that could be decided by a court—under equal protection to challenge the districting plan, and it remanded the case to the D.C. district court for a hearing on merits. Justice O'Connor instructed the lower court that in reviewing the challenges, it should adopt a strict scrutiny test, reflecting how the Court had begun handling affirmative action cases.

Justice O'Connor had compared the North Carolina First to a "bug splattered on a window," and in *Miller v. Johnson* (1995) the Court said that the shape of a district could be the subject of judicial scrutiny. In addition to North Carolina, other states under pressure to create majority-minority districts had drawn lines that practically defied description to get a black majority. One district ran through ten counties, dividing them and even the towns within them. That case came out of Georgia, and Justice Kennedy affirmed the lower-court decision that the Georgia Eleventh, under a strict scrutiny review, violated equal protection because the legislature had clearly subordinated traditional race-neutral principles to racial considerations: race had become the predominant and overriding consider-

Robinson Oscar Everett, the force behind the law-suits over majority-minority districting in North Carolina.

ation of the district's boundaries. Moreover, the plan failed another requirement of strict scrutiny in that it had not been narrowly tailored. Cleansing discrimination from the nation's political system, wrote Justice Kennedy, is a goal "neither assured nor well served . . . by carving electorates into racial blocs. . . . It takes a shortsighted and unauthorized view of the Voting Rights Act to invoke that statute . . . to demand the very racial stereotyping the Fourteenth Amendment forbids."

O'Connor in *Shaw,* however, had emphasized that "the Court never has held that race-conscious state decision-making is impermissible in *all* circumstances." A former state legislator herself (and the only member of the high court with that experience), she said a state legislature "always is *aware* of race when it draws district lines, just as it is aware of age, economic status, religious and political persuasion, and a variety of other demographic factors. That sort of race consciousness does not lead inevitably to impermissible race discrimination." This reminder would prove to be important when the Court finally reached its position on majority-minority districting.

On 13 June 1996, the Court announced two decisions—both by

5–4 majorities—that struck down four majority-minority districts in two states. The case from North Carolina, *Shaw v. Hunt (Shaw II)*, reversed the district court's finding that although the legislature had classified voters by race, the plan did not violate the Constitution and survived a strict scrutiny review. The Texas case, *Bush v. Vera*, affirmed a lower court ruling racial gerrymandering unconstitutional. The decisions in both cases cheered the critics of racial line drawing but drew bitter attacks from traditional civil rights groups. Legally, both rulings made clear that states faced added difficulties in justifying excessive use of race when drawing district lines. The rulings, however, left unclear at what point a racial districting plan crossed the line to become an improper racial gerrymander. It also gave the states no guidance on how they could comply with the 1965 Voting Rights Act.

Chief Justice Rehnquist's opinion in *Shaw II* again reiterated that when race is the predominant consideration in drawing electoral lines, strict scrutiny is the required test. The district court had erred in finding that the state had a compelling interest either in establishing majority-minority districts or in creating such strangely shaped districts. The opinion, however, still avoided the key substantive question: whether, under the proper circumstances, compliance with section 5 of the Voting Rights Act could be a compelling state interest.

In Texas, a new Thirtieth District started in predominantly black sections of Dallas but had narrow tentacles reaching into two neighboring counties and jagged edges to skirt around white neighborhoods. Two interlocking districts in Houston—the Eighteenth and Twenty-Ninth—were configured by means of jigsaw-puzzle geometry to include majority black and Hispanic populations, respectively. As in North Carolina, Texas used detailed racial census information and sophisticated computer mapping, and as in North Carolina the mapmakers tried to protect incumbents.

For Texas and North Carolina, the rulings posed a conundrum: whether to hold congressional elections in November under the redistricting plans that the Court had struck down or to try to draw new maps in time for the election. In North Carolina, the district court allowed the use of the existing lines for the November election, but in Texas the court drew up a new plan that changed thirteen districts altogether, including the three that the high court had ruled invalid.

———

GIVEN THE INABILITY of the nine justices to agree on any clear rationale in majority-minority districting—other than if race had been the primary consideration, then the plan had to be judged under strict scrutiny—there seemed little question that the issue would sooner or later come back to the Court. In fact, the issue came back the following term when the case it had remanded in *Miller v. Johnson* returned on appeal. On remand, the district court in Georgia reconsidered the constitutionality of the 1990 state apportionment plan. After the legislature had failed to develop a scheme that met with the court's approval, the district court fashioned its own plan, one that included only one majority-minority district. Critics attacked this scheme on the grounds that while the court had the power to draft such a plan, it had failed to follow the rules laid down by the Supreme Court in earlier decisions. More important, it had failed to follow the clear mandate of the Georgia General Assembly that wanted two black-majority districts.

In his dissent in *Bush v. Vera,* Justice Souter had warned that the Court's failure to provide clear guidelines on redistricting would lead to lower courts arrogating unto themselves the power that properly belonged to the legislature. Although the Rehnquist Court repeatedly avowed the principle of judicial deference to legislative policy making, in the case of race-conscious districting a majority of the justices consistently denied Congress power under the Enforcement Clauses of the Fourteenth and Fifteenth Amendments to impose a plan it deemed necessary to give minorities voting effectiveness. The justices also denied to the states their usual leeway in drawing less than compact or contiguous district lines.

Although the Court never explicitly declared majority-minority districts unconstitutional per se, its decision in *Abrams v. Johnson* (1997) made it questionable whether such districts could be created anyplace other than in large cities, where it would be almost impossible not to have them. Justice Kennedy, for a 5–4 majority, reaffirmed that race "must not be a predominant factor in drawing the district lines." While the task should always be left to the elected representatives of the people, the high court upheld the district court's plan as necessary, given the inability of the legislature to reach a decision.

The district court, according to Kennedy, had properly acted within its discretion in failing to defer to an alternative plan submitted by the legislature that had two majority-minority districts. The court's plan did not violate either section 2 of the Voting Rights

*Justice David Souter, appointed to the Court in
1990, supported majority-minority plans in
general, but he warned that the courts should
stay out of the planning and leave it to the appropriate state agencies.*

Act, notwithstanding the fact that the plan allegedly diluted minority votes, nor section 5, notwithstanding the claim that the plan
allegedly led to a retrogression in the position of racial minorities.

It is possible that states can create majority-minority districts,
provided such districts meet the traditional standards of being
compact, contiguous, and one-person, one-vote. It is possible that
if states do not make race the dominant criterion, they could even
stray somewhat from the compact and contiguous standards. Four
members of the bench, led by Justice Breyer, dissented in *Abrams,*
emphasizing that the lower court should not have been allowed to
disregard the Georgia legislature's wishes for two majority-black
districts and that such a wish would not be unconstitutional given
the legislature's belief that the Voting Rights Act mandated such a
plan. He also reiterated that he and the other dissenters—Stevens,
Souter, and Ginsburg—had consistently argued through all the districting cases that the majority's rule would prove unworkable and,
as a result, would shift responsibility for drawing district lines from
the legislature, where it belonged, to the courts, where it did not.

This "would prevent the legitimate use (among others, the remedial use) of race as a political factor in redistricting, sometimes making unfair distinctions between racial minorities and others."

That same term, a 5–4 majority upheld a redistricting plan in which once again a court had drawn the lines. After the 1990 census, the Florida legislature had drafted a plan that failed to meet Justice Department preclearance under section 2 of the Voting Rights Act. The legislature then proved unable to come up with a new plan, and the Florida Supreme Court devised one of its own. This plan included an irregularly shaped state senate district that comprised portions of four counties in the Tampa Bay area and had a 46 percent black voting population. Critics challenged the plan in federal district court on equal protection grounds, and a different plan was fashioned to meet the objections of several of the challengers. The district court then approved the plan without adjudicating the constitutionality of the state supreme court's proposal.

(The notion that racial districting is the electoral version of affirmative action is well borne out in this case, in which Judge Steven D. Merryday cited numerous opinions from the Supreme Court's decisions in affirmative action cases.)

Justice Souter, joined by all the dissenters in the *Shaw* line of cases and Chief Justice Rehnquist, found no procedural problem and no clear error (the traditional standards of review) in the Georgia district court's finding. What is of most interest is the majority's rejection of the claim that because the percentage of black voters in the district was higher than in any of the three counties it drew from, it should be invalidated because race had been the primary consideration. (The district had a 36.2 percent African American voting-age population.) To this, Souter in essence responded that the Court had never said race could not be a factor, only that it could not be the sole factor, the same standard it would adopt in the 2003 Michigan Law School affirmative action case.

THE CASES OF *Hunt v. Cromartie I* and *II* finally completed the long-running litigation that had begun after the 1990 census, when the North Carolina legislature reapportioned the state's congressional districts. Following *Shaw v. Hunt* (1996), the state redrew the district's boundaries in 1997, but a three-judge district court panel granted summary judgment to white challengers of the new plan. The lower court found that the 1997 boundaries had been created with racial considerations dominating all others. The Supreme Court reversed in *Hunt v. Cromartie* (1999), noting that the record did not clearly indicate that race had been the primary factor in drawing the district lines or whether it had been the intent of the legislature to protect a Democratic seat. If the latter, then that fell within the political latitude afforded legislatures in drawing district lines. The opinion by Justice Thomas, and supported by all the other justices, also chided the lower court for granting summary judgment in a case that clearly needed a hearing. The case went back to the district court, which again found that the legislature had used race-driven criteria in violation of the Equal Protection Clause.

Once again, the Supreme Court reversed. In a 5–4 opinion, Justice Breyer—joined by Stevens, O'Connor, Souter, and Ginsburg—found the district court's conclusion clearly erroneous. The facts as to the district's unusual shape, the splitting of towns and counties, and the high African American voting population did not, in and of themselves, prove that race was the primary motive. The lower court had looked only at voting registration rather than voting behavior, and thus did not accurately take into account the political realities of the district. Undisputed evidence showed that racial identification highly correlated with political affiliation, so districts with significant black populations would tend to vote Democratic. This and other evidence indicated that the legislature had drawn boundaries that, in general, placed more reliably Democratic voters inside the district while placing less reliably Democratic voters outside the lines.

DESPITE THE CLOSENESS of the vote, the case finally put an end to a decade of litigation, just prior to state legislatures having to redraw congressional as well as state assembly lines following the 2000 census. The majority seemed to say that if a legislature drew lines solely on the basis of race in order to achieve a majority-minority district, it would fall afoul of the Equal Protection Clause. But if the legislature overtly and with documentation could show that it was trying to create a district in which one party would clearly have the upper hand—and if at the same time it coincidentally created a majority-minority district—that map would survive judicial scrutiny.

The high court, however, failed to spell out the relationship between the state and the Equal Protection Clause, on the one hand, and the pressure from the Justice Department, on the other. The Voting Rights Act and its subsequent iterations have been held to be a constitutional exercise of power granted to Congress by the Enforcement Clauses of the Fourteenth and Fifteenth Amendments. While perhaps a color-blind constitution would be the ideal in a color-blind society, this country has certainly not achieved that goal.

The problem facing the courts in the redistricting cases, as well as in the affirmative action employment and university cases, has been to what extent it is legitimate public policy as well as constitutionally acceptable to take race into account. For decades, southern states denied African Americans the vote either through devices such as the poll tax and literacy tests or through out-and-out intimidation. Where blacks could register, they could rarely, except in some of the bigger southern cities, exercise any real political influence living in predominantly white districts. This is surely the electoral counterpart to decades of African Americans, women, and other minorities being shut out of jobs and universities.

The Voting Rights Act aimed at making sure not only that minorities could register and vote free from violence and coercion but also that their votes would count and that, as a group, African Americans would have enough political clout to elect minority candidates. Majority-minority districting appeared the only possible way to give African Americans influence in a South that still had minorities spread across large areas.

But what are the rights of whites in those areas? If one is a white Republican in a majority-minority district, does one's vote count very much? Blacks had to put up with electoral powerlessness for decades, and the deprivation whites may feel at least does not carry the threats of violence that blacks in the South faced prior to 1965.

At the heart of the issue, according to Abigail Thernstrom, is an argument about the nature of American society, as is the case with "all conflicts over affirmative action policies. Deliberately drawn majority-minority districts are racial classifications for familiar affirmative action ends." When affirmative action is applied to electoral processes, just as when it is applied in other areas, we get opposing views of "white racial attitudes, black opportunity, the nature of democratic representation, and the costs of race-conscious policies."

It is now more than half a century since Lyndon Johnson's Executive Order 11246 and the Voting Rights Act, and while the Supreme Court has seemingly allowed race to be a factor in employment, higher education admissions, and electoral districting, those questions are still unanswered.

CHAPTER 16

SEEKING DIVERSITY IN HIGHER EDUCATION

There's a lot of diversity here, so I think it's representative of the real world. . . . So, me being here for four years at a university with all these different cultures, I think has prepared me very well for what's to come. . . . Sometimes, like being a psychology major, just not having someone who looks like me in the class with me, sometimes can be distressing. I feel like I have to hold it down, hold down the fort for Black people. I have to watch what I say. I wish there were more like me.

—ROBERTO

Color blindness, for all its moral and political appeal, is not really a practical option. When asked point-blank, few conservatives are honestly willing to accept the widespread resegregation that would follow from a rigid ban on racial preferences. . . . The end of affirmative action would mean, in many cases, a return to lily-white universities.

—JEFFREY ROSEN

In the 1970s, many American universities felt themselves belea-guered by seemingly irrational demands from the federal government that they hire minorities and women so that their faculty would mirror the population. There existed a great deal of ignorance on the part of government officials over exactly how universities worked, what tenure meant, and the fact that relatively few women and minorities held doctorates at the time. Some of this pressure eased in the 1980s, in part because the Reagan and Bush administrations opposed affirmative action and because each year more and more women and minorities earned the advanced degrees needed to teach at research universities. Eventually, most schools had faculty that included people of color and women, although very few could say their faculty "looked like the population." At the end of the twentieth century, articles and news stories kept reporting on the difficulty of getting—and keeping—minorities on staff.

Federal agencies had no direct jurisdiction over school admissions policies—unless they overtly discriminated—but colleges and universities had made a commitment, often starting in the 1960s, to admit minorities, and many, but not all, previously single-sex schools decided to go coeducational. Some traditionally all-male schools, such as Hampden-Sydney in Virginia, or all-female schools, such as Barnard in New York, chose not to change. Most of the Ivy League went coed in the early 1980s, while West Point began admitting women in 1977. Moreover, the Supreme Court held that public colleges could only remain single sex if the state provided a truly equivalent education for the other gender.

Following the *Bakke* decision in 1978, which allowed admissions officers to take race into account as one of several considerations, schools all over the country began recruiting minority students. This proved to be a difficult task, because many minority teenagers—male and female—had attended inferior and often segregated schools, had little intellectual or emotional preparation for college work, or lacked the grades and test scores that the better colleges required of white applicants. The historically black colleges complained that northern schools cherry-picked their best students, luring them to Cambridge or New Haven with overly generous scholarship packages.

Things for the most part went better for white women. They had been attending college since the nineteenth century, and the land-grant universities west of the Appalachians had been coed from their founding or shortly thereafter. When the prestigious Ivy League schools decided to admit women, no problem of preparation or qualifications existed. While minority women faced the same handicaps as their brothers, white women applying to Columbia or Princeton had gone to the same public or private schools as their brothers, and their GPA and SAT scores competed on a par with male applicants.

Even with these qualifications, in some places it took a lawsuit to open the gates. John C. Lowe had a law practice in Charlottesville, Virginia, in the 1960s and asked his young office assistant, Virginia Scott, if she would be entering the University of Virginia in the fall. No, Scott replied. "Women aren't allowed at Virginia." A shocked

Lowe immediately undertook to get her in and with the help of the ACLU filed a lawsuit on behalf of Scott and three other women. At the hearing, a university lawyer cross-examined one of Lowe's expert witnesses, the feminist writer Kate Millett, and said there were very few women's restrooms in campus buildings. Millett shot back, "Sir, all you do is plant geraniums in the urinals and you've got a women's bathroom." Lowe and his clients won the case, the university agreed to admit 450 women in 1970, and 550 the following year. By 1972, special allowances were no longer required.

One should not ignore the fact that race and ethnicity are not the only consideration in a university admissions procedure. Geography is an important issue for many of the elite schools, which see themselves, and want to be seen, as national rather than provincial institutions. David Boonin, for example, believes he got into Yale because of its geographic affirmative action plan. He came from the West, had good grades and scores, and got into every college he applied to on the East Coast, but only one on the West Coast. In general, there seems to be acceptance of geographic diversity as a legitimate criterion for college and university admissions. Even the committee that awards Rhodes Scholarships divides the country into sixteen "districts" and chooses two persons from each.

In the elite private schools, who your parents are matters a great deal. In 1994, 40 percent of the children of Harvard alumni who applied to Harvard got in, compared with a 14 percent admission rate for students who did not have alumni parents. A Department of Education report also found that the SAT scores of alumni children averaged thirty-five points lower than those of other admitted applicants. One 1991 study on higher education concluded that far more whites enrolled at the ten most elite American colleges through "alumni preference" than the combined numbers of all the African Americans and Latinos entering through affirmative action.

A number of critics have attacked the legacy program, and it is crucial to Richard Reeves's thesis in *Dream Hoarders*. His argument is that legacy admits are usually less qualified by GPA and test scores than non-legacy students who are competing for a diminished number of openings. In fact, as Bowen and Bok showed many years ago, the number of legacy admits into the elite colleges is far larger than those brought in under affirmative action plans. Moreover, recent studies conclude that for young men and women who want to go to college, it is better to be born rich than naturally gifted. Most legacy students, whatever their natural abilities, benefit far more by being born into a well-to-do family. (This, of course, is far different from the scandal that erupted in early 2019 about wealthy families bribing college officials to get their children into elite schools. Coming from a well-to-do family gives a youngster many benefits that are just not available for those mired in poverty.)

Even when court decisions, such as *Hopwood* in Texas, or initiatives such as Proposition 209 in California, theoretically barred any use of race, gender, or ethnicity in university admissions, legislation and creative academic policies usually made it possible to get around the bans. In the quarter century following *Bakke,* the face of higher education in America changed, and the presence of significant numbers of minorities in the classroom became the norm. This did not mean, however, that the debate stopped; to the contrary, it intensified as colleges and universities changed the goal of their affirmative action programs. Originally, schools had seen affirmative action as a compensatory program, reaching out to take in groups hitherto excluded whether for race, gender, or ethnicity. They focused primarily on rectifying the past sins of discrimination, and while they expected there would be some benefits to the school from having minorities on campus, that did not constitute their primary justification.

At some point, academic leaders started talking about diversity and how having a diverse student body (and faculty) would be better for the education of all students. Having African Americans in the classroom while discussing racism, or having a woman professor talking about gender discrimination, would lead to a fuller understanding of the multiethnic, multicultural tapestry of the nation. The legal scholar Mark Killenbeck wrote that he had "been unable to find any mainstream higher education institution or advocacy group that does not believe that diversity is a fundamental educational value." An admissions officer at an Ivy League school made it quite plain: "We're after diversity. We ideally want a student body where racial and ethnic groups are represented according to their proportion in society." In 1997, the Association of American Universities, a group of sixty-two of the nation's leading research universities, came out in support of colleges using affirmative action in their admissions processes to secure a more diverse student body. The triumph of this approach came in the Michigan Law School case, *Grutter v. Bollinger* (2003).

———

WHEN LOOKING AT affirmative action programs in higher education—whether for compensatory or diversity reasons—the first questions one should ask concern the minority students: How were they chosen; why did they decide on a particular school; how did their GPA, SAT, and other scores compare with those of their white classmates; how did they do in school; and how did they see themselves as part of campus life? Unfortunately, there are no easy, one-size-fits-all answers. All we can do is look at some examples and see if we can tease out a pattern.

First of all, not all minority admissions fell into the preferential pool. By the 1960s, a small but growing black middle class existed, primarily north of the Mason-Dixon Line; their children went to the same public or private high schools as did those of their white neighbors and did comparatively well in their grades, their extracurricular activities, and their test scores. Colleges certainly took their race into account, but many in this group would have been admitted even in a race-blind admissions process. These students found themselves the object of what amounted to a bidding war as the Ivy League schools wooed them with financial aid packages that were often far more attractive than those offered to white students.

Yet even at elite schools, the stories are not of happy minority groups but of continuing racial tensions. In the late 1970s, Harvard established the Committee on Race Relations, headed by the dean of students and consisting of administrators, faculty, and students. It drew on the feedback from several open meetings, as well as the expertise of Harvard professors like Thomas Pettigrew, a social psychologist and nationally known authority on race relations. Most important, the committee sent out a sixteen-page, 251-question survey to all 6,000 Harvard-Radcliffe undergraduates and received 1,300 responses. Harvard, it should be noted, had been among the first universities to adopt an affirmative action policy and, while rejecting explicit quotas, had encouraged a slow but steady increase in black and Hispanic enrollments. From the mid-1970s on, black undergraduate enrollment had been consistent at around 7 percent and total minority enrollment at 14 percent.

Harvard students divided along racial lines over several issues. While white students said they valued and supported the goal of a racially diverse student body, they rejected any kind of quota arrangement. Three out of five opposed the idea that "the minimum number of minority students . . . should be in a proportion commensurate with their representation in the general population." In contrast, 69 percent of the black students agreed with this goal. White students appeared to take the idea of admission by merit far more seriously than did many of the opponents of affirmative action outside academia, while black students seemed far more supportive of quotas than did African Americans in the general population.

The survey also showed that black students labored under a distinct shadow of doubt as to their academic abilities. There was a "widespread assumption that the minorities accepted at Harvard were 'the best of the worst,' rather than the 'best of the best.' " While noting the long history of biological racism in the country, which assumed the inferiority of African Americans, the report also placed some of the blame on affirmative action. Although the report supported such policies, "it must be recognized that this issue has a negative side to it, that sometimes the impression is created that minorities at Harvard are less qualified." A high percentage of white students (54 percent) and an even higher proportion of black students (69 percent) agreed with the statement "Admissions policies that are thought to favor minorities generally often create doubt about their academic ability." In response to further questions, a majority of black students felt that their fellow students, administrators, and faculty all doubted their ability. Moreover, one out of six black students said that Harvard's admissions policy had created doubts *in their own minds* about minority abilities.

This would make more sense if the black students at Harvard had come from poor families and had attended inferior and/or segregated schools. But 70 percent of black undergraduates came from professional or managerial families, compared with 86 percent of white students. They did not come from disadvantaged backgrounds, and four out of five attended majority-white high schools. Yet for all that Harvard had to offer that made it one of the most sought-after schools in the country, a majority of the black respondents reported a rather negative experience at Harvard, and 40 percent agreed that "being at Harvard has influenced my attitude about whites negatively."

Negative reactions appeared among white students as well, and these did not result simply from prejudice. Many white students had "the perception that blacks at Harvard were being separatists: that they tended to segregate themselves from interacting with whites and sometimes even appeared hostile to various forms of interracial interaction." Three out of five believed that minority students isolated themselves from the mainstream of college life. This was no misperception, because many of the black students acknowledged this self-isolation.

This tension between black and white students could be found not just at Harvard but at other elite schools as well. At Stanford, where only 15 percent of seniors identified themselves as somewhat conservative, some faculty declared that relations between white and black students had made the campus a "racial tinder box." Campuses today, according to one University of Pennsylvania faculty member, "have the cultural diversity of Beirut. There are separate armed camps. The black kids don't mix with the white kids. The Asians are off by themselves. Oppression is the great status symbol." At Oberlin, which for well over a century had been the model of a racially integrated campus, students there "think, act, and live apart." Asians lived in Asia House, Jews in J-House, Latinos in Spanish House, and blacks in Afrikan Heritage House. Even the Lesbian, Gay, and Bisexual Union had broken into racial and gender factions.

Underlying much of the friction at Harvard and other schools was the undeniable fact that a completely race-blind, merit-only admissions process would keep many minority students out. As one article subtitle put it, "Can Elitism and Affirmative Action Coexist?" At Stanford, for example, as of 1994 entering black undergraduates had an average combined (math and verbal) SAT score of 1,164, a good score by national standards, putting them in the top sixth of all test takers in the country. But their white classmates had been admitted with a 1,315 average, putting them in the top 3 percent. As the African American scholar and affirmative action critic Shelby Steele argued, black students pay a heavy price for their letters of acceptance based on lower academic standards. Studies at Stanford, certainly one of the country's elite schools, showed the same tensions as at Harvard, the same sense that people looked down on minority students as not really qualified, and the same painful self-doubt.

No doubt the disparity in SAT scores underlines the sense that minority students did not really "belong" in some schools. For example, at the University of California at Berkeley, the mean SAT score for whites admitted was 1,256, for Asians 1,293, for Hispanics 1,032, and for blacks 994. At the University of Texas at Austin, the average SAT score for whites was 1,147, Asians 1,155, Hispanics 1,043, and African Americans 991. "Average" numbers, of course, do not tell us much about individuals, and we all know people who are very bright, creative, and well-read but do not do well on tests. Nonetheless, people of color admitted to these schools who looked at these numbers would probably have doubts as to whether they were "bona fide students," and so long as programs of racial preference utilized lower test scores, such doubts would persist.

And so would the suspicions of other students. Yolanda Cruz, a biology professor at Oberlin, told a story about her first year in graduate school at Berkeley. A second-year student greeted her and said that she had been looking forward to meeting the "twofer" who had been admitted that year. The student assumed that Cruz, a Filipino woman in a male-dominated field, had been admitted because the school included both Filipinos and women in its affirmative action program and that Cruz had therefore qualified on both grounds, ergo a "twofer." In fact, Cruz had been admitted solely on a sterling undergraduate academic record.

This sense of self-doubt affected not just students but minority faculty as well. Too often, charged Ernest van den Haag, universities hired black and Hispanic faculty members less academically qualified than their white colleagues. "Even well-qualified black degree holders," van den Haag claimed, "suffer from the public perception that they got their degrees without meeting the same standards as whites." The perception may be unfair in some cases, but it did not help self-esteem, and those who were in fact well qualified suffered as well as those who were not. "Affirmative action has thus done as much injury to black scholars as to black students."

Ella Bell of MIT's Sloan School of Management defended affirmative action but understood why other African Americans would not. "I think it's very difficult once we have achieved, and we have good educations, and we know we're good, we know we have the skills, and we run up against this brick wall," she said. She had been hired in part because of affirmative action, but MIT had not lowered its standards when hiring her. Too many blacks believed that because affirmative action played some role in gaining a position, then everyone else looked down on them as untalented and unskilled. In this dialogue, the whole issue of white racism had been ignored, because nobody wanted to think of themselves as prejudiced. "Nobody wants to be perceived as being a victim of racism, or prejudice. It hurts deeply." Bell, however, did not think that getting rid of affirmative action would ease the pain. "No matter what I do, I will still be perceived as a token until you bring in a significant number [of blacks]."

Many women faculty members tell a similar story, especially if they were part of the group that got their degrees in the 1970s and 1980s. One colleague of mine held an endowed chair at a major public university and had certainly earned it: she had published more than a dozen books and numerous articles and had also won prestigious awards and fellowships. But as she told me, every time she got a promotion or won an award, rumors abounded that she had succeeded because she had been sleeping with the department chair, the dean, or some other highly placed male administrator. Other women faculty members have told similar stories.

IT WOULD BE NICE if we had numbers that could tell us whether affirmative action actually worked, not just for the gifted, such as Sonia Sotomayor (Princeton and Yale Law), but for all minority students admitted. In July 2009, a piece by Helene Cooper lauded the success of affirmative action in creating a new elite and pointed to members of the recently installed administration who had benefited from affirmative action—Barack and Michelle Obama (Columbia, Princeton, Harvard Law), Eric Holder (Columbia), and Valerie Jarrett (Stanford, Michigan Law). Cooper, herself an affirmative action admission from Africa at the University of North Carolina, believed this new elite differed from the older WASP establishment in that even if they excelled in school and did well afterward, they never lost the sense of otherness, of not being the same, that they had experienced in school. This, she believed, was a good thing, because the country needed leaders sensitive to the problems of all groups. Theodore Cross, the editor of *The Journal of Blacks in Higher Education,* claimed that in the two decades between 1974 and 1994 affirmative action in higher education had "vaulted tens of thousands of young blacks into the upper and professional classes," an assertion that may be true but that lacks any empirical support. He also argued that a return to race-blind admissions would close that gateway for minorities into the middle class.

We do have some specific numbers. For example, in 1969–1970, approximately 3,000, or 4.4 percent, of the 68,386 students enrolled in American law schools belonged to minority groups. By 1982–1983, minority students accounted for 11,611, or 9 percent, of a law school population of 127,915. While the author of the article, a professor of law at the University of New Mexico, believed that law schools should continue—indeed increase—their affirmative action programs, he stated that he did not believe it necessary to discuss the positive values of such programs; everybody knew the importance of diversity in the legal profession.

Richard Sander put forward a far less optimistic view in his controversial study of the 27,000 students who entered law school in the fall of 1991. Drawing on data provided by the Law School Admission Council National Longitudinal Bar Passage Study, he could follow these students from admission through completion of law school, when they took the state bar exam and whether they passed. He also had access to supplemental studies on the employment experience of young black attorneys. He found that race-based preferences for black students in law school admissions resulted in a higher attrition from law school, lower bar passage rates, and subsequent problems in the job market compared with a race-blind system. In his most damning charge, Sander concluded that racial preferences produced fewer successful black lawyers each year than would come from a race-blind system.

In April 1991, a white Georgetown University law student, Timothy Maguire, set off a storm by questioning the academic qualities of black students admitted to the school. In an article in a student newspaper, Maguire charged that black law students were in general not as qualified as whites. They had lower scores on the Law School Admission Test and lower grade point averages, information he secured surreptitiously while working as a file clerk in the student records office. The article polarized the campus. Some demanded that Maguire be expelled for unethical behavior, while others saw him as a champion of free speech and truth. In the middle of this brouhaha, it became known that Maguire himself had a low LSAT score and had been admitted under a program for "low testers" as well as for his experience as a Peace Corps volunteer in Africa.

Results in medical schools proved disappointing. In 1970, the Association of American Medical Colleges, acknowledging a long history of racial discrimination, set a goal of having blacks represent 12 percent of total medical school entrants, a figure reflecting the African American percentage of the population. They never reached that goal. Twenty years later blacks made up 6 percent of first-year medical students, and in terms of doctors in practice only 3 percent of the 587,000 physicians in the country. So in 1991 the AAMC set itself a new goal, Project 3000 by 2000, in which there would be 3,000 so-called underrepresented minorities enrolled; of these, 1,900 would be African Americans, and the rest would include Mexican Americans, Puerto Ricans, and American Indians. Although over the next few years the numbers in the 126 member schools of the AAMC did go up, the vast majority of African American medical students still attended the two historically black medical schools. Howard University in Washington, founded in 1867, trained about 25 percent of all black doctors in the United States, while Meharry Medical College in Nashville, founded in 1876, graduated nearly 40 percent of all black doctors and dentists. The increase in numbers at previously exclusionary schools is significant, although still far from the rather high expectations of the AAMC. One unforeseen result has been the waning dominance of the historically black schools. Interestingly, a study of doctors trained at the University of California at Davis Medical School showed that over a twenty-year period those who had been admitted with special consideration for race or ethnicity had remarkably similar postgraduate careers as those admitted strictly on academic merit alone.

ONE CAN FIND a number of studies indicating a rise in minority applications and acceptances, but most of them have been limited, and even taking them all together does not lead to any consistent conclusions. In the largest study, *The Shape of the River* (1998), undertaken under the auspices of the Andrew W. Mellon Foundation, William Bowen, the former president of Princeton and an economist, and Derek Bok, the former president of Harvard and a political scientist, came out strongly in favor of affirmative action and what it had meant in American higher education.

Bowen and Bok began by noting that although some progress had been made by 1960 in terms of more blacks staying in and graduating from high school and even from college, little progress had occurred in opening up elite occupations to African Americans. The number of people of color who entered professions such as medicine or law, won elective office, or worked as managers or proprietors had all increased, but by small numbers. In 1960, only four people of color sat in the House of Representatives and none in the Senate. "In 1960, then, the outlook for blacks seemed highly uncertain." By the mid-1960s, with the rising concern for civil rights, more schools began recruiting and admitting black students, although the actual numbers remained low. As one critic noted, the top colleges "would rather be selective than integrated." Few blacks enrolled in the nation's top law schools, and of all African Americans in medical school three-fourths attended Howard and Meharry.

All this began to change as schools adopted affirmative action programs, and Bowen and Bok credit the "striking" changes that prevailed in the mid-1990s to this decision. Blacks now made up 8.6 percent of all male professionals and 13.1 percent of all female professionals (up respectively from 3.8 and 6.0 percent in 1960). In that thirty-year period, blacks almost doubled their share of the nation's doctors and tripled their share of attorneys and engineers. Black representation in Congress rose from 4 to 41 members, and the total number of black elected officials went from 280 in 1965 to 7,984 in 1993. Hispanics also made striking gains and from 1983 to 1996 increased their share of executives, managers, and administrators from 2.8 to 4.8 percent and their portion of professionals from 2.5 to 4.3 percent.

The two men examined grades, test scores, choice of majors, graduation rates, careers, and attitudes of 45,000 students at twenty-eight of the most selective schools in the country. Bowen and Bok admitted that they both favored affirmative action but wanted to test their hypotheses about its benefits. Having done the work, they believed their book ought to put to rest major objections to race-conscious preference policies.

A primary argument in the book was that affirmative action had moved beyond its original goal of compensating minorities for past discrimination to one of ensuring a healthier future for all segments of society. The diversity a person encountered in college would prepare her for the diversity she would meet in her career and in the real world for the rest of her life.

Bowen and Bok jumped right into the fray by acknowledging, at the beginning of their book, that most blacks who entered elite institutions did so with lower GPAs and test scores. Moreover, as they progressed through these schools, blacks received lower grades and graduated at a lower rate. But where many critics of affirmative action assumed that the problems minorities faced in school would determine the arc of their careers afterward, the new survey found that after graduation affirmative action students achieved notable success. They earned advanced degrees at about the same rate as their white classmates and were slightly more likely than their white classmates from the same institution to get professional degrees in law, medicine, and business. Once into their careers, minority members showed greater participation in civic activities than white graduates. In fact, the more selective the school, the more likely that black graduates would go on to earn advanced degrees and receive higher salaries.

As far as the authors of *The Shape of the River* could determine, these "affirmative action babies," whatever problems they might have had in college, went on to have successful careers in the professions and in business and became "the backbone of the emergent black middle class," with an influence that extended far beyond the workplace. They served as "strong threads in a fabric that binds their own community together and binds those communities into the larger social fabric as well." Bowen and Bok noted that by getting through these elite universities, minority graduates would earn 70 to 85 percent more than black graduates from non-elite schools. In this, they very much reflected the experience of whites, who had known for many years that a degree from Columbia or Duke meant not only greater earnings but entry into alumni networks that could facilitate useful and perhaps even lucrative contacts.

As for skeptics who might charge that the success of these students after college relied on racial preference policies in graduate schools and in corporations, Bowen and Bok noted that the students who had entered in 1976 were now about forty years old, and even if they had garnered favored entry into graduate school or business, once there they had to demonstrate that they were capable of doing the work. Someone who could not do so would flunk out of professional school or be fired for incompetence.

This had not happened. The authors took a closer look at 700 blacks who had been admitted under race-conscious policies in 1976: 225 obtained professional degrees or doctorates; 70 became doctors, 60 lawyers, 125 business executives, and more than 300 would be considered civic leaders. Their annual salaries averaged $71,000 (around $112,868 in 2019 dollars). If a race-neutral policy had been followed, the number of minorities in the top schools would have fallen from about 7 percent to 2 percent, and many of these now-middle-class professional, business, and civic leaders would not have had any chance at success.

The book also confronted charges raised in the 1981 Harvard report that affirmative action exacerbated race relations. In this survey, both blacks and whites said they had had substantial social interaction with each other in school and that this had helped prepare them to relate to different racial groups later in life.

A more troubling question, perhaps the key question, in the whole debate, involved white students displaced by affirmative action minority admissions. Would society have been better off if they had attended college and gone on to graduate schools and successful careers? "This is the central question," the authors note, "and cannot be answered by data alone." It is a question of "principle versus principle, not principle versus expediency." In this case, Bowen and Bok had chosen to come down on the side of the minority students, because society needed them.

They did, however, use some statistics based on an analogy proposed by Thomas J. Kane of the Brookings Institution involving handicapped parking spaces. Eliminating such spaces, according to Kane, would have only a minuscule effect on parking options for the nondisabled driver. "But the sight of the open space will frustrate many passing motorists who are looking for a space. Many are likely to believe that they would now be parked if the space were not reserved." Bowen and Bok point out that if half of the blacks accepted at the elite colleges had been rejected, the probability of another white getting in would rise only 2 percent, to 27 from 25 percent. Like handicapped parking places, race-conscious admissions policies have a major impact on the minorities, whereas eliminating them would have only a marginal benefit for the white majority.

In what was certainly one of the more interesting findings, Bowen and Bok claimed that they had focused on the twenty-eight elite schools to make an often-ignored point. The whole debate about race-conscious admissions applies to only about one-fourth of all colleges and universities in the country. The other 75 percent take nearly everyone who applies.

The book also contradicted the findings of Stephan and Abigail Thernstrom's influential book, *America in Black and White,* published the year before, which claimed that because black students admitted under preferential policies did not keep up with their white classmates, they ended up failed and stigmatized. "When students are given a preference in admission because of their race or gender," the Thernstroms claimed, "it means that they are jumping into a competition for which their academic achievements do not qualify them and many find it hard to keep up." Bowen and Bok pointed to their massive database and argued that their findings completely contradicted the Thernstroms' allegation.

ADVOCATES OF AFFIRMATIVE ACTION and diversity applauded the study. *The New York Times,* for example, praised the study for finally providing "striking confirmation of the success of affirmative action in opening opportunities and creating a whole generation of black professionals who are now leaders in their fields and their communities." The evidence collected "flatly refutes many of the misimpressions of affirmative action opponents." The authors clearly—and correctly—see that merit must be defined in terms not of test scores but of the institution's mission, and race must be considered in order to choose individuals who will become leaders in our society.

Bowen and Bok had rather naively hoped that their impressive data-laden brief would put to rest major objections to affirmative action, and in that hope they proved mistaken. One could provide reams of data printouts both for and against race-conscious policies, and it is doubtful if more than a very small number of people would change their minds. As Bok himself conceded, the debate was not between right and wrong, or right and expediency, but right against right. As we have seen, many of the most ardent opponents of affirmative action came not from the ranks of out-and-out bigots or die-hard segregationists or male chauvinists but from liberals and conservatives who believed that race- and gender-conscious programs, even when designed for a benign purpose, violated not only the Equal Protection Clause but common rules about fairness.

It did not take very long for the Thernstroms to respond. In an article published the following year, they marshaled their own data to show how badly affirmative action students did in elite schools and reiterated the claim they had made in earlier work that the great leap forward of African Americans in the previous quarter century had not come from policies of racial preference, but was part of a long-term change that began in the 1940s, well before the Civil Rights and Voting Rights Acts, and had nothing to do with affirmative action. (It should be noted that while the Thernstroms believed that African Americans had made a great deal of progress, they were not dismissive of the very real problems still facing the country in its search for a true racial equality and of the problems of minorities who suffered from racism.) Other opponents of affirmative action chimed in, each with his or her own horror story about how degrading and unfair affirmative action had proved.

In *The Shape of the River,* Bowen and Bok noted that when the Supreme Court decided *Brown v. Board of Education* in 1954, the justices had "relied heavily on social science studies." They hoped that their book would provide the needed data for the high court when, at some future point, it ruled on affirmative action. That opportunity came up sooner than many people had expected.

ON 26 JANUARY 1999, students on fifteen campuses across the country opened their school newspapers to a full-page advertisement with the headline "Guilty by Admission," and in bold print "Nearly Every Elite College in America Violates the Law. Does Yours?" The ad went on to condemn the "lingering presence of unlawful racial preferences" and urged students to send away for a free handbook on how to tell if their school had been breaking the law. A group called the Center for Individual Rights (CIR), a conservative public policy law firm in Washington, sponsored the ads. The campaign kickoff featured a news conference at which the former Reagan education secretary William Bennett, a conservative, as well as the liberal columnist Nat Hentoff spoke.

The CIR had been the driving force behind the suit that led to the *Hopwood* decision and now hoped that through the ad campaign it would find students willing to be plaintiffs against their schools. Terence J. Pell, the senior counsel at the center, charged that colleges were using racial preference "to get a certain mix in their student bodies, and that is illegal." Many colleges had reduced the notion of "diversity" to nothing more than skin color or ethnicity. Pell also noted that the CIR had decided to step up its campaign in response to the Bowen and Bok book, because the book had shifted the debate with its claims that race-conscious admissions had great benefits to society. The CIR already had some cases in the pipeline, including two against the University of Michigan, one against the undergraduate admissions process, and one against the law school.

THE UNIVERSITY OF MICHIGAN in Ann Arbor had admitted its first African American students, two men from Detroit, in 1868 with little fanfare. More controversy surrounded the first woman student admitted in 1870, but once that died down, women regularly attended the school; the first black woman enrolled in 1878. Prior to World War II, the campus usually had fewer than twenty black students; they were, as one historian put it, "passively accepted, with no direct intervention from the university to attract more." The numbers grew slowly, to 200 in 1954, and 400 by 1966, or a little over 1 percent out of a total enrollment of 32,000.

Michigan began affirmative action in the 1960s, well ahead of many other schools, but for the most part it flew under the radar. The university's president, Harlan Hatcher, and its vice president for academic affairs, Roger Heyns, initiated a program quietly, not sure how it would be received by a relatively conservative constituency. During the student unrest of the early 1970s, the program became public knowledge, and school officials no longer had to hide that they had a program, although they did not divulge details of how the race-conscious admissions policy worked. Several efforts by conservatives failed to derail the program, and even though Republicans controlled the state government, they could not get enough support to eliminate racially conscious programs. The Michigan state constitution at that time gave the University of Michigan more autonomy from the governor and state legislature than most other state universities had. Where Republican governors in California could stack the Board of Regents to kill affirmative action, Michigan governors could not.

Lee Bollinger, a supporter of affirmative action, had testified as an expert witness on behalf of the Texas Law School's admissions policy in *Hopwood,* and he became president of the University of Michigan in 1996. As he recalled, almost as soon as he took office, he faced a small but growing argument that achieving diversity by using race as a factor of admission constituted a form of discrimination. He "deeply disagreed" with this view but learned that some of the same groups that had backed the *Hopwood* suit in Texas and Prop 209 in California had targeted Michigan, and Bollinger spent much of his six years as president fighting the lawsuits.

During his tenure, defenders of affirmative action could claim that the Michigan plan had been a success. The Michigan psychology and women's studies professor Patricia Gurin's research concluded that "for most of Michigan's students, its residence halls are the most diverse environments they have ever encountered. . . . Rooming with a student from a different racial/ethnic background, though sometimes a genuine challenge . . . is potentially a very positive experience." By 1997, minority enrollment at Ann Arbor had reached 25 percent, although African American enrollment was 8 percent, only a little over half their statewide 14 percent of the population. Hispanics constituted 6 percent, twice their rate of the state's census, and Asians formed 10 percent of the student body, ten times their proportion in Michigan. Whites made up 83 percent of the state, but only three-quarters of the students, and some white parents wanted to know why their children could not get into a school supported by their taxes.

The story of the lawsuits that eventually went to the Supreme Court is quickly told. Two white students, Jennifer Gratz and Patrick Hamacher, applied to the University of Michigan's undergraduate college at Ann Arbor, Gratz in 1995 and Hamacher in 1997, but neither gained admission, and neither knew exactly why they had been rejected. The public information about the affirmative action program really did not say much about its actual workings, and so Carl Cohen, who had taught philosophy at the school for four decades, used a Freedom of Information request to obtain the confidential information. On reading it, he realized that his beloved university was using the same kind of policy he had criticized in a book he had written attacking racial preferences. Cohen forwarded what he had found out to Bollinger and to the regents; both ignored his findings.

Cohen had learned that undergraduate admissions depended on the number of points an applicant would get for different qualities, such as having alumni as parents, geographic location (it helped to come from the sparsely populated Upper Peninsula), grade point average, and test scores, with the maximum number of points one could earn set at 150. White applicants from Detroit, however, mostly had only their GPA and test scores to help them. Applicants were divided into two groups, in state and out of state, but in both groups minorities received 20 points just for being a minority, and these points for race overcame deficits in other areas. For example, nonminority applicants with GPAs of 3.2 or 3.3, SAT scores between 1,010 and 1,080 (maximum 1,600), or ACT scores of 22 or 23 (out of 36) were automatically rejected; minority applicants with these same scores gained acceptance. (Prior to 1997, the admissions office used four different grids, with two reserved for minorities.) Cohen, a former president of the Michigan ACLU, was horrified, and before long the Center for Individual Rights had secured a copy and filed suit on behalf of Jennifer Gratz and Patrick Hamacher in federal court. That same year, Barbara Grutter, a white law school applicant, received notice of rejection from the University of Michigan Law School, and the CIR filed suit on her behalf as well.

The CIR won the Gratz/Hamacher case in the district court. Judge Patrick Duggan invalidated the pre-1997 plan because it separated minorities and nonminorities into different pools for consideration and reserved seats for underrepresented minorities. He upheld the post-1997 index, which did not separate minorities out but gave them a twenty-point bonus, and said that it operated like Justice Powell's "race-as-a-plus model" in *Bakke*.

In the same district court, but with Judge Bernard Friedman presiding, the CIR on behalf of Barbara Grutter attacked the law school admissions process. The law school, one of the best in the country, did not set aside seats for minorities, nor did it use a point system. Rather, it used race as one factor in admission, seeking to put together a diverse student body. Friedman ruled that achieving a diverse student body was not a compelling governmental interest under the Fourteenth Amendment's equal protection analysis.

Both cases were appealed up to the Court of Appeals for the Sixth Circuit. The importance of the two cases moved the appeals court to hear the cases en banc, that is, with all the judges sitting, rather than the usual three-member panel. Chief Judge Boyce F. Martin Jr. spoke for a divided court, which by a 5–4 vote reversed the lower court's decision regarding the law school, but it could not reach a decision on undergraduate admissions. As would be expected, the CIR filed for a writ of certiorari to the U.S. Supreme Court in Grutter's case, but when the Sixth Circuit had not handed down an opinion in *Gratz* a year after it had been argued, the CIR appealed that one as well. The Supreme Court granted cert in both cases on 2 December 2002 and heard oral argument on 1 April 2003.

On that day, thousands of demonstrators paraded in front of the Marble Palace, with most of them expressing support for affirmative action. The men and women of the high court are used to demonstrations; one cannot, however, see or hear what is happening on the front steps from inside the courtroom. But they do pay attention to the briefs, not only those filed by the parties, but any filed by the solicitor general and, in this case, a remarkable number of amici—friend of the court—briefs, seventy-eight in favor of affirmative action and nineteen opposed. In each case there would be one hour of oral argument. In addition, Solicitor General Ted Olson would offer the federal government's argument.

Olson, however, had a problem. The Clinton administration had backed the university's affirmative action plan in the lower courts. Now George W. Bush sat in the White House, and the *Hopwood* decision, which he approved, had been handed down while he was governor of Texas. It had been his administration that came up with the "affirmative access" plan granting undergraduate admission to the top 10 percent of Texas high school graduates. Bush had gone on record as opposing the use of quotas and any racial or ethnic preferences in public education.

Bush's White House counsel and future attorney general, Alberto Gonzales, a Mexican American, as well as Deputy Attorney General Larry Thompson, an African American, did not want the administration to oppose affirmative action. Both men personally favored race and ethnic preference programs, and they pointed out the political costs involved if the administration opposed programs favoring minorities at the same time the Republican Party was attempting to woo them. Although opposition to "reverse discrimination" had long been a mainstay of the GOP, large corporations were on record as supporting diversity in the workforce. In the end, Olson and the conservatives in the administration won, and Bush announced that he would oppose the university's racial preferences, which he decried as "divisive, unfair, and impossible to square with the Constitution. . . . At their core, the Michigan policies amount to a quota system that unfairly rewards or penalizes prospective students based solely on their race." The brief produced by the government, however, was dismissed by most court watchers as anemic and not very helpful to the Court.

The nearly one hundred amici briefs amazed not only the justices but observers, especially the one that came to be known as the "military brief." It included such well-known generals as Norman Schwarzkopf, John Shalikashvili, Wesley Clark, William Crowe, former superintendents of the military academies, and the former defense secretary William Cohen. The brief began,

Based on decades of experience, amici have concluded that a highly qualified, racially diverse officer corps educated and trained to command our nation's racially diverse enlisted ranks is essential to the military's ability to fulfill its principal mission to provide national security. The primary sources for the nation's officer corps are the service academies and the ROTC, the latter comprised of students already admitted to participating colleges and universities. At present, the military cannot achieve an officer corps that is *both* highly qualified *and* racially diverse unless the service academies and the ROTC use limited race-conscious recruiting and admissions policies.

The military brief also quoted the nation's most celebrated product of ROTC, General Colin Powell, then serving as secretary of state. "In the military," he said, we "used affirmative action to reach out to those who were qualified but who were often overlooked or ignored as a result of indifference or inertia."

Most of the amici briefs supporting the Michigan plan, including those from General Motors, DuPont, IBM, and the AFL-CIO, all emphasized the need for diversity in colleges so that there would be diversity in the workforce and the professions. One could find occasional references to compensating minorities for past sins against them, but the main thrust of the pro-affirmative-action briefs talked about diversity, which by 2003 had become the major justification for racial and ethnic preference programs.

The law school's brief provided justices with statistics showing that a color-blind admissions process would not yield diversity. In 1997, when Barbara Grutter applied, only 67 minority applications had LSAT scores above 163, the range from which more than 90 percent of the applicants had been admitted. Had the law school insisted on merit alone, it would have had in the class of 400 only 16 African Americans, Hispanics, and Native Americans, as opposed to the 58 it took from these three "under-represented" groups. Moreover, the number varied each year, with minority students making up between 13.5 and 20.1 percent during the period the law school had an affirmative action plan, proof that there was no fixed quota.

As the political scientist Barbara Perry pointed out, the law school could appeal to the justices' understanding of the legal profession and the need for top law schools to produce "leaders of the profession and of our nation." This message was clearly aimed at Justice Sandra Day O'Connor, who had led the way for women in the legal field and who was especially concerned with training civic leaders. The law school brief also relied heavily on Justice Powell's decision in *Bakke,* and Michigan claimed that like Harvard it took race into account as one factor and not as the sole determinant. Here, too, the law school recognized how highly O'Connor regarded Powell.

The undergraduate program, while also insisting on diversity as its goal, had a much more difficult road to travel. The automatic award of twenty points to minorities—an amount that could overcome low GPA and test scores—did not make race one of many factors, but for many minority applicants it became *the* determining consideration.

Maureen Mahoney, a veteran Supreme Court litigator who had once clerked for Rehnquist, argued for the law school and easily held her own against the barrage mounted by Justice Scalia. When he tried to get her to admit that race did not enter into making Michigan an elite law school, she retorted, "I don't think there's anything in this Court's cases that suggests that the law school has to make an election between academic excellence and racial diversity."

Ted Olson, on the other hand, had tough going. The justices kept bringing up the brief submitted by the former military officers, and although Olson tried to say he was not prepared to deal with an amicus brief, the justices would not let go. Ruth Bader Ginsburg and Anthony Kennedy kept coming back to the fact that all the military academies—agencies of the federal government—had race preference programs. Ginsburg asked him point-blank if that was illegal. The justices, according to onlookers, sought not absolute answers but rather nuance. They did not support or oppose affirmative action per se but wanted to know how Michigan and other schools used it, whether diversity could be achieved in other ways, and how finely Michigan had tuned its admissions processes.

Opponents of affirmative action had easier going in the undergraduate case. The law school had clearly followed Powell's suggestions in *Bakke,* making race just one factor, while the college system had no subtlety at all and was simply numbers-driven. In truth, it would probably have been almost impossible for the undergraduate admissions office to have adopted a subtle, race-as-only-one-factor system. It had to process 25,000 applications to get an entering class of 5,000, and the only way it could handle that many was to set up some sort of numerical grid and award points for different attributes. The great mistake it made was to give so many points based on nothing more than the color of the applicant's skin.

The high court handed down its opinions on 23 June 2003, almost the last day of the term. Unlike *Bakke,* the Court majority had five votes in the law school case, and six in the undergraduate program. The justices filed a total of twelve opinions in the two cases.

In *Grutter v. Bollinger,* the Court by a 5–4 vote upheld the law school plan, ruling that diversity did constitute a compelling governmental interest and that the law school's plan, in which race was one of several considerations, did not violate the Constitution's Equal Protection Clause. In her opinion, O'Connor also responded to the Fifth Circuit's dismissal of Justice Powell's *Bakke* decision by reaffirming it, and thus in effect overruling *Hopwood*. O'Connor, whose questioning in the law school argument had made it clear she believed race could be a factor, wrote that the Constitution "does not prohibit the law school's narrowly tailored use of race in admissions decisions to further a compelling interest in obtaining the educational benefits that flow from a diverse student body." Reiterating what the Court had said in past decisions that even narrowly tailored affirmative action plans should not last forever, she declared, "We expect that 25 years from now the use of racial preferences will no longer be necessary to further the interests approved today," the clearest marker yet of how long the Court, at least, thought that such plans would be necessary.

Chief Justice Rehnquist dissented, joined by Scalia, Kennedy, and Thomas. Rehnquist argued that the law school's program bore little or no relation to its stated goal of achieving an undefined "critical mass" of minority students.

In the undergraduate case, *Gratz v. Bollinger*, the Court struck down

Lee Bollinger, then president of the University of Michigan, and Jennifer Gratz, the lead plaintiff challenging the university's undergraduate admissions policies, outside the Supreme Court after oral argument on 1 April 2003.

the 150-point scheme. O'Connor and Breyer joined the dissenters in the law school case to provide a 6–3 majority. Rehnquist acknowledged that the law school case demonstrated that government had a compelling interest in promoting racial diversity on campus, but the rigid point system was not the way to achieve it. Automatically awarding 20 points "solely on the basis of race, is not narrowly tailored to achieve the interest in educational diversity" that Michigan claimed justified the policy.

In her dissent, Justice Ginsburg noted that the country is not that "far distant from an overtly discriminatory past" and that it would take many years of effort to undo that damage. Because Michigan did not try to hide its point system, which was known to all who applied, she believed it an acceptable means designed to overcome the past effects of discrimination. Hers is a strange opinion, in that although past discrimination had been mentioned by Michigan, its emphasis, like that of the amici, had centered on diversity.

Linda Greenhouse called O'Connor's opinion in *Grutter* an "unapologetic embrace" of diversity as a compelling state interest, far beyond what Justice Powell had envisioned in *Bakke*. Greenhouse speculated that once the Court accepted the two Michigan cases, they recognized the high stakes at issue, especially after receiving the record number of amici briefs. The Court took a "societal reality check" and asked itself how it would look to the country if it struck down affirmative action, especially when the overwhelming majority of briefs—especially the ones from Fortune 500 companies and the military—favored it. Moreover, the nineteen amici briefs opposing affirmative action came from conservative interest groups, which many of the justices would have perceived as more partisan or ideological and less "real world" in their outlook.

For the nation's elite colleges and graduate schools, where race had been a factor in admissions since before *Bakke,* little would change. They already had a pool of well-qualified students, they had long looked at factors beyond GPA and test scores in picking a class, and race had been one of those considerations. Most of these had already met the criteria spelled out by Justice Powell in *Bakke* and confirmed by *Grutter.* Large state-sponsored schools like Michigan would definitely have to make changes in their undergraduate admissions policies, and while they could still seek diversity, they would have to come up with procedures far more subtle than awarding points for race or ethnicity. Anyone looking for some sort of general effect of the two decisions would be disappointed. As one article put it, "Impact on Universities Will Range from None to a Lot."

Reports from the American Council on Education and other groups noted that the Michigan undergraduate system was unique, and few other schools utilized it. A majority of schools took over 70 percent of their applicants and set relatively low minimum standards for test scores, GPA, and the like, an argument made by Bowen and Bok in *The Shape of the River.* The more selective schools, the tier just below the elite colleges, had already moved to provide a full-file review of all applicants. In such a review, race might be a factor but not the determining one. In this sense, as Barbara Perry notes, the work of the CIR and other opponents of rigid race-based admissions had already paid off.

In August 2003, Michigan announced a new affirmative action plan, discarding the previous point system, and said it would spend between $1.5 and $2 million to hire and train additional staff to read and evaluate all undergraduate applications. Applicants for the first-year class entering in the fall of 2004 as well as transfer students would be given the option of reporting their race or ethnicity, but if they did, that information would be considered "holistically," that is, as just one factor among many. A spokesperson for the university announced that "the changes in our admissions process did not signal any change in our commitment to having a diverse student body." A year after the Court's decisions, Michigan, Ohio State, and the University of Massachusetts at Amherst all scrapped point scores in their admissions, yet all reported only a slight decrease in minority enrollments. Since then, other schools have also abandoned SAT and other general tests. More than 125 schools and colleges featured in the *U.S. News & World Report* rankings have adopted test-optional admissions policies.

The fact is that schools committed to bringing in more minority students continued to do so. The vice-provost at the University of Missouri said that he and his colleagues were busy working to figure out "how we would continue to ensure diversity at our campus if we could not consider race." Mary Sue Coleman, the new president of the University of Michigan and a champion of affirmative action, told reporters, "Of course, you want to look at family income, and being the first in the family to attend college and those kinds of factors, of course we do that, but it doesn't get us to a racially diverse student body."

WHILE PROPONENTS OF affirmative action cheered the law school case, opponents did not sit by passively. Enter Ward Connerly, the architect of California's Prop 209. The Michigan Civil Rights Initiative (MCRI), or Proposal 2, went on the November 2006 ballot, where it easily passed by a vote of 58 to 42 percent, and became part of the state constitution. Jennifer Gratz, long since graduated from the University of Michigan at Dearborn and living in California, returned home to be the executive director of MCRI. Barbara Grutter also campaigned for the amendment as the founder of Toward a Fair Michigan based at Michigan State University in East Lansing. What Connerly had learned in California is that a constitutional amendment that on the face of it does no more than prohibit discrimination based on race would withstand court challenge.

The first two sections of Proposal 2 are the following:

1. The University of Michigan, Michigan State University, Wayne State University, and any other public college or university, community college, or school district shall not discriminate against, or grant preferential treatment to any individual group on the basis of race, sex, color, ethnicity, or national origin in the operation of public employment, public education, or public contracting.
2. The state shall not discriminate against, or grant preferential treatment to, any individual or group on the basis of race, sex, color, ethnicity, or national origin in the operation of public employment, public education, or public contracting.

Within a few months, the Coalition to Defend Affirmative Action filed suit, claiming Proposal 2 violated the federal constitution. In March 2008, Judge David Lawson of the federal district court dismissed the case. The Court of Appeals for the Sixth Circuit, however, overturned the lower-court ruling, holding that Proposal 2 placed special burdens on minority interests. The state's attorney general, Bill Schuette, appealed the decision to the Supreme Court, which granted cert on 25 March 2013, heard oral argument on 15 October 2013, and handed down its decision on 22 April 2014.

Justice Anthony Kennedy wrote a plurality opinion, joined by Chief Justice Roberts and Samuel Alito. Roberts, Scalia (joined by

*Justice Anthony Kennedy joined the Supreme
Court at the beginning of 1988 and would be the
"swing vote" on the Court after Justice O'Connor
retired, voting for affirmative action in the key
Michigan and Texas cases.*

Thomas), and Breyer also filed concurring opinions. As Kennedy put it, "There is no authority in the Constitution of the United States or in this Court's precedents for the Judiciary to set aside Michigan laws that commit this policy determination to the voters." Scalia, in his opinion, examined what he termed a "frighteningly bizarre question" of whether the Equal Protection Clause forbids what its text requires.

The opinion brought forth an angry dissent from Justice Sonia Sotomayor (joined by Ginsburg) that ran fifty-eight pages to Kennedy's eighteen-page opinion upholding the Michigan amendment. She was so mad that for the first time she took the step of reading portions from the bench. She chided her colleagues for ignoring the needs of people on the margins and challenged the contention of Chief Justice Roberts and other conservatives that it was time to look beyond race. "Race matters," she wrote, "because of the slights, the snickers, the silent judgments that reinforce that most crippling of thoughts: 'I do not belong here.'" The Michigan law placed a heavy burden—"selective barriers"—on just one group and noted that other groups seeking preferences in admissions, such as family alumni status, could and did lobby for such measures. In contrast, the only way to obtain race-based affirmative action would require winning a constitutional amendment to repeal Proposal 2.

There had been little chance that the high court would void Proposal 2. The Court has ruled invalid laws that appear neutral on their face but actually have and are meant to have a disparate impact on minorities. The Michigan law, however, fit in perfectly with the argument—made by both liberals and conservatives—that affirmative action is a form of racial discrimination and violates the Equal Protection Clause. Proposal 2 did, in fact, as both the Sixth Circuit and Sotomayor claimed, have a disparate impact on people of color. Not all disparate impacts, however, are illegal. A requirement for someone to be able to speak Spanish in a job that deals with Spanish-speaking clientele has a disparate impact on all non-Spanish speakers. A requirement that drivers of eighteen-wheel rigs have a special license bars anyone who does not have that license.

For the Court majority, and for the majority of white parents in Michigan, Proposal 2 established a level playing field. Diversity for its own sake mattered little to them; that people would be preferred for no other reason than the color of their skin mattered a lot. Of course, the history of our country had always preferred people of a particular skin color. But by 2014, a majority of the high court believed, as Chief Justice Roberts put it, "the way to stop discrimination on the basis of race is to stop discriminating on the basis of race."

BY THE TIME THE Supreme Court upheld Michigan's Proposal 2, voter initiatives had struck down affirmative action in California, Washington, and Michigan; a court decision had temporarily stopped Texas, and gubernatorial action had halted minority preferences at Florida universities.

Schools in these states employed various devices to continue accepting minority students whose GPA and test scores fell below those of their white applicants, and while all had some success, the fact remained that minority enrollments in all these state schools had decreased. The enrollment of black students at the University of California at Los Angeles stood at a thirty-year low. At Berkeley, the number of blacks in the freshman class plunged by half the year after Prop 209, and the number of Hispanics nearly that much.

Among minority students accepted by the California system, half declined the offer in order to attend private colleges and universities. At Stanford, for example, the minority numbers went up. The class entering in the fall of 2006 had 11 percent African Americans, up from 8 the year before, and an increase in Hispanics as well. In Texas, the Top 10 Percent Plan swamped the University of Texas's flagship school at Austin, but the plan never brought in that many minority students. At Ohio State, Mabel Freeman, the assistant vice president, said, "When we saw what was coming down the road, we started looking to other models, but no other model results in as much diversity." And at Michigan, Robert Sellers, the vice-provost for equity and inclusion, said that there were many ways to attract minority students, and the university had tried most of them. None, however, brought in as many—or enough—minority students as the older system. The result of Proposal 2 is that "we have one hand tied behind our back."

CHAPTER 17

WOMEN AND AFFIRMATIVE ACTION II

Young women currently being appointed to university positions are already suspect as a consequence of preferential hiring.

—DOREEN KIMURA

I am the perfect affirmative action baby.

—SONIA SOTOMAYOR

In early August 2017, James Damore, a software engineer at Google, posted a ten-page memo, "Google's Ideological Echo Chamber," on one of the company's internal message boards. Damore's screed on the "biological causes" of unequal gender representation and the "discriminatory" nature of diversity initiatives quickly went viral. He criticized Google for pushing mentoring and diversity programs and for "alienating conservatives." Damore claimed that women "prefer jobs in social and artistic areas," while men "may like coding because it requires systematizing." Biological differences explained why "we don't have 50% representation of women in tech and leadership."

Google's newly hired head of diversity, Danielle Brown, immediately responded that the company is "unequivocal in our belief that diversity and inclusion are critical to our success," and noted that change is hard and "often uncomfortable." CEO Sundar Pichai denounced the posting for "advancing harmful gender stereotypes" and fired Damore.

The memo and the firing immediately stirred up an enormous number of online comments from both progressives and conservatives. The incident came as Silicon Valley as a whole grappled with accusations of sexism and discrimination and when Google itself was in the midst of a Department of Labor investigation into whether it paid men more than women. While leading tech companies such as Google, Facebook, and Uber had said they were trying to improve hiring and working conditions for women, their diversity numbers had barely moved.

Facebook, which annually releases information on its employee demographic, reported that women made up 35 percent of its work-force in 2017, up slightly from 33 percent the year earlier, but they still accounted for less than one in five technical positions. The com-pany's technical, or STEM, roles, as well as its executive leadership, remained overwhelmingly male and white.

Over in Cupertino, California, Apple reported that it had made small but significant gains in hiring women and minorities. The Apple workforce now consisted of 32 percent women, 9 percent Afri-can Americans, and 12 percent Hispanics—a 1 percent increase in each category over 2015. The company has offices and plants around the world, and a total workforce of 125,000 people. Apple claimed that it had engaged in active recruiting everywhere, and 37 percent of new hires in the past twelve months had been women. Out of a U.S. workforce of 80,000, more than one in four new hires came from underrepresented minority groups. Although it did not give specific figures, Apple claimed that it had closed the wage gaps for female and minority workers.

The giant chip maker Intel releases an "annual diversity" report, as do many of the leading tech companies, and like those of Facebook, Google, and Apple these reports admit to lower numbers of women and minorities than white men. Intel in 2015, however, conducted a compensation analysis that went beyond its annual pay audit to examine gender pay parity for U.S. employees and then proudly announced that no pay gap existed between its male and its female employees within the same job-grade levels. Intel also boasted that it had exceeded its goal of 40 percent of new hires being women and minorities who had the job skills Intel needed. The company admit-ted, however, that although there had been an increase in the number of women in higher management positions, there was still a long way to go before Intel could claim parity.

The story of these tech giants also reflects the story of women in the last few decades. On the one hand, and in large part due to affirmative action programs, more women can be found at all levels in business and especially in academia, where they are the presidents of prestigious schools such as Harvard and William & Mary. On the other hand, although a few Fortune 500 companies have female CEOs, women are still notably absent from the executive suites and the boards of major corporations. While there are a few bright spots in some Wall Street firms, women still account for only one in five senior positions. The old 1960s slogan "You've come a long way, baby," may be partially true, but there is still a great deal further to go. The giant investment firm of Goldman Sachs acknowledged that its female workers in Great Britain make 56 percent less than men. CEO Lloyd Blankfein said that "while we have made progress in recent years . . . there is still significant progress to be made."

MUCH OF THE WRITING on affirmative action holds that white women benefited most from preferential programs. One analysis of employment data, for example, concluded that between 1980 and 1990 "white women have now reached their proportional share of management jobs, while minority women and men remain underrepresented in management." In 1980, white men occupied 65 percent of managerial positions, while white women held 27.1 percent. By 1990, the percentage for white men had dropped to 50.6 percent, while that for white women had jumped to 35.3 percent. In the federal government, the number of women in pay grades 9–11 rose from 16.65 percent of the workforce to 39.19 percent in 1980, while in pay grades 12–16 the percentage went from 5.37 to 14.27. In some agencies, women made up half or more of the grade 9–11 workforce. A somewhat mixed result could be gleaned from the EEO-1 forms required from federal contractors by the Office of Federal Contract Compliance. They showed a small decline in both white males and females from 1970 to 1980 (5 percent each) and a small increase for black men (a little over 1 percent). The big gains, about 12 percent, went to black women. One study showed that by the early 1990s African American women had virtually closed the historical gap between their earnings and those of white women.

Black women began organizing their own wing of the civil rights movement through such groups as the National Black Feminist Organization, and they learned to cooperate with other women's groups in lobbying government agencies to include women in affirmative action guidelines. The indomitable Pauli Murray predicted that "by asserting a leadership role in the feminist movement, the black woman can help keep it allied to the objectives of black liberation while simultaneously advancing the interests of all women."

We have already seen that for white women getting into college did not pose any great difficulty. For the most part, they went to the same schools as did their brothers and had—especially after Title IX—the same panoply of sports and extracurricular activities to bolster their applications. Once admitted, they earned grades as good as or better than the men in their classes. Black women, on the other hand, often suffered from the same disabilities as black men—poor schools, discrimination, and lack of training in the study habits and social skills that make for success in college and on jobs.

This narrative, however, has been challenged, and the literature on women—like that dealing with African Americans—is full of articles disparaging affirmative action as well as praising it. There are also stories told by strong, intelligent, and competent women who felt that their entry into graduate school or a good job was perceived as a result not of their ability but of preferential hiring. The historian Nell Irvin Painter, later to be president of the Organization of American Historians, recalled a conversation with a man in the 1970s who

Professor Nell Irvin Painter of Princeton and president of the Organization of American Historians in 2007–2008. As a young scholar she often faced charges that her success relied more on her color and gender than on talent.

had a degree in history but could not get a teaching job in higher education. Painter was just then finishing her doctorate at Harvard and had landed an assistant professorship at the University of Pennsylvania. The man told her, "It must be great to be black and female, because of affirmative action. You count twice." She later moved to the University of North Carolina and discovered when talking to black undergraduates that although they had gotten in because they had the grades, "white students and professors think we only got in because we're black." Moreover, when it came to African American faculty, black students as well as white doubted their abilities.

There has also been a fair amount of study on the psychological effects of affirmative action and how people saw women who supposedly benefited from affirmative action. One study concluded that the more people viewed a woman as an affirmative action hire, the less they saw her as competent. The black students at North Carolina apparently shared the same negative view of anyone—minority or female—suspected of being an affirmative action beneficiary. Nor was theirs a unique response. An African American student at the University of California said, "I feel like I have AFFIRMATIVE ACTION stamped on my forehead."

At about the same time that Professor Painter wrote her column, Midge Decter, an author and critic, attacked affirmative action on grounds similar to those of Painter's students. Preferential programs did not help those they had been designed to serve, namely, blacks and women. Both groups, she wrote, "are beginning to suffer from a new, and no doubt in many cases permanent and irrecoverable decline in self-respect. The advantages they have gained in employment and in school admissions appear to be bringing them little sense of either private or public satisfaction." They are beginning to realize, she claimed, that their special privileges, "having been unearned . . . are doing them, spiritually speaking, no good."

Thomas Sowell, a longtime critic of affirmative action, termed women "a special case" and noted that the real differential was not between men and women who shared the same work history but between men and those women who took time off from the workplace to have children. Take men and women who never marry, he suggested, and women earn 91 percent of the income of men who remain single in the twenty-five-to-sixty-four age bracket. In 1971, women who remained unmarried into their thirties and had worked continuously since high school earned slightly higher incomes than men who had done the same. Single women who had earned their doctorates in the 1930s had by the 1950s become full professors slightly more often than did male PhDs.

Marriage and children affected men and women differently. For men, marriage increased their rate of participation in the workforce, and the number of hours worked increased with each child. Just the opposite was true of women, who worked less after marriage and even less after having children. Married women living with their husbands earned only 25 percent of the annual income of men living with their wives. "The big difference is not between men and women," he claimed, "but between married women and everyone else."

While everyone ought to be free to enter any occupation for which they are qualified, many women tended to congregate in so-called female occupations such as schoolteacher, nurse, or librarian. According to Sowell, there is a perfectly good and non-prejudicial reason for this. Someone who is a good teacher or librarian today will be good at that occupation in five or six years, that is, after taking time off for childbearing and child care. But a tax attorney who missed five years of tax legislation and its judicial interpretations could not advise a client as well as someone who had been doing it continuously. This held true for other fields in which necessary skills or knowledge rapidly changed, such as aerospace.

Feminists, of course, rejected Sowell's argument, but they could not escape his facts, namely, that women did indeed take time off to have children; that many women voluntarily worked part-time; that part-time work earned less than full-time employment; and that many of the fields targeted by feminist activists where few women worked resulted less from male prejudice than from the fact that they required continuous work. Whatever argument about "equality" and "male chauvinism" there may be, for Sowell the basic facts of biology defeated rhetoric every time. Affirmative action, in his view, could never work.

Most feminists disagreed with Sowell, as did many beneficiaries of affirmative action. One of the most famous, the Supreme Court justice Sonia Sotomayor, proudly acknowledged that affirmative action helped her get into Princeton and then into Yale Law School. Without such a plan, she would have remained a bright Hispanic girl without the family resources to get ahead in the world. Affirmative action opened the world to her and gave her the opportunity to succeed on her own merits. As she herself often admitted, indeed boasted, "I am the perfect affirmative action baby." Yet even so, years after she became a justice, she said, "It's very hard for people who haven't lived my life to know what it's like to have your experiences looked down upon, to be viewed as inferior, to be viewed as not smart enough. You need to affirm that you have value."

CHANGING A CULTURE is difficult, even when the culture may be based upon an erroneous set of facts, assumptions, and even prejudices. This proved true at the Polaroid Corporation, which, eventually, came up with a plan that satisfied its female workers. But it took time and was certainly not easy.

Polaroid management began its efforts to bring its hiring and pay practices into line with new federal laws in the late 1960s and early 1970s. It issued position papers and memoranda; affirmed its commitment to equal opportunity and pay; and published not only a plan for women but some leaflets on the historic discrimination against women workers in the country. The company's annual reports of 1972 and 1973 showcased women in professional positions.

Polaroid, however, relied on the same techniques it had always used to handle budget requests and sales goals; edicts came from on high and were then left to middle and lower management to make them work. Without continuous oversight and pressure from the top, the lower ranks of managers did nothing. Women employees remained in the lowest-paying jobs and had to take unpaid maternity leaves, and only a handful enrolled in "female management training programs." Although a rather extensive affirmative action plan had been promulgated, women employees knew nothing about the document and its proposed action steps.

When women tried to talk to supervisors or even to the personnel department, they ran into a stone wall of indifference. One division head, encouraged to upgrade women in his area, promoted his secretary to an administrative post previously held by a man. After she had been on the job for two months, he gave her a rave review, telling her, "You're much better than your predecessor." Not until a year later did she learn that her salary was 40 percent less than that of the man who had held the position, and she filed an equal pay suit. "But she's earning good money for a woman," said her befuddled manager. Other women also filed suit, and as of November 1973 Polaroid had paid out $350,000 to settle cases and expected that it would cost a lot more to settle remaining suits.

The company then recognized that its earlier approach had not worked and this time asked women employees to research a report on their status within the company, what they found wrong, and how they thought it should be fixed. A divisional director, appointed by the top management, served as a liaison between it and the committee. The women set up five groups that studied company policies, company practices, benefits, pay differentials, and compliance with federal policy. Some of the recommendations seem trivial, such as the constant use of masculine pronouns in all written policy statements. Others were more substantial, such as that single women employees were not eligible for obstetrical coverage under the corporate health-care contract with Blue Cross. When the groups turned in their reports, top management took them seriously and began implementing a plan that met nearly all the objectives the women called for. It did not happen overnight, but this time around the implementers—middle management—knew that not only their bosses were looking over their shoulders, but their women employees as well. The company eliminated pay differentials for the same job and began an active recruiting campaign, as well as a training program for existing employees to qualify them for more skilled positions.

Despite such success stories, one study declared that "in 1973 the condition of women in the American labor market continues to be one of gross inequality." Statistics abound that support this view, of which the best known is that women's median income as a proportion of men's stood around 58 percent, that is, for every dollar a man made, a woman earned fifty-eight cents. Moreover, a Census Bureau report showed that the wages of white women entering the job market in 1980 were further behind the wages of comparable white men than they were in 1970, despite the growth of affirmative action and educational gains.

Yet a number of important considerations had to be taken into account. According to Labor Department figures, the majority of working women did so to support themselves or others. Of 37 million female workers in 1968, about 23 percent were single and 17 percent widowed, divorced, or separated. Of the latter group, a majority had the sole responsibility for rearing and supporting their children. Many of these women had few skills and worked in low-paying jobs. In 1970, one-third of all families headed by a woman lived in poverty, and as many had incomes barely above the poverty line. Thirty percent of all working women had husbands who earned between $3,000 and $7,000 at a time when the annual income neces-sary for a substandard level of living for an urban family of four was estimated by the government at $6,567. In 1968, median annual earnings for men were $7,664, while women received $4,457, well below the poverty line. One is dealing here with a group of unskilled and often poorly educated women, white as well as minority, who worked out of necessity, not choice, and because of their lack of skills had to take anything available, no matter how poorly it paid. The women who filed suit at Polaroid had some skills and some education, and affirmative action for them meant a real opportunity to earn more and to move into a position with greater responsibility and status.

A second problem in the 1970s did not pit one class of women against another but reflected the changing requirements of law. Ever since the Progressive Era, women had been the beneficiaries of pro-tective legislation, laws that guaranteed them minimum wages and maximum hours, factory safety, and the like. But as more women became educated, they began to look on these laws as limiting, or as one scholar put it, as "the chains of protection." They charged that these laws limited their opportunities, because they treated women as "persons with a disability" who needed special protection, with the disability being their gender. Gradually, the courts—which had approved these laws six decades earlier—began to agree, and eventu-ally either the states repealed them or they fell into desuetude.

But employers who wanted to hire and/or promote more women had to work their way around legal questions that had yet to be addressed by the courts. What constituted a BFOQ—a bona fide occupational qualification—that allowed an employer to designate certain jobs for men and others for women? How far could retail stores take into account customer preferences, such as women want-ing other women to wait on them in certain departments, such as lin-gerie or cosmetics? What did equality mean for a company's benefits plan? Did it have to include maternity leave? Could societal norms of morality play any role in job decisions?

Courts had already answered some of these questions in matters that may seem strange to us now. For example, in 1971 the Court of Appeals for the Fifth Circuit ruled that an airline violated Title VII when it refused to hire a male applicant as a flight attendant because a study showed that passengers overwhelmingly preferred to be served by female stewardesses. In another case that seemingly ignored accepted societal norms, a district court ruled that a hospital violated Title VII when it refused to permit registered male nurses to care for female patients. A court also invalidated a municipal ordinance that prohibited persons from massaging the bodies of persons of the opposite sex in massage parlors.

Victoria Eslinger wanted to be a page in the South Carolina Senate but ran into a rule that prohibited women working as pages. She sued under Title VII, and the district court agreed with Lovick Thomas, the clerk of the senate, that certain functions performed by pages on behalf of senators, such as running personal errands, packing their bags in hotel rooms, and cashing personal checks, were "not suitable under existing circumstances for young ladies and may give rise to the appearance of impropriety."

The court of appeals found this rationale "unconvincing. It rests upon the implied premise, which we think false, that on the one hand, the female is viewed as a pure, delicate and vulnerable creature who must be protected from exposure to criminal influences; and on the other hand, as a brazen temptress, from whose seductive blandishments the innocent male must be protected." Judge Harrison Lee Winter of the Fourth Circuit noted that his court had female secretaries and law clerks and that "an intimate business relationship, including traveling on circuit, between persons of different sex presents no 'appearance of impropriety.'" Eslinger was an adult and had the ability to act on her own judgment; South Carolina could not bar her or other women from being pages.

For all the problems, such as the differential in wages, the 1970s seemed to hold out promise for further gains. Then, in November 1980, the American people chose Ronald Reagan to be the fortieth president of the United States, and he made clear his hostility to affirmative action. Nell Painter worried that if he succeeded in dismantling preferential programs, African Americans and women would be pushed further back than they had been in the 1960s, subject to the old prejudices and stereotypes, but made even more bitter by the taste of opportunity affirmative action had provided.

THE 1970s WERE EXCITING times for women, and while the benefits of affirmative action did not go far enough for some, there is no question that new federal laws plus energetic enforcement opened many doors. Reagan seemed to be nothing but trouble for the women's movement. He opposed the Equal Rights Amendment, which died in 1982. He also opposed abortion, favored cutting the budgets of federal programs that helped women, such as a nurses' training program, and, as we have seen, wanted to kill off affirmative action. According to Representative (later Senator) Barbara Mikulski of Maryland, the Reagan administration was "a direct assault on women and children in this country." On the plus side, many women who had been politically neutral awoke to the fact that for the first time in their memory they had an administration in Washington that opposed women's issues. Eleanor Smeal, president of the National Organization for Women, reported that new member applications had jumped following Reagan's inaugural and by May 1981 were running at between nine and ten thousand a month. Spokesmen for the administration claimed that the Reagan budget would trigger an economic turnaround, and women would be the main beneficiaries. Few women bought that argument.

Reagan had to deal with a Democratic Congress that blocked some of his more extreme measures, and his Justice Department could not persuade courts, corporations, or local jurisdictions to abandon affirmative action. By the end of the Reagan-Bush era, as one story put it, these were the backlash years, when the administration trashed affirmative action, feminism went out of fashion, and media analysts told women they could not have it all. But "popular wisdom aside, women were big winners in the 1980s." From stock traders earning six-figure bonuses down to $5-an-hour store clerks, according to new studies done in the early 1990s by female economists who mined a great deal of data, women actually gained on men in the Reagan years. The median salary for men decreased 8 percent between 1979 and 1990, from $31,315 to $28,843, while the comparable salary for women rose 10 percent, from $18,683 to $20,636. The number of cents women earned for each dollar that men earned rose from fifty-eight to seventy-two. The studies showed a brighter future for younger women (aged twenty-four to thirty-five), who were now earning eighty cents for every dollar earned by a man, up from sixty-nine cents in 1980.

One might look at these numbers, compiled by the feminist Institute for Women's Policy Research in Washington, and see that women's pay, despite the gains, still lagged behind that of men. Why? According to the institute's director, Heidi Hartmann, women still entered the workforce in lower-paying occupations than men. They worked fewer hours, were less educated, and had less job experience and skills. But, she noted, the fifty-four million working women in America included several generations, from a thirty-three-year-old pharmacist with ten years on the job to her fifty-three-year-old mother who left the workforce at twenty to raise children and returned to a minimum wage job at a local five-and-dime. If one isolated groups who could be compared directly with men having the same qualifications, for example, men and women with PhDs in economics, women earned between 95 and 99 percent of the men, for all statistical purposes the same.

The optimism found in these reports derived from several factors. Many more women went to college, learned marketable skills, and chose not only to enter a profession but to stay in it longer. They had fewer children and, when they did, stayed out of the market for shorter periods of time. They might take a two- to six-month maternity leave and then return to their work. At the other end of the scale, the 1980s saw an enormous growth in service jobs, such as retail sales clerks, nurses, and hairdressers, populated primarily by women, while the traditional factory and mining jobs for men disappeared due to globalization.

Not everyone shared this rosy view. When Bill Clinton ran for president in 1992, the same motto was scribbled on the walls of all his field offices: "It's the Economy, Stupid." The growing recession in the Bush years threatened not only blue-collar men but pink- and white-collar women and male managers. John Kennedy's maxim that "a rising tide raises all boats" had a corollary: an ebb tide could beach those same boats. Pat Reuss, a lobbyist at NOW's legal defense fund, feared that if the hostile climate of the Reagan-Bush years continued, many of the gains could be wiped out.

Nonetheless, some economists believed that women had entered the third period when they would be making great economic gains. The first had been during the Industrial Revolution of the nineteenth century, when farm girls streamed into new factories in the cities. The second had been in the early twentieth century, when young, unmarried women went to work in offices. The third had begun in the 1970s, and economists believed that as more women earned advanced degrees and chose to stay in the labor market longer, they would move closer and closer to parity with men in the same fields.

Did affirmative action cause this? Certainly not any government-sponsored programs in the 1980s, but there is little doubt that the measures adopted in the 1960s and 1970s, such as the Equal Pay Act and Titles VII and IX, gave the cause of women's equality in college and the job market a great push. By 1990, the percentage of women graduating with advanced degrees in medicine, dentistry, pharmacy, law, and engineering had all risen sharply in the prior two decades. The theory had always been that affirmative action would do away with the old barriers against race, ethnicity, and gender, and then it would no longer be needed. By the early 1990s, it seemed, white women no longer needed affirmative action, or at least not as much as they had a decade or so earlier.

This is not to say that prejudice against women has disappeared, because it certainly has not. Whatever faults Hillary Clinton might have had as a candidate, there can be little doubt that misogyny played a large role in the visceral dislike, even hatred, that men who supported Trump felt against her. Some large data studies show that while there has been a decrease in the degree of blatant bias, it has persisted in other forms. One study found that while men's successes are attributed to high ability, women's successes are not. When thinking of leaders, people in general think of men, not women.

ONE MIGHT HAVE THOUGHT that under President Clinton women would have done very well, and many did. But when Marcia Greenberger, the co-president of the National Women's Law Center, testified before Congress in 1995, she claimed that barriers to women remained pervasive. While much had changed, she argued, women remained second-class citizens in many ways, and she gave several examples:

- Between 95 and 97 percent of the senior managers at the Fortune 500 companies were men. In the Fortune 200 industrial and service companies, which had many women employees, only 5 percent of the senior managers were women, and nearly all of them white.
- Contrary to the findings of economists only a few years earlier, Greenberger cited government studies that a wide earnings gap still existed. Women physicians, for example, earned 53.9 percent of the wages of male doctors, while women in sales earned only 59.5 percent of men in equivalent positions. On the whole, she placed the wage gap at 71.5 cents for every dollar earned by men.
- The gender gap in collegiate education had for the most part disappeared, and women earned roughly half of all bachelor's

and master's degrees. But they earned only a third of the doctorates and first professional degrees, 15.4 percent of undergraduate engineering degrees, and less than 22 percent of doctoral degrees in mathematics and the physical sciences.

· Of the 62 million working women in the United States, two-thirds of them earned less than $20,000 annually, and 38 percent less than $10,000.

· In a 1994 Labor Department study, 61 percent of women surveyed said they had little or no likelihood of advancement, and 14 percent of white women and 26 percent of minority women reported losing a job or promotion because of race or sex.

· The Glass Ceiling Commission found that one-quarter of women surveyed reported that "being a woman/sexism" was the biggest obstacle they had to overcome, and three out of five said they had personally experienced sexual harassment on the job.

The issue of sexual harassment became a front-page issue in 2016 and 2017 with accusations against such important entertainment figures as Bill Cosby and Harvey Weinstein, and against a number of political figures including Senator Al Franken of Minnesota. The hashtag #MeToo soon had hundreds of stories of women in almost every aspect of the job market facing harassment and even rape.

Judy L. Lichtman, the president of the Women's Legal Defense Fund, weighed in with equally disturbing figures. Among high wage earners (denoted as $52,364 or more annually), 16.4 percent of men made this much, compared with 3.8 percent of white women, 1.6 percent of black women, and 1.8 percent of Hispanic women. For the obverse, only 11.6 percent of men made less than $13,091 a year, compared with 21.1 percent of white women, 26.9 percent of black women, and 36.6 percent of Hispanic women. Hispanic women seemed to have the worst problem earning good money. A college-educated Hispanic woman typically earned $1,600 annually *less* than a white male high school graduate, and $16,000 less than a college-educated white man.

The answer, Lichtman argued, lay in more and more effective affirmative action programs. She especially praised universities and companies that had developed specialized counseling and training programs and heaped great praise on the Office of Federal Contract

Compliance, which created thousands of job opportunities for women in coal mining, banking, and myriad other industries by its insistence on federal contractors adopting goals. The results could be seen in the fact that women earned more, although still less than men (seventy-one cents on the dollar), more women were in the pipeline for middle- and upper-level-management jobs, and had moved into fields previously occupied solely by men, such as architecture, economics, and law.

In addition, affirmative action made sense in terms of dollars and cents. A recent study had found that the market performance of companies with good records of hiring and promoting women and people of color was 2.4 times higher than companies with poor records. The one hundred companies with the best records of diverse hiring earned an 18.3 percent average return on investment, while the one hundred lowest-ranked companies earned an average return of only 7.9 percent.

In early February 1996, more than three thousand women attended the first "Feminist Expo" in Washington, sponsored by a coalition of some three hundred groups headed by the Feminist Majority Foundation. Gloria Steinem was there, as was Molly Yard, the fiery past president of NOW, then in her eighties. The vast majority of those attending, however, were women in their twenties and thirties, and they responded to the call that they had to fight conservative efforts to roll back or even destroy affirmative action. Susan Gross, the director of the Upper Midwest Women's History Center, said the "Republicans have done us a tremendous favor by trying to turn back the clock. They've galvanized a whole new generation. . . . It's just a fascinating time in the feminist evolution."

BLACK WOMEN ALSO BENEFITED from affirmative action, seeing increased opportunities in employment and access to college, but not to the extent that white women benefited. Where Nell Painter's inquisitor said she was a "twofer," both female and black, and therefore poised to benefit doubly from affirmative action, many women of color found the twofer status doubly burdensome. As one lawyer put it, "The combination of being an attorney of color and a woman is a double negative in the legal marketplace, regardless of the type of practice or geographic region involved." Yet the fact remains that the number of female attorneys of color increased from 7,300 in the mid-1970s to 23,000 a decade later. The law professor Laura Padilla believed that nearly all the progress made by women of color in the law and in other professions resulted from affirmative action.

But she argued, and in this she was not alone, that women generally, and women of color in particular, had a long way to go. One newspaper article claimed that "minority women fare the worst. They have the lowest percentage of entry level jobs in law firms, following white men, white women, and minority men." An American Bar Association committee listed the reasons why women of color faced greater obstacles than either men of color or white women: "(1) stereotypes that limit job opportunities, (2) failure to be recognized as competent, (3) failure to advance as rapidly as others, (4) undue difficulties in attaining partnership status, (5) pay inequities, (6) insufficient mentoring, and (7) heightened scrutiny of hours, work product, and performance." The report also noted that multicultural women often felt ostracized by white women and believed they carried the responsibility of rectifying their own outsider status.

Since this report in the mid-1990s, conditions have improved a great deal for women of color in law. A recent visit to the premier law school in the country found not only numerous minority women students in classes but minority women teaching and mentoring them. The same may be said for other professions, such as medicine, and much of this is due to the impact affirmative action had on women of color in the 1980s and 1990s. Stories of how some minorities felt belittled by affirmative action are not to be dismissed. But for every Clarence Thomas who raged at his role as an affirmative action admit to the Yale Law School, there were more like Sonia Sotomayor, who grabbed the chance and went on to success, grateful for the opportunity.

WHEREAS EVERYONE COULD SEE the genesis and the need for affirmative action for African Americans, the prejudices and stereotypes and myths surrounding women made things less clear. Women had been discriminated against in the job market, yet special circumstances existed. Employers, for example, could legitimately wonder what the effect on their business would be if a woman in a key position took maternity leave. Some women wanted to "have it all"—job, husband, and children—and discovered that difficulties abounded everywhere. Were there, for example, certain jobs that seemed to belong to one sex or the other?

Justice Antonin Scalia caught some of this ambivalence in his dissent in the *Johnson* case, one of the very few decisions involving affirmative action for women:

> There are of course those who believe that the social attitudes which cause women themselves to avoid certain jobs and to favor others are as nefarious as conscious, exclusionary discrimination. Whether or not that is so (and there is assuredly no consensus on the point equivalent to our national consensus against intentional discrimination), the two phenomena are certainly distinct.

Social attitudes embedded in families, schools, religious institutions, and the media construct certain attitudes regarding women, some positive, others negative, but all strongly held. When the government tried to use its power to uproot some of these myths, people objected to what they saw as an attack on venerated social traditions. Alice Kessler-Harris, one of the doyennes of women's history, while supporting equal opportunities for women, also recognized the force of long-established social norms. Women, she wrote, would not only have to battle discrimination in the courts and in legislatures but also have to work to change the ideas and prejudices that made affirmative action necessary in the first place.

MENTION HAS BEEN MADE that for women in general, and for white women in particular, affirmative action seems to have grown less important in recent years. One historian of women, Nancy Woloch, has suggested that the peak interest by women appears to have been in the 1970s, when many schools went coed, women won a variety of gender discrimination cases, and companies began establishing affirmative action plans aimed at gender discrimination. The *Johnson* case in 1987 may, by this view, be seen more as a confirmatory footnote than one that blazed a new trail. In recent years, affirmative action, whether seen as compensatory or as providing diversity, seems to be more focused on race and ethnicity than on gender. The most recent cases have all involved higher education, an area in which white women grasped equality early.

Women in recent years have sought different forms of "equality," such as an end to sexual harassment, the provision of family leave, and more opportunities in which they can develop their skills. To take but one example, look at the Academy Awards presentation in early March 2018. Many of the participants, but especially the women, were still cheering the #MeToo movement, and particularly the disgrace and fall of Harvey Weinstein and other sexual predators. They believed, however, that women had far fewer chances than men to exercise their creativity in Hollywood.

Frances McDormand won the Best Actress Oscar for her stunning portrayal of a grieving, angry mother in *Three Billboards Outside Ebbing, Missouri*. In her acceptance speech, she asked every woman in the auditorium who had been nominated for an Oscar in any category to stand up. Quite a few women did. McDormand then asked the men in the room to look around.

"We all have stories to tell and projects we need financed. Invite us into your office in a couple of days, or you can come to ours, whichever suits you best, and we'll tell you about them." Then she signed off with a phrase that sent many viewers to Google: "I have two words to leave you with tonight, ladies and gentlemen: 'Inclusion rider.'"

An inclusion rider is one that actors, directors, and others who have employment contracts rather than daily or hourly wage packages can ask to have or—as McDormand suggested—insist on having added to their contracts. It is a stipulation that cast and crew in a film reflect real demographics, including proportionate numbers of women, minorities, LGBTQ individuals, and people with disabilities.

The idea had been developed by Stacy Smith of the University of Southern California, Kalpana Kotagal of the law firm Cohen Milstein, and the actor and producer Fanshen Cox DiGiovanni. Professor Smith first broached the proposal in a 2016 TED talk, and the idea has gained ground since. Of course, the only people who can really insist on an inclusion rider are stars like McDormand or directors like Guillermo del Toro who have clout with the financing studios, but apparently more and more of this group are calling for it in their contracts.

Needless to say, as in every other form of affirmative action, no sooner is such a proposal made than critics attack it, in this case claiming that McDormand and other proponents of the rider are calling for quotas. It will probably be a long time before some people will believe that inclusion of some does not mean exclusion of others.

CHAPTER 18

OTHER GROUPS, HERE AND ABROAD

These {Hispanic} newcomers have come to America to make a better life for themselves and their families, to enjoy the fruits of their labor, or to escape tyranny—all without the slightest notion that they deserved special privileges. And yet, they are eligible for affirmative action benefits immediately upon their arrival, despite the fact that they have no conceivable claim upon our nation's conscience.

—MARK KRIKORIAN

Will Vietnamese-Americans benefit by the elimination of affirmative action? Yes, I think so. But my concern is, are we then going to have a campus that's all Asian-American and white?

—PHAT CHIEM

In the summer of 1984, the great historian Salo W. Baron asked, "Is America ready for ethnic minority rights?" Well aware of the controversy swirling around affirmative action, Baron wanted his audience to think beyond the immediate impact of such programs on minorities and women. Affirmative action, as he—and many others—understood it, meant equal rights for *individual* blacks, Hispanics, and females, comparable to those rights as exercised by *individual* white males in the majority. Baron, however, knew European and Middle East history, and worried about what he termed "national minority rights" and how they had disrupted the social cohesion of many lands. Americans would see how deadly these passions could be when the former Yugoslavia exploded in 1992 and war broke out among the "national minorities." There would be equally bloody fighting in Somalia just a few years later. Baron worried not about individuals seeking equal opportunity but whether minority groups in the United States would ask for some form of legal recognition, whether African Americans, Hispanic Americans, Asian Americans, and others would seek a status similar to that accorded national minorities in other countries. If this happened, he feared, the United States would suffer great social turmoil.

Although there had been periodic efforts to foster a "black nationalism" in the twentieth century, first by Marcus Garvey and later by Malcolm X, it never caught on. Most ethnic groups that immigrated to the United States, even if they kept their own language for the first generation, wanted to become Americanized. To take one example, the children and grandchildren of Italian immigrants have remained proud of their ethnic heritage, and many return every year for the festival of San Gennaro in the Lower East Side of New York, but they speak English, have moved to the suburbs, and see themselves as Americans.

Yet as the problems of racial, ethnic, and gender discrimination remain, there has been a lively debate over how the United States

Marcus Garvey, shown here in 1923, whose advocacy of black nationalism enjoyed a short-lived fad in the early twentieth century.

should treat its minorities. A few African Americans believe that as a legally recognized group, they would be treated better. Others have bemoaned what they see as a growing tribalism.

Affirmative action, even while aiming to give minorities and women opportunities equal to those of white men, in practice did see "groups." Government agencies wanted federal contractors to hire veterans, blacks, Hispanics, and women. Private corporations, state and local governments, and universities set up goals that said we need so many from each of certain minority groups. And in turn, the white majority felt it had been belittled and spoke of people of color as a united group. "They all want to go to the head of the line. They are all like that."

We tend to think of affirmative action for the most part as directed toward African Americans, a device to compensate for more than three centuries first of slavery and then of segregation. We also think of women, and the prejudices they have faced in our society. There have been other groups, however, who have also been affected by or who have demanded affirmative action programs. This chapter is about some of them.

THE FASTEST-GROWING GROUP in the United States consists of Hispanics, sometimes called Latinos. New York has long had a significant Hispanic population, primarily from Puerto Rico. In Miami, refugees from Castro's Cuba make up an important and politically vocal part of the populace. In California and the Southwest, the dominant group came from Mexico and are often called Chicanos, although in the past decade or two there have been hundreds of thousands who have come—often illegally—from Central America.

According to the 2010 census, 50.3 million people, or one out of every six persons, listed themselves as Hispanics. Between 2000 and 2010, the Hispanic population grew 43 percent and is expected to account for one out of every three Americans by 2050. Whereas in 2010 almost 40 percent of Hispanics were foreign-born, projections indicate that nearly all the growth in the next three decades will come from native-born Americans of Hispanic descent. In this period, non-Hispanic white people will become demographically just another minority group, and within the workforce this shift to a no-majority America will happen sooner.

On the negative side, the poverty rate among Hispanics has been fairly constant since 1970, with about one in four living below the poverty line, about the same percentage as African Americans. The rate among whites is one in ten. Some analysts believe that the poverty rate will drop as a greater percentage of Hispanics are native-born. All projections do not take into account the alleged millions who are in the United States illegally.

(Hispanics, like African Americans, are often treated as one homogeneous group, and this tends to distort statistics. For example, the émigrés who came from Cuba tended to be "whiter" and better educated and for the most part have done well economically. Of all the Hispanic groups, they have been the only one to vote Republican. On the other hand, the Puerto Rican population has been the poorest and the least educated; in 1960, 87 percent of those over thirty-five had not completed high school, and less than 1 percent had a college degree. They tend to vote overwhelmingly Democratic and are most likely to cooperate with black activists, because the civil rights movement in New York, where most Puerto Ricans live, has long included demands for them as well.)

The 1964 Civil Rights Act and the 1965 Voting Rights Act (and its subsequent iterations) apply not only to race but to ethnicity as well. The Voting Rights Act made it possible for people literate in Spanish but not in English to cast a ballot, and areas of large Hispanic density have become majority-minority districts as well.

Opposition to affirmative action for Hispanics usually comes through a general animus against any preferential program. But some writers believe that only African Americans, because of the history of slavery and state-sponsored degradation afterward, deserve special treatment. "Hispanics have no claim of repressive treatment comparable to blacks," argues the sociologist Richard Tomasson. Yet, he claims, Hispanic leadership in the United States has managed to unite all the different Latino groups, and to both the leadership and the rank and file "affirmative action has become an inalienable right of being Hispanic."

There are many Hispanic activists who would take issue with Tomasson. Angelo Corlett says that "historic injustices toward [Latinos are] significantly stronger than some would admit." What he calls "anti-Latino racism" is and has been so harmful to Latinos that their claims for affirmative action are based not only on distributive justice but, like those of African Americans, on corrective justice as well. There is little question that Latinos in this country, even if they did not pass through the ordeal of slavery, have been unjustly and often viciously exploited, have faced perverse discrimination, and have been treated as second- or even third-class human beings. The anti-Latino tirades of Donald Trump in the 2016 presidential campaign could not have found such resonance with white voters had they not already shared that prejudice. The undeniable fact that many of the so-called illegal aliens in the United States have come here from south of the border has inflamed antagonism against the many Hispanics who are native-born or naturalized citizens or who hold a green card.

A major debate took place within the Chicano community in the 1960s as to whether Mexican Americans should see themselves as "whites" or "people of color." According to one activist, Bert Corona, most of the delegates to a 1960 convention of Chicano groups "were not prepared to come out front and state that we consider ourselves nonwhite." Moreover, this was not a new question but had been a "thorny issue for years." By the 1960s, Hispanics were, after blacks, the best organized minority in the country, with groups that included the League of United Latin American Citizens, the Community Service Organization, the Mexican American Political Association, and the American GI Forum, a veterans group that lobbied for good jobs.

When Senator Joseph Lieberman (D-Conn.) declared that "you can't defend policies that are based on group preferences as opposed to individual opportunities, which is what America has always been about," Juan A. Figueroa, head of the Puerto Rican Legal Defense and Education Fund, immediately jumped in to challenge him, noting that Hispanics had been among the people of color who had faced and continued to face discrimination in the United States. As the leading Hispanic constituency, Chicanos also accounted for nearly all of the "national origins" complaints filed with the EEOC. This last fact has often been overlooked because it has been overshadowed by the farmworkers campaign led by Cesar Chavez and Dolores Huerta.

Initially, Hispanics sought to distance themselves from African Americans, claiming to be white so as to avoid the stigma and persecution suffered by blacks. Latino leaders, however, discovered that even if they could be listed as "white" on census returns, they still suffered discrimination. One leader denounced doctors who used "the same rooms for the Mexican American people and the Negroes" and charged that the draft board classification of them as "nonwhite" was illegal. All this changed with the Civil Rights Act. Hispanics no longer had to choose sides in a situation in which aligning with blacks did them little good. They could now position themselves as the "brown" counterpart to blacks in a vigorous assertion of their own rights, including opportunities to get good jobs and a better education.

IN THE SPRING OF 1966, the new Equal Employment Opportunity Commission held a regional conference in San Francisco, and the agency's executive director infuriated the Mexican Americans in attendance. Asked why the EEOC did nothing about the discrimination facing Chicanos, Herman Edelsberg responded that Mexican Americans were "distrustful of agencies," so little could be done. He even told his audience that their people had no such proverb as "the wheel that squeaks loudest gets the grease," at which point one man jumped up and shouted, *"El que no grita, Dios no lo oye"*—"The one who doesn't cry, God doesn't hear." A few weeks later Edelsberg, joined by another commissioner who knew as little or perhaps even less about Hispanic problems, repeated his performance in Albuquerque, New Mexico. This so infuriated the activists who attended that they urged Lyndon Johnson to reorient the EEOC and institute affirmative action for Mexican Americans.

For many Latino activists, the Albuquerque meeting proved a turning point. According to one of the attendees, the EEOC people "had done us a favor by turning their backs on us, since many Mexican-American professional people and educators who had never before displayed their anger and disgust with the government were now coming out to protest." Like African Americans and women, Hispanics came to see good jobs—or at least fair access to good jobs—as a key indicator of full citizenship. Title VII, which explicitly forbade discrimination based on ethnicity, provided the key, and Hispanics had the example of blacks and women who had already begun using the law to fight employment discrimination.

For the first time, the various groups joined together in the Mexican-American Ad Hoc Committee on Equal Employment Opportunity and in early 1967 set up a picket line at the main Los Angeles Post Office to protest discrimination against Chicanos, American Indians, and Filipinos. Originally a one-day affair, the pickets stayed for over a month, and the Postal Service agreed to create an affirmative action program in which it would help 800 people prepare for the hiring exam; 640 passed and got jobs. Within a few months, West Coast Latinos could point to several similar training programs that would lead to better jobs at higher pay. Hector Garcia of the American GI Forum took his cue from the NAACP's Herbert Hill and aimed a constant stream of complaints at the EEOC, insisting that the government compel employers and unions to treat Hispanics fairly.

The newly activated civil rights consciousness in the Latino community drew attention from Washington. Lyndon Johnson, who as a young man had seen how poorly Chicanos lived in Texas, responded that the fundamental issue for the Hispanic community was "the need for good jobs and job training." He appointed Vicente T. Ximenes of the American GI Forum to the EEOC and also named him to head the cabinet-level Inter-agency Committee on Mexican American Affairs. When the EEOC held public hearings in El Paso in October 1967, it found the room flooded with Chicanos demanding to tell their stories of discrimination and oppression.

This new confrontational strategy paid off. The federal government began an affirmative action program to train less skilled workers so they could apply for more skilled and better-paying jobs. The program, run by two Latino activist groups, was called SER/Jobs for Progress and worked with private employers to prepare thousands of unskilled workers for better blue-collar and white-collar positions in cities across the Southwest and the West Coast. Ximenes would later tell an interviewer that he ranked affirmative action for Mexican Americans as their most important achievement in the 1960s.

The initiative, by all accounts, worked well as employers discovered that people they had earlier dismissed as "lazy" or "unteachable" proved eager to learn and worked hard. One woman, studying to become a nurse's aide, wrote to thank President Johnson "for the education I have received under your equal employment opportunity program. I have had to work since I was 9 years old. . . . I sent my three daughters to school by working in the fields, so this is the first time I have had a chance to learn to read and write English." Another Chicano from south Texas trained as a sheet metal worker and now had a job with an aerospace company. "Today, I look at my children and I know they will finish high school and maybe go to college," he wrote. "I see my family and I know the chains are broken."

JUST AS WITH African Americans and women, one could find within Hispanic ranks people firmly opposed to affirmative action. The former congressman Herman Badillo of the Bronx, the first Puerto

Rican elected to Congress, argued against special provisions for any minority and pointed to the success of the United States in assimilating wave after wave of immigrants in the eighteenth, nineteenth, and early twentieth centuries by insisting that all live up to the same set of standards, or as he titled his book, *One Nation, One Standard*. As head of the board for the City University of New York, Badillo led the fight to eliminate open admissions and to do away with remedial courses in the senior colleges.

Another vocal opponent has been Linda Chavez, whom President Reagan named staff director for the U.S. Commission on Civil Rights, where she made a name for herself as an outspoken foe of affirmative action. In 1991, following a three-day riot by black and Latino youth in the Mount Pleasant neighborhood of Washington, D.C., the commission (which Chavez had left several years earlier) determined that the way to avoid such riots in the future was for the mostly black District government to establish an affirmative action program for hiring Latinos for city jobs and provide them with a proportional share of city social services. At the time, approximately thirty-three thousand Latinos lived in the District, roughly 5 percent of the city's population.

What particularly incensed Chavez is that the commission did not distinguish between legal Hispanics—those born or naturalized citizens, or those with a green card—and the large if imprecise numbers of those in the country illegally. Latino citizens, she claimed, "are just as angry as blacks, and appear no more likely than blacks or whites to favor special treatment for Hispanic immigrants," however politically correct Hispanic advocacy groups claim it to be. The only way out of the impasse would be for those who are legally in the country to do what every other immigrant group had done, namely, get an education and work hard. As for the illegals, the federal government should find a solution to that problem rather than imposing additional financial burdens on states and localities.

Years ago, except for urban areas like New York, Miami, and Los Angeles, one did not hear Spanish spoken in banks, department stores, or hospitals outside the barrios. Today one can find Spanish speakers in all levels of commerce, education, and the government. When one calls an 800 number to place an order, discuss a bill, or just get information, after the "Welcome," the first thing one hears is *"Para continuar en español, oprima el 2"*—"To continue in Spanish, press 2." Years ago some firms recognized that before long Hispanics would be a large part of their market. As Marion Sandler of Golden West Financial explained, "The whole country is moving away from being white, Anglo, and Protestant to polyglot," especially in places like California and Texas where the company did business. "You have to recognize what's happening and be part of it." For Golden West, it made good sense to hire Latinos, who would then draw in other Latinos as customers.

Other companies, once they had adopted affirmative action plans, decided to stay the course, even when the Reagan administration and the Supreme Court were taking a more negative and at times a hostile view. In 1973, the American Telephone and Telegraph Company had signed a consent decree in which it paid $50 million to settle complaints of past discrimination and opened well-paying jobs to women and members of minorities, including Hispanics. US West, one of the "Baby Bells" created after the breakup of AT&T in 1984, continued and even expanded upon the affirmative action program it inherited. Located in the Southwest and Pacific coast states, where Hispanics are the largest minority, the company could be a textbook example of how to make affirmative action work. It has reached out to Hispanic groups, held job fairs in Latino neighborhoods, and provided paid training to make men and women qualified to hold skilled blue-collar and white-collar jobs.

Similarly, state and local governments in areas of high Latino population established affirmative action plans, sometimes after a lawsuit, but once in place they, like US West, made their intentions clear that they would stay the course, despite urging from the Reagan Justice Department to abandon the plans. In Los Angeles, for example, it took a lawsuit in 1973 to get the fire department to start hiring Hispanics, but once in place the plan proved a boon to the large Chicano community. Osbaldo Amparan recalled that when he grew up in East Los Angeles, there were no blacks or Hispanics in the fire department; by 1978, he and many other people of color had become firemen.

DURING THE REVOLUTIONARY WAR, a soldier came home without one arm. Congress offered William Douglass a pension at half pay but could not give this "useless" man a job. Douglass refused the pension and went about recruiting other men similarly disabled by the war and formed a special unit of ex-soldiers. They served as guards and called themselves the "Invalid Corps." The lesson: there is, after all, a job for everyone.

Congress wrote affirmative action for the handicapped into the Rehabilitation Act of 1973. Section 503 required that in any federal contract exceeding $2,500, the contractor "shall take affirmative action to employ and advance in employment qualified handicapped individuals." If people with handicaps believed that a contractor had discriminated against them, they could file a complaint with the Department of Labor. That law, together with the Americans with Disabilities Act of 1990, constituted the legal bases for providing people with disabilities not only with opportunities for jobs and education but with basic access to public and private buildings, transportation, and other parts of daily life that the fully abled take for granted.

Despite the wording of the law—"qualified handicapped individuals"—the affirmative action part of the 1973 law unfortunately took a one-size-fits-all approach, similar to how civil rights laws grouped people of color, women, and ethnic minorities as to some extent fungible. Section 504 held that "no otherwise qualified handicapped individual . . . shall, solely by reason of his handicap, be excluded from the participation in, or be denied the benefits of, or be subject to discrimination under any program or activity receiving federal financial assistance." Some people, however, suffered worse disabilities than others, and the Supreme Court recognized this in a 1979 case, *Southeastern Community College v. Davis.*

Frances Davis, for many years a licensed practical nurse, wanted to become a registered nurse by taking the necessary courses at Southeastern Community College in North Carolina. Davis was partially deaf, however, and while this did not create an insurmountable barrier for her work as a practical nurse (which did not require administering medicines), the school said it would debar her from many of the activities that a registered nurse would have to do. An audiologist at Duke Medical School examined her and reported that even an improved hearing aid would not allow her to understand normal spoken speech. Southeastern then turned to the North Carolina Board of Nursing, which concluded that Davis's disability would make it impossible for her to participate safely in the normal clinical training program or to practice as a registered nurse. As a result, the school turned her down, and she sued, claiming that she had been discriminated against in violation of section 504, and demanded that the college not only make allowances for her disability but take affirmative steps to qualify her. She won in the lower courts but lost in a unanimous Supreme Court decision.

Writing for the Court, Justice Lewis F. Powell chastised the lower court for assuming "that a person need not meet legitimate physical requirements in order to be 'otherwise qualified.'" Taken literally, Powell continued, the lower court's ruling "would prevent an institution from taking into account any limitation resulting from a handicap, however disabling." In short, handicaps are not fungible, and employers as well as educational institutions could take into account the severity of the disability compared with the requirements of a job or training program.

Interestingly, one of the most successful programs for bringing in physically handicapped people to the job market predated the Rehabilitation Act by nearly four decades. Under David E. Lilienthal, the New Deal's Tennessee Valley Authority almost from the beginning had an occupational medical services program that helped injured employees obtain workers' compensation benefits. TVA management realized that many of those injured on the job left the workforce completely, taking with them valuable knowledge and skills. Not only did this increase the cost of workers' compensation insurance, but only a few of the mostly men leaving had become totally disabled and thus unable to work. The agency began a vocational rehabilitation program and removed architectural, transportation, and communications obstructions, as well as working to change procedural and attitudinal barriers.

What the TVA found out, and what the ADA to some extent codified, is that for many, but certainly not all, basic "assistive technology" may be all that is required. Ramps, for example, will allow people using wheelchairs to enter a workplace and then use desks with adjustable heights. TTY allows people with impaired hearing to have telephone conversations. Casual barriers that most people go around can be removed, so that walkways are clear. Later, people with impaired vision would be able to use computers that respond to voice commands or that convert written text into spoken words. According to the president's committee that operated the Job Accommodation Network, the typical accommodation cost less than $50:

- A $26.95 timer with an indicator light allowed a deaf medical technician to perform the laboratory tests required for her job.
- A visually impaired receptionist received a light probe, costing $45, which allowed her to determine which lines on a telephone were ringing, on hold, or in use at her company.
- A $49.95 headset allowed an insurance salesperson with cerebral palsy to write while talking.

There is some question as to how successful the two laws have been. All new buildings have to have ramp access, curbs require cutouts at corners, traffic crossing signals have to emit warning sounds either in words or in beeps, and these accommodations have become so ubiquitous that most nondisabled people pay little or no attention to them. We have also become accustomed to having signers at many public and private events, signing for the hearing impaired. But have job opportunities improved? The greatest success has come in government, where there have been mandated goals to have a certain percentage of the workforce composed of people with disabilities. In the private sector, however, it has really been up to the employer, because aside from those with government contracts, there is no pressure to hire the disabled. When the idea of establishing goals came up in the George H. W. Bush administration, he opposed it as a quota bill, and the ADA, while it mandates a great deal, does not establish hiring quotas.

Two-thirds of the countries in the European Union have some form of quota system for the disabled, as does Japan. In France, for example, all companies—not just those with government contracts—with more than twenty employees must have 6 percent of their workforce people with disabilities. The average unemployment rate for the disabled in the European Union is about 5 percent of those who want to work and are capable of doing so; in the United States, the comparable unemployment rate is 80 percent.

There has not been the storm over affirmative action for the disabled anywhere near what we have seen for people of color, women, or ethnic groups. In part, because the range of disabilities is so wide, there are no organizations lobbying for the disabled comparable to the NAACP or NOW. The ADA itself has been described "as being the perfect bill for left and right to agree on," because aside from providing increased access and barrier removal, its main goal is to help disabled people achieve independence by getting an education or a job and living independently. For liberals, independent living means that people with disabilities can determine their own fate and live autonomously. Conservatives also applaud these goals and see disabled people as part of the workforce and paying taxes rather than living off a government subsidy. George H. W. Bush and others believed that most people with disabilities wanted to work and government should—at least in part—make it possible for them to do so. While the left would have liked to have had an enforcement clause, conservatives opposed it. Even on the liberal side, one did not find unanimous support. Labor unions, for example, did not favor some provisions of the ADA, especially if seniority might be trumped by a disability accommodation.

Critics of affirmative action in general oppose programs for African Americans, women, and others because they claim, among other things, that if these people were not lazy, they would be out there working to get a leg up. They make an exception for people in wheelchairs or with other physical disabilities. Employers have also learned, as did the TVA, that just because a person cannot do physical labor, he or she often has abilities that are useful, indeed valuable, for their business. An engineer can still check building specs at a desk or with a computer; a blind woman can handle business over a phone. The increased use of computers has given disabled people greater opportunities to work, either at home or at an office.

Unfortunately, discrimination against the disabled continues, and no matter how many ramps, Braille signs, or assistive technologies are used, prejudice remains, and in this the disabled faced a situation truly comparable to that suffered by people of color.

LINDA CHAVEZ, WHO HEADED the U.S. Commission on Civil Rights during the Reagan years and who remains a leading opponent of affirmative action, claims that "the biggest group of people who are [negatively] affected are Asian students." The largest concentration of Asian Americans is in California, and according to the latest census figures they constitute 14.7 percent of the state's total population of 39,250,000. Asian Americans make up 5.6 percent of the total U.S. population.

Within this number, which exceeds 15 million, the largest ethnic groups are Chinese (3.79 million), Filipino (3.41 million), Indian (3.18 million), Vietnamese (1.73 million), Korean (1.7 million), and Japanese (1.3 million). Some writers claim that the term "Asian

American" is mostly meaningless. "Nobody grows up speaking Asian-American, nobody sits down to Asian-American food with their Asian-American parents, and nobody goes on a pilgrimage back to their motherland of Asian-America." While non-Asians tend to lump all of these groups together, Asians see very real differences among the groups and tend to stay close to their particular ethnicity.

Although few cultures are as distinctly non-European as those of Asia, immigrants from China, Japan, and other countries have readily adapted to the free market economy and the open competition for education in this country. In fact, Asian Americans have been so successful that the University of California at Berkeley allegedly imposed a cap on the number of Asian Americans admitted. Similar charges have been made against the Massachusetts Institute of Technology. In 2005, the two thousand Asian Americans entering Berkeley accounted for nearly half the entering freshmen, and of this the largest group was Chinese Americans, numbering one thousand.

In 1982, Asian American applicants to Harvard had an average combined SAT score of 1,251 out of 1,600; Caucasian students who applied that year had a combined score of 1,258. One would say that the two groups seemed evenly matched. But when it came to admissions, Asian Americans whom Harvard accepted had a combined SAT of 1,467, while the whites admitted had a score of 1,355, or 112 points lower. Researchers found a similar pattern at Princeton for 1982 and 1983, and at Brown for classes entering from 1979 through 1983.

The problem, as cultural critic William Henry argues, is not, as is the case with African Americans and Hispanics, recruiting enough Asian Americans; rather, it is just the opposite—to keep Asians from crowding out the less accomplished children of donation-minded white alumni. Henry believes there is a private conversation among leaders of American society wondering why blacks and Hispanics cannot perform as Asians do, although it would be politically incorrect to ask this question publicly. In 1993, a study showed that Asians, who constituted 2.9 percent of the population, accounted for 19.5 percent of all engineering degrees and 11.2 percent of degrees in the physical sciences.

IN THE COURSE OF WRITING this book, I have asked colleagues, including some who teach in West Coast schools, why they think the children of Asian immigrants do so well. One response, I think, is noteworthy and sums up what others have said. "At the beginning of the twentieth century the largest immigrant group consisted of Jews escaping persecution in eastern Europe. Jews had always had a culture of learning; it was a religious obligation to study the Torah and the Talmud, and children were rewarded when they did well. When Jews came to America, they impressed upon their children the need to study the new torah, the idea that to assimilate and to succeed economically, they had to go to school, study hard, and get good grades." And they did. The children of Jewish immigrants became teachers, doctors, and lawyers and within one generation moved out of the ghetto and into the middle class.

Asian families in the late twentieth and early twenty-first centuries have many of the same characteristics as did Jewish families a century earlier, especially the belief that education is the key to success in America. And like Jews, their very success has bred resentment, and in some cases efforts to limit the number of Asian students have echoed the quotas used to restrict Jewish students beginning in the 1920s and, in some cases, lasting until after World War II.

If we look at a comparison of Asian groups and whites enrolled as students in schools and colleges, the numbers are rather amazing. In every age bracket except seven to fifteen (covering roughly most of elementary and middle school), Asians have more children in school than do whites. For the age bracket eighteen to nineteen (last year of high school and first year of college), 83.9 percent of Chinese and 61.6 percent of Japanese are in school, compared with 52.8 percent of whites, while in the age bracket twenty-two to twenty-four (college and beginning graduate school), only 17.4 percent of whites are enrolled, compared with over half of the Chinese and 38.9 percent of Japanese.

For a very brief time in the 1970s, schools looked at Asian students as another ethnic group, and also as people of color. Beginning in the mid- to late 1980s, conservatives began arguing that discrimination against Asian Americans reflected a deeper problem in the university, namely, affirmative action. According to conservatives, discrimination against Asians was the logical, indeed inevitable, result of policies favoring other minorities, namely, blacks and Hispanics. Although Asian groups initially denounced conservative attacks, eventually the conservative argument won out; affirmative action policies harmed not only white students but gifted Asian students as well.

Initially, in the early 1980s, when Asian Americans learned of quotas at elite schools, they framed the problem in terms of "racial discrimination," akin to the policies that had previously kept blacks and Hispanics—and earlier Jews—out of the better schools. University officials, faced with proof that such discrimination in fact existed, tried to shift the conversation away from why limits existed on Asian students and toward the idea that the caps represented an effort to achieve a truly diverse student body. Asians had no problem with diversity, but not at their expense, and by the late 1980s conservatives had shifted the debate back to the problems with affirmative action.

Interestingly, many white students who resented affirmative action did not view Asians as part of the problem. A white coed at Berkeley said, "Every time I see a black person, *not an Asian,* but any other person of color walk by, I think, affirmative action. It's like that's your first instinct. It's not, maybe that person was smart; it's gotta be Affirmative Action. They don't even belong here." Governor Pete Wilson, in praising the University of California regents for eliminating race as a consideration for admissions in 1995, called it the "right decision" and declared that "racial preferences are by definition racial discrimination. They were wrong 30 years ago when they discriminated against African-Americans. And they're wrong today, when they discriminate against Asian or Caucasian Americans."

YET EVEN AS MANY PRAISED the academic ability of Asian students, the debate over affirmative action found those of Asian descent torn between two camps. On the one hand, conservatives praised Asians for their work ethic and their determination to succeed, and claimed that, as it did to whites, affirmative action kept many well-qualified Asians out of schools. In 1988, a writer for *The New Republic,* James Gibney, claimed that a "zero-sum relation" existed between Asian admissions and affirmative action. In his view, Asians and African Americans were each other's main opponents in the admissions sweepstakes. Asians' underrepresentation based on their test scores resulted from affirmative action for other minorities. Daniel Seligman, writing in *Fortune,* saw Asian admissions as a continuation of reverse discrimination toward whites. "Racial preferences in college admissions," he charged, "is now being used against the wrong people. Affirmative action logic states firmly that Asian Americans should now suffer reverse discrimination, just as the whites have suffered it for years."

In many ways, the qualifications of Asian Americans allowed conservatives to deny that they are racists. "You see," they seemed to say, "we do not oppose affirmative action because we are against blacks and Hispanics. Asians are also nonwhite, but they deserve to succeed because of their efforts. They are qualified to go to Harvard or Stanford. Affirmative action hurts not only whites but qualified people of color as well."

If people on the right saw Asians as a "model minority," and pitted them against other racial minorities, then advocates of affirmative action on the left wanted Asians to join other people of color and become part of a united front against whites.

This dichotomy, of course, did not and does not work. While we may lump people from the eastern side of the Pacific as Asians, they are in fact a diverse group, some from China and Japan, some from India and elsewhere. Similarly, we often make the mistake of lumping all women into one group, all African Americans, all Hispanics, and indeed all whites. Asian American educational achievement subverts the claims of both the left and the right. Some members of the right, including Governor Pete Wilson and Ward Connerly, the father of Prop 209, have argued for the substitution of class preference for that of race in California admissions, believing that this will help poorer whites who are currently boxed out. The idea of class preferences also appeals to some on the left, who anticipate that because so many African Americans and Hispanics are poor, that will ensure a larger number of them getting into the university.

Here again, the Asian American community confounds both assumptions. Should the University of California—or other schools— adopt a class-based preference program, it would give Asian Americans a clear advantage. While many of the Asian groups have done well in America, many of them are first generation and socioeconomically are in the poorer brackets. Officials at the University of California estimate that if socioeconomic status is used as an admissions criterion instead of race, the Asian enrollment will increase by 15–25 percent, while African American enrollment will drop 40–50 percent, Hispanic enrollment will drop 5–15 percent, and the white percentage will stay about the same.

At the time California voters were considering Prop 209, *The New*

York Times sent a reporter out to the University of California's Irvine campus to interview Asian students and see what they thought of affirmative action. For the most part, the students agreed that in the absence of preferential programs Asian Americans as a group would do better. Binh Nguyen, whose family fled Saigon in 1975, hoped to be a doctor, but despite having a good GPA, he worried that as an Asian he would have trouble getting into medical school. "Without affirmative action, it would help me get into med school." But then he went on, "Affirmative action is kind of needed, but for me as an applicant, I would personally not support it." His good friend Phat Chiem agreed that Vietnamese Americans, as a group, would benefit by the elimination of affirmative action: "But my concern is, are we then going to have a campus that's all Asian-American and white? When you have a campus where the population of African-Americans is 2 percent, it's hard to say we should eliminate affirmative action to increase the number of Asian-Americans."

Asian Americans, although marked to some extent by skin color, have had vastly different experiences than have African Americans and Hispanics. Although they have certainly faced prejudice and dislocation (nearly all of the Vietnamese segment consists of refugees who fled here at the end of the war, bringing very little in terms of personal wealth or even belongings), the culture of Asian Americans as a group makes it impossible to categorize them as "white" or "other" in the debate over affirmative action. As a group, they do not need it; as individuals, they do not want to be penalized by preferences for other groups.

This is not an issue that will soon go away. In May 2015, a coalition of sixty-four Asian American associations filed a complaint with the Justice Department alleging racial discrimination against Asians at a particular university, which, although unnamed, appeared to be Harvard. Lawyers in the Civil Rights Division refused to pursue the complaint, and in the summer of 2017 the Justice Department posted a call for "volunteers" to investigate. On 2 August 2017, Attorney General Jeff Sessions announced his intention to go after any school whose affirmative action plan discriminated against other groups.

A few days later, Edward Blum, the president of the Students for Fair Admissions, weighed in to praise Sessions for going after Harvard. The university had a long history of discrimination; in the 1920s, it had adopted something called "holistic" admissions, deliberately designed to keep Jews out. Now Harvard was using a holistic policy to keep the number of Asian Americans at a stable level; from 1992 to 2013, the number of Asian Americans admitted into the undergraduate program had remained at 19 percent or less. Blum charged that the other Ivy League schools also had a cap on the number of Asian Americans they admitted, and directly rebutted the claim for diversity: "A university is more than the sum of its ethnic parts. It is comprised of individuals—some black, white, Asian and Hispanic—who should be admitted or rejected without their race or ethnic heritage making any difference. Let's hope the Justice Department agrees."

AFFIRMATIVE ACTION IS NOT a uniquely American phenomenon, but can be found in many countries around the world, and a number of studies can be referenced on programs in Europe, Asia, and Africa. In all of them, the basic issue is the same as in the United States: a particular group has faced discrimination in the past, and the current government wants to do something to atone for the past and improve prospects for the future. Perhaps the largest program can be found in South Africa, where the end of apartheid nonetheless left millions of black people in a situation similar to African Americans after *Brown.* In New Zealand, the targeted group are the aboriginal Maori; in Canada, programs aim to help women, Native tribes, and the disabled.

The debates in these countries for the most part parallel ours, with one group arguing that merit and only merit should guide determinations of employment or education, and opponents calling for justice to those who had suffered through decades or even centuries of persecution. Thomas Sowell, well known for his opposition to affirmative action in the United States, found the same moral and pragmatic problems afflicting programs in other countries.

In no other country, however, has affirmative action become the divisive issue it is in the United States, and that is due to the unique circumstances driving programs here.

CHAPTER 19

BUSH, OBAMA, AND FISHER

As we work to address the wrong of racial prejudice, we must not use means to create another wrong, and thus perpetuate our division.

—GEORGE W. BUSH

We have to think about affirmative action and craft it in such a way where some of our children who are advantaged aren't getting more favorable treatment than a poor white kid who has struggled more.

—BARACK OBAMA

There were people in my class with lower grades who weren't in all the activities I was in, who were being accepted into UT, and the only other difference between us was the color of our skin. I was taught from the time I was a little girl that any kind of discrimination was wrong. And for an institution of higher learning to act this way makes no sense to me.

—ABIGAIL FISHER

The contested 2000 election, the attacks on the World Trade Center and the Pentagon on 11 September 2001, the devastation Hurricane Katrina wrought in Louisiana, and the wars in Afghanistan and Iraq have overshadowed just about everything else that occurred during the eight years (2001–2009) that George W. Bush occupied the White House. (Of course, the 9/11 attack did not stop right-wing instigators like Ann Coulter, who, in her usual restrained manner, penned a screed titled "Affirmative Action for Osama." In it she charged that "each of the 12,000 boys born in Pakistan the pre-

Justice Samuel Alito Jr. replaced Sandra Day O'Connor in 2006 but, unlike her, opposed all forms of affirmative action.

vious year named 'Osama' would be granted preferential treatment over American-born whites.")

Bush, like most Republicans, opposed affirmative action, although, because of the other and more pressing matters, he paid little attention to it. The president named two men to the Supreme Court, John Roberts and Samuel Alito, and others who opposed affirmative action to places in his government, yet no one in his administration attacked it the way Ed Meese had done during the Reagan years.

Ironically, Bush himself had benefited from a preferential policy in gaining admission to Yale in 1964. Colleges call it a "legacy" system, and it provides favored treatment for the children of alumni, or as one reporter called it, "the quintessential example of the 'old boys network.'" Colleges—both public and especially private—view the system as a way to tap the pockets of alumni: admit their children, and the alumni parents will increase their donations to their alma mater, or at the least maintain a level of giving.

Although Bush never released his grades from Andover, the elite prep school that both he and his father attended, *The New Yorker* managed to get hold of Bush's Yale record and learned that he had scored 566 on the verbal and 640 on the math SAT, a total of 1,206, or 180 points below the median score for his Yale classmates. Had he not been a legacy (both his father and his grandfather had been "Elis"), and had not three of the seven members of the admissions committee been members of Skull and Bones (the exclusive club to which his father and grandfather belonged and to which he would be tapped in his junior year), George W. would never have gotten in. He had mediocre grades, no special talents, was not an outstanding athlete, and, in fact, had little going for him other than an accident of birth. His record at Yale was mediocre, a C average that put him in the bottom fifth of his class. When he spoke at Yale's commencement ceremony in 2001, he joked, "To the C students I say, you, too, can be president of the United States."

Bush's record on diversity is not bad. In his first term, he named Colin Powell as secretary of state, the first African American to hold that position, and in his second term Condoleezza Rice, who had been national security adviser in the first four years, became the first black woman to head the State Department. In 2005, he named Alberto Gonzales as the first Hispanic to be attorney general. He appointed so many African Americans to subcabinet and agency positions that an editorial writer said that Bush had "assembled what may be the blackest administration in American history." He also appointed more women to his cabinet than Bill Clinton and was the first Republican president to name an openly gay man to serve in his administration, Scott Evertz, as director of the Office of National AIDS Policy. His nominee as ambassador to Romania, Michael E. Guest, became the first openly gay man to be confirmed by the Senate as a U.S. ambassador.

On the other hand, his first-term choices for attorney general, John Ashcroft, and health and human services secretary, Tommy Thompson, were both longtime opponents of affirmative action. He named an African American foe of affirmative action, Gerald A. Reynolds, to head the Department of Education's Office for Civil Rights. When Reynolds ran into opposition from civil rights groups and in the Senate, Bush waited until Congress went home for a break and gave Reynolds the position on a recess appointment. At the beginning of his second term, Bush named Reynolds to be chairman of the U.S. Civil Rights Commission. Reynolds described himself this way: "I am not a civil rights activist. I've never been a civil rights activist." He further antagonized leaders of civil rights groups when he declared that the federal government did not do enough to use "race neutral" programs as alternatives to "race conscious" undertakings. In the rush of congressional sentiment to support Bush immediately after the 9/11 attacks, the Senate confirmed Brian Jones, the former president of the Center for New Black Leadership and a longtime opponent of both affirmative action and much of the civil rights agenda, as general counsel of the Department of Education despite opposition from civil rights groups. Gerald Reynolds had also come from the center, as well as Peter Kirsanow, who received a high-ranking appointment to the National Labor Relations Board.

At the start of Bush's second term, the Labor Department suspended requirements that government contractors have an affirmative action plan for women, minorities, Vietnam veterans, and the disabled, if the companies were first-time contractors working on reconstruction in the wake of Hurricane Katrina. There seems to have been little response from civil rights groups, primarily because the exemption applied to a limited number of companies and for only three months, the time estimated that they would be at work in Louisiana. The step aimed to speed up reconstruction efforts and to offset some of the criticism the administration faced for its slow response to the crisis caused by the storm.

The administration immediately inherited an affirmative action case from the Clinton administration. Adarand Constructors had submitted the low bid for a Department of Transportation project, but the contract had gone to a minority-owned company as part of the department's "disadvantaged business enterprise" program. Adarand sued, and by a 5–4 vote the Supreme Court ruled that federal programs involving race had to be narrowly tailored and meet the test of strict scrutiny. It sent the case back to a lower court to see if the federal program met those standards.

In September 2000, the Court of Appeals for the Tenth Circuit ruled that the program did meet strict scrutiny and was therefore constitutional. In addition, the program had been revised so that even white-owned small businesses could apply for consideration as a disadvantaged business. The new system also discontinued the practice of awarding financial bonuses to prime contractors who subcontracted parts out to minority firms. Adarand appealed to the high court, and in the last days of the Clinton administration the Justice Department filed a brief arguing that the program now met constitutional standards and that the Court should decline to reopen the matter.

The Bush Justice Department filed a fifty-page brief in August 2001, agreeing with its predecessor that the program no longer violated constitutional requirements, and also seemingly accepting one of the basic underlying premises of affirmative action, namely, that some businesses have suffered as a result of their minority ownership. (Bush was careful to clarify that the Justice Department acted out of concern for upholding federal law rather than support for affirmative action.) The brief aroused the ire of longtime foes of preferential policies. After all, had not Bush during the 2000 campaign said he opposed quotas and that considering an applicant's race in college admissions "amounts to a quota system that unfairly rewards or penalizes prospective students based on their race"? Indeed he had, but he had also spoken of the need for some affirmative action programs. The Supreme Court heard arguments in October and the following month dismissed the case as improvidently granted.

Clint Bolick, head of the anti-affirmative-action Institute for Justice, gave the president a pass because of the "institutional need of defending federal statutes." Others were far less charitable. Linda Chavez, head of the Center for Equal Opportunity and an unsuccessful Bush nominee for secretary of labor, reacted strongly to what she deemed the administration's failure to fight affirmative action. Chavez claimed that guilt about opposing the first civil rights laws in the 1960s, and now the politics of attracting Latino voters, led the "Republican establishment controlling the White House" to avoid moving against racial preferences. She told her audience at the Federalist Society, "I'm hoping and looking to the courts to bail us out."

That opportunity came just a few years later. In January 2003, the president announced that the administration would file briefs opposing affirmative action policies in the University of Michigan cases, which the Supreme Court would hear that spring. He charged that both the undergraduate and the law school programs essentially used racial quotas, and while the goal of diversity might be worthwhile, at Michigan the "result is discrimination and that discrimination is wrong." Diversity can be achieved without quotas, he said, and pointed to systems in California, Florida, and Texas to show that diversity could be achieved in innovative and race-neutral ways. The leading African American in his administration, Colin Powell, distanced himself from the president on this question, arguing that race could and should be one of several factors in the admissions process. Condoleezza Rice tried to straddle the issue, saying that race might be a factor, but she believed that the president had come out strongly for diversity while opposing quotas.

When the Supreme Court handed down its decisions in the Michigan cases on 23 June 2003, Bush immediately issued a statement praising the Court for "recognizing the value of diversity on our Nation's campuses. Diversity is one of America's greatest strengths." The two decisions created a "careful balance" between the goal of diversity and the "fundamental principle of equal treatment under the law." Again, he declared that race-neutral alternatives existed, and interpreted the Court's decisions as requiring universities to engage in them. He did admit, however, that race remained a "reality" in American life, and he looked forward to the day when "America will truly be a colorblind society."

All in all, despite the appointments of men and women opposed to preferential policies, little happened during the Bush years to really set back the cause of affirmative action. Congress refused to do away with small-business programs that benefited minority contractors. The Supreme Court in the Michigan cases allowed colleges and universities to take race into account in their admissions processes provided they did not use quotas or make race the dominant consideration. In the private sector, affirmative action had become a way of doing business for large corporations, and while too few women and minorities had reached the top rungs of management, the companies themselves no longer needed prodding from the federal government. This is not to say all was rosy for racial and gender diversity. Efforts by state and local governments often ran into legal challenges, and civil rights and gender activists still fought against prejudice. Yet the fears that the Bush administration would dismantle affirmative action proved groundless, much to the despair of conservative groups like the Federalist Society. Then, in 2008, the American people elected Barack Hussein Obama as the forty-fourth president of the United States.

OBAMA LATER SAID that his first experience with affirmative action came when he was a boy in Hawaii. The Punahou Academy had been founded in 1841 by missionaries and in the latter half of the twentieth century had grown into a prestigious prep school, an "incubator for the island elites." His mother wanted him to go there, but in addition

President Barack Obama, shown here prior to winning his second term in 2012.

to the high cost there was a long waiting list. The school considered him only because his grandfather's boss, an alumnus, interceded on his behalf; it not only accepted him but gave him a scholarship. "My first experience with affirmative action," he later said, "had little to do with race." In fact, it had a lot more to do with contacts, a situation very similar to that of George W. Bush at Andover and Yale.

Obama entered Occidental College in the fall of 1979 and two years later transferred to Columbia, graduating from the college in 1983. There is no record that would indicate whether either school took him because of affirmative action. After graduation, he went to Chicago, where he worked as a community organizer until he decided to go to law school. Did Harvard take his race into account? Obama did not list his race on his application, although it would not have been too hard for the admissions committee to learn. Even if they did take race into account, as one article noted, "he is perhaps the ideal example of the policy gone right." He graduated magna cum laude, his peers selected him as president of the *Harvard Law Review,* and he impressed classmates and professors with his smarts. He later said he did not know if he had been admitted to Harvard Law or to the *Review* because of a preferential program, but "if I was, then I certainly am not ashamed of the fact, for I would argue that affirmative action is important precisely because those who benefit typically rise to the challenge when given an opportunity."

Some controversy surrounded his selection as an editor and later president of the prestigious *Harvard Law Review*. He apparently was the only editor to be selected without any published articles, and charges flew that he had been chosen only because of his race. As one right-wing conservative charged, "Affirmative action is the only reason a man of average grade and moderate intellect would be considered for Harvard and the *Law Review*." Aside from the fact that Obama had a superior intellect and honor-level grades, selection for the *Review* is a double-blind process, where students are chosen on the basis of both grades and writing (although the writing need not be a published article). Once the first group of students had been chosen, the remaining positions would be filled by an affirmative action plan that had been in effect for several years. If the first batch had people of color, women, and other disadvantaged groups, there would be no need for the plan. If not, then the selection committee could take race, gender, physical handicaps, and other considerations into account. "In no event," Obama wrote, "is the Selection Committee required to meet any set quotas."

Obama was particularly vexed by charges that he had been chosen as an editor and then as president of the *Review* solely because of his race, and in November 1990 he and other officers responded to articles in the school newspaper that selection of unqualified people, solely on the basis of race or gender, diminished the position as well as the school. In his letter, Obama defended the selection process for the diversity of views it brought to the editorial room. "The vigor of debate and the wide range of perspectives that results from our current selection process have not been purchased at the price of any 'lower standard' of editorial excellence; in fact, our program argues for the proposition that diversity can and should be the companion of quality legal scholarship."

Obama added what he called a personal note, in response to a letter from Jim Chen objecting to the *Law Review*'s affirmative action policy and its stigmatizing effects. He did not doubt Chen's sincerity, but "as someone who has undoubtedly benefited from affirmative action programs during my academic career, and as someone who may have benefited from the *Law Review*'s affirmative action policy when I was selected to join the *Review* last year, I have not personally felt stigmatized either within the broader law school community or as a staff member of the *Review*." In fact, he believed that his selection as president would indicate "that at least among *Review* staff, and hopefully for the majority of professors at Harvard, affirmative action in no way tarnishes the accomplishments of those who are members of historically underrepresented groups." (A dozen years later, as an Illinois state senator, he spoke with empathy about accomplished minority students at elite universities who sometimes lived "under a cloud they could not erase.")

In the 2008 election, the Republican Party platform denounced any form of discrimination based on sex, race, age, religion, creed, disability, or national origin, and stated, "We ask all to join us in rejecting the forces of hatred and bigotry." And "precisely because we oppose discrimination, we reject preferences, quotas, and set-asides, whether in education or in corporate boardrooms. The government should not make contracts on this basis, and neither should corporations."

Where the Republicans avoided using the phrase, the Democrats came right out and said, "We support affirmative action, including in federal contracting and higher education, to make sure that those locked out of the doors of opportunity will be able to walk through those doors in the future." Yet the Democratic candidate seemed to distance himself from this plank in the platform.

Although Obama opposed ballot measures that would have prohibited state universities from taking race into account, he seemed lukewarm at best to affirmative action. It would not be a long-term solution to the problems of race, because "if you've got 50 percent of African-American or Latino kids dropping out of high school, it doesn't matter what you do in terms of affirmative action. Those kids aren't going to college." He also said, much to the dismay of some civil rights leaders, that his two daughters, Malia and Sasha, should not be given preferential treatment. They had a relatively privileged upbringing, and what the government should do is craft a policy where children of color who are advantaged do not get better treatment "than a poor white kid who has struggled more."

This statement is consistent with what some commentators saw as Obama's shift from race to class. During the years he worked as a community organizer, he worked with poor people—black, Hispanic, and white. Gerald Kellman, who hired Obama to help organize poor families in Chicago, said that Obama "never had much inclination to use affirmative action as a tool then. He wanted to level the playing field by providing early childhood education programs and access to good schools."

In office, Obama appointed African Americans, women, and Hispanics to many governmental positions, especially in the judiciary. Both of his appointments to the Supreme Court were women: Sonia Sotomayor, the Court's first Hispanic member, and Elena Kagan, the former dean of Harvard Law then serving as solicitor general. In addition to the high court, there are federal district courts and circuit courts of appeal with a total of nearly nine hundred judges. Every year some of these men and women die, retire, or resign, so that over the course of two terms a president can significantly affect

Justice Elena Kagan, who as dean of the Harvard Law School (2003–2009), U.S. solicitor general (2009–2010), and a justice on the high court since 2010, supported affirmative action programs.

the makeup of these courts, where the lion's share of federal judicial business gets done. (These lower courts hear thousands of cases each year, of which only about seventy-five will be heard on appeal at the Supreme Court.)

In his two terms, Obama appointed over a third of the federal bench. By late 2014, he had nominated and the Senate had confirmed 53 judges to the courts of appeals and 223 to federal district courts. When he took the oath of office in 2009, Republican appointees controlled ten of the thirteen circuit courts of appeals; midway through his second term, Democratic appointees controlled nine. Even in his last two years, the Senate continued to confirm lower-court nominees, so that the final tally for eight years included 2 Supreme Court justices, 55 judges of the courts of appeal, and 268 district court judges.

Obama took great pride that his judicial appointments looked different from their predecessors. In an interview with Jeffrey Toobin, Obama said that some groups had historically been underrepresented on the bench, especially Latinos and Asian Americans, who each year represent a larger proportion of the population. "And so for them to be able to see folks in robes that look like them is going to be important. When I came into office, I think there was one openly gay judge who had been appointed. We've appointed ten."

In the same interview, Obama took a stance on affirmative action that closely paralleled that of Justice Sandra Day O'Connor, who wrote opinions in both the *Adarand* case and that of the Michigan Law School. "If the University of Michigan or California decided that there is a value in making sure that folks with different experiences in a classroom will enhance the educational experience of the students, and they do it in a careful way," the practice should be allowed. But, he added, "most of the time the law's principal job should be as a shield against discrimination, as opposed to a sword to advance a social agenda, because the law is a blunt instrument in these situations." African Americans face not only racism but poverty, and "the single most important thing I could do for poor black kids is to make sure they're getting a good K-through-12 education. Then they'll be able to compete for university slots and jobs."

In 2011, the Departments of Justice and Education issued a new "guidance document" to replace an earlier one issued by the George W. Bush administration. The earlier document stated that the Department of Education "strongly encourages the use of race-neutral methods for assigning students to elementary and secondary high schools." The Obama statement informed elementary and secondary schools as well as colleges that the Supreme Court had established diversity as a compelling interest and "has made clear [schools] can include taking account of the race of individual students in a narrowly tailored manner."

Although it received little attention at the time, a rule that Obama proposed in January 2016 would have required companies to share pay data with the EEOC based on race, gender, and ethnicity, giving the federal government a way to monitor pay discrepancies. While the data would not be made public, it could have opened employers to lawsuits in which they would be publicly named. Obama hoped that by having to share the data, companies would be led to do away with discrepancies based on race or gender. Those companies with good records could boast about it, helping them with recruitment and making points with consumers, whom polls showed were increasingly concerned about how employers treated their workers. Few companies outside Silicon Valley showed any enthusiasm, but tech giants such as Intel and Apple have for the past few years issued an annual "diversity" report that includes facts on pay rates between whites and people of color, and between men and women.

THE HOPE THAT Obama's election would mark the end of overt racism in the country soon proved groundless. A CNN poll early in his administration showed that while 55 percent of African Americans thought discrimination remained a serious problem, only 17 percent of whites felt that way. In another 2009 poll by the Pew Research Center, 80 percent of blacks said equality had not been achieved, and 43 percent thought there was still "a lot of discrimination," but only 13 percent of whites believed there was much antiblack bias. Within a few years, however, polls began showing increased white resentment against blacks. In a 2012 Associated Press poll, 51 percent of respondents expressed explicit antiblack attitudes, up from 48 percent shortly before Obama's election. It is no surprise that 64 percent of Republicans held this attitude, a fact that would become crystal clear in Donald Trump's 2016 presidential campaign and his actions once in office.

Interestingly, people who analyzed the polls considered antiblack attitudes not equivalent to racism. What they saw, as one person explained it, is not so much racism as white resentment. "A lot of people honestly think they have been significantly deprived of various things because of minorities. . . . It's not so much the animosity toward people who are different—it's the animosity of the aggrieved. They feel like victims."

Republicans in general opposed Obama's first Supreme Court appointment, Sonia Sotomayor, but had little to use that could have derailed her confirmation. She had excelled both at Princeton and at Yale (having been an affirmative action admit at both schools), had worked as a prosecutor and as a circuit court judge, where she had gained the thanks of millions of people by averting a strike that would have canceled the Major League Baseball season. So they jumped on her for her role in an affirmative action case she had heard as part of a three-judge panel on the Second Circuit, *Ricci v. DeStefano.*

The City of New Haven had given a test for firemen seeking promotion and then had discarded the results of that test because no African American and only two Hispanics had qualified for the rank of lieutenant or captain. The city contended that the test format had been flawed and feared that it would be sued by minority firefighters who could argue that they had been disproportionately and unlawfully barred from promotion. The basis of their case would be that under the Supreme Court's ruling in *Griggs v. Duke Power Company* (1971), companies could not utilize tests that had a disparate impact on minorities, an idea codified by the 1991 Civil Rights Act.

When the tests had been given, 118 applicants took the written and oral exams (both of which had been drawn up by a firm the city had hired to avoid any bias in the testing). Of the 41 firefighters applying for captain, 25 were white, 8 black, and 8 Hispanic; 77 men sought promotion to lieutenant: 43 white, 19 black, and 15 Hispanic. Several white applicants had passed with high enough grades to get promoted, only to see the city discard the results. A group of white firefighters sued the city for discrimination, but their claim had been rejected by a federal district court, which accepted the city's disparate-impact claim.

Sotomayor and two other judges heard Frank Ricci's appeal but could not agree on the proper rationale, and so they issued a brief order on a Friday afternoon affirming the lower-court decision. This brought a sharp reaction from the senior judge, José Cabranes, who had at one time been Sotomayor's mentor in law school and then her colleague on the bench for the ten years since she had been appointed by Bill Clinton. He wanted the whole circuit to rehear the case en banc, that is, with all the Second Circuit judges hearing the case, but he lost that bid by a narrow 7–6 vote. Newspapers were all over the split among the judges, and then the U.S. Supreme Court took the case on appeal and heard oral argument on 22 April 2009, just a few months after Barack Obama became president.

The Obama administration tried to walk a narrow path in its brief filed in the case. The Justice Department contended that the city had acted lawfully in discarding the test results and urged the justices to return the case to the lower courts because neither the district judge nor the circuit court panel had "adequately considered" whether the city's fear of lawsuits had been a pretext for racial discrimination. Critics of the New Haven decision, including Justice Samuel Alito, emphasized that not even the Obama administration endorsed the Second Circuit's one-paragraph dismissal of the suit.

In the end, a 5–4 Court rejected the city's position and sided with the white firefighters. Justice Anthony Kennedy held that an employer must have "a strong basis in evidence" that, had it not taken the action, it would have been liable under Title VII. New Haven had no evidence—much less the required "strong evidence"—that the tests were flawed and not job related. Fear of litigation failed to justify the city's actions, and as a result the city had intentionally discriminated against the white firefighters.

By this time, White House lawyers were watching the case very closely. Sotomayor's place on the short list of possible Supreme Court nominees would be jeopardized if it appeared that she had not done an adequate job in reviewing the case. Did she take it seriously or simply engage in a politically expedient move? The White House counsel, Gregory Craig, wanted to know, "Did she phone it in?" In the end, Obama did name her, knowing that even if Republicans attacked her for some of her decisions, they would be in a political bind if they voted against the first Hispanic named to the high court.

The *Ricci* case did come up in her confirmation hearings, not so much for the results as for the minimal decision that seemed to some to have casually dismissed an important reverse discrimination claim. She responded that as far as she was concerned, the city faced the real threat of lawsuits over the results of the test and New Haven had taken necessary steps to avoid that problem. The only real question the Second Circuit had to answer was whether the city did what it was required to do. As for the brevity of the opinion, she kept reminding the senators that the district judge had written a very thorough seventy-eight-page opinion that relied on what was then accepted precedent. In the end, the Senate voted to confirm her, 68–31, with all the Democrats and nine Republicans voting yea.

BOTH GEORGE W. BUSH and Barack Obama watched closely as the Supreme Court heard one of the most important affirmative action cases of the new century, *Fisher v. University of Texas*—Bush because as governor he had endorsed the plan now used by the University of Texas, and Obama because a hostile opinion could threaten all government-sponsored affirmative action plans.

Abigail Noel Fisher wanted to go to the University of Texas in Austin, the flagship school in the state's higher education system, one that her father and sister had attended. As her lawyer's brief claimed, she had done everything right; she had worked hard, received good grades, and rounded out her high school years in suburban Sugar Land, Texas, with an array of extracurricular activities. Fisher, who ranked 82nd out of a class of 674, just missed out under the Texas Top 10 Percent Plan, as well as the "holistic" review that allowed the school to look at the entire portrait of students who did not make the 10 percent cutoff.

The case of *Fisher v. Texas* went to the Supreme Court twice, but before we look at what the justices decided in June 2016, we should recall what happened in Texas twenty years earlier after the Fifth

Abigail Fisher, the lead plaintiff in the University of Texas case, with her lawyer, Bert Rein (left), and Edward Blum (right) outside the Supreme Court on 10 October 2012.

Circuit ruled in *Hopwood v. Texas* that the University of Texas could not use race as a factor in admissions.

Hopwood immediately affected university enrollments. In 1996, the UT Law School admitted 65 blacks; the following year it accepted 11, and of these only 4 decided to enroll. Where there had been 70 Mexican Americans in 1996, the following year the school accepted 34, with 26 deciding to enroll. Numbers for the undergraduate program also showed a decline, but not as steep. The class admitted in 1996 had 421 black members, that of the following year 314, while the number of Mexican Americans went from 1,568 to 1,333. During that year, white enrollment in the law school rose from 370 to 424, and Asian Americans from 30 to 45. In the undergraduate program, the number of whites admitted increased from 6,854 to 7,140, and Asian Americans from 1,553 to 1,715. It was the first decline in minority enrollment since UT had begun keeping such records in 1975. Moreover, state colleges and universities in Texas reported that minority interest plummeted after the Fifth Circuit decision, the same situation that had arisen in California after Prop 209.

The *Hopwood* decision had led to the Top 10 Percent Plan, whereby the top 10 percent of every high school graduating class in Texas was guaranteed admission to one of the state universities. All who supported the Top 10 Percent Plan had one goal in common—get minority enrollments back to where they had been at the time of *Hopwood,* and the plan seemed to work. In the seven years following its passage, the University of Texas system witnessed a 15 percent increase in African American students and a 10 percent jump in Latinos. The thirty-five schools involved also became more regionally diverse and saw a rise not only in minority enrollment but also in students from poor rural areas and cities. Students entering through the plan seemed to do as well as those admitted under regular criteria.

The admissions office revamped its procedures to take in as many factors as possible aside from the standard GPA and SAT scores. The Austin campus developed a "personal achievement index" that included extracurricular activities, awards and honors, work experience, service to the school and community, and special circumstances, such as socioeconomic status and the language spoken at home. By 2002, the pre-1996 minority undergraduate levels had for the most part been achieved. The Top 10 Percent Plan did not, of course, apply to graduate school, and while Hispanic registration at UT Law returned to its pre-*Hopwood* level, the percentage of African Americans dropped. In other schools in the system, both Latino and black enrollments, while increasing, had still not achieved their pre-1996 levels.

FOLLOWING THE SUPREME COURT'S decision in the Michigan Law School case in 2003, UT reestablished an affirmative action plan. While it still took the top 10 percent automatically, it looked "holistically" at applicants who missed that cutoff, evaluating a wide range of considerations, including extracurricular activities, service to school and community, and race. Race and ethnicity were not assigned any specific numerical value, but UT openly committed itself to increasing minority enrollment with the goal of achieving what it called a "critical mass."

It was into this system that Abigail Fisher applied to the University of Texas, seeking admission to the class entering in the fall of 2008. That year, 29,501 people applied, and from this group the school admitted 12,843, of which 6,715 accepted and enrolled. Fisher did not get admission, leading her to contact Edward Blum. Fisher challenged not the Top 10 Percent Plan, which was facially race neutral, but the holistic review, which included race as a factor.

Edward Blum, a former stockbroker, ran a one-man show, the Project on Fair Representation. Funded by conservative donors, Blum sought out plaintiffs to challenge minority preference programs. He had been looking in vain for almost three years when his old friend Richard Fisher called to tell him that Abigail had not been admitted, and they believed it was because she was white. Blum put the Fishers into contact with a high-priced but politically sympathetic Washington lawyer, Burt W. Rein, who agreed to work for a lower than normal rate that would be billed to the Project on Fair Representation's sponsors.

Blum, a 1973 UT graduate, operates out of a simple two-story frame house on Penobscot Bay, Maine, and also holds an unpaid fellowship with the conservative American Enterprise Institute in Washington. A self-admitted former liberal, over time Blum came to believe that race-based programs violated the very equality they supposedly addressed. As for affirmative action, he claims that it treats whites unfairly and stigmatizes minorities.

In an interview with Adam Liptak of *The New York Times,* Blum said it was difficult to get plaintiffs, because most teenagers want to avoid the high level of scrutiny a case will engender, and so he was delighted to get Abigail Fisher. He also explained that he had started a series of websites seeking plaintiffs. "Were you denied admission to the University of North Carolina?" one asks. "It may be because you're the wrong race." The site features a picture of a student who appears to be Asian American. Blum also had sites targeting Harvard and the University of Wisconsin at Madison.

There is more than a little irony in the fact that the University of Texas refused Abigail Fisher admittance not because of her race but because of her grades. In fact, in all of the legal filings by Rein and his associates, there is no argument that race cost Fisher her spot at UT; instead, they attacked the holistic part of the UT process that took race into account and claimed that it did not meet the strict standard of scrutiny that the Supreme Court required in any program using racial classification. Blum and his allies worked very hard to make Abigail Fisher out as a victim of racial prejudice. They claimed she had done everything right—worked hard, earned good grades, engaged in a variety of extracurricular activities—and had been denied admission for one reason only, her race.

The year Fisher applied turned out to be one of stiff competition

Justice Sonia Sotomayor, appointed by President Obama in 2009, is a self-proclaimed "affirmative action baby" and has become the Court's most forceful voice in upholding diversity plans.

for admission to UT, with students admitted under the Top 10 Percent Plan taking up 92 percent of the available seats. Fisher had not graduated in the top 10 percent, so she had to compete for one of the remaining 841 openings. The school's rejection rate for applicants applying for these seats proved to be higher than the turndown rate for students trying to get into Harvard.

Fisher had a grade point average of 3.59 and SAT scores of 1,180, good but not great for the highly selective UT-Austin campus. It is true that UT offered provisional admission to some students with lower test scores and grades than Fisher. Five of them were black or Latino; 42 were white. Blum and Rein also did not mention that 168 black and Latino students with grades as good as or better than Fisher's had also been denied admission that year. They also ignored the fact that Fisher turned down a standard UT offer under which she could have transferred to the Austin campus in her sophomore year if she maintained a 3.2 GPA at another UT school in her freshman year. Even Blum had to admit to a reporter that "there are some Anglo students who had lower grades than Abby who were admitted also, but litigation like this is not a black and white paradigm."

THE UNIVERSITY OF TEXAS argued that its admissions procedures, which took race into account for only one part of the entering class, met the standard the Supreme Court had set in the Michigan Law School case, and asked for summary judgment—that is, the judge hearing the case to find for the university without holding a full trial. The district court agreed and termed the university's use of race as "a factor of a factor of a factor." The Court of Appeals for the Fifth Circuit affirmed, holding that the *Grutter* decision required courts to give substantial deference to the university, both in defining its compelling interest of diversity and in deciding if its plan had been narrowly tailored to achieve that result. Fisher asked for a rehearing en banc—that is, with all of the Fifth Circuit's judges hearing the case—and over the dissent of seven justices the court denied that request. Fisher then appealed to the U.S. Supreme Court, which granted cert and heard oral argument on 10 October 2012.

Although the inner workings of the high court are usually shrouded in secrecy, every now and then the veil is pulled aside. Thanks to Joan Biskupic, part of the band of Supreme Court reporters, we know what happened in the eight and a half months between oral argument and the announcement of the decision on 24 June

2013. The Court's membership at the time included Samuel Alito, appointed by President George W. Bush and considered by some the most conservative justice, more so even than Antonin Scalia, Clarence Thomas, or Chief Justice John Roberts. It also included two Obama appointees, Sonia Sotomayor and Elena Kagan, but Kagan had to recuse herself because she had worked on the case during the time she had served as solicitor general. The formal opinion showed a 7–1 majority, but all it did was send the case back to the lower courts, instructing them not to defer to the university but to apply the same standard used in all racial classification cases, strict scrutiny.

According to Biskupic, the original vote stood at 5–3 to void the Texas plan. The chief justice assigned the majority opinion to Anthony Kennedy. Justices Ginsburg, Breyer, and Sotomayor voted to uphold UT, and as the senior justice in dissent Ginsburg assigned Sotomayor the opinion that would speak for three of them. Sotomayor then circulated a passionate and polarizing draft, one that essentially charged the majority with being racist. Then, Biskupic reported, there followed a long series of negotiations, with "Sotomayor as agitator, Breyer as broker, and Kennedy as compromiser," working out a minimalist opinion that Sotomayor could accept. Seven members signed on to Kennedy's brief opinion. Scalia and Thomas also concurred to make clear they would welcome the opportunity to overturn the Court's affirmative action precedents. Only Justice Ginsburg held out and in a lone dissent said she thought the UT plan constitutional.

BY THIS TIME, Abigail Fisher had graduated from another school and entered the workforce, and Justice Sotomayor had in fact raised that issue during oral argument: Was there still a case or controversy, or had the case become moot? Rein had responded that so long as UT used race, it violated the Constitution, and the conservative justices agreed. So back it went, and although the reasoning now used the standard of strict scrutiny, the lower-court results were the same. Without remanding it further, the Court of Appeals for the Fifth Circuit again affirmed summary judgment for the university. The circuit court spoke through Judge Patrick E. Higginbotham, who had been appointed to the bench in 1982 by President Reagan and was one of the federal judiciary's most respected senior judges. His forty-one-page opinion carefully examined and explained UT's rationales for its choices.

The Top 10 Percent Plan, although not under attack, had been mentioned in Justice Ginsburg's dissent in *Fisher I,* and Higginbotham explained why the university, once it had accepted students under that plan, had to go further. Although the plan is racially neutral, it is "exquisitely race-aware" and produced diversity only because so many public schools in Texas are overwhelmingly white or black/Hispanic. In Dallas, for example, only 4.6 percent of the students in public schools were white. As a result, some highly qualified students from good schools (such as Fisher claimed to be) miss the cutoff and may be excluded, and some of the top students from underfunded, low-achieving schools may arrive at Austin poorly prepared to do college-level work. "The reality is that the strength of the Top Ten Percent Plan," Higginbotham noted, "is also its weakness, one that with its single dimension of selection makes it unworkable alone." Therefore the university, in order to achieve diversity, had to go beyond the automatic admissions and reach into the remaining pool of applicants to seek minority as well as nonminority students with good records. Here, the university did look at race, but in a minor and very limited way that met the requirements of strict scrutiny.

As Higginbotham framed the issue, the case presented not a broad question of affirmative action but a far narrower one of a Texas-specific plan, and a small portion of that plan. Once UT went beyond the automatic admits, it used a holistic review on a very small part of its entering class. Should the Supreme Court find this aspect of the plan unconstitutional, how would that square with its decision in the Michigan Law School case, where it upheld a fully holistic review? Higginbotham's opinion gave the Court a much different perspective from that put forward by Abigail Fisher's legal team.

The Supreme Court heard oral argument on 9 December 2015, and it looked as if the vote would go 5–3 against the university, with Justice Kagan still recusing. Justice Scalia riled many supporters of affirmative action when he raised the mismatching theory and questioned whether black students admitted to top-tier schools suffer because the courses are too difficult. "There are those who contend that it does not benefit African-Americans to get into the University of Texas, where they do not do well, as opposed to having them go to a less-advanced school, a slower-track school where they do well," he suggested. Citing one of the briefs, he noted that "most of the black scientists in this country don't come from schools like the University of Texas. They come from lesser schools where they do not feel they're being pushed ahead in classes that are too fast for them." The comments led to an outcry from UT's African American students, and on the other side spurred the creation of the Twitter hashtag #StayMadAbby.

Then, on 13 February 2016, Antonin Scalia, who had served on the Court since 1986, suddenly died, and the Republican leader of the Senate, Mitch McConnell of Kentucky, declared that the Senate would not even consider an Obama appointment to replace Scalia. The Court would have to make do with eight justices until "the people have spoken" in the 2016 presidential election. This still left, it appeared, four votes against the UT plan, three in favor, and Kagan recusing.

The Court did indeed hand down a 4–3 decision, but one upholding the UT plan. Justice Anthony Kennedy wrote the majority opinion, joined by Ginsburg, Breyer, and Sotomayor. Justice Alito, joined by Chief Justice Roberts and Clarence Thomas, dissented, and Thomas also entered a separate dissent.

Kennedy explained that the opinion in *Fisher I* had set out three controlling principles: first, there had to be strict scrutiny of all affirmative action admissions processes; second, courts should defer to a university's "reasoned explanation" of why it chose to pursue student body diversity; and third, courts should not defer to university claims that the admissions process is narrowly tailored, but must examine that claim under strict scrutiny standards. He then noted the unique nature of UT's combination of the Top 10 Percent Plan and holistic evaluation of other applications. The Court found the data on resulting diversity limited and suggested that UT should regularly evaluate available data and make changes when necessary.

As for the plaintiff's four arguments, Kennedy found them unconvincing. First, the Court held the university's rationale for diversity goals sufficiently articulated. Second, in the seven years between *Hopwood* and the implementation of the new system, the race-neutral policies and increased outreach programs had failed to achieve the desired diversity. Third, while UT did take race into account, its use "has had a meaningful, if still limited, effect on the diversity of the University's freshman class," and such a limited effect should be seen as "a hallmark of narrow tailoring, not evidence of unconstitutionality." Finally, the petitioners had failed "to offer any meaningful way in which the University could have improved" its prior race-neutral efforts to achieve diversity.

Samuel Alito's lengthy fifty-one-page dissent, joined by Roberts and Thomas, dismissed the university's efforts at diversity as "shifting, unpersuasive, and, at times, less than candid." "This is affirmative action gone berserk," he charged, "based on offensive and unsupported stereotypes." Justice Thomas's separate and brief dissent repeated the ideas he had expressed in his *Fisher I* concurrence, namely, that "a State's use of race in higher education admissions decisions is categorically prohibited by the Equal Protection Clause."

The big question is why did Anthony Kennedy switch sides? As Justice Alito pointed out in his dissent, in 1989 Kennedy, who had joined the Court in 1988, had written in an affirmative action case that "the moral imperative of racial neutrality is the driving force of the Equal Protection Clause." In 2003, Kennedy criticized the affirmative action program at the University of Michigan. "Racial and ethnic distinctions of any sort are inherently suspect and thus call for the most exacting judicial examination." In fact, prior to his opinion in *Fisher II,* Kennedy had voted against every race-based affirmative action program that had come before the high court in his tenure. Theories abounded, but this was not the first time Kennedy had shifted to the left. Court watchers believe that one of the trademark characteristics of Kennedy's jurisprudence was a willingness to reexamine old doctrines, and in fact a biography of him is titled *The Tie Goes to Freedom.*

PREDICTABLY, REACTION TO the decision depended on how one viewed preferential programs. Justin Driver, who had been a law professor at UT when the case began and then moved to Chicago, believed the decision "signals that affirmative action is safe not only at the University of Texas but around the country." He had thought that the unique nature of the Top 10 Percent Plan and the holistic review would have made the UT plan vulnerable in the courts. But if it could survive this much judicial scrutiny, then it is doubtful that the court would strike down any other plan in the near future.

Marisa Bono, a lawyer with the Mexican American Legal Defense and Educational Fund, hailed the decision as a "green light" for colleges to proceed with race-conscious admissions policies. *Fisher II* sends "a clear and resounding message that UT and other institutions of higher education may consider race in the admissions process," provided they can show a narrow tailoring.

President Obama also praised the ruling and said that the high court had "upheld the basic notion that diversity is an important value in our society. . . . We are not a country that guarantees equal outcomes, but we do strive to provide an equal shot to everybody." The Education and Justice Departments put out another guidance document regarding the Court's findings and urged schools to strive for a more diverse student body.

When contacted, Abigail Fisher expressed disappointment that the Court had approved UT's different treatment of applicants because of race. "I hope the nation will one day move beyond affirmative action."

Edward Blum of the Project on Fair Representation called the decision a "sad step backward for the original, color-blind principles in our civil rights laws." At the time, Blum was also sponsoring challenges to the admissions policies at Harvard and the University of North Carolina and described the *Fisher II* ruling as narrow enough that other lawsuits could be successful.

One month after the decision, two scholars released the results of their study regarding race relations in the country, and one of their conclusions was that whites now thought that bias against white people constituted more of a problem than bias against blacks.

CHAPTER 20

YES...AND NO...AND TRUMP

There are instances where affirmative action is essential and times when it is unnecessary. There are techniques of affirmative action that are highly questionable and means that are easily defended. A meaningful discussion of affirmative action must therefore focus on context. Unfortunately, that is what has been all too often lacking in debates about affirmative action.

—DEAN ERWIN CHEMERINSKY

All the pieces of the affirmative action puzzle do not, unfortunately, fit neatly together so that one can offer the reader a coherent picture at the end. For all the studies done over the past half century, there are still gaps for which no reliable data exists. The Supreme Court has heard many cases involving race- or gender-specific plans in education and the workplace and has been unable to come to any definite rule on what is constitutional. As of this writing, the Court has recognized diversity as a "compelling" interest, and race can be one factor of a holistic assessment in seeking a varied student body. But both the Michigan and the Texas cases were decided by a one-vote margin, and the addition of one or more conservative justices could easily reverse that holding. Politicians have been no help, and once you say that as a rule Democrats support compensatory programs and diversity while Republicans oppose them, that is the limit of any generalities one can make. Recent polls show that conservatives, by wide margins, believe enough has been done to help African Americans.

Do people of color, women, and other minority groups support affirmative action? Yes . . . and No, depending on how the questions are phrased and who the respondents are.

Have white males been victimized by affirmative action programs?

Have whites in general been deprived of jobs or places in universities because of a push for diversity? Again, Yes . . . and No.

Have women, blacks, and other minorities benefited from compensatory programs or efforts to achieve diversity? Yes . . . and No.

Nearly everyone claims that affirmative action is a "temporary" measure, but how long should it last? Justice Sandra Day O'Connor, in the Michigan Law School case, thought the goals would be reached in twenty-five years; Justice Thurgood Marshall is reported to have said one hundred years. Benjamin Hooks of the NAACP believed that it should be a permanent part of our society.

Do affirmative action programs demean their beneficiaries, leading minorities and women to feel inferior and making the white male population see them that way as well? Apparently, for some women and minority members the answer is Yes, while for others it is No. This is an area where all we have are anecdotes and accusatory essays, but no hard and reliable data.

Can we expect the social and political divisions over affirmative action to continue into the foreseeable future? Will some politicians continue to use affirmative action as a wedge issue to further deepen the chasms in our society? Even historians like myself who normally avoid predicting what is ahead would have to answer Yes to both questions.

THE MOST IMPORTANT INQUIRY is whether African Americans—whose plight called affirmative action into existence—have benefited.

Art Fletcher, the assistant secretary of labor in the Nixon administration and its point man for affirmative action, claimed that one-third of black Americans used the Civil Rights Act and presidential orders "to position themselves in middle-class America." The only ones who did not make it, he charged, were those who did not try.

Professor Orlando Patterson of Harvard also believes that affirmative action has worked to foster an African American and Latino middle class. Corporate America "has . . . embraced the policy, mostly by choice. As a result, minorities make up a large part of the middle and top ranks at many of the country's most recognizable firms." *Fortune* magazine's 2003 poll of the fifty best companies for minorities found that one out of every four managers and officials were people of color. Patterson credited affirmative action for transforming the American military, making it "the most ethnically varied at all levels of its organization of all the world's great forces."

Anecdotal evidence, of which there is plenty, attests to the successes of affirmative action, but anecdotes cut both ways. In the early 1980s, for example, Harvard, under pressure from the U.S. Department of Education, coerced its programs into hiring women and minorities. The economics department had never had a person of color or a woman as a tenured professor, but orders were orders. The search committee found an African American the department was willing to hire as a tenured professor. Glenn Loury, a full professor at the University of Michigan with a PhD from MIT, accepted Harvard's offer. Apparently, Loury never felt "at home" in the department and he resented that deeply, believing his colleagues disliked him for racist reasons. He transferred to another department and eventually left Harvard altogether. He complained loudly about how affirmative action had injured him, and he became a bitter critic of the program. It is difficult to sort out whether affirmative action, racism, or just a clash of personalities caused Loury's trouble.

There have, of course, been studies done—hundreds of them. Several found that the employment of African Americans by federal contractors grew more rapidly than in firms that did not have such contracts and were therefore free from government oversight. Prior to the 1970s, minority employment usually meant working in unskilled and lower-paying positions, such as pick-and-shovel jobs or as janitors. That changed so that, at least in firms under compliance contracts, people of color could be found in nearly all occupational categories except the highly technical and in some crafts where union rules shut them out. Moreover, studies found less job discrimination in firms adhering to federal guidelines.

Harry Holzer of Georgetown University and David Neumark of Michigan State performed the most systematic exploration of whether affirmative action worked. The two economists reviewed over two hundred serious scientific studies of the topic and conceded that because of different methods and goals the evidence remained murky in spots. Nonetheless, they found that affirmative action produced tangible benefits for women, minority entrepreneurs, students, and workers for the overall economy. Employers who adopted the program—either voluntarily or under government pressure—increased the number of women and people of color by between 10 and 15 percent. Affirmative action had boosted the percentage of blacks attending college by a factor of three, and those enrolled in medical school by a factor of four since the early 1960s. Between

1982 and 1991—the Reagan-Bush years—the number of federal contracts going to black-owned businesses rose by 125 percent, even though the total number of federal contracts rose in that period by less than 25 percent. In addition, even when employers hired blacks and Hispanics who lagged on credentials (such as education) compared with whites, within a short time they were performing as well as nonminority employees.

Despite these findings, opponents of affirmative action claimed that it has not worked at all. Abigail and Stephan Thernstrom maintain that the real progress took place earlier. Between 1948 and 1973, the gross national product grew at an average of 2.3 percent a year, a third higher than the average for the preceding eight decades. "Millions of working people, white and black, saw their incomes rise above the poverty level." In addition to the boom times, African Americans benefited from increased educational opportunities as well as the Second Great Migration, in which millions of blacks moved out of rural poverty in the South and into bustling northern cities with their great opportunities unmarked by Jim Crow. In fact, black economic strides continued until affirmative action became widespread, and progress in reducing black poverty ground to a halt. While affirmative action is not the only cause of contemporary black poverty, the Thernstroms do not believe it has helped any but a few talented African Americans who would in any case have made it on their own.

(The Thernstroms' view, it should be noted, runs counter to the classic study of race relations in the North during and after the Great Migration. Professor Arnold Hirsch detailed the abuse and discrimination African Americans faced in Chicago and how racism permeated every stratum of American society. According to Ta-Nehisi Coates, if one wants to understand the current racial unrest in northern cities, "Arnold Hirsch is telling you why.")

Thomas Sowell was, and remains, the foremost African American critic of affirmative action, and especially how governmental agencies—including the Supreme Court—ignored the plain language of the Civil Rights Act as well as of the Fourteenth Amendment's Equal Protection Clause to transform a legitimate effort at outreach (what I have termed "soft") into quotas ("hard") that were expressly forbidden by the law and the Constitution. Like the Thernstroms, he believes that African Americans had done well before 1964: "The percentage of employed blacks who were professional and technical workers rose less in the five years following the Civil Rights Act of 1964 than in the five years preceding it. The percentage of employed blacks who were managers and administrators was the same in 1967 as in 1964—and in 1960." The history of Asians and Hispanics, he claims, also showed long-term upward trends that began years before 1964.

Although they list many things they believed "wrong" about affirmative action, Carl Cohen and James Sterba considered one of its greatest sins the lingering sense of inferiority it gave to minority candidates seeking jobs or admission to school. Others, like the Yale professor Stephen L. Carter, do not shy away from the problems that he and other black professionals face, but at the same time he believes that without affirmative action they would not have had the opportunities they did. He received advanced professional training at one of the finest law schools in the country, and "I like to think that I have made the most of this privilege. So, yes, I *am* an affirmative action baby, and I do not apologize for that fact."

The problem is that there is absolutely no data on how many African Americans, women, Hispanics, or people with disabilities gained entrance to college or secured a job because of affirmative action. Not every woman, person of color, or wheelchair user is an affirmative action admit or hire. If a college employed what I have called a "soft" plan, consisting entirely of outreach to groups that had previously been barred or just not considered and then found minorities with the GPA and test scores that would qualify for admission, or if a company found someone with abilities that the firm needed, they certainly should not be considered affirmative action admits or hires. The bank that employs a Latina may do so for no other reason than that it needs someone who speaks fluent Spanish at one of its branches. The company that hires a person using a wheelchair may have a policy of giving preference to veterans. While it is possible that others see the Latina or the veteran as less qualified, that is another part of the puzzle that cannot be answered. There are many anecdotes, but they are hardly reliable evidence. Moreover, people who are currently admitted to college or to a job may very well be second-generation college goers from a middle-class family or have successfully completed a program that makes them eminently qualified for a job.

What about students or people offered jobs as a result of a "hard" program, with goals or quotas? Many companies say that they no longer use quotas, because they have plenty of qualified minorities applying for jobs and sufficient minorities already on the payroll to show new job seekers that the company does not discriminate. Under *Fisher II,* the last case decided by the Supreme Court on affirmative action, colleges may use race as one of several factors that go into the admissions process, but it cannot be the only or even the main consideration. Given the *Fisher* decision, it would be foolhardy if not out and out stupid for schools to do what they did back in the 1970s, putting minority applications in a special pile and using less stringent criteria for them.

College admissions, with a few exceptions, have never been simple. Schools field athletic teams and have a daily newspaper, a strong dramatics program, and many other activities. They may also have a long-standing legacy program, and these days it is far more likely that a student will get into a college with below-average scores not because she is a minority but because one or both of her parents attended that school.

(Interestingly, now that there are more and more minority candidates whose parents are college graduates, they could well be considered part of the legacy pool. Ashton Lattimore, a lawyer in Philadelphia, believes that her race probably served as a plus factor in her admission to Harvard. She agrees that in theory legacy admissions should be considered wrong, but should her son, if he applies to Harvard, be denied the benefit of legacy because Harvard admits the children of its alumni at a rate more than five times that of non-legacies?)

While the goal of diversity has been criticized by opponents of affirmative action, diversity in education is a value worth respecting. The whole purpose of a liberal arts education is to make a person think, to try to understand ideas and cultures different from his or her own, and to see people with a different-colored skin not as an "Other" to be feared but as a person with values worth knowing.

Proponents of economic analysis say that affirmative action reduces economic efficiency in two ways: it forces firms to allocate resources to comply with regulations that yield little in the way of tangible benefits, and it compels employers to hire minority workers less qualified than nonminority workers. Peter Brimelow and Leslie Spencer argue that affirmative action reduced the country's gross national product by a whopping 4 percent! Glenn Loury also believes that affirmative action makes no sense economically, because it has blocked minorities from acquiring the skills they need to succeed in jobs or schools. Few economists have gone this far, and there are plenty of studies that have argued just the contrary—that affirmative action has increased the productivity of the workforce.

But affirmative action has always been far more than an economics program. The criticisms of the people just mentioned are unfortunately typical of the way many economists look at social, political, and cultural problems, as if they were distractions from an economic paradigm that is the only reliable guide. If nothing else, affirmative action can only be understood in a multidimensional context. Moreover, there are studies demonstrating that affirmative action hires quickly become useful members of the workforce and increase a company's productivity.

We can acknowledge that because of affirmative action some minorities got jobs they might not otherwise have secured or received a letter of admission from a college that might not otherwise have taken them, but the fact remains that after more than half a century of race-conscious programs, there still is no economic parity between African Americans and whites.

A 2017 study by the Kaiser Family Foundation found an overall level of poverty in the United States of 13 percent. (The Census Bureau defines the poverty threshold for a family with two adults and one child as $20,160.) While 9 percent of whites fell below this line, 22 percent of blacks and 20 percent of Hispanics were classified as poor. In some states, black poverty ran even higher—29 percent in Arkansas and Indiana, 30 percent in Louisiana, 36 in Mississippi, and 38 in Minnesota. All told, of the 41 million Americans known to be living in poverty in 2016, 8.7 million were black and 11.3 million Hispanic, percentages well above their share of the population.

According to a study released by the Economic Policy Institute in February 2018, little has changed in the fifty years since the Kerner Commission Report in 1968 identified "white racism" as the key cause of "pervasive discrimination in employment, education, and housing." In some areas, African Americans are worse off today than before the civil rights movement. The black unemployment rate stood at 7.5 percent in 2017, compared with 6.7 percent in 1968, in both instances roughly twice that of white unemployment. The rate of black home ownership has remained virtually unchanged, at 40 percent, thirty points behind whites. The median net worth of white families, $171,000, is ten times that of black families.

Another marker that clearly shows the economic discrepancy between whites and people of color is the distribution of wealth in the United States. Aside from the debate over the 1 percent versus everyone else, the country has a huge and growing racial wealth gap, a fact that even opponents of affirmative action concede. According to the latest studies (2017), white households in the middle-income quintile own nearly eight times as much wealth as middle-income black earners, and ten times as much as middle-income Latinos.

Nor is this a new phenomenon. During the Jim Crow years, a majority of African Americans lived on southern farms, often as tenants subject to ruthless exploitation by white landowners. Beginning in the New Deal and on into the postwar years, the federal government invested heavily to help ordinary Americans buy homes through programs like the Federal Housing Administration and the GI Bill, but very little of this assistance went to people of color. Redlining by banks and government agencies prevented many black Americans from buying homes, and in a thirty-year period just 2 percent of FHA loans went to black families, while the GI Bill disproportionately benefited white veterans. If you have less wealth to start with, any additional income goes to paying down debt rather than saving or investing. A 2013 study found that for white families every dollar increase in income yields an increase of $5.19 in wealth, while for black households the figure is just sixty-nine cents.

Since 1983, black and Latino families have seen their wealth fall considerably from $6,800 and $4,000, respectively, to just $1,700 and $2,000 in 2013. Even though white households took a hit during the 2008 financial crisis, they still had a median wealth of $116,800 in 2013. Moreover, the gap is widening. Researchers project that by 2024 black wealth will decline 30 percent, Latinos will experience a 20 percent drop, while white households will have a five-point increase. If current trends continue, it will take 228 years for the average middle-class black family to reach the same level of wealth that white families have today, and 84 years for Latinos.

The figures are even more dismal for earnings. In the lowest quintile, white earnings rose from $20,000 to $26,000 between 1967 and 2015 (numbers in 2015 dollars), while black earnings went from $11,000 to $14,000. In terms of black income as a percentage of white income, in three out of the five quintiles the gap worsened. Even in the highest group, where the median black family income was $150,000, the difference has grown greater, not smaller. Black income ranges from 53 percent in the lowest quintile to 67 percent in the highest. Michelle Singletary, a columnist for *The Washington Post,* has a son in college, and she is worried about his future, because every study indicates that 99 percent of black youth, even those from two-parent middle-class households, will grow up to earn less than white boys.

There are, however, some positive figures as well. In the decade before Barack Obama became president, the Census Bureau reported that the number of African American adults with advanced degrees had doubled. Half a million more black students were in college in 2008 than in the early 1990s. Between 1989 and 2008, the median income of black families had increased more than 16 percent in constant dollars. The gap in test scores between black and white students had narrowed. The black middle class had never been so large. All of this may be true, but the overall figures on income and wealth make these numbers appear as a rosy anomaly rather than a general rule.

So, did affirmative action work? Yes, for some minority members— and there were many of them—who were able to get jobs that they probably would not have gotten otherwise, or who entered colleges that previously would have barred them, or who had test scores that might not otherwise have qualified them. But did it raise all African Americans to a near parity with their white neighbors? Did it eliminate the huge economic gulf in education and earnings that has afflicted black America? To this the answer must be No.

DO AMERICANS IN GENERAL support affirmative action, and more specifically do women and people of color? In the African American community, there are clearly powerful voices in opposition—Justice Clarence Thomas, Thomas Sowell, Shelby Steele, and Glenn Loury, to name a few. Their argument, as noted before, is not only does it not work, but it demeans the men and women who get jobs or places in a school because others will assume that affirmative action hires or admits have inferior intelligence or skills, no matter how bright and talented they may be. Loury believes that enough strides have been made by the black middle class that "the time has come for us to let go of the ready-made excuse that racism provides [for failure]. It is time to accept responsibility for what we and our children do, and do not, achieve."

Nonetheless, the most recent polls (2003–2017) found not only blacks and Hispanics in favor of affirmative action but a majority of whites as well. In the general population, in 2003, 60 percent thought affirmative action to help "blacks, women and other minorities" a "good" thing, and 30 percent considered it "bad." In 2014, 63 percent rated it "good," and 30 percent "bad." By 2017, 71 percent favored affirmative action, and only 22 percent opposed. In the 2014 poll, 55 percent of whites supported and 36 percent opposed; the comparable numbers for African Americans were 84 and 8, and for Hispanics 80 and 15. While conservative Republicans oppose any further programs for people of color, overall 61 percent of Americans in 2017 believe that minorities still need some forms of compensatory aid.

But if a majority of Americans agree that affirmative action in general is good, they differ when the pollsters ask about preferential treatment for women and minorities. Even when the questions do not use the word, for most people the phrase "preferential treatment" means "quotas." Two out of three respondents opposed special treatment, and among whites three out of four were against. African Americans, however, were in favor by a 58–36 margin, and Hispanics by 53–35. As one commentator noted, "The degree to which people in general are in favor of affirmative action largely depends on how that policy is described."

There are also differences when the questions are about affirmative action for women. A majority of Americans believe that discrimination against blacks and Hispanics is worse than that suffered by women. A November 2014 poll said that 68 percent of African Americans face "a lot or some discrimination," while only 57 percent said the same about women. Yet a Gallup poll in August 2015 found that every group—men, women, whites, blacks, and Hispanics—all favored affirmative action for women more than they did for minorities. Even African Americans favored plans for women over those for minorities 80–77, and so did Republicans, 51–38, and while Democrats strongly supported both, they favored women 83–76.

Although the conventional wisdom has it that women—especially white women—benefited the most from affirmative action, the numbers show that women of any color have not yet achieved parity with white males. In 2013, American women made eighty-two cents for every dollar a man made, and eighty cents for every dollar made by a white male, up from seventy-nine and seventy-seven cents, respectively, in 2012. White and Asian people, male or female, make more than African Americans and Hispanics, regardless of their gender.

Having a college education or an advanced degree certainly increased opportunity for whites and Asians, but in both instances women lagged behind, although Asian women outearned white women.

A study in the *Harvard Business Review* also demolished the myth that companies paid more to secure women of color, because "twofers" could be counted in more than one category for affirmative action reports to the federal government. In fact, black and Hispanic women stood in last place on the earnings pyramid at every educational level. When corporations undertake pay equity analyses, the employees whose salaries are greater than two standard deviations higher than their predicted pay (based on job-related variables) are invariably white men.

Black women report that while it is certainly easier to get through the door and be hired, many of them claim that it is tough to work in what remains a primarily white environment. It is not overt harassment so much as women feel they are always on display, always being tested. Earlier we spoke of how white students believed that their black classmates had gotten into college on affirmative action and therefore did not meet regular standards. It is less that white men harass black women or put them down than that they ignore them, don't say hello back, or do not hold an elevator. As Ymani Wince wrote, "At a time when companies are hiring a more diverse crop of employees, it's difficult to feel like I belong in such a space, when being at work feels like the outside world, just more closeted and muted."

THERE IS NO QUESTION that affirmative action programs have benefited some women—white, black, and Hispanic—just as they have benefited some African American and Hispanic males. As one writer suggested, just look at the pictures of graduating classes in law and medical schools from a generation ago and today, the former nearly all male and white, the latter with women and people of color.

This does not mean that there were no problems for women who are in previously all-male positions. As Barbara Bergmann points out, we do not know how often women, blacks, Latinos, and other minorities face hostility, because it is impossible to gather those statistics. There is, however, sufficient anecdotal evidence to show that it happens often enough. The reaction is not limited to blue-collar work, but occurs in pink-collar, white-collar, and professional levels as well.

Moreover, while we can point to numerous instances of the "first" woman to enter law school or become a highway repair dispatcher or a hog buyer, the influx of women into schools and jobs that had heretofore been closed to them coincided not only with the government's adoption of affirmative action for federal contractors but also with hundreds of thousands of women flooding into the job market as a result of better education, the women's movement, or the need to help with family finances. For this reason, any statistical study of, say, federal contract compliance regarding women can lead to mixed results. For example, one study reported that contract compliance improved women's access to previously male jobs, while another showed that white women (as well as black women and men) were significantly less likely to hold white-collar jobs for federal contractors than for non-contractors. One review of all the studies on women and federal contract compliance simply concluded that the results were mixed.

White women, for the most part, do not share the views of African Americans and Hispanics on affirmative action and do not believe that their own principal interests would be at risk if either the federal government abandoned the program or courts found it unlawful. One significant difference is that unlike the stories told by people of color of their white colleagues or classmates questioning their abilities, only 8 percent of white women stated that their "colleagues at work or school privately questioned" their qualifications due to affirmative action, compared with 19 percent of black women and 28 percent of black men. Less than one in five white women in the poll listed workplace discrimination as a "major problem," compared with 41 percent of African Americans and 38 percent of Latinos. In fact, 40 percent of white women declared job discrimination as "not being a problem" at all. As one writer concluded, these results may explain why liberal feminist leaders and their primarily white middle-class constituencies have been relatively less vocal than blacks and Hispanics in defending affirmative action.

For all the strides women have made, the glass ceiling still exists. As of 2017, there were thirty-two female CEOs among the Fortune 500 companies, meaning 6.4 percent of the nation's biggest companies (by revenue) were run by women. This is the highest proportion of female CEOs in the sixty-three-year history of *Fortune*'s listing. They ran a diverse range of companies, from consumer goods (PepsiCo) to defense contractors (Lockheed Martin), but of the thirty-two only two were people of color, Geisha Williams of PG&E and Indra

Nooyi of PepsiCo; none of them were African American. One can, of course, look at this number in two ways: one is that women have come a long way in getting to the top, and the other is to ask why there are not more women in executive suites.

In a previous chapter, I mentioned the memorandum at Google charging that women were biologically unsuited to be engineers, and the firing of its writer, James Damore. One would, however, want to know why Silicon Valley, which claims—indeed boasts of—how it rewards innovation, thinks outside the box, provides wonderful day-care facilities, and so on, is nonetheless, in the words of one writer, "so awful to women." Although the major tech companies annually post the steps they have made in hiring women and other minorities, how they are closing the pay gap, and how they are spending hundreds of millions of dollars to improve conditions for their female employees, women leave the tech companies at twice the rate that men do. The reasons given are that they are not taken seriously and that men doubt their abilities and, whenever possible, will avoid working with a woman.

A typical story is told by Bethanye Blount, then a veteran software engineer holding a senior position at Linden Lab, the company that runs Second Life, the online virtual world. One day she interviewed a job applicant who, although he knew her job title, essentially blew her off whenever she asked him a question. Afterward, Blount spoke to another top woman—a vice president—who said he had treated her the same way. But the applicant was still there, and they had a new employee, a man, who needed practice doing interviews. So they sent him in, and when he came out, he had a funny look on his face. "I don't know what just happened," he said. "I went in there and told him I was new, and all he said was he was so glad I was there: 'Finally, somebody who knows what's going on.'" Blount now says she can laugh at the experience, but it was a reminder that as a woman in a tech company she had to be prepared to have her authority and ability questioned at any moment. A survey titled "Elephant in the Valley" found that nearly all the two-hundred-plus senior women in the tech industry had experienced sexist interactions.

Where people of color seem to believe that racism is so extensive that only with the help of affirmative action can they get through the door into college or a job, women recognize that it isn't sexism that keeps them outside the door. They can get in easily enough—into college, grad school, and desirable jobs. Rather, it is once they are through that door, they find that sexism within companies—even supposedly forward-looking tech firms—is still to be fought, and affirmative action programs can do very little at that point. Did affirmative action open some opportunities for women? Yes. Have they become truly equal in getting into college and professional schools? Here again, a definite Yes. Are they treated as equals in the job market? No, even among those companies who boast about how many women they have and how well they pay them. The glass ceiling is still strong and still in place.

If any proof were needed that even if women can get through the door they still face formidable obstacles to success, one only had to look at a post on LinkedIn in early December 2018. Paul, Weiss, one of the nation's most prominent—and profitable—law firms, was "pleased to announce" its new partner class. In the image, twelve very happy new partners smiled at the world, and all but one of them was a white male! The exception was a white woman. The outburst of criticism led Paul, Weiss to take the picture down and to apologize for the "gender and racial imbalance" of its 2019 partner class.

ACCEPTED WISDOM IS THAT education is key to success in life. One study after another shows that men and women with advanced degrees earn more than those with only a college education, who in turn make more than those with just a high school diploma. Higher education will probably be the sticking point in the continuing debate over affirmative action, because in many instances admission *is* a zero-sum game. If a medical school has one hundred seats for its entering class, then if Mary gets in—for whatever reason—Johnny does not. If Mary has been accepted on any basis other than pure merit, Johnny and others like him will attack affirmative action.

Professor Randall Kennedy of Harvard believes that if the nation went back to a completely color-blind system, not only for colleges, but for many jobs, we would soon wind up with essentially an all-white police force or freshman class, a situation that many people would find "inconceivable." Most Americans, he believes, want to escape from the country's "ugly racial past. If affirmative action is required to effectuate that ambition, they will accept it, albeit in disguise." He points out that in three states that abolished color-conscious admissions and instituted a percentage basis—Texas, Florida, and California—the state schools have managed to attract and admit minorities. This is only partially true, however; the percentage of people of color at public universities in these three states is still well below what it had been earlier.

The debate on color-blind merit versus race-conscious policies is really a fruitless one. William G. Bowen and Derek Bok have argued that "merit," like "preference" and "discrimination," has taken on so much "baggage" that it is almost meaningless. Clearly schools do not want to admit applicants who lack merit; college resources are too precious to waste on someone who cannot take advantage of the educational opportunities offered. As to the argument that candidates with higher test scores and GPAs are more deserving, have worked harder, and are more intelligent, they answer that (a) test scores are not a reliable indicator of success and (b) a college education is more than getting good grades.

The College Board, which owns the Scholastic Aptitude Test (SAT), has for a number of years recognized that the test had a cultural bias that favored white, middle- and upper-class students, and has tried to remedy that. In 2019, the Board announced that it would now have an "adversity score" that would give college admissions officers information on the socioeconomic background of applicants. Using a scale of 1 to 100, with 50 as the average, the higher numbers will indicate that the student comes from a poorer background, that the area in which he or she lives is difficult or even dangerous, that the school system is poor, and so on. Lower numbers, on the other hand, will indicate that the applicant comes from a wealthier environment, one with good schools and safe streets. Whether this "adversity score" catches on is difficult to predict. William R. Fitzsimmons, the dean of admissions and financial aid at Harvard, says that the extremely careful holistic review in use there gets into many facets not only of the applicant's academic abilities, but his or her socioeconomic background as well. A fair number of schools, however, are deciding not to use standardized tests at all.

In August 2015, George Washington University, the largest school in the nation's capital, announced that it would no longer require either of the two standard admissions tests, the SAT or the ACT. GW had used a holistic admissions process for many years, and the dean of admissions, Karen Stroud Felton, explained that low SAT and ACT scores discouraged students who could succeed based on their GPAs and other factors. By this time, more than 125 private colleges and universities featured in the *U.S. News & World Report* rankings had either abandoned the tests or made them optional.

One year later, George Washington boasted that it now had the most racially diverse student body in its nearly two-hundred-year history. Of 2,523 freshmen, the African American share stood at 8.8 percent, up from 4.7 percent the year before. The Hispanic share climbed to 10.5 percent from 9.2. At the same time, the median grade point average edged up slightly, from 3.64 to 3.66, indicating there had been no decline in the quality of the new class. Interestingly, the portion of first-generation college students, many from low-income families, rose to 13.9 percent from 11.9. Nearly 60 percent of GW's students receive grants and scholarships to defray the school's annual tuition of $52,000.

In their plans for diversity, many schools are also reaching out to students from low-income families and have found that this group, whatever their color or gender, have initial adjustment problems unfamiliar to administrators. Provost Richard Locke of Brown University described how Brown, like many schools, closed its dorm and eating facilities over the Thanksgiving holiday. Brown assumed that students would want to be with their families, as they had been when they were in high school. Then a scholarship student told him that he and others did not have the money to travel home, and so they had to scramble to find places to stay and eat for the long weekend. Brown quickly rectified this problem, and it now keeps dorms and cafeterias open.

Dean Nitin Nohria of the Harvard Business School relates that it took him a long time to realize problems faced by scholarship students. Harvard and many other private schools have adopted an admissions policy that completely ignores the ability of the applicants' families to pay. Once students are admitted, the schools provide grants and scholarship aid that cover all or part of tuition, fees, books, room, and board, a number that at some schools is approaching $70,000 per year. Aside from the normal problems of students adjusting to a new environment, it seems that the scholarship students often felt excluded from campus life, for the simple reason that they had no money for social costs. Nohria says this may seem like a petty concern, but he argues that if we really want to integrate all these diverse students, then we must be inclusive; we have to give them the resources to participate in all aspects of campus life, not just the classroom.

Other schools have picked up on this theme. Princeton, for example, always considered the preppiest school in the Ivy League, has taken steps to be "less preppy" so that students who do not come from well-to-do backgrounds will not feel excluded. The school also has self-interest involved. "If we're going to be excellent, we're going to need to bring in talent from all backgrounds," according to President Christopher Eisgruber. Jonathan Haynes, an African American, is part of a group of students there pushing the university to admit more people from low-income backgrounds. Columbia, another Ivy school, and American University in Washington have also indicated that they want to diversify not just by race but by socioeconomic background as well.

"Diversity," which for a long time meant efforts to get more people of color, has in fact morphed at many American colleges into an effort to get a student body that reflects the country, in terms of not just race and gender but socioeconomic status as well. Richard Kahlenberg, a senior fellow at the Century Foundation, has long pushed to have class-based admissions replace race-based policies. He believes a race-neutral plan would create not only socioeconomic diversity but racial diversity as well.

Has affirmative action worked to make colleges and graduate schools more open to women and minorities? The answer is clearly Yes. Walk around any major school, anywhere in the country, and you will find a rainbow of colors, ethnic origins, and backgrounds, not only among students, but also among faculty and administrators.

But is all well? Alas, there the answer must be No. Schools are still learning what is necessary to integrate this rainbow into a seamless experience in which all students will not only learn in the classroom but just as important learn from their peers. And there are some dark clouds on the horizon.

A front-page story in *The New York Times* on how different colleges are trying to diversify their student bodies also notes that because different schools have different ways of holistically evaluating applications, many applicants not only are confused but believe the system is against them. Asian Americans feel that they are being held to a higher standard; white students feel similarly penalized; and people of color complain that the system is so opaque that if they do get into a good school, it must be because of their color, a marker that will trail them well after graduation. Jonathan Haynes recalls that when he told people he was going to Princeton, it was not uncommon to hear "Oh, you're going to Princeton because you are black."

Columbia accepted Daniel Alvarez, and he admits part of his

success may be due to an affirmative action plan. But he also had a sterling GPA, as well as the type of extracurricular record that schools look for. "People can think what they will, but in the end, I'm never going to really be able to know" whether race helped. "I feel like the true measure of whether or not it was really part of it will depend on how I do there. If I get there, and I'm struggling, and this isn't the sort of school that I belong at, then maybe I'll reconsider."

Schools in states that have prohibited using race, such as Michigan, Washington, California, and Florida, are trying different ways to attract minority students, and while the numbers have rebounded somewhat, in each state the number of minority students remains well below earlier percentages. Latinos, for example, make up 52 percent of high school graduates in California but only a third of students enrolling in one of the ten UC schools. In the class entering Berkeley in the fall of 2016, blacks made up only 3 percent of all undergraduates, Asian Americans 39 percent, and whites 26 percent. Ward Connerly, who engineered Proposition 209, charges that the California system's emphasis on holistic review and efforts to get in more students from low-income areas is just a smoke screen to get more African Americans.

Similar statistics apply to other states that mandate color-blind admissions. At the flagship University of Florida, the class entering in the fall of 2015 consisted of 6 percent African Americans, down from 12 percent in 2000; about 17 percent of Florida's population is black. Florida has also tried different programs to reach a wider socioeconomic base, but so far these efforts have not improved African American enrollment.

Edward Blum, whose group financed Abigail Fisher's case against the University of Texas, is now suing Harvard University over its alleged discrimination against Asian Americans. Blum claims that Harvard's holistic admissions process is primarily a means to screen out or limit undesirable groups. In fact, according to Blum, Harvard invented the holistic system to keep out Jews in the 1920s by favoring such subjective factors as "leadership" and "sociability." And it worked; Jewish enrollment plummeted.

The main statistic that Blum uses is that Asian enrollment at Harvard from 1992 to 2013 has been "remarkably stable," 19 percent of the freshman class in the earlier year, and 18 percent in the latter. This stability is "remarkable" because the number of Asian applicants to elite schools has jumped immensely in the last quarter of a

"Were You Denied Admission to Harvard?" website of Edward Blum's Students for Fair Admissions.

century, and according to Blum, Asians "make up a large percentage of the most qualified applicants." Harvard is not alone; the same flat rate of Asian admissions is seen at all the Ivy League schools, ranging between 12 and 18 percent.

Compare this with the California Institute of Technology, Blum urges, where thanks to Prop 209 race cannot be a consideration for admission. The Asian enrollment at Caltech has grown from 25 percent in 1992 to nearly 43 percent in 2013. Blum crowed with delight that the Justice Department had begun to examine claims of racial discrimination against Asian Americans in university admissions.

Researchers have found that Asian Americans need SAT scores 140 points higher than white students—all other things equal—to get into elite colleges. Moreover, teenage girls seem to study harder and get better grades and test scores than white boys, yet the college admission rate for girls was 13 percent lower than for boys. In 2014, a *Washington Post* story reported that sixty-four elite schools, including Brown, Amherst, and Wesleyan, made it harder for girls than for boys to get in. The ironic result is that the bias against Asian Americans and women essentially constitutes affirmative action for white males!

If, in fact, Harvard and other schools are deliberately holding down their percentages of Asian American students, it will be very difficult for them to rationalize it on the basis of diversity. But Harvard is a private school, admittedly one with millions of dollars in government contracts, while Caltech is public and subject to California law. According to colleagues in the California system, the big beneficiaries of Prop 209 were not white men or women but Asians. Blum had a strong advocate on his side in Trump's then attorney general, Jeff Sessions, who would have liked nothing better than to successfully sue an elite private school, one that he no doubt saw as a hotbed of liberalism.

Donald Trump is the first Republican since the civil rights revolution to reach the White House without campaigning against affirmative action. In a *Meet the Press* interview, he told Chuck Todd, "I'm fine with affirmative action. We've lived with it for a long time." When a few months later Chris Wallace on *Fox News Sunday* asked him how that view squared with conservative doctrine, Trump responded that he thought perhaps affirmative action had "served its time" and it would "be a wonderful thing" if its necessity faded. He even joined in denouncing Antonin Scalia when the justice suggested that African Americans might be better off at "less advanced schools."

On the face of it, it would appear that Trump assumed his base did not really care about affirmative action during the campaign. In fact, Trump ran the most racist campaign since that of George Wallace in 1968, but in a far more clever manner. He seemingly tried to keep arm's distance from the former Ku Klux Klan leader David Duke, but unlike just about every other national politician he never condemned Duke's views. When asked about Duke's support, Trump's answers ran along the lines of "I would do that [repudiate Duke] if it made you feel better." In an interview with Bloomberg's John Heilemann in 2015, Trump went on seemingly disingenuously to note that Duke said "I was absolutely the best of all candidates." In early 2016, Duke on his radio program declared, "I do support his candidacy, and I support voting for him. . . . I hope he does everything we hope he will do." At a news conference the next day, Trump brushed aside a question about the endorsement: "David Duke endorsed me? Okay, all right. I disavow, okay?"

Trump's vicious attack on Mexican immigrants as "rapists and murderers," his promise to build a wall on our southern border, his long-standing attacks on Barack Obama, his embrace of the white-nationalist "alt-right," and his closeness to one of its leaders, Steve Bannon—all made clear to his followers that Trump wanted to "make America great again" by returning to an older age when white males ruled the roost, people of color served them and kept quiet, and women were essentially invisible, quiet, and sex toys. Trump did not have to attack affirmative action in the campaign; his followers knew that he stood with them in opposing it.

Trump instinctively knew who would support him, and during the campaign, without overtly making racist remarks he played to their hopes but above all to their fears. In a 2013 book, Michael Kimmel described the people who would be at the heart of the Trump movement as "angry white men." According to Kimmel, one of the enduring images of the 2012 campaign was the demise of the white male voter as a dominant force in the political landscape. On right-wing radio, white men—both the show hosts and those calling in—complained that the benefits they had long known and enjoyed had been snatched away from them. They lost their jobs, their families disintegrated, their women were no longer docile, and as they looked around, people unlike them had become the favorites of society. They lamented—and Trump picked up on this—that they had always done the "right thing," that is, they had worked hard, and they had not received the rewards that had always gone to those who worked hard and lived by accepted norms. Instead of getting ahead, they had lost their jobs and their status to women, people of color, and immigrants.

Other Republican presidents, such as Reagan and the two Bushes, openly opposed affirmative action, but not in an outwardly racist manner. As we have seen, there is a principled way to oppose compensatory programs, and politicians and intellectuals across the political spectrum have done so without denigrating people of color, women, and other minorities. No other major party candidate ever made fun of people with disabilities, declared that prisoners of war or soldiers killed in combat were not heroes, or said that his Democratic opponent should be criminally investigated and sent to jail.

Neither his Republican opponents in the primaries, the Democratic candidate Hillary Clinton, nor anyone else in the general election ever fully realized that Trump would not play by the accepted norms of civility or even telling the truth. If he did not like some accusation, he labeled it "fake news." He gave his opponents demeaning nicknames, such as "Little Marco [Rubio]" or "Crooked Hillary," and his supporters ate it up. He was different; he seemed to care about the white lower class that modern economic trends had left behind. He promised to make coal king again, even though a majority of the country's power-generating plants had already switched over to gas because it was both cleaner and cheaper, and many coal jobs had become automated. He would open all those closed factories in the Rust Belt, whose closure he blamed on the Democrats, even though globalization, not Barack Obama, had sent those jobs overseas. As he once admitted, his followers believed whatever he told them. If he shot and killed someone in the middle of Fifth Avenue, they would still vote for him!

For those familiar with Isaac Asimov's classic *Foundation* series, Trump is the Mule, a mutant with powers that defy the accepted rules of history that have guided the Foundation for centuries. The Mule flouts the conventions, and his followers rejoice because he seemingly attacks the powers that be that have caused their problems and loss of status. For Trump's primarily white and working-class followers, it did not matter whether he could actually deliver on his promises. Some studies indicated that even when they recognized his lies, his supporters did not care. He was attacking the establishment that had taken away their status and had apparently made minorities and women more successful economically and important socially.

On Saturday, 12 August 2017, a white-nationalist rally in Charlottesville, Virginia (that included members of neo-Nazi groups and the Klan), got out of hand and led to rioting between them and protesters. A car driven by one of the white nationalists slammed into the protesters, killing one person and injuring nineteen others; two state troopers also died when their helicopter crashed. Nearly everyone immediately blamed the white nationalists for the violence—everyone, that is, except Donald Trump, who said that those who protested against the white nationalists were equally to blame for the violence. When some southern cities began thinking about taking down statues commemorating Confederate leaders—nearly all of them erected during the Jim Crow era—Trump made fun of the efforts. "This week it's Robert E. Lee. I noticed that Stonewall Jackson is coming down. I wonder, is George Washington and Thomas Jefferson [because they owned slaves] the week after?" Only after a huge outcry against his comments—how could he equate people protesting against the Klan and neo-Nazis with the white hooligans themselves—did he back down, but only a little. David Duke tweeted thanks to the president for his comments.

The riot occurred just a few weeks after the Justice Department announced a new project to investigate and sue universities over affirmative action policies that discriminated against white applicants.

The project would be based out of the Civil Rights Division, but not the place where such suits usually originate, the Educational Opportunities Section. Apparently, the civil service attorneys there refused to cooperate, and so the project would be run out of the front office of the division. Jeff Sessions's aides began looking to hire lawyers interested in working on "investigations and possible litigation related to intentional race-based discrimination in college and university admissions."

If Trump's followers had apparently not cared about affirmative action during the campaign, conservatives and Republican operatives quickly jumped to Sessions's defense. Linda Chavez, a foe of affirmative action since the Reagan era, called opposition to race-based programs "a long-standing conservative approach." One study found that 44 percent of people who voted for Trump saw "whites losing out because of preference for blacks and Hispanics" and that this was a bigger problem than minorities losing out. Stephen Miller and Steve Bannon, both at that time still in the White House and both part of the racist alt-right, praised Sessions. For the most part, commentators saw the move and its endorsement by senior Republican officials as one more step in trying to cement Trump's support among disaffected whites.

JOURNALIST ELLIS COSE recalled a conversation he had with a young white man, a student at Harvard, shortly after a Supreme Court case had upheld an affirmative action plan. The young man was choleric at the notion that "unqualified minorities" would dare to demand preferential treatment. "Why . . . couldn't they compete like everyone else? Why should hardworking whites like himself be pushed aside for second-rate affirmative action hires? Why should he be discriminated against in order to accommodate *them?*"

The attitude Cose described is not unique and, at least according to some sources, is widespread among white male college students. Here are two samples from students at large public universities:

> I don't think that special treatment of minorities or giving them preference is any answer [to past discrimination]. Just because someone is a woman or black or whatever doesn't mean they should get an advantage. That is reverse discrimination and is just as bad as discrimination.
>
> I'm all for helping whoever needs help, but I don't think it

should be based on a history of oppression. I know a lot of bad
things happened in history to minority groups, but . . . my
generation did not inflict any of this on your generation. . . .
I really believe that [college admission] should be based on
meritocracy . . . on who's more qualified.

The belief that affirmative action harms white men shows up in
many places, although Steven Farron's *Affirmative Action Hoax* (2005)
is probably an extreme. In his book, Farron claims there has been
a "vicious anti-White discrimination that has pervaded American
society since the 1960s." As for affirmative action, he argues that if
we are going to practice racial discrimination to please minorities, it
would be far easier to just set quotas and have it all out in the open.
The usual arguments for affirmative action—compensation for past
injustice or diversity—are "shameless frauds and blatant lies," all
aimed at demeaning white men.

Just as it is "accepted wisdom" that white women and Asian
Americans are the prime beneficiaries of affirmative action, so it is
equally accepted that white males are the main losers. Every time a
white male fails to get into a school or be hired for a job, the blame is
often put on affirmative action. A cartoon by Signe Wilkinson shows
five students admitted to a college: one is the daughter of an alum,
the second the son of a big donor, the third a soccer player, the fourth
a young woman raised in a distant state, and the fifth simply labeled
"minority." To the side is a white man who did not get in, pointing
to the minority and yelling, "It's HIS fault!"

At this point, one could introduce dozens of polls about white
and black reactions to affirmative action, and whether any of the
white participants had ever in fact been the "victim" of affirmative
action, but it would be a waste of time. The polls have widely diver-
gent responses depending on what questions are asked and how the
results are interpreted. Several polls found that one in ten white
men reported they had lost a job opportunity or a promotion to a
woman or minority, yet if one looks at the overwhelming number of
white males in management (the main readership of *Forbes,* which
sponsored one of the polls), in the case that 10 percent of them lost
out to a minority, then there should be four or five times the number
of women and minorities in management positions, and they are not
there.

I am not claiming that no white man has ever lost an opportunity because of his race; I am suggesting that we have absolutely no idea if and how many white males actually failed to get into a college or professional school or obtain a job because of affirmative action. It is a lot easier to document years of discrimination against people of color and women turned away from college or factory doors because of race or gender.

One of the problems in trying to assess and understand affirmative action is distinguishing between groups and individuals. The Constitution does not grant group rights, and neither does the 1964 Civil Rights Act. Yet we have talked about programs that favor women, people of color, and other minorities. The same is true of white men, the "Other" that minorities claim has long shut them out of educational and employment opportunities. It is much easier documenting the long history of discrimination against African Americans, Hispanics, and women, and thousands of EEOC cases over the years show that such discrimination, even if no longer as overt as it used to be, still exists. There have been very few cases involving white men, but there have been some, and a few of these, such as those of Allan Bakke, Brian Weber, and Paul Johnson, have made it to the high court. But aside from saying that "yes, there have been some documented examples of reverse discrimination," one finds it impossible to get any accurate picture of how many white men have actually been victimized.

Some authors have attempted to pierce this fog, and what they have found is like much of the landscape of affirmative action, hazy and contradictory. Studies of alleged backlash find that in some instances there is white resentment and in others that it is almost nonexistent. Similarly, the idea that all minority students are from impoverished backgrounds may be a myth. Even early on, black students who went to college, especially the historically black schools, often came from what was at that time a small African American middle class. Since then, that group has grown, and its children have gone to better secondary schools, and many are admitted under regular standards. For example, even during the 1990s, only about a third of the black freshmen entering Berkeley could be considered low income. In Bowen and Bok's *Shape of the River,* the largest survey of minority students at selective universities, only one in seven came from homes earning less than $22,000 a year.

There is one area where the numbers do indeed tell a story. We looked at some of the figures regarding income and wealth, and on this there is no dispute: whites earn more and have greater wealth in every income bracket. Whites also have more of the skilled, managerial, and executive positions; they have more education and lower unemployment rates than do blacks. Nonetheless, in poll after poll, a large number of whites regard reverse discrimination as a greater social problem than discrimination against minorities. A 2009 Pew survey found that 80 percent of black respondents felt equality had not been achieved, 43 percent thought there was still "a lot of discrimination," but only 13 percent of whites agreed that there was a lot of antiblack prejudice. On the obverse side, 54 percent of whites believed the country had made the necessary changes to give African Americans rights equal to whites, compared with only 13 percent of blacks. While it is true that the black unemployment rate fell to 6.8 percent at the beginning of 2018, that of whites dropped to 3.7 percent, about the same differential it had been at the time of Trump's election.

The fact that there are a lot of angry white men in this country cannot be denied; they elected Donald Trump in 2016. Blue-collar workers had actually begun deserting the old New Deal coalition years before. Some had become so-called Reagan Democrats, and in 2012 they voted for Mitt Romney against Barack Obama. While some studies would indicate that this group believes minorities are getting too much at their expense, in fact the problem is not that blacks or women took their jobs so much as that their jobs disappeared. It is somewhat hard, however, to blame globalism, with no identifiable villains, as the cause of the departure of jobs; it's far easier to say affirmative action gave good jobs away to women, blacks, and Hispanics.

THE DEBATE OVER affirmative action, its justification, its values, and its methods will not end soon. The Trump administration has not only announced that it wants to sue universities who allegedly discriminate against white students but also proposed doing away with the Labor Department division that has policed discrimination among federal contractors, the Office of Federal Contract Compliance Programs. This comes at a time when the administration is reducing the federal government's role in fighting discrimination and protecting minorities, by cutting budgets, dissolving programs, and appointing officials unsympathetic to civil rights. Few African Americans supported Trump in 2016, and he feels no obligation to them, while opposing affirmative action will appeal to his followers. (Recent polls, however, show support for the president in the black community is rising and has doubled from 8 to 16 percent since Trump's election, although three-fourths of blacks still oppose him.)

In his first eighteen months in office, the president continued to say nothing about affirmative action. The Office of Management and Budget did propose cutting money from certain agencies, and of course then attorney general Sessions said he wanted to sue Harvard. Then, on 3 July 2018, without any advance indication, the Education and Justice Departments announced plans to abandon Obama administration policies that urged universities to consider race as a factor in diversifying their student bodies. From now on, the government would champion race-blind admissions standards. Devin O'Malley, a Justice Department spokesman, declared that the "executive branch cannot circumvent Congress or the courts by creating guidance that goes beyond the law." Secretary of Education Betsy DeVos, in a separate statement, noted that the Supreme Court "has determined what affirmative action policies are constitutional. . . . Schools should continue to offer equal opportunities for all students while abiding by the law."

Why did the administration choose to do so at this time? Sev-

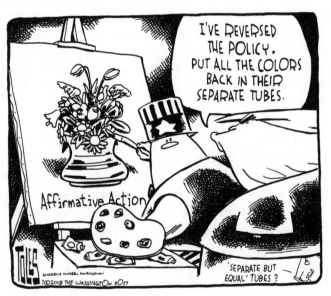

Cartoon comment on Trump's reversal of government guidelines on affirmative action.

eral reasons come to mind. First of all, Anthony Kennedy, who had been the swing vote in *Fisher II,* announced his retirement, and the appointment of the very conservative jurist Brett Kavanagh could tip the balance not only against affirmative action but also against *Roe v. Wade.* Second, the suit against Harvard had begun to pick up steam, although the bulk of the work was still being done by private law groups such as the conservative Center for Equal Opportunity. Third, the intense opposition to a number of Trump policies, especially the horrific separation of immigrant children from their parents, had many Republicans worrying about a backlash at the polls in the 2018 midterm elections that could give Democrats control of one or both houses of Congress. It was time to feed the base.

The document in question had been issued in 2011, with the Education and Justice Departments informing schools that "the compelling interests" established by the Court included diversity, and the Court "has made clear such steps can include taking into account the race of individual students in a narrowly tailored manner." The Education Department reaffirmed its position on affirmative action in 2016 after the *Fisher II* decision. The Trump administration did not issue a new policy statement, but essentially returned the government's policies to those of the George W. Bush era, and in fact formally reissued the Bush guidance document, which stated, "The Department of Education strongly encourages the use of race-neutral methods for assigning students." These documents do not have the force of law, but they do represent the official view of the federal government, so that school officials who kept race-conscious policies in place would be aware that they might become the subject of a Justice Department investigation.

Conservatives cheered; others did not. Nancy Pelosi, the House Democratic leader who would become Speaker after the 2018 elections, charged that the "rollback of vital affirmative action guidance offends our national values" and called it "yet another clear Trump administration attack on communities of color." Ted Mitchell, president of the American Council on Education, declared that the Trump administration was sending "precisely the wrong message to institutions that are committed to following four decades of Supreme Court precedent." Some colleges, such as Duke and Bucknell, said they would wait to see if any new guidelines would appear or what the courts would say. Melodie Jackson, a Harvard spokesperson, said the university would "continue to vigorously defend its right, and that of all colleges and universities, to consider race as one factor among many in college admissions, which has been upheld by the Supreme Court for more than forty years." Attorney General Sessions indicated that he would take a tough line against such views, and federal prosecutors would investigate and sue universities over "discriminatory" admissions policies.

Although people on the right cheered and those on the left booed, in fact the action really changed nothing, at least for the moment. The Court's decision in *Fisher II* remains the law of the land, and in it the majority clearly held that diversity constituted a "compelling interest" to justify schools taking race into account in their admissions policies. That decision applied to public universities, which fall under the command of the Fourteenth Amendment's Equal Protection Clause. Schools like Harvard and Duke are private, although each receives millions annually in federal support for research. The Court has never ruled on what private schools can do, although Justice Powell pointed to Harvard as a model in the *Bakke* decision. Even if the suit against Harvard and a later one against Yale go forth, it will take two to three years before they might reach the high court. And by then there could be a different administration in Washington.

IN THE FIFTY YEARS SINCE affirmative action became a public policy, it has embedded itself in America's corporate culture, where it will survive regardless of what the Trump administration does. If the OFCCP is abolished, there will be some firms who may revert to a racist or sexist policy, but these, I believe, will be relatively few. Big companies like ExxonMobil have publicly vowed that they are taking affirmative action seriously, not just in the United States but around the world. ExxonMobil has, it claims, benefited greatly from the diversity of its workforce and is pledged to providing equal opportunity in employment and promotion. For a company with branches in nearly every country in the world, it would be a major public relations disaster to abandon its promises of equality. Moreover, while tooting one's horn is always good business, to do so about a controversial program is something else. Nor is ExxonMobil alone. Major League Baseball, for whom Jackie Robinson was the first African American player seven decades ago, has pledged itself to diversity, not only among the players but also in the managerial and executive suites. Kim Ng, a woman of Asian American origin, is now senior vice president for baseball operations.

Nor should we expect colleges and universities to abandon diversity. The days are gone—one hopes—when colleges and professional schools put all applications from people of color or women into one pile and those from white males into another. Even if the Justice Department sues Ivy League schools over their alleged limits on Asian Americans, it is far from certain that the suit would win, and even if it did, we have seen how schools have managed to diversify their student bodies even in the face of state constitutional amendments or laws. Just as it would be poor business policy for companies to suddenly turn their backs on long-established programs, so, too, it would not be in the universities' best interest to revert to policies that overtly favored the white children of alumni over everyone else.

But even if we concede that affirmative action is here to stay in corporations, in higher education, and in state and local governments, the debate over it will not go away.

On the one hand, there is no question that the groups targeted for affirmative action—women, people of color, the handicapped—are acknowledged by all sides of the argument to have been victims not only of past injustice but in many cases of current discrimination as well. Hardly anyone would argue that racism and sexism have disappeared in the United States.

While nearly everyone would prefer a race-blind program, the fact is that out of practical necessity the country moved to a race-conscious one. The premise of the color-blind model was that once the country embraced it in law, freedom from discrimination would bring about equality of treatment and then positive economic results for minorities. That very quickly proved to be wishful thinking, and the race-conscious plan seemed the only viable way ahead.

Affirmative action has worked in that hundreds of thousands of people who would have been barred from colleges or from the workplace have gotten in, have gotten an education or a job, and while there is still much too great an economic gulf between whites on the one hand and African Americans and Hispanics on the other, that gulf would be even greater without preferential programs. There are black and Hispanic and female students in schools that in 1960 were all male and all white.

The Voting Rights Act of 1965, sections of which I have treated as involving affirmative action, has transformed the political landscape, with literally thousands of African Americans, Hispanics, and women in state and local governments. The fact that a county has a black sheriff means a great deal to people who remember when the white sheriff was an enforcer of Jim Crow.

Nor has affirmative action harmed white males. True, a very few have been shut out of a school or job, but compared with the very many people of color and women shut out earlier, it is a minuscule number. One of the best analogies of this is one mentioned earlier, the reserving of some parking spaces for the handicapped. While the able driver may be annoyed that she cannot park there, the chances are overwhelming that she will find another spot.

Any social policy that had such far-reaching goals as affirmative action could not have succeeded without ruffling feathers, without discomforting some people, or even depriving some of benefits they had previously taken for granted. Along with *Brown v. Board of Education* (1954) and its progeny, the Civil Rights Act (1964), and the Voting Rights Act (1965), affirmative action has caused a major social upheaval in this country, which for the first time allows women and people of color to have a fair shot at succeeding in our society. Many would say that for all these benefits the price paid has been quite small.

It has made America less segregated in educational and occupational spheres. It is a rare white student today who does not know or have classes with African Americans, Asians, or Latinos, which was not true of the generation that went to college before the Civil Rights Act. There is more mixing in the workplace as well, and while there is still rampant sexism, there is less open misogyny than existed a few decades back.

On the other hand, critics of affirmative action have their own list of negative effects that the policy has had on the country and its inhabitants, black and brown as well as white. For them "the policy is wrong on moral grounds, mistaken on legal grounds, and against the American grain; it is ineffective on practical grounds, destructive on political grounds; and basically unnecessary."

No doubt the biggest criticism has been of quotas, even when disguised as "goals." The very idea of blocking out everyone else and holding seats in medical school or in job training programs strikes most Americans as wrong, even those groups—women and people of color—who benefit from such tactics. If we now condemn the Jim Crow era for punishing people solely on the basis of their skin color, then morally there is no difference in rewarding them because they are black or brown or female.

While outreach ("soft" affirmative action) is acceptable, "hard" programs involving numerical goals/quotas violate not only the Equal Protection Clause of the Fourteenth Amendment but the 1964 Civil Rights Act, whose sponsors promised that Title VII would prohibit employment quotas. Moreover, by treating people as part of a group—African American, Hispanic, disabled, female—we have gone against one of the basic tenets of American democracy and the constitutional order, namely, that rights are individual.

Allowing less qualified people into college or professional school or jobs demeans the institutions themselves. How much faith can we have in the graduates of a medical school when we learn that its affirmative action admits had considerably lower qualifications than the norm? How good is a college we believed to be one of the best in the country when it favors letting in men and women who—were they not people of color or female—would never have been admitted because they could not meet the entrance requirements?

One very disturbing recent news story reports on the failure of many black students who not only do not complete their undergraduate degree in six years but do not graduate at all. Stretching out time in college seems to be the new norm, with only 40 percent of all students graduating in four years and 59 percent getting it done in six years. The then Texas governor, Rick Perry, raised a ruckus over these numbers, and the UT system had to pour millions into providing coaching and other assistance, primarily to students of color admitted under the Top 10 Percent Plan. At Wayne State University in Detroit, less than a third of its undergraduate admits were able to graduate in six years; for African American students, only one in eight admits managed to graduate. Wayne State had its own version of an open admissions plan, and far too many of those it admitted were ill-prepared to do college-level work.

This leads to another criticism, namely, that affirmative action demeans its so-called beneficiaries. Other students will look askance at those they believe were admitted because of their color, or faculty hired because of theirs, whether the individual student or professor has sterling credentials or not. Moreover, this "stain" will stay with the student well after graduation and make her doubt her own abilities and accomplishments.

The unfairness of affirmative action is to blame, at least in part, for the tremendous upswelling of racism, misogyny, and plain crude bigotry that Donald Trump rode to the White House and that he has exacerbated as president. He did not cause these things, but programs like affirmative action did in part, and he, like any politician, took advantage of what he saw.

It should be clear by now that the real problem, and one which affirmative action cannot solve, is the deep-seated racism in the country, and there will be no solution to that until all Americans, and both political parties, face up to the fact that America remains a racist country. Ta-Nehisi Coates, arguably one of the leading African American public intellectuals today, believes affirmative action is on its last legs, primarily because it has neither addressed nor solved the problem of racism and what is owed to black people for centuries of slavery and Jim Crow.

ONE COULD GO ON AND ON, citing one "statistic" against another, one argument in favor against one opposed, and in fact this is happening every day. I once read that a poem is never done; the poet writes and revises and revises until she reaches a point where, willingly or not, it goes out to the world, even though she believes it could be revised even more. Since I started this work, I have had to add and revise constantly, because nearly every week—and sometimes more frequently—there is an article in the media about minorities and women, the discrimination they still face, the efforts of some companies and schools to recruit or pay equally, and that in some instances affirmative action is indeed a zero-sum game.

Everyone, from the Supreme Court on down, has held that affirmative action—whether to compensate for prior discrimination or to achieve diversity in the classroom or in the corporation—is a "temporary" measure. At some point, there would be no further need because the playing field would be level. Minority children would go to schools as good as those of white students; they would thus be as prepared to apply to college or for a job; employers would treat minorities and women fairly; and we would then see a workforce that "looked like the country," with women and minorities spread throughout not only the factory floor but the executive suite as well. That day, however, is not in sight.

I mentioned earlier that only a bigot could oppose a soft affirmative action, one that reached out to different groups but made the decision for admission or hiring solely on merit. Much of the uproar has come because of hard programs involving quotas and goals. I remain conflicted about the hard version, and especially how a government agency—the Equal Employment Opportunity Commission—disregarded the plain wording of Title VII of the 1964 Civil Rights Act and imposed a hard policy on the nation's employers and, together with the Department of Education, on the country's schools. Some people have cogently argued that the depth of racism and misogyny in this country made it impossible for the soft program to work; there had to be stronger policies, a hard affirmative action.

Arguments over affirmative action will not be quickly settled, and even as you read this book, there have undoubtedly been new developments. The puzzle is far from solved.

ACKNOWLEDGMENTS

As my family and friends can attest, this has been a difficult book to write. Aside from the moral ambiguities, it often seemed as if each day a new development appeared in the media. Donald Trump's first attorney general, Jeff Sessions, had long been an opponent of affirmative action, and during his tenure managed to get a lawsuit going against Harvard—that bastion of liberalism—for allegedly discriminating against Asian-American applicants. That case has still not been decided, but when it is, there is little doubt that it will be appealed to a higher court.

Several friends endured the task of reading all or part of the manuscript. Mark R. Killenbeck of the University of Arkansas Law School, Jonathan Lurie of Rutgers, and Nancy Woloch of Barnard not only saved me from errors, but made me rethink arguments so that, at the very least, they would be intelligible to the reader. Whatever problems remain, I am afraid, all belong to me.

Thanks to my friend Alan Kraut, I had the good fortune to have Terumi Rafferty-Osaku (now Dr. Rafferty-Osaku) as my research assistant. Terumi was not only diligent in tracking down printed materials, but he brought me into the twenty-first century and educated me in the way one can access online material through a home computer.

This is the third book I have done with Victoria Wilson at Pantheon, and one could not ask for a more knowing and sympathetic editor. Recognizing that events were taking place that could not be ignored, she encouraged me to get as much as possible into the book. By definition, it will not be completely au courant when it appears, but there is a lot more in the book now than when I thought it would be finished.

It is a pleasure working with the people at Pantheon. Marc Jaffee, Vicky's assistant, answered numerous questions for me so that production could proceed with minimal fuss. My thanks also go to the managing editor, Altie Karper; Lisa Montebello, production manager; Betty Lew, designer; and Adalis Martinez, who designed the cover. Jessica Purcell, the publicist, and Julianne Clancy in marketing have done their best to get this book into your hands. Over a decade ago I had the good fortune to have Ingrid Sterner copyedit my book on Louis Brandeis, and I wrote there that I would be happy to have her as copy editor on any other book I would do for Pantheon. She has done it again, and I thank her for the care and skill she brought to the job.

I am also grateful to my agent, Nick Mullendore of Loretta Barrett Books, for taking care of all the things agents do, and with panache.

Finally, this book is dedicated to my family—toute la famille—but my wife, Susan, deserves special mention. Over the years she has kindly and graciously allowed me to become slightly berserk when writing, and afterwards leading me back to normal.

Gaithersburg, Maryland

NOTES

INTRODUCTION

ix **the same story:** *Johnson v. Transportation Agency, Santa Clara County,* 480 U.S. 616 (1987); the book is *A Conflict of Rights: The Supreme Court and Affirmative Action* (1991).

x **equally stalwart conservatives:** See, for example, Thomas Sowell, *Affirmative Action Around the World: An Empirical Study* (2004), and Stephan Thernstrom and Abigail Thernstrom, *America in Black and White: One Nation, Indivisible* (1997). Sowell is one of the leading African American conservatives, while the Thernstroms are, in most areas, liberal. All three strongly oppose affirmative action.

x **"Koch deeply believed several things":** Peter L. Zimroth Memoir, Columbia Oral History Collection, Columbia University, New York.

xii **covered by its policies:** U.S. Commission on Civil Rights, *Affirmative Action in the 1980s: Dismantling the Process of Discrimination* (1981), 3–5.

xii **"It is both transient and permanent":** Nancy Woloch to author, 15 March 2018.

xiii **some form of affirmative action:** See Elaine Kennedy-Dubourdieu, ed., *Race and Inequality: World Perspectives on Affirmative Action* (2006), and Sowell, *Affirmative Action Around the World.*

xiii **more recently, diversity:** Lincoln Caplan, *Up Against the Law: Affirmative Action and the Supreme Court* (1997), 17–18.

xiii **"We expect that 25 years from now":** *Grutter v. Bollinger,* 539 U.S. 306 (2003).

xiv **"I realize that the bright":** Stephen L. Carter, *Reflections of an Affirmative Action Baby* (1991), 5.

xiv **"You do not take a person":** *Public Papers of the Presidents of the United States: Lyndon B. Johnson: 1965* (1966), 2:636.

xv **an ongoing discrimination:** *United States v. Paradise,* 480 U.S. 149 (1987).

xvi **"Minorities Getting Slice of Contract Pie":** *Washington Post,* 22 April 2015. The contract involved building the MGM casino in a Maryland suburb of the nation's capital. MGM had to agree not only to seek minority workers and subcontractors but also to hire residents of Prince Georges County.

xvi **"Intel Diversity Report Shows":** *Washington Post,* 4 February 2016.

xvii **effect a quota:** The Supreme Court has not conflated "quotas" and "goals," but I think it will be clear that in many programs forced on colleges and employers, the two are pretty much treated as the same.

1. AFFIRMATIVE ACTION BEFORE KENNEDY

4 **"When a man has emerged"**: Randall Kennedy, *For Discrimination: Race, Affirmative Action, and the Law* (2013), 24; *Civil Rights Cases,* 109 U.S. 3, 25 (1883).

5 **"if they can be voted for"**: Cited by Lawrence H. Fuchs, "The Changing Meaning of Civil Rights, 1954–1994," in *Civil Rights and Social Wrongs: Black-White Relations Since World War II,* ed. John Higham (1997), 60.

5 **"most prefigured the race conscious remedies"**: Jo Ann Ooiman Robinson, "Affirmative Action in the United States," in *Race and Inequality: World Perspective on Affirmative Action,* ed. Elaine Kennedy-Dubourdieu (2006), 12.

5 **out of business in 1872**: Paul A. Cimbala, *The Freedmen's Bureau: Reconstructing the American South After the Civil War* (2005); Mark Graber, "The Second Freedmen's Bureau Bill's Constitution," 94 *Texas Law Review* 1361 (2016).

6 **"Do nothing with us"**: Quoted in Philip F. Rubio, *A History of Affirmative Action, 1619–2000* (2001), 38–39.

6 **In 1883, the Supreme Court**: *Civil Rights Cases,* 109 U.S. 3 (1883); *Plessy v. Ferguson,* 163 U.S. 537 (1896).

7 **during the emergency**: This section is based primarily on Ronald M. Benson, "Searching for the Antecedents of Affirmative Action: The National War Labor Board and the Cleveland Women Conductors in World War I," 5 *Women's Rights Law Reporter* 271 (1979).

8 **for scraps of food**: Robert S. McElvaine, *The Great Depression: America, 1929–1941* (1993); Dalton Conley, "40 Acres and a Mule," *National Forum* (Spring 2000): 23.

9 **supervised by white officers**: John A. Salmond, *The Civilian Conservation Corps, 1933–1942: A New Deal Case Study* (1967).

9 **"FHA set itself up"**: Charles Abrams, quoted in Rubio, *History of Affirmative Action,* 97.

9 **"No Rights at All"**: *Id.,* 100.

10 **Tennessee Valley Authority**: Robinson, "Affirmative Action in the United States," 15–16.

10 **"take such affirmative action"**: 29 U.S.C. 151, §§ 160b, 160c (1935). See Richard C. Cortner, *The Wagner Act Cases* (1964).

10 **"part of the white labor establishment"**: Rubio, *History of Affirmative Action,* 92–93; Nancy MacLean, *Freedom Is Not Enough: The Opening of the American Workplace* (2006), 40–41.

11 **no able-bodied males**: Terry H. Anderson, *The Pursuit of Fairness: A History of Affirmative Action* (2004), 14–15.

11 **"the policy of nondiscrimination"**: J. Edward Kellough, *Understanding Affirmative Action: Politics, Discrimination, and the Search for Social Justice* (2006), 23.

11 **well as political change**: A good overview of this scholarship is the review essay by Nelson Lichtenstein in 35 *Law and Social Inquiry* 243 (2010).

11 **earlier declared unconstitutional**: In *Bailey v. Alabama,* 219 U.S. 219 (1911), the Court attacked peonage that led to labor on a chain gang as

a restriction on personal rights and a violation of the Thirteenth Amendment. Three years later, in *United States v. Reynolds,* 235 U.S. 133 (1914), the Court struck down another Alabama statute that assigned a prisoner's labor to private parties. Not until *Pollock v. Williams,* 322 U.S. 4 (1944), did the Court finally invalidate the last vestiges of peonage.

12 **1950s and 1960s:** Risa L. Goluboff, *The Lost Promise of Civil Rights* (2007). See also Harvard Sitkoff, *A New Deal for Blacks* (1978), and Richard Dalfiume, "The 'Forgotten Years' of the Negro Revolution," 55 *Journal of American History* 90 (1968), where the idea of a "long" movement dating back to the 1930s was first expressed.

12 **discrimination in the North:** Martha Biondi, *To Stand and Fight: The Struggle for Civil Rights in Postwar New York City* (2006); Glenda Gilmore, *Defying Dixie: The Radical Roots of Civil Rights, 1919–1950* (2008); and Robert Korstad, *Civil Rights Unionism: Tobacco Workers and the Struggle for Democracy in the Mid-twentieth Century South* (2007).

12 **pitifully low wages:** Abigail Thernstrom and Stephan Thernstrom, "Black Progress," in *The African American Predicament,* ed. Christopher H. Foreman Jr. (1999), 31.

12 **of whites at $6,107:** Virginia Willis, *Affirmative Action: The Unrealized Goal* (1973), 29, based on figures from a 1972 report by the U.S. Census Bureau.

13 **"The desire for fair and equitable":** *New Negro Alliance v. Sanitary Grocery Co.,* 303 U.S. 552, 561 (1938).

15 **a view held by many employers:** Anderson, *Pursuit of Fairness,* 2, 20.

16 **"Now, Therefore, by virtue of the authority":** David Lucander, *Winning the War for Democracy: The March on Washington Movement, 1941–1946* (2014).

16 **helping black workers:** Merl E. Reed, *Seedtime for the Modern Civil Rights Movement: The President's Committee on Fair Employment Practice, 1941–1945* (1991).

16 **Little progress had been made:** Kellough, *Understanding Affirmative Action,* 23–27; Kennedy, *For Discrimination,* 27.

16 **during the 1940s:** The best book on this subject is Nicholas Lemann, *The Promised Land: The Great Black Migration and How It Changed America* (1991).

16 **especially in employment:** Although conditions in the North regarding African Americans proved far better than they had been in the South, it was not the Garden of Eden many thought it would be. For the extent of racism and the obstacles placed in front of the black migrants, see the classic work by Arnold R. Hirsch, *Making the Second Ghetto: Race and Housing in Chicago, 1940–1960* (1983).

17 **"Discrimination is the rule":** Gunnar Myrdal, *An American Dilemma: The Negro Problem and Modern Democracy* (1944), 1005.

17 **to maintain order:** Bryan K. Fair, *Notes of a Racial Caste Baby: Color Blindness and the End of Affirmative Action* (1997), 116–17.

18 **of the 1960s began:** David M. Kennedy, *Freedom from Fear: The American People in Depression and War, 1929–1945* (1999), 776–81.

19 **1930s and 1940s:** Paul D. Moreno, *From Direct Action to Affirmative Action: Fair Employment Law and Policy in America, 1933–1972* (1997), 268.

19 **"If Lucky had yielded to the demands"**: *Hughes v. Superior Court of Contra Costa County,* 32 Cal. 2d 850, 856 (1948). It is noteworthy that four decades later Lucky, which by then had 188 stores in Northern California, settled a class-action gender bias case for $75 million and agreed to change its personnel and pay policies in order to cease discrimination against women. *New York Times,* 17 December 1993.

19 **"To deny California the right to ban"**: *Hughes v. Superior Court of California for Contra Costa County,* 339 U.S. 460, 464 (1950).

20 **which the NAACP stood:** For the disagreements within the NAACP, see Mark V. Tushnet, *The NAACP's Strategy Against Segregated Education, 1925–1950* (1987), as well as his *Making Constitutional Law: Thurgood Marshall and the Supreme Court, 1961–1991* (1997), 116–19.

21 **into the larger culture:** Manning Marable, *Beyond Black and White: Transforming African-American Politics* (2009), 82–83.

21 **"The recruiter looked at me"**: Both Franklin and Byrd are quoted in Ira Katznelson, *When Affirmative Action Was White: An Untold History of Racial Inequality in Twentieth-Century America* (2005), 80–81.

21 **"the hysterical cries of the preachers"**: W. E. B. Du Bois, "Now Is the Time Not to Be Silent," *Crisis,* July 1940.

21 **treatment of Negroes in the army:** Lucille Milner, "Jim Crow in the Army," *New Republic,* 13 March 1944. For further examples of the racial bias in the military during World War II, see Katznelson, *When Affirmative Action Was White,* 89–112.

23 **known as the GI Bill:** PL 78-346 (1944). See Keith Olson, *The G.I. Bill, the Veterans, and the Colleges* (1974), and Michael J. Bennett, *When Dreams Came True: The G.I. Bill and the Making of Modern America* (1996).

24 **white male veterans:** Karen Brodkin Sacks, "The GI Bill: Whites Only Need Apply," in *Critical White Studies: Looking Behind the Mirror,* ed. Richard Delgado and Jean Stefanic (1997), 310–13.

24 **veteran would be hired:** John David Skrentny, *The Ironies of Affirmative Action: Politics, Culture, and Justice in America* (1996), 37.

24 **"the law was deliberately designed"**: Katznelson, *When Affirmative Action Was White,* 114; see also Neil A. Wynn, *The Afro-American and the Second World War* (1976).

25 **not evenly distributed:** Hilary Herbold, "Never a Level Playing Field: Blacks and the GI Bill," 6 *Journal of Blacks in Higher Education* 104 (Winter 1994).

25 **black middle class:** Sacks, "GI Bill," 313.

25 **recalled in 1994:** Katznelson, *When Affirmative Action Was White,* 120–21.

25 **subject of many books:** See, among many others, Richard Kluger, *Simple Justice: The History of* Brown v. Board of Education *and Black America's Struggle for Equality* (1976), Mark V. Tushnet, *Making Civil Rights Law: Thurgood Marshall and the Supreme Court, 1936–1961* (1994), and Risa L. Goluboff, *The Lost Promise of Civil Rights* (2007). A good overview is James T. Patterson, *Grand Expectations: The United States, 1945–1974* (1996), which puts the civil rights struggle in the context of other developments in the country at the time.

25–26 **"When those problems are solved"**: Thurgood Marshall to Noah W. Griffin, 9 May 1946, cited in Risa L. Goluboff, *"Brown v. Board of Edu-*

cation and the Lost Promise of Civil Rights," in *Civil Rights Stories,* ed. Myriam E. Gilles and Risa L. Goluboff (2007), 25–40, 31.

27 **the next generation:** President's Committee on Civil Rights, *To Secure These Rights* (1947).

27 **integration in the armed forces:** Michael R. Gardner, *Harry Truman and Civil Rights: Moral Courage and Political Risks* (2002).

28 **largely as a "study group":** Kellough, *Understanding Affirmative Action,* 27–28.

28 **and restrictive covenants:** *Mitchell v. United States,* 313 U.S. 80 (1941); *Smith v. Allwright,* 321 U.S. 649 (1944); *Steele v. Louisville & Nashville Rail Road,* 323 U.S. 192 (1944); *Morgan v. Virginia,* 328 U.S. 373 (1946); *Bob-Lo Excursion Co. v. Michigan,* 333 U.S. 28 (1948); and *Shelley v. Kraemer,* 334 U.S. 1 (1948).

28 **equal separate facilities:** *Sweatt v. Painter,* 339 U.S. 626 (1950).

28 **"that in the field of public education":** 347 U.S. 483 (1954). *Brown* covered the four states and relied on the Equal Protection Clause of the Fourteenth Amendment. Because the federal government had authority over the District of Columbia, the Court issued a separate opinion in *Bolling v. Sharpe,* 347 U.S. 497 (1954), which relied on the Fifth Amendment's Due Process Clause. For the cases, see Robert J. Cottrell et al., Brown v. Board of Education: *Caste, Culture, and the Constitution* (2003).

29 **"humane, among the most humane moments":** J. Harvie Wilkinson, *From Brown to Bakke* (1979), 39. Wilkinson refers to footnote 11, which cited Gunnar Myrdal's *American Dilemma,* as well as a controversial study by Kenneth B. Clark about negative self-image among black children. Wilkinson's view about the nobility of the decision remains the dominant view of the case.

29 **"the lights of reason and tolerance":** C. Vann Woodward, *The Strange Career of Jim Crow,* 3rd ed. (1974), 165.

29 **"had set back progress in the South":** Emmet John Hughes, *The Ordeal of Power: A Political Memoir of the Eisenhower Years* (1963), 201.

30 **to enforce black rights:** Tony A. Freyer, *Little Rock on Trial:* Cooper v. Aaron *and School Desegregation* (2007).

30 **not to enforce nondiscrimination:** Executive Order 10479, 18 Fed. Reg. 4899 (1953). Over the next four years, Eisenhower issued five more orders amending and refining the government's policy on employment. Kellough, *Understanding Affirmative Action,* 28–29.

30 **on the basis of equality:** Fair, *Notes of a Racial Caste Baby,* 118.

2. KENNEDY AND JOHNSON

31 **"Yes, it is a good idea":** Lawrence H. Fuchs, "The Changing Meaning of Civil Rights, 1954–1994," in *Civil Rights and Social Wrongs: Black-White Relations Since World War II,* ed. John Higham (1997), 65.

31 **African American press:** Arthur M. Schlesinger Jr., *Robert Kennedy and His Times* (1978), 216–18.

32 **occupied his presidency more:** Much of the following is based on James N. Giglio, *The Presidency of John F. Kennedy* (1991), chap. 5, and Carl M. Brauer, *John F. Kennedy and the Second Reconstruction* (1977).

32 **other southern cities:** For this very important aspect of the civil rights

era, see Mary L. Dudziak, *Cold War Civil Rights: Race and the Image of American Democracy* (2000).

32 **Congress should address:** Giglio, *Presidency of John F. Kennedy,* 161.

34 **in the top grades by 88.2 percent:** Roy Wilkins Oral History transcript, Kennedy Library, cited in Brauer, *Second Reconstruction,* 163; Arthur M. Schlesinger, *A Thousand Days: John F. Kennedy in the White House* (1965), 777.

34 **Johnson as its chair:** Brauer, *Second Reconstruction,* 67; 26 Fed. Reg. 1977 (1961). For more on the order and its provisions, see Ricardo José Pereira Rodrigues, *The Preeminence of Politics: Executive Orders from Eisenhower to Clinton* (2007), 41–43.

35 **"carrot and stick provisions":** Ruth P. Morgan, *The President and Civil Rights: Policy-Making by Executive Order* (1970), 47.

35 **on behalf of civil rights:** Hugh Davis Graham, *The Civil Rights Era: Origins and Development of National Policy, 1960–1972* (1990), 41.

35 **"vastly strengthened machinery":** *Public Papers of the Presidents: John F. Kennedy: 1961* (1962), 67, 150.

36 **"affirmative action":** Graham, *Civil Rights Era,* 41; Mark R. Killenbeck, "Affirmative Action and the Courts: From *Plessy* to *Brown* to *Grutter,* and Back?," in *Social Consciousness in Legal Decision Making: Psychological Perspectives,* ed. Richard L. Wiener et al. (2010), 91–120, at 96.

36 **agreed to the conditions:** *New York Times,* 21 April 1961. Holleman also served as executive vice chairman of the committee.

36 **0.001 percent of the workforce:** Giglio, *Presidency of John F. Kennedy,* 172.

37 **prior to Plans for Progress:** Bernard E. Anderson, "Affirmative Action Policy Under Executive Order 11246: A Retrospective View," in *Civil Rights and Race Relations in the Post Reagan-Bush Era,* ed. Samuel L. Myers Jr. (1997), 51. The Kennedy brothers privately blamed Johnson for the committee's shortcomings.

37 **in many instances:** Michael I. Sovern, *Legal Restraints on Racial Discrimination in Employment* (1966), 103–12, 117–18.

37 **"The Republican-conservative-southern Democratic coalition":** Harris Wofford, *Of Kennedys and Kings: Making Sense of the Sixties* (1980), 136.

38 **"it will be a hollow victory":** The figures are taken from a U.S. Census report, "The Social and Economic Status of the Black Population in the United States, 1972," cited in Virginia Willis, *Affirmative Action: The Unrealized Goal* (1973), 29. See also Graham, *Civil Rights Era,* 101–2.

38 **"then who among us would be content":** *Public Papers of the Presidents: John F. Kennedy: 1963* (1964), 469.

39 **"it also had integrity":** Herman Belz, *Affirmative Action from Kennedy to Reagan: Redefining American Equality* (1984), 1.

39 **"after which the actual selection":** Thomas Sowell, *Civil Rights: Rhetoric or Reality?* (1984), 39.

40 **special training for them:** Nancy MacLean, *Freedom Is Not Enough: The Opening of the American Workplace* (2006), 54.

41 **Most unions out and out refused:** Dennis Deslippe, *Protesting Affirmative Action: The Struggle over Equality After the Civil Rights Revolution*

(2012), 18–19. More than two-thirds of labor organizations contacted by the federal government about racial membership refused to return the surveys.

41 **"In most states," Miller concluded:** Herman P. Miller, *How Our Income Is Divided* (1963), expanded into *Rich Man, Poor Man* (1964), 84–124.

42 **War on Poverty:** Schlesinger, *Thousand Days,* 62, 777–78; James T. Patterson, *Grand Expectations: The United States, 1945–1974* (1996), 542–43.

42 **"All I have," he said:** *Public Papers of the Presidents: Lyndon B. Johnson: 1963–1964* (1965), 8–10.

43 **protective legislation:** For women, as the historian Nancy Woloch has said, Title VII is "a big deal." See Cynthia Deitch, "Gender, Race, and Class Politics and the Inclusion of Women in Title VII of the 1964 Civil Rights Act," in *Race, Class, and Gender: Common Bonds, Different Voices,* ed. Esther Ngan-Ling et al. (1996), 288–307.

43 **to the Senate:** Smith had been a sponsor of the Equal Rights Amendment. For the strange bedfellows the proposal made, see Hugh Davis Graham, *Civil Rights and the Presidency: Race and Gender in American Politics, 1960–1972* (1992), 75–77. Originally, Title VII also banned age discrimination, but that provision was deleted during committee hearings. When Johnson learned that age discrimination would not be in the final bill, he issued Executive Order 11141 on 12 February 1964, declaring a government policy against discrimination based on age. 29 Fed. Reg. 2477 (1964).

43 **2 July 1964:** 78 Stat. 241 (1964). For the passage of the bill and its provisions, see Clay Risen, *The Bill of the Century: The Epic Battle for the Civil Rights Act* (2015).

44 **"An antidiscrimination law is the antithesis":** Clint Bolick, *The Affirmative Action Fraud: Can We Restore the American Civil Rights Vision?* (1996), 41.

44 **courts would misconstrue it:** *Id.,* 42; Sowell, *Civil Rights,* 40–41.

45 **upheld its provisions:** *Heart of Atlanta Motel v. United States,* 379 U.S. 241 (1964); *Katzenbach v. McClung,* 379 U.S. 294 (1964).

45 **service-based employment:** Hugh Davis Graham, *Collision Course: The Strange Convergence of Affirmative Action and Immigration Policy in America* (2002), 25–26; Willis, *Affirmative Action,* 29.

45 **James Farmer:** The best study is August Meier and Elliott Rudwick, *CORE: A Study in the Civil Rights Movement, 1942–1968* (1973).

45 **would be nonwhite:** Gertrude Ezorsky, *Racism and Justice: The Case for Affirmative Action* (1991), 31.

46 **New York, and Detroit:** Deslippe, *Protesting Affirmative Action,* 20.

47 **"'preferential hiring' system":** Anderson, *Pursuit of Fairness,* 77.

47 **"is necessary and appropriate":** Graham, *Civil Rights Era,* 105–6; MacLean, *Freedom Is Not Enough,* 56.

48 **his private convictions:** Graham, *Civil Rights Era,* 111–12.

48 **"do not aim to perpetuate":** Herman Belz, *Equality Transformed: A Quarter-Century of Affirmative Action* (1991), 10.

48 **"does not require 'racial balance'":** Anderson, *Pursuit of Fairness,* 77.

48 **"do not dare put":** Belz, *Equality Transformed,* 26.

48 "contrary to the allegations": Kennedy, *For Discrimination,* 37–38.

49 "to fail or refuse to hire": Public Law 88-352, Title VII (1964); 42 U.S.C. 2000e, § 703(a).

49 "Nothing contained in this subchapter": 42 U.S.C. 2000e, § 701(h).

50 "their disavowal of preferential treatment": Kennedy, *For Discrimination,* 39.

51 "equal rights were a personal thing": Richard N. Goodwin, *Remembering America: A Voice from the Sixties* (1988), 214; Joe B. Franz, "Opening of a Curtain: The Metamorphosis of Lyndon B. Johnson," 65 *Journal of Southern History* 3, 21 (1979).

51 "But freedom is not enough": *Public Papers of the Presidents of the United States: Lyndon B. Johnson, 1965* (1966), 2:635–40.

52 include his vice president: Executive Order 11197, 30 Fed. Reg. 1721 (1965); Rodrigues, *Preeminence of Politics,* 51–52; Graham, *Civil Rights Era,* 161–62, 183–85.

53 include gender discrimination: Executive Order 11246, 24 September 1965, 30 Fed. Reg. 12319 (1965); Executive Order 11247, 24 September 1965, 30 Fed. Reg. 12327 (1965); Executive Order 11375, 13 October 1967, 32 Fed. Reg. 14303 (1967).

53 as "soft plus": Mark Killenbeck to author, 13 February 2018.

54 "there is no fixed and firm definition": Deslippe, *Protesting Affirmative Action,* 22–23.

55 "This is not the case": *Id.,* 23.

55 more minorities hired: Kellough, *Understanding Affirmative Action,* 33; Graham, *Collision Course,* 30.

56 troops to the war: The best single book on the conflict is George C. Herring, *America's Longest War: The United States and Vietnam, 1950–1975,* 4th ed. (2002).

56 "It looks like Berlin in 1945": Patterson, *Grand Expectations,* 662–63.

3. AFFIRMATIVE ACTION SPREADS—AND MUTATES

58 in their movements: Richard A. Epstein, *Forbidden Grounds: The Case Against Employment Discrimination Laws* (1992), 395–96; Randall B. Woods, *Prisoners of Hope: Lyndon B. Johnson, the Great Society, and the Limits of Liberalism* (2016), 11.

58 in apprentice programs: Hugh Davis Graham, *The Civil Rights Era: Origins and Development of National Policy, 1960–1972* (1990), 114.

60 medieval guild system: *New York Times,* 27 July 1963; Ray Marshall, *The Negro and Organized Labor* (1965), 234–35.

60 about quotas appeared: *New York Times,* 18 December 1963.

61 probably included quotas: *New York Times,* 9 October 1963.

61 an end in 1965: This view has been challenged by Professor David Chappell, who claims that civil rights activism continued after the two laws and the assassination of Martin Luther King, and he cites the Fair Housing Act of 1968 as an example. He concedes, however, that there were no major landmark laws and that the leadership of the movement was in disarray. *Waking from the Dream: The Struggle for Civil Rights in the Shadow of Martin Luther King Jr.* (2016).

61 of overt discrimination: Epstein, *Forbidden Grounds,* 395.

62 **poor and elderly people:** Woods, *Prisoners of Hope*, 392. Segregation never fully ended, but de jure apartheid could no longer be enforced.

62 **the American economy:** Stephan Thernstrom and Abigail Thernstrom, *America in Black and White: One Nation, Indivisible* (1997), 81–82.

62 **"remained far behind whites":** *Id.*, 83. One reason the 1940 unemployment rate was so low compared with whites is that during the Depression black men in the rural South could usually find someone to take them on as a farmhand, and so they never appeared in the statistics.

63 **"rights wanted by almost all Negroes":** Lee Sigelman and Susan Welch, *Black Americans' Views of Racial Inequality: The Dream Deferred* (1991), 126–27.

63 **"we can no longer evade":** All quoted in John David Skrentny, *The Ironies of Affirmative Action: Politics, Culture, and Justice in America* (1996), 70.

65 **"the best point . . . at which":** Daniel Patrick Moynihan, *The Negro Family: The Case for National Action* (1965); Woods, *Prisoners of Hope*, 184–85. For the impact of the report, see Daniel Geary, *Beyond Civil Rights: The Moynihan Report and Its Legacy* (2015).

65 **the Coleman Report:** James S. Coleman, *Equality of Educational Opportunity* (1966). Coleman had long been a leader in trying to assess which factors affected educational quality.

67 **Rumford Fair Housing Act:** A year later, the California Supreme Court reinstated the Fair Housing Act in *Reitman v. Mulkey*, 64 Cal. 2d 529 (1966), affirmed, 387 U.S. 369 (1967). For a detailed study, see Gerald Horne, *Fire This Time: The Watts Uprising and the 1960s* (1995).

67 **in the black ghettos:** Skrentny, *Ironies of Affirmative Action*, 73.

69 **Negro lieutenant to captain:** *Id.*, 88–89.

69 **hands of the government:** Alfonso J. Cervantes, "To Prevent a Chain of Super-Watts," 45 *Harvard Business Review* 55 (September/October 1967).

69 **"would be to ease discontent":** Skrentny, *Ironies of Affirmative Action*, 89–91.

70 **staffed their banks:** Anne B. Fisher, "Businessmen Like to Hire by the Numbers," *Fortune*, 16 September 1985, 26.

70 **"There should be no legal obstacle":** Epstein, *Forbidden Grounds*, 396.

71 **form of affirmative action:** Howard McGary, *Race and Social Justice* (1999), chap. 8, discusses the various alternatives for implementation, all of them fraught with difficulties.

71 **other employment practices:** Hugh Davis Graham, *Civil Rights and the Presidency: Race and Gender in American Politics, 1960–1972* (1992), 120–21.

72 **re-advertised the contract:** The details can be found at 33 Fed. Reg. 7804, revised 21 May 1968, effective 1 July 1968.

72 **"more" minorities:** Harry Downs, "Equal Employment Opportunity: For Whom?," 21 *Labor Law Journal* 274, 275. Downs, an attorney in Cambridge, Massachusetts, nonetheless defended the regulations as the only pragmatic approach to a long-smoldering problem.

73 **"do to get results":** Lemann, "Taking Affirmative Action Apart," 49; Herman Belz, *Equality Transformed: A Quarter-Century of Affirmative Action* (1991), 30–31.

74 **"poor enfeebled thing":** Richard K. Berg, "Equal Employment Oppor-

tunity Under the Civil Rights Act of 1964," 31 *Brooklyn Law Review* 62 (1964); Michael I. Sovern, *Legal Restraints on Racial Discrimination in Employment Law* (1966), 83.

74 **complaints rose to 77,000:** Graham, *Civil Rights and the Presidency,* 102–3; Finis Welch, "Affirmative Action and Its Enforcement," 71 *American Economic Review* 127, 129 (1981).

74 **not last very long:** Thernstrom and Thernstrom, *America in Black and White,* 425.

74 **"The history of the period":** Dennis Deslippe, *Protesting Affirmative Action: The Struggle over Equality After the Civil Rights Revolution* (2012), 25.

75 **each occupational level:** Thernstrom and Thernstrom, *America in Black and White,* 425; Alfred W. Blumrosen, *Black Employment and the Law* (1971), 53, 58.

76 **Sonia Pressman:** Later Sonia Pressman Fuentes. See her *Eat First—You Don't Know What They'll Give You: The Adventures of an Immigrant Family and Their Feminist Daughter* (1999).

76 **"Less time [could] be devoted":** Graham, *Civil Rights and the Presidency,* 104. Graham goes on to note that from the perspective of the male establishment in the Kennedy-Johnson years, prejudice primarily meant racism, and secondarily ethnoreligious, that is, anti-Semitism or anti-Catholicism. "Sexism" still had no place in the public discourse. During 1963 and 1964, Congress produced hundreds of hours of hearings and thousands of pages of testimony relating to racial inequality, but there were no committee hearings or reports on gender inequality at all.

77 **"the EEOC revised the basic principles":** Belz, *Equality Transformed,* 27.

78 **its founding statute:** Graham, *Civil Rights and the Presidency,* 122.

79 **implied, was "quotas":** Belz, *Equality Transformed,* 28–29.

79 **H. Rap Brown:** *Report of the National Advisory Commission on Civil Disorders* (1968); Skrentny, *Ironies of Affirmative Action,* 92–100.

80 **required by Title VII:** The Supreme Court adopted the disparate-impact test in *Griggs v. Duke Power Company,* 401 U.S. 424 (1971), in which the Court twice cited the Kerner Commission Report as part of its justification.

4. NIXON AND THE PHILADELPHIA PLAN

81 **Darth Vader of American politics:** The literature on Nixon and his presidency is large and expanding. See, among many others, Stephen E. Ambrose, *Nixon,* 3 vols. (1987–1991); Herbert Parmet, *Richard Nixon and His America* (1990); Joan Hoff, *Nixon Reconsidered* (1994); and Melvin Small, *The Presidency of Richard Nixon* (1999). Nixon also penned a two-volume autobiography, *Six Crises* (1962), and *RN: The Memoirs of Richard Nixon* (1978). The newest, and in many ways the best, examination of the man and his career is John A. Farrell, *Richard Nixon: The Life* (2017).

82 **their own standards:** Dean J. Kotlowski, "Richard Nixon and the Origins of Affirmative Action," 60 *Historian* 523, 524 (1998).

82 **"*Any* small business has a 75% chance":** Dean J. Kotlowski, *Nixon's Civil Rights* (2001), 134.

82 **only went to minorities:** Executive Order 11458, 34 Fed. Reg. 4937

(1969); Small, *Presidency of Richard Nixon*, 174; Terry Eastland, *Ending Affirmative Action: The Case for Colorblind Justice* (1996), 54.

83 **in low esteem:** Kotlowski, *Nixon's Civil Rights*, 129–30. Johnson had also wanted to help minority entrepreneurs, and the 1967 antipoverty amendments increased the SBA budget and required that half its loans go to blacks and whites in poverty areas.

83 **"Nothing much is happening":** Hugh Davis Graham, *Civil Rights and the Presidency: Race and Gender in American Politics, 1960–1972* (1992), 137–38.

83 **"runners of other colors":** Eastland, *Ending Affirmative Action,* 55–56.

84 **civil rights leaders:** Farrell, *Nixon,* 257–58.

84 **"through positive action, make it possible":** Executive Order 11478, 34 Fed. Reg. 12985 (1969); *Public Papers of the Presidents: Richard Nixon: 1969* (1971), 635–36.

84 **"the majority of Americans":** John D. Ehrlichman, *Witness to Power: The Nixon Years* (1982), 222.

84 **secretary of labor:** Shultz served as labor secretary for eighteen months. See his *Learning from Experience* (2016).

86 **"appalling unemployment experience":** Hugh Davis Graham, *The Civil Rights Era: Origins and Development of National Policy, 1960–1972* (1990), 322–23.

86 **in the craft unions:** This long-standing problem is detailed in "Trade Union Bias Found Unchecked," *New York Times,* 1 June 1967.

86 **"most international unions have failed":** Both quoted in Michael J. Graetz and Linda Greenhouse, *The Burger Court and the Rise of the Judicial Right* (2016), 278–79.

86 **"I had to wait my turn":** Kotlowski, "Nixon and Origins," 528.

87 **Model Cities Act:** *New York Times,* 3 April and 4 September 1969.

87 **apprentices in the country:** Nixon, *Memoir,* 437.

87 **opportunity for growth:** Joseph Debro, "The Minority Builder," 21 *Labor Law Journal* 298, 299 (1970).

88 **"I am deeply interested":** Kotlowski, *Nixon's Civil Rights,* 103. An editorial in *The New York Times* on 12 August 1969 not only lauded Shultz for trying to break down the bars against minority employment but applauded Nixon and Attorney General Mitchell for backing him.

88 **"a political dilemma for the labor union leaders":** Ehrlichman, *Witness to Power,* 228–29.

88 **African American Republican:** "Arthur A. Fletcher, Civil Rights Advocate and Affirmative Action Pioneer, Dies at 80," *New York Times,* 14 July 2005. Fletcher stayed with the Labor Department for only a few years, then resigned to become executive director of the United Negro College Fund. President George H. W. Bush named him to head the U.S. Commission on Civil Rights from 1990 to 1993.

88 **gentle persuasion:** For the extent of building trade union hostility to civil rights, see Thomas J. Sugrue, "Affirmative Action from Below: Civil Rights, the Building Trades, and the Politics of Racial Equality in the Urban North, 1945–1969," 91 *Journal of American History* 145 (2004).

88 **"It had sixteen craft unions":** Arthur A. Fletcher, "A Personal Footnote

in History," in *The Affirmative Action Debate,* ed. George E. Curry (1996), 25–30, at 27.

89 **"reasonable percentage of the working hours":** *Id.,* 27–28. Joseph Debro, the executive director of the National Association of Minority Contractors, charged that the large, white-owned firms would promise anything, "with the full knowledge that any excuse for non-performance will be accepted once the job is underway." "Minority Builder," 300.

90 **National Historical Park:** Graham, *Civil Rights and the Presidency,* 155–56.

91 **lose their contracts:** *New York Times,* 12 June 1969.

92 **at the same level:** See Avril V. Adams, Joseph Krislov, and David R. Lairson, "Plantwide Seniority, Black Employment, and Employer Affirmative Action," 26 *Industrial and Labor Relations Review* 686 (1972).

92 **regulatory powerhouse:** Hugh Davis Graham, *Collision Course: The Strange Convergence of Affirmative Action and Immigration Policy in America* (2002), 68–69.

92 **"whether the black leadership":** Nixon, *Memoirs,* 438.

93 **not set in stone:** Kotlowski, *Nixon's Civil Rights,* 105.

93 **"we went on to spread":** *Id.,* 72–73.

94 **with the government:** Ervin later claimed that the administration had lied to his committee, claiming that the Philadelphia Plan was limited in its application and would require only good faith efforts by construction contractors; there would be no set minority quotas. Graham, *Civil Rights and the Presidency,* 167–68.

94 **"Politically, I don't think":** Maurice Stans, *One of the President's Men* (1995), 69.

94 **affirmative action policy completely:** *Id.,* 140; see below, chapter 11.

95 **"Job tests and promotion criteria":** Graham, *Collision Course,* 78.

95 **a high school diploma:** 401 U.S. 424 (1971). The Duke Power Company had actively discriminated against blacks prior to the Civil Rights Act and had limited African Americans to the lowest-paying unskilled positions. Neither of the two tests the company used was intended to measure specific skills required by any of the jobs for which the employees sought promotion.

97 **"The destiny of minority group employment":** *Contractors Association of Eastern Pennsylvania v. Secretary of Labor,* 311 F. Supp. 1002, 1012–13 (E.D. Pa., 1970).

97 **lower-court rulings:** *Contractors Association of Eastern Pennsylvania v. Secretary of Labor,* 442 F.2d 159 (3d Cir. 1971); cert. denied, 404 U.S. 854 (1971).

98 **affirmative action plans:** A Nixon appointee, Brown proved a strong proponent of affirmative action. While it is hard to determine if Nixon wanted the EEOC to go as far as it did, starting in early 1973 the president and his close aides found more and more of their time taken up by Watergate, leaving agency heads pretty much unsupervised by the White House.

98 **"a way of life here":** Anne B. Fisher, "Businessmen Like to Hire by the Numbers," *Fortune,* 16 September 1985, 26; Peggy Simpson, "Why the Big Backlash Is a Big Bust," *Working Woman,* November 1986, 165; *New York Times,* 3 March 1986.

99 **affirmative action basis:** David H. Rosenbloom, "The Civil Service Commission's Decision to Authorize the Use of Goals and Timetables in the Federal Equal Employment Opportunity Program," 26 *Western Political Quarterly* 236 (June 1973). Rosenbloom was an academic fellow at the commission during this time, and his article is an eyewitness account of what happened.

99 **a decade earlier:** Minnie H. Freeman, "Blacks Making Their Mark in Legal Profession," 38 *Negro History Bulletin* 440 (August 1975).

99 **"getting the plan written into law":** Nixon, *Memoirs,* 438.

100 **the following table:** Virginia Willis, *Affirmative Action: The Unrealized Goal* (1973), 112. Willis has numerous tables illustrating the dearth of minority workers in various skilled trades.

100 **be completely warranted:** Thaddeus H. Spratlen, "The Record and Rhetoric of Black Economic Progress," 4 *Review of Black Political Economy* 1 (Spring 1974).

101 **the executive suites:** Bernard E. Anderson, "Affirmative Action Policy Under Executive Order 11246: A Retrospective View," in *Civil Rights and Race Relations in the Post Reagan-Bush Era,* ed. Samuel L. Myers Jr. (1997), 47–59, at 54–55.

102 **who did not try:** Stephan Thernstrom and Abigail Thernstrom, *America in Black and White: One Nation, Indivisible* (1997), 449; Fletcher is quoted in Alan Farnham, "Holding Firm on Affirmative Action," *Fortune,* 13 March 1988, 88.

102 **"If you've got the atom bomb":** "Acting Affirmatively to End Job Bias," *Business Week,* 27 January 1975, 94. The magazine declared that because of its potential power—even if rarely exercised—"no other agency matches the OFCC in the breadth of its influence."

102 **"the mortar binding CEOs to affirmative action":** Farnham, "Holding Firm on Affirmative Action," 88.

5. PREJUDICE PERSISTS, AFFIRMATIVE ACTION GROWS

105 **"Exclusion in the craft unions":** Nancy MacLean, *Freedom Is Not Enough: The Opening of the American Workplace* (2006), 90–91.

106 **to go to court:** *New York Times,* 3 April 1969.

107 **street corner society:** MacLean, *Freedom Is Not Enough,* 91–92.

107 **racial discrimination:** *New York Times,* 11 September 1977.

107 **"rational" economic theory:** The work of Becker and other economists trying to take discrimination into account is examined in William Darity, "Economic Theory and Racial Economic Inequality," 5 *Review of Black Political Economy* 225 (1975).

107 **"the vital accumulation of knowledge":** Thomas Sowell, "Economics and Black People," 2 *Review of Black Political Economy* 3 (1971).

108 **chance of success:** William Howard Quay Jr., *The Negro in the Chemical Industry* (1969).

108 **by the mid-1970s:** Minnie H. Freeman, "Blacks Making Their Mark in Legal Profession," 38 *Negro History Bulletin* 440–41 (1975).

108 **racial considerations:** Harry Gilman, "Economic Discrimination and Unemployment," 55 *American Economic Review* 1077 (1965). See also Marvin J. Levine, "The Conflict Between Negotiated Seniority Provisions and

Title VII of the Civil Rights Act of 1964: Recent Developments," 29 *Labor Law Journal* 352 (1978).

109 **Caucasian employees:** Avril V. Adams, Joseph Krislov, and David R. Larson, "Plantwide Seniority, Black Employment, and Employer Affirmative Action," 26 *Industrial and Labor Relations Review* 686 (1972).

109 **"for black people in American society":** Alexis Marcus et al., "An Economic Bill of Rights," 3 *Review of Black Political Economy* 1, 28 (1972); see also Louis Henri Bolce III and Susan H. Gray, "Blacks, Whites, and 'Race Politics,'" 61 *Public Interest* 61 (1979).

109 **"a surefire moneymaker like me":** A. Barry Rand, "Diversity in Corporate America," in *The Affirmative Action Debate,* ed. George E. Curry (1996), 66.

110 **goals or quotas:** *Id.,* 68–72.

111 **significant minority presence:** "Aerospace Concerns Hiring More Negroes," *New York Times,* 13 October 1968.

112 **for their policies:** Peggy Simpson, "Why the Big Backlash Is a Big Bust," *Working Woman,* November 1986, 165; *New York Times,* 3 March 1986.

112 **office or kitchen:** The antitrust suit that led to the company's breakup is explored in Peter Temin, *The Fall of the Bell System: A Study in Prices and Politics* (1987).

112 **Civil Rights Acts of 1866:** The Supreme Court in the *Civil Rights Cases* (1883) had struck down the 1875 Civil Rights Act, the last effort by Congress to act against state-sponsored discrimination. However, many parts of the 1866 bill remained on the books, although dormant until a century later. Civil rights lawyers discovered them and began using §§ 1981 and 1982 in civil suits regarding equal protection and property rights.

113 **higher management positions:** Full details are in the consent decree, *Equal Employment Opportunity Commission v. American Telephone and Telegraph et al.,* 365 F. Supp. 1105 (E.D. Pa. 1973). See also the views of William J. Kilberg, the solicitor of labor who played a major role in the negotiations, in "Progress and Problems in Equal Employment Opportunity," 24 *Labor Law Journal* 651 (1973).

114 **"The Consent Decree was necessary":** *McAleer v. American Telephone and Telegraph Co.,* 416 F. Supp. 435, 440 (D.C. Dist. 1975). McAleer and AT&T settled out of court for $14,000, of which $6,500 went to legal fees for his attorney. Tom Beauchamp, "McAleer v. AT&T," www.stephen hicks.org. Gesell, incidentally, had chaired the President's Committee on Equal Opportunity in the Armed Forces from 1962 to 1964.

114 **"The use of employment goals":** *Equal Employment Opportunity Commission v. American Telephone and Telegraph Co. et al.,* 556 F.2d 167, 180 (3d Cir. 1977); cert. denied, 438 U.S. 915 (1978). See also *Washington Post,* 4 July 1978. The three unions were the CWA, the telephone section of the International Brotherhood of Electrical Workers, and the Alliance of Independent Telephone Unions.

116 **14 Hispanics:** Elliot E. Slotnick, "Lowering the Bench or Raising It Higher? Affirmative Action and Judicial Selection During the Carter Administration," 1 *Yale Law and Policy Review* 270 (1983); Jon Gottschall,

"Carter's Judicial Appointments: The Influence of Affirmative Action and Merit Selection on Voting on the U.S. Courts of Appeals," 67 *Judicature* 165 (1983).

116 **EEOC intervention:** Obituary of Smith in *Washington Post,* 21 February 2018.

116 **"an ideological litmus test":** Phyllis Schlafly, "It's Time to Reform the 'Imperial' Judiciary," in *Taking Sides: Clashing Views on Controversial Political Issues,* ed. George McKenna and Stanley Feingold (1983), 119.

116 **"quiet mobilization of a comprehensive regime":** Hugh Davis Graham, "Civil Rights Policy in the Carter Presidency," in *The Carter Presidency: Policy Choices in the Post–New Deal Era,* ed. Gary M. Fink and Hugh Davis Graham (1998), 202–23, at 203.

116 **they wanted more:** Stuart Eizenstat, *President Carter: The White House Years* (2018), 839–42, 845.

117 **"It is through such programs":** John Dumbrell, *The Carter Presidency: A Re-evaluation* (1993), 93; *Public Papers of the Presidents: Jimmy Carter* (1979), 1320.

117 **"a fresh faith in the old dream":** Ricardo José Pereira Rodrigues, *The Preeminence of Politics: Executive Orders from Eisenhower to Clinton* (2007), 67; *Public Papers of the Presidents: Jimmy Carter* (1978), 1.

117 **"the single most important action":** *Public Papers: Carter* (1979), 398–406.

117 **Labor to the EEOC:** Executive Order 12086, 43 Fed. Reg. 46501, 5 October 1978. The same day, Carter issued Executive Order 12068, 43 Fed. Reg. 28971, transferring all responsibility for litigation under § 707 of Title VII of the 1964 Civil Rights Act, as amended, regarding litigation against any public-sector employer.

118 **"be accomplished by executive order":** Executive Order 12086, 43 Fed. Reg. 46501, 5 October 1978; *Public Papers: Carter* (1978), 404.

118 **responsibilities to the EEOC:** Executive Order 12106, 44 Fed. Reg. 1053, 28 December 1978, and Executive Order 12144, 44 Fed. Reg. 37193, 22 June 1979.

118 **consistency in federal policy:** Executive Order 12250, 45 Fed. Reg. 72995, 2 November 1980.

118 **charting new directions:** A *U.S. News & World Report* survey in the summer of 1977 of House and Senate members gave Carter high marks for his executive action and efforts to streamline the bureaucracy. However, most of those polled, including Democrats, rated his effectiveness in working with Congress as "below average." Cited in Rodrigues, *Preeminence of Politics,* 71.

119 **nothing more than commonsense fairness:** Brent Staples, "What the United States Army Teaches Us About Affirmative Action," *New York Times,* 6 January 2003. Staples also notes the racism that characterized the army in the two world wars and had still not dissipated by the time Alexander took office.

119 **regarding affirmative action:** Section 103 (f) (2) of 91 Stat. 116 (1977). One should note that most large contractors already subcontracted part of their jobs. For example, a company building a hospital might well subcontract out plumbing, electrical work, painting, and other specific

tasks to smaller firms. Usually, however, these primarily white-owned companies had a track record known to the prime contractor.

120 **"we more often encounter a business system"**: This section is based primarily on Graham, "Civil Rights Policy," 206–9.

121 **on 2 July 1980**: *Fullilove v. Klutznick,* 448 U.S. 448 (1980). See Felicity Hardee, *"Fullilove* and the Minority Set Aside: In Search of an Affirmative Action Rationale," 29 *Emory Law Journal* 1127 (1980).

122 **affirmative action cases**: Despite the Nixon and Ford appointments—Burger, Blackmun, Powell, Rehnquist, and Stevens—the Burger Court did not depart greatly from the standards set by the Warren Court, thanks in large measure to the effective—one might even say brilliant—leadership of William Brennan. The far more conservative appointments of Reagan and Bush—O'Connor, Scalia, Kennedy, and Thomas—had little sympathy for affirmative action.

122 **would be necessary**: EEOC, *Affirmative Action and Equal Employment: A Guidebook for Employers* (1974), 1:16–61.

126 **grudgingly follow suit**: "Where Is Shannon Faulkner Now?," *Charleston Post and Courier,* 20 October 2012. For the VMI case, see *United States v. Virginia,* 518 U.S. 515 (1996). An excellent study, which shows how VMI avoided the Citadel debacle, is Philippa Strum, *Women in the Barracks: The VMI Case and Equal Rights* (2002).

126 **and household help**: Elmer E. Wells, "Affirmative Action: Dead or Alive?, 1970–1980," 48 *Negro History Bulletin* 49–58 (October 1985).

127 **compared with white men**: M. V. Lee Badgett, "The Impact of Affirmative Action on Public-Sector Employment in California, 1970–1990," in *Impacts of Affirmative Action: Policies and Consequences in California,* ed. Paul Ong (1999), 83–102.

127 **excluding the southern states**: If there is little or no impetus politically to recruit minorities, there will be little opportunity created for them, and at least in the 1970s southern states had little interest. See Kenneth J. Meier, "Constraints on Affirmative Action," 7 *Policy Studies Journal* 208 (1978).

127 **lagged behind women**: Gregory B. Lewis, "Progress Toward Racial and Sexual Equality in the Federal Civil Service," 48 *Public Administration Review* 700 (1988); see also "Black Men Are Last," *New York Times,* 14 March 1980.

127 **gains in the early 1980s**: Gregory B. Lewis and David Nice, "Race, Sex, and Occupational Segregation in State and Local Governments," 24 *American Review of Public Administration* 393 (1994).

127 **circumvent the glass ceiling**: I can attest to this by personal knowledge. The governor of Virginia, Gerald Baliles, appointed Susan L. Urofsky to head the Department of Rehabilitative Services, the first woman to hold that position, and she was reconfirmed in that office by Baliles's successor, L. Douglas Wilder. The advisory board had not been consulted and would have preferred someone else.

128 **white females of 58 and 73**: Andrew Hacker, *Two Nations: Black and White, Separate, Hostile, Unequal* (1995), 259.

129 **as much as men**: Numbers vary depending on the methodology used, but there is general agreement that despite some gains, despite the Equal

Pay Act, and despite affirmative action, women were still paid less than men for comparable work. In 1970, according to one study, white women made about 86 percent of white male salaries, and that number slipped to 83 percent a decade later. *New York Times,* 16 January 1984. The National Research Council report is in *Science,* 31 January 1986, 449.

6. MARCO DEFUNIS, ALLAN BAKKE, AND BRIAN WEBER

130 **Marco DeFunis:** Information about DeFunis can be found in the obituary in *The Seattle Times,* 18 January 2002, and in Howard Ball, *The Bakke Case: Race, Education, and Affirmative Action* (2000), 22–25.

131 **When Charles E. Odegaard became president:** Odegaard (1911–1999), the nineteenth president of the university, made a number of changes and is credited with turning a complacent local school into a major university. During his fifteen-year tenure, the student population grew from sixteen thousand to thirty-four thousand, thirty-five new buildings opened, and the university budget went from $37 million to over $400 million.

132 **also denied admission:** The entering class also had 22 veterans and another 16 who had mitigating factors that offset low PFYA scores. Details about the law school's plan and the numbers involved can be found in Justice Douglas's dissent in *DeFunis v. Odegaard,* 416 U.S. 312, 320 (1974).

134 **"Where the purpose is to promote":** *DeFunis v. Odegaard,* 507 P.2d 1169 (Wash. 1973).

136 **attention at the time:** See Arval A. Morris, "Equal Protection, Affirmative Action, and Racial Preferences in Law Admissions," 49 *Washington Law Review* 1 (1973), written by a faculty member at the law school shortly after the state supreme court handed down its decision; and Larry M. Lavinsky, "*DeFunis v. Odegaard:* The Non-decision with a Message," 75 *Columbia Law Review* 520 (1975).

136 **Equal Protection Clause:** *New York Times,* 27 February 1974.

137 **"will receive his diploma regardless":** *DeFunis,* 416 U.S. at 317, 320. There is an exception to the mootness doctrine for cases that "are capable of repetition but evading review." This was not available here, because it is usually limited to the same litigant, such as in *Roe v. Wade,* where "Jane Roe" could have gotten pregnant again.

138 **"the Court clearly disserves the public interest":** *Id.* at 345, 350 (Brennan, J., dissenting).

138–39 **the university's plan:** When asked why he had written such a strong dissent from a per curiam, Douglas, who was then seventy-five, said it was simple: "I might not be around next time this issue comes up." In fact, Douglas suffered a debilitating stroke the next year and reluctantly resigned from the Court in November 1975.

139 **"To the contrary, the school appears":** *Id.* at 320, 331.

139 **"The Equal Protection Clause commands":** *Id.* at 342.

140 **shy of his fifty-third birthday:** *Seattle Times,* 18 January 2002. According to his family, DeFunis ran about five times a week.

140 **African Americans, Chicanos, Asians, and American Indians:** It is somewhat strange that the program included Asians as a minority need-

ing special attention. In 1973 and 1974, students of Asian origin gained 10 percent of the slots under the regular admissions program, although Asians at the time made up less than 3 percent of the California population. Robert M. O'Neil, "*Bakke* in Balance: Some Preliminary Thoughts," 67 *California Law Review* 171, 183 (1979).

140 **maximum to 600:** R. A. Maidment, "The US Supreme Court and Affirmative Action: The Cases of Bakke, Weber, and Fullilove," 15 *Journal of American Studies* 341, 345 (1981); a critical view of the Davis plan is John H. Bunzel, "*Bakke v. University of California,*" *Commentary,* March 1977, written before the Supreme Court granted cert. Bunzel, a well-known conservative, was then the president of San Jose State University.

142 **be able to practice:** In 1971, Bakke inquired of a dozen medical schools about their age policy and received near-uniform replies. Davis told him that "when an applicant is over thirty, his age is a serious factor which must be considered. . . . An older applicant must be unusually highly qualified." Ball, *Bakke Case,* 46–47; John C. Jeffries Jr., *Justice Lewis F. Powell Jr.* (1994), 455–56.

142 **students who gained admission:** For example, the MCAT science range for the minority students ran from 35 to 83; Bakke scored 97.

142 **admission to the medical school:** This might have been true if one compared Bakke only with those admitted in the "regular" group of eighty-four, and other white applicants with higher scores than his had also been rejected. But it was also quite clear that he had far higher scores than nearly all of those admitted under the set-aside. See Michael Novak, "The Gap Between Bakke and Those Who Got In," *Human Events,* 14 January 1978, 36.

143 **"the issue to be determined":** *Bakke v. Regents of the University of California,* 18 Cal. 3d 34, 48 (1976).

143 **"We do not hesitate to reject":** *Id.* at 50.

143 **for his legal expenses:** Only one judge, Mathew Tobriner, dissented, agreeing with the university's rationale for affirmative action. 18 Cal. 3d at 64 (Tobriner, J., dissenting). One has to assume that Judge Mosk wanted this case to go to the U.S. Supreme Court. He could have reached the same conclusion relying on the equal protection guarantees of the California state constitution. The Supreme Court will not review a state decision based on adequate state law grounds; once a lower court invokes a constitutional protection, as Mosk did here, the high court can, if it wishes, review it.

144 **no role to play:** Jeffries, *Justice Powell,* 459–60.

144 **in professional schools:** *New York Times,* 12 and 25 October 1977.

145 **"We are here—at least I am":** Earl M. Maltz, *The Chief Justiceship of Warren Burger, 1969–1986* (2000), 204.

146 **did the justices:** For the views of the justices during deliberations and opinion writing, see especially Jeffries, *Justice Powell,* chap. 14; Powell considered *Bakke* the most important opinion he wrote during his tenure. See also Seth Stern and Stephen Wermiel, *Justice Brennan: Liberal Champion* (2010), 445ff.; Tinsley E. Yarbrough, *Harry A. Blackmun: The Outsider Justice* (2008), 265–69; Linda Greenhouse, *Becoming Justice Blackmun: Harry Blackmun's Supreme Court Journey* (2005), 129–33; Charles L.

Zelden, *Thurgood Marshall: Race, Rights, and the Struggle for a More Perfect Union* (2013), 161–67; Bill Barnhart and Gene Schlickman, *John Paul Stevens: An Independent Life* (2010), 268–70.

146 "the nation's debt to black people": Mark V. Tushnet, *Making Constitutional Law: Thurgood Marshall and the Supreme Court, 1961–1991* (1997), 121.

146 "Both were intellectually coherent": Jeffries, *Justice Powell*, 463.

146 "Our Constitution is color-blind": *Plessy v. Ferguson*, 163 U.S. 537, 559 (1896) (Harlan, J., dissenting).

146 "The lesson of the great decisions": Alexander M. Bickel, *The Morality of Consent* (1975), 132–33.

147 "There can be no blinking the enormous": McGeorge Bundy, "Issue Before the Court: Who Gets Ahead in America?," *Atlantic Monthly,* November 1977.

147 percentage of the population: *United States v. Paradise*, 480 U.S. 149 (1987).

147 eight months later: The best narrative, although told primarily through the lens of Lewis Powell, is Jeffries, *Justice Powell,* chap. 14. One should also look at Stern and Wermiel, *Justice Brennan,* 445–55. When Brennan first saw Powell's draft, he suggested that Powell split his opinion so as to condemn quotas but uphold the use of race, a strategy already latent in Powell's draft.

148 that quotas could not: *Regents of the University of California v. Bakke*, 438 U.S. 265 (1978).

149 "You can do whatever you like": Jeffries, *Justice Powell,* 484.

150 "racists of reverse discrimination": Both quoted in Ball, *Bakke Case,* 15, 142.

150 "BAKKE—WE LOST": All cited in William J. Bennett and Terry Eastland, "Why Bakke Won't End Reverse Discrimination: I," *Commentary,* September 1978.

151 "You say this is fudging the issue?": *New York Times,* 29 June 1978; Meg Greenfield, "How to Resolve the Bakke Case," *Newsweek,* 24 October 1977.

151 "work things out": Joan Biskupic, *The Chief: The Life and Turbulent Times of Chief Justice John Roberts* (2019), 50.

151 comment on the case: David J. Bodenhamer, "Allan Paul Bakke," in *100 Americans Making Constitutional History,* ed. Melvin I. Urofsky (2004), 3–5; *New York Times,* 13 July 1988; Stern and Wermiel, *Justice Brennan,* 455.

152 *United Steelworkers of America v. Weber:* 443 U.S. 193 (1979).

153 affirmative action plan: The Southeastern Legal Foundation and the Anti-defamation League of B'nai B'rith filed amicus briefs supporting Weber.

153 of prior discrimination: *Weber v. Kaiser Aluminum and Chemical Corporation and United Steelworkers of America,* 563 F.2d 216 (5th Cir. 1977); Judge Wisdom's dissent is at 227.

154 "intention of its makers": Citing *Holy Trinity Church v. United States,* 143 U.S. 457, 459 (1892).

154 on the basis of race: Richard A. Epstein charged that Brennan not only

misread the intent of these sections but in his citation from the congressional debate truncated some of the quotations so as to justify his position. *Forbidden Grounds: The Case Against Employment Discrimination Laws* (1992), 403.

155 **war with Eastasia!:** 443 U.S. at 219, 222 (Rehnquist, J., dissenting). Two members of the Court did not participate, Justices Powell and Stevens; Justice Blackmun entered a concurrence.

155 **constitutionally applied:** *New York Times,* 29 June 1979; "Note: Insights on *Weber:* Its Implications and Application in Public and Private Affirmative Action Programs, Labor Unions, and Educational Institutions," 23 *Howard Law Journal* 521 (1980); William E. Boyd, "Affirmative Action in Employment: The *Weber* Decision," 66 *Iowa Law Review* 1 (1980).

155 **action plans in employment:** *EEOC v. American Telephone and Telegraph Co. et al.,* 556 F.2d 167 (3d Cir. 1977), cert. denied, 438 U.S. 915 (1978); *Washington Post,* 4 July 1978.

155 **"We reject the contention":** *Fullilove v. Klutznick,* 448 U.S. 448, 482, 483 (1980).

156 **previously been excluded:** Writing a year after the decision, Terry Leap and Irving Kovarsky predicted that *Weber* would have enormous influence on the private sector. "What Is the Impact of *Weber* on Collective Bargaining?," 31 *Labor Law Journal* 323 (1980). A year later, Dean Ronald D. Johnson predicted that human resources administrators "might do well to prepare themselves for a decade of affirmative action." "Voluntary Affirmative Action in the Post-*Weber* Era," 32 *Labor Law Journal* 609 (1981).

7. CHANGING ACADEMIA

157 **after twelfth grade:** According to a 2012 Pew Research study, the average high school graduate with no further education will earn about $770,000 over a forty-year work life. A person with just a bachelor's degree, and no advanced degree, will earn about $1.4 million. www.pewresearch.org.

158 **of whom 945 enrolled:** James Cass, "Can the University Survive the Black Challenge?," *Saturday Review of Literature,* 21 June 1969.

158 **graduate and professional schools:** Thomas E. Weisskopf, *Affirmative Action in the United States and India: A Comparative Prospective* (2004), 135.

159 **class entering in 1989:** The Mellon Foundation figures can be found in "College and Beyond," distributed by the foundation. The following section is based on William G. Bowen and Derek Bok, *The Shape of the River: Long-Term Consequences of Considering Race in College and University Admissions* (1998).

160 **number of minority students:** Some scholars have taken issue with these estimates and argue that in fact both the percentages and the actual numbers are higher. Weisskopf, *Affirmative Action in the United States and India,* 139.

160 **across New York State:** While Cornell is primarily a private school in the Ivy League, its College of Agriculture and Life Sciences is also the New York State land-grant college, so that in launching programs like this, the school would naturally look to fulfill its mission within the state. Cornell had admitted women since 1884, although one scholar claims that the school discriminated against women and provided them with

an inferior education. Charlotte Williams Conable, *Women at Cornell: The Myth of Equal Education* (1977).

160 **SAT scores altogether:** Anthony S. Chen and Lisa M. Stulberg, "Racial Inequality and Race-Conscious Affirmative Action in College Admissions: A Historical Perspective on Contemporary Prospects and Future Possibilities," in *Beyond Discrimination: Racial Inequality in a Postracist Era,* ed. Frederick C. Harris and Robert C. Lieberman (2013), 105–34, at 115.

161 **partake of the offerings:** Robert Pollack, "Farewell Letter to Columbia College Students," 8 May 1989.

161 **4.6 to 2.4 percent:** Cited in Weisskopf, *Affirmative Action in the United States and India,* 139; Susan Welch and John Gruhl, *Affirmative Action and Minority Enrollment in Medical and Law Schools* (1998).

161 **Admission decisions to undergraduate institutions:** David Boonin, *Should Race Matter? Unusual Answers to the Usual Questions* (2011), chap. 4, notes that these and other criteria used by schools rarely raise complaints and, although in some ways as "fair" or "unfair" as using race as a criterion, do not invoke heated moral arguments pro or con.

162 **type of school:** The University of Virginia's president, Edgar Shannon, hired a politically astute aide, Paul Saunier, to ease the transition of integration, and he was for the most part successful. See Ernie Gates, "Integrating from Behind the Scenes," *Virginia Magazine* (Summer 2017), 46–49.

162 **the expense of excellence:** Aside from references to newspapers and other sources, this section relies on "The History of Open Admissions and Remedial Education at the City University of New York," a study commissioned by the city, and available at www.nyc.gov.

163 **in the city system:** Diane Ravitch, *The Great School Wars* (1974), 180. See also James Traub, *City on a Hill: Testing the American Dream at City College* (1994).

163 **been previously admitted:** During this time, women's groups were also raising the issue of why there were not more females in tenured ranks or in administration. *New York Times,* 22 April 1972.

164 **"I was telling people":** Martin Mayer, "Higher Education for All?," *Commentary,* February 1973, 40. There is some question about just how effective the protests might have been among students, many of them first- or second-generation descendants of Catholic and Jewish immigrants. Engineering students, for example, set up a counterprotest against the administration allowing the disruption of their classes. "City College Rebellion," *New York Times,* 23 April 1969.

164 **second-class status:** *New York Times,* 27 and 29 May 1969; on 30 May, the CCNY Faculty Senate rejected the dual plan.

165 **mayoral election agreed upon:** Editorial, "Speeding Open Enrollment," *New York Times,* 12 September 1969.

165 **abetting black racism:** Various stories in *New York Times,* 17 September, 12 and 23 October, 6 and 17 November 1969.

166 **would do to CUNY:** *New York Times,* 14 December 1969.

166 **whites and others, 57.8 percent:** *New York Times,* 19 December 1975.

166 **poor but bright students:** *New York Times,* 19 April and 14 June 1970.

167 **on most campuses:** *New York Times,* 26 and 28 March 1971.

167 **Brooklyn College "new life"**: *New York Times,* 12 September 1971. Actually, the numbers really moved very little. Some faculty at the time believed that the president of Brooklyn had adopted a policy of passive resistance, so that the school never had a very high percentage of minorities who could not meet regular requirements. As a result, when the great experiment ended, Brooklyn was among the first to recover some semblance of its former self.

167 **"Many of the kids who came"**: Morris Dickstein, a longtime CUNY professor and well-known literary critic, to author, 25 August 2016. When administrators gave the entering class the standard assessment tests, they were reportedly "shocked" to learn that one-fourth of the students—now in college under open admissions—were reading at or below the ninth-grade level and an additional 40 percent scored between the ninth and the eleventh grades. *New York Times,* 14 September 1970 and 19 December 1975.

167 **"Many of them had not been"**: Philippa Strum to author, 22 February 2018.

167 **eight students failed**: Herman Badillo, *One Nation, One Standard: An Ex-liberal on How Hispanics Can Succeed Just Like Other Immigrant Groups* (2006), 122–23. A study at this time reported that one in three students in the system needed remedial work.

167 **more remedial work**: *New York Times,* 19 September 1971; Solomon Resnik and Barbara Kaplan, "Report Card on Open Admissions: Remedial Work Recommended," *New York Times Sunday Magazine,* 9 May 1971.

168 **hoped would be equality**: *New York Times,* 18 January 1972.

168 **"Even if only 15 or 20 percent"**: *New York Times,* 15 July 1973.

168 **went bankrupt in 1975**: See Martin Shefter, *Political Crisis/Fiscal Crisis: The Collapse and Revival of New York City* (1992).

168 **"and the required courses"**: Dickstein to author, 25 August 2016.

169 **picked up the story**: *New York Times,* 19 February 1974.

169 **administrators, adjuncts, and nontenured faculty**: *New York Times,* 4 October 1975.

170 **nearly five thousand people**: The system let go 1,842 full-time teachers, 2,632 part-time faculty, and 1,900 nonteaching professionals. *New York Times,* 9 September 1976.

170 **the old CUNY**: *New York Times,* 22 February 1978.

170 **the same playbook**: *New York Times,* 6 May and 19 June 1978. Another study around this time reported that one in every three students in the system needed remedial work.

170 **all of their requirements**: Badillo, *One Nation, One Standard,* 122–23.

170 **much more democratic**: For a contrary view, see the CUNY philosophy professor Barry R. Gross's *Discrimination in Reverse: Is Turnabout Fair Play?* (1978).

170 **can claim success**: Virginia Commonwealth University in Richmond tried an open admissions policy in the 1970s and had to abandon it as well.

171 **"bar like discrimination in the future"**: *Albemarle Paper Co. v. Moody,* 422 U.S. 405 (1975).

171 **"a sharing of the burden"**: *Franks v. Bowman Transportation Co.*, 424 U.S. 747 (1976).

171 **sometimes conflicting rules**: William A. Kaplan and Barbara A. Lee, *The Law of Higher Education*, 2 vols. (2006), § 5.4, Affirmative Action.

171 **of how to do so**: Robert A. Ibarra, *Beyond Affirmative Action: Reframing the Context of Higher Education* (2001), 237.

172 **0.3 percent were "Other"**: Alan E. Bayer, *College and University Faculty: A Statistical Description* (1970), 12. These results came from a sampling of 303 institutions, including 57 junior/community colleges, 168 four-year colleges, and 78 universities, and relied on questionnaire responses from 60,028 faculty.

172 **the name of equality**: See, for example, Nathan Glazer, "Regulating Business and the Universities: One Problem or Two?," *Public Interest* 43 (Summer 1979). Glazer's fears were not unfounded. See Gwendolyn H. Gregory, "Making the Affirmative Action Plan Work," 1 *Journal of College and University Law* 16 (1973).

172 **on detailing minutiae**: George C. Roche III, "What Is Affirmative Action?," *Human Events*, 1 June 1974, 9.

174 **as they had previously**: Carol Greitzer, "Women in the Universities: They Don't Rate," *New York Times*, 22 April 1972. Greitzer was a member of the New York City Council.

175 **had to be fought fiercely**: Sidney Hook, "The Road to a University 'Quota System,'" *Human Events*, 15 April 1972, 9, 12; the piece originally appeared in *Freedom at Issue*, the official publication of Freedom House in New York. Hook and a number of other faculty formed the Committee on Academic Nondiscrimination and Integrity, which consistently opposed the HEW pressure on colleges and universities. *New York Times*, 8 December 1974.

175 **"are suddenly waking up"**: John Chamberlain, "Academic Liberals Are Getting Wise to Quotas," *Human Events*, 2 December 1972, 14.

175 **and not a job**: I was chair of the department of history at VCU at the time and recall how the administration—president, provost, and deans—kept hammering to hire women and minorities.

176 **in their teaching areas**: Justus van der Kroef, "Another Threat to Our Universities," *Human Events*, 20 January 1973, 18–19. The HEW guidelines came out on 4 October 1972, and their chief interpreter was the same J. Stanley Pottinger who aroused Dr. Hook's ire. Van der Kroef was chair of the political science department at the University of Bridgeport.

176 **"Seldom has a good cause"**: *New York Times*, 11 August 1975.

176 **affirmative chaos**: *New York Times*, 2 August and 14 September 1975.

177 **"have yet to say what the Government"**: Dr. Ezorsky would remain an outspoken defender of affirmative action. See her book, *Racism and Justice: The Case for Affirmative Action* (1991).

177 **"end the numbers games"**: *New York Times*, 27 February 1975.

178 **be more effective**: Rodney J. Reed, "Affirmative Action in Higher Education: Is It Necessary?," 52 *Journal of Negro Education* 332 (1983).

178 **larger society as well**: See, for example, Bruce A. Kimball, "An Historical Perspective on the Constitutional Debate over Affirmative Action Admissions," 7 *Journal of Law and Education* 31 (1978).

178 "It is like being angry": Tom Wicker, "A Misplaced Anger," *New York Times,* 30 June 1974.

8. BACKLASH AND DEFENSE

180 **"Americans ought to honor"**: Cited in Frederick R. Lynch, *Invisible Victims: White Males and the Crisis of Affirmative Action* (1989), 2–3. See also the editorial "The Complaints of White Men," *New York Times,* 27 November 1977.

181 **small-business owners**: For a very good example of the angst of white intellectuals over affirmative action, see Midge Decter, "Benign Victimization," *Policy Review* (Summer 1980): 65–72.

181 **ideas of equal opportunity**: Polls among African Americans in the late 1960s showed overwhelming support for moderate groups such as the NAACP, Martin Luther King Jr., and Roy Wilkins and very little support for perceived radicals such as Malcolm X, Stokely Carmichael, and Rap Brown. A summer 1966 survey of blacks found that only one in twenty approved of "Black Nationalism." Stephan Thernstrom and Abigail Thernstrom, *America in Black and White: One Nation, Indivisible* (1997), 170.

182 **demand for a giveaway**: See, for example, Nancy MacLean, *Freedom Is Not Enough: The Opening of the American Workplace* (2006), 339.

182 **"Do you think that Negroes/blacks"**: Elaine B. Sharp, *The Sometime Connection: Public Opinion and Social Policy* (1999), 73–74.

183 **community strongly rejected**: *New York Times,* 19 and 21 February 1979; "A New Racial Poll," *Newsweek,* 26 February 1979, 48.

183 **help particular groups**: Loan Le and Jack Citrin, "Affirmative Action," in *Public Opinion and Constitutional Controversy,* ed. Nathaniel Persily, Jack Citrin, and Patrick J. Egan (2008), 162–83, at 166. See also Louis Henri Bolce III and Susan H. Gray, "Blacks, Whites, and 'Race Politics,'" *Public Interest* (Winter 1979): 61–75, for additional evidence of the complex results of polling.

183 **craft unions**: For organized labor's resistance from 1960 to 1974, see Dennis Deslippe, *Protesting Affirmative Action: The Struggle over Equality After the Civil Rights Revolution* (2012), chap. 1.

183 **much they disliked**: A sampling of conservative views can be found in American Enterprise Institute, *Affirmative Action: The Answer to Discrimination?* (1975), and Herman Belz, *Equality Transformed: A Quarter-Century of Affirmative Action* (1991).

184 **between 1971 and 1974**: Deslippe, *Protesting Affirmative Action,* 180–81.

184 **"few federal programs are now"**: Carnegie Council on Policy Studies in Higher Education, *Summary of Reports and Recommendations* (1980).

184 **"a widespread feeling that the process"**: Deslippe, *Protesting Affirmative Action,* 181–82.

185 **"in order to meet it admitted"**: Joseph Adelson, "Living with Quotas," *Commentary,* May 1978, 23, 26. There is no definitive data for whether affirmative action worked, with some studies reporting gains by minorities in the workplace and others showing little impact. See J. Edward Kellough, *Understanding Affirmative Action: Politics, Discrimination, and the Search for Social Justice* (2006), chap. 7.

185 **denounced his comments:** Bernard D. Davis, "Academic Standards in Medical Schools," 294 *New England Journal of Medicine* 1118–19 (13 May 1976).

185 **"meritocracy tends to create":** John C. Livingston, *Fair Game? Inequality and Affirmative Action* (1979), 153; see his chap. 12, "Meritocracy and Racism." See also Eric Schnapper, "New White Rights—the Transformation of Affirmative Action Jurisprudence," in *Old Rights and New*, ed. Robert A. Licht (1993), 112–47, at 115–16.

186 **"would meet with strong objections":** Smith, a scholar of Asian politics, had made his prediction based on how a form of affirmative action had worked in India. Quoted in Paul Seabury, "The Idea of Merit," *Commentary*, December 1972, 44. Seabury noted that Smith's predictions were "somewhat out of date."

187 **equality of results:** Lee Sigelman and Susan Welch, *Black Americans' Views of Racial Inequality: The Dream Deferred* (1991), 119, 126–34. The authors cite and analyze various polls on attitudes toward school integration, affirmative action, and other issues in chapter 7.

187 **in a 1984 survey:** *Id.*, 128–29.

187 **affirmative action as well:** The difference between black and white responses is most dramatic when asked whether black applicants should be given special treatment because of past discrimination. A Gallup poll in 1984 found half of blacks agreeing with this statement, while less than one in ten whites agreed.

188 **"a fair shake":** Charlotte Steeh and Maria Krysan, "Trends: Affirmative Action and the Public," 60 *Public Opinion Quarterly* 128 (1996), also notes that there appear to have been contradictory views in the 1970s, but consistency in the opposition to both prejudice against minorities and quotas.

188 **black community wanted:** Thomas Sowell, "A Black 'Conservative' Dissents," *New York Times*, 8 August 1976.

189 **hiring women and minorities harder:** *Id.;* see also his "Black Progress Can't Be Legislated," *Washington Post*, 12 August 1984.

189 **"The truly disadvantaged—those with little":** Thomas Sowell, " 'Affirmative Action' Reconsidered," *Public Interest* (Winter 1976): 47–65. Sowell has been criticized for arguing that political action is irrelevant to black economic advancement, other than to the extent that it removes governmental impediments to the free market. He does not believe that there may be a connection between political success and economic progress or that a different kind of politics (other than deregulation) could help black Americans. W. Avon Drake and Robert D. Holsworth, *Affirmative Action and the Stalled Quest for Black Progress* (1996), 114.

189 **help as patronizing:** On this point, see the exchange between Charles Murray and Derek Bok in the 31 December 1984 and 4 February 1985 issues of *The New Republic*. See also, "Blacks Debate the Costs of Affirmative Action," *New York Times*, 10 June 1990.

189 **"the drive to get a good-looking":** In 1984, the California State University system lowered admissions standards slightly so as to get a larger applicant pool, especially of minorities. At the same time, a Cal State official noted that black and Latino students appear to have more trouble

than other students in finishing required high school courses. Lynch, *Invisible Victims*, 36.

189 **"distract the subordinate group"**: In the symposium "Race, Class, and the Contradictions of Affirmative Action," *Black Law Journal* 270, 275 (1980). See also his book, *And We Are Not Saved: The Elusive Quest for Racial Justice* (1987).

190 **"the liberal white is increasingly uneasy"**: Murray Friedman, "The White Liberal's Retreat," *Atlantic Monthly,* January 1963, 42.

190 **legally mandated segregation:** The prejudice against people of color in the North has been well documented. After the Civil War, blacks in the North did not face the extreme measures taken in the former Confederate states, but there was segregation in many public facilities and restrictions on voting. Most of these disappeared in the post–World War II era, but major discrimination still existed. See Arnold R. Hirsch, *Making the Second Ghetto: Race and Housing in Chicago, 1940–1960* (1983).

190 **"In the North, Negroes would be demanding"**: Anthony Lewis, "Concern Grows over 'White Backlash,'" *New York Times,* 10 May 1964. The animus against blacks erupted in many places, such as the rioting in Boston after a court ordered busing to end de facto school segregation.

191 **white person did not:** This is, to some extent, too simple an explanation, but it does get at the heart of the matter. For a more sophisticated version based on polling and social science nomenclature, that is, "competitive self-interest," see James R. Kluegel and Eliot R. Smith, "Affirmative Action Attitudes: Effects of Self-Interest, Racial Affect, and Stratification Beliefs on Whites' Views," 61 *Social Forces* 797 (1983).

191 **"When receiving an application"**: Letter to *Los Angeles Times,* 2 October 1983, quoted in Lynch, *Invisible Victims*, 5–6.

191 **"hard data" is unreliable:** For more examples, see Darien A. McWhirter, "Victims of Affirmative Preference," in *The End of Affirmative Action: Where Do We Go from Here?* (1996). McWhirter argues that affirmative action programs have "sometimes meant hiring or promoting people who were not qualified" because of their race or gender, but admits that it is impossible to say how often this has happened.

191 **reverse discrimination:** Lynch, *Invisible Victims*, 7.

192 **by the government:** "Affirmative Action at the Crossroads," *Nation's Business,* March 1968; *New York Times,* 3 March 1986.

192 **against union activists:** This section relies heavily on Marvin J. Levine, "The Conflict Between Negotiated Seniority Provisions and Title VII of the Civil Rights Act of 1964: Recent Developments," 29 *Labor Law Journal* 352 (June 1978). See also Karen G. Kramer, "Voluntary Affirmative Action in the Private Sector—Are Seniority Overrides for Layoffs Permissible?," 35 *Hastings Law Journal* 379 (1983).

193 **"Resentment among minorities and women"**: *New York Times,* 19 March 1975.

193 **appear to be race or gender neutral:** *Griggs v. Duke Power Company,* 401 U.S. 424 (1971).

194 **plant as a whole:** *Local 189, United Papermakers v. United States,* 416 F.2d 980 (5th Cir. 1969); cert. denied, 397 U.S. 919 (1970).

194 **other government agencies:** "Seniority Squeezes Out Minorities in Lay-offs," *Business Week,* 5 May 1975.

194 **heavily on minorities:** *Waters v. Wisconsin Steel Works of International Harvester Corp.,* 502 F.2d 1309 (7th Cir. 1974), and *Jersey Central Power & Light Co. v. International Brotherhood of Electrical Workers, Local 327,* 508 F.2d 687 (3d Cir. 1975).

194 **contractual obligations:** *Watkins v. Steel Workers Local 2369,* 516 F.2d 45 (5th Cir. 1975); see also *United States v. Hayes International Corp.,* 456 F.2d 112 (5th Cir. 1972).

194 **during a layoff:** *Wygant v. Jackson Board of Education,* 476 U.S. 267 (1986). The Court did hear some other cases involving seniority, but for the most part avoided a hard-and-fast ruling, focusing on technical details or sending the case back to the lower courts for rehearing.

195 **"industry-wide lawsuit could lead":** Deslippe, *Protesting Affirmative Action,* 42–43. Under the terms of the decree, neither steel companies nor the union had to admit violations of workers' rights and were exempt from further class-action lawsuits. Minority men and women as well as white women came into the mills taking jobs once held by white men. It proved to be a Pyrrhic victory, however, because a stagnant economy and the growth of imported steel led to the loss of thirty thousand jobs in steel, thinning and weakening the union ranks.

195 **"part of the moral economy":** Nelson Lichtenstein, *State of the Union: A Century of American Labor* (2002), 206. There were, of course, occasions when both union leaders and employers had violated the seniority principle, most notably in regard to women workers at the end of World War II, when they invented departmental or unit seniority to shut women and minorities out of higher-paying jobs.

195 **cared about them:** For a particularly bitter account, see Lynch, *Invisible Victims;* Herbert Hill of the NAACP had little sympathy for either unions or male blue-collar workers' complaints that they had become the victims of discrimination. See Hill, "Affirmative Action and the Quest for Job Equality," 6 *Review of Black Political Economy* 263 (1976).

195 **through one lens:** This section is based on Drake and Holsworth, *Affirmative Action and the Stalled Quest for Black Progress,* chap. 5. The process, however, had begun earlier with Nixon's southern strategy.

196 **"Some previously quite controversial":** Albert Karnig and Susan Welch, *Black Representation and Urban Policy* (1980), 9. A few years later, Paul Burstein noted and applauded evidence of recent declines in prejudice but said there was no way to know whether that trend would continue or reverse. Paul Burstein, *Discrimination, Jobs, and Politics: The Struggle for Equal Opportunity in the United States Since the New Deal* (1985), 159.

197 *individual* **white males:** While *Bakke* supposedly barred outright quotas, it did not take very much ingenuity to establish a "goal" that in fact was a quota.

197 **"The fate of young men and women":** Editorial, "Disadvantaged Groups, Individual Rights," *New Republic,* 15 October 1977, 7.

198 **"institutionalized division of the pie":** Morris Abram, letter to the

editor, *Atlantic,* January 1978, 77; see also the interview with him in *U.S. News & World Report,* 27 May 1985, 50. The effect of affirmative action in general, and quotas in particular, on relations between Jews and African Americans is discussed in the next chapter.

198 **"A racial quota derogates"**: Alexander Bickel, *The Morality of Consent* (1975), 133.

199 **"Klan did in a century"**: MacLean, *Freedom Is Not Enough,* 236. Other conservatives adopted the color-blind approach and tried to put distance between it and segregationist ideas. In fairness, Kilpatrick ultimately acknowledged that segregation was a lost cause and reexamined his earlier defense of it. His comments, however, bear an eerie resemblance to those of Chief Justice John Roberts: "The way to stop discrimination on the basis of race is to stop discriminating on the basis of race." *Parents Involved in Community Schools v. Seattle School District No. 1,* 551 U.S. 701, 748 (2007).

199 **"is not the Department of Health"**: John H. Bunzel, "Affirmative Action Must Not Result in Lower Standards or Discrimination Against the Most Competent Students," *Chronicle of Higher Education,* 1 March 1989.

199 **"now attach[es] benefits and penalties"**: See also Alan H. Goldman, *Justice and Reverse Discrimination* (1979), who argued that compensatory programs are owed only to individuals who have been the actual victims of discrimination, and not to any group.

200 **not just morally**: For a debate on the moral aspects, see William T. Blackstone, "Reverse Discrimination and Compensatory Justice," 3 *Social Theory and Practice* 263 (1975), and Tom Beauchamp, "Blackstone and the Problem of Reverse Discrimination," 5 *Social Theory and Practice* 227 (1979).

201 **into American life**: See Nathan Glazer, *We Are All Multiculturalists Now* (1997), chap. 6.

202 **affirmative action worked**: "Battle Heats Up over Sex, Race Bias in Jobs," *U.S. News & World Report,* 27 May 1985, 49; "Assault on Affirmative Action," *Time,* 25 February 1985, 20.

202 **perceived as just**: Daniel C. Maguire, "Unequal but Fair: The Morality of Justice by Quotas," *Commonweal,* 14 October 1977, 648–49.

202 **"past and present degeneration"**: Herbert O. Reid Sr., "Assault on Affirmative Action: The Delusion of a Color-Blind America," 23 *Howard Law Journal* 381, 382, 428 (1980).

202 **"The occupational spheres where blacks"**: Stephen Steinberg, *Turning Back: The Retreat from Racial Justice in American Thought and Policy* (1995), 167.

203 **"he owes a debt to legal justice"**: Maguire, "Unequal but Fair," 649.

203 **"my family came over on the *Mayflower*"**: Paul R. Spickard, "Why I Believe in Affirmative Action," *Christianity Today,* 1 October 1986, 12.

204 **"I received 300 pieces of hate mail"**: Spickard to author, 1 December 2016.

9. BLACKS AND JEWS DIVIDE

206 **NAACP for decades:** Mark V. Tushnet, *The NAACP's Legal Strategy Against Segregated Education, 1925–1950* (1987), 16–25; Jack Greenberg, *Crusaders in the Courts: Legal Battles of the Civil Rights Movement* (2004).

206 **opportunities for minorities:** *New York Times,* 30 June 1974.

207 **should be merit:** *New York Times,* 10 and 16 September 1972 and 25 March 1973.

207 **"this group appears to have":** Nancy MacLean, *Freedom Is Not Enough: The Opening of the American Workplace* (2006), 187–88.

208 **tensions between the two:** Cheryl Lynn Greenberg, *Troubling the Waters: Black-Jewish Relations in the American Century* (2006).

208 **to do the same thing:** See Melvin I. Urofsky, ed., *Why Teachers Strike: Teachers Rights and Community Control* (1970).

209 **in fact destroyed it:** Paul Seabury, "The Idea of Merit," *Commentary,* December 1972. So-called critical race theorists denounced notions of merit as manipulable and based on culture, and objected to the success that certain groups, such as Americans of Asian ancestry and especially Jews, enjoyed in a society dominated by white gentiles. See Daniel A. Farber and Suzanna Sherry, "Is the Radical Critique of Merit Anti-Semitic?," 83 *California Law Review* 853 (1995).

209 **category of "Other White":** Two years earlier, the school board had—without any protest—implemented a policy seeking minority members for a program of training so they would be better prepared to compete whenever administrative openings occurred.

210 **all that mattered:** Earl Raab, "Quotas by Any Other Name," *Commentary,* January 1972.

211 **all white ethnics:** Kevin P. Phillips, "'Affirmative Action' Decrees Are Getting out of Hand," *Human Events,* 15 January 1977, 7. Phillips believed that in the mid-1970s "Eastern European and Mediterranean ethnic groups really aren't much further up the executive ladder than non-whites."

211 **its admissions policy:** While there are several works about the *numerus clausus* in Europe, there is relatively little on its American history. Beginning in the 1930s, the *American Jewish Year Book,* sponsored by the American Jewish Committee, began tracking the number of Jewish students in the leading American colleges and professional schools. See the article in the 1955 *Year Book* by Oscar Handlin and Mary Handlin at 75–77. See also Marcia Graham Synnott, "Anti-Semitism and American Universities: Did Quotas Follow Jews?," in *Anti-Semitism in American History,* ed. David A. Gerber (1986), 233–71. For the Ivy League, see Jerome Karabel, *The Chosen: The Hidden History of Admission and Exclusion at Harvard, Yale, and Princeton* (2005).

211 **general American population:** Stanley Lieberson and Mary C. Waters, *From Many Strands: Ethnic and Racial Groups in Contemporary America* (1988), 138–39; Sidney Goldstein, "Profile of American Jewry," 1992 *American Jewish Year Book* 77, 110–11.

212 *The Public Interest:* While this group was certainly conservative, at least as compared with the liberal wing of the Democratic Party, they

differed from the conservatives whose intellectual leader was William Buckley, the editor of the *National Review*. They objected to Buckley's defense of Senator Joseph McCarthy, the opposition to civil rights, and the embrace of biological racism. For the most part, the early neocons still had a continuing commitment to the New Deal welfare state, opposed McCarthyism, and supported civil rights. Led by Kristol and Podhoretz, they developed a new conservatism devoted to classic liberal ideas. See Irving Kristol, *Neoconservatism: The Autobiography of an Idea* (1999), and Norman Podhoretz, *The Norman Podhoretz Reader* (2004).

212 "American liberals are now divided": "Liberalism and the Negro: A Round-Table Discussion," *Commentary*, March 1964, 25–42.

212 "Is it good for the Jews?": Norman Podhoretz, "Is It Good for the Jews?," *Commentary*, February 1972, 7–12.

213 to do just that: Nathan Glazer, *Affirmative Discrimination: Ethnic Inequality and Public Policy* (1975).

213 "I liked John Kennedy": Jonathan Rieder, *Canarsie: The Jews and Italians of Brooklyn Against Liberalism* (1985), 109.

214 made it on their own: For more on affirmative action in Canarsie, see *id.*, 107–19.

214 the total population: MacLean, *Freedom Is Not Enough*, 199; Stephen Steinberg, *The Academic Melting Pot: Catholics and Jews in American Higher Education* (1974), 122–23; Charles E. Silberman, *A Certain People: American Jews and Their Lives Today* (1985), 144.

214 Jewish defense organizations: For the *DeFunis* case, see chapter 6.

215 "Jews have said, 'Let's make sure'": MacLean, *Freedom Is Not Enough*, 201.

215 "We cooked up a real storm": *Id.*, 202–3.

215 the liberal tradition: Norman Podhoretz, *Breaking Ranks: A Political Memoir* (1979), 305, 334.

216 "illegal and immoral": Daniel Bell, "On Meritocracy and Equality," *Public Interest* (Fall 1972): 31ff.; Paul Seabury, "HEW and the Universities," *Commentary*, February 1972, 97–112; Nathan Glazer, "Jews and Blacks: What Happened to the Grand Alliance?," in *Jews in Black Perspectives: A Dialogue*, ed. Joseph R. Washington (1984), 108; Carl Cohen, "Why Racial Preference Is Illegal and Immoral," *Commentary*, June 1979, 40–51.

216 doors by themselves: Seymour Martin Lipset called African Americans "the great exception to the American Creed." "A Unique People in an Exceptional Country," in *American Exceptionalism: A Double-Edged Sword* (1996), 151–75.

216 proven more than enough: Stephen Steinberg, *The Ethnic Myth: Race, Ethnicity, and Class in America* (1981).

216 "are deprived not of their rights": Samuel Walker, *In Defense of American Liberties: A History of the ACLU* (1990), 305–6.

217 always defending the plans: Interview with the longtime ACLU board member Philippa Strum, Washington, D.C., 1 July 2015.

217 affect Jews adversely: See the discussion in MacLean, *Freedom Is Not Enough*, 207ff.

217 "it is self-deluding to advocate": Walter T. Hubbard Jr. was one of the leaders of the Black Catholic Movement.

218 **escape the quota system:** Seabury, "Idea of Merit," 41.

218 **resentment among whites:** Numbers can be found in Richard B. Freeman, *Black Elite: The New Market for Highly Educated Black Americans* (1976), 195–213.

218 **The third prong reflected:** Nathan Glazer, "The Exposed American Jew," *Commentary*, June 1975; MacLean, *Freedom Is Not Enough*, 209; Norman Podhoretz, "A Certain Anxiety," *Commentary*, February 1972, 10.

218 **common in that era:** The sole exception, of course, was Hadassah, the American women's Zionist organization, which readily recognized talented women among its members and moved them into positions of responsibility.

219 **"affirmative action for [white] women":** MacLean, *Freedom Is Not Enough*, 192.

220 **"Jews were far and away":** Joan Steinau Lester, *Eleanor Holmes Norton: Fire in My Soul* (2003), 151.

221 **"They use the very system":** MacLean, *Freedom Is Not Enough*, 213–16, has many examples of black anger and a feeling of betrayal.

222 **lobby for Israel:** Andrew De Roche, *Andrew Young: Civil Rights Ambassador* (2003); "The Fall of Andy Young," *Time*, 27 August 1979.

222 **agreement on affirmative action:** Arthur Hertzberg, "Jews, Blacks, and Affirmative Action," *New York Times*, 5 September 1979.

223 **"The son of a judge":** Seymour Siegel, "'Affirmative Action' Programs Spawn Grievous Injustices," *Human Events*, 9 September 1978, 744.

223 **"For many years now":** "Liberalism and the Jews: A Symposium," *Commentary*, January 1980, 15–82, at 15. As noted before, even though *Bakke* prohibited overt quotas, the editors believed that the euphemism "goals" actually meant quotas.

223 **condemn the plan as unconstitutional:** *Wesberry v. Sanders*, 376 U.S. 1 (1964).

225 **"relations between American blacks and Jews":** Glenn C. Loury, *One by One from the Inside Out: Essays and Reviews on Race and Responsibility in America* (1995), 83–85.

10. WOMEN AND AFFIRMATIVE ACTION

227 **eliminate sex discrimination:** *New York Times*, 3 December 1971.

228 **housekeeper, nurse, or stenographer:** Victor Riesel, "Government Wants More Blue-Collar Women," *Human Events*, 24 December 1977, 8.

228 **discrimination in the fire department:** Nancy MacLean, "The Hidden History of Affirmative Action: Working Women's Struggles in the 1970s and the Gender of Class," in *No Permanent Waves: Recasting Histories of U.S. Feminism*, ed. Nancy A. Hewitt (2010), 356–78, at 356–57. For a similar story of a woman trying to join the all-male Alabama State Police, see Gillian Thomas, *Because of Sex: One Law, Ten Cases, and Fifty Years That Changed American Women's Lives at Work* (2016), chap. 2. It eventually took a lawsuit to end discrimination against black firefighters. See David A. Goldberg, *Black Firefighters and the FDNY* (2017).

228 **safety regulations:** Samuel Leiter and William M. Leiter, *Affirmative Action in Antidiscrimination Law and Policy: An Overview and Synthesis*

(2002), 32–33; Nancy Woloch, *A Class by Herself: Protective Laws for Women Workers, 1890s–1990s* (2015), chaps. 1–4.

229 **private educational institutions:** Executive Order 11375, issued on 13 October 1967, amending Executive Order 11246, 32 Fed. Reg. 14303 (1967); Title IX is at 20 U.S.C. §§ 1681–88 (1972).

229 **Kennedy administration:** Equal Pay Act, amending the Fair Labor Standards Act, 77 Stats. 56 (1963).

230 **"for a wife anymore":** *Wall Street Journal,* 22 June 1965; *New York Times,* 3 July and 20 August 1965.

231 **160-year history:** MacLean, *Freedom Is Not Enough,* 140–41; Lindsey Van Gelder, "Women vs. the New York Times," *Ms.,* September 1978, 66–68. Abramson was fired in May 2014, to be replaced by Dean Baquet, the paper's first African American executive editor. *New York Times,* 14 May 2014.

231 **"the message came through clearly":** Frances Reuissman Cousens, *Public Civil Rights Agencies and Fair Employment* (1969), 13, and Aileen C. Hernandez, *E.E.O.C. and the Women's Movement, 1965–1975* (1975), 6–7, both quoted in Hugh Davis Graham, *Civil Rights and the Presidency: Race and Gender in American Politics, 1960–1972* (1992), 107.

232 **were not "feminists":** Betty Friedan, *It Changed My Life: Writings on the Women's Movement* (1976), 75–86.

233 **hiring and firing:** EEOC, *First Annual Report* (1966), 6. Most sex discrimination complaints came from women, but some came from men seeking to enter traditionally female jobs such as nursing.

233 **to name a few:** See Woloch, *Class by Herself.* The Supreme Court effectively put an end to protective legislation in *United Auto Workers v. Johnson Controls,* 499 U.S. 187 (1991).

234 **nineteen job categories:** The Supreme Court had previously had little difficulty with such laws. In *Goesaert v. Cleary,* 335 U.S. 464 (1948), six justices voted to uphold a Michigan law prohibiting women from working as barmaids, unless their husbands or fathers owned the bar, and in *Hoyt v. Florida,* 368 U.S. 57 (1961), sustained a Florida law keeping women off juries, a necessity to spare women from this obligation in light of their place at "the center of home and family life."

234 **"Shades of suffragettes!":** *Wall Street Journal,* 22 May 1967.

234 **had been resolved:** See Woloch, *Class by Herself,* 261–72.

234 **African Americans demanded:** Leiter and Leiter, *Affirmative Action in Antidiscrimination Law and Policy,* 51; James P. Scanlan, "Employment Quotas for Women?," *Public Interest* (Fall 1983): 106–12.

234 **"the belated feminist conversion":** See Graham, *Civil Rights and the Presidency,* chap. 6, for a more detailed analysis of the changes that took place in EEOC policy.

235 **"foundational questions about gender":** MacLean, *Freedom Is Not Enough,* 124–25.

235 **the usual "women's work":** MacLean, "Hidden History," 369.

236 **involved African Americans:** See Nancy DiTomasso, *The American Nondilemma: Racial Inequality Without Racism* (2013), chap. 8.

236 **its peaceful transition:** *United States v. Virginia,* 518 U.S. 515 (1996).

The case, its background, and its aftermath are well explicated in Philippa Strum, *Women in the Barracks: The VMI Case and Equal Rights* (2002).

236 **better social situation:** James T. Patterson, *Restless Giant: The United States from Watergate to Bush v. Gore* (2005), 53–54.

238 **departmental meetings:** For more on the status of women in academia, see Blanche Linden-Ward and Carol Hurd Green, *American Women in the 1960s: Changing the Future* (1993), 68–83.

238 **front of the classroom:** *New York Times,* 28 December 1975.

239 **not promoting them:** William E. Reif, John W. Newstrom, and Robert Monczka, "Exploding Some Myths About Women Managers," 17 *California Management Review* 72 (Summer 1975). It should be noted that the authors did not share these views, and the article cites numerous sources that conclude that the differences between men and women in managerial positions is far less than their similarities.

239 **needed for ratification:** Although Congress extended the deadline from 1979 to 1982, the ERA failed to pick up any further states, and in fact five states rescinded their ratification. Ironically, the opposition was led by a woman, Phyllis Schlafly. See Jane J. Mansbridge, *Why We Lost the ERA* (1986).

240 **decedents' estates:** *Reed v. Reed,* 404 U.S. 71 (1971). Although the then professor Ruth Bader Ginsburg did not argue this case, she helped guide the writing of Mrs. Reed's brief and arguments.

240 **leave if pregnant:** *Nashville Gas Co. v. Satty,* 434 U.S. 136 (1977); *Cleveland Board of Education v. LaFleur,* 414 U.S. 632 (1974). But if a woman could not be penalized for being pregnant, the employer did not have to reward her either. Pregnancy is not a disability, and state disability income plans could exclude pregnancy without violating equal protection (*Gedulgig v. Aiello,* 417 U.S. 484 [1974]); similarly, private employers could omit pregnancy from their disability coverage (*General Electric Co. v. Gilbert,* 429 U.S. 125 [1976]). Congress later reversed these two rulings through statute.

240 **prohibited by law:** *Phillips v. Martin Marietta Corp.,* 400 U.S. 542 (1971).

240 **their male counterparts:** *Frontiero v. Richardson,* 411 U.S. 677 (1973). Under the existing law, men automatically received a housing allowance and health-care benefits for their civilian wives; women received these benefits only if they supplied three-fourths of the family's support (all of their own and one-half of the husband's).

240 **and the Fourteenth (equal protection):** *Taylor v. Louisiana,* 419 U.S. 522 (1975).

240 **not to a widower:** *Weinberger v. Wiesenfeld,* 420 U.S. 636 (1975). See Ruth Bader Ginsburg, "Gender in the Supreme Court: The 1973 and 1974 Terms," 1975 *Supreme Court Review* 1.

240 **did not discriminate:** *Califano v. Goldfarb,* 430 U.S. 199 (1977), and *Wengler v. Druggists Mutual Insurance Company,* 445 U.S. 142 (1980).

241 **31 December 1979:** Thomas, *Because of Sex,* chap. 6.

241 **in Hishon's favor:** One should note that at the time of this case the Court had its first female justice, Sandra Day O'Connor. She had gradu-

ated magna cum laude from Stanford and third in her class at Stanford Law (William Rehnquist was first), yet the large law firms she applied to in the early 1950s offered her only a legal secretary position.

241 **not apply to it:** *Hishon v. King & Spalding,* 467 U.S. 69 (1984). Apparently, the sexism at King & Spalding took only a temporary hit. At a summer retreat in North Carolina, some of the men thought it would be "fun" to stage a wet T-shirt contest starring the firm's female associates, but then backed down and substituted bathing suits.

242 **$100,000 and more:** William Plummer, "Women Lawyers Agree That If Justice Is a Lady, She Has a Right to Make Partner," posted 2 July 1984 on www.people.com.

242 **that happened:** See Sheila K. Johnson, "It's Action, but Is It Affirmative?," *New York Times Magazine,* 11 May 1975, with the subtitle "Applying for Two Jobs, He Lost Out to Women Who Were Less Qualified." The story deals with the affirmative action plan the University of California signed with HEW.

11. THE REAGAN PRESIDENCY

246 **"it is hard to imagine":** Ronald Reagan, "Affirmative Action: Retailer Bites Bureaucrats," *Human Events,* 24 February 1979, 16.

246 **"fought and lost a holy war":** Quoted in Mark V. Tushnet, *Making Constitutional Law: Thurgood Marshall and the Supreme Court, 1961–1991* (1997), 121.

246 **"This promise," he explained, "wasn't meant":** Quoted in Howard Ball and Kathanne Greene, "The Reagan Justice Department," in *The Reagan Administration and Human Rights,* ed. Tinsley E. Yarbrough (1985), 1–28, at 14, 15.

246 **"becoming quota systems":** News Conference, 29 January 1981, Public Papers of the President, www.presidency.ucsb.edu.

247 **"was determined to revise":** Nicholas Laham, *The Reagan Presidency: In Pursuit of Colorblind Justice and Limited Government* (1998), 19.

247 **affirmative action:** For a very strong taste of this black conservatism, see Walter Williams, *The State Against Blacks* (1983). Williams, a professor of economics at George Mason University, argued that government intervention in the economy, and not racism, led to the underrepresentation of blacks in the workforce. See also Allan C. Brownfeld, "For Blacks, Government Is the Enemy, Not the Savior," *Human Events,* 5 March 1983, 11.

247 **"people who purport to represent":** Dona Cooper Hamilton and Charles V. Hamilton, *The Dual Agenda: Race and Social Welfare Policies of the Civil Rights Organizations* (1997), 208–9. See also Edwin Meese III, *With Reagan: The Inside Story* (1992), 314–15, where Meese overtly argues that Reagan's (and his) view of freedom and equal opportunity ran directly counter to that of the established civil rights organizations.

248 **its previous positions:** Robert Pear, "Smith's Term: Vast Changes Under a Conservative," *New York Times,* 23 January 1984.

249 **"last four decades":** William Bradford Reynolds, "Tending the Civil Rights Garden," 25 *Wake Forest Law Review* 197 (1990); and William Bradford Reynolds, "An Experiment Gone Awry," in *The Affirmative Action Debate,* ed. George E. Curry (1996), 130–36.

249 **"our country is not a group"**: William Bradford Reynolds, "The 'Civil Rights Establishment' Is All Wrong," *Human Rights* (Spring 1984): 40; Ball and Greene, "Reagan Justice Department," 21. See Reynolds's defense of how the Justice Department enforced Title VII in 34 *Labor Law Journal* 259 (May 1983).

249 **Executive Order 11246**: "EEOC Transition Team: End Affirmative Action," *Human Events,* 7 February 1981, 114.

249 **personnel cut in half**: Compliance review dropped sharply, although in the eight Reagan years it claimed to have completed a record number of reviews. According to one study, nearly all of these were "perfunctory and incomplete." During the four years of Carter's presidency, the office used its ultimate sanction—debarment from future federal contracts—thirteen times, but only four times during Reagan's eight years.

250 **sued for discrimination**: See, for example, *Washington v. Seattle School District No. 1,* 458 U.S. 457 (1983), challenging a Washington State initiative that prohibited busing for the purpose of racial integration. The lower courts held the initiative unconstitutional, and the Supreme Court affirmed.

250 **"breeds public distrust of the legal profession"**: Clifford Freed, "Ethical Considerations for the Justice Department When It Switches Sides During Litigation," 7 *University of Puget Sound Law Review* 405, 421 (1983). Freed also noted a 1976 American Bar Association report that a change of position by the government breeds "a substantial credibility gap in the minds of the public."

250 **not been fully investigated**: Ricardo José Pereira Rodrigues, *The Preeminence of Politics: Executive Orders from Eisenhower to Clinton* (2007), 76–77.

250 **could not keep up with its caseload**: James P. Smith, "Affirmative Action and the Racial Wage Gap," 83 *American Economic Review* 79 (May 1993).

251 **enforced existing rules**: *New York Times,* 25 August 1981.

251 **"quality and thoroughness"**: Bernard E. Anderson, "Affirmative Action Policy Under Executive Order 11246: A Retrospective View," in *Civil Rights and Race Relations in the Post Reagan-Bush Era,* ed. Samuel L. Myers (1997), 47–59, at 57.

252 **"Reagan Sends Mixed Signals on Civil Rights"**: *New York Times,* 16 July 1981.

252 **"an assault upon America"**: *New York Times,* 18 May 1981.

253 **"is dedicated and devoted"**: News Conference, 17 December 1981, Public Papers of the Presidents, www.presidency.ucsb.edu.

253 **"wrongly decided"**: *New York Times,* 30 December 1981. The *Weber* case is discussed above at pp. 151–156.

253 **"I have been on the side"**: News Conference, 20 January 1982, Public Papers of the Presidents, www.presidency.ucsb.edu.

253 **"bringing us together"**: Chester E. Finn Jr., "'Affirmative Action' Under Reagan," *Commentary,* April 1982.

254 **"The President and I are firmly behind"**: *Id.,* 24.

254 **"than affirmative action"**: "Affirmative Action: Will the Commitment Hold Firm?," 7 *Journal of Academic Librarianship* 3 (March 1981); Michael Kinsley, "Equal Lack of Opportunity," *Harper's,* June 1983.

254 **the following year:** Ball and Greene, "Reagan Justice Department," 13.

255 **action or not?:** Finn, "'Affirmative Action' Under Reagan," 26.

255 **December 1980:** The New Coalition apparently faded away in less than a decade. The IRS revoked the organization's tax-exempt status in 1993 after it had failed to file the necessary Form 990 for three consecutive years.

255 **"We believe the answer to black poverty":** Sophia Z. Lee, *The Workplace Constitution from the New Deal to the New Right* (2014), 243.

256 **shaped his views:** See Clarence Thomas, "Affirmative Action Goals and Timetables: Too Tough? Not Tough Enough!," 5 *Yale Law and Policy Review* 402 (1987).

256 **administration in general:** *Los Angeles Times,* 3 July 1991.

256 **any political traction:** Carter A. Wilson, "Exploding the Myths of a Slandered Policy," 17 *Black Scholar* 19 (May/June 1986).

257 **his report as well:** The gist of his report can be found in Harold Orlans, "Affirmative Action in Higher Education," *AAPSS Annals,* September 1992, 144–58.

258 **it did not work:** *New York Times,* 19 June 1983.

258 **a number of academic studies:** See Jonathan S. Leonard, "What Was Affirmative Action?," 76 *American Economic Review* 359 (May 1986). Leonard, a professor at Berkeley, worked with the Department of Labor and published in this piece his findings that affirmative action worked. Affirmative action also seems to have worked at the state level, surprisingly enough, in South Carolina. See also James Heckman and Brook Payner, "Determining the Impact of Federal Antidiscrimination Policy on the Economic Status of Blacks: A Study of South Carolina," 79 *American Economic Review* 138 (March 1989), and Susan D. Clayton and Faye J. Crosby, *Justice, Gender, and Affirmative Action* (1992), 99.

259 **"despite its name, this body":** Editorial, *New York Times,* 15 May 1987.

259 **other city agencies:** A consent decree is an agreement by a defendant to cease activities that the government has asserted are illegal. Upon approval by the court, the government's action against the defendant is dropped.

259 **negotiated with the city:** *Firefighters Local Union No. 1784 v. Stotts,* 467 U.S. 561 (1984). In the time between the first firings and the appeal to the Supreme Court, the city's fiscal problems had eased, and all of the white employees laid off had been hired back. The Court could easily have avoided this case by declaring it moot, but at least four justices wanted to deal with the issue, and under the rule of four the Court granted certiorari. For the impact of the case, see Theresa Johnson, "The Future of Affirmative Action: An Analysis of the *Stotts* Case," 36 *Labor Law Journal* 782 (October 1985).

260 **even resembling quotas:** Although the administration initially seemed eager to challenge the fifty-one existing consent decrees, it soon backed off. Reynolds, in an address to the American Bar Association, said they would challenge some but not all of them. *New York Times,* 13 August 1986.

260 **beneficial to minorities:** *New York Times,* 1 February 1985 and 13 June 1984; Charles Krauthammer, "In Defense of Quotas," *New Republic,* September 1985.

260 **race and sex discrimination:** *New York Times,* 13 June 1984.

260 **had been a party:** *New York Times,* 18 July and 16 June 1984.

261 **their vested interests:** *New York Times,* 14 June and 1 July 1984.

261 **discrimination in hiring:** *Van Aken v. Young,* 750 F.2d 43 (6th Cir. 1984).

261 **argued against it:** *United States v. Paradise,* 480 U.S. 149 (1982), confirming 767 F.2d 1514 (5th Cir. 1985).

261 **believed in such programs:** *New York Times,* 28 July 1984.

262 **secretary of education:** Lemann, "Taking Affirmative Action Apart," 49–50.

262 **agencies in the Labor Department:** In a speech at the NAACP convention in June, Brock told the delegates that the country would "have some form of affirmative action for the foreseeable future." *New York Times,* 25 June 1985.

262 **"evolved into precisely the sort":** Robert R. Detlefsen, "Affirmative Action and Business Deregulation: On the Reagan Administration's Failure to Revise Executive Order No. 11246," in *Presidential Leadership and Civil Rights Policy,* ed. James W. Riddlesperger Jr. and Donald W. Jackson (1995), 59–70, at 62.

263 **contractors to use them:** *New York Times,* 18 August and 12 September 1985.

263 **the idea of voiding 11246:** Nicholas Laham, a conservative independent scholar, strongly supported Reagan's opposition to affirmative action as well as the Meese plan. In his book *The Reagan Presidency and the Politics of Race: In Pursuit of Colorblind Justice and Limited Government* (1998), chap. 2, he details the many civil rights and political groups that opposed the Meese plan.

264 **"the dismantling of a pervasive system":** MacLean, *Freedom Is Not Enough,* 306–7.

264 **his other programs:** Laham, *Reagan Presidency and the Politics of Race,* 20.

264 **government requirements:** *New York Times,* 19 September 1985 and 17 January 1988; Detlefsen, "Affirmative Action," 66.

264 **not have gone quietly:** In fact, personnel officers in private industry across the country did not sit passively by but actively fought back both by working with civil rights groups and by touting the success of equal opportunity and affirmative action programs. See Kevin Kelly and Frank Dobbin, "How Affirmative Action Became Diversity Management: Employer Response to Antidiscrimination Law, 1961–1996," in *Color Lines: Affirmative Action, Immigration, and Civil Rights Options for America,* ed. John David Skrentny (2001), 87–117, 88.

264 **"Once a company has":** Detlefsen, "Affirmative Action," 68. Professor Detlefsen also notes a major split in business between large corporations, associated with the National Association of Manufacturers, and small businesses, who spoke through the U.S. Chamber of Commerce. The former overwhelmingly wanted to keep government requirements, while the latter, who had small personnel offices and no "entrenched bureaucracy," found OFCCP regulations expensive and intolerable.

265 **"will be harmful and destructive":** MacLean, *Freedom Is Not Enough,* 307.

265 **while opposing quotas:** Charlotte Steeh and Maria Krysan, "Affirma-

tive Action and the Public, 1970–1995," 60 *Public Opinion Quarterly* 128 (Spring 1996).

265 **goals and timetables:** *New York Times,* 23 October and 1 November 1985. In a speech to the Rotary Club in Wilmington, Delaware, Reynolds continued his public tirade against affirmative action. *New York Times,* 1 November 1985.

266 **other, more important things:** *New York Times,* 29 October 1985; Lemann, "Taking Affirmative Action Apart," 49. Shortly afterward, the Senate Judiciary Committee refused to recommend Reynolds for associate attorney general because of his opposition to affirmative action.

266 **Office of Federal Contract Compliance:** Lemann, "Taking Affirmative Action Apart," 49.

266 **to their efforts:** Iran-contra is outside the scope of this volume, but for details see Haynes Johnson, *Sleepwalking Through History: America in the Reagan Years* (1991), 245–371.

267 **almost all these decrees:** *New York Times,* 3 April 1985. The Justice Department initially did not want to release the names of the jurisdictions, but finally handed the list over to reporters after a Freedom of Information request.

267 **view echoed by others:** *New York Times,* 30 April, 1 and 8 May 1985.

267 **requirements from its plan:** *New York Times,* 4 and 5 May 1985.

268 **less precedential value than *Stotts*:** *Wygant v. Jackson Board of Education,* 476 U.S. 267 (1986). The National Education Association, the largest teachers' union in the United States, over strenuous objections from some of its members, had issued a statement in support of affirmative action in 1983 that even suggested seniority could be downgraded in certain cases. *New York Times,* 6 July 1983.

268 **"to read *Stotts* to prohibit":** *Local 28, Sheet Metal Workers International Assn. v. EEOC,* 478 U.S. 431 (1986).

268 **"the voluntary action available":** *Local 93, International Association of Firefighters v. City of Cleveland,* 478 U.S. 501 (1986).

268 **held only by men:** See next chapter.

268 **"very little impact" on the case:** *New York Times,* 1 April 1987.

269 **"deserves less credit":** 104 Stat. 327 (1990); John Robert Greene, *The Presidency of George Bush* (2000), 74–75.

270 **passage of the ADA:** Americans with Disabilities Act of 1990, *Wikipedia,* en.wikipedia.org. The crawl occurred on 12 March 1990.

270 **eager and capable workers:** There has been some debate over whether the ADA helped or hindered employment of the handicapped, and there are conflicting statistical studies about the rate of employment. A 2005 study found that the rate of employment among disabled people had increased to 45 percent of the disabled population. For assistive technology, see Karen F. Flippo, Katherine J. Inge, and J. Michael Barcus, *Assistive Technology: A Resource for School, Work, and Community* (1995), which reflected the latest thinking and devices available at the time.

271 **gates of opportunity:** For an overview of the law, its provisions, and its subsequent history, see Lennard J. Davis, *Enabling Acts: The Hidden Story of How the Americans with Disabilities Act Gave the Largest U.S. Minority Its Rights* (2015).

12. THE COURT CHANGES ITS MIND

272 **beyond its predecessor:** For comparisons between the Warren and the Burger Courts, see Vince Blasi, ed., *The Burger Court: The Counter-revolution That Wasn't* (1985), and Melvin I. Urofsky, *The Continuity of Change: The Supreme Court and Individual Liberties, 1953–1986* (1991), both of which emphasize similarities outweighing the differences.

274 **affirmative action programs:** These cases are discussed in the previous chapter, pp. 259ff.

274 **position was lawful:** *Johnson v. Transportation Agency, Santa Clara County, California, and Service Employees International Union Local 715,* 770 F.2d 752 (9th Cir. 1984). For details of the case, see Melvin I. Urofsky, *A Conflict of Rights: The Supreme Court and Affirmative Action* (1991).

274 **"whether the consideration of the sex":** *Johnson v. Transportation Agency, Santa Clara County,* 480 U.S. 616 (1987).

276 **have to pay for it:** *Id.,* at 657, 658 (Scalia, J., dissenting). Rehnquist and White joined Scalia's dissent, and White also wrote separately.

276 **against the court order:** *NAACP v. Allen,* 340 F. Supp. 703 (M.D. Ala. 1972); *Paradise v. Prescott,* 767 F.2d 1514 (11th Cir. 1985).

277 **forbidden by the Constitution:** *United States v. Paradise,* 480 U.S. 149 (1987).

277 **standards of strict scrutiny:** *Id.,* at 196 (O'Connor, J., dissenting), joined by Rehnquist and Scalia; Justice White filed a two-sentence dissent to the effect that he agreed with O'Connor and believed the district court exceeded its equitable power.

277 **violated the Constitution:** See Stuart Taylor Jr., in *New York Times,* 27 and 29 March 1987.

277 **undesirable as well:** George Rutherglen and Daniel R. Ortiz, "Affirmative Action Under the Constitution and Title VII: From Confusion to Convergence," 35 *UCLA Law Review* 467 (1988).

277 **"The central question in the national debate":** Robert Belton, "Reflections on Affirmative Action After *Paradise* and *Johnson,*" 23 *Harvard Civil Rights–Civil Liberties Law Review* 115, 116–17 (1988).

278 **Congress wanted overturned:** These cases are discussed at length in M. Ali Raza, A. Janell Anderson, and Harry Glynn Custred Jr., *The Ups and Downs of Affirmative Action Preferences* (1999), chap. 3.

278 **Brenda Patterson sued the credit union:** *Patterson v. McLean Credit Union,* 491 U.S. 164 (1989).

278 **In a 1971 case:** *Wards Cove Packing Co. v. Atonio,* 490 U.S. 642 (1989).

278 **violated Title VII:** *Griggs v. Duke Power Company,* 401 U.S. 424 (1971).

279 **Ann Hopkins, a senior manager:** *Price Waterhouse v. Hopkins,* 490 U.S. 228 (1989).

279 **AT&T had agreed to allow women:** *Lorance v. AT&T Technologies, Inc.,* 490 U.S. 900 (1989).

279 **Seven white firefighters sued the city:** *Martin v. Wilks,* 490 U.S. 755 (1989).

279 **"the good ol' boy network":** *New York Times,* 22 June 1989.

280 **"will lead inevitably to racial quotas":** William Laffer III, "Why Kennedy-Hawkins Will Mean Quotas," Heritage Foundation, 2 July

1990, www.heritage.org; George H. W. Bush, "Statement on Civil Rights Legislation," 20 October 1990, Public Papers of the Presidents, www .presidency.ucsb.edu.

281 **"introduce the destructive forces"**: Veto Message, 22 October 1990, Public Papers of the Presidents, www.presidency.ucsb.edu.

281 **the gubernatorial race**: Green, *Presidency of George Bush,* 66; see also Anthony Lewis on the danger posed by Duke, *New York Times,* 11 November 1991.

281 **"following a new trail of racial resentment"**: *New York Times,* 7 December 1990. Although the stratagem worked in some races, in the election that fall the Democrats increased their majority in the Senate from 55 to 58 seats, and in the House from 251 to 270.

281 **broad bipartisan support**: By this time, not only liberal Democrats but also moderate Republicans supported affirmative action. In the business world, as a newspaper headline put it, "Affirmative Action Plans Are Now Part of the Normal Corporate Way of Life," *New York Times,* 22 November 1991.

281 **21 November 1991**: 105 Stat. 1071 (1991).

283 **Title VII did not apply**: *EEOC v. Arabian American Oil Company,* 499 U.S. 244 (1991); Raza, Anderson, and Custred, *Ups and Downs,* 43–46.

283 **on the basis of race, color, or gender**: The practice had been around for years in the U.S. Employment Service, where the General Aptitude Test Battery was widely used for vocational counseling and job referrals. Before the practice was banned in 1991, an estimated three million people had been hired by employers based on race-normed scores. Many universities also used race norming in their admissions policies.

283 **upward in organizations**: Raza, Anderson, and Custred, *Ups and Downs,* 43–46.

283 **"The debate about its passage"**: Glen D. Nager, "Affirmative Action After the Civil Rights Act of 1991: The Effects of a 'Neutral' Statute," 68 *Notre Dame Law Review* 1057. The article is part of a symposium on the 1991 act.

283 **"impermissible reverse discrimination"**: The statements are at various places in the *Congressional Record* and are cited in Ronald Turner, "Affirmative Action and the Civil Rights Act of 1991," 44 *Labor Law Journal* 615, 618 (1993).

284 **expenses associated with a trial**: Nager, "Affirmative Action After the Civil Rights Act," 1075.

284 **most important case of the 1989 term**: *City of Richmond v. J. A. Croson Co.,* 488 U.S. 469 (1989). This section of the case relies heavily on my chapter on *Croson* in *Virginia and the Constitution,* ed. A. E. Dick Howard and Melvin I. Urofsky (1992), 192–207.

285 **admitted overt discrimination**: The American Subcontractors Association had no African Americans among eighty Richmond members; the Professional Contractors Estimators Association had sixty members, one of whom was black; and the National Electrical Contractors Association had two blacks among its eighty-one Virginia members.

287 **atone for discrimination**: Joan Biskupic, *Sandra Day O'Connor: How*

the *First Woman on the Supreme Court Became Its Most Influential Justice* (2005), 206.

287 **"While there is no doubt"**: *Croson,* 488 U.S. at 499.

287 **opposed affirmative action:** *Id.* at 520 (Scalia, J., concurring). The quotation at the beginning of the chapter is at 527–28.

288 **"The standard of review":** *Id.* at 494; Linda Greenhouse, "Signal on Job Rights," *New York Times,* 25 January 1989.

288 **whether they would survive:** Leslie A. Nay and James E. Jones Jr., "Equal Employment and Affirmative Action in Local Governments: A Profile," 8 *Law and Inequality* 103 (1989). "We estimate that there are many more affirmative action in contracting programs currently in operation than is commonly believed, and that minority set-aside programs are also prevalent." See also Martin J. Sweet, *Merely Judgment: Ignoring, Evading, and Trumping the Supreme Court* (2010), 124–25.

288 **could be documented:** *New York Times,* 24 January 1989.

289 **could be settled:** *New York Times,* 27 January and 3 March 1989.

289 **none of them on appeal:** Docia Rudley and Donna Hubbard, "What a Difference a Decade Makes: Judicial Response to State and Local Minority Business Set-Asides Ten Years After *City of Richmond v. J. A. Croson,*" 25 *Southern Illinois University Law Journal* 39 (2000).

289 **participated by phone:** The attendees were a Who's Who of American constitutional scholarship. The deans of Columbia, Harvard, Yale, Michigan, and Stanford Law Schools, as well as such well-known scholars as Barbara Black, Walter Dellinger, Norman Dorsen, John Hart Ely, Yale Kamisar, Robert O'Neil, and Cass Sunstein. The full list of attendees is appended to Joint Statement, "Constitutional Scholars' Statement on Affirmative Action After *City of Richmond v. J. A. Croson Co.,*" 98 *Yale Law Journal* 1711, 1714–16 (1989).

290 **efforts to do so:** The statement elicited a response from Professor Charles Fried of Harvard Law, solicitor general during the Reagan administration, who interpreted the *Croson* decision as far less amenable to the types of affirmative action steps proposed by the scholars group. His response is at 99 *Yale Law Journal* 155 (1989), and this in turn brought a further response from the original scholars group, at *id.,* 163.

290 **"This is a time for healing":** Anthony Lewis, "A Time for Healing," *New York Times,* 6 April 1989.

290 *Federal Communications Commission:* 497 U.S. 547 (1990), decided along with *Astroline Communications Company Limited Partnership v. Shurberg Broadcasting of Hartford.*

291 **"source of corruption":** *New York Times,* 4 July 1990.

291 **programs of the federal government:** *Adarand Constructors, Inc. v. Peña,* 515 U.S. 200 (1995).

292 **"The unhappy persistence of both":** *Id.* at 237.

292 **"We are just one race":** *Id.* at 239 (Scalia, J., concurring in part and concurring in the judgment).

292 **"ultimately be decided":** Linda Greenhouse, *New York Times,* 14 June 1995, and Charles Krauthammer, *Washington Post,* 16 June 1995. An editorial in *The New Republic,* 3 July 1995, calling for an end to all racial

preferences said that "this historic decision should be announced not by Sandra Day O'Connor but by the Congress of the United States."

292 **"in celebration or dismay"**: Quoted in Neal Devins, *"Adarand Constructors, Inc. v. Peña* and the Continuing Irrelevance of Supreme Court Affirmative Action Decisions," 37 *William and Mary Law Review* 673, 678 (1996).

293 **action for women:** Justice Department memorandum on *Adarand,* 28 June 1995, from Assistant Attorney General Walter Dellinger to general counsels, quoted in Gerald W. Heany, "The Political Assault on Affirmative Action," in *Civil Rights and Race Relations in the Post Reagan-Bush Era,* ed. Samuel L. Myers Jr. (1997), 217–26, at 223.

293 **be little affected:** Devins, "Adarand Constructors."

294 **grounds of discrimination:** In fact, the Bush Justice Department began the process on her behalf, and she joined the suit as an intervenor. After she had won in district court, however, the Clinton Justice Department declared that the previous government position was wrong and secured the court's permission to withdraw. The Third Circuit heard the case with Taxman as the sole plaintiff.

294 **for upholding diversity:** *Taxman v. Piscataway Township Board of Education,* 91 F.3d 1547 (3d Cir. 1996).

295 **plus attorneys' fees:** *New York Times,* 22 November 1997.

295 **had been admitted:** The numbers unearthed in the case indicate that without racial preferences only one out of 380 black applicants to the University of Texas Law School in 1992 had scores high enough to be admitted through the regular process. Out of all minority applicants to all law schools in the country, only 289 blacks and 96 Hispanics had scores high enough to put them in the discretionary zone for white applicants to Texas. Only 88 blacks and 52 Hispanics in the country had scores higher than the median for white students at Texas. Jeffrey Rosen, "A Reversal of Affirmative Action," 9 *Academic Questions* 15, 17 (Fall 1996).

295 **go to court:** There were three other plaintiffs, all recruited by an Austin lawyer, Steven Smith, who had filed a Freedom of Information request in 1992 as part of his own investigation into what he believed to be reverse discrimination at UT. *New York Times,* 13 July 1994.

296 **from minority applicants:** Michael J. Sandel, *Justice: What's the Right Thing to Do?* (2009), 167–68.

296 **reapply without a fee:** *Hopwood v. Texas,* 861 F. Supp. 551 (W.D. Tex., 1994).

296 **plan had to fall:** *Hopwood v. Texas,* 78 F.3d 932 (5th Cir. 1996). See Rosen, "Reversal of Affirmative Action," for a contemporaneous appraisal of the case.

296 **to integrate in 1950:** *Sweatt v. Painter,* 339 U.S. 626 (1950), in which the Court—four years before *Brown*—ordered the all-white University of Texas Law School to admit African American students.

297 **5.6 percent, respectively:** Samuel Ray Riley, "The Impact of Anti–Affirmative Action Lawsuits: A Case Study of the University of Texas Law School from 1996 to 2003" (EdD thesis, University of Texas at Austin, 2014). Dr. Riley is now director of admissions at the law school. I am indebted to my friend Professor Scot Powe, who put me in touch with

Jane A. O'Connell, the deputy director of the Tarlton Law Library, who provided this information.

297 **this important issue:** The denial of cert and Justice Ginsburg's concurrence are at 518 U.S. 1033 (1996).

13. MEND IT, DON'T END IT—OR NOT

298 **presidency in 1992:** A good overview of the Clinton presidency is Patrick J. Maney, *Bill Clinton: Gilded Age President* (2016).

298 **"I am honored to be thought of":** Marc Morano, "Clinton Honored . . . ," CBS News, 7 July 2008, www.cnsnews.com.

298 **"the American marketplace":** Joan Biskupic, "America's Longest War," *Washington Post,* 22 January 1993; Steve Roberts, "Affirmative Action on the Edge," *U.S. News & World Report,* 13 February 1995.

299 **"a surrogate for unsolved problems":** Lincoln Caplan, *Up Against the Law: Affirmative Action and the Supreme Court* (1997), 29.

299 **or ethnic classifications:** Robert K. Robinson, Ross L. Fink, and Billie Morgan Allen, "Affirmative Action in the Public Sector: The Increasing Burden of 'Strict Scrutiny,'" 49 *Labor Law Journal* 801, n.3 (January 1998).

299 **in jobs and schools:** A Zogby poll earlier in the year showed 77 percent of Americans, including 52 percent of blacks, 71 percent of Hispanics, and 67 percent of liberals, opposing racial preferences in school admissions. Ted Halstead and Michael Lind, *The Radical Center: The Future of American Politics* (2001), 249n.

299 **help African Americans:** James H. Kuklinski et al., "Racial Prejudice and Attitudes Toward Affirmative Action," 41 *American Journal of Political Science* 402 (1997).

299 **during his two terms:** "The Greening of America's Black Middle Class," *New York Times,* 18 June 1995.

300 **local governments:** James T. Patterson, *Restless Giant: The United States from Watergate to Bush v. Gore* (2005), 305–6; Sharon M. Collins, "The Making of the Black Middle Class," 30 *Social Problems* 369 (April 1983); James P. Pinkerton and Kristin Dunlap Godsey, "Why Affirmative Action Won't Die," *Fortune,* 13 November 1995.

301 **White House advisory positions:** Deborah L. Rhode, "Affirmative Action," *Kappa Phi Journal* (Spring 1997): 12.

301 **any of his predecessors:** Christopher Edley Jr., *Not All Black and White: Affirmative Action, Race, and American Values* (1996), 179ff.

301 **"ending discrimination on the basis":** "Memorandum for Secretary of Defense," 29 January 1993, Public Papers of the Presidents, www.presidency.ucsb.edu.

301 **at the Pentagon:** In his memoirs, Clinton said that although the issue of gays in the military took up only a small part of his time, the news media blew it out of proportion. "If we had thought more about this challenge and worked harder on it during the transition, I'm sure we would have handled it better." Bill Clinton, *My Life* (2004), 468.

301 **resisted the idea:** See *id.,* 483–86. The chiefs of navy, army, and air force opposed the idea on what they saw as practical grounds, but General Carl Mundy, commandant of the marines, went far beyond practicality;

he believed homosexuality was immoral and, if gays served openly, the military would be condoning immoral behavior and would no longer be able to attract the finest young Americans.

302 **in the armed forces:** Ricardo José Pereira Rodrigues, *The Preeminence of Politics: Executive Orders from Eisenhower to Clinton* (2007), 93–94; *New York Times,* 25 March 2004; 10 U.S.C. § 654.

303 **minorities and the poor:** The idea of using affirmative action to help poor people as well as blacks and women had been around for a while, but Gingrich was the first Republican leader to embrace the idea. Gingrich, however, wanted to do away with affirmative action for women and blacks and use it just for the poor. *New York Times,* 17 June 1995.

303 **"The people in America":** *New York Times,* 7 February 1995.

304 **supported affirmative action:** *New York Times,* 24 and 25 February 1995.

305 **its intellectual elite:** Daryl A. Carter, *Brother Bill: President Clinton and the Politics of Race and Class* (2016), 149–50.

305 **been treated unfairly:** *New York Times,* 30 May 1995. Ironically, a number of studies showed that white males had not actually suffered that much. The majority of court cases, even before the arrival of the Reagan-Bush appointees, had protected white men already employed and kept them secure under seniority systems. They continued to hold 75 percent of the highest-earning occupations and 95 percent at the very top.

306 **racist, sexist, and heartless:** *New York Times,* 29 June, 14 and 19 July 1995.

306 **on 19 July 1995:** See Edley's humorous recollections of his work on this topic at the White House and trying to get the president to focus. *Not All Black and White,* 5–40.

306 **"The job is not done":** Clinton, "Remarks on Affirmative Action," 19 July 1995, Public Papers of the Presidents, www.presidency .ucsb.edu.

307 **minority-owned businesses:** *New York Times,* 1 May and 22 October 1995.

307 **disguised as goals:** *New York Times,* 12 April 1995, 8 March 1996, and 21 January 2000.

308 **lives of African Americans:** "Race Initiative Outreach Meeting," 19 December 1997, Public Papers of the Presidents, www.presidency .ucsb.edu.

308 **plants and offices:** This and other examples can be found in a 1995 Labor Department report.

309 **together they worked:** Richard F. Tomasson, Faye J. Crosby, and Sharon D. Herzberger, *Affirmative Action: The Pros and Cons of Policy and Practice* (1996), 58–59.

309 **dropped dramatically:** *New York Times,* 31 March 1995.

309 **founded in 1991:** The commission had its origin in 1990, when Elizabeth H. Dole, secretary of labor in the George H. W. Bush administration, initiated a department-level investigation into the issue of the glass ceiling. Her husband, Senator Bob Dole, then the minority leader, sponsored the legislation establishing the commission as a bipartisan panel, comprising ten Democrats and ten Republicans—lawmakers, workplace

experts, and executives—plus an ex officio chair, the secretary of labor, who in 1995 was Robert B. Reich.

309 **"because of the perception of many"**: Glass Ceiling Commission, "Good for Business: Making Full Use of the Nation's Human Capital" (1995), *New York Times*, 16 March 1995.

310 **in two decades**: See the various polls summarized in "Mass Opinion on Affirmative Action," *USA Today*, 24 March 1995, and "Middle Class Views in Black and White," *Washington Post*, 9 October 1995.

310 **"Just as football teams need"**: Max Frankel, "Reaffirm the Affirmative," *New York Times Magazine*, 26 February 1995.

311 **less danger of a backfire here**: Executive Order 13087, 63 Fed. Reg. 30097, 28 May 1998.

311 **Gingrich as Speaker**: Lawrence C. Dodd and Bruce Oppenheimer, eds., *Congress Reconsidered*, 7th ed. (2001), 36.

311 **March 1998**: An NBC–Wall Street Journal poll in 1998 showed that 66 percent of African Americans approved of Clinton's presidency. All they had to do was compare the attitude of the president with that of the House Republicans.

312 **"Two facts are clear"**: Michael Hughes, "Symbolic Racism, Old-Fashioned Racism, and Whites' Opposition to Affirmative Action," in *Racial Attitudes in the 1990s: Continuity and Change*, ed. Steven A. Tuch and Jack K. Martin (1997), 45–75.

14. PROP 209

313 **continuous upward mobility**: Christopher Newfield, *Unmaking the Public University: The Forty-Year Assault on the Middle Class* (2008), 81.

314 **medical, and welfare programs**: California voters approved Prop 187 by a wide margin, 59 percent to 41 percent. A number of groups immediately challenged it, and a federal district judge issued a permanent injunction against its implementation (*Los Angeles Times*, 15 November 1997). Governor Wilson wanted to appeal the decision, but he was replaced by Gray Davis, who withdrew the appeal and thus effectively killed 187.

314 **to his campaign**: Neil J. Smelser, "Problematics of Affirmative Action: A View from California," in *Promise and Dilemma: Perspectives on Racial Diversity and Higher Education*, ed. Eugene Y. Lowe Jr. (1999), 169–92, at 184–85.

314 **113 community colleges**: A tenth university center for UC was created in 2005.

315 **Mexico—and Asians**: The story of increasing minorities prior to Prop 209 is in Joseph O. Jewell, "An Unfinished Mission: Affirmative Action, Minority Admissions, and the Politics of Mission at the University of California, 1868–1997," 69 *Journal of Negro Education* 38 (2000). For a critical portrait of affirmative action at the most prestigious of the UC schools, see John H. Bunzel, "Affirmative-Action Admissions: How It 'Works' at UC Berkeley," 20 *Public Interest* 111 (Fall 1988).

315 **"he is trying to keep in place"**: *Los Angeles Times*, 20 July 1995. For Wilson's views on affirmative action, see his "Minority-Majority Society," in *The Affirmative Action Debate*, ed. George E. Curry (1996), 167–74. Wilson had already vetoed an affirmative action bill passed by the assembly.

315 **"take all necessary action"**: The regents responded not only to Wilson's order and what they believed to be public opposition to affirmative action but also to events within the system that upset numerous faculty members. These events included salary supplements for "underrepresented" faculty, identified as minority, female, or disabled; and the adoption of a new standard for promotion and tenure at Cal State Chico that did away with credits for teaching and research and replaced them with "ability to relate to an ethnically diverse student population." M. Ali Raza, A. Janell Anderson, and Harry Glynn Custred Jr., *The Ups and Downs of Affirmative Action Preferences* (1999), 93–95.

315 **before the regents met**: A detailed account of the regents' meeting is in Brian Pusser, *Burning Down the House: Politics, Governance, and Affirmative Action at the University of California* (2004), chap. 7.

315 **"Ensuring Equal Treatment of Admissions"**: The regents had begun to explore the problem of affirmative action through a special committee starting in January. *New York Times,* 25 January 1995.

315–16 **"A law, Hinnissey, that might look"**: Finley Peter Dunne, "Mr. Dooley on the Power of the Press," *American Magazine,* October 1906.

316 **"Believing California's diversity to be an asset"**: For an analysis of SP-1, see Daniel R. Ortiz, "Self-Defeating Identities," in *Race and Representation: Affirmative Action,* ed. Robert Post and Michael Rogin (1998). See also Paul Takayama, UC Fact Sheet, Implementation SP-1, UC Office of the President, UCLA, 1996.

316 **the word "race"**: Marianne Constable, "The Regents on Race and Diversity: Representations and Reflections," in Post and Rogin, *Race and Representation,* 185–92.

316 **plan by two academics**: Custred was an anthropology professor at Cal State Hayward, while Wood, a former philosophy professor, now headed the California Association of Scholars, a Berkeley-based group of conservative educators.

317 **Civil Rights Initiative**: This clever name, according to the pollster Louis Harris, muddied the waters, because a majority of Americans supported affirmative action (which I have called the "soft" version) but opposed preferential treatment (so-called hard policy). "Affirmative Action and the Voter," *New York Times,* 31 July 1995.

317 **"We can do that"**: Rich Lowry, "Quitting Quotas," *National Review,* 20 March 1995, 26; *New York Times,* 26 March 1995.

317 **UC Board of Regents**: Connerly has written a memoir about the fight against affirmative action, titled *Creating Equal: My Fight Against Race Preference* (2000); chap. 8 is about Prop 209. Other good accounts of the struggle are Lydia Chávez, *The Color Bind: California's Battle to End Affirmative Action* (1998), and Bob Zelnick, *Backfire: A Reporter's Look at Affirmative Action* (1996), chap. 17.

317 **"I've always believed that people"**: Zelnick, *Backfire,* 348. Connerly also added, "Which people am I betraying?" He had a full-blooded Choctaw Indian as his maternal grandmother, a French grandfather, and a white great-grandfather.

317 **in the first part**: Other sections allowed bona fide qualifications based on sex, the priority of consent decrees in force at the time, actions needed

to qualify for federal funds, and severability, meaning that if one section were found unconstitutional, the others would remain in force.

318 **in support of 209:** *New York Times,* 29 October 1996.

318 **enough will win:** Chávez, *Color Bind.*

318 **"As a liberal Democrat":** Paul Craig Roberts and Lawrence M. Stratton, *The New Color Line: How Quotas and Privilege Destroy Democracy* (1995), 2.

319 **white men agreed:** Newfield, *Unmaking the Public University,* 93.

319 **"Tonight, my friends, we celebrate":** Francis J. Beckwith and Todd E. Jones, eds., *Affirmative Action: Social Justice or Reverse Discrimination?* (1997), 64.

319 **The Supreme Court denied cert:** *Coalition for Economic Equity v. Wilson,* 1996 U.S. Dist. LEXIS 18486; same litigants, 122 F.3d 692 (9th Cir. 1997); cert denied, 522 U.S. 963 (1997); *New York Times,* 22 December 1996.

319 **regents had acted hastily:** *New York Times,* 3 June 1996.

320 **the admissions process:** *New York Times,* 22 March 1996. The investigation had been initiated in 1988 after a complaint had been filed claiming that the Berkeley campus maintained illegal quotas for black and Hispanic students. It was exactly the kind of case that the Reagan administration would have loved to have proven but could not.

320 **planned to attend:** Richard H. Sander, "A Systematic Analysis of Affirmative Action in American Law Schools," 57 *Stanford Law Review* 367 (2004).

320 **"when I taught *Brown v. Board*":** Winkler to author, 11 March 2018.

320 **26.8 percent in 2010:** Office of Institutional Research, "Ethnic Group Enrollment Percentages in First-Year Enrollment at the University of California," 11 August 2011; see also Andrea Guerrero, *Silence at Boalt Hall: The Dismantling of Affirmative Action* (2002), 147ff.; *New York Times,* 29 November 1997. These numbers refer to the ten university centers that make up the UC system.

320 **Asian Americans held steady:** *New York Times,* 18 March 1998; Tavis Smiley, *Hard Left: Straight Talk About the Wrongs of the Right* (1996), 107. The numbers at UC's flagship school, Berkeley, are dramatic. The number of entering African Americans in 1997, the year before Prop 209 went into effect, was 257, and it dropped to 126 the following year. Comparable numbers for other groups are American Indians, 23 to 14, and Chicanos, 389 to 189. Asian American numbers improved, from 1,468 to 1,562, while whites went from 1,017 to 1,090. Grace Carroll, Karolyn Tyson, and Bernadette Lumas, "Those Who Got in the Door: The University of California–Berkeley's Affirmative Action Success Story," 69 *Journal of Negro History* 128, 132 (2000).

321 **$22,000 a year:** John H. McWhorter, *Losing the Race: Self-Sabotage in Black America* (2000), 167.

321 **The greatest loser, Belknap claims:** Belknap to author, 2 June 2017.

321 **"I am not yet ready to concede":** *New York Times,* 24 July 1995.

321 **"You have to distinguish between":** *New York Times,* 28 November 1997.

321 **and go to college:** Roger Clegg, "Beyond Quotas: A Color-Blind Vision for Affirmative Action," *Policy Review,* May 1998, 12, 14.

322 **more than 10 percent:** James Traub, "The Class of Prop. 209," *New York Times Magazine,* 2 May 1999, which is highly laudatory of developments at UC. In contrast, see Richard Sander and Stuart Taylor, *Mismatch: How Affirmative Action Hurts Students It's Intended to Help, and Why Universities Won't Admit It* (2012), esp. chap 10, subtitled "The Evasion of Prop 209 at the University of California."

322 **enrollments stayed low:** *New York Times,* 5 April 2000.

322 **"The goal here is to increase":** *New York Times,* 22 September 2000.

322 **"But all the minority firms were wiped out":** Ellis Cose, "The Color of Change," *Newsweek,* 13 November 2006, 52–53.

323 **"We believe the vote in California":** *New York Times,* 10 November 1996.

323 **the coming generation:** *New York Times,* 12 April 1998.

324 **except in Seattle:** *New York Times,* 5 November 1998; Andorra Bruno, "Affirmative Action in Washington State: A Discussion and Analysis of Initiative 200," in *Affirmative Action Revisited,* ed. Patricia M. Nelson (2001), 107–14.

324 **a constitutional amendment:** Unlike Frop 209 in California, opposition to Initiative 200 was strong and well funded because the proponents, and the Democratic governor, Gary Locke, worked hard to defeat the measure. The campaign by the backers might have been more convincing to voters, but analysts could not figure out why so many people opposed affirmative action when it applied to so relatively few minorities.

324 **half to 38 percent:** *New York Times,* 7 November 1998; Washington Higher Education Coordinating Board, *Diversity in Washington Higher Education,* September 2006, www.wsac.wa.gov.

324 **from every high school:** Apparently, one reason behind Bush's decision is that he did not want Ward Connerly putting an affirmative action referendum on the November 2000 Florida ballot. That ballot, it was widely presumed, would feature George W. Bush as the Republican nominee for president. Florida was a crucial swing state and in fact turned out to be *the* most important state. A Connerly referendum would probably bring out droves of African Americans, overwhelmingly Democratic voters who would oppose the measure and, at the same time, probably vote against Jeb's big brother. *Washington Post,* 8 January 2016. Efforts to bring Connerly into Florida apparently ran into a wall of opposition. *New York Times,* 7 June 1999.

325 **Texas plan work:** In Texas, the universities actively recruited and did mentoring and tutoring, and the state pushed local schools to do better. Public schools in Texas now have to keep academic achievement records by race, and the state penalizes schools that allow black and Latino students to fall behind. "After Affirmative Action," *New York Times,* 20 May 2000.

325 **"diversifying the student body":** *New York Times,* 11 November 1999.

325 **less stringent admissions requirements:** The first class admitted after Bush's order actually showed an increase in minorities across the entire system. Like California, minority students turned away from the flagship schools, and Hispanics especially helped make up a minority population of 40 percent in the system. *New York Times,* 30 August 2000.

326 **if their plans have succeeded:** *Washington Post,* 6 April 2015.

326 **in the community:** *New York Times,* 12 April 1998.

327 **would be undermined:** Glazer's book showed a very unhappy soul, and he insisted on referring to affirmative action as a form of discrimination rather than as a measure that enhanced both minority opportunities and the health of the polis. He also insisted that Americans were overwhelmingly hostile to affirmative action, but polls showed that women, who made up slightly more than half the electorate, liked it a lot. See Brent Staples, "The Quota Bashers Come in from the Cold," *New York Times,* 12 April 1998. Glazer's sadness over the change can be seen in an interview by James Traub, "Nathan Glazer Changes His Mind, Again," *New York Times Magazine,* 28 June 1998.

327 **striking that balance:** John H. Bunzel, "Affirmative Action, Race, and the Pragmatic Temper," 10 *Academic Questions* 20 (Spring 1997), an expansion of an article Bunzel had written for the *Los Angeles Times* Opinion Section, 8 December 1996.

15. AFFIRMATIVE ACTION AND ELECTIONS

328 **convention in Chicago:** John Dittmer, *Local People: The Struggle for Civil Rights in Mississippi* (1994); Allen Matusow, *The Unraveling of America: A History of Liberalism in the 1960s* (1984).

329 **less than 3 percent in 1968:** Byron Shafer, *Quiet Revolution: The Struggle for the Democratic Party and the Shaping of Post-reform Politics* (1983).

329 **women won the toss:** *New York Times,* 18 December 1979.

330 **and to the world:** David Garrow, *Protest at Selma: Martin Luther King Jr. and the Voting Rights Act of 1965* (1978).

330 **"a simple, uniform standard":** Lyndon Baines Johnson, "Speech to Congress," 15 March 1965, Public Papers of the Presidents, www.presidency.ucsb.edu.

331 **treated African Americans:** 79 Stat. 437 (1965). For details, see Richard M. Vallely, ed., *The Voting Rights Act: Securing the Ballot* (2006). For results, see Steven F. Lawson, *In Pursuit of Power: Southern Blacks and Electoral Politics, 1965–1982* (1985).

331 **a near-unanimous Court upheld the law:** *South Carolina v. Katzenbach,* 383 U.S. 301 (1966). Justice Black dissented on one minor point. Soon afterward, the Court overturned poll taxes in state elections, following the Twenty-Fourth Amendment's ban in federal elections, *Harper v. Virginia Board of Elections,* 383 U.S. 663 (1966); struck down literacy tests in *Katzenbach v. Morgan,* 384 U.S. 641 (1966); and upheld the provision that people literate in Spanish but not in English could not be denied the ballot.

331 **1980 census returns:** Much of this section relies on Tinsley E. Yarbrough, *Race and Redistricting: The Shaw-Cromartie Cases* (2002).

331 **the disputed districts:** 590 F. Supp. 345 (E.D.N.C. 1984).

331 **"First, the minority group must be":** *Thornburg v. Gingles,* 478 U.S. 30 (1986).

332 **"perhaps the most basic affirmative-action issue":** *New York Times,* 20 April 1995.

332 **Justice Department preclearance:** Following passage of the act, Attorney General Nicholas Katzenbach identified Alabama, Alaska, Georgia,

Louisiana, Mississippi, South Carolina, Virginia, thirty-four counties in North Carolina, and isolated counties in Arizona, Hawaii, and Idaho as jurisdictions that had prevented minorities from voting. In those states, the local registration requirements could be suspended, federal marshals would take over the job of registering voters, and there could be no changes in congressional or assembly legislative district lines without preclearance (that is, approval) from the Justice Department.

333 **white Republicans to office:** Yarbrough, *Race and Redistricting,* 9–10.

334 **"It wanders from the Virginia border":** *Id.,* 21.

335 **"continued frustration of the will":** *Davis v. Bandemer,* 478 U.S. 109 (1986). Justice White spoke only for a plurality, but three other justices also concluded that partisan gerrymandering raised the kinds of political questions the Court had traditionally not considered appropriate for judicial resolution.

336 **case a full hearing:** *Pope v. Blue,* 809 F. Supp. 392 (W.D.N.C. 1992); judgment affirmed, 506 U.S. 801 (1992).

336 **to elect black candidates:** *Rogers v. Lodge,* 458 U.S. 613 (1982).

337 **apportionment should as well:** The Reagan administration, as we have seen, strongly opposed the notion of group rights, and its antipathy to affirmative action extended to race-conscious districting. Apportionment, however, is primarily a state function, even when the locality came under section 5 jurisdiction. As a result, in many states civil rights advocates and their allies managed to win significant victories.

337 **misapportionment itself:** *League of Women Voters v. Pennsylvania,* J-1-2018 (Supreme Court of Pennsylvania, 7 February 2018). The Supreme Court cases decided on technicalities are *Benisek v. Lamone,* 585 U.S. ___ (2018), from Maryland, and *Gill v. Whitford,* 585 U.S. ___ (2018), from Wisconsin. In *Rucho v. Common Cause,* 588 U.S. ___ (2019), the Court held political gerrymandering nonjusticiable.

338 **continued the battle:** Yarbrough, *Race and Redistricting,* 27–29.

338 **dealing with the merits:** *Shaw v. Barr,* 808 F. Supp 461 (E.D.N.C. 1992).

338 **only that white citizens:** The Court said not that *only* white citizens could sue but rather that white citizens who felt harmed by the majority-minority plan could sue under an equal protection claim.

338 **affirmative action cases:** *Shaw v. Reno,* 509 U.S. 630 (1993). Timothy G. O'Rourke, "*Shaw v. Reno:* The Shape of Things to Come," in *Affirmative Action and Representation: Shaw* v. Reno *and the Future of Voting Rights,* ed. Anthony A. Peacock (1997), chap. 3.

339 **"neither assured nor well served":** *Miller v. Johnson,* 515 U.S. 900 (1995).

340 **a strict scrutiny review:** *Shaw v. Hunt,* 861 F. Supp. 408 (E.D.N.C. 1994).

340 **racial gerrymandering unconstitutional:** *Bush v. Vera,* 517 U.S. 952 (1996).

340 **compelling state interest:** *Shaw v. Hunt,* 517 U.S. 899 (1996).

340 **had ruled invalid:** For criticism of these rulings, see Morgan Kousser, *Color-Blind Injustice: Minority Voting Rights and the Undoing of the Second Reconstruction* (1999).

341 **one majority-minority district:** *Johnson v. Miller,* 922 F. Supp. 1556 (S.D. Ga. 1995).

342 **position of racial minorities:** *Abrams v. Johnson,* 521 U.S. 74 (1997).

343 **"racial minorities and others":** *Id.* at 103, Breyer dissenting.

343 **state supreme court's proposal:** *Scott et al. v. U.S. Department of Justice,* 920 F. Supp. 1248 (M.D. Fl. 1996).

343 **Law School affirmative action case:** *Lawyer v. Department of Justice,* 521 U.S. 567 (1997).

344 **needed a hearing:** *Hunt v. Cromartie,* 526 U.S. 541 (1999).

344 **Equal Protection Clause:** *Cromartie v. Hunt,* 133 F. Supp. 2d 407 (E.D.N.C.).

344 **outside the lines:** *Easley/Hunt v. Cromartie,* 532 U.S. 234 (2001).

345 **across large areas:** One effort to statistically evaluate the impact of majority-minority districting is Ronald Keith Gaddie and Charles S. Bullock III, "Voter Turnout and Candidate Participation: Effects of Affirmation Districting," in *Southern Parties and Elections: Studies in Regional Political Change,* ed. Robert P. Steed, Lawrence W. Moreland, and Tod A. Baker (1997), chap. 2. The study finds that the creation of majority black districts substantially increased the participation of black candidates, but only in new or open seats; the authors claim that it did not substantially affect black voter turnout.

345 **"all conflicts over affirmative action":** Abigail Thernstrom, "More Notes from a Political Thicket," in Peacock, *Affirmative Action and Representation,* chap. 4, at 116–17.

16. SEEKING DIVERSITY IN HIGHER EDUCATION

346 **"There's a lot of diversity here":** "Roberto" is the name Latty Goodwin gave to a first-generation immigrant from Jamaica, and a first-generation college student at "Ivy University." *Graduating Class: Disadvantaged Students Crossing the Bridge of Higher Education* (2006), 45.

347 **minorities on staff:** Elizabeth Kolbert, "The Scramble for Black Professors," *New York Times,* 8 January 1989, reporting that "the real issue," according to school officials, "is retaining such faculty members and granting them tenure." For law school faculty, see the empirical study in Deborah Jones Merritt and Barbara F. Reskin, "Sex, Race, and Credentials: The Truth About Affirmative Action in Law Faculty Hiring," 97 *Columbia Law Review* 199 (1997).

347 **the other gender:** In *United States v. Virginia,* 518 U.S. 515 (1996), a 7–1 Court, speaking through Justice Ruth Bader Ginsburg, held that the Virginia Military Institute had to admit women because the Commonwealth could not do for its sons what it did not do for its daughters. Earlier, a more narrowly divided Court ruled that the nursing school at the Mississippi University for Women had to admit Joe Hogan. *Mississippi University for Women v. Hogan,* 458 U.S. 718 (1982). In both cases, the Court held that the state could sponsor single-sex schools, but only if equivalent education experiences were available to the other sex.

347 **generous scholarship packages:** See Terese Loeb Kreuzer, "The Bidding War for Top Black Students," *Journal of Blacks in Higher Education* (Winter 1993/1994): 114–18.

348 **no longer required:** Obituary of John C. Lowe, *Washington Post,* 27 October 2017. I have been told, however, that there was more resistance at Virginia to admitting women than to admitting blacks.

348 **two persons from each:** David Boonin, *Should Race Matter? Unusual Answers to Unusual Questions* (2011), 140, 177.

348 **through affirmative action:** Both studies noted in Judy L. Lichtman, Jocelyn C. Frye, and Helen Norton, "Why Women Need Affirmative Action," in *The Affirmative Action Debate,* ed. George E. Curry (1996), 175–83, at 183n16.

348 **A number of critics have attacked:** Richard V. Reeves, Dream *Hoarders* (2017), 143–47; *Washington Post,* 10 October 2018. For details of the scandal, see the front-page story in *The Washington Post,* 13 March 2019.

349 **"been unable to find any mainstream":** Mark R. Killenbeck, "Affirmative Action and the Courts: From *Plessy* to *Brown* to *Grutter,* and Back?," in *Social Consciousness in Legal Decision Making: Psychological Perspectives,* ed. Richard L. Wiener et al. (2010), 91–120, at 93.

349 **diverse student body:** Shelby Steele, *The Content of Our Character: A New Vision of Race in America* (1990), 114; *New York Times,* 24 April 1997.

350 **race-blind admissions process:** In 1993, according to the College Board, approximately fifty-four hundred African American students applying for admission scored 600 or better on either the verbal or the math section of the SAT, and this number represented 5.3 percent of the African American students taking the test. This compared with 29.2 percent of the white students taking the exam.

350 **to white students:** All the Ivy schools grant financial aid packages based on need, not merit, and these consist of two parts. The first is scholarship money, which need not be repaid. The second is "self-help" and consists of work-study and low-interest loans, the latter requiring repayment. To attract minority students, the package would be skewed to include more scholarship money and less self-help, so black students would have more time to study and would leave school with a far lower student debt. See Kreuzer, "Bidding War."

350 **total minority enrollment at 14 percent:** The Harvard story has unique aspects because it is seen as the nation's preeminent institution of higher education and has the largest endowment and is therefore able to provide help to minority students that might not be available at "poorer" schools. But the racial tensions at Harvard could be found at many of the better schools in the country. See "Deep Racial Divisions Persist in New Generation at College," *New York Times,* 22 May 1989.

352 **this self-isolation:** The document is *A Study of Race Relations at Harvard College* (1981) and is discussed at length by Peter Skerry, "Race Relations at Harvard," *Commentary,* January 1981, 62–64.

352 **"racial tinder box":** Stephan Thernstrom and Abigail Thernstrom, *America in Black and White: One Nation, Indivisible* (1997), 387.

352 **racial and gender factions:** Arthur M. Schlesinger Jr., "The Disuniting of America: Reflections on a Multicultural Society," in *Campus Wars: Multiculturism and the Politics of Difference,* ed. John Arthur and Amy Shapiro (1995), 227.

352 **"Can Elitism and Affirmative Action Coexist?":** R. Fred Zuker, "Col-

lege Admissions Crisis: Can Elitism and Affirmative Action Coexist?," *USA Today Magazine,* March 1996, 66–68.

352 **top 3 percent:** One might also note that so-called legacy students, that is, those who have a parent or other close relative graduate from the school, also get preferential treatment at many of the country's elite schools. For example, while only 14 percent of Harvard's ordinary applicants were admitted, a whopping 40 percent of alumni offspring got an acceptance letter, even though many had weaker scholastic records than the people they replaced. Andrew Hacker, "An Affirmative Vote for Affirmative Action," 5 *Academic Questions* 24 (Fall 1992).

352 **painful self-doubt:** Shelby Steele, "The Recoloring of Campus Life: Student Racism, Academic Pluralism, and the End of a Dream," in Arthur and Shapiro, *Campus Wars,* 176–87. The article includes many examples of African American students feeling—or being made to feel—inferior to their white classmates. See also Edmond Costantini and Joel King, "Affirmative Action: The Configuration, Concomitants, and Antecedents of Student Opinion," 16 *Youth and Society* 499 (1985).

352 **African Americans 991:** Terry Eastland, *Ending Affirmative Action: The Case for Colorblind Justice* (1996), 85. The Berkeley numbers are for the class entering in the fall of 1994; the Texas numbers are for the fall of 1993.

353 **undergraduate academic record:** *Id.,* 86.

353 **"Even well-qualified black degree holders":** Ernest van den Haag, "Affirmative Action and Campus Racism," 14 *Engage Social Action* 66, 67–68 (March 1986). Van den Haag was professor of law at Fordham University.

353 **"I think it's very difficult":** Bell is quoted in Ellis Cose, "Affirmative Action and the 'Dilemma of the Qualified,'" 25 *Black Enterprise* 158, 159–60 (October 1994).

354 **problems of all groups:** Helene Cooper, "Meet the New Elite, Not Like the Old," *New York Times,* 26 July 2009. Cooper at that time was the White House correspondent for the *Times.*

354 **any empirical support:** Theodore Cross, "What If There Was No Affirmative Action in College Admissions?," *Journal of Blacks in Higher Education* (Autumn 1994): 52.

355 **the legal profession:** Leo M. Romero, "An Assessment of Affirmative Action in Law School Admissions After Fifteen Years: A Need for Recommitment," 34 *Journal of Legal Education* 430 (1984). However, while applauding the rise in minority numbers, the assistant dean at the University of Oregon Law School, Charles L. Finke, pointed out that such students, far more than white students, need a great deal of academic support to graduate. "Affirmative Action in Law School Academic Support Programs," 39 *Journal of Legal Education* 55 (1989).

355 **race-blind system:** Richard H. Sander, "A Systematic Analysis of Affirmative Action in American Law Schools," 57 *Stanford Law Review* 367 (2004). For a more complex study of how minority students fare in higher education, and one with mixed conclusions, see Thomas J. Espenshade and Alexandria Walton Radford, *No Longer Separate, Not Yet Equal: Race and Class in Elite College Admission and Campus Life* (2009), chap. 6. A

study in 1998 by the Law School Admission Council found that although blacks passed the bar at a lower rate than whites, 78 percent to 92 percent, the difference was not as great as some critics made it out to be. *New York Times,* 20 May 1998. Sander has also been attacked for the statistical model that he used to support his claim that blacks would do better if they went to lower-quality schools.

355 **volunteer in Africa:** Ellis Cose, *The Rage of a Privileged Class* (1993), 113–14.

356 **historically black schools:** Milton Moskowitz, "The Black Medical Schools Remain the Prime Training Ground for Black Doctors," *Journal of Blacks in Higher Education* (Autumn 1994): 69–70.

356 **academic merit alone:** *New York Times,* 8 October 1997.

356 **American higher education:** The following section is based on William G. Bowen and Derek Bok, *The Shape of the River: Long-Term Consequences of Considering Race in College and University Admissions* (1998).

356 **even from college:** In 1960, the proportion of blacks aged twenty-five to twenty-nine who had graduated from high school increased from 12.3 to 38.6 percent over the 1940 level, and those graduating from college went from 1.6 to 5.4 percent. Although significant increases, in 1960 still only one out of three African Americans had graduated from high school, and one in twenty college.

357 **schools in the country:** The twenty-eight institutions were Barnard College, Bryn Mawr College, Columbia University, Denison University, Duke University, Emory University, Hamilton College, Kenyon College, Miami University (Ohio), Northwestern University, Oberlin College, Pennsylvania State University, Princeton University, Rice University, Smith College, Stanford University, Swarthmore College, Tufts University, Tulane University, the University of Michigan at Ann Arbor, the University of North Carolina at Chapel Hill, the University of Pennsylvania, Vanderbilt University, Washington University, Wellesley College, Wesleyan University, Williams College, and Yale University.

359 **society needed them:** One scholar has examined this issue carefully and concluded that black gains in higher education did not come at the expense of whites. Hugh A. Wilson, "Does Affirmative Action for Blacks Harm Whites? Some Evidence from the Higher Education Arena," 22 *Western Journal of Black Studies* 218 (1998). The study came out too late for Bowen and Bok to use.

359 **"When students are given a preference":** Thernstrom and Thernstrom, *America in Black and White.*

360 **leaders in our society:** "The Facts About Affirmative Action," *New York Times,* 14 September 1998.

360 **with affirmative action:** Abigail Thernstrom and Stephan Thernstrom, "Black Progress," in *The African American Predicament,* ed. Christopher H. Foreman Jr. (1999), 29–44. They had also written a sharply critical review, "Reflections on *The Shape of the River,*" 46 *UCLA Law Review* 1583 (1999).

361 **action had proved:** See, for example, Hacker, *Two Nations,* 134; James Kilpatrick, "'Affirmative Action' Lunacy," *Human Events,* 14 July 1990, 9;

Gertrude Himmelfarb, "Stanford and Duke Undercut Classical Values," *New York Times,* 5 May 1988.

361 **benefits to society:** *New York Times,* 26 January 1999. The fifteen schools were the University of Chicago, Columbia, Dartmouth, Duke, James Madison, North Carolina, Pennsylvania, Pittsburgh, Rutgers, Stanford, Virginia, Wake Forest, George Washington University, Washington University (St. Louis), and the College of William and Mary. The list of primarily elite colleges included some second-tier schools, where the center hoped to find students who had been rejected from the better schools because of affirmative action.

362 **total enrollment of 32,000:** Barbara A. Perry, *The Michigan Affirmative Action Cases* (2007), 52; this section relies on her fine narrative and analysis.

362 **conservative constituency:** For the early history of affirmative action at Michigan, I am indebted to Matthew J. Johnson, who shared several chapters of his dissertation with me. "The Origins of Diversity: Managing Race at the University of Michigan, 1963–2006" (Temple University, 2011).

362 **fighting the lawsuits:** Lee Bollinger, Columbia Oral History Collection, Columbia University, New York. Bollinger left Michigan in 2002 to become president of Columbia University.

363 **attacking racial preferences:** Carl Cohen, *Naked Racial Preference: The Case Against Affirmative Action* (1995).

364 **her behalf as well:** For the three students and how they wound up as plaintiffs, see Greg Stohr, *A Black and White Case: How Affirmative Action Survived Its Greatest Legal Challenge* (2004), chap. 3.

364 **"race-as-a-plus model" in** *Bakke: Gratz et al. v. Bollinger et al.,* 122 F. Supp. 2d 811 (E.D. Mich., 2000).

364 **equal protection analysis:** *Grutter v. Bollinger,* 137 F. Supp. 2d 821 (E.D. Mich., 2001).

364 **undergraduate admissions:** *Grutter v. Bollinger,* 288 F.3d 732 (6th Cir. 2002). The nine judges delivered seven opinions.

365 **"reverse discrimination":** Throughout this book, I have used "reverse discrimination" primarily as a reflection of what most conservatives and quite a few liberals saw as the problem, and have also cited instances in which whites, usually male, complained that they had been denied a job or college admission because of reverse discrimination. There is, however, no solid studies on the extent of reverse discrimination; nearly all of what we have is anecdotal (although some of the stories are probably true). Fred L. Pincus argued that reverse discrimination was essentially a social construct created by the opponents of affirmative action and that white males had not suffered at all. See his *Reverse Discrimination: Dismantling the Myth* (2003).

365 **"divisive, unfair, and impossible to square":** George W. Bush, "Remarks on the Michigan Affirmative Action Case," 15 January 2003, Public Papers of the Presidents, www.presidency.ucsb.edu.

365 **helpful to the Court:** *New York Times,* 17 January 2003.

366 **"indifference or inertia":** In addition, what the reporter Linda Green-

house called the "establishment voices" all supported affirmative action, as did the alma maters of every member of the Court, and dozens of Fortune 500 companies. See Schmidt, *Color and Money,* chap. 12, which he titles "Voices from on High: The Establishment Speaks," discussing the amici briefs.

367 **its admissions processes:** *New York Times,* 2 April 2003.

367 ***Grutter v. Bollinger:*** 539 U.S. 306. In addition to Justice O'Connor's opinion for the Court (joined by Stevens, Souter, Ginsburg, and Breyer), there was a concurring opinion by Ginsburg (joined by Breyer), an opinion concurring in part and dissenting in part by Scalia (joined by Thomas) and one by Thomas (joined by Scalia), and a dissenting opinion by Rehnquist (joined by Scalia, Kennedy, and Thomas).

368 **plans would be necessary:** Very few people, conservative or liberal, agreed with this assessment. It had been nearly fifty years since *Brown v. Board of Education* (1954), and racism still poisoned much of American society. One writer believed that while the problem of discrimination against women seemed to be correcting itself, thanks in large part to affirmative action, the same could not be said for African Americans. He believed it would be a long time before the country could abandon programs, especially in the universities, where there would be a dearth of minority faculty members for the foreseeable future. Andrew Oldenquist, "Remarks on Affirmative Action," in *The Affirmative Action Debate,* ed. Steven M. Cahn, 2nd ed. (2002).

368 **In the undergraduate case:** *Gratz v. Bollinger,* 539 U.S. 244 (2003). Rehnquist wrote the opinion of the Court (joined by O'Connor, Scalia, Kennedy, Thomas, and Breyer); with concurring opinions by O'Connor (joined by Breyer), Thomas, and Breyer; and dissents from Stevens (joined by Souter), Souter (joined by Ginsburg), and Ginsburg (joined by Souter).

369 **past effects of discrimination:** *Id.* at 298, Ginsburg dissenting.

369 **in their outlook:** *New York Times,* 25 June 2003.

370 **"Impact on Universities Will Range from None to a Lot":** *Id.*

370 **had already paid off:** Perry, *Michigan Cases,* 160.

370 **in minority enrollments:** *New York Times,* 10 July 2003 and 13 April 2004.

370 **test-optional admissions policies:** *Washington Post,* 28 July 2015.

370 **"Of course, you want to look":** Espenshade and Radford, *No Longer Separate, Not Yet Equal,* 340.

371 **the state constitution:** In the wake of the Michigan victory, Connerly started talking about a "Super Tuesday" in 2008, where anti-affirmative-action measures would be on the ballot in all states that permitted voter referenda.

371 **on minority interests:** *Coalition to Defend Affirmative Action v. Regents of the University of Michigan,* 701 F.3d 466 (6th Cir. 2012).

371 **Samuel Alito:** *Schuette v. Coalition to Defend Affirmative Action,* 134 S.Ct. 1623 (2014). Justice Alito took Justice O'Connor's seat; Justice Kagan recused because she had worked on the case during her time as solicitor general.

373 **family alumni status:** In fact, at this time there was an effort to do away with so-called legacy admissions, a fight that has continued but has so

far been unsuccessful. See *New York Times,* 29 February 2004 and 30 September 2010, and *Washington Post,* 10 April 2017.

373 **repeal Proposal 2:** 134 S.Ct. at 1651. Sotomayor, a self-described affirmative action baby, opposed the conservatives in both this case and the *Fisher* case (see below, pp. 426ff.). See also Joan Biskupic, *Breaking In: The Rise of Sonia Sotomayor and the Politics of Justice* (2014), 210–12.

373 **"the way to stop discrimination":** *Parents Involved in Community Schools v. Seattle School District No. 1,* argued and decided with *Meredith v. Jefferson County Board of Education,* 551 U.S. 701, 748 (2007).

374 **"When we saw what was coming":** *New York Times,* 26 June 2007.

374 **"we have one hand tied":** *Washington Post,* 9 December 2015.

17. WOMEN AND AFFIRMATIVE ACTION II

375 **Danielle Brown, immediately responded:** *Washington Post,* 8 August 2017.

375 **and fired Damore:** *Washington Post,* 7 August 2017. Google reported in early 2019 that it had employed fewer white males in 2018 as compared to 2017. There were more Asian American males, and a smaller increase in women and people of color. *Washington Post,* 4 April 2019.

376 **sexism and discrimination:** At the end of April 2018, a group of black congressmen visited Silicon Valley and made a direct appeal to the firms there to make a greater effort to achieve a truly diverse workforce. *Washington Post,* 1 May 2018.

376 **had barely moved:** Liza Mundy, "Why Is Silicon Valley So Awful to Women?," *Atlantic,* April 2017. Google, like many tech companies, has far fewer women in technology slots than men. Its workforce as of August 2017 was 56 percent white, 35 percent Asian, 4 percent Hispanic, and 2 percent black.

376 **male and white:** *Forbes,* 2 August 1917. The company's workforce is 49 percent white and 40 percent Asian; senior leadership is predominantly white (70 percent) and male (72 percent), and of women in this group 68 percent are white.

376 **female and minority workers:** *Washington Post,* 4 August 2016.

376 **could claim parity:** *Washington Post,* 4 February 2016.

377 **five senior positions:** Bethany McLean, "Wall Street Diversifies Itself," *Atlantic,* March 2017. The article deals with women making up 50 percent of an important function on Wall Street, getting new stocks listed on exchanges around the world.

377 **further to go:** Philip Morris (later Atria) introduced Virginia Slims cigarettes in 1968 and targeted women smokers with the ad "You've come a long way, baby."

377 **"while we have made progress":** *Washington Post,* 17 March 2018.

377 **from preferential programs:** For a contrary, and for the most part minority, view, see James Button, Ryan Bakker, and Barbara A. Rienzo, "White Women and Affirmative Action in Employment in Six Southern Cities," 43 *Social Science Journal* 297 (2006).

377 **jumped to 35.3 percent:** Heidi Hartmann, "Who Has Benefited from Affirmative Action in Employment?," in *The Affirmative Action Debate,* ed. George E. Curry (1996), 77–96, at 78–79. During this period, minority

men and women, who held small percentages to begin with, also benefited, especially minority women, who saw their share of managerial jobs
double from 3.2 to 6.9 percent.

377 **grade 9–11 workforce:** J. Edward Kellough, "Federal Agencies and
Affirmative Action for Blacks and Women," 71 *Social Science Quarterly* 83,
85 (March 1990). In no agency did women even come near the halfway
mark in the higher pay grades. The highest they reached was 26.4 percent
in Health and Human Services. Blacks also made gains but lagged behind
women in almost every agency.

377 **went to black women:** June E. O'Neill and David M. O'Neill, *The
Declining Importance of Race and Gender in the Labor Market: The Role of
Employment Discrimination Policies* (2012), 181.

377 **those of white women:** Gerald Horne, *Reversing Discrimination: The Case
for Affirmative Action* (1992), 59.

377 **"by asserting a leadership role":** Nancy MacLean, *Freedom Is Not Enough:
The Opening of the American Workplace* (2006), 152–53.

379 **"It must be great to be black":** Nell Irvin Painter, "Whites Say I Must
Be on Easy Street," *New York Times,* 10 December 1981. Painter would
later teach at Princeton.

379 **affirmative action beneficiary:** Faye J. Crosby, *Affirmative Action Is Dead;
Long Live Affirmative Action* (2004), chap. 5; reported by Troy Duster, a
sociologist at UC, in *Time,* 27 May 1991.

379 **"are beginning to suffer":** Midge Decter, "On Affirmative Action and
Lost Self-Respect," *New York Times,* 6 July 1980. See also Katty Kay and
Claire Shipman, "The Confidence Gap," *Atlantic,* May 2014, which argues
that women have less confidence in themselves than men do.

380 **such as aerospace:** Thomas Sowell, *Civil Rights: Rhetoric or Reality?*
(1984), chap. 5. In a far less confrontational manner, see the arguments
put forward by Elizabeth Fox-Genovese, "Women's Rights, Affirmative
Action, and the Myth of Individualism," 54 *George Washington Law Review*
338 (1986).

381 **"It's very hard for people":** Sonia Sotomayor, *My Beloved World* (2013),
119; Joan Biskupic, *Breaking In: The Rise of Sonia Sotomayor and the Politics
of Justice* (2014), 129.

382 **more skilled positions:** Susan C. Ells, "How Polaroid Gave Women the
Kind of Affirmative Action Program They Wanted," *Management Review*
62, no. 11 (November 1973): 11–15.

382 **"in 1973 the condition of women":** Eudora Pettigrew, L. Thomas
Keith, and Homer C. Hawkins, "Sex Discrimination and the American
Labor Market: A Perspective," 7 *Sociological Focus* 71 (Winter 1973). This
article is replete with figures showing the disparity between male and
female wages.

382 **and educational gains:** *New York Times,* 16 January 1984. The numbers are rather startling. In 1970, white women entering the labor force
earned, on average, 86 percent of the average wage paid to white men; in
1980 that number dropped to 68 percent.

383 **government at $6,567:** Women's Bureau, U.S. Department of Labor,
"Who Are the Working Mothers?" (1972).

383 **"the chains of protection":** Judith Baer, *The Chains of Protection* (1978).

383 **fell into desuetude:** Nancy Woloch, *A Class by Herself: Protective Laws for Women Workers, 1890s–1990* (2015). A good example of the high court moving away from this attitude is the unanimous decision in *Automobile Workers v. Johnson Controls, Inc.,* 499 U.S. 187 (1991).

383 **What constituted a BFOQ:** BFOQs did not arise in the 1990s but dated back to Title VII and early EEOC decisions in the 1960s.

383 **in job decisions?:** These issues, and court responses to them, are discussed in Harry T. Edwards, "Sex Discrimination Under Title VII: Some Unresolved Issues," 24 *Labor Law Journal* 411 (1973).

383 **by female stewardesses:** *Diaz v. Pan American World Airways,* 442 F.2d 385 (5th Cir. 1971).

384 **in massage parlors:** *Wilson v. Sibley Memorial Hospital,* 340 F. Supp. 686 (D.D.C. 1972); *Corey v. City of Dallas,* 352 F. Supp. 977 (N.D. Texas 1972).

384 **"not suitable under existing circumstances":** *Eslinger v. Thomas,* 340 F. Supp. 886 (D.S.C. 1972).

384 **"an intimate business relationship":** *Eslinger v. Thomas,* 476 F.2d 225 (4th Cir. 1972).

385 **bought that argument:** "Sisterhood Is Braced for Reaganauts," *New York Times,* 10 May 1981.

385 **"popular wisdom aside, women":** The "conventional wisdom" is epitomized in Susan Faludi's best-selling *Backlash: The Undeclared War Against American Women* (1991).

385 **sixty-nine cents in 1980:** Sylvia Nasar, "Women's Progress Stalled? Just Not So," *New York Times,* 18 October 1992. For additional statistics, see Hartmann, "Who Has Benefited from Affirmative Action in Employment?"

386 **could be wiped out:** Nasar, "Women's Progress Stalled?"

386 **in the same fields:** See Claudia Dale Goldin, *Understanding the Gender Gap: An Economic History of American Women* (1990), and Francine D. Blau and Marianne A. Ferber, *The Economics of Women, Men, and Work* (1992).

387 **felt against her:** It is ironic that Clinton had difficulty attracting young women, and during the primary season polls found that young Democratic women mostly supported Bernie Sanders, while older women flocked to the Hillary banner. One analysis suggested that the younger women had not faced years of sexism at work, and therefore did not appreciate what Clinton had overcome. *New York Times,* 21 February 2016.

387 **men, not women:** Many of these studies are discussed in Crosby, *Affirmative Action Is Dead,* 182–89.

387 **Between 95 and 97 percent:** Marcia D. Greenberger, "Affirmative Action and Women," in S. N. Colamery, *Affirmative Action: Catalyst or Albatross?* (1998), 165–75, at 167–79.

388 **college-educated white man:** Judy L. Lichtman, Jocelyn C. Frye, and Helen Norton, "Why Women Need Affirmative Action," in Curry, *Affirmative Action Debate,* 175–83. Frye and Norton also worked at the Women's Legal Defense Fund.

388 **especially praised universities:** For universities, see Nancy E. Carriuolo, "Recruiting and Retaining Women and Minority Faculty," 27 *Journal of Developmental Education* 18 (Winter 2003).

389 **of only 7.9 percent:** Lichtman, Frye, and Norton, "Why Women Need
     Affirmative Action," 181, citing Glass Ceiling Commission, *Good for
     Business* (1995), 14, 61.

389 **"Republicans have done us":** "New Cause Helps Feminists Appeal to
     Younger Women: Rallying for Affirmative Action," *New York Times,* 5
     February 1996.

390 **from affirmative action:** Laura M. Padilla, "Women of Color Face Two
     Barriers," in *Issues on Trial: Affirmative Action,* ed. Justin Karr (2008), 30–
     37, at 31.

390 **for the opportunity:** In 1989, *Sex Roles* ran a special issue on African
     American women's struggles against racism and sexism and included
     several articles on the impact of affirmative action.

391 **"There are of course those who believe":** *Johnson v. Transportation
     Agency, Santa Clara County,* 480 U.S. 616 (1987).

391 **in the first place:** Alice Kessler-Harris, "Feminism and Affirmative
     Action," in *Debating Affirmative Action: Race, Gender, Ethnicity, and the
     Politics of Inclusion,* ed. Nicolaus Mills (1994), 68–79, at 79.

391 **grasped equality early:** Woloch to author, 5 March 2018. Professor
     Woloch believes that "even if education is still unequal, there is more
     equality in education than in other areas of life."

392 **calling for quotas:** *Washington Post,* 6 March 2018.

18. OTHER GROUPS, HERE AND ABROAD

394 **great social turmoil:** Salo W. Baron, "Is America Ready for Ethnic
     Minority Rights?," 46 *Jewish Social Studies* 189 (Summer 1984).

394 **never caught on:** See William Van Deburg, *Modern Black Nationalism:
     From Marcus Garvey to Louis Farrakhan* (1996).

394 **themselves as Americans:** Hispanics seem not to have followed this
     pattern, and many Latinos have kept Spanish as their primary language,
     even while learning English. However, a number of studies confirm that
     marriage to non-Latinos and erosion of ethnic identity tend to increase
     with each generation of Latinos, just as they did in the case of European
     immigrant diasporas in the United States in the past.

395 **about some of them:** One group that is not mentioned here is the LGBT
     community, which in recent years has been fighting more to escape preju-
     dicial laws and attitudes than to have special programs. See Michael Ruse,
     "Gay Rights and Affirmative Action," 55 *Analysis* 271 (October 1995),
     for reasons why affirmative action would not be good for homosexuals.
     Another group has been fighting the prejudice of "ageism," but so far has
     not mounted any sustained drive to become one of the groups to benefit
     from affirmative action. See Lydia DePillis, "Baby Boomers Are Taking
     On Ageism—and Losing," *Washington Post Magazine,* 4 August 2016.

396 **United States illegally:** Pia Orrenius and Madeline Zavodny, "Trends in
     Poverty and Inequality Among Hispanics," in *The Economics of Inequality,
     Poverty, and Discrimination in the 21st Century,* vol. 1, *Causes,* ed. Robert
     S. Rycroft (2013), chap. 12. Here again one has to be careful about over-
     arching generalities. As Orrenius and Zavodny show, poverty rates differ
     among groups that came over a generation ago and newcomers, as well
     as by age and by where they live in the country.

396 **districts as well:** See the attack on this development by Linda Chavez, "Hispanics, Affirmative Action, and Voting," 523 *AAPSS Annals* 75 (1992), taken from her *Out of the Barrio: Toward a New Politics of Hispanic Assimilation* (1991).

396 **"Hispanics have no claim":** Richard F. Tomasson, Faye J. Crosby, and Sharon D. Herzberger, *Affirmative Action: The Pros and Cons of Policy and Practice* (1996), 207, 213.

396 **"historic injustices toward":** J. Angelo Corlett, *Race, Racism, and Reparations* (2003), 122.

397 **third-class human beings:** Many Latinos, especially in the Southwest, continue to suffer from discrimination, poor schools, limited job opportunities, and police hostility. See Frances Contreras, *Achieving Equity for Latino Students: Expanding the Pathway to Higher Education Through Public Policy* (2011), chap. 1.

397 **The anti-Latino tirades:** During the later 1970s, the evangelist/politician Pat Robertson declared that one reason to oppose abortion was racial power. In the absence of sufficient white fecundity, he warned on his *700 Club* television show, within a couple of generations the majority of the U.S. population would derive from Asia, Africa, and Latin America and would "lack our Anglo-Saxon heritage and values." That stream of racial prejudice has never disappeared, although it had become somewhat more discreet until Trump. William A. Henry III, *In Defense of Elitism* (1994), 63. For a recent article on "white rage," see Carol Anderson, "The Policies of White Resentment," *New York Times,* 6 August 2017.

397 **lobbied for good jobs:** This all happened after World War II. Prior to that, there was no Hispanic equivalent of the NAACP, and whereas blacks had looked to the federal government ever since Reconstruction for aid, Hispanics, especially Chicanos, had a history of the American government going to war with Mexico and taking almost half of its territory. For the story of one activist lawyer who fought for Latino rights, see the obituary of Joaquin Avila in *The Washington Post,* 15 March 2018.

397 **the United States:** Lieberman is in *The New York Times,* 10 March 1995; the Figueroa letter to the editor, titled "Affirmative Action Keeps Door Open for All," is in the 18 March 1995 issue of the paper.

397 **Dolores Huerta:** For a good general discussion of the Latino awakening, see F. Arturo Rosales, *Chicano! A History of the Mexican American Civil Rights Movement,* 2nd ed. (1997).

398 **a better education:** This section is drawn primarily from Nancy MacLean, *Freedom Is Not Enough: The Opening of the American Workplace* (2006), chap. 5. MacLean also includes numerous examples of how Mexicans were discriminated against even as they were imported into the country to do farmwork in California and Texas.

399 **He appointed Vicente T. Ximenes:** Ximenes could trace his American roots back to when the United States had taken much of the Southwest and California from Mexico.

399 **"the chains are broken":** Ibid., 171–72.

400 **the senior colleges:** Herman Badillo, *One Nation, One Standard: An Ex-liberal on How Hispanics Can Succeed Just Like Other Immigrant Groups* (2006).

400 **the city's population:** A far larger number, roughly a quarter of a million Hispanics, lived in the metropolitan Washington area, which included nearby counties in Virginia and Maryland. The number of Hispanics living in these counties is even larger today than in 1991.

400 **states and localities:** Linda Chavez, "Just Say Latino," in *Debating Affirmative Action: Race, Gender, Ethnicity, and the Politics of Inclusion,* ed. Nicolaus Mills (1994), 174–79. In *Plyler v. Doe,* 457 U.S. 202 (1982), a narrowly divided Court ruled that states had to allow the children of illegal immigrants into their public schools.

401 **Latinos as customers:** Alan Farnham, "Holding Firm on Affirmative Action," *Fortune,* 13 March 1989, 88.

401 **white-collar jobs:** *New York Times,* 16 June 1995.

401 **had become firemen:** *New York Times,* 18 November 1978.

402 **a job for everyone:** Diane P. Jackson, "Affirmative Action for the Handicapped and Veterans: Interpretive and Operational Guidelines," 29 *Labor Law Journal* 107 (February 1978).

402 **Department of Labor:** Public Law 93-112 (1973). Within a few years, Congress amended the law, and while the basic premise of § 503 remained, the regulations for implementing it changed. See Bernard E. DeLury, "Equal Job Opportunity for the Handicapped Means Positive Thinking and Positive Action," 26 *Labor Law Journal* 679 (November 1975).

402 **take for granted:** Public Law 101-336 (1990). For the law, see Leonard J. Davis, *Enabling Acts: The Hidden Story of How the Americans with Disabilities Act Gave the Largest US Minority Its Rights* (2015). During the 1980s, the Reagan administration paid no more attention to the problems of disabled people than it did to civil rights in general. See Otis H. Stephens, "Discrimination, Affirmative Action, and the Disabled," in *The Reagan Administration and Human Rights,* ed. Tinsley E. Yarbrough (1985), 157–79.

402 **disabilities than others:** See U.S. Commission on Civil Rights, *Accommodating the Spectrum of Individual Abilities* (September 1983), 4.

403 **"that a person need not meet":** *Southeastern Community College v. Davis,* 442 U.S. 397 (1979). See the analysis of the case by Thomas J. Flygare, "Schools and the Law," 61 *Phi Delta Kappan* 63 (September 1979).

403 **and attitudinal barriers:** Gopal C. Pati and Edward F. Hilton Jr., "A Comprehensive Model for a Handicapped Affirmative Action Program," 59 *Personnel Journal* 99 (February 1980).

403 **cost less than $50:** Maureen Harrison and Steve Gilbert, eds., *The Americans with Disabilities Act Handbook* (1992), 16–17.

404 **rate is 80 percent:** Davis, *Enabling Acts,* 244.

405 **them to do so:** Various studies have shown that two-thirds of working-age people with disabilities who are not working want to do so. According to a Harris poll, 82 percent of people with disabilities said they would give up their government benefits in favor of a full-time job. Harrison and Gilbert, *Americans with Disabilities Act Handbook,* 15.

405 **a disability accommodation:** Davis, *Enabling Acts,* 244–45.

405 **or at an office:** This section has, for the most part, dealt with physically disabled people who could work if given the proper settings and assistive technology. There are many people, however, with mental conditions

that make it far more difficult, and expensive, to provide them with jobs.

405 **"the biggest group of people"**: *Washington Post,* 3 August 2017.

406 **"Nobody grows up speaking Asian-American"**: Jay Caspian Kang, "Not Without My Brothers," *New York Times Magazine,* 13 August 2017, 34.

406 **Massachusetts Institute of Technology**: See Dana Y. Takagi, "From Discrimination to Affirmative Action: Facts in the Asian American Admissions Controversy," 37 *Social Problems* 578 (November 1990).

406 **numbering one thousand**: *New York Times,* 6 November 2005. Whites accounted for 31 percent of the class, Hispanics 11 percent, and African Americans 3 percent.

406 **combined score of 1,258**: The Asian average verbal score was 594, while the average white verbal score was 618. The verbal score discrepancy may be due to the fact that many of the Asians were either immigrants or the children of immigrants.

406 **1979 through 1983**: John H. Bunzel and Jeffrey K. D. Au, "The Asian Difference," in *Racial Preference and Racial Justice: The New Affirmative Action Controversy,* ed. Russell Nieli (1991), 465–73, at 463.

406 **this question publicly**: William A. Henry III, *In Defense of Elitism* (1994), 69.

406 **in the physical sciences**: Tomasson, Crosby, and Herzberger, *Affirmative Action,* 202.

407 **after World War II**: In-house reviews at Brown and Stanford, as well as the Education Department's review of several California schools, found evidence of discrimination against Asian students. Dana Y. Takagi, *The Retreat from Race: Asian-American Admissions and Racial Politics* (1992), 9.

407 **38.9 percent of Japanese**: Bunzel and Au, "Asian Difference," 459. The authors list six Asian groups—Chinese, Filipino, Indians, Japanese, Korean, and Vietnamese—and all of these groups outperformed whites in most age brackets, although the starkest difference was between Chinese and Japanese, on one hand, and whites, on the other.

408 **"Every time I see a black person"**: Takagi, *Retreat from Race,* 110; italics added.

408 **"racial preferences are by definition"**: Michael Omi and Dana Y. Takagi, "Situating Asian Americans in the Political Discourse on Affirmative Action," in *Race and Representation: Affirmative Action,* ed. Robert Post and Michael Rogin (1998), 271–80, at 272.

409 **"suffered it for years"**: Both quoted in Takagi, *Retreat from Race,* 115–16.

409 **India and elsewhere**: In June 1995, Governor Wilson described his conversation with a Vietnamese senior at the prestigious Lowell High School in San Francisco. The young woman, he reported, was "deeply troubled" that Vietnamese students were admitted to UC with lower scores than Chinese students. The student cited by Wilson bears more than a passing resemblance to African American students cited by conservatives, who claim that affirmative action undermines the self-esteem and sense of worth of minority students admitted because of racial preference.

409 **stay about the same**: Omi and Takagi, "Situating Asian Americans," 277–78.

410 **"Without affirmative action, it would help me"**: Norimitsu Onishi, "Affirmative Action: Choosing Sides," *New York Times Magazine,* 31 May 1996.

410 **against other groups:** *Washington Post,* 3 August 2017. Sessions's statement came at a time when the Trump administration was in turmoil, and directly appealed to the Republican base, which opposed affirmative action.

411 **"A university is more than the sum"**: Op-ed, *Washington Post,* 8 August 2017. Shortly after filing the suit against Harvard, the Justice and Education Departments announced an investigation into whether Yale discriminated against Asian Americans.

411 **Affirmative action is not a uniquely American:** See Elaine Kennedy-Dubourdieu, ed., *Race and Inequality: World Perspectives on Affirmative Action* (2006); Graham K. Brown et al., eds., *Affirmative Action in Plural Societies* (2012); and Harish C. Jain et al., *Employment Equity and Affirmative Action: An International Comparison* (2003). There are many other sources dealing with affirmative action in specific countries.

411 **afflicting programs in other countries:** Sowell first looked at other countries in the 1980s, "Affirmative Action: A Worldwide Disaster," *Commentary,* December 1989, and took a more extensive appraisal fifteen years later in *Affirmative Action Around the World: An Empirical Study* (2004). In both cases, he found much to disapprove.

19. BUSH, OBAMA, AND FISHER

412 **"Affirmative Action for Osama"**: Posted 12 October 2001, on town hall.com.

413 **and Samuel Alito:** Roberts, who had been a clerk to William Rehnquist, replaced him as chief justice, and jurisprudentially did not differ greatly from his predecessor. Alito took Sandra Day O'Connor's seat and has proven to be far more conservative. Moreover, where O'Connor supported some affirmative action programs, Alito seems to be opposed to all of them.

414 **"To the C students"**: Peter Dreier, "How George W. Bush Benefited from Affirmative Action," *The Blog, Huffington Post,* 13 September 2013, www.huffingtonpost.com. Nicholas Kristof had actually uncovered much of this earlier and also learned that Andover, seeking some diversity in its student body, had awarded Bush three extra points on a twenty-point scale for being from Texas. According to reports, young Bush flourished at Andover and was proof that diversity admits could do well. "A Boy and His Benefits," *New York Times,* 24 January 2003.

414 **"assembled what may be the blackest"**: *New York Times,* 1 February 2003.

414 **U.S. ambassador:** The first openly gay ambassador, James Hormel, received a recess appointment from Bill Clinton after the Senate failed to confirm the nomination.

415 **"race conscious" undertakings:** *New York Times,* 27 June 2001 and 30 March 2002; *Washington Post,* 17 January 2005.

415 **Labor Relations Board:** See Lee Cokorinos, *The Assault on Diversity: An Organized Challenge to Racial and Gender Justice* (2003), 126–27, for other

Bush appointments who opposed either affirmative action or the main tenets of the civil rights agenda.

415 **caused by the storm:** *New York Times,* 20 September 2005.

415 **met those standards:** *Adarand Constructors, Inc. v. Peña,* 515 U.S. 200 (1995).

415 **therefore constitutional:** *Adarand Constructors, Inc. v. Slater,* 228 F.3d 1147 (10th Cir. 2000).

416 **for affirmative action:** Rachel Kranz, *Affirmative Action* (2002), 23.

416 **some affirmative action programs:** *New York Times,* 11 August 2001.

416 **improvidently granted:** *Adarand Constructors, Inc. v. Mineta,* 534 U.S. 103 (2001).

416 **"to bail us out":** Cokorinos, *Assault on Diversity,* 121, 123. Chavez and others on the right had long complained about the failure of the Reagan and George H. W. Bush administrations to roll back civil rights protections as well as affirmative action.

416 **race-neutral ways:** "Remarks on the Michigan Affirmative Action Case," 15 January 2003, www.presidency.ucsb.edu.

417 **while opposing quotas:** *New York Times,* 19 January 2003. At the 2000 GOP convention, Powell had told delegates that "some in our party" are ready to condemn affirmative action for a few thousand black kids, "but you hardly hear a whimper when it's affirmative action for lobbyists who load our federal tax code with preferences for special interests." *New York Times,* 3 August 2000.

417 **"America will truly be a colorblind society":** "Statement on the Supreme Court Decision on the Michigan Affirmative Action Cases," 23 June 2003, www.presidency.ucsb.edu. Interestingly, the Office of the Press Secretary also released a Spanish-language version of this statement.

419 **with his smarts:** Conor Friedersdorf, "Barack Obama: Affirmative Action's Best Poster Child?," Politics and Policy Daily, *Atlantic,* 28 April 2011, www.theatlantic.com.

419 **"if I was, then I certainly am not ashamed":** Quoted in David Paul Kuhn, "Obama Shifts Affirmative Action Rhetoric," *Politico,* 10 August 2008.

419 **"Affirmative action is the only reason":** Posted 23 April 2014 on "The Last Refuge," theconservativetreehouse.com.

419 **had been chosen:** In the first go-around, about half are chosen solely on their writing, and the other half on a weighted scale of 70 percent grades and 30 percent writing.

420 **"underrepresented groups":** Barack Obama, letter to the editor, *Record,* 16 November 1990.

420 **"under a cloud they could not erase":** *New York Times,* 3 August 2008.

420 **"We ask all to join us":** 2008 Republican Party Platform, 1 September 2008, American Presidency Project, www.presidency.ucsb.edu.

420 **"We support affirmative action":** 2008 Democratic Party Platform, 25 August 2008, American Presidency Project, www.presidency.ucsb.edu.

420 **"than a poor white kid":** Kuhn, "Obama Shifts Affirmative Action Rhetoric." Obama said this several times, both in interviews with reporters and in a televised debate with his opponent, Senator John McCain.

422 **In an interview with Jeffrey Toobin:** Jeffrey Toobin, "The Obama Brief," *New Yorker*, 27 October 2014.

422 **"strongly encourages the use":** *New York Times*, 4 July 2018.

423 **treated their workers:** *Washington Post*, 4 February 2016.

423 **"A lot of people honestly think":** Sheryll Cashin, *Place, Not Race: A New Vision of Opportunity in America* (2014), 9–12.

424 ***Ricci v. DeStefano:*** 530 F.3d 88 (2d Cir. 2008). A good analysis of the case and Sotomayor's role is Joan Biskupic, *Breaking In: The Rise of Sonia Sotomayor and the Politics of Justice* (2014), chap. 8.

424 **disparate-impact claim:** *Ricci v. DeStefano*, 554 F. Supp. 2d 142 (D. Conn., 2006).

425 **the white firefighters:** *Ricci v. DeStefano*, 557 U.S. 557 (2009).

425 **"Did she phone it in?":** Biskupic, *Breaking In*, 149.

427 **factor in admissions:** See *Hopwood v. Texas*, discussed above at 295–297.

427 **such records in 1975:** Enrollments from 1983 to 2002 are posted at tarltonguides.law.utexas.edu.

428 **their pre-1996 levels:** Robert Zelnick, *Swing Dance: Justice O'Connor and the Michigan Muddle* (2004), 80–82; Jim Yardley, "The 10 Percent Solution," *New York Times Magazine*, 14 April 2002. Yardley profiled several minority students and the successes and problems they faced in college. A study undertaken at Harvard found that the Top 10 Percent Plan, and another percentage plan in Florida, were not securing the diversity in state colleges that had been the goal. *New York Times*, 11 February 2003.

428 **case in 2003:** *Grutter v. Bollinger*, see above, pp. 361–376.

428 **and stigmatizes minorities:** For more on Blum's background and activities, see Joan Biskupic, "Behind U.S. Race Cases, a Little-Known Recruiter," Reuters, 4 December 2012, www.reuters.com. Blum also maintains a website that lists the cases currently under way: www.project onfairrepresentation.org.

428 **In an interview with Adam Liptak:** *New York Times*, 7 April 2014.

430 **"there are some Anglo students":** Nikole Hannah-Jones, "What Abigail Fisher's Affirmative Action Case Was Really About," ProPublica, 23 June 2016, reprinting the original story filed by Hannah-Jones on 18 March 2013. Fisher knew that even if she won her case, it could take several years, and she chose not to sit by idly. She entered and graduated from Louisiana State University and took a job in finance well before the case had been resolved in the high court.

430 **"a factor of a factor":** *Fisher v. Texas*, 645 F. Supp. 2d 587, 608 (W.D. Tex., 2009).

430 **to achieve that result:** *Fisher v. Texas*, 631 F.3d 213 (5th Cir. 2011).

431 **strict scrutiny:** *Fisher v. Texas*, 133 S.Ct. 2411 (2013).

431 **with being racist:** Although Sotomayor withdrew her dissent, it reappeared in a slightly different form the following year in *Schuette v. BAMN*, in which the Court upheld a Michigan voter-approved ban on affirmative action in the state's public universities. See Biskupic, *Breaking In*, chap. 11. One might also note that at this time nearly all the Court's clerks were white and male. Tony Mauro, "Shut Out," *National Law Journal*, 11 December 2017.

431 **"Sotomayor as agitator, Breyer as broker":** Biskupic, *Breaking In*, 201.

432 **of strict scrutiny:** *Fisher v. Texas,* 758 F.3d 633 (5th Cir. 2014).

433 **a separate dissent:** A good discussion of the justices and the decision-making process involved in *Fisher II* is Laurence Tribe and Joshua Matz, *Uncertain Justice: The Roberts Court and the Constitution* (2014), 26–32.

433 **to achieve diversity:** *Fisher v. Texas,* 136 S.Ct. 2198 (2016).

434 **"the moral imperative of racial neutrality":** *City of Richmond v. J. A. Croson Co.,* 488 U.S. 469, 518 (1989) (Kennedy, J., concurring).

434 **"Racial and ethnic distinctions":** *Grutter v. Bollinger,* 539 U.S. 306, 388 (2003) (Kennedy, J., dissenting).

434 ***The Tie Goes to Freedom:*** Helen J. Knowles, *The Tie Goes to Freedom: Justice Anthony M. Kennedy on Liberty* (2009). For different views on why Kennedy changed his mind, see Tony Mauro, "Justice Kennedy's Startling Shift on Affirmative Action," *National Law Journal,* 23 June 2016.

435 **could be successful:** *Washington Post,* 24 June 2016.

435 **bias against blacks:** Samuel Sommers and Michael Norton, "What Whites Mean When They Say Race Relations Are Bad," *Washington Post,* 24 July 2016.

20. YES . . . AND NO . . . AND TRUMP

436 **Recent polls show that conservatives:** "Race and Discrimination," 24 October 1917, Pew Research Center.

437 **part of our society:** Marshall and Hooks are quoted in Arch Puddington, "What to Do About Affirmative Action," *Commentary,* June 1995. Puddington in another article claims that "many in the new black middle class have come to look on it as an entitlement—much as the elderly view Medicare or farmers regard crop subsidies." "Will Affirmative Action Survive?," *Commentary,* October 1995.

437 **"to position themselves in middle-class America":** Quoted in Alan Farnham, "Holding Firm on Affirmative Action," *Fortune,* 13 March 1989, 88.

437 **"has . . . embraced the policy":** Orlando Patterson, "Affirmative Action: The Sequel," *New York Times,* 22 June 2003.

438 **caused Loury's trouble:** Barbara Bergman, *In Defense of Affirmative Action* (1996), 136–37. For Loury's views, see his *One by One from the Inside Out: Essays and Reviews on Race and Responsibility* (1995), and "Who Cares About Racial Inequality?," 27 *Journal of Sociology and Social Welfare* 133 (March 2000).

438 **federal guidelines:** A number of these studies are cited in Barbara Reskin, *The Realities of Affirmative Action Employment* (1998), 46–47.

439 **nonminority employees:** Michael Weinstein, "A Reassuring Scorecard for Affirmative Action," *New York Times,* 17 October 2000. The study originally appeared in the *Journal of Economic Literature* (2000).

439 **made it on their own:** Stephan Thernstrom and Abigail Thernstrom, *America in Black and White: One Nation, Indivisible* (1997), 234–35.

439 **"Arnold Hirsch is telling you why":** Arnold R. Hirsch, *Making the Second Ghetto: Race and Housing in Chicago, 1940–1960* (1983). The book and its findings sent a jolt through the field of urban history, and it "remains a touchstone for historians, sociologists, and journalists." *Washington Post,* 28 March 2018.

439 **"The percentage of employed blacks"**: Thomas Sowell, *Civil Rights: Rhetoric or Reality?* (1984), 49–50.

440 **admission to school**: Carl Cohen and James P. Sterba, *Affirmative Action and Racial Preference: A Debate* (2003), 110–11.

440 **"I like to think that I have made"**: Stephen L. Carter, *Reflections of an Affirmative Action Baby* (1991), 4–5.

441 **that of non-legacies**: Ashton Lattimore, "Legacy Admissions Are Wrong, but It's Tricky for Black Alums," *Washington Post,* 12 August 2018.

441 **values worth knowing**: See the perceptive op-ed by Max Boot, "A Diverse Student Body Adds Value to Campus Life," *Washington Post,* 21 June 2018. See also the study by Patrick T. Terenzini in the *Journal of Education* (September/October 2001).

442 **in jobs or schools**: Peter Brimelow and Leslie Spencer, "When Quotas Replace Merit, Everybody Suffers," *Forbes,* 15 February 1993; Glenn C. Loury, "Incentive Effects of Affirmative Action," 523 *AAPSS Annals* 19 (September 1992), and his "Who Cares About Racial Inequality?"

442 **of the workforce**: Cecille A. Conrad argues the pro economic case in "The Economic Cost of Affirmative Action," in *Economic Perspectives on Affirmative Action,* ed. Margaret C. Simms (1995), 33–53. See also "Where Credit Is Due," *Spectrum* (Winter 1997): 2, showing that affirmative action does not create a less productive workforce.

442 **in a multidimensional context**: For a critique of attempts to make affirmative action fit an economic theory, see William Darity, "Economic Theory and Racial Economic Inequality," 5 *Review of Black Political Economy* 225 (1975).

442 **share of the population**: Kaiser Family Foundation, "Poverty Rate by Race/Ethnicity," www.kff.org. The report, released in 2017, was based on U.S. Census Bureau figures of 2016.

442 **that of black families**: *Washington Post,* 27 February 2018.

443 **middle-income Latinos**: Similar studies by two progressive think tanks, CFED and the Institute for Policy Studies, found white households own, on average, seven times as much wealth as African Americans and six times as much as Latino households.

443 **just sixty-nine cents**: James Surowiecki, "The Hidden Cost of Race," *New Yorker,* 10 October 2016, 39. The study was co-authored by Melvin L. Oliver and Thomas M. Shapiro, who also wrote *Black Wealth, White Wealth: A New Perspective on Racial Inequality* (2006). A study in the late 1990s came up with similar findings, indicating that the problem is not new. See Dalton Conley, "40 Acres and a Mule," 80 *National Forum* 21 (Spring 2000). Redlining, initially used by government agencies and then adopted by private banks, drew a red line through predominantly poor and black neighborhoods and would not issue mortgages for houses in those areas.

443 **84 years for Latinos**: Niall McCarthy, "Racial Wealth Inequality in the U.S. Is Rampant," *Forbes,* 14 September 2017, www.forbes.com; Paul F. Campos, "White Economic Privilege Is Alive and Well," *New York Times,* 30 July 2017.

444 **67 percent in the highest**: Campos, "White Economic Privilege Is Alive and Well." White income in the ninety-fifth percentile was $225,000.

444 **less than white boys:** *Washington Post,* 21 March 2018.

444 **never been so large:** Stephen L. Carter, "Affirmative Distraction," *New York Times,* 6 July 2008.

444 **answer must be No:** While different analysts have found differing rates of inequality, they have all found a gap between black and white earnings. See Thomas N. Maloney and Ethan Doetsch, "What Explains Black-White Economic Inequality in the United States in the Early 21st Century? The Effects of Skills, Discriminatory Legacies, and Ongoing Discrimination," in *The Economics of Inequality, Poverty, and Discrimination in the 21st Century,* vol. 1, *Causes,* ed. Robert S. Rycroft (2013), 161–76.

444 **"the time has come for us":** Glenn C. Loury, "How to Mend Affirmative Action," *Public Interest* (Spring 1997): 33, 43.

445 **of whites as well:** Changes in polling can be traced in Charlotte Steeh and Maria Krysan, "Affirmative Action and the Public, 1970–1995," 60 *Public Opinion Quarterly* 1 (1996), which acknowledges that one of the difficulties interpreting the numbers is, as they so tactfully put it, "the spottiness of the survey record."

445 **30 percent "bad":** In 2013, a CBS/*New York Times* poll found 53 percent of the respondents supporting affirmative action, and 38 percent opposed. Of those in favor, two out of three gave the reason as compensating for past discrimination.

445 **compensatory aid:** "Race and Discrimination," 24 October 2017, Pew Research Center.

445 **Hispanics by 53–35:** Polls from 2003 to 2017 are at www.pewresearch.org. For earlier polls, showing that African Americans supported preferential policies far more than whites, see Cardell K. Jacobson, "Black Support for Affirmative Action Programs," 44 *Phylon* 299 (December 1983). Nonetheless, according to the Times Mirror Center for the People and the Press, while black support for affirmative action remained consistently in the 60 percent range between 1987 and 1994, white support in that period inched up from 18 to 25 percent, a significant change.

445 **"The degree to which people":** James P. Sterba, *Affirmative Action for the Future* (2009), 31.

445 **favored women 83–76:** Gallup poll reported in *Washington Post,* 28 August 2015. The polls also uncovered a gender gap between white men and white women. The latter are far more supportive of affirmative action in general, 66–26, compared with white men, 48–41.

446 **invariably white men:** Deborah Ashton, "Does Race or Gender Matter More to Your Paycheck?," *Harvard Business Review* online, 10 June 2014, hbr.org.

446 **"At a time when companies are hiring":** Ymani Wince, "I'm a Black Woman in Corporate America. I Know I Always Have to Be Ready to Prove Myself," The Lily, *Washington Post* online, 31 May 2018.

446 **people of color:** Michele Goodwin, "The Death of Affirmative Action, Part I," *Chronicle of Higher Education,* 15 March 2012.

446 **professional levels as well:** Barbara R. Bergmann, *In Defense of Affirmative Action* (1996), 133.

447 **the results were mixed:** Barbara Reskin, *The Realities of Affirmative Action Employment* (1998), 47–48.

447 **defending affirmative action:** Manning Marable, *Beyond Black and White: Transforming African-American Politics* (2009), 85. The poll cited was a joint *USA Today*/CNN/Gallup undertaking.

447 **As of 2017, there were thirty-two female CEOs:** "These Are the Women CEOs Leading Fortune 500 Companies," *Fortune,* 7 June 2017, www.fortune.com.

447 **run by women:** On 15 August 2018, Wells Fargo, after a disastrous scandal-plagued year, named Elizabeth Duke to become the first female chairman of a top American bank. It then began an intense public relations campaign featuring Duke and the promise that Wells Fargo would "rededicate" itself to its customers' best interests. Money.cnn.com, 15 August 2018.

448 **closing the pay gap:** In its annual "Diversity Report," Intel proudly announced there was no longer any pay gap between men and women in comparable jobs. *Washington Post,* 4 February 2016. A few months later Apple reported that its workforce showed a bit more diversity than the year before, with an "uptick" in hiring blacks and Hispanics. *Washington Post,* 4 August 2016.

448 **experienced sexist interactions:** Liza Mundy, "Why Is Silicon Valley So Awful to Women?," *Atlantic,* April 2017.

449 **"gender and racial imbalance":** In fact, the firm actually did have a varied group of partners, with six African Americans in the senior partner range, and 23 percent of its more than a thousand lawyers were women. *New York Times,* 7 February 2019.

449 **"ugly racial past":** Randall Kennedy, *For Discrimination: Race, Affirmative Action, and the Law* (2013), 140–41; see also Michelle Adams, "Isn't It Ironic? The Central Paradox at the Heart of 'Percentage Plans,'" 62 *Ohio State Law Journal* 1729 (2001).

450 **getting good grades:** See William G. Bowen and Derek Bok, *The Shape of the River: Long-Term Consequences of Considering Race in College and University Admissions* (1998).

450 **William R. Fitzsimmons, the dean:** *Washington Post,* 17 May 2019 and 18 October 2018.

450 **made them optional:** *Washington Post,* 28 August 2015.

451 **tuition of $52,000:** *Washington Post,* 23 November 2016.

451 **not just the classroom:** Nitin Nohria, "We've Gotten Better at Diversity. Now We Need Inclusion," *Washington Post,* 21 May 2017.

452 **socio-economic background as well:** *Washington Post,* 24 October 2017; Neil Kerwin, president of American University, to all faculty and administrators, "Immediate Actions to Build a More Diverse and Inclusive University," 29 February 2016; Sally Lee, "Bold Ideas, Real Impact," an interview with Columbia president Lee C. Bollinger, *Columbia Magazine* (Summer 2017): 38ff.

452 **racial diversity as well:** Professor Tomiko Brown-Nagin of Harvard Law has also argued that the focus of affirmative action should shift away from color and gender and toward groups that are economically disadvantaged and thus face problems of social mobility. "Rethinking Proxies for Disadvantage in Higher Education: A First Generation Students' Project," 2014 *University of Chicago Legal Forum* 433 (2014).

453 **African American enrollment:** "Colleges Seek Diversity Ideal, but Choose Different Paths to Achieve It," *New York Times,* 6 August 2017.

454 **43 percent in 2013:** Kathy Svitil, a spokesperson for Caltech, claims, "We are as close to a meritocracy as is possible." In the freshman class entering in the fall of 2016, of the 235 students, there were 77 Asians, 70 whites, and only 4 African Americans.

454 **in university admissions:** *Washington Post,* 8 August 2017.

454 **for white males!:** Jonathan Zimmerman, "Who's Benefiting from Affirmative Action? White Men," *Washington Post,* 12 August 2017. For a defense of affirmative action by an Asian American, see Young Jean Lee's op-ed in *The New York Times,* 10 February 2019.

455 **"less advanced schools":** Charles Lane, "Why Restart the Affirmative-Action War?," *Washington Post,* 3 August 2017. Scalia's comment came during oral argument on *Fisher II* and immediately stirred up a hornet's nest of criticism and defense. See *Washington Post,* 11 December 2015.

455 **"I was absolutely the best":** Interview on Bloomberg Politics, 26 August 2015.

456 **women, people of color, and immigrants:** Michael S. Kimmel, *Angry White Men: American Masculinity at the End of an Era* (2013).

456 **not in an outwardly racist manner:** This is not to say that blacks, Hispanics, and women agreed with their policies, but no one believed that Reagan and the two Bushes were out-and-out racists.

457 **for his comments:** Andrew Rafferty, Marianna Sotomayor, and Daniel Arkin, "Trump Says 'Two Sides' Share Blame for Charlottesville Rally Violence," NBC News, 16 August 2017, www.nbcnews.com.

458 **"investigations and possible litigation related":** *Washington Post,* 1 August 2017. As of this writing, according to an attorney in the Civil Rights Division, nothing really has happened in terms of government lawyers entering a suit.

458 **among disaffected whites:** *Washington Post,* 3 August 2017.

458 **"Why . . . couldn't they compete":** Ellis Cose, *The Rage of a Privileged Class* (1993), 111.

458 **"I don't think that special treatment":** Both quoted in Faye J. Crosby, *Affirmative Action Is Dead; Long Live Affirmative Action* (2004), 40–41.

459 **Steven Farron's *Affirmative Action Hoax*:** The subtitle of his book is *Diversity, the Importance of Character, and Other Lies.* His arguments are laid out on xv–xvi.

459 **"It's HIS fault!":** For more of this view, see the screed by Scott Greer, *No Campus for White Men: The Transformation of Higher Education into Hateful Indoctrination* (2017), and the epilogue, "Trump Wins and Campus Insanity."

459 **they are not there:** See Cose, *Rage of a Privileged Class,* 111–13.

460 **it is almost nonexistent:** Marylee C. Taylor, "White Backlash to Workplace Affirmative Action: Peril or Myth?," 73 *Social Forces* 1385 (June 1995).

461 **13 percent of blacks:** Sheryll Cashin, *Place, Not Race: A New Vision of Opportunity in America* (2014), 9–10; see also Samuel Sommers and Michael Norton, "What Whites Mean When They Say Race Relations Are Bad," *Washington Post,* 24 July 2016.

461 **time of Trump's election:** money.cnn.com/2018/01/05. Asian unemployment was 2.5 percent, that of Hispanics 4.9 percent.

461 **coalition years before:** See Carol M. Swain, *The New White Nationalism in America: Its Challenge to Integration* (2002); Nicholas Kristof, "When Whites Just Don't Get It, Revisited," *New York Times,* 3 April 2016.

461 **women, blacks, and Hispanics:** See Carol Anderson, "The Policies of White Resentment," *New York Times,* 6 August 2017. She believes Trump won on the politics of racial backlash and has made it part of his agenda.

461 **unsympathetic to civil rights:** *Washington Post,* 30 May 2017.

462 **still oppose him:** the federalist.com/2018/18/05.

462 **"has determined what affirmative action":** *New York Times,* 4 July 2018.

464 **admissions policies:** *Id.;* "Affirmative Action Guidelines Dropped by Trump Administration," *Politico,* 3 July 2018. For further comments both pro and con, see *CNN Politics,* 3 July 2018, and the editorial in *The Washington Post,* 4 July 2018.

464 **program is something else:** "Taking Affirmative Action," ExxonMobil advertisement, *New York Times,* 28 February 2003, A25.

464 **for baseball operations:** *Washington Post,* 14 December 2016.

465 **all male and all white:** See the recollection of the noted historian Eric Foner, who graduated from Columbia College in 1963. "Hiring Quotas for White Males Only," *Nation,* 26 June 1995.

466 **"the policy is wrong on moral grounds":** Quoted in Lincoln Caplan, *Up Against the Law: Affirmative Action and the Supreme Court* (1997), 31. It should be noted that Caplan completely disagrees with this view.

467 **college-level work:** *New York Times,* 4 March 2018.

468 **slavery and Jim Crow:** Ta-Nehisi Coates, "The Case for Reparations," *Atlantic,* June 2014. Stephen Carter, a self-confessed affirmative action baby, also agrees that unless the problem of racism is addressed, affirmative action will in the end yield little to people of color. *New York Times,* 6 July 2008.

INDEX

NOTE: Page numbers followed by *f* indicate a figure.

ILLUSTRATION CREDITS

Etching of a soldier protecting former slaves: Library of Congress
Frederick Douglass: Library of Congress
A. Philip Randolph: Library of Congress
Jessie May Turner: Library of Congress
Levittown, Pennsylvania: Library of Congress
Thurgood Marshall and Spottswood W. Robinson III: Library of Congress
Martin Luther King Jr.: Library of Congress
Lyndon Johnson: Lyndon Johnson Presidential Library
James Farmer: Library of Congress
Sit-in in Nashville, 1960: Library of Congress
Adam Clayton Powell: Library of Congress
Daniel Patrick Moynahan: Library of Congress
Watts, Los Angeles, after riots, 1965: Library of Congress
Richard Nixon, George Meany, and George Schultz: Richard Nixon Library
Richard Nixon and Arthur Fletcher: Richard Nixon Library
Jimmy Carter: Library of Congress
Parren J. Mitchell: Library of Congress
Marco De Funis: University of Washington, Special Collections
William O. Douglas: Photograph by Harris & Ewing, Collection of the Supreme
    Court of the United States
Allan Bakke: Bettmann/Getty Images
Drawing of Archibald Cox: Library of Congress
Lewis F. Powell: Photograph by Joseph Bailey, National Geographic, courtesy of
    the Supreme Court of the United States
William Brennan: Supreme Court of the United States
William G. Bowen: University Archives, Princeton University Library
Derek Bok: Harvard University Archives
Professor Sidney Hook: New York University Archives Photograph Collection
William F. Buckley and Thomas Sowell: Firing Line Broadcast Records, Hoover
    Institution Archives
Professor Nathan Glazer: Harvard University Archives
Professor Paul Spickard: University of California at Santa Barbara

Rabbis Maurice Eisendrath and Abraham Heschel: American Jewish Archives

Bella Abzug: Library of Congress

Andrew Young: Library of Congress

Betty Freidan: Library of Congress

Ruth Bader Ginsburg: Collection of the Supreme Court of the United States

Edwin Meese, Ronald Reagan, and William French Smith: Courtesy of the Ronald Reagan Library

Ronald Reagan and Linda Chavez: Courtesy of the Ronald Reagan Library

Edwin Meese: Courtesy of the Ronald Reagan Library

George Bush: George H.W. Bush Presidential Library

William H. Rehnquist: Photograph by Dane Penland, Smithsonian Institution, Courtesy of the Supreme Court of the United States

Antonin Scalia: Photograph by Steve Petteway, Collection of the Supreme Court of the United States

Jesse Helms: Courtesy of the State Archives of North Carolina

Harvey Gantt: Courtesy of the State Archives of North Carolina

Sandra Day O'Connor: Photograph by Dane Penland, Smithsonian Institution, courtesy of the Supreme Court of the United States

Bill Clinton and Janet Reno: Library of Congress

Bill Clinton with his Joint Chiefs of Staff: Library of Congress

Bob Dole: Library of Congress

Bill Clinton and Al Gore: Clinton Presidential Library

Voting rights demonstration in Selma, 1965: Library of Congress

Dan T. Blue: Courtesy of *The News and Observer* (Raleigh, N.C.)

Map of North Carolina's Twelfth Congressional District: Courtesy of the author

Robinson Oscar Everett: Duke University School of Law

David Souter: Photograph by Joseph Bailey, National Geographic Society, courtesy of the Supreme Court of the United States

Lee Bollinger: Diego M. Radzinschi/© 2018 ALM Media Properties, LLC

Anthony Kennedy: Photograph by Robin Reid, Collection of the Supreme Court of the United States

Professor Nell Irvin Painter: University Archives, Princeton University Library

Marcus Garvey: Library of Congress

Samuel Alito: Photograph by Steve Petteway, Collection of the Supreme Court of the United States

Barack Obama: Library of Congress

Elena Kagan: Photograph by Steve Petteway, Collection of the Supreme Court of the United States

Abigail Fisher: Diego M. Radzinschi/© 2018 ALM Media Properties, LLC

Sonia Sotomayor: Photograph by Steve Petteway, Collection of the Supreme Court of the United States

Edward Blum's website landing page: by permission of Edward Blum

Cartoon: TOLES © The Washington Post, July 2018. Reprinted with permission of Andrews McMeel Syndication. All rights reserved.